A SUFFOLK BIBLIOGRAPHY

A
SUFFOLK
BIBLIOGRAPHY

Compiled by
A. V. STEWARD

1979
SUFFOLK RECORDS SOCIETY
Distributed by The Boydell Press

VOLUME XX

Compilation and editorial matter © A. V. Steward 1979

First published 1979 by The Suffolk Records Society

Distributed for the Society by The Boydell Press Ltd, PO Box 24, Ipswich IP1 1JJ

British Library Cataloguing in Publication Data

Steward, A V
    A Suffolk bibliography. – (Suffolk Records Society.
    Publications; vol.20).
    1. Suffolk, Eng. – History – Bibliography
    I. Title   II. Series
    016.9426′4   Z2025.S/

ISBN 0 85115 115 9

Filmset by Northumberland Press Ltd, Gateshead, Tyne & Wear
Printed in Great Britain by Fletcher & Son, Norwich

To the memory of my daughter Susan
1937–1974

Foreword

The proposal for the compilation and publication by the Suffolk Records Society of a bibliography of Suffolk was put forward as long ago as September 1964, when a sub-committee for the purpose of achieving that object first met at my then home at the Old Rectory, Newbourne.

If this seems (as it doubtless may) a long time ago, regard must in fairness be had to the temerity of the enterprise in times and circumstances which were less than propitious to the activities of local publishing societies, and when large-scale undertakings of this kind have taxed the resources of larger and better endowed organisations. It may well be imagined that the progress of the work encountered its due share of problems and difficulties, and some credit may reasonably be claimed by the Society for having travelled hopefully for so long, and for having at length arrived so satisfactorily at the intended destination.

Credit in such a work as this must be widely shared, and this has been duly acknowledged by the compiler in his introduction. What modesty may well forbid him to state, however, and what we all know to be true, is that far the major responsibility has been his alone and that accordingly far the greater credit must fall to his own indefatigable endeavours, and I welcome the opportunity to pay him due tribute here. In other words, and with every allowance for the assistance he acknowledges, he has for twelve years and more borne the chief and daily burden, and the volume which is now before you is above all the product of his industry and his dedication.

That it is a volume worthy of the care, accuracy, and patience that have been devoted to it, and that it will be of great and lasting value to Suffolk local studies I have not the least doubt. It is my great pleasure to welcome its appearance.

LESLIE DOW

Introduction

The Rev. James Ford (1779–1850), Vicar of Navestock, Essex, and Perpetual Curate of St. Lawrence, Ipswich, transcribed the title-pages of Suffolk books over a number of years ending in 1842. The loose sheets, covered with his firm, legible script, were gathered together in a portfolio with a descriptive title-page as follows:

NOTITIA SUFFOLCIENCIS; or, A bibliographical list of the printed works, engraved views, portraits, maps, plans, arms, seats, etc., relating to, and illustrative of, the history, topography, antiquities, biography, customs, charities, and natural history of the county of Suffolk. With biographical notices of its historians, illustrators, and collectors. 1842.

This first attempt at a bibliography of Suffolk was purchased for the sum of £10 by the Ipswich Public Library at W. H. Booth's sale in April, 1906. Pasted inside the cover is the printed extract from the bookseller's catalogue:

"The most cursory glance at the contents of this portfolio is sufficient to warrant the conviction that it represents the results of enthusiastic, indefatigable, and life-long labours. What the cause of the author's failing to carry out his design to completion may have been, is needless to enquire. The fact, however, remains, and can hardly fail to be a subject of deep regret for the Literati of Suffolk today, that this valuable contribution to their County Bibliography (one of the most important ever made) exists in manuscript only."

Claude Morley (1874–1951), entomologist and antiquarian of Monk Soham, contributed, in April 1918, the first of several titles to a list of Suffolk books in the East Anglican Miscellany, at the same time expressing the opinion that "the difficulty of a compilation of the literature bearing upon this county is very great, and there is no guide whatever upon the subject". The entries appeared until 1958, and an alphabetical index was subsequently compiled by Sir Guy Hambling.

After the formation of the Suffolk Records Society in 1958 further thought was given to the matter with the object of including a Suffolk Bibliography in its series of annual publications. Eventually a meeting was held at the Old Rectory, New-bourne, under the chairmanship of Mr. Leslie Dow, to consider "Proposals for a bibliography of the history and topography of the county of Suffolk" drafted by Mr. James Campbell. Those proposals envisaged a comprehensive bibliography, an ideal which has had to be modified as printing costs escalated and in view of the sheer bulk of the entries collected. The need to observe reasonable limits in size and cost has resulted in a series of compromises and some degree of arbitrariness in the final selection both of subjects and entries.

COVERAGE

At the outset it was decided that the requirements of the bibliophile—details of size, pagination, illustrations, portraits, maps, diagrams, variations in editions—could not be met. Later decisions excluded most Acts of Parliament, Local and Personal Acts, and Statutory Instruments, indexes to which are available in record offices and reference libraries; sale catalogues; train and omnibus time-tables; many post-1945 district, town, and church guides. However, in compensation for the above exclusions, a liberal policy has been adopted towards articles from periodicals. Their importance is unquestioned and yet they are rarely indexed in classified form. Approximately 2,000 articles from 185 periodicals are included, but even so many minor articles remain in manuscript-slip form. These, together with other excluded entries for books and pamphlets, and the original manuscript-slips for the 8,123 printed entries, have been classified in loose-leaf binders and deposited in the Suffolk Record Office.

General works From the numerous eighteenth- and nineteenth-century national topographies and histories a few have been included which have substantial sections on Suffolk. The same principle has been applied to general books on various subjects.

Manuscripts This is essentially a bibliography of printed and published works, but in the absence of a companion list of Suffolk manuscripts it was decided to include entries for important collections of manuscript material by Fitch, Glyde, Redstone, and others, and also selected unpublished genealogies, university theses, and other typescript, cyclostyled, and photo-copied material.

Books printed before 1700 The relevant numbers are given from Pollard and Redgrave's *Short-title catalogue of books printed in England ...*, 1475–1640 (1926; 2nd edn. v 2, I–Z. 1976), and Wing's *Short-title catalogue of books printed in England ...*, 1641–1700 (New York, 1945–51; 2nd edn. v 1, A–England, New York, 1972).

Non-book material Separate maps, plans, and prints have been excluded, but a few collections of newspaper cuttings, playbills, photographs, and views have been listed.

Grangerized copies A number have been included as they are fruitful sources of views, portraits, and supplementary material.

Incomplete sets Certain categories of material, notably almanacs, newspapers, and church and school magazines, have not been systematically preserved by institutions or individuals, and it has not been possible to give precise dates of first and last issues in many cases. It was felt, however, that the practical value of identifying an item, even by an incomplete entry, outweighed other considerations. The term "extant" indicates that copies are known to exist for the dates given. "Incomplete" at the end of an entry indicates that some of the issues are missing. Further search might reveal additional copies. The incumbents of parishes and the head teachers of schools were circularized, with uneven results. Completed questionnaires have been deposited in the Suffolk Record Office.

Natural history Botany and zoology are not included.

Geography and geology   The regions of Breckland, Broadland, and Fenland are dealt with in the *Bibliography of Norfolk History* (1975). The section on geology is limited, with a bias towards works of some historical relevance.

Local government   The minutes and reports of local councils, the annual reports of officers, and many other local government items vary in format, regularity of issue, and consistency of preservation and location. Researchers are referred to the extensive collections held in the Suffolk Record Offices, and to local government offices throughout the county. The University of East Anglia booklet entitled *Periodicals and sets relating to British history in Norfolk and Suffolk libraries* (1971), is a useful guide to this material.

Sermons   Published sermons are very numerous. Only a few have been included, such as Assize sermons and those preached at the funerals of local notabilities.

Imaginative literature   Fiction and poetry by Suffolk writers, or with a local setting, have been largely excluded.

Clubs and societies   In the main, entries have been restricted to the older clubs and societies, and to those with intellectual or historical interests rather than sports and hobbies.

Biography   From the numerous families and persons having some connection with the county the selection is of necessity limited, as is the selection of books on the major figures such as Constable, FitzGerald, or Wolsey. Critical assessment of writers is omitted. Biographical articles in newspapers, such as "Suffolk and Ipswich worthies", "Suffolk and Ipswich pulpit", have not been indexed. Bound collections of these are available in the Suffolk Record Office.

Reference is made where a family or person appears in one or more of the following works: *Dictionary of National Biography* –1900, 22v. (1885–1901). –1960, 6v. (1912–71); Cockayne's *Complete peerage* . . . , 13v. (1910–59); Howard and Crisp's *Visitation of England and Wales*, 35v. (1893–1921); Emden's *Biographical register of the University of Oxford to A.D. 1500*, 3v. (1957–9). . . . *A.D. 1501–1540*, (1974); Watson's *New Cambridge bibliography of English literature*, 4v. (1969–74).

Place of publication   This is given only in the case of items published outside London.

Cross-references   These have been inserted freely to link related subjects, using entry numbers.

Terminal date   The terminal date was originally 31 December 1970. Although it has not been possible to extend the search of periodicals beyond that date, a number of important books and pamphlets published up to 1977 have been included.

ARRANGEMENT

The scheme of classification is outlined on pages xv–xx. To a large extent the classification is uniform with the *Bibliography of Norfolk history* (1975), compiled and published by the University of East Anglia as a memorial volume to the late Mr. R. W. Ketton-Cremer. The two bibliographies complement each other, and will often be used concurrently by students. As many books and articles deal jointly with Norfolk and Suffolk, and with the wider area of East Anglia, some duplication has been unavoidable.

Under each subject heading the items general in scope appear first, followed by entries on specific aspects of the subject. Thereafter the arrangement is chronological by date of publication, except where an historical sequence seemed appropriate.

Newspapers and periodicals, biographies and family history, are arranged alphabetically.

Localities   Under the names of towns, villages, and parishes the entries have been arranged in accordance with the main classification, with some variation when this is imposed by the nature of the material. The form of name, Bealings, Great, and Bealings, Little has been preferred, but Brent Eleigh, Monks Eleigh, North Cove, South Cove, and similar names have not been transposed. The border towns of Thetford, Gorleston (and Southtown), are dealt with in the *Bibliography of Norfolk history*.

LOCATIONS

Most books and pamphlets will be found in the Suffolk Record Office, Ipswich, which now contains the local history collections formerly housed in the Ipswich Central Library. Locations, where known, are given for items not held at Ipswich.

ACKNOWLEDGEMENTS

This bibliography owes its inception to Mr. James Campbell, Fellow of Worcester College, Oxford, who formulated the original proposals, and persuaded the Borough Librarian of Lowestoft to act as compiler after his retirement. The magnitude and complexity of the task soon became apparent. Without Mr. Campbell's sustained encouragement and critical appraisal, and his invaluable participation in its compilation by undertaking the extraction of articles from periodicals, it is doubtful whether the project would have been brought to a successful conclusion. The advice and time of Professor G. H. Martin, of the University of Leicester, have been freely given throughout, and particularly in the later stages of the work.

Of the numerous collaborators, to whom gratitude is warmly expressed, no one was more meticulous and assiduous than Miss D. M. White, formerly Chief Librarian of Ipswich. With Miss M. I. Maynard, formerly Local History Librarian in the Suffolk Record Office, Ipswich, she checked the Ipswich entries and those Suffolk items held only in Ipswich. At Bury St. Edmunds Mr. A. M. Tupling, and Mr. A. K. Robertson, checked the Bury and West Suffolk entries. The staff of the Reference Library at Lowestoft tolerated the frequent intrusions, and dealt with the persistent enquiries of their former chief. Miss K. M. Sharkey, and latterly the present Reference Librarian, Mr. D. Wright, were particularly helpful.

The Council of the Suffolk Records Society maintained its faith in the ultimate completion of the bibliography. Mr. Leslie Dow, founder Chairman of the Society until 1975, appreciated more than most the necessity for a county bibliography and suggested many additions. During its lengthy preparation the Honorary Secretaries of the Society, Mr. D. Charman, and then Mr. W. R. Serjeant, gave support and advice, answering frequent enquiries in their capacities as successive County Archivists.

Introduction

Mr. Henry Hallam, of the Bodleian Library, checked the Gough and other local history collections in Oxford, and inserted the STC and Wing numbers.

In their special fields the following contributed advice and additions: Miss Joan Corder, genealogy and heraldry; Mr. S. F. Watson, printing and Freemasonry; Mr. P. G. M. Dickinson, town and village guides; Mr. and Mrs. H. W. Wilton, transport and postal history; Rev. J. A. Fitch, church guides.

In the later stages Dr. J. M. Blatchly, and Mr. A. T. Copsey, of Ipswich contributed several additional items. Finally, Miss S. McIntyre, who collaborates with Professor Martin in the *Bibliography of British and Irish municipal history*, scrutinised the entries in relation to the Suffolk material in the British Library and the Bodleian Library.

At all times during the twelve years devoted to this work my wife, Mary, gave unfailing support and encouragement.

The Suffolk Records Society gratefully acknowledges the grants towards the cost of this volume from the Suffolk County Council, The British Library, and the Oxford Modern History Board.

CONCLUSION

In a work of this nature sundry omissions and unnoticed errors are inevitable. The compiler accepts responsibility and craves indulgence. Additions and corrections to be incorporated in any future supplement should be sent to the County Archivist, Suffolk Record Office, County Hall, Ipswich.

A. V. STEWARD
March, 1978.

Classification

Classification

Classification

Abbreviations

AASJ	Arms and Armour Society Journal
AB	Analecta Bollandiana
AHRJ	Army History Research Journal
ANL	Archaeological News Letter
Ant	Antiquity
Ant J	Antiquaries Journal
Arch	Archaeologia
Arch J	Archaeological Journal
BA	British Archivist
BIHR	Bulletin of the Institute of Historical Research
BL	British Library
BL-T	British Library-Thomason Tracts
BMQ	British Museum Quarterly
BNJ	British Numismatic Journal
BQ	Baptist Quarterly
Brit	British
BTH	Beccles Town Hall
Bull	Bulletin
Burl	Burlington Magazine
CA	Coat of Arms
CAGB	Colchester Archaeological Group Bulletin
CB	Church Builder
CBEL	Cambridge Bibliography of English Literature
CHST	Congregational Historical Society Transactions
CL	Country Life
Conn	Connoisseur
cont.	continued
CP	Complete Peerage
CRS	Catholic Record Society
CTetG	Collectanea Topographica et Genealogica
CU	Cambridge University Library
Cur A	Current Archaeology
DAR	Devon Association Report [& Transactions]
DNB	Dictionary of National Biography
EADT	East Anglian Daily Times
EAM	East Anglian Magazine
EA Misc	East Anglian Miscellany
E Ang	East Anglian
EAST	Essex Archaeological Society Transactions

Eccl	Ecclesiologist
ECCT	English Ceramic Circle Transactions
Ec Geog	Economic Geography
EcHR	Economic History Review
ECM	Eastern Counties Magazine
Ed.	Editor, compiler, transcriber, translator
edn(s)	edition(s)
EDP	Eastern Daily Press
EHR	English Historical Review
Emden	Biographical Register of the University of Oxford to A.D.1540 (Emden)
EN	Essex Naturalist
EPCT	English Porcelain Society Transactions
ER	Essex Review
ERO	Essex Record Office
et al.	and others
ff	following
FHSJ	Friends' Historical Society Journal
Frag Gen	Fragmenta Genealogica (Crisp)
Gen	Genealogist
Geog	Geographical
Geol	Geological
GLSJ	Gypsy Lore Society Journal
GM	Gentleman's Magazine
GU	Glasgow University
HC	House of Commons Papers
HS	Harleian Society
HSLP	Hugenot Society of London Proceedings
HTM	History Teachers' Miscellany
incorp.	incorporated
IBGT	Institute of British Geographers Transactions
IFCJ	Ipswich and District Field Club Journal
INHSJ	Ipswich and District Natural History Society Journal
IS	Ipswich School
JAABI	Journal of the Antiquarian Association of the British Isles
JBAA	Journal of the British Archaeological Association
JMGP	Journal of the British Society of Master Glass-Painters
Jour	Journal
JRAI	Journal of the Royal Anthropological Institute
JTH	Journal of Transport History
LA&LHS	Lowestoft Archaeological and Local History Society
Lib	Library
LSE	London School of Economics
MA	Medieval Archaeology
Mem	Memoir(s)
MGetH	Miscellanea Genealogica et Heraldica
MJ	Museum Journal
MM	Mariner's Mirror
MS	Manuscript(s)

NA	Norfolk Archaeology
N&Q	Notes and Queries
NC	Numismatic Chronicle
NCL/GY	Norfolk County Library, Great Yarmouth
NCL/N	Norfolk County Library, Norwich
nd	no date of publication given
NEH&GR	New England Historical and Genealogical Register
NGM	National Geographic Magazine
NIMT	Norfolk Installed Masters' Lodge Transactions
nl	no location
NNA(GY)	Norfolk and Norwich Archaeological Proceedings (Gt. Yarmouth Branch)
no(s)	number(s)
np	no place of publication given
nr	near
NRO	Norfolk Record Office
NRS	Norfolk Record Society
NS	New Series
NST	Newcomen Society Transactions
O	Bodleian Library, Oxford
obit	obituary
PCAS	Proceedings of the Cambridge Antiquarian Society
PPS	Proceedings of the Prehistoric Society
PPSEA	Proceedings of the Prehistoric Society of East Anglia
PRI	Proceedings of the Royal Institution
Proc	Proceedings
PRS	Pipe Roll Society
PSA	Proceedings of the Society of Antiquaries
PSIA	Proceedings of the Suffolk Institute of Archaeology
PTRS	Philosophical Transactions of the Royal Society
publ	published, publisher, publication(s)
Publ CAS	Publications of the Cambridge Antiquarian Society
QJSIA	Quarterly Journal of the Suffolk Institute of Archaeology
Quart	Quarterly
RBA	Report of the British Association
REMI	Register of English Monumental Inscriptions
Rev	Review
rev	revised
Rev Anthr	Revue Anthropologique
RIBAJ	Royal Institute of British Architects Journal
RIBAT	Royal Institute of British Architects Transactions
RM	Railway Magazine
rp	reprint, reprinted
SAAP	Suffolk Archaeological Association Original Papers
SAJ	Society of Archivists Journal
SBVC	Saga Book of the Viking Club
SC	Suffolk Chronicle
SCL	Suffolk County Library

SCL/L	Suffolk County Library, Lowestoft
Ser	Series
SGB	Suffolk Green Book
SIMT	Suffolk Installed Masters' Lodge Transactions
SM	Southwold Museum
Soc	Society
SPF	Société Préhistorique Française, Congrès Préhistorique de France
SR	Suffolk Review
SRO/B	Suffolk Record Office, Bury St. Edmunds
SRO/I	Suffolk Record Office, Ipswich
SRS	Suffolk Records Society
STC	Short-title catalogue of books ... 1475–1640 (Pollard and Redgrave)
Supp	Supplement
TG	Topographer and Genealogist
TMBS	Transactions of the Monumental Brass Society
TNNS	Transactions of the Norfolk and Norwich Naturalists Society
TPR	Town Planning Review
Trans	Transactions
TRHS	Transactions of the Royal Historical Society
TSNS	Transactions of the Suffolk Naturalists Society
UEA	University of East Anglia Library
var	various
VCH	Victoria County History
VE&W	Visitation of England and Wales (Howard and Crisp)
Vet M	Vetusta Monumenta
Wing	Short title catalogue of books ... 1641–1700 (Wing)
YAJ	Yorkshire Archaeological Journal

Directories

See also **477**, *and* entries under individual localities

1 Bailey's British directory ... for ... 1784, and 1785. 4v. Suffolk, v 4. BL

2 Universal British directory of trade, commerce, and manufacture ... 5v. 1790–98. Suffolk, v 2–5. BL

3 Holden's triennial directory for 1805, 1808, 1809, 1811. BL

4 Pigot and Co's London and provincial new commercial directory for 1823–4. Suffolk, 454–82. BL

5 Traveller's Suffolk directory, containing an alphabetical list of towns and villages ... Also a list of fairs. Beccles, [1830?]. BL

6 Pigot and Co's national commercial directory, comprising a directory ... of the merchants, bankers, professional gentlemen, manufacturers, and traders in all the cities, towns, ... and principal villages in ... Bedfordshire, ... Suffolk ... 1830. Suffolk, 739–88. BL

7 Pigot and Co's royal national and commercial directory and topography of the counties of Bedford ... Suffolk ... 3pts. 1839. Suffolk, 527–84

8 Robson's commercial directory of the six counties forming the Norfolk circuit. 1839. Suffolk, 1–102

9 Pigot and Co's royal national, commercial, and street directory of London for 1840 ... To which are added directories of the counties of Bedford ... Suffolk ... BL

10 **White, W.** [Proposal for his history, gazetteer, and directory of Suffolk]. Sheffield, [1843]. O

11 **White, W.** History, gazetteer, and directory of Suffolk. Sheffield, 1844. 1855. 1874. 1885. 1892. 1844 edn rp 1970

12 Kelly's directory of Suffolk. 1846. 1853. 1858. 1865. 1869. 1875. 1879. 1883. 1888. 1892. 1896. 1900. 1904. 1908. 1912. 1916. 1922. 1925. 1929. 1933. 1937. [Sometimes bound with edns for other counties]

13 Slater's royal, national, and commercial directory and topography of the counties of Bedfordshire ... Suffolk. Manchester 1850, 1851. BL

14 Hunt's directory of East Norfolk with part of Suffolk ... 1850. NCL/N

15 Post Office directory for Norfolk and Suffolk ... Norwich, [1852]. 1865. O

16 Melville's directory and gazetteer of Norwich ... Ipswich, 1856. NCL/N

17 Harrod's postal and commercial directory of Norfolk and Norwich, including Lowestoft in the county of Suffolk. 1863. 1868. 1872. 1877. 1879. NCL/N

18 Harrod's postal and commercial directory of Suffolk, with Newmarket. 1864

19 Morris's commercial directory and gazetteer of Suffolk, with Great Yarmouth and Newmarket. Nottingham, 1868

20 Harrod's postal and commercial directory of Suffolk and Cambridgeshire. 2nd edn Norwich, 1873. O

21 Deacon's Cambridgeshire, Norfolk, and Suffolk Court guide and county blue book: a fashionable record, professional register, etc. 1886. 1892. 1893. NCL/N

22 Bennett's business directory: Norfolk, Suffolk, Cambridgeshire. 1889. NCL/N

23 **Trades' Directories Ltd.** Eastern counties of England trades' directory. 1910–. Edinburgh

24 Aubrey's Cambridgeshire, Norfolk, and Suffolk directory. 1916. 1922. 1925. 1932. Walsall. NCL/N

25 **Town and County Directories Ltd.** Norfolk and Suffolk trades' directory ... 1933/4–. Edinburgh

26 Kelly's directory of the wireless and allied trades, 1934; chemical industries, 1935; wine, spirit, and brewing trades, 1935; cabinet, furnishing, and upholstery trades, 1936; engineering, hardware, and motor trades, 1936; leather trades, 1937; building trades, 1939. [Suffolk sections only]

27 County directories for the year ... Suffolk, 1951/2–. Hornchurch. BL

28 Burkett's trades directory of Suffolk: classified trades and professions, 1957/8 . Needham Market

29 **County Publicity Services.** D. A. Yates county directory of Suffolk of trades, professions, etc. 1964/5–. Hunstanton

Almanacs, Annuals, Handbooks

See also entries under individual localities

30 Shave's memorandum book for the year of our Lord 1768, peculiarly useful to the gentlemen and tradesmen of Ipswich and Suffolk. Extant 1768–88. Ipswich

31 Suffolk and Norfolk ladies' own memorandum book . . . for the years 1785–94. NCL/N

32 Rackham's Suffolk ladies' memorandum book, 1787–1824. Bury St. Edmunds

33 Gedge's town and country ladies' own memorandum book; or, Fashionable companion for the year. 1803–16. Bury St. Edmunds. BL

34 Bransby's Suffolk memorandum book; or, Gentleman's pocket ledger [c.1804–c.1815]. Ipswich

35 Raw's ladies' fashionable repository, 1809–34. Ipswich

36 Raw's Suffolk gentleman's pocket book, 1814–35. Ipswich

37 Norfolk, Suffolk, Essex, and Cambridge gentleman's pocket book. Ipswich. Extant 1817–38. NCL/N

38 Norfolk, Suffolk, Cambridgeshire, Isle of Ely, . . . almanack. Extant 1822–94. BL

39 Fulcher's ladies' memorandum book, 1825–93. Sudbury

40 Frost's new town and country ladies' memorandum book, and fashionable repository, 1835–6. Bury St. Edmunds. BL

41 Pawsey's ladies' fashionable repository, 1836–1914. Ipswich

42 East Anglian handbook, yearbook, and scrapbook, 1860–77. *Cont. as* East Anglian handbook and agricultural manual, 1878–93. Norwich

43 Knights' Suffolk almanack and county handbook for . . . 1869. *Cont. as* County handbook and Suffolk almanack, 1870–1902. *Cont. as* Suffolk county handbook and official directory, 1903–39. Ipswich

44 Hodson and Hollier's illustrated almanack and directory for West Suffolk, etc. Extant 1873–8. Sudbury. BL

45 Lambert's Family almanack, 1857–1917. Framlingham and Woodbridge

46 East Anglian holiday annual. 1877, 1879, 1887. Norwich. NCL/N

47 Jarrold's Norfolk and Suffolk companion to the almanack. 1877, 1881, 1884–1908. Norwich. NCL/N

48 Jarrold's Norwich and Eastern Counties handbook. 1879, 1888–9, 1890, 1893–4. Norwich. NCL/N

49 Glyde's Suffolk almanac, annual, and official directory. 1880–90. *Incorp. with* County handbook and Suffolk almanack [Knights']

50 Jarrold's Norwich and Eastern Counties almanack, advertiser, and magazine list. 1882–3, 1885–94. Norwich. NCL/N

51 **Lucia, T. F.** Bury and West Suffolk almanack and year book . . . for 1884. Bury St. Edmunds. 1884. SRO/B

52 Knights' Norfolk and Norwich annual and East Anglian gleaner, 1886–9. Norwich. NCL/N

53 Jarrold's Norfolk and Suffolk handbook, 1909, 1910, 1913, 1915–17. Norwich. NCL/N

54 East Anglian and Essex countryside annual, 1964–. Ipswich

Newspapers and Periodicals

For regimental magazines, house journals, etc., *see* the appropriate sections *below. For* parish magazines, *see under* Localities

55 Aldeburgh, Leiston, and Saxmundham Times, Aug 4, 1900–. *Cont. as* Leiston Observer and Aldeburgh, Saxmundham, and Thorpeness Mercury, 1904–. Ipswich. BL

56 Beccles and Bungay Gazette, May 23, 1969–. nl

57 Beccles and Bungay Journal, 1933–. nl

58 Beccles and Bungay Weekly News. Extant 1861. nl

59 Beccles Gazette, Jan 14, 1965–May 15, 1969

60 Beccles Record, Feb 6, 1896–May 1899. *Cont. as* North Suffolk Advertiser, Aug 25, 1899–Aug 22, 1920. BL

61 Beccles Weekly News, 1857–67. *Cont. as* East Suffolk Gazette, June 11, 1867–March 1, 1926. BL

62 Budget; or, Norfolk, Suffolk, and Essex Entertaining Weekly Miscellany, May–June, 1779. NCL/N
Bungay. *See* Beccles and Bungay Gazette
        Beccles and Bungay Journal
        Beccles and Bungay Weekly News

63 Bury Advertiser, nos 1–7, Oct–Dec 1973. SRO/B

64 Bury Advertising Gazette, 1853–March 15, 1856. *Cont. as* Bury Gazette to 1857. *Incorp. in* Bury Free Press. BL
Bury and Norwich Post. *See* Bury Post
Bury and Suffolk Herald. *See* Suffolk Herald

65 Bury and Suffolk Press, March 21, 1832–June 26, 1833. BL

66 Bury and Suffolk Standard, March 9, 1869–March 29, 1887. *Incorp. in* Bury and Norwich Post. BL

67 Bury and West Suffolk Advertiser, Oct 30, 1886–Sept 27, 1907. BL

68 Bury and West Suffolk Journal, Oct 30, 1886–Feb 21, 1890. BL

69 Bury Free Press and West Suffolk Observer, July 14, 1855–. BL

70 Bury Free Press: Suffolk century story, 1855–1955. Bury St. Edmunds, 1955. SRO/B.
Bury Gazette *See* Bury Advertising Gazette

71 Bury Gazette; or, Bury, Ipswich, and Norwich Advertiser, Sept 20, 1821–March 1827. SRO/B

72 Bury Philosophic Album, including a variety of original articles, etc., 1827. SRO/B

73 Bury Post, 1782–5. *Cont. as* Bury and Norwich Post, 1786–Dec 25, 1931. *Incorp. in* Bury Free Press from Jan 2, 1932. SRO/B. *See also* **2886**

74 Bury Post [Bury Free Press supplement]. nos 1–48, Sept 18, 1973–Sept 10, 1974. *Discontinued.* SRO/B

75 Bury St. Edmunds and District Advertiser, Aug 1955–Nov 1956. SRO/B

76 Carlton, a weekly review and record of news for East Anglia, Feb 17– April 21, 1883. Norwich. NCL/N

77 Daily Herald and East of England Advertiser, Dec 30, 1897–July 30, 1898. *Incorp. in* Evening Star

Daily Ipswich Journal. *See* Ipswich Journal

Daily Journal. *See* Ipswich Journal

78 Deben Bulletin, 1947–54. nl

79 East Anglia Life 1961–. *Formerly* Norfolk Life. NCL/N

80 East Anglian, a magazine of literary and miscellaneous information for the counties of Suffolk, Norfolk, Essex, and Cambridge. [Ipswich]. 5 parts only, Jan–May 1814. [*Includes* History of Suffolk, by T. Harral and W. Betham, 1–108]

81 East Anglian; or, Norfolk, Suffolk, Cambridgeshire, Norwich, Lynn, and Yarmouth Herald, Oct 12, 1830–April 16, 1833. *Incorp. in* Bury and Norwich Post. NCL/N

82 East Anglian Circular; or, Literary and General Advertiser, April 2, 1839–44 Ipswich. BL

East Anglian Daily Times. *See* Ipswich Express

83 East Anglian Daily Times. Jubilee souvenir, 1874–1924. [Ipswich], [1924]

84 East Anglian Daily Times. Souvenir of the East Anglian Daily Times. On the inauguration of the new press, Feb 24, 1936. Ipswich, [1936]

85 East Anglian Echo, June 5, 1869–Sept 23, 1870. Bury St. Edmunds. BL

86 East Anglian Magazine, Jan–Oct 1909. Ipswich. 4 pts [no more published]

87 East Anglian Magazine, v 1 no 1, Summer 1935–v 5 no 6, April 1941; v 6 no 1, Sept 1946–. Index 1935–60 by T. Mollard. Ipswich. [index 1960–70. SRO/B]

88 East Anglian Miscellany upon matters of history, genealogy, archaeology, folk-lore, literature, etc., relating to East Anglia. Notes 1–285, from March 2, 1901 to Dec 28, 1901, and index. *Rp from* East Anglian Daily Times. Ipswich, 1965. [only first year reprinted. 1902–06 in newspaper, newspaper cuttings, and micro-film. SRO/I]

89 East Anglian Miscellany ... General index 1901–06 [By *Sir* G. Hambling]. [Typescript]

90 East Anglian Miscellany ... 1907–58. Ipswich. *Rp from* East Anglian Daily Times

91 East Anglian Miscellany ... General index, 1907–58 and 1901. By *Sir* G. Hambling [includes an alphabetical catalogue of over 1000 Suffolk books listed in the East Anglian Miscellany between April 1918 and Dec 1958, and an index to wills and families]. 3v. [Typescript]

92 East Anglian Miscellany. Alphabetical list of pen-names used by contributors ... By H. R. Lingwood. Sept 1960. [Typescript]

93 East Anglian Spectator, 1814. [4 issues only]

94 East Coast Mail. Extant 1872. Norwich. BL

95 East Coast Visitor, Feb 22–March 29, 1871. Lowestoft. BL

96 East Coast Visitor, June 1904–Sept 1906. Norwich. BL

97 Eastern Counties Daily Press, Oct 10, 1870–May 2, 1871. *Cont. as* Eastern Daily Press, May 3, 1871–.

Eastern Counties Gazette. *See* Ipswich Free Press

98 Eastern Counties Magazine and Suffolk Note-Book. *Ed.* by M. Henniker. Aug 1900–May 1902. 2v. [no more published]

Eastern Daily Press. *See* Eastern Counties Daily Press

99 Eastern Times. Extant 1864–March 11, 1871. *Cont. as* Lowestoft News and Eastern Times, March 18, 1871–July 10, 1875. *Cont. as* Lowestoft News and Observer and Eastern Times, July 17, 1875–Feb 22, 1895. BL

East of England Advertiser. *See* Daily Herald and East of England Advertiser

East Suffolk Gazette. *See* Beccles Weekly News

100 East Suffolk Mercury, 1858–Sept 13, 1862. [Publ. Lowestoft 1858–60, then Ipswich]. *Cont. as* Suffolk Mercury, Sept 20, 1862–July 1, 1876. *Cont. as* Suffolk Times and Mercury, July 8, 1876–Aug 18, 1899. *Incorp. in* Suffolk Chronicle

101 Essex and Suffolk Co-operative Citizen, 1932. nl

102 Essex and Suffolk Mercury. Extant 1838. nl

Essex and Suffolk News. *See* Suffolk and Essex News (Sudbury)

103 Essex and Suffolk Press (Chelmsford), 1832. *Incorp. in* Essex Independent, 1832–3. *Incorp. in* Colchester Gazette, and *cont. as* Essex and Suffolk Times, 1837–41. nl

Essex and Suffolk Times. *See* Essex and Suffolk Press

104 Essex and West Suffolk Gazette, 1852–73. nl

105 Essex, Herts, and Suffolk Mercury, 1843. nl

106 Essex, Herts, and Suffolk Times, 1841. nl

107 Essex Notebook and Suffolk Gleaner, Oct 1884–Nov 1885. BL

108 Evening Herald, Sept 1, 1897–Dec 29, 1897. *Cont. as* Daily Herald and East of England Advertiser, Dec 30, 1897–July 30, 1898. *Incorp. in* Evening Star

109 Evening Star, May 31, 1893–. Ipswich

Eye. *See* Framlingham and Eye Mercury

110 Felixstowe and Walton Free Press, July 16–Oct 1, 1881. BL

111 Felixstowe Post. Extant 1896. BL

112 Felixstowe Times and Mercury, April 19, 1930–

113 Felixstowe Times and Visitors' List, May 8, 1920–Oct 26, 1929. [Weekly, distributed with EADT]

114 Felixstowe Visitors' List, June 21 1890–[1914?]. [Weekly during holiday season, distributed with EADT]

115 Framlingham and Eye Mercury, 1972–

116 Framlingham Weekly News. Extant 1869–1900. BL

117 Free Press (Sudbury), July 5–Aug 23, 1855. *Cont. as* West Suffolk and North Essex Free Press, 1855–6. *Cont. as* Suffolk and Essex Free Press, June 19, 1856–1949. *Cont. as* Suffolk Free Press, 1949–. BL

118 **Taylor, R. R.** Bogey's rag: a brief history of the Suffolk Free Press, 1855–1949. 1970. SRO/B

119 Hadleigh Weekly News and South Suffolk Mercury, Sept 30, 1966–. Ipswich

120 Halesworth Times and Southwold Mercury, July 17, 1855–. BL
Haverhill Echo. *See* South-West Suffolk Echo

121 Haverhill Weekly News, 1889–1910. *Incorp. in* Cambridge Weekly News. nl
Independent. *See* Ipswich Independent.

122 Ipswich Advance, no 1, July 3, 1885–no 11, Nov 20, 1885. Ipswich. [No more published]

123 Ipswich Advertiser. Extant 1938–40

124 Ipswich Advertiser; or, Illustrated Monthly Miscellany, 1855–66

125 Ipswich and Colchester Times, 1858–? nl

126 Ipswich Express, Aug 1839–Oct 6, 1874. nl *Cont. as* East Anglian Daily Times, Oct 13, 1874–. *See also* **113, 114**

127 Ipswich Free Lance. Extant 1870–71. BL

128 Ipswich Free Press, 1872–June 19, 1886. *Cont. as* Eastern Counties Gazette, June 26, 1886–March 20, 1889. BL

129 Ipswich Gazette, 1719. *Incorp. in* Ipswich Journal Aug 13, 1720. *See* Ipswich Journal

130 An Ipswich newspaper of the olden time: Ipswich Gazette, 1734–6. 22 parts in Ipswich Journal 1867–8

131 Ipswich Independent, Nov 14, 1908–April 1, 1910. *Cont. as* Suffolk Standard, April 8–July 7, 1910. *Cont. as* Independent, July 15, 1910–Nov 3, 1911. BL

132 Ipswich Journal, or, the Weekly Mercury, Aug 13, 1720–Oct 12, 1734. *Issued as* Ipswich Gazette, Oct 19, 1734–Feb 10, 1738/9; *then* the Original Ipswich Journal, Feb 17, 1738/9–1774; *then* the Ipswich Journal, 1774–June 29, 1886; *then* Daily Ipswich Journal, July 1, 1886–Sept 17, 1887 and Weekly Ipswich Journal, Nov 5, 1886–Sept 17, 1887; *then* Daily Journal, Sept 19, 1887–July 21, 1888 and Weekly Journal, Sept 23, 1887–Aug 10, 1888; *then* Ipswich Journal, Aug 17, 1888–July 26, 1902

133 Ipswich Journal when first established [1720]. Being copies of four old Ipswich Journals . . . no 20, Dec 24, 1720; no 22, Jan 7, 1721; no 24, Jan 21, 1721; no 31, March 11, 1721. [Ipswich], 1881

134 Critical review of the Ipswich Journal; or, Candid remarks on the disputes both religious and political, which occur in that paper for the month of January [Feb–March] 1790. [3 numbers]. Ipswich, 1790. BL

135 Ipswich Journal. No 34 in The Provincial Press Series from Effective Advertiser, Dec 1, 1888; Jan 1, 1889. nl

136 Ipswich Magazine for the year 1799 [monthly, Feb 1799–Jan 1800]. *Ed.* by J. Bransby. Ipswich

137 Ipswich Monthly Visitor, Jan–Feb 1847. Ipswich. BL

138 Ipswich Observer. Extant 1906–09

139 Ipswich Phono-Press, Aug 1845–Dec 1846 [Phonographically ·printed]. Ipswich. [No more published]. BL

140 Ipswich Review. v 1, no 1, May 1885–v 3, no 27, June 1887. *Ed.* by C. T. Roberts *and* H. Turner. Ipswich. [No more published]

141 Ipswich Times. Extant 1865–Oct 9, 1874. *Incorp. in* East Anglian Daily Times. BL

142 Ipswich Weekly Mercury, no 1, Feb 22, 1734/5. [only known issue]

Leiston Observer. *See* Aldeburgh, Leiston, and Saxmundham Times

Long Melford Gazette. *See* Sudbury Post and Long Melford Gazette

143 Lowestoft Advertiser, no 1, Oct 17, 1853. BL

Lowestoft Journal and Mercury. *See* Lowestoft Weekly Journal

144 Lowestoft Mercury. Extant 1871–6. BL

145 Lowestoft Mercury, 1936–9. SCL/L

Lowestoft News and Eastern Times. *See* Eastern Times

Lowestoft News and Observer and Eastern Times. *See* Eastern Times

146 Lowestoft Observer, July 2, 1870–July 3, 1875. *Incorp. in* Lowestoft News and Observer and Eastern Times. BL

147 Lowestoft Standard, Feb 11, 1882–Dec 24, 1904. *Cont. as* Lowestoft Weekly Standard, Dec 31, 1904–Oct 20, 1916. BL

148 Lowestoft Weekly Journal, July 26, 1873–July 14, 1877. *Cont. as* Lowestoft Journal and Mercury, July 21, 1877–. SCL/L

149 Lowestoft Weekly Press, Jan 2, 1886–1941. BL

Lowestoft Weekly Standard. *See* Lowestoft Standard

Lowestoft. *See also* Yarmouth and Lowestoft Dove
Yarmouth and Lowestoft Era

150 Lynn and Wisbech Packet; or, Norfolk, Suffolk, Cambridge, and Lincolnshire Advertiser. Extant 1800–02. NCL/N

151 Moonraker, with which are incorporated The Essex Calf and Norfolk Dumpling, no 1, Nov 2, 1886—no 22, March 29, 1887. Ipswich. NCL/N

152 Newmarket Advertiser, 1882– [Local edn. of Cambridgeshire Times (March)]. Newmarket. BL

153 Newmarket Free Press, 1927–31. nl

154 Newmarket Journal, 1872–. BL

155 Newmarket Monthly Illustrated Journal and Advertiser, etc. 1872–82. BL

156 Newmarket Sporting News, May 17, 1889–Nov 18, 1933. BL

157 Newmarket Sporting Telegraph, Sept 4, 1897–March 20, 1899. BL

158 Newmarket Weekly News, April 27, 1889–Oct 28, 1910 [Local edn of Cambridgeshire Weekly News]. BL

159 Nightlight, Oct 29, 1888–Feb 4, 1889. Ipswich. BL

160 Norfolk and Suffolk Journal, 1864–. nl

161 Norfolk and Suffolk Monthly Advertiser. Extant Jan–Feb 1854. Gt. Yarmouth. BL

Norfolk Life. *See* East Anglia Life

162 Norfolk Mail and Norwich, Yarmouth, and Lowestoft Conservative Reporter, July 11, 1876–Dec 28, 1886. Norwich. BL

Norfolk Suffolk Advertiser. *See* Beccles Record

163 Norwich Gazette and Norfolk Weekly Advertiser [later ... or, Norfolk and Suffolk Advertiser July 1761–July 1764]. Norwich. NCL/N

164 Norwich Mercury and Yarmouth, Lynn, and Ipswich Herald. Extant 1823–7. nl

165 Norwich Penny Magazine and Eastern Counties' Literary, Scientific, and Critical Review, Jan–Aug 1870. NCL/N

Original Ipswich Journal. *See* Ipswich Journal

166 Orwell Phonographer. *Ed.* by C. W. Rand. v 1–5, 1887–9. Ipswich. BL

167 Provincial Spectator, nos 1–8, 1821. Bury St Edmunds. [SRO/B nos 4–6 only]

168 Pulpit and Literary Magazine for the Eastern Counties, May 1, 1881. Norwich. NCL/N

Saxmundham. *See* Aldeburgh, Leiston, and Saxmundham Times

169 Searcher; or, Norwich, Norfolk, and Suffolk Humourist and Fashionable Gazetteer, Sept 1839. Norwich. NCL/N

170 South Suffolk Beacon, no 1, March 1910. *Cont. as* Suffolk Beacon, no 2, April 1910–no 28, June 1912. Sudbury. BL

171 South-West Suffolk Echo, North Essex, and East Cambs Observer, 1888–1962. *Cont. as* Haverhill Echo, West Suffolk, North Essex, and East Cambs Observer, 1963. *Cont. as* Haverhill Echo, 1970–. BL

Southwold. *See* Halesworth Times and Southwold Mercury

172 Star of the East, Feb 17, 1885–May 30, 1893. *Incorp. in* Evening Star

173 Stour Valley Reporter, July 6–Dec 28, 1876. Sudbury. BL

174 Stowmarket Chronicle and Mercury, Oct 4, 1963–. Ipswich

175 Stowmarket Courier. Extant 1868–97. BL

176 Stowmarket Weekly Post, Dec 7, 1905–Dec 27, 1917

177 Sudbury Express, Aug 31, 1871–Jan 18, 1872. BL

178 Sudbury Herald and South Suffolk Pioneer, nos 1–2, March, June, 1904. BL

179 Sudbury Post and Long Melford Gazette. Extant 1919–31. BL

Sudbury. *See also* Free Press (Sudbury)

Suffolk and Essex Free Press. *See* Free Press (Sudbury)

180 Suffolk and Essex News (Sudbury), 1857–9. *Cont. as* Essex and Suffolk News, 1859–1921. *Incorp. in* Suffolk and Essex Free Press. BL

Suffolk Beacon. *See* South Suffolk Beacon

181 Suffolk Chronicle, April 4, 1801–July 17, 1802; May 5, 1810–99. *Cont. as* Suffolk Chronicle and Mercury, 1899–1961. *Cont. as* Suffolk Mercury, 1961–

182   Suffolk Chronicle: supplement. Extant 1858–60
      Suffolk Chronicle and Mercury. *See* Suffolk Chronicle
183   Suffolk Examiner, Feb 13–June 12, 1866. Ipswich
184   Suffolk Express, July 4, 1839–March 1840. Ipswich. BL
185   Suffolk Fair, v 1, no 1, Oct–Nov 1970–. Brundall
186   Suffolk Free-Lance, and Cambridgeshire, Norfolk, and Essex Critic, Feb 21,
      1888–May 22, 1888. Bury St. Edmunds. SRO/B
      Suffolk Free Press. *See* Free Press (Sudbury)
187   Suffolk Herald, March 28, 1827–June 25, 1828. *Cont. as* Bury and Suffolk
      Herald, July 2, 1828–Dec 26, 1849. *Incorp. in* Bury and Norwich Post. Bury St.
      Edmunds. SCL/B. *See also* **2886**
188   Suffolk Literary Chronicle. A collection of miscellaneous literature, and of . . .
      papers relating to the county. v 1 and 2, nos 1–14, June 1837–8. Ipswich. BL
189   **Harris, H. A.** "Suffolk Literary Chronicle" [1837–8]. N&Q 11th Ser 5, 1912,
      246
      Suffolk Mercury. *See* Suffolk Chronicle
190   Suffolk Mercury; or, St. Edmundsbury Post, 1714–40? SRO/B
      Suffolk Standard. *See* Ipswich Independent
191   Suffolk Temperance Recorder for the Eastern Counties of England. Ipswich.
      Extant 1840–41. O. NS no 1, May 1841–no 15, July 1842
      Suffolk Times and Mercury. *See* East Suffolk Mercury
      Thorpeness. *See* Aldeburgh, Leiston, and Saxmundham Times
      Walton. *See* Felixstowe and Walton Free Press
192   Waveney Chronicle, Nov 7, 1935–. Extant Oct 3, 1940. Beccles. nl
      Weekly Ipswich Journal. *See* Ipswich Journal
      Weekly Journal. *See* Ipswich Journal
      Weekly Mercury. *See* Ipswich Journal
      West Suffolk and North Essex Free Press. *See* Free Press (Sudbury)
      Wickham Market. *See* Woodbridge Reporter and Wickham Market Mercury
193   Woodbridge Reporter and Wickham Market Mercury, 1859–. Ipswich. BL
194   Yarmouth and Lowestoft Dove, no 1, Sept 1874. BL
195   Yarmouth and Lowestoft Era and People's Advocate, June 14–Nov 8, 1871. BL
196   **Mander, R. P.** The local paper [early Norfolk and Suffolk newspapers].
      EAM 10, 1951, 473–8

Geography, Landscape, and Climate

GENERAL FEATURES   *See also* 349, 1636

197   **Engleheart, F.** Physical aspects of Suffolk: 1. TSNS 3, 1935/7, 1–6
198   **Morley, C.** Physical aspects of Suffolk: 2. TSNS 6, 1946/8, 86–94
199   **Steers, J. A.** Physiography of East Anglia. TNNS 15, 1939/43, 231–58

GEOLOGY   *See also* 586, 1059–60, 1062, 2188, 2192, 6789

200   **Clarke, W. B.** Extracts from a memoir on the geological structure and phenomena of the county of Suffolk, and its physical relations with Norfolk and Essex. 1837

201   **Phear, J. B.** On the geology of some parts of Suffolk, particularly of the valley of the Gipping. Trans. Cambridge Philosophical Soc. 9, 1854

202   Memorials on sand deposits at Landguard Point. HC 1861, 38. Suffolk, 391–400

203   Great chalk formation in Suffolk. E Ang 1, 1858/63, 323–4

204   **Prestwich,** *Sir* **J.** On the structure of the crag-beds of Norfolk and Suffolk . . . 1871

205   **Gunn, J.** On the prospect of finding productive coal-measures in Norfolk and Suffolk. RBA 1873, 102–03

206   **Taylor, J. E.** Sketch of the geology of Suffolk. *In* White's History, gazetteer, and directory of Suffolk. 1874, 1885

207   **Whitaker, W.,** *et al.* Geology of the NW part of Essex and the NE part of Herts. With parts of Cambridgeshire and Suffolk. Mem Geol Survey. 1878

208   **Whitaker, W.,** *et al.* Geology of the neighbourhood of Stowmarket. Mem Geol Survey. 1881

209   **Bennett, F. J.** Geology of the country around Diss, Eye, Botesdale, and Ixworth. Mem Geol Survey. 1884

210   **Whitaker, W.,** *et al.* Geology of the country around Ipswich, Hadleigh, and Felixstowe. Mem Geol Survey. 1885

211   **Bennett, F. J.,** *et al.* Geology of the country between and south of Bury St. Edmunds and Newmarket. Mem Geol Survey. 1886

212   **Dalton, W. H.** Geology of the country around Aldborough, Framlingham, Orford, and Woodbridge. *Ed.* with some additions by W. W[hitaker]. Mem Geol Survey. 1886

213   **Whitaker, W.** Geology of Southwold and of the Suffolk coast from Dunwich to Covehithe. Mem Geol Survey. 1887

214 Whitaker, W., *and* Dalton, W. H. Geology of the country around Halesworth and Harleston. Mem Geol Survey. 1887

215 Blake, J. H. Geology of the country near Yarmouth and Lowestoft. Mem Geol Survey. 1890

216 Whitaker, W., *et al*. Geology of parts of Cambridge and Suffolk. Mem Geol Survey. 1891

217 Taylor, J. E. Relation of the geology of East Anglia to its archaeology. PSIA 8, 1892/4, 51–4

218 **Eastern Counties' Coal-Boring and Development Syndicate, Ltd.** List of Provisional Committee, etc. Proposed prospectus, geological reports, etc. Ipswich, 1893. BL. *See also* **7506**

219 Holmes, T. V., *et al*. Boring in search of coal in Suffolk and Essex. EN 9, 1895/6, 213, 253; 10, 1896/7, 9, 136

220 Harmer, F. W. Glacial geology of Norfolk and Suffolk ... [1910]. SCL/L

221 Lydekker, R. Palaeontology. *In* VCH Suffolk 1, 1911, 31–46

222 Woodward, H. B. Geology. *In* VCH Suffolk 1, 1911, 1–30

223 Boswell, P. G. H. Age of Suffolk valleys with notes on the buried channels of the drift. Quart Jour Geol Soc 69, 1913, 581–620

224 Boswell, P. G. H. Notes on the chalk of Suffolk. IFCJ 4, 1913, 17–26

225 Boswell, P. G. H. On the occurrence of the North Sea Drift (lower glacial) and certain other brick-earths in Suffolk. Proc Geol Assoc 25, 1914

226 Boswell, P. G. H. Geology of the Woodbridge district. IFCJ 5, 1916, 1–11

227 Boswell, P. G. H. Geology of the country around Ipswich. Mem Geol Survey. 1927

228 Boswell, P. G. H. Geology of the country around Woodbridge, Felixstowe, and Orford. Mem Geol Survey. 1928

229 Boswell, P. G. H. Geology of the country around Sudbury. Mem Geol Survey. 1929

230 Chatwin, C. P. East Anglia and adjoining areas. Mem Geol Survey. 1937. 2nd edn 1948. 3rd edn 1954. 4th edn 1961

231 Spencer, H. E. P. New inter-glacial beds at Ipswich. ANL 5, 1954, 4

232 Spencer, H. E. P. Contribution to the geological history of Suffolk. 5pts and suppl. TSNS 13, 1964/7, 197–209, 290–313, 366–89; 15, 1969/72, 148–96, 279–363, 517–19

WEATHER   *See also* **6790–92, 7387, 7825**

233 Whistlecraft, O. The magnificent and notably hot summer of 1846 ... 1846

234 Whistlecraft, O. Rural gleanings, or facts worth knowing as recorded for many years' natural observations in the Eastern counties. Ipswich, 1851

235 Whistlecraft, O. Weather record of 1856. [Thwaite], [1857]. BL

236 Whistlecraft, O. Weather almanac for the years 1857–1886. Ipswich, 1857–86. 30v

237 **Whistlecraft, O.** Variations in the seasons in the eastern parts of England, as observed at Thwaite. Norwich, [1883]

FLOODS, STORMS, ETC. *See also* **6792**

238 Wonderfull and straunge newes, which happened in the countye of Suffolke and Essex the first of February . . . where it rayned wheat, for the space of VI or VII miles compass. Written by William Averell, student in divinitie. 1583. STC 982.5. BL

239 **B, E. E.** The great flood of 1607. E Ang NS 1, 1885/6, 107–08.

240 **Eastern Electricity Board.** East coast floods of 1953: the restoration of electricity supplies. 1954

241 Flood of 31 Jan–1 Feb 1953: collection of newspapers . . . and Weather, 8, no 3, March 1953

242 **Grove, A. T.** Sea flood on the coasts of Norfolk and Suffolk. Geography 38, 1953, 164–89

243 **Institution of Civil Engineers.** Conference on the North Sea Floods of 31 Jan–1 Feb 1953; a collection of papers presented at the Institution in Dec 1953. 1954. SCL/L

244 **Janson, H.** Britain's great flood disaster. 1953

245 **Lord Mayor of London's National Flood and Tempest Distress Fund.** The sea came in: the history of the . . . National Flood and Tempest Distress Fund. [1959]

246 **Steers, J. A.** The East coast floods, 31 Jan–1 Feb 1953. Geog Jour 119, 1953, 280–98

247 **Women's Voluntary Services.** Report on help given by East Suffolk W.V.S. in flood relief work after the storm and tempest of the night of 31 Jan–1 Feb 1953. 1953. SCL/L

248 **Roy, A. E.,** *and* **Stones, E. L. G.** The record of eclipses in the Bury Chronicle. BIHR, 43, 1970, 125–33

249 **Meldola, R.,** *and* **White, W.** Report on the East Anglian earthquake of 22 April 1884. Essex Field Club Special Memoirs, 1, 1885

WATER RESOURCES *See also* **3562, 5598, 5996–9, 6727**

250 **Child, S. T.** Water finding and the divining rod (so-called). Ipswich, [1902]

251 **Whitaker, W.,** *et al.* Water supply from underground sources with records of sinkings and borings. Mem Geol Survey. 1906

252 **East Suffolk County Council.** Report on water resources and services in the administrative county of East Suffolk. Ipswich, 1945

253 **Woodland, A. W.** Water supply from underground sources of the Cambridge–Ipswich district. Pts 1–9 Well catalogues. 1942–5. Pt 10 General discussion. 1946. Water supply: Mem Geol Survey. 1942–6

254 East Anglian hydrological survey. Hydrometric area nos 34 and 35. 1963

255 **East Suffolk County Council.** Underground water resources: report. Ipswich, 1963

256 **Cole, M. J.,** *et al.* Record of wells in the area of new series one-inch (geological) Eye sheet 190. Geol Survey and Museum. 1964

257 **Cole, M. J.,** *et al.* Record of wells in the area of new series one-inch (geological) Sudbury sheet 206. Geol Survey and Museum. 1965

258 **Davies, M. C.,** *et al.* Record of wells in the area of new series one-inch (geological) Ipswich sheet 207 and Woodbridge sheet 208. Geol. Survey and Museum. 1966

259 **Standon-Batt, L.,** *et al.* Records of wells in the area of new series one-inch (geological) Colchester 224 and Felixstowe 225 sheets. 1969. Institute of Geological Sciences

260 **East Suffolk and Norfolk River Authority.** Water Resources Act, 1963. First survey of water resources and demands. v 1, pts 1–6 and appendices. v 2. Tables, diagrams and maps. Norwich, 1971. SCL/L

REGIONS   *See also* 349, 351, 355, 364, 414, 750, 1087, 1093, 1101–02

261 **Miller, S. H.,** *and* **Skertchly, S. B. J.** Fenland past and present. 1878

262 **Miller, S. H.** Handbook to the Fens; being a brief account of all the towns, villages ... [1889]. SCL/L

263 **Dutt, W. A.** By sea-marge, marsh, and mere. [1899]. BL

264 **Harris, C. D.** Geography of the Ipswich–Orford area. Thesis, Oxford, Lincoln College, 1936

265 **Darby, H. C.** Draining of the Fens. 1940. 1956 2nd edn

266 **Darby, H. C.** Medieval Fenland. Cambridge, 1940

267 **Burrell, E. D. R.** Historical geography of the Sandlings of Suffolk, 1600 to 1850. M.Sc. thesis, London, 1960

268 **Whiting, N. E.** Changes in the agricultural geography of the Suffolk Sandlings since 1930. MA thesis, London, 1967

269 **Armstrong, P. H.** Heathlands of the Suffolk Sandlings in their setting: a systems approach to landscape study. Thesis, Cambridge College of Arts and Technology, 1970

COAST AND EROSION   *See also* 239–47, 925–6, 930, 4720–21, 7353

270 **Redstone, V. R.** Suffolk coast delineated in the thirteenth century. PSIA 18, 1922/4, 70–71

271 An ordinance for reviving and continuing an Act of Parliament for recovery of many thousand acres of ground in Norfolk and Suffolk surrounded by the rage of the sea. 2 Sept 1654. BL-T

272 **Baker, J.** Imperial guide, v 2. Guide to the picturesque scenery, subjects of antiquity ... throughout the coast of Suffolk to Yarmouth. [Also contains General description of Lowestoft and its vicinity]. 1802

273 Walcott, M. E. C. Guide to the coasts of Essex, Suffolk, & Norfolk descriptive of scenery, historical, legendary, & archaeological. [pp 1–120 of The East coast of England, with different title-page, preliminaries, and index]. 1860

274 Redman, J. B. The East coast between the Thames and the Wash estuaries. Proc. Institute of Civil Engineers 23, 1863/4. 1865

275 Varden, J. T. Round the East Anglian coast: tourist notes between the Orwell and the Wash. Norwich, 1894

276 Spiller, J. Recent coast erosion—Southwold and Covehithe. RBA 1895, 678–9

277 Spiller, J. Recent coast erosion—Dunwich to Covehithe. RBA 1905, 544–5

278 Notes relating to coast erosion in Essex and Suffolk. [From a British Assoc report]. EN 12, 1905/6, 221–4

279 Eastern Daily Press. Royal Commission on Coast Erosion tour from Lynn to Lowestoft, 1907. Norwich, 1907. SCL/L

280 First, Second, and Third reports of the Royal Commission on Coast Erosion. HC. 1907, 34; 1909, 14; 1911, 14. 3v. Suffolk, *passim*

281 Dutt, W. A. Norfolk and Suffolk coast. 1909

282 Cooper, E. R. Suffolk coast. INHSJ 1, 1925, 49–68

283 Steers, J. A. Suffolk coast: Orford Ness. Proc Geol Assoc 37, 1925, 300–325

284 Steers, J. A. Suffolk shore: Yarmouth to Aldeburgh. PSIA 19, 1925/7, 1–14

285 Steers, J. A. Suffolk coast: Orford Ness. PSIA 19, 1925/7, 117–40

286 Steers, J. A. Orford Ness: a study in coastal physiography. Geol Mag 64, 1927, 46–7

287 Cooper, E. R. Suffolk coast garland. 1928

288 Evans, H. M. Sandbanks of Yarmouth and Lowestoft. MM 15, 1929, 251–70

289 White, A. Tideways and byways in Essex and Suffolk. 1948

290 Steers, J. A. Notes on erosion along the coast of Suffolk. Geol Mag 88, 1951, 435–9

291 Eastern Daily Press. Sea defence in East Anglia. Supp Feb 19, 1959. SCL/L

292 Green, C. East Anglian coast-line levels since Roman times. Ant 35, 1961, 21–8

293 Orford Ness: a selection of maps mainly by John Norden. Presented to J. A. Steers. Cambridge, 1966

294 Coasts of East Anglia: report of the Regional Coastal Conference held at Ipswich on March 16, 1967. 1968

295 Greensmith, J. T., *et al*. Estuarine region of Suffolk and Essex. Colchester, 1973

296 Strugnell, K. W. Seagates to the Saxon shore. Lavenham, 1973

297 Palmer, T. Suffolk coast: birds, boats, beaches—and Britten. Clacton-on-Sea, 1976

298 Suffolk County Council. Suffolk heritage coast; draft plan. [Ipswich], 1976

PLACE-NAMES   *See also* 3714, 4504, 4783, 6321, 6815, 7019, 7066, 7090, 7826, 8094, 8104

299   Charnock, R. S. Fluvial etymology of Suffolk. E Ang 1, 1858/63, 235–6, 247–8, 265

300   Rye, W., *and* "Rusticus", *pseud*. Pronunciation of East Anglian Localities. E Ang 4, 1869/70, 23, 44

301   Gowers, E. Suffolk place-names, classified and compared. E Ang NS 3, 1889/90, 316–18, 352–4; NS 4, 1891/2, 43–6, 70–71

302   Candler, C. On the significance of some East Anglian field-names. NA 11, 1892, 143–78

303   Barber, H. N. Place-names of East Anglia: Suffolk. E Ang NS 6, 1895/6, 196–9, 237–40, 281–5

304   Skeat, W. W. Place-names of Suffolk. Cambridge, 1913

305   Zachrisson, R. E. River-names in Suffolk and North Devonshire. Studia Neophilogica 5, 1933, 70–76

306   Arnott, W. G. Place-names of the Deben valley parishes. Ipswich, 1946

307   Baron, M. C. Study of the place-names of East Suffolk. MA thesis, Sheffield, 1952

308   Williams, F. Place-names: Lowestoft area. LA&LHS 1969/70, 20–24

GEOGRAPHY   *See also* 1636

309   Fussell, G. E. Suffolk in 17th- and 18th-century geography. SR 1, 1957, 60–64

310   Morris, D. Geography of Suffolk for use in schools. 1872. BL

311   Lawson, W. Geography of the county of Suffolk. [1874]. BL

312   Sortwell, H. T. Geography of the county of Suffolk. [c.1880]. SRO/B

313   Dutt, W. A. Suffolk. 1909

314   Keyte, V. C., *Ed*. Field excursions in Eastern England. 1970. SCL/L

POPULATION   *See also* 3616, 4769, 5879, 7214

315   [Census of Great Britain, 1801]. 1801/02. 2v

316   [Census of Great Britain, 1811]. 1812. 2v

317   [Census of Great Britain, 1821]. 1822. 2v

318   [Census of Great Britain, 1831]. 1834. 3v

319   Census of Great Britain, 1841. 1841/4. 4v

320   Census of Great Britain, 1851. 1852/4. 5v

321   Census of England and Wales, 1861. 1862/3. 4v in 3

322   Census of England and Wales, 1871. 1871/3. 5v

323   Census of England and Wales, 1881. 1881/3. 3v

324   Census of England and Wales, 1891. 1891/3. 5v

325   Census of England and Wales, 1901. 1901/03. 54v

326 Census of England and Wales, 1911. 1912/17. 14v

327 Census of England and Wales, 1921. 1921/7. 62v

328 **General Register Office.** Census of England and Wales, 1931. 1931/50. 55v

329 **General Register Office.** Census 1951, England and Wales. 1951/9. 60v

330 **General Register Office.** Census of England and Wales, 1961. 1961/[8]. 92v

331 **General Register Office.** Sample census. 1966. England and Wales county report: East Suffolk, West Suffolk. 1967. 2v

332 **Office of Population Censuses and Surveys.** Census 1971: East Suffolk. 3pts. 1973

333 **Office of Population Censuses and Surveys.** Census 1971: West Suffolk. 3pts. 1973

334 **Office of Population Censuses and Surveys.** Census 1971: Report for the county of Suffolk as constituted on 1 April 1974. 1976

335 **Marshall, J.** Account of the population in each of 6,000 of the principal towns and parishes in England and Wales ... 1801, 1811, and 1821. 1831

336 Population [of Great Britain]. Comparative account of the population of Great Britain ... 1801, 1811, 1821, and 1831. 1831

337 **Minchin, G. S.** Table of population, 1801–1901. *In* VCH Suffolk 1, 1911, 683–95

338 List of the several parishes and hamlets in the county of Suffolk ... with the treasurers of each Division, the population of each parish as taken in 1821 ... Ipswich, [1822]. BL

339 **Partridge, C.** Rural population in Suffolk, 1844. N&Q 193, 1948, 75–7

340 Return of the following information in respect of each parish ... not within the limits of any city or parliamentary borough, for the year ended at Lady-Day 1856, viz: 1. Name; 2. Population; 3. Gross estimated rental of the property assessed to the Roor Rate; 4. Rateable value, etc. HC 1857/8, 50

341 Registrar-General's statistical review of England and Wales, 1921–

SETTLEMENT PATTERNS   *See also* **677, 1657, 4805–07, 6967**

342 **Dickinson, R. E.** Distribution and functions of the smaller urban settlements of East Anglia. Geography 17, 1932, 19–31. [Ph.D. thesis, London, 1933]

343 **Dickinson, R. E.** Town plans of East Anglia. Geography 19, 1934, 37–50

344 **Carter, G. G.** Forgotten ports of England. 1951. Suffolk, 1–91

345 **Corke, J.** Growth and change in the Suffolk village. 1967. SRO/B

346 **Dymond, D. P.** Suffolk landscape. *In* East Anglian studies. *Ed.* by L. M. Munby. Cambridge, 1968. 17–47

347 **Cranbrook, *Earl of.*** Structure of Suffolk villages. SR 4, 1971, 3–7

348 **Jobson, A.** Suffolk villages. 1971

349 **Scarfe, N.** Suffolk landscape. 1972

350 **Armstrong, P.** The changing landscape: the history and ecology of man's impact on the face of East Anglia. Lavenham, 1975

Guide Books and Descriptive Works

See also **451, 548, 550, 750,** *and* individual localities

351 Chorography of Suffolk [c.1602]. *Ed.* by D. N. J. MacCulloch. Ipswich, 1976. SRS 19

352 **Defoe, D.** Tour through the Eastern counties of England, 1722. 1888. With an introduction by R. A. N. Dixon; Ipswich, 1949

353 **Defoe, D.** Tour through the whole island of Great Britain. 1724–27, and var edns. Suffolk, v 1, 57–118

354 Description of the Diocese of Norwich: or, The present state of Norfolk and Suffolk. By a gentleman of the Inner Temple and a native of the diocese of Norwich [T. Gurdon]. 1735. NCL/N

355 **Kirby, J.** Suffolk traveller; or, A journey through Suffolk. Ipswich, 1735. 2nd edn. [*Ed.* by R. Canning] Woodbridge, 1764. 1765 and var edns

356 **Price, J.** Original diary of Rev. J. Price, Keeper of the Bodleian Library, during a tour through Norfolk and Suffolk in 1757. MS. NCL/N

357 **Gilpin, W.** Observations on several parts of the counties of Cambridge, Norfolk, Suffolk, and Essex ... made in the year 1769 ... [and] 1773. 1809

358 **Gough, R.** British topography. 1780. Suffolk v 2, 241–60

359 [**Beatniffe, R.**] The Norfolk tour or, Traveler's pocket companion: being a concise description of all the principal towns, noblemen's and gentlemen's seats, and other remarkable places ... 1772 and later edns. Suffolk, 97–9, 208–30

360 **Hodgkinson, J.** County of Suffolk surveyed [map publ 14 Aug 1783]. *Ed.* with introduction by D. P. Dymond. Ipswich, 1972. SRS 15

361 **Cooke, G. A.** Topographical and statistical description of the county of Suffolk ... [c.1805]. BL

362 **Shoberl, F.** Topographical and historical description of the county of Suffolk. [A re-issue of v 14, pt 1, of Brayley and Britton's Beauties of England and Wales]. 1813. 1820

363 Excursions in the county of Suffolk: comprising a brief historical and topographical delineation of every town and village ... 2v. 1818–19

364 Topographical and historical description of the county of Suffolk ... embellished with prints and a map of the county [By J. Kirby]. Woodbridge, 1829

365 **Tymms, S.** Family topographer: being a compendious account of the antient and present state of the counties of England. v 3. Norfolk circuit [Suffolk, 179–223]. 1833

366 **Page, A.** Supplement to the Suffolk traveller; or, Topographical and genealogical collections concerning that county. Ipswich, Large paper, 5v. 1843. IV. 1844. Grangerized copy by M. Reeve, 6v

367 **Page, A.** Topographical and genealogical history of the county of Suffolk. Compiled from authentic records. Ipswich, 1847. Grangerized copies. 5v. [c.1850]. 7v. [c.1853]

368 **Hunt, G.** Norfolk, Suffolk, Cambridge, and Essex: being an authentic list of all boroughs, towns, parishes, villages, and hamlets in the above counties. Norwich, [c.1865]. NCL/N

369 **White, W.** Eastern England, from the Thames to the Humber. 1865

370 **Taylor, A.** Papers in relation to the antient topography of the Eastern counties of Britain and the right means of interpreting the Roman itinerary. 1869

371 **Waugh, E.** A green nook of old England. Manchester, 1874. nl

372 **Murray, J.** Handbook for Essex, Suffolk, Norfolk, and Cambridgeshire. 1870. 2nd edn 1875. 3rd edn 1892

373 **Kelly, E. R.,** *Ed.* County topographies: Suffolk. 1875. BL

374 **Pearson's** gossipy guide to Great Yarmouth, Lowestoft, Cromer, Southwold, etc. [c.1880]

375 **Ritchie, J. E.** East Anglia: personal recollections and historical associations. 1883. BL. 2nd edn 1893

376 **Taylor, J. E.** Tourist's guide to the county of Suffolk ... 1887. BL. 2nd edn 1892

377 **Hissey, J. J.** Tour in a phaeton through the Eastern counties. 1889

378 **Dutt, W. A.** Highways, byways, and waterways of East Anglia: a collection of prose pastorals, etc. Lowestoft, 1899. BL

379 **Dutt, W. A.** Highways and byways in East Anglia. 1901. 1904. 1923

380 **Dutt, W. A.** Suffolk. 1904, and var edns

381 **Tompkins, H. W.** In Constable's country. 1906

382 **Vincent, J. E.** Through East Anglia in a motor car. 1907

383 **Hooper, J.** County guide to Suffolk, with notes on industries, antiquities, etc. Norwich, 1919

384 **Valleys** of the Stour and Colne: official guide to the Constable country. Croydon, [c.1920]

385 **Clarke, W. G.** Norfolk and Suffolk. 1921

386 **Morley, F. V.** Travels in East Anglia. 1923

387 **Home, G. C.** Through East Anglia. 1925

388 **Cooper, A. H.** Suffolk water-colours. 1926

389 **Maxwell. D.** Unknown Suffolk. 1926

390 **Meyrick, F. J.** Round about Norfolk and Suffolk. Norwich, 1926

391 **Thornton, G. A.** Suffolk. Cambridge, 1928. BL

392 **Meredith, H.** East Anglia, etc. [1929]. BL

393 **James, M. R.** Suffolk and Norfolk. A perambulation of the two counties with notices of their history and their ancient buildings. 1930

394 Baker, B. G. Blithe waters: sheaves out of Suffolk. 1931

395 Cooper, E. R. Mardles from Suffolk: tales of the South folk. 1932. SCL/L

396 Cornish, H. Constable country, a hundred years after John Constable, R.A. v 1. only publ. 1932

397 Reeves, B. Rambles in Suffolk. [1934]. SCL/L

398 Wellbanks, O. R. Suffolk, my county, with something of Fleet Street, being the random recollections of an "emigrant". 1934

399 Constable, W. G. Constable country. Geographical Mag. 8, 1937, 373-84

400 Tennyson, C. J. Suffolk scene: a book of description and adventure. 1939. Rp 1973

401 Wallace, D. East Anglia. A survey of England's eastern counties, etc. 1939. 1942

402 Mee, A. Suffolk. 1941. 1949

403 Arbib, R. S. Here we are together: the notebook of an American soldier in Britain. 1946

404 Palmer, A., *Ed.* Recording Britain. 4v. Oxford, 1947. Suffolk v 2, 49-89

405 Appleby, J. T. Suffolk summer. Ipswich, 1948. 1960

406 Cook, O. Suffolk. 1948

407 Jobson, A. North-east Suffolk. Wrotham, [1948]

408 Rickword, G. O. Constable country: a guide to the vale of Dedham. Colchester, 1948 and later edns. nl

409 Messent, C. J. W. Suffolk and Cambridgeshire. Harmondsworth, 1949

410 Tompkins, H. W. Companion into Suffolk. 1949

411 Addison, W. W. Suffolk. 1950

412 County of Suffolk: an historical, descriptive, and industrial survey of the county of Suffolk. Gloucester, [1951] and later edns

413 Dickinson, P. G. M. Suffolk: based on the original guide by W. A. Dutt. 1957

414 Scarfe, N. Suffolk: a Shell guide. 1960. 2nd edn 1966. 3rd edn 1976

415 East Anglian Daily Times. Royal visit souvenir: a pictorial record of Her Majesty the Queen's visit to Suffolk July 21, 1961. Ipswich, 1961

416 Forrest, A. J. Under three crowns. Ipswich, 1961

417 Glorious Suffolk. Norwich, 1962

418 Miller, A. G. There's life in the old land yet. Ipswich, 1962

419 Rotheroe, J. [W.] Discovering East Suffolk; with contributions by W. G. Arnott, R. A. Campbell. Tring, [1962 and later edns]

420 Brooke, J., *and* E. Suffolk prospect. 1963

421 Boumphrey, G. M., *Ed.* Suffolk. [1964]

422 Burn, R., *et al.* The two counties of Suffolk: a pictorial study by R. Burn and other East Anglian photographers. Introduction by J. Venmore-Rowland. Lavenham, 1967

423 Court, A. N. Suffolk in colour. [1967]

424 Jobson, A. In Suffolk borders. 1967

425 **Rotheroe, J.[W.]** Discovering West Suffolk: a guide to places of interest. Tring, 1967
426 **Strutt, C.** Setting for a Suffolk festival: a pictorial study. Lavenham, 1968
427 **Jennett, S.**, *Ed.* Suffolk and Essex. [1970]
428 **Pawsey, J. T.** Constable country. Ipswich, [1970]
429 **Rolfe, W. E.** East Anglia, including Cambridge. 1970
430 **Seymour, J.** Companion guide to East Anglia. 1970
431 **Burke, J.** Suffolk. 1971
432 **Jobson, A.** Portrait of Suffolk. 1973
433 **Burke, J.** Suffolk in photographs. 1976
434 **Fincham, P.** The Suffolk we live in. Norwich, 1976
435 **Jennings, C.** John Constable, in Constable country. East Bergholt, 1976
436 **Smart, A.,** *and* **Brook, A.** Constable and his country. 1976
437 **Salmon, J.** Suffolk-Essex border. Ipswich, 1977

VIEWS *See also* 433

438 Four views of Orwell Park, Woolverstone Park, and Broke Hall in the county of Suffolk, and of Harwich, Essex [Ipswich], [1834?]. BL
439 Suffolk, illustrated in a series of nearly one hundred views. 1834. nl
440 **Fitch, W. S.** Pictorial illustrations of the county of Suffolk. 31v. [c.1850]. MS
441 West Suffolk in retrospect: collotype reproductions of old prints. Bury St. Edmunds, 1974

General and Political History

BIBLIOGRAPHIES AND HISTORICAL AIDS

442 **Ford, J.** Index to Suffolk MSS: Harleian MSS and Cottonian MSS deposited at the British Museum. [c.1840]. MS

443 **Ford, J.** Notitia Suffolciencis; or, A bibliographical list of the printed works, engraved views, portraits, maps, ... relating to and illustrative of the history, topography, antiquities, biography, ... of the county of Suffolk, with biographical notices of its historians, illustrators, and collectors. 1842. MS

444 **Fitch, W. S.** Catalogue of Suffolk manorial registers, royal grants and deeds ... and other documents collected for the purpose of illustrating a history of the county, in the possession of W.S.F. Pt 1. [No more published]. Gt. Yarmouth, 1843. 50 copies. *See also* **502–3, 2864**

445 Catalogue of the books in the library of the Bury St. Edmunds Athenaeum and Suffolk Institute of Archaeology and Natural History ... Bury St. Edmunds, [c.1856]. SRO/B

446 **Levien, E.** MS. collections relating to Suffolk in the British Museum. JBAA 21, 1865, 5–21

447 **Rix, S. W.** MS. collections relating to the county of Suffolk [Glemsford, Loes Hundred, Brampton]. JBAA 21, 1865, 144–58

448 **Golding, C.** Suffolk scarce tracts, 1595 to 1684 [A catalogue of tracts preserved in the library of C. Golding. Half-title reads "Suffolk early tracts"] Norwich, 1873

449 Calendar of charters and rolls preserved in the Bodleian Library. *Ed.* by W. H. Turner. Oxford, 1878. Suffolk 410–547, 665–6. O

450 **Everitt, A. T.,** *and* **Perceval, C. S.** Documents relating to Suffolk and Norfolk. PSA 2nd Ser 10, 1883/5, 97–105

451 **Sanderson, R. P.** Topography of Suffolk: references to MSS in the British Museum. E Ang NS 4, 1891/2, 183–5, 262–6; NS 5, 1893/4, 361

452 **Liebermann, F.** Ueber ostenglischen Geschichtsquellen des 12–14. Jahrhunderts ... Neues Archiv 18, 1892, 225–67

453 Catalogue of books, MSS etc, in the library of the Suffolk Institute of Archaeology. PSIA 10, 1898/1900, 97–124

454 Descriptive catalogue of ancient deeds in the Public Record Office: Suffolk notices. PSIA 10, 1898/1900, 251–344, 399–413

455 **Glyde, J.** Account of the Davy and Jermyn MSS in the British Museum. [c.1900]. MS

456 **Copinger, W. A.** Davy's Suffolk collections: BL Additional MS. 19172. E Ang NS 8, 1899/1900, 373–6; NS 9, 1901/02, 9–12, 21–3, 56–8, 70–72, 88–9

457 Suckling MSS. E Ang NS 8, 1899/1900, 334, 352; NS 9, 1901/02, 16

458 **Rivett-Carnac, J. H.** Suffolk MS. collections. E Ang NS 9, 1901/02, 12–14

459 **Copinger, W. A.,** *Ed.* County of Suffolk: its history disclosed by existing records and other documents, being materials for the history of Suffolk. 5v. 1904–05

460 **[Copinger, W. A.].** Index nominum et locorum, being an index of names of persons and places mentioned in Copinger's County of Suffolk ... Compiled by H. B. Copinger. Manchester, 1907

461 **Livett, R.** Suffolk MSS. E Ang NS 12, 1907/08, 161–2

462 **Partridge, C.** Some Suffolk unprinted material: suggestions. E Ang NS 13, 1909/10, 160

463 **Wayman, H. W. B.** Coleman's Suffolk deeds. E Ang NS 13, 1909/10, 328–9

464 Suffolk county records. PSIA 15, 1913/15, 144–51

465 Descriptive catalogue of the charters, rolls, deeds, pedigrees, pamphlets, newspapers, monumental inscriptions, maps, and miscellaneous papers forming the Jackson Collection at the Sheffield Public Libraries. Compiled by T. W. Hall and A. H. Thomas Sheffield, 1914. Suffolk, 206–46

466 **[De Castre, W.]** Handlist of some MS. indexes to Norfolk and Suffolk works. Great Yarmouth, [1920]

467 **Bloom, J. H.** Calendar of broadsides and single sheets relating to the county of Suffolk. 1921

468 **Bloom, J. H.** Early Suffolk tracts, pamphlets, and printed sheets: a bibliography, v 1. 1473–1650. [Re-issued as v 1 of English tracts ... early period, 1473–1650. 2v 1922–3]. 1921. 50 copies

469 **McColvin, L. R.,** *and* **Harrison, W. E.** Bibliography, Suffolk: A list of books on Suffolk. Ipswich, 1927. 2nd edn 1929

470 **Farrer, E.** List of deeds recently acquired by the [Suffolk] Institute [of Archaeology]. PSIA 20, 1928/30, 73–9

471 **Redstone, L. J.** Suffolk MS. books [chiefly on a MS. Canterbury Tales in the British Library, Harl. MS. 7335]. PSIA 20, 1928/30, 80–92

472 Catalogue of books in the library [of the Suffolk Institute of Archaeology] at the Athenaeum, Bury St. Edmunds. Bury St. Edmunds, 1933

473 **Redstone, L. J.** Inventory of the records deposited by the Suffolk Institute of Archaeology at the Ipswich Borough Library. PSIA 23, 1937/9, 187–201

474 **East Suffolk County Library.** Suffolk scene in books and maps [A catalogue of an exhibition: Aldeburgh Festival of Music and the Arts]. [Ipswich], 1951

475 **Fearn, H.** List of unpublished writings [theses] on Suffolk history. PSIA 26, 1952/4, 61–2

476 **Library Association.** Suffolk regional list. Entries extracted from the Subject Index to Periodicals, continued as the British Humanities Index. 1954–66 [no more published]. [Typescript]

477 Fussell, G. E. Old directories as source books. SR1, 1958, 184–7

478 **Library Association.** Eastern Branch. East Anglian bibliography: a checklist of publications not in the British National Bibliography. No 1, July 1960–. Quarterly. Norwich. [Typescript]

479 **Dow, L.** List of unpublished writings [theses] on Suffolk history. PSIA 31, 1967/9, 206–07

480 East Anglian Miscellany: an alphabetical catalogue by authors of over 1,000 Suffolk books listed in the East Anglian Miscellany between April 1918 and December 1958 ... Compiled by *Sir* G. Hambling. Ipswich, 1968. [Typescript]

481 Catalogue of books in the library [of the Suffolk Institute of Archaeology] at Moyse's Hall Museum, Bury St. Edmunds. Bury St. Edmunds, 1968. [Typescript]. *See also* **4224–9**

482 **Charman, D.** Historical Manuscripts Commission centenary, 1869–1969. Historical records of Suffolk towns: Ipswich, Eye, Aldeburgh, Orford, Dunwich. Ipswich Information: Supplement. May–June, 1969. Ipswich, 1969

483 **Suffolk Local History Council.** Suffolk local history: a short bibliography. Ipswich, 1970

484 **University of East Anglia.** Centre of East Anglian Studies. East Anglian history and archaeology: work in progress in summer, 1970–. Norwich, 1970–

485 **University of East Anglia.** Centre of East Anglian Studies. History collections in Norfolk and Suffolk libraries: a handbook. Norwich, 1971

486 **University of East Anglia.** Centre of East Anglian Studies. Periodicals and sets relating to British history in Norfolk and Suffolk libraries: a finding-list. Norwich, 1971

487 **University of East Anglia.** Centre of East Anglian Studies. East Anglian history: theses completed. Norwich, 1972

488 **Blatchly, J.** [M.], *Ed.* Topographers of Suffolk. Ipswich, 1976. [Typescript]

COLLECTIONS OF MANUSCRIPTS AND PAMPHLETS

489 **Gillingwater, E.** Topographical history of the county of Suffolk. To which is added a general account of the civil, ecclesiastical, and natural history of the said county. 13v. 1790/1813. MS. nl

490 **Fitch, W. S.** Collection of manuscripts relating to the history of the Hundreds of Suffolk. 30v. [c.1850]. MSS

491 **Glyde, J.** Materials for a history of Suffolk [Illustrations, cuttings, and MSS "gathered over the years"]. 9v. [c.1900]

492 **Raven, J. J.** Pamphlets. [Bound in 27v. Mainly 18th- and 19th-century sermons, theological tracts, topographical material on Suffolk and Cambridgeshire, and political pamphlets]. SRO/B

493 Redstone Collection. [30 boxes of MS. notes, transcripts, etc., mainly relating to Suffolk, collected by V. B. *and* L. J. Redstone]

494 **Wodderspoon, J.** MSS of J. Wodderspoon. [c.1855]. MS

495 Woolnough Collection. Cuttings, MSS, photographs, and drawings mainly of Suffolk and Ipswich. 191 v.

496 Collection of miscellaneous papers, political, topographical, parochial, etc., relating to the county of Suffolk [1756–1825]. BL

497 Collections for Suffolk. 22v. c.1825–30. MSS

498 Collection of the proposals for publishing various engravings and books relating to Suffolk; together with advertisements of agricultural machines [1770?–1845?]. BL

499 Prospectuses, advertisements, and other notices relating to ... Suffolk [1835, etc.] BL

SALE CATALOGUES OF PRIVATE LIBRARIES

500 Catalogue of the valuable library, containing upwards of 2,000 books, ... engravings, and drawings made and designed for the illustration of a county history, by the late Henry Jermyn ... June 1821. Halesworth, [1821]. BL. *See also* **3079–82**

501 Catalogue of books on sale ... by John Loder, Woodbridge. Woodbridge, [1825]. [1847]. [1848]. BL

502 Printed books and manuscripts illustrative of the history of the county of Suffolk [belonging to W. S. Fitch]. Puttick and Simpson, London, 1855. Ross, Ipswich, 1859. *See also* **2864**

503 Remaining library of the late W. S. Fitch ... works relating to Suffolk ... with his manuscript collections illustrative of the county ... Sotheby and Wilkinson, London, 1859. *See also* **2864**

504 Rare books, manuscripts, and illustrative works relating to the county of Suffolk [belonging to W. P. Hunt]. Ipswich, 1873. Sotheby, Wilkinson, and Hodge, London, 1879

505 Library [belonging to S. W. Rix]. Spelman, Beccles, 1894. BL

506 Library [belonging to J. Glyde]. Garrod, Turner, Ipswich, 1900

507 Suffolk collection of printed books, MSS, etc., [belonging to W. E. Layton], illustrative of the literature, art, topography, and family history of the county. Tregaskis, London, 1907. SRO/B

SOCIETIES AND PERIODICALS *See also* **4902**

508 **Suffolk Archaeological Association.** Original papers. Pt 1, Oct 1846, Pt 2, June 1847, Pt 3, Nov 1848. Ipswich

509 **Suffolk Archaeological Association.** List of members ... [Ipswich?], [1847?] BL

510 **Bury and West Suffolk Archaeological Institute** Proceedings, v 1. 1848/53. *Cont. as* **Suffolk Institute of Archaeology, Statistics, and Natural History** Proceedings, v 2. 1854/9, v 3. 1860–3. *Cont. as* **Suffolk Institute of Archaeology and Natural History** Proceedings, v 4. 1864/74–. v 1. Bury St. Edmunds. v 2 & 3. Lowestoft. v 4 & 5. Bury St.

Edmunds. v 6 onwards. Ipswich. [**Suffolk Institute of Archaeology and History** since 1976]

511 **Suffolk Institute of Archaeology and Natural History.** Quarterly Journal, Jan 1869 and June 1869 [no more issued]. Bury St. Edmunds, 1869

512 **Dow, L.** Short history of the Suffolk Institute, with an index to articles v 1–24, list and index of excursions and meetings 1848–1948, tables of contents of the Quarterly Journal, Jan and June 1869, and the Suffolk Archaeological Association Original Papers, 1846–8, 3pts. PSIA 24, 1946/48, 129–62

513 East Anglian: or notes and queries on subjects connected with the counties of Suffolk, Cambridge, Essex, and Norfolk. v 1–4. *Ed.* by S. Tymms. Lowestoft, 1858–70. New Series, *ed.* by C. H. E. White. 13v. Ipswich, 1885–1910

514 Eastern Counties Collectanea, being notes and queries on subjects relating to the counties of Norfolk, Suffolk, Essex, and Cambridge. *Ed.* by J. L'Estrange. v 1. 1872–73. Norwich. [Connecting link between the 1st and 2nd Series of East Anglian Notes and Queries]

515 **Suffolk Local History Council.** Bulletin no 1, Sept 1953–No 8, April 1956. *Cont. as* Suffolk Review 1 (1), July 1956–. Ipswich

516 **Suffolk Local History Council.** Local history record (notifications), 1954–. Ipswich

517 **Suffolk Local History Council.** West Suffolk local history recording scheme. Reports 1954–65. Bury St. Edmunds. [Typescript]. SRO/B

518 **Suffolk Records Society.** Publications, v 1, 1958–. Ipswich

519 **Suffolk Local History Council.** Reports of annual general meetings, 1961–. Ipswich. [Typescript]

520 **Lowestoft Archaeological and Local History Society.** News Sheet, May 1966–April 1969. Monthly Review, v 1, no 1, May 1969–. Annual report, 1966/7–.

521 **Suffolk Local History Council.** Newsletter 1969–. Ipswich

522 **Suffolk Local History Council.** Local history recording scheme. Ipswich, 1970

523 **Suffolk Institute of Archaeology (and History,** since 1976]. Newsletter. Bi-annually from Autumn 1975. [Typescript]. Ipswich

HISTORY, GENERAL

524 **Cox, T.,** *and* **Hall, A.** Magna Britannia et Hibernia, antiqua et nova; or, A new survey of Great Britain. 1720–31. 6v. Suffolk, v 5, 171–344

525 **Ipswich Journal.** Suffolk notes from 1729, reprinted from the Ipswich Journal [covers period 1729–1864]. Ipswich, 1883–4

526 **Gentleman's Magazine Library.** Topographical history of Staffordshire and Suffolk: a classified collection of the chief contents of "The Gentleman's Magazine" from 1731–1868. *Ed.* by G. L. Gomme. 1899. Suffolk, 169–295

527 **Glyde, J.** Chronological digest of some of the contents of the "Ipswich Journal" 1800–1810, and the "Suffolk Chronicle" 1810–1847. [c.1900]

528 **Harral, T.**, *and* **Betham, W.** Part 1 of the History of Suffolk. [108 pages only, then discontinued. Ipswich, 1814]. Also appended to "The East Anglian, a magazine of literary and miscellaneous information". *See also* **80**

529 **Partridge, C.**, *and* **Clemence, J. L.** "The East Anglian" of 1814, and Harral and Betham's "History of Suffolk". E Ang NS 12, 1907/08, 228, 260

530 **Pinnock, W.** History and topography of Suffolk. 1818. SCL/L

531 **Wodderspoon, J.** Historic sites and other remarkable and interesting places, in the county of Suffolk. Ipswich, 1839. 2nd edn 1841

532 **Suckling, A. I.** [Proposal for printing his Memorials of the antiquities of the county of Suffolk]. Beccles, 1845. O

533 **Suckling, A. I.** History and antiquities of the county of Suffolk, with genealogical and architectural notices of its several towns and villages. v 1, 1846. Wangford, Mutford, Lothingland Hundreds. v 2. 1848. Lothingland [cont.], Blything Hundreds. Grangerized copy. 6v

534 An index to the history and antiquities of the county of Suffolk by the Reverend Alfred Suckling. Ipswich, 1952. 100 copies

535 **Clarke, J.** Suffolk antiquary: containing a brief sketch of the sites of ancient castles, abbeys . . . also, notices of ancient coins, and other antiquities found in the county . . . [in verse]. Woodbridge, 1849

536 **Chester, G. J.** Antiquities of the valleys of the Waveney and Yare. NA 4, 1855, 310–16

537 **Nall. J. G.** Great Yarmouth and Lowestoft . . . chapters on the archaeology, natural history, etc., of the district, a history . . . of the East Coast herring-fishery, and an etymological and comparative glossary of the dialect of East Anglia. 1866

538 **Hervey,** *Lord* **A. C.** Plea for a history of Suffolk. Arch J 26, 1869, 197–208

539 **Bayne, A. D.** Royal illustrated history of Eastern England . . . including a survey of the Eastern counties . . . description of antiquities, etc. 2v. Great Yarmouth, [1872–3]

540 **Boswell, G. J.** Eastern counties chronology; or, Book of dates. Ipswich, 1877. Var edns incl 1891, 1922, and 1931 *Ed.* by V. C. Boswell

541 **Groome, F. H.**, *Ed.* Suffolk notes and queries, 1877–78, from Ipswich Journal [Includes list of Suffolk authors to 1850]. Ipswich

542 **"Gippeswyche,"** *pseud.* [i.e. **C. Golding**] Old Suffolk: facts, scraps, notes, and traditions of local history. From Suffolk Chronicle 1882–4. 22pts. Ipswich

543 **Watling, H.** Antiquities of Suffolk. EADT 1886–7

544 **Aldred, H. W.**, *Ed.* New history of Suffolk, entitled "The Suffolk records". 11 monthly parts, Jan–Dec 1888 [Pt 8–9 Aug–Sept is a double number]. 1888

545 **Raven, J. J.** History of Suffolk. 1895

546 **Copinger, W. A.** Manors of Suffolk: notes on their history and devolution. 7v. 1905–11. [Typescript index. 1965. NCL/N]. *See also* **366–7**

547 **Walters, [J.] C.**, *Ed.* Bygone Suffolk: its history, romance, legend, folklore, etc. [1900]

548 **Barker, H. R.** West Suffolk, illustrated . . . Bury St. Edmunds, 1907

549 Victoria History of the County of Suffolk. *Ed.* by W. Page. v 1, 1911; v 2, 1907. 2v. Rp 1975

550 **Barker, H. R.** East Suffolk illustrated [assisted by V. B. Redstone ... the account of Ipswich written by F. Woolnough]. Bury St. Edmunds, 1908–09

551 **Redstone, V. B.,** *Ed.* Memorials of old Suffolk. 1908

552 **Round, J. H.** Essex and Suffolk border. PSIA 18, 1922/4, 244–6

553 **Morley, C.** Suffolk villages [Parish histories from the time of Domesday, with pronunciation of village names]. [c.1930]. [Typescript]

554 **Redstone, L. J.** Suffolk. 1930

555 **Redstone, L. J.** Our East Anglian heritage. 1939. 2nd edn 1951

556 **Munby, L. M.,** *Ed.* East Anglian studies: essays by J. C. Barringer *et al.* Cambridge, 1968

557 **Harris, J. R.** East Anglia and America. Ipswich, 1973

558 **Bates, M.** East Anglia. Reading, 1974. Regional Military Histories

559 **Wilson, D.** Short history of Suffolk. 1977

ARCHAEOLOGY, GENERAL

560 **Tymms, S.** Contributions to Suffolk archaeology: papers read at meetings of the Suffolk Institute of Archaeology ... Bury St. Edmunds. 1861. SRO/B

561 Proceedings of the Annual Meeting of the Royal Archaeological Institution held at Ipswich, 25 July–1 Aug 1899. Arch J 56, 1899, 388–406

562 **Wall, J. C.** Ancient earthworks. *In* VCH Suffolk, 1, 1911, 583–631

563 Suffolk "finds". PSIA includes lists for the years 1923, 18, 164–6; 1924, 18, 253; 1927, 19, 364; 1928, 20, 112; 1933, 21, 263; 1947, 24, 257

564 Archaeology in Suffolk. PSIA include reports for the years 1954/5, 27, 41–6; 1956, 27, 112–19; 1957, 27, 178–85; 1958, 28, 90–96; 1959, 28, 161–7; 1960, 28, 290–96; 1961, 29, 91–102; 1963, 29, 348–54; 1964, 30, 116–23; 1965, 30, 188–97; 1966, 30, 275–83; 1967, 31, 72–83; 1968, 31, 188–201; 1969, 31, 318–30; 1970, 32, 92–107; 1971, 32, 205–14; 1972, 32, 282–91; 1973, 33, 94–102; 1974, 33, 212–24; 1975, 33, 322–8

565 **British Archaeological Association.** Programme of 85th annual congress, June 25–30, 1928, at Ipswich. 1928. nl

566 **Fox,** *Sir* **C.** Archaeology of the Cambridgeshire region [includes N.W. Suffolk]. 1948

567 **Maynard, G.** Recent archaeological field-work in Suffolk. PSIA 25, 1949/51, 205–16

568 **Norwich Castle Museum.** Archaeological discovery in East Anglia, 1851–1951. Catalogue of Exhibition ... 9 June–1 July 1951. Norwich

569 Ancient monuments in Suffolk (scheduled under the Acts of 1913 and 1931). PSIA 26, 1953/4, 233–4

570 **Smedley, N.** Recent archaeological work in Suffolk. LA&LHS 1966/7, 29–38

571 **Dow, L.** List of ancient monuments in Suffolk (scheduled since 1954). PSIA 31, 1967/9, 208–09

572 **Clarke, H.** East Anglia. 1971
573 **Scole Committee.** Report [on] the problems and future of East Anglian archaeology. 1973. SRO/B
574 **Suffolk County Council.** Planning Committee. East Anglian archaeology. Report nos 1 & 3. Suffolk. Ipswich, 1975. 1977. [In progress, alternate years]

PREHISTORY AND HISTORY, BY PERIOD
See also individual localities, *below*

EARLY MAN
575 **Prehistoric Society of East Anglia, 1908–34. Prehistoric Society, 1935–.** Proceedings
576 **Greenwell,** *Canon, et al.* Examination of Suffolk tumuli [Seven Hills, Ampton; Barton Hill] QJSIA 1, 1869, 19–21, 40–42
577 **Moir, J. R.** A defence of the 'humanity' of the pre-river valley implements of the Ipswich district. PPSEA 1, 1908/14, 368–74
578 **Holden, J. S.** Existence of an early Palaeolithic bed beneath the glacial boulder clays in South West Suffolk. PSIA 14, 1910/12, 6–8; Man 10, 1910, 43–64
579 **Sturge, W. A.,** *et al.* Early man. *In* VCH Suffolk 1, 1911, 235–77
580 **Moir, J. R.,** *and* **Keith, A.** Account of the discovery and characters of a human skeleton found beneath a stratum of chalky boulder clay near Ipswich. JRAI 42, 1912, 345–79
581 **Dixon, S. E.** Some earthworks and standing stones in East Anglia in relation to a pre-historic solar cultus. PPSEA 2, 1914/18, 171–3
582 **Clarke, W. G.** Two North-West Suffolk floors [Eriswell and Barnham Common]. PPS 2, 1915, 39–41
583 **Moir, J. R.** Human and animal bones, flint implements, etc., discovered in two ancient occupation levels in a small valley near Ipswich. JRAI 47, 1917, 367–412
584 **Moir, J. R.** A series of ancient floors in a small valley near Ipswich. PPSEA 3, 1918/22, 559–79
585 **Morley, C.** Suffolk 'Dane stones' [Halesworth and Hunston]. PSIA 17, 1919/21, 93–6
586 **Moir, J. R.** Geological age of the Red Crag and of its underlying detritus bed. PPSEA 4, 1922/4, 235–6
587 **Moir, J. R.** Man and the ice age. Man 24, 1924, 17–20
588 **Dutt, W. A.** Ancient mark-stones of East Anglia: their origin and folklore. Lowestoft, 1926. BL
589 **Moir, J. R.** Antiquity of man in East Anglia. Cambridge, 1927
590 **Fox, C.** Note and sketch-map of the dykes of Norfolk and Suffolk. Ant 3, 1929, 145
591 **Moir, J. R.** Ancient man in the Gipping-Orwell valley. PPSEA 6, 1929/32, 182–221
592 **Hudson, H.** Ancient sun alignments. PSIA 21, 1932–3, 120–38

593   **Clarke, R. R.** Prehistoric and Roman Suffolk. Arch Jour 108, 1951, 129–31

594   **Clarke, R. R.** East Anglia. 1960. Rp 1971

595   **Collings, H. D.** Prehistoric Easton Bavents ... LA&LHS 1969/70, 57–9

596   **Dutt, W. A.** Waveney valley in the Stone Age, Lowestoft, 1905

597   **Dutt, W. A.** New Palaeolithic site in the Waveney valley. Man 8, 1908, 41–2, 168–9

598   **Layard, N. F.** Ancient land surface in the river terrace at Ipswich and palaeoliths from a gravel pit in the valley of the Lark. Man 8, 1908, 171–2

599   **Moir, J. R.** Early Mousterian floor discovered at Ipswich. Man 18, 1918, 98–100

600   **Moir, J. R.** Pre-Palaeolithic man, Ipswich, [1919]

601   **Moir, J. R.** Upper Palaeolithic man in East Anglia. PPSEA 5, 1925/8, 232–47

602   Discoveries in Suffolk: Stone Age. JBAA NS 31, 1926, 246–7

603   **Moir, J. R.** Culture of Pliocene man [in Suffolk]. PPSEA 7, 1932/4, 1–17

604   **Paterson, T. T.,** *and* **Fagg, B. E. B.** Studies in the Palaeolithic succession in England: The Upper Breckland Acheul (Elveden, Hoxne, High Lodge, Warren Hill). PPS NS 6, 1940, 1–29

605   **Hancox, E. R. H.** Neolithic Suffolk. PSIA 11, 1901/03, 200–04, 335–6

606   **Moir, J. R.** Discovery of some bones, etc., of neolithic and later date in the Ipswich district. Man 16, 1916, 97–102

607   **Caton, L. L. F.** Spade-work in North-West Suffolk [Bronze Age barrow; Romano-British midden at Fakenham Magna]. PPS 2, 1914/18, 35–8

608   **Clarke, R. R.** Late Bronze and Early Iron Ages in Norfolk and Suffolk. ANL 2, 1948, 16–17

609   **Perkins, J. B. W.** Iron Age sites in Suffolk. Ant J 17, 1937, 195–7

610   **Clarke, R. R.** Iron Age in Norfolk and Suffolk. Arch J 96, 1939, 1–113, 223–5

611   **Cunliffe, B. W.** Early pre-Roman Iron Age communities in Eastern England. Ant J 48, 1968, 175–91

ARTEFACTS   *See also* Coins and tokens,
       and individual localities, *below*, especially Brandon

612   **Whincopp, W.** Important discoveries which have led to the elucidation of the deposit of flint implements in France and England [mainly in Suffolk Crag]. Woodbridge, 1861. 1863. 1865

613   **Brigg, H.** Flint implements in the gravel of the Little Ouse valley at Thetford and elsewhere [Brandon, Santon]. RBA 1867, 50–51

614   Exhibition of objects obtained from the beds of drift or tertiary gravel in various countries, including 42 specimens from the valley of the Little Ouse, Norfolk and Suffolk, and 5 from the valley of the Lark, Suffolk. PSA 2nd Ser 5, 1870/73, 165–70

615   **Charlesworth, E.** Objects in the Red Crag formation of Suffolk. JRAI 2, 1873, 91–4

616   **Hancox, E. R. H.** Some Suffolk arrowheads. Antiquary 43, 1907, 88–91

617 Moir, J. R. Flint implements of the Sub-Crag man [Ipswich]. PPSEA 1, 1908/14, 17–24, 24–43

618 Moir, J. R. Flint implements of man from the middle glacial gravel and the chalky boulder clay of Suffolk. PPSEA 1, 1908/14, 307–19; Man 13, 1913, 36–7

619 Moir, J. R. Further discoveries of flint implements of man beneath the base of the Red Crag of Suffolk. PPSEA 2, 1914/18, 12–31; 3, 1918/22, 389–433

620 Moir, J. R. Series of mineralized bone implements of a premature type from below the base of the red coralline crags of Suffolk. PPSEA 2, 1914/18, 116–31

621 Layard, N. F. Coast finds by Major Moore at Felixstowe Ferry. PPSEA 2, 1914/18, 132–4

622 Moir, J. R. Ancient flint implements of Suffolk. PSIA 16, 1916/18, 99–134

623 Haward, F. N. Origin of the Rostro-Carinate implements and other chipped flints from the basement beds of East Anglia. PPSEA 3, 1918/22, 118–49

624 Sollas, W. J. A flaked flint from the Red Crag [near Ipswich]. PPSEA 3, 1918/22, 261–7

625 Moir, J. R. Humanly-fashioned flints, etc., in the "Middle Glacial" gravel at Ipswich. JRAI 49, 1919, 74–93

626 Moir, J. R., *and* Howorth, H. H. Piece of carved chalk from Suffolk. Man 19, 1919, 17–18, 68–70, 95–6, 183–6

627 Moir, J. R. Flint implements of man in the glacial chalky boulder clay of Suffolk. JRAI 50, 1920, 135–52

628 Moir, J. R. Four Suffolk flint implements. Ant J 2, 1922, 114–17

629 Moir, J. R. Further flint implements of the Pliocene age discovered in Suffolk [Foxhall and Bramford]. PPSEA 4, 1922/4, 46–56

630 Moir, J. R., *and* Burchell, J. P. T. Diminutive flint implements of Pliocene and Pleistocene Age. Ant J 15, 1935, 119–29

631 Moir, J. R. Series of Solutré blades from Suffolk and Cambridgeshire. PPSEA 4, 1922/4, 71–81

632 Moir, J. R. Solutrean flint implements found in Suffolk. Man 25, 1925, 23

633 Clark, J. G. D. Beaker pottery of Ipswich Museum. PPSEA 6, 1929/32, 356–61

634 Moir, J. R. Further Solutré implements from Suffolk. Ant J 12, 1932, 257–61

635 Moir, J. R. Hand-axes from glacial beds at Ipswich. PPSEA 7, 1932/4, 178–84

636 Moir, J. R. The age of the pre-crag flint implements. Man 35, 1935, 45; JRAI 65, 1935, 343–74

637 Smith, W. G., *and* Prigg, H. Eoliths in Suffolk. Man 8, 1908, 49–50

638 Dutt, W. A. Paleolithic implements in East Suffolk. Antiquary 44, 1908, 60–64

639 Sturge, W. A. Implements of the late paleolithic 'cave' periods in East Anglia. PPSEA 1, 1908/14, 210–32

640 Dutt, W. A. East Suffolk neoliths. PSIA 11, 1901/03, 326–34

641 Peabody, C. Les silex néolithiques, à égratinures, du Suffolk. SPF 8, 1912, 459–69

642 **Charlesworth, E.** Collection of bronze instruments found in Suffolk. PSA 2nd Ser 7, 1876/8, 426

643 **Prigg, H.** Recent discovery of a bronze sword at Chippenham, Cambs, with notices of similar discoveries in the western district of Suffolk. PSIA 6, 1883/8, 184–94

644 **Moore, E. S. F.** Bronze objects found in Suffolk. PSA 2nd Ser 11, 1885/7, 98–9

645 **Cane, L. B.** Socketed celts. PSIA 23, 1937/9, 79–82.

646 **Clarke, R. R.** Bronze cauldron and other antiquities from North-East Suffolk. PSIA 23, 1937/9, 219–23

647 **Smedley, N.,** *and* **Owles, E. J.** Pottery of the early and middle Bronze Age in Suffolk. PSIA 29, 1961/3, 175–97, 355–6

648 **Edwardson, A. R.** Bronze-Age metal work in Moyes Hall Museum, Bury St. Edmunds. Bury St. Edmunds, 1969. SRO/B

649 **Suffolk Archaeological Unit.** Introductory guide to pottery and worked flints in Suffolk. Ipswich, 1976. SRO/B

ROMAN PERIOD   *See also* Coins and tokens,
     and individual localities, *below*, especially Mildenhall

650 **Whincopp, W.** British and Roman ornaments of bronze and other materials found at Colchester and other places in Essex and Suffolk. PSA 1, 1843/9, 84

651 **Irving, G. V.** Camps, Roman roads, pavements, etc., in Suffolk. Collectanea Archaeologia 2, 1861, 241–50

652 Vexillum found in Suffolk. PCAS 11, 1903/06, 177–8

653 **C, J. C.** Romans in Suffolk. E Ang 2, 1864/6, 29

654 **Raven, J. J.** The locations of 'Camboricum', 'Janus', and the 'Villa Faustini' [Cambridge, Ixworth, and Stoke Ash]. Arch J 50, 1893, 176–7

655 **Fox, G. E.** Roman Suffolk. Arch J 57, 1900, 89–165

656 **Corder, J. S.** Romano-British pottery, near Ipswich. PSIA 11, 1901/03, 337–8

657 **Barham, G. B.** Discoveries of Roman remains at Sicklesmere [Whelnetham] and Villa Faustini. Antiquary 42, 1906, 248–50

658 **Compton, C. H.** Villa Faustini. JBAA NS 12, 1906, 43–50

659 **Fox, G. E.,** *and* **Smith, R. A.** Roman-British Suffolk. *In* VCH Suffolk 1, 1911, 279–323

660 **Moore, I. E.** Roman Suffolk. PSIA 24, 1946/8, 163–81

661 **Clarke, R. R.** Romano-Saxon pottery in East Anglia. Arch J 106, 1949, 69–71

ANGLO-SAXON PERIOD   *See also* Coins and tokens,
     and individual localities, *below*, especially Sutton Hoo

662 **Whincopp, W.** Two supposed Saxon ornaments, a silver ear-ring found near Bury St. Edmunds, and a gold ear-ring also found in Suffolk. PSA 1, 1843/9, 116–17

663 **Tymms, S.** Devil's Dyke, Newmarket. PSIA 1, 1848/53, 166–76

664 **Smith, C. R.** Two Anglo-Saxon or Frankish fibulae of bronze and gold, and a bronze fibula found in Suffolk. PSA 2, 1849/53, 93

665 **Cuming, H. S.** On the kings of East Anglia. JBAA 21, 1865, 22–31

666 **Planché, J. R.** Earls of East Anglia. JBAA 21, 1865, 91–103

667 **Morgan, T.** On East Anglian history in Saxon times. JBAA 36, 1880, 185–200

668 **Green, W. C.** Norsemen in Suffolk. SBVC 2, 1899, 147–50

669 **Smith, R. A.** Anglo-Saxon remains. *In* VCH Suffolk 1, 1911, 325–55

670 **Hudson, W.** Status of "villani" and other tenants in Danish East Anglia in pre-Conquest times. TRHS 4th Ser 4, 1921, 23–48

671 **Morley, C.** Historica Saxonica Suffolciensis: an attempt to recover the history of the county of Suffolk during Anglo-Saxon times. [Prospectus of unpublished work, dated 1925, and typescript]

672 **Lethbridge, T. C.** East Angles, an acount of recent field-work in Cambridgeshire and Suffolk. Ipek 5, 1930, 69–76

673 **Lethbridge, T. C.,** *Ed.* Recent excavations in Anglo-Saxon cemeteries in Cambridgeshire and Suffolk. A report, etc. Publ CAS, Quarto Ser NS 3, 1931. SCL/L

674 **Lethbridge, T. C.** Huts of the Anglo-Saxon period: 1, Huts of the pagan period at Waterbeach and West Row. PCAS 33, 1931/2, 133–7

675 **Bruce-Mitford, R. L. S.** Anglo-Saxon Suffolk. Arch J 108, 1951, 132–3

676 **Davis, R. H. C.** East Anglia and the Danelaw. TRHS 5th Ser 5, 1955, 23–9

677 **Lethbridge, T. C.** Anglo-Saxon settlement in Eastern England. *In* Dark-age Britain: studies presented to E. T. Leeds. *Ed.* by D. B. Harden. 1956. 112–22

678 **Homans, G. C.** Frisians in East Anglia. EcHR 2nd Ser 10, 1957/8, 190–201

679 **Stenton, F. M.** East Anglian kings of the seventh century. *In* The Anglo-Saxons; studies presented to Bruce Dickins. *Ed.* by P. Clemoes. 1959. Rp *in* Stenton's Preparatory to Anglo-Saxon England. Oxford, 1970. 394–402

680 **Smedley, N.,** *and* **Owles, E. J.** Some Anglo-Saxon animal brooches [from the collections in the museums of Dunwich and Ipswich]. PSIA 30, 1964/6, 166–74

681 **Holland, C. G.** Battle of Ringmere, 1010. SR 3, 1966, 122–31

682 **Hart, C. J. R.** Early charters of Eastern England. Leicester, 1966

MEDIEVAL PERIOD

See also individual localities, particular elections, Agriculture, Trade and Industry, Coins and tokens, *and* Local government, *below*

683 **Richardson, H. G.** A twelfth-century Anglo-Norman charter [relating to Leyland castle, Suffolk]. Bull. John Ryland's Lib 24, 1940, 168–72

684 East Anglia and the Barons' War. E Ang NS 7, 1897/8, 63–4

685 **Sperling, C. F. D.** Three thirteenth-century charters preserved at Redgrave Hall, Suffolk. EAST NS, 1925/7, 139–40

686 **Round, J. H.** The landing of Queen Isabella in 1326 [Orwell]. EHR 14, 1899, 104–05

687   **Glasscock, R. E.** Distribution of wealth in East Anglia in the early fourteenth century. IBGT 32, 1963, 113–23

688   Suffolk notes from the Calendar of French Rolls of the reign of Henry VI in the Public Record Office. E Ang NS 13, 1909/10, 105–08

Domesday Book   See also **2384, 6467**

689   Domesday Book; or, The great survey of England of William the Conqueror ... facsimile of the part relating to Suffolk. Southampton, 1863

690   **Hamilton, N. E. S. A.,** *Ed.* Inquisitio Comitatus Cantabrigiensis, subjecitur Inquisitio Eliensis [or description of the monastic lands of Ely]. 1876. BL

691   Suffolk Domesday – to be translated by Lord John Hervey. E Ang NS 3, 1889/90, 12, 146, 225–6

692   Suffolk Domesday ... the Latin text extended and translated into English ... By J. H. [*Lord* J. W. N. Hervey]. 25pts. Bury St. Edmunds, 1888–91

693   Suffolk Domesday: the Carlford and the two Babergh Hundreds. E Ang NS 3, 1889/90, 97–8

694   **Bedell, A. J.** Suffolk Domesday: Samford Hundred. E Ang NS 3, 1889/90, 25–6

695   **Pearson, W. C.** Suffolk Domesday: Hundreds of Blything, Claydon, Carlford, Colneis, and Samford. E Ang NS 4, 1891/2, 233–8

696   **Pell, O. C.** Upon libere tenentes, virgatae, and carucae in Domesday in six counties [including Suffolk]. PCAS 6, 1884/8, 17–40

697   **Lees, B. A.** Introduction to the Suffolk Domesday, and translation adapted from the translation by the late Lord Hervey. *In* VCH Suffolk 1, 1911, 357–582

698   **Darby, H. C.** Domesday woodland in East Anglia. Ant 8, 1934, 211–15

699   **Darby, H. C.** Domesday geography of Norfolk and Suffolk. Geog Jour 65, 1935, 432–52

700   **Dodwell, B.** Free peasantry of East Anglia in Domesday. NA 27, 1941, 145–57

701   **Darby, H. C.** Domesday geography of Eastern England. Cambridge, 1952. 2nd edn 1957. 3rd edn 1970

702   **Finn, R. W.** The Inquisitio Eliensis re-considered. EHR 75, 1960, 385–409

703   **Finn, R. W.** Domesday studies: the eastern counties. 1967

Land Tenure and Ownership, and Manorial History
    See also **444, 546, 700, 1065, 4282,** *and* Enclosures and commons, *below*

704   Rotuli Hundredorum tempore Hen. III and Edw. I in Turre Lond' et in curia receptae scaccarii Westm. asservati. 1818. Suffolk, v 2, 142–200

705   On the Abbey lands, etc., in order to ascertain how far they are available to the necessities of the State. Bury St. Edmunds, 1831. SRO/B

706   **Corner, G. R.** On the custom of Borough English, with a list of the manors and places in Suffolk in which customary descent is to the youngest son. PSIA 2, 1854/9, 227–41

707 'Epizetetes' *pseud*. Whereabouts of manor rolls of various Suffolk manors. N&Q 4th Ser 6, 1870, 197, 262

708 **Stedman, A. E.** East Anglian manor court rolls. E Ang NS13, 1909/10, 22–4

709 **Nichols, F. M.** Court-roll of the manor of Hollesley with the arms of Stanhope. PSA 2nd Ser 3, 1864/7, 260–64

710 'Memorandum' of ancient measurements: a Knight's Fee. E Ang NS 1, 1885/6, 29–30

711 **Rye, W.** Notes from Suffolk fines. E Ang NS 1, 1885/6, 65–6

712 List of Knight's Fees of the Honors of Lancaster and Leicester in the county of Suffolk; from the Ipswich Great Domesday volume, Book 6. E Ang NS 1, 1885/6, 86

713 **Gerish, W. B.** Map by Randulphus Agas: survey of the manors of Tangleham, Buttlie, and Boyton ... 1594. E Ang NS 5, 1893/4, 154

714 Inventory of the goods and chattels, together with the rents and farms, of the college of Stoke, 2 Edw. III. E Ang NS 6, 1895/6, 329–31. *See also* **7419**

715 **Rye, W.** Calendar of the Feet of Fines for Suffolk. Ipswich, 1900

716 **Hudson, W.** Three manorial extents of the thirteenth century [including one for Wykes manor in Bardwell]. NA 14, 1899/1901, 1–56

717 **Copinger, W. A.** Feet of Fines, Suffolk. E Ang NS 9, 1901/02, 15

718 **Redstone, V. B.** Nomina villarum, co. Suffolk, 1316. PSIA 11, 1901/03, 173–99

719 **Douglas, D. C.** Social structure of medieval East Anglia. Oxford, 1927

720 **Nichols, J. F.** Custodiae Essexiae: a study of the conventual property held by the priory of Christ Church, Canterbury, in the counties of Essex, Suffolk, and Norfolk. Ph.D. thesis, London, 1929–30. Thesis summary. BIHR 9, 1931/2, 116–20

721 **Dodwell, B.** The Sokeman of the southern Danelaw in the eleventh century. M.A. thesis, London, 1936

722 **Lennard, R.** An unidentified twelfth-century custumal of Lawshall, Suffolk. EHR 51, 1936, 104–07

723 **Dodwell, B.** East Anglian commendation. EHR 63, 1948, 289–306

724 Feet of Fines for the county of Norfolk ... [and] for the county of Suffolk for the reign of King John, 1199–1214 ... *Ed*. by B. Dodwell. PRS NS 32. Reading, [1959]

725 **Blake, E. O.,** *Ed*. Liber Eliensis. Camden Soc 3rd Ser 92. 1962

726 **Dodwell, B.** Holdings and inheritance in medieval East Anglia. EcHR 2nd Ser 20, 1967, 53–66

727 Suffolk Chancery proceedings, *temp.* James I. E Ang NS 4, 1891/2, 120–22

728 **Stanford, C. M., and Son.** Beaumont collection of Lordships of manors in the counties of Essex, Suffolk, and Norfolk: Catalogue of sale, 3 Nov 1954

729 **Stanford, C. M., and Son.** Second auction of Lordships of manors in the counties of ... Suffolk, Norfolk, ... Catalogue of sale, 7 Dec 1955. SCL/L

730 **Stanford, C. M., and Son**. Third auction of Lordships of manors in the counties of Essex, Suffolk, ... Catalogue of sale, 30 Sept 1964

731 **Stanford, C. M., and Son**. Fourth auction of Lordships of manors in the counties of Essex, Suffolk, Norfolk, ... Catalogue of sale, 1 Dec 1965

Other Medieval Topics
See also **266, 1178,** *and* Local government, social services, and justice, *below*

732 **Raven, J. J.** Serfdom in Suffolk in the reign of Edward I. E Ang NS 5, 1893/4, 193, 236, 251

733 **Davenport, F. G.** Decay of villeinage in East Anglia. TRHS NS 14, 1900, 123–41

734 **Warren, F. E.** Slavery and serfdom in England, with special reference to East Anglia. PSIA 15, 1913/15, 183–99

735 **Jessopp. A.** Black Death in East Anglia. *In his* The coming of the friars and other essays. 1889. 166–261

736 **Mander, R. P.** Black Death and other plagues in East Anglia. EAM 7, 1948, 292–8

737 **Cole, L. G.** Black Death in East Anglia. EAM 18, 1959, 554–8. *See also* 4292

738 **Powell, E.** Account of the proceedings in Suffolk during the Peasants' Rising in 1381. TRHS NS 8, 1894, 203–49

739 **Powell, E.** The rising in East Anglia in 1381, with an appendix containing the Suffolk Poll Tax lists for that year. Cambridge, 1896

740 **Redstone, V. B.** Social condition of England during the Wars of the Roses. TRHS NS 16, 1902, 159–200

LATER HISTORY
16th Century *See also* Local Government, Social Services, and Justice, *below*

741 **Bullen, R. F.** Records of the Court of Star Chamber: Suffolk, *temp*. Henry VIII. E Ang NS 13, 1909/10, 233–6, 253–6, 269–72, 294–5

742 **Simpson, A.** Wealth of the gentry 1540–1660: East Anglian studies. Cambridge, 1961

743 **Patten, J. H. C.** Urban structure of East Anglia in the 16th and 17th centuries. Ph.D. thesis, Cambridge, 1972

Elizabethan Period

744 Spanish invasion of 1588 and the eastern coast. E Ang NS 2, 1887/8, 325–8

745 Kempe's nine daies wonder: performed in a daunce from London to Norwich. 1600. STC 14923. BL. *Ed.* by A. Dyce. Camden Soc. 1st Ser 11, 1840

746 **Bullen, R. F.** Calendar of Exchequer depositions by commission during the reigns of Elizabeth and James I, relating to the county of Suffolk. PSIA 14, 1910/12, 9–56

747 **Churchyard, T.** A discourse of the Queenes Maiesties entertainement in Suffolk and Norffolk ... [1578]. STC 5226. BL

748 **Churchyard, T.** The Queenes Majestie's entertaynemente in Suffolke and Norffolke; with a description of many things then presently seen. Series of tracts on British topography, 3. 1851. 60 copies. BL

17th Century

749 **Hervey, *Lord* F., *Ed*.** Glimpses of Suffolk in past time: County business in the XVII century; Old scenes, old buildings, old families, old questions, old manners, and other old rates and expenses. Bury St. Edmunds, [1907]

750 **Reyce [Ryece], R.** Suffolk in the XVII century. The breviary of Suffolk, by Robert Reyce, 1618, now published for the first time from the MS. in the British Museum, with notes by *Lord* Francis Hervey. 1902

751 **Gurdon, W. B.** The Gurdon papers. E Ang NS 4, 1891/2; NS 5, 1893/4, *passim*

752 **M, J. J.** A Suffolk directory: *temp*. James I [List of Suffolk lenders to the Crown]. E Ang NS 8, 1899/1900, 289–95

753 **Hopper, C.** Suffolk emigrants to New England in 1634. JBAA 21, 1865, 180–83

754 **Tyacke, N. C. P.** Migration from East Anglia to New England before 1660. Ph.D. [Econ] thesis, London, 1951. *See also* **7131**

755 **Fea, A.** The 'Merry Monarch' in Suffolk. PSIA 23, 1937/9, 1–5

756 **Jones, A. G. E.** Sick and wounded in Suffolk in the 1670's. SR 1, 1957, 59–60. *See also* **934, 937**

757 Proposed repeal of the test and penal statutes by King James II in 1688. SR 1, 1958, 190–91

758 **Casley, H. C.** French refugees in East Anglia. E Ang NS 1, 1885/6, 81–2 99–102

The Civil War

759 **Kingston, A.** East Anglia and the Great Civil War. The rising of Cromwell's Ironsides in the associated counties of Cambridge, Huntingdon, Lincoln, Norfolk, Suffolk, Essex, and Hertford. 1897. 1902

760 **Everitt, A. M., *Ed*.** Suffolk and the Great Rebellion, 1640–60. Ipswich, 1961. SRS 3

761 **[Bradley, K. R.]** Suffolk in the Civil War (1642–46). Ipswich, [1975]

762 **Partridge, C. S.** Suffolk royalists of the Great Rebellion. E Ang NS 7, 1897/8, 48

763 **Raven, J. J.** Some Long Parliament notes of expenditure: Hundred of Hartismere. E Ang NS 9, 1901/02, 217–18

764 **Davies, G.** Army of the Eastern Association, 1644–5. EHR 46, 1931, 88–96

765 **Holmes, C.** The Eastern Association. Ph.D. thesis, Cambridge, 1970. NCL/N

766 **Holmes, C.** The Eastern Association in the English Civil War. Cambridge, 1974

767 To the Honourable the Knights, citizens, and burgesses in the House of Commons in Parliament the humble petition of sundry of the Knights ...

and others of the inhabitants of the county of Suffolke ... 31 Jan 1641 [for the removal of popish lords, etc.]. Wing T 1458. O

768 Humble petitions of the bailifes, port-men, and other of the inhabitants of Ipswich, in the county of Suffolke. 1641. Wing H 3590A. BL-T

769 Letter sent by Sir John Suckling, from France, deploring his sad estate and flight ... 1641. [verse] Wing S 6131. O

770 Foure petitions of Huntingdonshire, Norfolk, Suffolk, and Essex, joyntly concerning the liberty of the subjects, to the ... High Court of Parliament; unanimously concurring to the rooting out of Papists, etc. 1642. Wing F 1664. BL

771 To the ... Lords and Commons ... the ... petition of the inhabitants of the associated counties of Norfolk, Suffolk, etc., [for the payment and disbanding of the army in Ireland, and for the reduction of the assessments on those counties, etc.]. [1642?]. BL

772 Two petitions. The one ... to the Kings ... Majesty ... the other to the ... Justices of the Peace ... at the assizes holden at Bury St. Edmunds ... for ... Suffolk. The ... petitions of the Chiefe-Constable, and the Freeholders, inhabitants in the said county attending the service there [both praying for the reconciliation between the King and Parliament]. 1642. Wing T 3521. BL-T. Photostat SRO/B

773 Humble petition of the bailiffs, port-men, and inhabitants of Ipswich [against the Bishops]. 1642, [Feb]. Wing H 3483. BL

774 His Majesties speech to the Committee, when they presented the declaration of both Houses at New-Market, 1641/2., March 9. Wing C 2800. BL-T

775 His Majesties declaration to Parliament, in answer to that presented to him at Newmarket. 1641/2, March 9. Wing C 2226–73. BL-T

776 A declaration of the noble resolution of the Earle of Essex, concerning his intention in the defence of King and Parliament. 1642, Sept 9. Wing D 722. BL-T

777 A declaration of Parliament for the raising of forces. Together with certain instructions for the Lord Lieutenants in the county of Norfolk, Suffolk, Essex ... Also the resolution and association of the aforesaid counties. 1642, Dec 22. Wing E 1429. BL-T

778 A declaration and ordinance of the Lords and Commons assembled in Parliament, for the associating of the severall counties of Norfolk, Suffolk ... for the mutuall defence and preservation of themselves from all rapines, plundrings, and spoylings of papists. 1642/3. Wing E 1299. BL

779 **Dowsing, W.** The journal of W.D., of Stratford, Parliamentary Visitor, appointed ... for demolishing the superstitious pictures and ornaments of churches ... within the county of Suffolk, in the years 1643–1644. [*Ed.* by R. Loder]. Woodbridge, 1786. Woodbridge, 2nd edn 1818. Oxford, 1840. London, 1844. Ipswich, 1885. *Ed.* by C. H. E. White

780 **White, C. H. E.** Journal of William Dowsing, Parliamentary Visitor appointed to demolish church ornaments, etc., within the county of Suffolk [With Dowsing pedigrees]. PSIA 6, 1883/8, 236–95. *See also* **2801–3**

781 Eight special orders of Parliament for associating to the county of Huntingdon with Herts, Cambridge, etc. ... 1643, June 2. Wing E 1529. BL-T

782 An ordinance of the Lords and Commons ... concerning the names of the committee for the associated counties of Norfolk, Suffolk ... together with instructions for the said committee. 1643, Aug 8. Wing E 1827. BL-T

783 An ordinance of Parliament for the speedy pressing of 20,000 souldiers for the six associated counties. 1643, Aug 16. Wing E 2047. BL-T

784 An ordinance of Parliament wherein the county of Lincolne is added in the association of Norfolke, Suffolke, Essex ... for mutual defence against the the Popish army under the Marquess of Newcastle ... 1643, Sept 20. Wing E 2107. BL-T

785 Londons love to her neighbours in generall and in particular to the six associated counties. Wherein is plainly laid open the danger which is like to fall upon them, unless they withstand the blood-thirsty Cavaliers. 1643, Oct 20. [By Capt. John Williams]. Wing W 2744. BL-T

786 Ordinance of the Lords and Commons ... to inable the ... Earle of Manchester, to put in execution all former ordinances for sequestering delinquents estates ... and other ordinances for raising of monies within the associated counties ... 1643, Nov 17. Wing E 2095. BL

787 To the honnorable committee at Bury. The humble pitticion of the cheife inhabitants of the liberty of St. Ethelrids and of Hoxon Hundred, on behalfe of themselves and others well-affected within the countye of Suffolk. 1643, Dec 12. Wing I 5. BL-T

788 A catalogue of remarkable mercies conferred upon the seven associated counties, viz Cambridge ... Suffolk ... and appointed to be published in the severall parish churches of the aforenamed counties [First item "The quenching that fire kindled at Laystaff]. Cambridge, 1643/4. Wing C 1365. BL-T

789 An ordinance of Parliament for the maintaining of the forces of the seven associated counties under Edward, Earl of Manchester. 1644, May 14. Wing E 1990. BL-T

790 An ordinance of Parliament for putting the associated counties and the cities of Lincoln and Norwich into a posture of defence. 1644, July 5. Wing E 1903. BL-T

791 An ordinance of Parliament for maintaining the forces of the seven associated counties under the Earl of Manchester. 1644, Oct 10. Wing E 1991. BL-T

792 An ordinance of Parliament for the raising of moneys for maintaining of five-hundred horse to be raised out of the Eastern association. 1645, July 10. Wing E 2018. BL-T

793 An ordinance of Parliament for the speedy raising of money in the Easterne association for the maintenance of the forces imployed in reducing the garrison of Newarke. 1645, Aug 12. Wing E 2059. BL-T

794 Petition of the inhabitants of the county of Suffolke. 1646. Wing P 1805

795 A perfect relation [signed L.M.] of the horrible plot of the malignant party of Edmondbury in Suffolk for the murdering of Mr. Lauceter and other

well-affected persons for opening of their shops upon Christmas-day, also the apprehending of the chief ring-leaders. 1646, Jan 4. Wing M 54. BL-T. Photostat. SRO/B

796 The humble petition of the inhabitants of the county of Suffolke, presented to the rt. hon. House of Peers, Feb 16, 1646. With their answer thereunto. 1646. Wing H 3524. BL-T

797 An ordinance of Parliament for £20,000 to be paid out of the Excise to the forces raised by the Easterne Association for blocking up Newarke. 1645/6 Feb 28. Wing E 2073. BL-T

798 Strange signs from heaven; seen and heard in Cambridge, Suffolke, and Norfolke, in and upon the 21 day of May ... 1646 ... 1646, May 21. Wing S 5918A. BL-T

799 Humble petition of the Ministers of the counties of Suffolke and Essex concerning church government presented to the ... House of Peers on Fryday, May 29, 1646, with their answer thereunto [in favour of Presbyterianism and against toleration]. 1646, May 29. Wing H 3564. BL-T

800 Sad newes from the Eastern parts, or a true relation of the spectacles and signes in the Eastern association ... 1646, July 14. Wing S 257. BL-T

801 The faith of the army reviving; or, Some fresh buddings of the armies ... at New-market and Triplo Heath, 1647. 1649. Wing F 259. nl

802 Humble petition of the ... inhabitants of the counties of Norfolk and Suffolk ... to the Hon House of Commons, etc. 1647. Wing H 3566. BL

803 To the ... Knights, citizens, and burgesses ... in ... Parliament ... the ... petition of diverse inhabitants in Norfolke, Suffolk, etc. [1647?] BL

804 Red-ribboned news from the army. In a discourse between a minister and a souldier of the State. Written from thence by a Minister ... in the county of Suffolk [By T. Coxcombe]. Wing C 6711A BL

805 Two letters of his Excellencie Sir Thomas Fairfax sent to both Houses of Parliament; with the humble advice of the Councel of Warre (held at St. Edmunds Bury in Suffolke, Satterday, 29 May 1647). 1647. Wing F 248. BL

806 Another letter from Sir Thomas Fairfax to the Speaker, of His Majesties removall from Childersley to New-Market and the grounds thereof ... 1647, June 8. Wing F 134. BL-T

807 Four petitions to Sir Thomas Fairfax from the inhabitants of Essex, Norfolk, and Suffolk ... [against the disbandment of the army] June 1647. 1647, June 12. Wing F 1665. BL-T

808 Account of the arbitrary exactions, taxations, impositions which have been leavied in these late warres, out of the associate counties, viz. Essex, Suffolke, Norfolke ... 1647, June 28. Wing A 235. Bl-T

809 To his excellency Sir T. Fairfax, ... the humble petition of the peaceable and well-affected inhabitants of the counties of Norfolk and Suffolk, ... earnestly endeavouring after the prosperity of ... Parliament ... 1647, July 2. Wing H 3566. BL-T

810 Bloody newes from Colchester concerning the late fight ... between the forces under the command of Sir Charles Lucas and the Suffolk forces ... Lord

Generall's propositions ... touching a generall peace. 1648. Wing B 3265. BL

811 England's complaint; or, A sharp reproof to the inhabitants thereof against that now raigning sin of rebellion. But more especially to the inhabitants of the county of Suffolk ... By Lionel Gatford, B.D., the true, but sequestered Rector of Dennington ... 1648. Wing G 332. BL-T

812 To the ... Knights and gentlemen committees for the county of Suffolke ... that the county may receive satisfaction that the moneys raysed upon them, hath been imployed for their own defence ... Signed Peter Fisher. [1648]. Wing F 1045. BL-T

813 To the Parliament of England, the petitions and expostulations of some gentlemen and freeholders of the Easterne association ... 1648, April 12. [By N. Ward]. Wing N 791. BL-T

814 The resolution of the Prince of Wales, concerning the landing of his army in the Isle of Loving-Land, within the county of Suffolk. [By J. Burdet]. 1648, July 29. Wing B 5619. BL

815 The hunting of the foxes from New-Market and Triploe Heaths to White-Hall, by five small beagles [late of the armie], of the grandie-deceivers unmasked ... 1649. By J. Lilburne. Wing L 2115. BL

816 Several proposals offered to the consideration of the keepers of the liberties of the people of England, in reference to a settlement of the peace and truth in this nation. As also a narrative ... to make known two or three sums of money concealed and many of the actings of the proposer. Samuel Duncon, late of Ipswich ... from the year 1640 to the year 1652. July 6, 1659. Wing D 2607. BL-T

817 The remonstrance of the noblemen, knights, gentlemen, and commons of the late Eastern, Southern, and Western associations, who desire to shew themselves faithfull to the good old cause. 1659, [Nov 16]. By W. Prynne. Wing P 4051

818 Letter agreed unto and subscribed by the gentlemen, ministers, and freeholders of Suffolk, presented to Generall Monck. 1659/60. Wing L 1344. BL-T

18th Century

819 **Partridge, C. S.** East Anglian Jacobites of the eighteenth century. E Ang NS 7, 1897/8, 48

820 **Partridge, C.** A Suffolk Jacobite tradition. E Ang NS 12, 1907/08, 212

821 Case of the counties of Norfolk, Suffolk, city of Norwich, and the county of the same, against the corporation of Great Yarmouth. [1705]. BL

822 Suffolk queries; or, Some questions sent from Ipswich to a friend in London for a just solution. Ipswich, 1710. SRO/B

823 List of subscribers of the county of Suffolk for the support of His Majesty's person and government ... on the occasion of the Rebellion; with the sum subscribed, etc. Ipswich, 1746

824 **Brierley, G. H.** East Anglia in the Annual Register, 1758–90. E Ang NS 3–5, 1889/94, *passim*

825 **La Rochefoucauld, F. A. F. De.** A Frenchman in England, 1784: being the "Mélanges sur l'Angleterre" ... New edn from the Ms with an introduction by Jean Marchand ... translated with notes by S. C. Roberts. Cambridge, 1933

826 Serious address to the members of the House of Commons and gentlemen residing in the counties of Suffolk, Norfolk, and Essex. 1790. NCL/N

827 Suffolk to wit. Notice to the Inn-Holders and Ale-House-Keepers in the Hundred of Mutford and Lothingland in the said county of Suffolk. [Signed S. Cooper, Fras. Bowness, warning them against harbouring illegal clubs and associations]. [1792]. BL

828 Remarks on the temper of the present times, addressed to the gentlemen, yeomanry, and common people, by a clergyman of Suffolk. Ipswich, 1792. nl

19th Century

829 **Singleton, F.** Captain Swing in East Anglia. Bull Soc for the Study of Labour History 8, 1964, 13–15

830 **Johnston, L.** Town and country in East Anglia one-hundred-and-fifty years ago. SR 2, 1964, 249–59

831 Extracts from various writers on emigration with authentic copies of letters from emigrants from Norfolk, Suffolk, and Sussex, now settled in Upper Canada. Norwich, 1834. NCL/N

832 **Fearn, H.** Chartism in Suffolk. MA thesis, Sheffield, 1952

833 **Fussell, G. E.** Potatoes to the rescue in 1894. SR 1, 1956, 8–10

834 **Jobson, A.** Victorian Suffolk. 1972

835 **Harrison, C.** Victorian and Edwardian Suffolk. 1973. [Mainly photographs]

20th Century

836 **Stokes,** *Sir* **W.** Short record of the East Anglian Munitions Committee in the Great War, 1914–18. 1919

837 **East Anglian Munitions Trust.** Origin and activities of the East Anglian Munitions Trust, 1921–61. [1964]

838 **Imperial War Graves Commission.** War graves of the British Empire: the register of the names of those who fell in the Great War and are buried in the cemeteries and churchyards in ... East and West Suffolk. 1931

839 Queen Mary in Essex and Suffolk [June 1938]. ER 47, 1938, 155–8

840 **Northway, B. S.,** *Ed.* History of 107 Squadron [at Wattisham]. 1963. SCL/L

841 **Imperial War Graves Commission.** War dead of the British Commonwealth and Empire: Memorial register 6, Lowestoft naval memorial. 2v. 1953

842 **Commonwealth War Graves Commission.** War dead of the Commonwealth: the register of the names of those who fell in the 1939–45 War and are buried in cemeteries and churchyards in the county of Suffolk. 1961

843 Suffolk garland for the Queen, 1961, ... on the occasion of the Royal Progress of Her Majesty Queen Elizabeth II through the county of Suffolk. *Ed.* by J. Hadfield and W. G. Sanford. Ipswich, [1961]

PARLIAMENTARY REPRESENTATION
GENERAL
See also Parliamentary history under individual localities (boroughs) *below*

844 **Brown, M. C.** Political history. *In* VCH Suffolk 2, 1907, 157–98

845 **John, E. L. T.** Parliamentary representation of Norfolk and Suffolk, 1377–1422. MA thesis, Nottingham, 1959

846 **Willis, B.** Notitia Parliamentaria, containing an account of the first returns and incorporations of the cities, towns, and boroughs ... that send members to Parliament, their returning officers, number of electors, and coats of arms. 1750. 3v

847 [**Carew, T.**] Historical account of the rights of elections of the several counties, cities, and boroughs ... to the year 1754 ... [includes Aldborough, Dunwich, Ipswich, St. Edmund's Bury, Sudbury]. 1755. 2v. BL

848 Letter agreed unto and subscribed by the gentlemen, etc., of Suffolk. Presented to ... the Lord General Monck [in favour of a free and full Parliament] ... delivered at St. Albans, Jan 28, 1659/60. Wing L 1344A. BL

849 Letter agreed unto and subscribed by the gentlemen, ... freeholders, and seamen of ... Suffolk ... to the ... Lord Mayor, aldermen, and common councell of the citty of London [for a free and full Parliament]. 1659/60. Wing L 1344. BL

850 Letter agreed unto by the county of Suffolk, presented to the Lord Mayor of London, 30 Jan [praying for a free Parliament]. 1659/60. Wing L 1344. BL-T

851 Parliamentary representation: reports from commissioners on proposed division of the counties and boundaries of boroughs. HC 1831/2, 40. Pt 2. Suffolk, 21–32

852 List of districts for the Eastern Division of the county of Suffolk, with the polling places, appointed by the Justices at special sessions assembled. Woodbridge, [1832]. BL

853 Report of the select committee on franchise. HC 1860. 12. Suffolk, 546–7

854 Redistribution of Seats Act, 1885 [contents of county divisions]. HC 1884/5, 63. Suffolk, 167–74

855 Report of the Boundary Commission. HC 1917/18, 13

856 Report of the Boundary Commission under House of Commons (Redistribution of Seats) Act, 1944. HC 1947/8, 15. Suffolk, 835

857 Boundary Commission. Report with respect to the areas comprised in the constituencies of ... Ipswich, Eye, Sudbury, and Woodbridge ... HC 1952/3, 7. Suffolk, 537–8

POLL BOOKS, ETC.
858 Suffolk Poll books. E Ang NS 4, 1891/2, 383: NS 5, 1893/4, 14–15, 143

859 **Bullen, R. F.** List of Suffolk poll books. N&Q 11th Ser 1, 1910, 306

860 List of Suffolk poll books. 1953. [Typescript]. SRO/B

861 Poll books, 1698–1730
862 Knights of the Shire, 1702. SRO/B
863 Members of Parliament, 1705. SRO/B
864 Knights of the Shire, 9 May 1705. nl
865 Knights of the Shire, 18 Oct 1710. SRO/B
866 Index to voters, 1710. [Typescript]
867 Knights of the Shire, 30 Aug 1727
868 Index to voters, 1727. [Typescript]
869 Knights of the Shire, 7 April 1784. SRO/B
870 Knights of the Shire, 29 and 30 June 1790. [includes list of Knights of the Shire, 1297–1471; 1542–1790]
871 Knights of the Shire, 10 Aug 1830
872 Woodbridge District, the poll for the knights of the shire for the Eastern Division of the county of Suffolk ... 17 and 18 Dec 1831. Woodbridge, [1831]. BL
873 Eastern Division, 17 and 18 Dec 1832
874 Western Division, 21 and 22 Dec 1832
875 Close of the poll [at the election of members for East Suffolk]. First day. Woodbridge, 1835. BL
876 Eastern Division, 13 and 14 Jan 1835
877 Western Division, 19 and 20 Jan 1835
878 Western Division, 4 and 5 Aug 1837. nl
879 Eastern Division, 12 and 13 July 1841
880 Western Division, 12 and 13 July 1841. SRO/B
881 Eastern Division 21 and 22 April 1843
882 Eastern Division, 1859
883 Western Division, 1859
884 Eastern Division, 1863
885 Eastern Division, 1868
886 Western Division, 1868
887 Register of electors for East Suffolk, 1843–

PARTICULAR ELECTIONS, POLITICAL CONTROVERSY
888 **Virgoe, R.** Three Suffolk parliamentary elections of the mid-fifteenth century. BIHR 39, 1966, 185–96
889 **Fitch, W. S.** Election expenses of Sir John Howard and Thomas Brewse: election for Knights of the Shire, 20 April 1467. SAAP Pt 2, June 1847, 4–6. Further note. PSIA 2, 1854/9, 206–07
890 An election to the Long Parliament [of members for the county of Suffolk, in October 1644]. By T. Carlyle. 1844. BL
891 Trial between Sir Samuel Barnardiston, Bart., plaintiff, and Sir William Soame, Knt., Sheriff of Suffolk, defendant, for damages he sustained, against

the defendant's making a double return at an election for a Knight of the Shire for Suffolk.... 1674. SCL/L

892 Tryal and conviction of Sr. Sam. Barnardiston, Bart. for high-misdemeanor ... before the Right Honorable Sir George Jeffreys ... on Thursday, 14 Feb 1683. 1684. Wing T 2164

893 The late Lord Chief Justice North's argument. In the case between Sir William Soames ... and Sir Sam. Barnardiston, etc. 1689. Wing G 2114. BL

894 **Barnardiston,** *Sir* N. A defence of the late Lord Russel's innocency ... Together with an argument in the great case concerning elections of members of Parliament, between Sr. Samuel Barnardiston, Bart. plaintiff, and Sr. Will. Soames, Sheriff of Suffolk, defend. etc. 1689. Wing A 4136. BL

895 An argument of a learned Judge [i.e. Lord Chief Justice North] ... wherein Sir Samuel Barnardiston was plaintiff against Sir William Soames ... defendant, wherein the privilege of the House of Commons, in determining matters relating to the right of elections of their own members is justified, etc. 1704. BL

896 [**Tollemache, L.** *Earl of Dysart*]. An election song in favour of Lord Dysart, who represented the county of Suffolk in the House of Commons from 1685 [to 1710]. [1705]. BL

897 **Ross, T. B.,** *Ed.* Collection of printed political squibs and papers relating to the county of Suffolk and the borough of Ipswich from 1736 [to 1900]

898 History of the last four elections for the county of Suffolk [1747–68], to which is added Mr Sawbridge's intended motion 'For shortening the duration of parliaments.' 1772

899 O ye freeholders of Suffolk! [An electioneering squib against Sir John Rous] By a Blunt Freeholder. Bury St. Edmunds, 1790. BL

900 To all saddlers who are Suffolk freeholders, as no other will be employed. [An election squib against Sir John Rous]. Bury St. Edmunds, 1790. BL

901 Rous for ever [An election song]. [Bury St. Edmunds], [1790]. BL

902 Observations on the cause, conduct, and effects of the late contested election for the county of Suffolk. Ipswich, 1790

903 Versification of ... affidavit ... inserted in the Ipswich Journal ... addressed to the ... committee for conducting Sir J. Rous's and Sir C. Bunbury's election. [Ipswich?], 1791. BL

904 Address to the independent freeholders of the county of Suffolk, on the approaching election, by a Suffolk freeholder. 1802. BL

905 [Advertisement for the sale of] the Old Treasury Hulk, the Sir Thomas. [An election squib]. [Ipswich?], 1830. BL

906 **Gooch,** *Sir* T. S. [Address] to the gentry, clergy, and freeholders of the county of Suffolk. Ipswich, 1830. BL

907 The peace of the county. A letter to the freeholders of Suffolk, on ... the election of two independent representatives. [Signed W.P.S., i.e. William Pitt Scargill?]. Bury St. Edmunds, 1830. BL

908 Electors of East Suffolk, What have the Tories done? [An election placard signed "A True Englishman"]. Ipswich, 1832. BL

909 To the electors of the Eastern Division of the county of Suffolk [an address, in verse]. [Woodbridge?], [1832]. BL

910 To the electors of the Eastern Division of the county of Suffolk [an address, in verse, in support of the Whig candidates]. Woodbridge, [1832]. BL

911 To the electors of East Suffolk [an address, in verse, in support of the Whig candidates. Dec. 8, 1832]. Woodbridge, [1832]. BL

912 Half measures do no good [an address to the electors of East Suffolk] Woodbridge, [1832]. BL

913 Election ballad for the electors of East Suffolk. [Ipswich?], [1835]. BL

914 Freeholders: an election ballad for East Suffolk. Woodbridge, [1835]. BL

915 To the electors of East Suffolk [an address, in verse, in support of the Conservative candidates] Woodbridge, [1835]. BL

916 A trumpet call to every elector in the Division of East Suffolk. A song. Woodbridge, [1835]. BL

917 Collection of election squibs, songs, placards, etc., printed during the elections of Members of Parliament for East Suffolk, in 1837, 1839, 1841, and 1843. 28 items. Ipswich, Bury St. Edmunds, Woodbridge, Framlingham. BL

918 To the electors of East Suffolk [an address, signed A. Shafto Adair, Flixton Hall]. 1840. O. 1841. O

919 Newspaper cuttings relating to the candidature and election as Member of Parliament for North-east Suffolk of F. S. Stevenson, 1884-92. 2v

920 Address of *Mr* X.Y.Z., M.P., to the electors of East Anglia ... [By T. W. O. Junr., i.e., T. W. Offin, Junr.] Chelmsford, [1885]. BL

921 Letters to the electors of the Eye Division of Suffolk, by a friend and neighbour [i.e. Foster B. Zincke]. 4th Ser Political searchlights. Ipswich, 1892. BL

922 North Suffolk Election, Dec 1910. Verbatim report of the libel action, Foster v. Beauchamp, in the High Court ... 19 and 20 July 1911. Lowestoft, 1911. SCL/L

MARITIME HISTORY   *See also* **1544**, *and* individual localities (seaports) *below*

923 **Norfolk Nautical Research Society.** Norfolk Sailor, No 1, 1958– [East Coast Mariner from No 17, 1970–]. Norwich. NCL/N. No 17, 1970–. SRO/I

924 **Port of Lowestoft Research Society.** Newsletter, No 1, Feb 1965–. SCL/L

925 **Oppenheim, M.** Maritime history. *In* VCH Suffolk 2, 1907, 199-246

926 **Ipswich Nautical Research Society.** East Coast maritime exhibition: the Naze to the Ness ... Art Gallery, High Street, Ipswich. 11–30 May 1953. Ipswich

927 **Benham, H.** Once upon a tide. [Account of East-coast shipping and seamen from the seventeenth to the nineteenth centuries]. 1955. 2nd edn 1971

928 **Malster, R.** [**W.**] Maritime East Anglia. Great Yarmouth, 1969

929 **Webb, J.** [**G.**] Elizabethan piracy: the evidence of the Ipswich Deposition Books. SR 2, 1961, 59-65

930 Malster, R. [W.] Brief history of the 19th-century East Anglian coast. LA&LHS, 1969/70, 50–56

NAVAL HISTORY   *See also* **1484** *and* individual localities (seaports) *below*
931 **Capper, D. P.** Moat Defensive: a history of the waters of the Nore Command, 55BC to 1961. 1963. SCL/L

932 **Clemence, J. L.** Private building of ships to the increase of the navie, 1599. Edward Stephens, shipwright, of Lowestoft. E Ang NS 5, 1893/4, 64

933 Contributions towards the equipment of vessels in the public service, *temp.* Elizabeth. E Ang NS 7, 1897/8, 352, 367–8

934 **Jones, A. G. E.** Sick and wounded in Ipswich during the First Dutch War, 1651–1654. SR 1, 1956, 1–7

935 **Keevil, J. J.** Medicine and the navy, 1200–1900. [v 2, 1649–1714, contains references to Suffolk in the Dutch Wars]. 1958

936 Journals of Sir Thomas Allin, 1660–1678. *Ed.* by R. C. Anderson. 2v. 1939. 1940. Navy Records Soc 79, 80. SCL/L

937 **Jones, A. G. E.** Sick and wounded in Ipswich during the Second Dutch War, 1665–1666. SR 1, 1956, 26–31. *See also* **756**

938 **Corbett, J. S.** Note on the drawings in the possession of the Earl of Dartmouth illustrating the Battle of Sole Bay, 28 May 1672. 1908 Navy Records Soc

939 Journals and narratives of the Third Dutch War. 1946. Navy Records Soc 86. SCL/L. *See also* **7342**

940 County of Suffolk subscribes for a man-of-war, to which Lord Keppel gives £300 ... GM 1st Ser 52, 1782, 450, 549

941 Two letters addressed to Sir Thomas Charles Bunbury, Member of Parliament for the county of Suffolk, in Feb 1781, previous to the late subscriptions raised ... for building a ship of the line ... By a Freeholder of Suffolk. Doncaster, 1782. BL

942 List of subscribers for ... building a ship of war for the service of the public, pursuant to the resolution of a general meeting of the county of Suffolk, held at Stowmarket, Aug 5, 1782. Ipswich, 1782

943 Lists of subscribers in Suffolk, for building a man-of-war of 74 guns for the use of the Government. 1782. [Cuttings from the Ipswich Journal]

944 The following reasons of several persons in the town of Ipswich for not subscribing towards building a ship of war, shew that some people when called upon for money, be the purpose ever so laudable, are not in want of an excuse. [Ipswich c.1782]

945 **Young, A.** An enquiry into the legality and expediency of increasing the Royal Navy by subscriptions for building county ships ... Correspondence between Arthur Young and Capel Lofft ... with a list of subscribers to the Suffolk man-of-war ... Bury St. Edmunds, 1783. BL

946 **Hall, A.,** *and* **Gildersome-Dickinson, C. E.** Office of Vice-Admiral of Suffolk, N&Q. 7th Ser 12, 1891, 51, 448

947 **Mallett, A. E.** Lowestoft and the Royal Navy. *In* Official programme of the

Lowestoft and Lothingland Warship Week, 18–25 Oct 1941. Lowestoft. SCL/L

948 **Scott, P. M.** Battle of the narrow seas. A history of the Light Coastal Forces in the Channel and North Sea, 1939–45. [1945]

949 **Summers, D. L.** H.M.S. Ganges, 1866–1966: one hundred years of training boys for the Royal Navy. Shotley, 1966

TYPES OF VESSEL   *See also* **4751, 5661–2, 6628, 6631,** *and* Sutton Hoo, *below*

950 **Carr, F.** Sailing barges. 1931. 1951

951 **Benham, H.** Last stronghold of sail. 1948

952 **Bennett, A. S.** Tide time. 1949

953 **Roberts, A. W.** Coasting bargemaster. 1949

954 **Benham, H.** Down tops'l: the story of the East Coast sailing-barges. 1951. 2nd edn 1971

955 **March, E. J.** Sailing drifters ... the story of the herring luggers of England, etc. [1952]. Rp Newton Abbot, 1969

956 **March, E. J.** Sailing trawlers ... the story of deep-sea fishing with long line and trawl. [1953]. Rp Newton Abbot, 1970

957 **Moffat, H. W.** Emigrant ships of the 1830's. SR 1, 1956, 46–7

958 **Roberts, A. W.** Last of the sailor men. 1960

959 **Moffat, H. W.** Vessels shown in John Cleverley's paintings of Ipswich. SR 2, 1964, 240–41

960 **Simper, R.** East coast sail: working sail, 1850–1970. Newton Abbot, 1972

LIFEBOATS, LIGHTHOUSES, AND LIGHTSHIPS

See also **6640–42, 6914, 7344, 7356–7**

961 **Suffolk Association for Saving the Lives of Shipwrecked Seamen.** List of the subscribers. Bury St. Edmunds, [1824]. BL

962 **Suffolk Humane Society and Life-Boat Association.** Rules. Lowestoft, 1838. List of subscribers, 1841, 1845. Lowestoft. O

963 **Cooper, E. R.** Suffolk and Norfolk beach yawls. MM 13, 1927, 213–18

964 **Cooper, E. R.** Storm warriors of the Suffolk coast, etc. 1937

965 **Malster, R. W.** Suffolk lifeboats – the first quarter-century. MM 55, 1969, 263–80

966 **Rose, J.** The old beach companies and their yawls. LA&LHS, 1970/71, 9–13

967 **Malster, R. W.** Saved from the sea: the story of life-saving services of the East Anglian coast. Lavenham, 1974

968 **Miller, C. D.** East Anglian beachmen. History Diploma thesis, Ruskin College, Oxford, 1975. [Typescript]. SCL/L

969 Report of the select committee on lighthouses. HC 1834, 12; 1845, 9

970 **Welch, C. E.** Sir Edward Turnour's lighthouses at Orford. PSIA 28, 1958/60, 62–74

971 **Carter, G. G.** Looming lights. 1945

SMUGGLING

972 **Cobbold, R.** History of Margaret Catchpole. 3v. 1845 and later edns

973 **Cooper, E. R.,** *and* **Herrington, J. C.** In the old smuggling days: yarns of the Suffolk coast. 1929. SCL/L

974 **Chandler, L.** Smuggling at Sizewell Gap ... Leiston, 1922. [1960]

975 **Thompson, L. P.** Smugglers of the Suffolk coast. Hadleigh, 1968

MILITARY HISTORY   *See also* **558, 4734–4, 4930–32, 5025, 5574, 5576**

976 **Redstone, V. B.** Suffolk under arms. PSIA 15, 1913/15, 255–66

977 **Bedell, A. J.** Unpublished muster-roll of the reign of Richard I: Norfolk and Suffolk. E Ang NS 4, 1891/2, 225–9

978 **Powell, E.** Muster-rolls (Suffolk) of the Territorials in Tudor times. PSIA 15, 1913/15–19, 1925/7, *passim*

979 **W[ayman], H. W. B.** Commission concerning musters, etc., *temp.* Henry VIII: Babergh Hundred. E Ang NS 12, 1907/08, 385

980 Babergh Hundred muster-roll and valuation, 1522. MS

981 **Cottesloe,** *Lord.* Warrant for musters in Suffolk [c.1605]. AHRJ 3, 1924, 172–5

982 **Wayman, H. W. B.** Muster-roll of two hundred footmen from the Hundreds of Hoxon and Plomesgate under Sir Thomas Glemham, Knight, A.D. 1631. E Ang NS 13, 1909/10, 132–5, 150–51, 163–4

983 Able men in Suffolk, 1638. Transcribed from the original [muster-roll] in the Public Record Office ... *Ed.* by C. E. Banks. [Washington, D.C.], 1931

REGIMENTS, MILITIA, ETC.

984 **Cannon, R.,** *Ed.* Historical record of the Twelfth, or the East Suffolk Regiment of Foot; containing an account of the formation of the regiment in 1685, and of its subsequent services to 1847. 1848

985 East Suffolk Gazette [The regimental newspaper of the 12th, or East Suffolk Regiment]. No. 1, 1863. Dublin. BL

986 The 2nd Suffolk Gazette: a journal of the Second Battalion, the Suffolk Regiment, 1890–. BL

987 **Bayly, R.** Diary of Colonel Bayly, 12th Regiment, 1796–1830. 1896. SRO/B

988 **Frost, H.** Short historical record of the 4th Battalion, the Suffolk Regiment, late Cambridgeshire Militia. Cambridge, [1896]. SRO/B

989 The 2nd Battalion, the Suffolk Regiment, illustrated with brief historical account of the services of the Regiment. Quetta, 1899

990 Suffolk Regimental Gazette: the journal of the Suffolk Regiment, the old 12th Foot, 1904–65. SRO/B. Incomplete. 1911–. SRO/I

991 **G[ardiner], C. H.** Annals of the Twelfth East Suffolk Regiment. Bury St. Edmunds, 1908. SCL/L

992 1st Battalion, the Suffolk Regiment: Malta, 1909 [Reproductions of photographs]. Paris, [1909] BL

993 Standing orders of the Suffolk Regiment (12th Foot). Aldershot, 1910. BL

994 **Gardiner, C. H.** Centurions of a century, among which are many who have soldiered in the Twelfth, or the Suffolk Regiment of Foot ... Brighton, [1911]

995 1st Battalion, the Suffolk Regiment: Cairo, 1912 [Reproductions of photographs]. Paris, 1912. nl

996 **Webb, E. A. H.** History of the 12th (the Suffolk) Regiment, 1685–1913. Including a brief history of the East and West Suffolk Militia, the latter being now the 3rd Battalion, Suffolk Regiment. 1914

997 Suffolk Regiment: its history and achievements, including details of recent fighting at Le Cateau. Rp from East Anglian Daily Times. [c.1915]. NCL/N

998 Short history of the Suffolk 12th Regiment ... souvenir of the help given to the Field Glass Fund for Suffolk Soldiers during the Great War. From EADT. nd

999 8th Battalion, the Suffolk Regiment [1914–18]. np. nd. SCL/L

1000 Short history of the Suffolk Regiment (12th Regiment of Foot),. 1921. BL

1001 **Fair, A.,** *and* **Wolton, E. D.** History of the 1/5th Battalion, the Suffolk Regiment [1859–1921]. [1923]

1002 Record of the foreign service tour of the 1st Battalion, the Suffolk Regiment, 1907–26, compiled from the Digest of Service of 1st Battalion and the Suffolk Regimental Gazette. Published by Capt. J. S. D. Lloyd. [1926]

1003 March of the 1st Battalion, the Suffolk Regiment, through the county of Suffolk, 16–23 Aug 1927. Arranged by Lieut. W. M. Lummis. Ipswich, [1927]

1004 **Murphy, C. C. R.** History of the Suffolk Regiment, 1914–27. [1928]

1005 The Suffolk Regiment XII Foot [Title on cover: A short history of the Suffolk Regiment]. Aldershot, 1933. nl

1006 Illustrated record of the 12th Foot for 250 years, 23 June 1685–23 June 1935. [Bury St. Edmunds], 1935

1007 Suffolk Regiment. 250th anniversary. Portfolio containing various pamphlets and other material. [1935]. SRO/B

1008 **Nicholson, W. N.,** *et al.* Suffolk Regiment, 1928–46. Ipswich, [1948]

1009 **Pocock, R.** The Suffolks: a history of the 12th Foot, the Suffolk Regiment. BBC script, produced by F. Dillon, transmitted 24 April 1953. [Typescript]

1010 **Monier-Williams, H. B.** Story of the colours, 1685 to 1954. [Inset to the Suffolk Regimental Gazette]. Bury St. Edmunds, 1954

1011 1st Battalion, the Suffolk Regiment. Historical report, Jan 1952–March 1954. [1954]. [Typescript]. BL

1012 1st Battalion, the Suffolk Regiment. Presentation of colours by Her Royal Highness, the Princess Margaret. Aldershot, 1955. SRO/B

1013 **Moir, G.** Suffolk Regiment (the 12th Regiment of Foot). 1969

1014 **Slack, J.** History of the late 73rd (West Suffolk) Regiment. 1884

1015 Loyal Suffolk Hussars Gazette. v 1, June–Dec 1896. Yeomanry Record. v 2–3, Jan 1897–Oct 1898. Ipswich. nl

1016 Regiments represented in Ipswich early in the [nineteenth] century. E Ang NS 8, 1899/1900, 209

1017 **Harvey, J. R.** History of the Suffolk Yeomanry, 1793–1901, *being* chapters 9 and 10 *of his* Records of the Norfolk Yeomanry Cavalry ... 1780 to 1908. nl

1018 C.B., being the Christmas Bulletin of the 2/6th Cyclist Battalion, the Suffolk Regiment. Skegness, 1915. BL

1019 Suffolk Punch, regimental magazine of the Loyal Suffolk Hussars, No 1, 1942–. Hinchley

1020 [**Mardon, J. K. L.**] 67th (Suffolk) Medium Regiment Royal Artillery (T.A.) campaign in North West Europe, 6 June 1944 to 5 May 1945. [1945]. nl

1021 Britannia and Castle: the journal of the 1st East Anglia Regiment, 1960–64. Morecambe. NCL/N

1022 Castle: the journal of the Royal Anglian Regiment, v 1, no 1, April 1965–. SRO/B

1023 **Adair, R. A. S.** Memoir on the defence of East Suffolk by a force composed of militia artillery. [1855]. [1860]. SCL/L

1024 **Cooper, E. R.** Suffolk militia: its history and performances. Rp from EADT, 8 Jan 1926. Ipswich

1025 **Cooper, E. R.** The militia: an address to the Militia Club, 21 April 1926. Ipswich [1926]

1026 **Cooper, E. R.** Suffolk militia, the militia, and militia notes. [Three papers:- Rp from EADT 8 Jan 1926, and addresses to the Militia Club, 1926 and 1927]. Ipswich, [1927]

1027 **Cooper, E. R.** Volunteers in Suffolk. Rp from EADT and the Suffolk Regimental Gazette. Bury St. Edmunds, 1935. *See also* **2020**

1028 **Suffolk Volunteer Regiment.** 4th (Woodbridge) Battalion. Battalion magazine, 1–3, 1915–18. Ipswich

1029 Naval and Military Magazine, v 4, no 1, Jan 1899. East Anglian Territorial number

1030 Suffolk Territorials and the Great War: a brief history of the Territorial Force Association. Ipswich, 1920. nl

1031 **Suffolk Regiment Old Comrades Association.** Annual reports, 1923, 1926, 1928, 1933. County Supplement, no 7. Suffolk. *In* Defence: the Territorial Mag Oct 1938, 25–34

1032 Battalion souvenir: a short account of the activities of the 11th Suffolk Home Guard. Ipswich, 1945

AVIATION *See also* **6806**

1033 **Rowe, A. P.** One story of radar [An account of the work of the Telecommunications Research Establishment]. Cambridge, 1948

1034 **Elliott, C.** Aeronauts and aviators: an account of man's endeavours in the air over Norfolk, Suffolk, and East Cambridgeshire between 1785 and 1939. Lavenham, 1971

1035 **Kinsey, G.** Aviation: flight over the Eastern counties since 1937. Lavenham, 1977

Economic History and Communications

AGRICULTURE

1052 **Royal Agricultural Society of England**. Catalogue of the ninety-third annual exhibition at Ipswich, 3–7 July 1934. Gloucester. Also posters, publicity material, etc

1053 **East Anglian Magazine**. Suffolk and Norfolk Shows supplement: Suffolk Show 2 and 3 June 1938 at Bury St. Edmunds; Norfolk Show 15 and 16 June 1938 at Hunstanton. Ipswich, 1938

1054 **Suffolk Agricultural Association**. Catalogues of the Suffolk county show: 1952, Shrubland Park; 1956, 1961–4, 1968–9, Permanent showground, Bucklesham Road, Ipswich

1055 **Fussell, G. E.** Suffolk farmers and 'The Bath and West'. SR 2, 1959, 13–17

1056 Bury and Suffolk Farmers' Journal, 21 Aug 1844–26 Feb 1845. Bury St. Edmunds. BL

1057 Suffolk Farmers' Journal, 1944–[?]

1058 Suffolk Farmer, 1971–

GENERAL   *See also* **268, 4130, 5193, 6256**

1059 **Alexander, H.** Soils of East Suffolk, considered geologically. [East Suffolk Agricultural Association prize essay]. Woodbridge, [1840]. BL

1060 **Alexander, H.** Treatise on the nature and properties of the soils of Norfolk, Suffolk, and Essex, chemically and geologically considered in relation to agricultural purposes, etc. 1841

1061 **Bond, R.** Essay on the improvement of the pasture farming of Suffolk. Ipswich, 1861

1062 **Bennett, F. J.** The Geological Survey and its relations to agriculture. Paper read before the Ixworth Farmers' Club. Diss, [1879]. BL

1063 **Biddell, H.** Sketch of the agriculture of Suffolk. *In* White's History, gazetteer, and directory of Suffolk. Sheffield, 1874. 23–31

1064 **Biddell, H.** Agriculture. *In* VCH Suffolk, 2, 1907, 385–402

1065 **Postgate, M. R.** Field systems of East Anglia. *In* Studies of field systems in the British Isles. *Ed.* by A. R. H. Baker and R. A. Butlin. Cambridge, 1973. 281–324

1066 **Allison, T. M.** Note on a "lutchet", or wooden barn shovel and a Suffolk corn dibbler. Proc Soc Antiq Newcastle-on-Tyne 3rd Ser 3, 1907/08, 93–4

1067 **Fussell, G. E.** Farmer's tools, 1500–1900. The history of British farm implements, tools, and machinery before the tractor came. 1952

1068 **Fairclough, J. C., Ed.** The farming year in Suffolk: the use of some agricultural tools at the Museum of East Anglian Life, Stowmarket. Ely, 1977

1069 **Fussell, G. E.** Suffolk livestock: the making of the breeds. SR 2, 1962, 139–63

1070 **Kerridge, E.** Turnip husbandry in High Suffolk. EcHR 2nd Ser 8, 1955–6, 390–92

1071 **Cox, J. C.** Forestry. *In* VCH Suffolk, 2, 1907, 403–09

1072 **Green, H. T.** Two Suffolk forests. PSIA 19, 1952/7, 241–3

1073 **Forestry Commission.** East Anglian forests. *Ed* by H. L. Edlin. 1972

To c.1750

1074 **Mitchell, J. B.** Suffolk agriculture in the Middle Ages. RBA 1938, 445

1075 Agrarian history of England and Wales. v 4, 1500–1640. *Ed.* by J. Thirsk. Cambridge, 1967. Suffolk, *passim*

1076 **Tusser, T.** A hundreth good pointes of husbandrie. 1557. STC 24372. BL And later edns

1077 **Tusser, T.** Five hundredth points of good husbandry. 1573. STC 24375. BL. And later edns

1078 **Tusser, T.** Five hundred pointes of good husbandrie ... *Ed.* by W. Payne *and* S. J. Herrtage. 1878

1079 **Tusser, T.** Thomas Tusser ... his good points of husbandry. *Ed.* by D. Hartley. 1931

1080 **Tarlton, J.** Thomas Tusser in Essex and Suffolk. ER 47, 1938, 15–18

1081 **Spratt, J.** Agrarian conditions in Norfolk and Suffolk, 1600–50. MA thesis, London, 1935. Thesis summary BIHR 15, 1937/8, 113–16

1082 **'Rusticus,"** *pseud.* On the method of letting farms in Suffolk. GM 1st Ser 22, 1752, 452–3

1083 **Baker, G. B.** Bungay Club books, 1739–82; cattle plague. E Ang 2, 1864–6, 332–3

1084 Reports of the Commission on Cattle Plague. HC 1866, 22

1750–1850: The Agricultural Revolution

1085 **Kerridge, E.** The agricultural revolution. 1967

1086 **Walsh, N.** The agrarian revolution in East Anglia in its geographical aspects. MA thesis, Liverpool, 1933–4

1087 **Young, A.** Farmer's tour through the East of England, being the register of a journey through the various counties of this kingdom, to enquire into the state of agriculture. 4v. 1771

1088 **Young, A.** Minutes relating to the dairy farms, etc., of High Suffolk, taken at Aspall, the seat of the Rev. Mr. Chevallier, in Jan 1786. Annals of Agriculture, no 27, 193–224. Rp SRO/B

1089 **Young, A.** General view of the agriculture of the county of Suffolk, with observations on the means of its improvement. 1794. 1797. 3rd edn 1804. 1813 edn rp 1969

1090 Wheat, barley, and malt exported from Suffolk and Essex, 1780–86. HC General Collection 1731–1800, 77, 440

1091 **Fussell, G. E.** Some land and produce prices in late eighteenth-century Suffolk. PSIA 26, 1952/4, 137–43

1092 **Marshall, W.** Review and abstract of the county reports to the Board of Agriculture ... v 3. Eastern Department. [Includes General view of the agriculture of ... Suffolk. 1797, 404–67.] 1811. 1818. Rp 1968

1093 **Thirsk, J.,** *and* **Imray, J. M.,** *Eds.* Suffolk farming in the nineteenth century. Ipswich, 1958. SRS 1

1094 Plan offered to the consideration of the publick for letting farms, etc. Ipswich, 1804. BL

1095 Minutes of evidence before the select committee on petitions complaining of the depressed state of agriculture. HC 1821, 9

1096 Suffolk County Meeting, for Feb 6, 1830. An address to the agriculturists, by a Suffolk farmer [on their condition, and that of the nation in general]. Ipswich, 1830. BL

1097 To the farmers of Suffolk . . . against the Bill of Reform. [By a Suffolk farmer]. Ipswich, [1832]. BL

1098 Minutes of evidence taken before the select committee on agriculture and report. HC 1833, 5. Suffolk, 108

1099 Minutes of evidence before the select committee on the state of agriculture and report. HC 1837, 5

1100 **Henslow, J. S.** Letters to the farmers of Suffolk, etc. Hadleigh, [1843]

1101 **Raynbird, W.,** *and* **H.** On the agriculture of Suffolk; including the report to which the prize was awarded by the Royal Agricultural Society, 1–69. 1849

1102 **Raynbird, W.,** *Ed.* Suffolk agriculture; or, Essays and notes on some of the chief points connected with the county . . . forming a brief supplement to Messrs Raynbird's work on the 'Agriculture of Suffolk', 1849. Bungay, 1867

Enclosures and Commons   *See also* **3880, 4483, 4619, 5083, 7164, 7779**

1103 **Tate, W. E.** Handlist of Suffolk enclosure Acts and awards. PSIA 25, 1949–51, 225–63

1104 **Bury St. Edmunds and West Suffolk Record Office.** Handlist of inclosure awards and maps. Rev edn [1961]. [Typescript]. SRO/B

1105 **Lavrovsky, V. M.** Parliamentary enclosures in the county of Suffolk (1797–1814). EcHR 1st Ser 7, 1936/7, 186–208

1106 Inclosures. Return of the acreage of – 1, Waste lands subject to the right of common; 2, Common field lands in which the tithes have been commuted, etc. HC 1874, 52

1107 **Tye, W.** Common lands of East Suffolk. SR 1, 1957, 97–101

1108 Royal Commission on common lands, 1955–58. Report. 1958. Suffolk *passim*

After 1850

1109 Minutes of evidence taken before the select committee on agricultural customs. HC 1866, 6. Suffolk, 97–100, 191–9

1110 **Raynbird, W.,** *Ed.* The East Anglian agriculturist; or, A collection of papers by various authors, forming a compendium of rural proceedings for the half-year ending July 1867. 1867

1111 Return . . . of every owner of one acre and upwards . . . with the estimated extent of common and waste lands. HC 1874, 72, pt 1. Suffolk, 1–45

1112 **Royal Commission on Agriculture.** HC 1881, 15, 16. Preliminary report: Assistant commissioners' reports. HC 1880, 18. Final report: Minutes of evidence. HC 1882, 14. Assistant commissioners' reports. HC 1882, 15. Suffolk, 338–49

1113   **Fussell, G. E.** Suffolk prize farms in 1886. SR 1, 1957, 118–22

1114   **Royal Commission on the Agricultural Depression.** First report [with] minutes of evidence. HC 1894, 16

1115   **Trist, P. J. O.** Short history of the Saxmundham Experimental Station, 1899–1959. 1959

1116   **East Suffolk County Council.** Report on the visit of Suffolk farmers to Denmark, June 1901. [By C. J. Steward and W. E. Watkins]. Ipswich, [1901]

1117   **Haggard,** *Sir* **H. R.** Rural England. Being an account of agricultural and social researches carried out in the years 1901 & 1902. 2v. 1902. 1906

1118   **Maxton, J. P.,** *Ed.* Regional types of British agriculture. 1936

1119   **Agricultural Land Commission.** Lakenheath Fen investigation report. 1952

1120   **Fisons Ltd.** Levington Research Station. 1958

1121   **Young, J.** Farming in East Anglia. 1967

1122   **Trist, P. J. O.** A survey of the agriculture of Suffolk. 1971

Agricultural Labour

1123   **Fussell, G. E.** The English rural labourer: his house, furniture, clothing, and food from Tudor to Victorian times. 1949

1124   **Fussell, G. E.,** *and* **K. R.** The English countryman: his life and work. A.D.1500–1900. 1955

1125   **Fussell, G. E.,** *and* **K. R.** The English countrywoman: a farmhouse social history, A.D.1500–1900. 1953

1126   **Peacock, A. J.** Bread or blood: a study of the agrarian riots in East Anglia in 1816. 1965

1127   **Peacock, A. J.** "The revolt in the field" in East Anglia. *In* The Luddites and other essays. *Ed.* by L. M. Munby. 1971. 161–90

1128   Minutes of evidence taken before the select committee on agricultural distress. HC 1836, 8, pt 2

1129   Marriages of labourers ... Norfolk and Suffolk. HC 1837/8, 18, pt 1. Suffolk, 498–9

1130   **Kay, J. P.** Earnings of agricultural labourers in Norfolk and Suffolk. Jour Royal Statistical Soc 1, 1838, 179–83

1131   **Dymond, D. P.** Suffolk in the 1840's: the employment of women and children in agriculture. SR 3, no 2, 1965, 16–20

1132   Reports of the Special Assistant Poor Law Commissioners on the employment of women and children in agriculture. HC 1843, 12. Suffolk ... [Denison's report], 215ff

1133   **Henslow, J. S.** Suggestions towards an enquiry into the present condition of the labouring population of Suffolk. Hadleigh, 1844

1134   **Colchester, B.** Hints on the employment of agricultural labourers, etc., respectfully offered to his brother farmers. Ipswich, 1849

1135 **Suffolk Agricultural Association.** Two prize essays ... on the elevation, improvement, and education of the labouring classes, by G. K. Cooper ... and R. Bond. Ipswich, 2nd edn [1859]. BL.

1136 Children's Employment Commission: 6th report. Organized agricultural gangs ... in the Eastern counties. HC 1867, 16

1137 Royal Commission on the employment of children, young persons, and women in agriculture. HC 1867–8, 17

1138 **Clifford, F.** Agricultural lock-out of 1874, with notes upon farming and farm-labour in the eastern counties. 1875. NCL/N

1139 **Royal Commission on Labour.** Assistant commissioners' reports on agricultural labourers. HC 1893–4, 35, pt 3

1140 **Glyde, J.** Autobiography of a Suffolk farm labourer, 1816–76. [Cuttings from Suffolk Mercury, 1894]

1141 **Cooper, E. R.** Farmhouse life fifty years ago. INHSJ 1, 1923/35, 235–45

1142 **Barrett, H.** Early to rise: a Suffolk morning. 1967

1143 **Bell, A. H.** Men and the fields. 1939

1144 **Bell, A. H.** Sunrise to sunset. 1944

1145 **Bell, A. H.** Flower and the wheel. 1949

1146 **Bell, A. H.** Path by the window. 1952

1147 **Bell, A. H.** Music in the morning. 1954

1148 **Bell, A. H.** Suffolk harvest. 1956

1149 **Bell, A. H.** Street in Suffolk. 1964

1150 **Bell, A. H.** Countryman's notebook. Ipswich, 1975

1151 **Day, J. W.** New yeomen of England. 1952

1152 **Evans, G. E.** Ask the fellows who cut the hay. 1956

1153 **Evans, G. E.** Village recordings. SR 1, 1956, 37–40

1154 **Evans, G. E.** Horse in the furrow. 1960. 1967

1155 **Evans, G. E.** Pattern under the plough: aspects of the folk-life of East Anglia. 1966

1156 **Evans, G. E.** Farm and the village. 1969

1157 **Evans, G. E.** Where beards wag all: the relevance of the oral tradition. 1970

1158 **Evans, G. E.** The days that we have seen. 1975

1159 **Jobson, A.** Suffolk yesterdays. 1944. Rp 1968

1160 **Jobson, A.** This Suffolk. 1948

1161 **Jobson, A.** An hour-glass on the run. 1959

1162 **Jobson, A.** Window in Suffolk. 1962

1163 **Jobson, A.** Under a Suffolk sky. 1964

1164 **Jobson, A.** Suffolk calendar. 1966

1165 **Jobson, A.** Suffolk remembered. 1969

1166 **Jobson, A.** Suffolk miscellany. 1975

1167 **Steward, B. A.** Farm down the lane. [1946]

FISHERIES   *See also* individual localities, *below*

1168   **Nall, J. G.** History ... of the East coast herring fishery. *In his* Great Yarmouth and Lowestoft ... 1866, 258–414

1169   **De Caux, J. W.** The herring and the herring fishery, with chapters on fishes and fishing, and our sea fisheries of the future. Norwich, 1881

1170   **Hodgson, W. C.** The herring and its fishery. 1957

1171   **Green, C.** Herring-nets and beatsters: an essay in industrial archaeology. NA 34, 1969, 419–28

1172   **Cherry, P.,** *and* **Westgate, T.** Roaring boys of Suffolk. Hadleigh, 1970

1173   **Gerish, W. B.** Christ's half dole [extracted from Yarmouth Mercury, 10 Sept 1898, and Folk-lore 9, 1898, 245–50]. SCL/L

1174   **Millican, P.** Christ's dole. NA 28, 1945, 83–6

1175   **Jones, A. G. E.** Southern whale fishery. SR 3, 1966, 119–21

TRADE AND INDUSTRY

GENERAL

1176   **Unwin, G.,** *and* **Hewitt, E. M.** Industries. *In* VCH Suffolk 2, 1907, 247–300

1177   **Bygott, J.** Eastern England: some aspects of its geography, with special reference to economic significance. 1923. SCL/L

1178   **Haward, W. I.** Economic aspects of the Wars of the Roses in East Anglia. EHR 41, 1926, 170–89

1179   **Jenkins, R.** Industries of Suffolk: a historical sketch. NST 19, 1940, 173–84

1180   **Jones, A. G. E.** Suffolk bankruptcies in the 18th century. SR 2, 1959, 4–10

1181   Industries of Norfolk and Suffolk. Birmingham, [1890]. BL

1182   **Eastwood, T. B.** Industry in the county towns of Norfolk and Suffolk. Being the report of a survey carried out in 1946–7, etc. 1951

1183   **Sant, M. E. [C.]** Geography of business cycles: a case study of economic fluctuations in East Anglia, 1951–68. LSE Geographical Papers, 5. 1973

1184   **Central Office of Information.** Eastern Region: Industrial trends in the Eastern Region: looking ahead to new factors. 1958. SCL/L

1185   **Board of Trade.** Report on the census of distribution and other services, 1961. Pt 6, Area tables: Eastern region. 1964. NCL/N

1186   **West Suffolk County Council.** Planning Dept. Industry thrives in West Suffolk. Bury St. Edmunds, 1965

1187   **General Register Office.** Sample census 1966, England and Wales: Economic activity county leaflet: Suffolk. 1968

1188   **Sant, M. E. C.** Age and area in industrial location: a study of manufacturing establishments in East Anglia. Regional studies, 4, 1970, 349–58

1189   **Office of Population Censuses and Surveys.** Census 1971: Economic activity county leaflet. East Suffolk. 1975

1190   **Office of Population Censuses and Surveys.** Census 1971: Economic activity county leaflet. West Suffolk. 1975

PORTS

1191   Pfeiffer, H. Ports of East Anglia in the twelfth and thirteenth centuries. MA thesis, Reading, 1971

1192   Williams, N. J. Maritime trade of the East Anglian ports, 1550–90. D.Phil. thesis, Oxford, 1952

1193   Return of dues and charges on shipping and goods imported at each port in the U.K. HC 1846, 46

1194   Pieters, L. J. Hundred years of sea communication between England and the Netherlands. JTH 6, 1964, 210–21

1195   Eastern Daily Press. The maritime province. Supplement May 31, 1961. Norwich. SCL/L

1196   Wren, W. J. Ports of the Eastern counties. Lavenham, 1976

MARKETS AND FAIRS

1197   [Caraccioli, C.] Historical account of Sturbridge, and Bury, and the most famous fairs in Europe and America. Cambridge, 1773

1198   Kemble, W. H. Kemble's list of fairs in Norfolk and Suffolk ... Swaffham, [c.1830]. NCL/N

1199   Raven, J. J. Notes on Suffolk fairs. ECM 1, 1900/01, 92–6

1200   Scarfe, N. Markets and fairs in medieval Suffolk. SR 3, no 1, 1965, 4–11

1201   Scarfe, N. Markets and fairs in 17th-century Suffolk. SR 3, no 2, 1965, 11–15

1202   Royal Commission on Market Rights and Tolls. First report: Appendix. HC 1888, 53. Statistics relating ... markets owned by local authorities. HC 1890–91, 39

1203   Dickinson, R. E. Markets and market areas of East Anglia. EcGeog 10, 1934, 172–82

STEELYARDS   *See* **3967, 4575, 8012**

COINS AND TOKENS

1204   Montagu, H. Find of ancient British gold coins in Suffolk. NC 3rd Ser 6, 1886, 23–37

1205   Account of some Saxon coins found in Suffolk. PTRS 16, 1688, 356–61

1206   W, W. Remarks on some Saxon coins found in Suffolk. PTRS 16, 1688, 361–6

1207   Haigh, D. H. Essay on the numismatic history of the ancient kingdom of the East Angles. Leeds, 1845. SRO/B

1208   H[aigh], D. H. On the coins of East Anglia. NC 2, 1840, 47–51

1209   Haigh, D. H. Remarks on the numismatic history of East Anglia during the seventh, eighth, and ninth centuries. NC 4, 1842, 34–41, 195–200

1210   Conder, J. An arrangement of provincial coins, tokens, and medalets issued in Great Britain ... within the last 20 years; from the farthing to the penny size. 2v. Ipswich, 1798. 2v. 1799. *See also* **2678**

1211 **Fitch, W. S.** Notices of coins and antiquities found in Suffolk. JBAA 1, 1846, 257; 2, 1847, 190, 268, 279, 345, 347; 3, 1848, 254; 21, 1865, 14–15

1212 **Golding, C.** Coinage of Suffolk: consisting of the regal coins, leaden pieces, and tokens of the 17th, 18th, and 19th centuries. 1868. SRO/I copy interleaved with extra illus. and newspaper cuttings

1213 **Seaby, W. A.** Mid-fifteenth-century hoard from Suffolk. BNJ 35, 1967, 195–8

1214 One hundred and seventy Suffolk tradesmen's tokens, engraved on seventeen plates for the late W. S. Fitch, Esq. Lowestoft, 1836

1215 **Boyne, W.** Tokens issued in the seventeenth century in England, Wales, and Ireland, by corporations, merchants, tradesmen, etc. 1858. New edn. Trade tokens, *Ed.* by G. C. Williamson. 2v. 1889–91. Suffolk v 2, 1061–1106. Rp 1967

1216 **Baker, G. B.** Suffolk tradesmen's tokens. E Ang 1, 1858/63, 267

1217 **Skinner, E.** Trade and other tokens for Norfolk and Suffolk. E Ang NS 3, 1890/91, 35–6

1218 **Wall, S. D.** Casting-counters or tokens from Suffolk. ER 52, 1943, 52–4

1219 **Cranbrook,** *Earl of.* Some tradesmen's tokens of the seventeenth century. PSIA 24, 1946/8, 20–24, 63–99

1220 **Atkins, J.** Tradesmen's tokens of the eighteenth century. 1892

1221 **Dalton, R.** *and* **Hamer, S. H.** Provincial token-coinage of the 18th century. 1910. Suffolk, 244–51. Rp 1967

1222 **Blunt, C. E.** St. Edmund memorial coinage. PSIA 31, 1967/9, 234–55

PARTICULAR TRADES, FIRMS, ETC

Agricultural Machinery Manufacture　　　　*See also* **1067, 5706–7, 5713, 5716–25**

1223 **Lines, C. J.** Development and location of the specialist agricultural engineering industry, with special reference to East Anglia. M.Sc. (Econ.) thesis, London, 1961

1224 **Fussell, G. E.** Suffolk farm-machinery industry. SR 2, 1964, 217–31

Apprenticeship   See **1508, 3838–9, 5658–60**

Auctioneers, Estate Agents, and Surveyors　　　　　　　　*See also* **5732**

1225 [**Shuttleworth, C. E.**] Professional excursions by an auctioneer. Pt 1, Essex, Suffolk, ... 1843. [No more publ.] BL

1226 Seven centuries of surveying in Suffolk: an exhibition arranged by the Ipswich and East Suffolk Record Office in association with the Royal Institution of Chartered Surveyors, held at Christchurch Mansion, 1954. Ipswich

1227 **Scarfe, N.** Whitney and Read: two Regency estate agents (with a short account of the Worlingham estate, 1755–1851). PSIA 28, 1958/60, 185–96

Banking and Insurance

1228 **Bidwell, W. H.** Annals of an East Anglian bank (Gurney and Co.). Norwich, 1900

1229 **Matthews, P. W.** History of Barclays Bank, Ltd. *Ed.* by A. W. Tuke. 1926

1230 **Jones, A. G. E.** Early banking in Suffolk. N&Q 199, 1954; 200, 1955, *passim*

1231 **Drew, B.** "The Fire Office" . . . the history of the Essex and Suffolk Equitable Insurance Society, 1802–1952. 1952

1232 **Halls, H.** Essex copper plate . . . the copper fire-plates issued by the Essex and Suffolk Insurance Co. Ltd. between 1802 and 1829. [1968]

1233 **Halls, H.** British fire marks and plates (with special reference to the Lowestoft area). LA&LHS 1970/71, 32–9

Bellfounding See **2262, 4138–9, 5695**

Brewing See **4141–2, 5696–7, 6835**

Brick Making See **7208, 7283**

Building Societies See **4137, 5698–702**

Clockmaking

1234 **Ford, J. C.** Grandfather clocks of East Anglian construction. E Ang NS 2, 1887/8, 109–11, 160

1235 **Haggar, A. L.,** *and* **Miller, L. F.** Suffolk clocks and clockmakers. Ramsgate, 1975

Coachbuilding See **5703–4, 6644**

Engineering See also **5705–26, 6437**

1236 **Fletcher, W.** Steam locomotion on common roads. Ipswich, 1891

1237 **Clark, R. H.** Steam-engine builders of Suffolk, Essex, and Cambridgeshire. Norwich, 1950

1238 **Clark, R. H.** Eastern Counties and its outstanding steam engines. NST 27, 1956, 31–42

1239 **Pratt, R. G.** Suffolk and the traction engine. SR 1, 1957, 50–53, 76–80

Flint Knapping See also Brandon, *below*

1240 **Skertchly, S. B. J.** On the manufacture of gun flints, the methods of excavating for flints, the age of palaeolithic man, and the connection between Neolithic art and the gun flint trade. Mem Geol Survey. 1879

1241 **Knowles,** *Sir* F. H. S., *and* **Barnes, A. S.** Manufacture of gunflints. Ant 11, 1937, 201–07

Pottery and China Manufacture See **3629, 5349–50, 5577–8, 7082, 7842–4, 7904–5,** *and* Lowestoft

Printing See also **2770, 3724–5, 5727–31**

1242 Printing in East Anglia exhibition [at Aldeburgh Festival]: a survey tracing the development ... 16th century to the early years of the 19th century, drawn from the collection of S. F. Watson. Ipswich, [1950]

1243 **Watson, S. F.** Early print in East Anglia. Brit Fed of Master Printers: Members' Circular 50, 1951, 181–3

1244 Early print in East Anglia: an exhibition ... arranged by S. F. Watson. Brit Fed of Master Printers Congress, Eastbourne, 1951

1245 **Goffin, J. H.** Early East Anglian printers. EAM 19, 1952, 18–24

1246 **Blake, N. F.** William Caxton and Suffolk. PSIA 29, 1961/3, 139–53; 30, 1964/6, 112–15

Retail Trade See **5733–5, 6972**

Salt Making

1247 **Cooper, E. R.** Salt-pans in Suffolk. NST 19, 1940, 213–15

1248 **Cooper, E. R.** Old-time saltworks in Suffolk. PSIA 24, 1946/8, 25–9

Shipbuilding See **5660, 6684–6**

Tea and Coffee

1249 **Jones, A. G. E.** Messrs Twining's ledgers [Tea and coffee merchants – Suffolk references]. SR 2, 1961, 65–72

Textiles See also **7982**

1250 **Benton, G. M.** Yarn industry in Suffolk. E Ang NS 13, 1909/10, 289

1251 **Gowers, W. R.** Cultivation of flax and hemp in Suffolk in the 14th century. E Ang NS 5, 1893/4, 180–83, 200–02

1252 **Meek, M.** Hempen cloth industry in Suffolk. SR 2, 1961, 82–5

1253 **Wilton, H. E.** Suffolk hemp industry, some further observations. SR 2, 1961, 121–5

1254 **McClenaghan, B.** Suffolk cloth trade in the 15th and 16th centuries. JAABI 2, 1931/2, 8–11

1255 **Pilgrim, J. E.** Cloth industry in Essex and Suffolk, 1558–1640. M.A. thesis, London, 1940. Thesis summary, BIHR 17, 1940, 143–5

1256 Humble petition of the clothiers of the county of Suffolk and Essex, delivered to his Majesty at Greenwich, Feb 10, with the King's most gracious answer to their petition Feb 11. 1641. Wing H 3491. BL

1257 To the ... House of Commons ... the ... petition of the clothiers, and others, inhabitants of the countie of Suffolk, now attending this hon. House, and of the townes of Dedham and Langham in Essex [in relation to the customs duty on certain cloths, etc.]. 1642. Wing T 1439. BL

1258 Clothiers petition to his Majestie, with his Majestie's gracious answer: To the kings most excellent majestie the humble petition of the clothiers of Suffolk, and the townes of Dedham and Langham in Essex [on the decay of trade] 10 Feb 1641/2. Wing C 4735. BL-T

1259   To the rt. hon. the Parliament ... the humble petition of the real lenders upon the public faith, the clothiers and all others in the counties of Essex and Suffolk, in behalf of themselves and all others the like that are unpaid [praying for payment]. 1657, [April]. Wing T 1706. BL-T

1260   **Courtauld, S. A.** East Anglia and the Huguenot textile industry. HSLP 13, 1923/9, 125–53

1261   Letter to ... the Duke of Grafton upon the Bill [28 Geo III, c.38] now depending in Parliament "For preserving the exportation of live sheep, wool, etc." [Subscribed: "The wool growers in the county of Suffolk"]. Ipswich, 1787. BL

1262   **Heard, N.** Wool, East Anglia's golden fleece. Lavenham, 1970

Thatching

1263   **Haslam, S. M.** The reed: a study of *Phragmites communis Trin*, in relation to its cultivation and harvesting in East Anglia for the thatching industry. Norwich, 1969. 2nd edn 1972

TRANSPORT AND COMMUNICATIONS

SOCIETIES

1264   **Ipswich and District Historical Transport Society.** Handbooks No 1, 1967–8; No 2, 1970; No 3, 1972. Capel St. Mary. Monthly bulletin, 1963–70, then bi-monthly. Ipswich. [Typescript]

1265   **Ipswich and District Historical Transport Society.** Exhibition catalogue. The story of transport ... 11–14 Aug 1965, St. Peter's Hall, Ipswich. Ipswich, 1965. [Typescript]

1266   **Ipswich Land Transport Society,** later **Ipswich Transport Society.** Monthly Newsletter, no 1, Oct 1964–no 14, Nov 1965; Anglia Transport Journal, Jan 1966–April 1966; Ipswich Transport Journal, May 1966–

TRACKS

1267   **Thomas, E.** Icknield Way. 1913. SRO/B

1268   **Clarke, W. G.** Icknield Way in East Anglia. PPSEA 2, 1914/18, 539–48

1269   **Hill, H. C.** Part of the Peddar Way in Suffolk. PSIA 18, 1922/4, 211–21

1270   **Knocker, H. W.** Ancient 'greenways' of Suffolk. Manorial Soc Publ 15, 1928, 3–6

1271   **Dunt, R. C.** Local markstones, roads, and trackways [Beccles and district]. JAABI 1, 1930/1, 167–70

ROADS

1272   **Raven, J. J.** Roman roads in the East of England. Arch J 35, 1878, 80–84

1273   **Napper, H. F.** Roman roads of Eastern England in the Itinerary of Antoninus. E Ang NS 2, 1887/8, 278, 283

1274   **Napper, H. F.** Roman roads in Eastern Britain. Ickworth as site of Villa Faustini. E Ang NS 3, 1889/90, 69–70, 77–8, 166

1275 Beaumont, G. F., *et al.* Ninth Iter of Antoninus. E Ang NS 5, 1893/4, 289–98, 321–3

1276 Dewhurst, P. C. Leman's suggested Roman road from New Buckenham to Burgh Castle. Norfolk Research Committee Bull 10, 1958, 4–5

1277 Margary, I. D. Roman roads in Britain. 1967 *See also* 651, 3695–6, 3873, 6283, 7055, 7239

1278 J, C. An order of the Suffolk justices for fixing the rates for land carriage. GM 1st Ser 19, 1749, 265–6

1279 Observations made in a survey of the road leading from Woodbridge to Debenham ... the plan of which accompanies this paper. Woodbridge, 1800. BL

1280 Report from the select committee appointed to consider the Acts now in force regarding turnpike roads and highways. HC 1821, 4. Suffolk, 206–11

1281 Copies of the several accounts transmitted to the clerks of the peace of the ... counties ... from the clerks of ... the several turnpike trusts ... HC 1824, 20. Suffolk, 668–79

1282 Ipswich Turnpike. General statement of the income and expenditure ... 1825–43. Halesworth, 1843 BL. 1844, 1846, O

1283 Aldeburgh Turnpike. General statement of the income and expenditure ... 1832–3, 1835–44. Ipswich. BL

1284 Abstract of the general statements of the income and expenditure of the several turnpike trusts, 1834–82. HC 1836, 83

1285 Report of the select committee on railroads and turnpike trusts. HC 1839, 9. Suffolk, 429–32

1286 Report of the commissioners for inquiring into the state of the roads in England and Wales. HC 1840, 27

1287 Abstract of the general statements of the receipts and expenditure on account of the highways of the several parishes, townships, etc., in England and Wales, 1850–83. HC 1852–83

1288 Return of turnpike trusts, continued by annual continuance Acts in 1864, 1865, 1866, and 1867, giving name of trust and county, date of expiry of last local Act, amount of interest per cent payable, etc. HC 1867–8, 62. Suffolk, 455–7

1289 Return showing the several highway districts in each county ... constituted under the Highway Acts 1862 and 1864, and the names of the parishes comprised in each district. HC 1873, 58. Suffolk, 154, 239–41, 336–7

1290 Return of the names of the several turnpike roads which have become disturnpiked between 31 Dec 1870 and 30 June 1878 in each county, etc. HC 1878, 66. Suffolk, 679, 690, 697

1291 Harper, C. G. The Norwich road: an East Anglian highway. 1901

1292 Harper, C. G. The Newmarket, Bury, Thetford, and Cromer road: sport and history on an East Anglian turnpike ... 1904

1293 Partridge, C. Tolls of the turnpike road, Worlington. E Ang NS 12, 1907/08, 254

1294 **Bullen, R. F.** St. Edmundsbury coach. [*from* Bury Post]. 1913. SCL/B

1295 **Thompson, L. P.** Suffolk coaching days. 1966

1296 **Serjeant, W. R.,** *and* **Penrose, D. G.** Suffolk turnpikes. Ipswich, 1973. Suffolk documents, 1

BRIDGES   *See also* **1322, 3914, 5278, 6252, 6636, 6907, 6930–31, 7062**

1297 List of county bridges in the Eastern division of the county of Suffolk, adopted by the Court of Quarter Sessions at Ipswich, 6 Jan 1881

1298 **Jervoise, E.** Ancient bridges of Mid- and Eastern England. 1932

RIVERS   *See also* Place-names, *above, and* Yachting, *below*

1299 Rivers of the East coast: descriptive, historical, pictorial. 1902

1300 Rivers Orwell, Deben, and Alde and the coast 'twixt Felixstowe and Southwold. Croydon, nd. NCL/N

1301 **Turner, J.** Rivers of East Anglia. 1954

1302 **Barringer, J. C.** Rivers of Norfolk and North Suffolk. *In* East Anglian studies. *Ed.* by L. M. Munby. Cambridge, 1968. 1–16

Alde

1303 **Arnott, W. G.** Alde estuary: the story of a Suffolk river. Ipswich, 1952. 2nd edn 1961. Rp 1973

Blyth   *See also* Dunwich, Southwold, *and* Walberswick, *below*

1304 Reports ... on the embarkments and encroachments upon the Crown lands of the river Blyth and harbour of Southwold, etc. [1845]. BL

Deben

1305 **M, J. S.,** *and* **Josselyn, J. H.** "Gofforde", an allegedly lost town, suggested to be connected with Gosford Haven, near Woodbridge. N&Q 9th Ser 8, 1901, 63, 151

1306 **Arnott, W. G.** Suffolk estuary: the story of the river Deben. Ipswich, 1950 Rp 1955, 1968, 1973

Orwell   *See also* Ipswich, *below, and* **1361, 4887, 4891**

1307 **Myers, W.** Account of the river Orwell or Orewell in the county of Suffolk and of the town and harbour of that name. Arch 10, 1792, 350–59

1308 **Fulcher, T.** Hints for a plan of the intended improvement of the river Orwell. Ipswich, 1803. SRO/B

1309 **Barton, B.** Triumph of the Orwell, with dedicatory sonnet, etc. Woodbridge, [1817]. BL

1310 The Orwell, a descriptive poem. Written by A Gentleman [John Cordingley] and published for the benefit of a poor family. Ipswich, 1826

1311 Ipswich Steam Packet companion; containing a description of all objects worthy of notice, between London and Ipswich, with historical remarks. Ipswich, 1834. 1840

1312 [**Wodderspoon, J.**] Steam-boat guide, between Ipswich and London, ... being a complete companion for the steam-boat traveller. Ipswich, [1842?]

1313 **Hurwood, G.** Port of Ipswich: report on the proposed channels ... [river Orwell]. Ipswich, [1845]

1314 **Hurwood, G.** River Orwell and port of Ipswich. Ipswich, 1862

1315 **Dorling, E.** Steam-packet guide between London and Ipswich. Ipswich, 1865

1316 Handbook for the river Orwell. Harwich, new edn [1870]. BL

1317 King's guide to the river Orwell. Ipswich, 2nd edn [c.1880] 5th edn [c.1892]

1318 Ipswich to Harwich: King's penny guide to the river Orwell. [Ipswich?], 2nd edn [1883?]. 5th edn 1888

1319 **Thompson, L. P.** Cruising down the Orwell: a companion to your river cruise. Ipswich, 1952

1320 **Arnott, W. G.** Orwell estuary: the story of Ipswich river, with Harwich and the Stour. Ipswich, 1954

1321 **Ipswich Corporation.** Museum Committee. The story of the Orwell: an exhibition. Ipswich, 1959

Stour

1322 **Hodson, W. W.** Ballingdon [Essex] bridge and the Sudbury Stour. PSIA 8, 1892/4, 21–30

1323 Committee on river Stour improvement. Report, with Engineer's reports. 1914

1324 **Waller, A. J. R.** Suffolk Stour. Ipswich, 1957

1325 **Inland Waterways Association.** The Essex and Suffolk river Stour. 1974

Waveney See also **1332**

1326 **Robberds, J. W.** Scenery of the rivers of Norfolk, comprising the Yare, the Waveney, and the Bure, from pictures by ... J. Stark; with historical and geological descriptions. 1834. SCL/L

1327 **Edwards, G.** River Waveney: did it ever reach the sea via Lowestoft? Lowestoft, 1879. SCL/L

1328 **Baker, B. G.** Waveney. 1924

1329 **Pursehouse, E.** Waveney valley studies: gleanings from local history. Diss, [1966]

1330 **Butcher, D. R.** Waveney valley. Ipswich, 1975

INLAND WATERWAYS

1331 **Fenn, E. A. H.** Origin of the inland waterways of East Anglia. 1934. NCL/N

1332 **Mathew, F.** To His Highness Oliver, Lord Protector ... is ... presented a mediterranean passage by water between ... Lynn and Yarmouth, upon two rivers, the Little Owse and Waveney. 1656. Wing M 1317. 1670. Wing M 1318. BL

1333 **Phillips, J.** Treatise on inland navigation: illustrated with a whole-sheet plan, delineating the course of an intended navigable canal from London to Norwich and Lynn. 1785. BL

1334   Act, for making and maintaining a navigable communication between Stow-market and Ipswich, 1790. 1793

1335   Proposals ... by the committee appointed to promote the making of a navigable canal from Bury St. Edmund's to Mistley, for raising the money necessary for the said work. Bury St. Edmunds, [1791]. BL

1336   [Nichols, J.] Dialogue between M., N., and O., wrote by a Suffolk ploughboy. [Scheme for a canal from Diss to Bungay, Beccles, and Yarmouth]. Norwich, [1817]

1337   Prospectus of the intended Diss and Bungay junction navigation company. nd. O

1338   Diss and Bungay navigation. Jan 1818. Yarmouth. O

1339   Smith, [–]. Statement of facts relative to the Bungay Navigation. 1818. nl

1340   Report and pamphlets on the subject of Norwich a port; from ... 1818, to the passing of the Norwich and Lowestoft Navigation Act in 1827. Lowestoft, [1830?] BL

1341   Speech of Alderman Crisp Brown, delivered at the public meeting held at the Guildhall at Norwich on Tuesday, 8 Sept 1818, together with Mr. Cubitt's report upon a plan for making the river from Norwich to Yarmouth navigable. Norwich, 1818. SCL/L

1342   Cubitt, W. Second report ... to the committee, appointed for taking into consideration the best means of making Norwich a port, by joining the rivers Yare and Waveney, and opening a harbour at Lowestoft. Norwich, [1820]

1343   Remarks on the intended measure of making Norwich a port, and opening a harbour at Lowestoft. Great Yarmouth, 1822. SCL/L

1344   Barrett, H. Warning voice to the projectors, subscribers, and supporters of the plan for making Norwich a port ... Great Yarmouth, 1823. NCL/N

1345   Bevan, B. Report made 16 Feb 1824 on the plan for making a ship navigation from the sea at Lowestoft to Norwich. Norwich, 1826. NCL/N

1346   Nicholls, G. Report ... upon the projected plan of opening a navigable communication for ships of burthen between the city of Norwich and the sea at Lowestoft. Norwich, 1825. O

1347   Reports on the report of Captain George Nicholls addressed to the proprietors of lands on the level with the rivers Yare, Waveney, and Bure [signed Gariensis]. Norwich, [1825]. O

1348   Walker, J. Report made 19 Jan 1826 to the corporation of Great Yarmouth, on the plan for making a ship navigation from the sea at Lowestoft to Norwich. Yarmouth, 1826. O

1349   Abstract of the minutes of evidence taken before a committee of the House of Commons, during the session of 1826, on a bill for making a navigable communication ... between the city of Norwich and the sea at or near Lowestoft ... Norwich. HC, 1826, 4

1350   Act for making and maintaining a navigable communication for ships ... between the city of Norwich and the sea, at or near Lowestoft ... 7 & 8 Geo. IV, XIII, 1827. Amended by 2 & 3 Will. IV, II, 1832. SCL/L

1351   Cubitt, W. Report and estimate on the river Waveney between Beccles Bridge and Oulton Dyke, towards making Beccles a port ... Beccles, 1829. O

1352   Cole, W. Poetical sketch of the Norwich and Lowestoft navigation works, from their commencement at Lake Lothing, to the opening of the harbour, 10 Aug 1831, in three cantos, with notes. Norwich, 1833. SCL/L

1353   Body, G., *and* Eastleigh, R. L. Norwich and Lowestoft navigation. EAM 28, 1968, 30–31

1354   Burnell, G. R. Report ... on the navigation of the river Lark to Bury St. Edmunds, May 1863. 1863. SRO/B

1355   East Suffolk and Norfolk River Board. Annual reports 1952/3–1964/5, *cont. as* East Suffolk and Norfolk River Authority. Annual reports 1965/6–. Norwich

1356   East Suffolk and Norfolk River Board. Byelaws 1963. Norwich. NCL/N

1357   Hull, J. S. River Stour Navigation Company. PSIA 32, 1970/72, 221–54

1358   Inland Waterways Association Ltd. London and Home Counties Branch. Essex and Suffolk river Stour, Sudbury to Brantham Lock: a handbook of historical and general information on the river with a detailed description of the navigation, and map. [1966]. SRO/B

1359   East Anglian Waterways Association Ltd. Newsletter no 1, 1968–

1360   Clark, R. Black-sailed traders: the keels and wherries of Norfolk and Suffolk. 1961

1361   Jones, A. G. E. Wherries on the Orwell. SR 2, 1963, 202–06

1362   Malster, R. [W.] Wherries and waterways: the story of the Norfolk and Suffolk wherry and the waterways on which it sailed. Lavenham, 1971

RAILWAYS
1363   Simmons, J. Railways of Britain: an historical introduction. 1961. Suffolk, 197–209

1364   Thomas, D. St. J., *Ed*. Regional history of the railways of Great Britain. v 5, Eastern counties, *by* D. I. Gordon. Newton Abbot, 1968

1365   Joby, R. S. Forgotten railways: East Anglia. Newton Abbot, 1977

1366   Saunders, J. F. Railways in the Eastern Counties district. 1852. BL

1367   Doble, E. History of the Eastern Counties railway in relation to contemporary economic development. Ph.D. thesis, London, 1939

1368   Gordon, D. I. East Anglian Railways Company: a study in railway and financial history. Ph.D. thesis, Nottingham, 1964

1369   Body, G., *and* Eastleigh, R. L. East Anglian Railway. Walthamstow, 1967. Transport History Ser. no 3

1370   Meik, H. Eastern Union Railway. RM 25, 1909, 513; 26, 1910, 43

1371   Hilton, H. F. Eastern Union Railway, 1846–62. 1946

1372   Allen, C. J. Great Eastern Railway. 1955 and later edns

1373   Riley, R. C. Great Eastern album. 1968. SCL/L

1374   Great Eastern Railway Magazine, v 1–12, Jan 1911–Dec 1922; *cont. as* Great

Eastern Magazine, v 13–16, Jan 1923–Dec 1926; *incorp. in* London and North Eastern Railway Magazine, Jan 1927–Dec 1947

1375 **Crump, N.** By rail to victory: the story of the LNER in wartime. 1947. SCL/L

1376 **Allen, C. J.** London and North Eastern Railway. 1966

1377 **Stephenson, B.** LNER album. 2v. 1970. SCL/L

1378 **Railway Invigoration Society.** East Suffolk railway line: an historical outline. Thame, 1965

1379 **Clark, R. H.** Short history of the Midland and Great Northern Joint Railway. Norwich, 1967

1380 **Wrottesley, A. J. F.** Midland and Great Northern Joint Railway. Newton Abbot, 1970

1381 **Mitchell, (–.)** Railways in and about Lowestoft. LA&LHS 1966–7, 15–17

1382 **Driver, G.** Growing up with a railway. SR 3, 1968, 212–15

1383 Great Chesterford and Newmarket Railway. RM 49, 1921, 422. *See also* **6971**

1384 **Brown, K.** Newmarket and Chesterford Railway. RM 87, 1941, 488, 533–6

1385 **Walsh, B. D. J.** Sudbury and Haverhill line, Eastern Region. RM 97, 1951, 616–20

1386 **Norfolk, Suffolk, and Essex Railroad Company.** Prospectus, dated 8 March 1825. BL

1387 **Eastern Counties Railway.** Minutes of proceedings before the committee on the Eastern Counties Railway Bill. 1836

1388 **Eastern Counties Railway.** Proceedings of the first general meeting ... held at the London Tavern, Bishopsgate Street, Monday 26 Sept 1836

1389 **Robertson, J. C.** Letter to Henry Norcutt Ward, Esq., on the progress and prospects of the Eastern Counties Railway Company. 1837

1390 Lowestoft to Reedham railway. Report of the speeches delivered in the Town Hall, Lowestoft on Saturday, 28 Sept 1844 ... Lowestoft, 3rd edn [1844]. NCL/N

1391 Report of the railway department of the Board of Trade on the schemes for extending railway communication in the counties of Norfolk and Suffolk. HC 1845, 39. SCL/L

1392 Minutes of evidence taken before the select committee on railway labourers. HC 1846, 13

1393 Railway reports: Colchester, Stour valley, Sudbury, and Halstead; Eastern Union; Halesworth, Beccles, etc.; Ipswich, Bury St. Edmund's, and Newmarket. HC 1847, 31

1394 **Eastern Counties Railway.** Official guides. Norwich, 1847, 1851, 1857

1395 Report of the committee of investigation to the shareholders of the Eastern Counties Railway Company. 1849. BL

1396 Report from the select committee on the Eastern Counties Railway Company. HC 1849, 10

1397 **Whitehead, J.** Key to railway investment: Pt 4, The Eastern Counties Railway. 1850. nl

1398 **Castle, H. J.** A few words to the shareholders of the Eastern Counties Railway Company. [1851]. BL

1399 **Eastern Counties Railway.** Report of the committee of investigation, and minutes of evidence ... together with the documents in relation thereto. 1855. BL

1400 Time-tables for the Eastern Counties, Norfolk, Newmarket, East Anglian, Eastern Union ... Railways, no 1–90; *cont. as* Time tables of the Great Eastern Railway. Stratford. BL

1401 Eastern Counties Railway. Why it does not pay? 1859. NCL/N

1402 **East Suffolk Railway.** Banquet at the Royal Hotel, Lowestoft, ... 14 June 1859. BL

1403 **Eastern Counties Railway.** A few facts and figures omitted from "Why it does not pay?", being an exposure of the palpable misrepresentations and falsehoods contained in the pamphlet. 1860. NCL/N

1404 A word or two about "E. U." [i.e. Eastern Union Railway], being an appeal to the President of the Board of Trade by an Old Aquaintance. 1860. BL

1405 **Great Eastern Railway.** Official guides. 1864–1923. BL

1406 Report of the committee of the Great Eastern Railway Shareholders' Association. 1866. BL

1407 **Great Eastern Railway Company** ... Reports of the directors. Ninth, 1867– Seventieth, 1897 [incomplete]. BL

1408 Cowell's model timetables and monthly handbooks, Nov. 1874–. Ipswich

1409 **Bass, M. T.** Circular from M. T. Bass, Esq., M.P., on the Great Eastern Railway, with a financial report. 1876. nl

1410 **Stebbings, A.** Model railway time-table, and travellers' guide, Aug 1878–June 1883, Oct 1885. [Lowestoft]. BL

1411 **Great Eastern Railway.** Rules and regulations, 1 June 1904. SCL/L

1412 **Great Eastern Railway.** Time-tables, July, Aug, and Sept 1913. SCL/L

1413 **British Railway Board,** Eastern Region. Heads of information in connection with the proposal to alter the passenger services between Cambridge and Ipswich. 1965. [Typescript]. SRO/B

1414 **Midland and Great Northern Joint Railway Society.** East Anglian branch line farewell rail-tour to mark the last day of through services on the Stour Valley and St. Ives branch lines, Saturday 4 March 1967. Sheringham, 1967. SRO

1415 **Long, P. D.** Bus or train? A commentary on the 1965 proposal to close the East Suffolk railway passenger services. 1968

1416 **Joby, R. S.** Felixstowe railway centenary, 1877–1977. Norwich, 1976

1417 **Prentice, K. R.,** *and* **Proud, P.** Locomotives of the LNER, 1923–37. 1941. SCL/L

1418 **Aldrich, C. L.** Locomotives of the Great Eastern Railway, 1862–. 1944 and later edns

1419 **Williams, A.,** *and* **Percival, D.** *Eds.* B.R. Steam locomotives from nationalisation to modernisation ... v 4, Eastern Region. 1967. SCL/L

Light Railways

1420 **Tonks, E. S.** Southwold railway. 1950. 2nd edn, with A. R. Taylor. [1965]

1421 **Jenkins, A. B.** Memories of the Southwold railway. Southwold, 1964 and later edns.

1422 **Jenkins, A. B.** Southwold railway. LA&LHS 1970/71, 21–4

1423 **Southwold and Lowestoft Light Railway.** Book of reference, May 1899. Plans and sections, 1899. SCL/L

1424 Southwold Railway timetable, 9 July–23 Sept 1928. SCL/L

1425 Mid-Suffolk Light Railway Order by the Light Railway Commissioners, authorising the construction of a light railway in the county of Suffolk. 1900. Amended 1902. nl

1426 Mid-Suffolk Light Railway: album of photographs and press notices of the ceremony of cutting the first sod at Westerfield Junction, Saturday, 3 May 1902, by H.R.H. the Duke of Cambridge

1427 **Comfort, N. A.** Mid-Suffolk Light Railway. Lingfield, Surrey, 1963

BUSES AND TRAMS   *See also* **5714,** Ipswich, *and* Lowestoft, *below*

1428 **Brewster, D. E.** Motor buses in East Anglia, 1901–31. Lingfield, Surrey, 1974. NCL/N

1429 **Eastern Counties Omnibus Co.** Motor coach services in the Eastern counties: an official handbook, 1937 and later edns. Gloucester. BL

1430 **P.S.V. Circle and Omnibus Society.** Eastern Counties Omnibus Company, Ltd., and the corporations of Great Yarmouth, Ipswich, and Lowestoft. [1958]. [1961]

1431 A.B.C. British bus fleets. No 4. East Anglia, by B. C. Kennedy and P. J. Marshall. 1962 and later edns

1432 **P.S.V. Circle and Omnibus Society.** Small stage-carriage operators of Essex and Suffolk. 1967. SCL/L

1433 **Everett, C. G. G.** From Tilling to National Bus Company: the story of Eastern Counties Omnibus Company, Ltd. Thesis, Keswick Hall College of Education, 1970. [Typescript]. SCL/L

1434 **Taylor, G. H.** Tramways of East Anglia. 1950

1435 **Anderson, R. C.** Tramways of East Anglia. 1969

POSTAL HISTORY

1436 **Driver, G.** Early days of the post-mail transport in East Anglia. Stamp Lover 59, May–June 1967

1437 **Driver, G.** Early days of the post. Stamp Lover 59, July–Aug 1967

1438 **Driver, G.** Early days of the post-charges and delays. Stamp Lover 61, Jan–Feb. 1969

1439 **East Anglia Postal History Study Circle.** Bulletins 1, Nov 1962–. [First 2 Bulletins as Norfolk Postal History Study Circle]. [Typescript]

1440 **Ipswich Philatelic Society.** East Anglia Philex: souvenir programme ... Ipswich, 9–10 Dec 1966. Ipswich, 1966

Local Government, Social Services, and Justice

GENERAL ADMINISTRATION

MEDIEVAL PERIOD

1441 **Gowers, W. R.** Where did the Thing of Suffolk meet? E Ang NS 3, 1899/90, 268–70

1442 **Cane, L. B.** Reeves and greaves. PSIA 26, 1952/4, 148–54, 233

1443 **Dymond, D. P.** The Chilton "bulge" [early mapping of Suffolk hundreds]. PSIA 33, 1973/5, 318–21

1444 **Cam, H. M.** The King's government, as administered by the greater abbots of East Anglia. PCAS 29, 1926/7, 25–49. *Rp in* Liberties and communities in medieval England. Cambridge, 1944

1445 **Ainsley, H.** Local administration and the maintenance of peace in Eastern England in the latter half of the thirteenth century. Ph.D. thesis, Wales, 1968

1446 **Morey, G. E.** Administration of the counties of Norfolk and Suffolk in the reign of Henry IV. M.A. thesis, London, 1941. Thesis summary. BIHR 19, 1944, 91–3

1447 **Page, A.** Charter of exemption from the office of Sheriff, etc., [1401]. PSIA 1, 1848/53, 140–41

1448 **Virgoe, R.** Government and society of Suffolk in the later Middle Ages. LA&LHS 1967/8, 28–32

1500–1800

1449 **Whitfield, J. H.** Evolution of local government authorities and areas in Suffolk, 1555–1894. MA thesis, Kent, 1970

1450 Lord Lieutenancy of Suffolk under the Tudors. PSIA 20, 1928/30, 227–31

1451 Extracts from the Sessions Order Book, 1639–51. PSIA 15, 1913/15, 152–82

1452 **Cullum, G. G. M. G.** Some of Sir Jasper Cullum's shrievalty expenses, etc., 1721–2. E Ang NS 3, 1888/9, 37–41

19TH AND 20TH CENTURIES

1453 Municipal Corporations Select Committee report. Minutes of evidence. HC 1833, 13

1454 First report of the commissioners appointed to inquire into municipal corporations in England and Wales. Appendix, pt 4. Eastern and north-western circuits. HC 1835, 26. Aldborough, 5ff.; Beccles, 69ff.; Bury St. Edmunds, 91ff.; Dunwich, 139ff.; Eye, 149ff.; Ipswich, 213ff.; Orford, 431ff.; Southwold, 441ff

1455 Boundaries and wards of certain boroughs and corporate towns: reports of commissioners. HC 1837, 26. Beccles, 65ff.; Bury St. Edmunds, 163ff.; Eye, 391ff. 27. Ipswich, 93ff. 28. Southwold, 187ff.; Sudbury, 233ff

1456 Reports of the Local Government Board, 1871–2: Eastern counties. Annual 1–48. 1871/2–1919

1457 **Municipal Corporations Commission.** Reports to the commissioners appointed to inquire into municipal corporations not subject to the Municipal Corporations Acts, together with minutes of evidence. HC 1880, 31. Aldeburgh, 15ff.; Dunwich, 44ff.; Orford, 100ff

1458 Report (supplementary report) of the Boundary Commissioners, 1885. HC 1884/5, 19

1459 **Local Government Boundaries Commission.** Report HC 1888, 51. Suffolk *passim*

1460 **East Suffolk County Council.** Reports of the meetings of the council and of the committees. Jan 1889–. Ipswich

1461 **West Suffolk County Council.** Reports of the meetings of the council and of the committees. Feb 1889–. Bury St. Edmunds

1462 **County Councils Association.** Jubilee of County Councils 1889 to 1939: fifty years of local government. [Localised edn has 16pp on East Suffolk County Council]. 1939

1463 **East Suffolk County Council.** Local Government Act, 1929. First genera! review of county districts … Ipswich, 1932

1464 **East Suffolk County Council.** Year-book, 1949/50. Ipswich, [1949]

1465 **East Suffolk County Council.** Guide to county services … Ipswich, 1950

1466 **West Suffolk County Council.** Survey of the work of the West Suffolk County Council, April 1958–March 1961. Bury St. Edmunds, 1961 and later edns. SRO/B

1467 **East Suffolk County Council.** Allocation of resources, 1970–75. Ipswich, 1970

1468 **[Suffolk] County Liaison Committee.** Management and structure in the new Suffolk. [Ipswich], 1973

1469 **Marsh, W. M.** Arms and seals of the several corporations in the county of Suffolk. E Ang 4, 1869/70, 165–7

1470 **Hope, W. H. St. J.** Description of the maces of Orford, Southwold, and Ipswich, lent for exhibition to the Society of Antiquaries. PSA 2nd Ser 12, 1887/9, 180, 183, 186, 188

1471 Suffolk Punch. Journal of the East Suffolk Branch of NALGO., 1956–1961. Ipswich

FINANCE AND TAXATION
See also individual localities, especially boroughs, *below*

MEDIEVAL

1472 **Potter, G. R.,** *Ed.* Translation of so much of the Pipe Roll of 31 Henry I as refers to Norfolk and Suffolk [Rye's Norfolk handlists, 2nd Ser 2]. Norwich, 1925

1473 **Munday, J. T.** A feudal aid roll for Suffolk, 1302–03. Bury St. Edmunds, 1973

1474 **Wickham, W. A.** "Nonarum Inquisitiones" for Suffolk. PSIA 17, 1919/21, 97–122

1475 **Powell, E.** Subsidy Roll, Suffolk: Hundred of Lackford and Half Hundred of Exning. E Ang NS 4, 1891/2, 170–71

1476 Suffolk Subsidy Roll, 1327: Hundred de Lacford. E Ang NS 5, 1893/4, 51–3, 87–90, 135–7, 169–71

1477 Suffolk in 1327, being a subsidy return. [*Ed.* by S. H. A. H(ervey)]. Woodbridge, 1906. SGB 9

1478 **Powell, E.** Suffolk return for the Three-Groat Poll Tax of 1381. E Ang NS 5, 1893/4, 369–70

1479 **Demarest, E. B.** "Consuetudo Regis" in Essex, Norfolk, and Suffolk. EHR 42, 1927, 161–79

1500–1800

1480 Suffolk in 1524: being the return for a subsidy granted in 1523, with a map of Suffolk in Hundreds. [*Ed.* by S. H. A. Hervey]. Woodbridge, 1910. SGB 10

1481 Subsidy Roll: Suffolk. 8 Elizabeth. E Ang NS 3, 1889/90, 241–4

1482 Suffolk in 1568: being the return for a subsidy granted 1566, with a map of Suffolk in Hundreds. [*Ed.* by S. H. A. Hervey]. Bury St. Edmunds, 1909. SGB 12

1483 **Wayman, H. W. B.** Loans from Suffolk, 1627. E Ang NS 13, 1909/10, 6–7

1484 **Redstone, V. B.,** *Ed.* Ship-money returns for the county of Suffolk, 1639–40: Harl. MSS 7,540–7,542. Ipswich, 1904. *See also* **4766**

1485 Suffolk in 1674: being the Hearth Tax returns. [*Ed.* by S. H. A. H(ervey)], Woodbridge, 1905. SGB 11

1486 **Jones, A. G. E.** Suffolk Hearth Tax return, 1674. SR 2, 1959, 31–5

1487 **Biden, L. M.** Index to the particulars of fee-farm rents reserved upon grants from the Crown and remaining in the Augmentation Office. E Ang NS 10, 1903/04, 249–53, 274–6, 286–9, 305–07

1488 **Biden, L. M.** Deeds relating to certain fee-farm rents vested in Lord Hawley ("The Hawley schedule"), Suffolk [temp. Charles II]. E Ang NS 11, 1905/06, 122–3

19TH AND 20TH CENTURIES *For* the statutory published accounts of local authorities, *see* individual localities, *below*

1489 Accounts ... from the treasurers of counties ... of the several sums received by them for county rates during the last 7 years. HC 1823, 15. Suffolk, 46–7

1490 Report from the select committee appointed to enquire into the expenditure of county rates, 1792 to 1823. HC 1825, 6. Suffolk, 425–54

1491 Comparative statement of the expenditure of the county rates in several counties of England ... 1792, 1802, 1812, 1822, and 1832. Report, Select Committee of the House of Lords appointed to inquire into the charges of the county rates. HC 1835, 14. Suffolk, 196–203

1492 Accounts from the respective treasurers of the counties in England and Wales, of the several sums received by them for county rates, during 1821 [–1832]. HC 1833, 32. Suffolk, 106–13

1493 An account of the latest valuation of every parish, township, or place. HC 1831/2, 44. Suffolk, 326–8

1494 Second report of the commissioners ... [on] county rates in England and Wales. HC 1836, 27

1495 Suffolk. Woodbridge Division. County rate, printed by order of the Magistrates. Woodbridge, [1840]. BL

1496 Report and minutes of evidence taken before the select committee on the burdens affecting real property. HC 1846, 6, pt 1

1497 Returns of the amount levied for the purposes of the county rate ... in each of the last seven years, showing the amount per cent levied on property assessed to the county rate ... and of the number of head of cattle ... and of any income derived by any county ... from any other source than the county rate. HC 1867, 58. Norwich diocese, 194–214

1498 Rating Act, 1874. Return (with respect to the several hereditaments rendered rateable by the above Act, etc.) HC 1877, 71. Suffolk, 270–75

SOCIAL WELFARE

GENERAL

1499 **East Suffolk County Council**. Social services: ten-year development plans, 1973/83. [Ipswich], 1973

POOR LAW TO 1834 *See also* individual localities, especially Ipswich, **5837** and other references, *below*

1500 **Gillingwater, E.** Essay on parish workhouses: containing observations on the present state of English workhouses, with some regulations proposed for their improvement. Bury St. Edmunds, 1786

1501 **"A Suffolk Gentleman"**, *pseud.* Letter to Sir T. C. Bunbury, Bart., one of the Members of Parliament for the county of Suffolk, on the poor rates, and the high price of provisions, with some proposals for reducing both. Ipswich, 1795

1502 Abstract of returns relative to the expense and maintenance of the poor. HC 1804, Pt 2. Suffolk, 477–500

1503 Abstract of returns relative to the expense and maintenance of the poor. HC 1818, 19

1504 Poor-rate returns. HC 1820, 12. Suffolk, 40. 1835, 47. Suffolk, 367–75

1505 To the Rt. Hon. the Lords Spiritual and Temporal of Great Britain and Ireland, in Parliament assembled, etc., [draft of a petition to the House of Lords, from agricultural labourers of Suffolk against the Poor Law Amendment Act]. MS. note. [Woodbridge?], [1834?]. BL

1506 Women as parish officials in Suffolk. E Ang NS 7, 1897/8, 304, 320

1507 **Fearn, H.** Financing of the poor-law incorporation for the Hundreds of Colneis and Carlford ... 1758–1820. PSIA 27, 1955/7, 96–111

1508 **Fearn, H.** Apprenticing of pauper children in the incorporated Hundreds of Suffolk. PSIA 26, 1952/4, 85–97

POOR LAW AFTER 1834
1509 **Priestley, E. H.** Nineteenth-century poor law migration from Suffolk. SR 1, no 6, 1957, 123–9

1510 Report from ... commissioners for inquiring into ... the poor laws. Appendix A: Reports. HC 1834, 28; Appendix B 1: Answers to rural queries. 5pts. HC 1834, 30–34; Appendix B 2: Answers to town queries. 5pts. HC 1834, 35–6; Appendix D: Labour rate. HC 1834, 38. Suffolk, *passim*

1511 Annual reports of the commissioners under the Poor Law Amendment Act. 1st Report, Appendix D: List of unions. HC 1835, 26. 2nd Report, Appendix B: Suffolk and Norfolk, by J. P. Kay. HC 1836. Appendix D: List of unions. HC 1836, 29, pt 1. Appendix F: Expenditure 1835–6. HC 1836, 29, pt 2. 3rd Report, Appendix D: Expenditure 1837. HC 1837, 31. 4th Report, Appendix D: Expenditure 1838. HC 1840, 18. Suffolk, *passim*

1512 Committee on the Poor Law Amendment Act, 1838. HC 1837–8, 18, pt 1. Appendix A: Return respecting children maintained and educated in workhouses in Norfolk and Suffolk, in the week ending 9 Dec 1837. Appendix B: The period in which children have resided in workhouses in Norfolk and Suffolk, in answer to a circular issued 3 Jan 1838. Appendix D: Answers to a circular concerning the number of various classes of paupers maintained in the week ending 2 Jan 1838. Appendix I: Mortality in the workhouses of Norfolk and Suffolk from 31 Dec 1836 to 25 March 1837

1513 Poor rates. A return showing the total value, 1844: and the amount of money levied ... from 1839 to 1842. HC 1844, 40. Suffolk, 510–18

1514 Return of all debts, liabilities, and engagements claimed against the poor rates of any parish at the passing of the Act, 4 & 5 Will. IV, c.76. HC 1842, 35

1515 "An Evangelical Reformer", [*pseud.*, i.e. **J. Glyde**] Another plea for the poor: a letter addressed to Christians of all denominations, on the condition of the people, and the only effectual remedy. Ipswich, [c.1843]

1516 Report presented by Sir John Walsham ... on certain alleged abuses in the administration of the poor law in Norfolk and Suffolk. HC 1846, 36. Suffolk, 365–6

1517 Reports to the Poor Law Board on the laws of settlement, and removal of the poor. HC 1850, 27. Suffolk, *passim*

1518 Return showing the amount of property assessed to the relief of the poor ... for the year ending 25 March 1850. HC 1852, 45

1519 Returns from the several parishes, etc., of the number of separate assessments in the rate for the relief of the poor ... HC 1852, 45

1520 Return of all parishes ... into which ... any public railway passes; showing

... the gross amount of Poor's rate collected in each parish in 1851, 1852, and the amount contributed by the railway property to the Poor's rate of each parish. HC 1852–53, 97

1521 Return of the names of the different unions ... into which, for the purposes of the Poor Law, the counties are divided; specifying the parishes included in each union, together with the population and extent, the sums of money raised for the relief of the poor in each parish, for the year ending 25 March 1852. HC 1854, 55

1522 Returns of the number, in the last week of Sept 1852 and in the last week of Jan 1853, in each workhouse in England and Wales, of the paupers of each religious denomination; specifying ... the religious accommodation ... and the provision made for the religious instruction of the children within the workhouse; and, of the number of children placed or farmed out in any establishment. HC 1854, 55

1523 Return of the following information in respect of each parish ... not within the limits of any city or parliamentary borough, for the year ended at Lady-Day 1856, viz. 1, Name; 2, Population; 3, Gross estimated rental of the property assessed to the poor rate; 4, Rateable value, etc. HC 1857–8, 50

1524 Number and ages of paupers on district and workhouse medical officers' relief books at Lady-Day 1870. HC 1870, 58

1525 Returns relating to the consumption of liquor in workhouses. HC 1872, 51

1526 First annual report of the Local Government Board. Appendix: Pauperism. HC 1872, 28. Annually to 1919

1527 **Glyde, J.** Benefit clubs of Suffolk, their present position and future prospects. A letter to the nobility, gentry, and clergy of Suffolk. Ipswich, [1874]

1528 Minutes of evidence taken before the Royal Commission on the Aged Poor, and report. HC 1895, 14

1529 **East Anglian Joint Vagrancy Committee.** Constitution and functions, with a list of casual wards and other related information. Ipswich, 1936

CHARITIES   *See also* individual localities, *below*

1530 **Clubbe, J.** Sermon preached before the Incorporated Society for the relief of the widows and orphans of clergymen ... of Suffolk, at their anniversary meeting ... Ipswich, 1751

1531 **Suffolk Clergy Charity.** Constitution by charter, and rules for the better government, of the ... charity for the relief of ... poor widows and orphans of ... clergymen. Bury St. Edmunds, 1776. BL. 1818. nl

1532 Abstract of returns of charitable donations, 1786–8. HC 1816, 16

1533 Laws of the Society for the relief of widows and orphans of medical men in the county of Suffolk, instituted in the year 1787. Bury St. Edmunds, 1794. nl

1534 Benevolent society ... for the relief of necessitous widows and orphans of Protestant Dissenting ministers in Suffolk: statement of the Treasurer's accompt ... 1799. Bury St. Edmunds, [1799]. BL

1535 Plan of a benevolent society for the relief of necessitous widows and orphans of Protestant Dissenting ministers and also of ministers ... incapacitated for public service in the county of Suffolk. Bury St. Edmunds, 1811. BL

1536 Reports of the commissioners appointed ... to enquire concerning charities and education of the poor. HC 1815, 39. [SCL/L. A made-up vol. for Suffolk]

1537 Charitable donations so far as relates to rents and profits of messuages, lands, tenements, etc. HC 1820, 6. Suffolk, 113–19

1538 **Suffolk Clergy Charity.** The state of the charity for the relief of poor widows and orphans of clergymen in Suffolk for the years 1822–29, 1831, 1833–6, 1838–43. Ipswich, [1822–43]. BL

1539 List of the counties reported upon and not reported upon by the commissioners of inquiry into charities, with the income of each charity. HC 1828, 21. Suffolk, 248–9

1540 Charities and charitable donations registered with the clerks of the peace. HC 1829, 20. Suffolk, 346–59

1541 Stoke and Melford Union Association, or Benefit Society and Sickness Club [Prospectus], Sudbury, [1830?]. BL

1542 Returns of corporation charitable funds and corporate officers who have become magistrates. HC 1834, 45. Aldeburgh, 13; Bury St. Edmunds, 59; Dunwich, 155ff.; Eye, 255ff.; Ipswich, 300ff.; Orford, 396ff.; Southwold, 460ff.; Sudbury, 474

1543 Analytical digest of the reports made by the commissioners on inquiry into charities. HC 1835, 40. Pt 2, HC 1843, 18. Suffolk, 944–53

1544 Suffolk, Essex, and Norfolk Sailors' Orphan Asylum. [Proposals for the formation of an orphanage]. Ipswich, 1838. O

1545 Charities to be distributed to the poor. HC 1843, 18

1546 **Suffolk Clergy Charity.** Centenary fund committee: [An address]. [Ipswich?], [1843?] BL

1547 Digest of endowed charities mentioned in the 14th report of the Charity Commissioners. HC 1875, 57, pt 5, 87–198

1548 **West Suffolk County Council.** Account of the endowed charities in West Suffolk, prepared for the county council. Ipswich, 1895

1549 Registers of East and West Suffolk charities (excluding educational) maintained in accordance with the Charities Act, 1960

1550 **Blaker, E. H.** Report on the review of parochial charities in East Suffolk. 1974

1551 **Waveney District Council.** Waveney District charities. Lowestoft, 1975. [photostat]. SCL/L

PUBLIC HEALTH AND MEDICAL SERVICES
General

1552 **Hollingsworth, A. G.** Medical, surgical, and pharmaceutical archaeology of Suffolk. PSAI 1, 1848/53, 253–67

1553 **Jones, A. G. E.** Plagues in Suffolk in the 17th century. N&Q 198, 1953, 384–6

1554 Van Zwanenberg, D. F. Geography of disease in East Anglia. Jour Royal College of Physicians of London 8, 1974, 145–53

1555 **Suffolk Benevolent Medical Society.** State of the Suffolk Benevolent Medical Society. [Bury St. Edmunds?], [1790]. BL

1556 Fourth report of the medical officer of the Privy Council. Appendix. Dr. Buchanan's inquiry in Norfolk and Suffolk. HC 1862, 22

1557 **Stracey, W. J.** Illegitimacy in Norfolk and Suffolk: its extent, causes and suggested remedies. A paper read at the 21st General Meeting of the Pastoral Work Association ... 1873. Norwich, 1884. NCL/N

1558 **Cory, J. W. E.** Short history of the Suffolk General Hospital [Bury St. Edmunds, 1826–1948]. Bury St. Edmunds, 1973. SRO/B

1559 Rules and orders for the government of the Suffolk General Hospital established at Bury, 1825. Bury St. Edmunds, 1825. BL

1560 **Dewhurst, C.** Suffolk General Hospital: a sermon preached for the benefit of this institution, 9 March 1828, at the Independent chapel, in Whiting Street, Bury St. Edmunds. Bury St. Edmunds, 1828

1561 **East Suffolk and Ipswich Hospital.** Annual reports, 1837–1947

1562 **East Suffolk and Ipswich Hospital.** Final and one-hundred-and-eleventh annual report 1947, also record of events to the dissolution of the voluntary hospital system ... 5 July 1948; Souvenir illustrated report, with history of the hospital 1837 to 1948, by A. Griffiths. Ipswich, 1948

1563 Programme of the official opening of the War Memorial wing at the East Suffolk and Ipswich Hospital, 28 July 1924. [Ipswich], [1924]

1564 **East Suffolk and Ipswich Hospital.** Brief history of the institution prepared on the occasion of the opening of the new wing, 7 June 1934, by A. Griffiths. Ipswich, 1934

1565 **East Suffolk County Council.** Reports of sub-committee appointed to consider reports of the Medical Officers of Health ... 1891, 1893–9. Ipswich. BL

1566 **East Suffolk County Council.** Annual reports of the Medical Officer of Health, 1926–. Ipswich

1567 **East Suffolk County Council.** Annual reports of the School Medical Officer, 1927–. Ipswich

1568 **West Suffolk County Council.** Abstract of Medical Officers' reports, 1889–1910. *Cont. as* Report of the Medical Officer of Health, 1918–

1569 **West Suffolk County Council.** Annual report of the School Medical Officer, 1931–. BL

1570 **Ipswich and East Suffolk Group Hospital Management Committee.** Account of the National Health Service and the Ipswich and East Suffolk Hospital Management Committee ... by H. Moxon. Ipswich, 1962

1571 **Norwich, Lowestoft, and Great Yarmouth Hospital Management Committee.** Annual reports, 1950–. Norwich

1572 Van Zwanenberg, D. F. The last epidemic of plague in England? Suffolk, 1906–1918. Medical History, 14, 1970

Asylums

1573 **Suffolk Lunatic Asylum, Melton.** Reports, 1st 1838–48th 1885. Wood-bridge. *See also* **6825–6**

1574 **Eastern Counties Asylum for Idiots.** Annual reports, 1859–1918, Colchester

EMERGENCY SERVICES
Civil Defence

1575 **East Suffolk County Council.** Civil defence in East Suffolk. Ipswich, 1948

Fire Service See also **4173, 5881–2, 6900, 8083**

1576 **Suffolk and Ipswich Fire Authority.** Annual report of the Chief Fire Officer, 31 March 1948–

1577 **Suffolk and Ipswich Fire Authority.** Suffolk and Ipswich Fire Service. 1963

EDUCATION

1578 **Ipswich and East Suffolk Record Office.** List of records relating to the history of education. Ipswich, 1968. [Typescript]

1579 **Carlisle, N.** Concise description of endowed grammar schools in England and Wales. 1818. Suffolk, 508–58

1580 **Venn, J.** Matriculation or admission books of Gonville and Caius College, Cambridge: East Anglian admissions from 1560. E Ang NS 1, 1885/6; NS 2, 1887/8, *passim*

1581 **Leach, A. F.,** *and* **Hutton, E. P.** Schools. *In* VCH Suffolk, 2, 1907, 301–55

1582 **Clegg, M. E.** Some eighteenth-century schools in Suffolk. SR 1, 1957, 55–8

1583 **Raven, J. J.** Remarks on the history of education in East Anglia. PSIA 9, 1895/7, 77–84

1584 **Suffolk Society for the Education of the Poor.** Society for the Education of the Poor in the Principles of the Established Church. Ipswich, 1812. BL

1585 **Norwich Diocesan Society for the Education of the Poor in the Principles of the Established Church.** Annual reports, 1813–53. [40th 1852; 41st 1853 SRO/I]

1586 Digest of parochial returns made to the Select Committee . . . on the education of the poor. HC 1819, 9

1587 **Deanery of Lothingland.** District Committee of the Society for Promoting Christian Knowledge [Statement of the objects of the Society]. Great Yarmouth, [1820] BL

1588 Reports of the District Committee for the Deaneries of Lothingland, Wangford, Dunwich, and South Elmham for the years 1821, 1823, 1825. Great Yarmouth. BL

1589 **Deanery of Lothingland.** Report of the sub-committee appointed by the District Committee . . . 12 Dec 1839, to consider the return already made as to the state of education in each parish of the district. Lowestoft, [1839]. SCL/L. 1840, 1841. O

1590 **Suffolk Archdeaconry.** Diocesan Society for Promoting Education in the Principles of the Established Church. Annual reports, 1840–72

1591 **Sudbury Archdeaconry.** Diocesan Society for Promoting Education in the Principles of the Established Church. Annual reports 1840–47

1592 **Deanery of Lothingland.** Reports of the District Committee of Education, 1840–45

1593 Digest of schools and charities for education. HC 1843, 18. Suffolk, 111–16

1594 Minutes and reports of the Committee of Council on Education. HC 1850–1901

1595 Report of the Royal Commission on Popular Education in England. HC 1861, 21, pt 2, Suffolk, 143–72

1596 Return related to endowed grammar schools. HC 1865, 43. Suffolk, 238–45

1597 Return ... of the number of children in inspected schools in the year ending the 31 Aug 1867, distinguishing how many of such children belong to the families which are considered as poor. HC 1867–8, 53. Suffolk, 161–4

1598 Report of the Schools Inquiry Commission. 21v. HC 1867–8, 28. v 13, Eastern counties. Suffolk, pt 11, 121–287

1599 **East Suffolk County Council.** Education Committee. Centenary circular, 1870–1970. [Ipswich], [1970]

1600 Return of all public elementary schools under inspection, relating to school fees (England and Wales). HC 1875, 59. Suffolk, 298–301.

1601 List of school boards and school attendance committees, 1882–1902. HC 1882, 1902

1602 Return of all public elementary schools examined ... giving denomination, number of scholars ... 1889, 1893, 1899. HC 1890, 56; 1894, 65; 1900, 65. Suffolk, *passim*

1603 **Imray, J. M.** Scholarships awarded by the Technical Instruction Committee of the East Suffolk County Council, 1893–1903. SR 3, no 1, 1965, 18–24

1604 Report of the Royal Commission on Secondary Education. HC 1895, 43–9

1605 **Swinburne, A. J.** Souvenir of the 21st anniversary of the East Suffolk Prize Scheme. 1901. *See also* **3371**

1606 An experiment in rural re-organisation [Reydon]. 1933. Board of Education. Educational Pamphlets no 93. SCL/L

1607 **East Suffolk County Council.** Education Committee. Education development plan. Ipswich, 1947

1608 **East Suffolk County Council.** Education Committee. East Suffolk county handbook of religious instruction ... Ipswich, 1952

1609 **West Suffolk County Council.** Education Committee. Five years' achievement, 1955–1960. Bury St. Edmunds, 1960. SRO/B

1610 **East Suffolk County Council.** Education Dept. Organisation of secondary education. Ipswich, [1966]

1611   **East Suffolk County Council.** Education Dept. Scheme of further education awards. Ipswich, 1969 and later edns

1612   **Workers' Educational Association.** Eastern District. Suffolk Federation Quarterly, *cont. as* The Suffolk Punch, v 1, no 1, Sept 1948–

1613   **Neill, A. S.** That dreadful school [Summerhill, Leiston]. 1937

1614   **Neill, A. S.** Summerhill: a radical approach to education. 1962

1615   **Neill, A. S.** Talking of Summerhill. 1967

1616   **Walmsley, J.** Neill and Summerhill: a man and his work. 1969

1617   **Segefjord, B.** Summerhill diary. 1970

1618   **Dunn, G.** Simon's last year: the story of a village school. 1959

MUSEUMS

1619   **Smedley, N.** Museum of Rural Life, Stowmarket. SR 3, 1966, 91–3

1620   Abbot's Hall Museum of Rural Life, Stowmarket: an introduction to the collections. SR 3, no 5, 1967, 1–28

1621   Friends of Abbot's Hall Museum. The open-air museum of rural life of East Anglia. Ipswich, [1967]

1622   Abbot's Hall Museum of Rural Life, Stowmarket. An introduction to the collections. Ipswich, 1967 and later edns. [Since 1975, Abbot's Hall Museum of East Anglian Life]

1623   Edgar's farmhouse [Combs Lane, Stowmarket]. Appeal by the Friends of Abbot's Hall Museum. 1971. [Typescript]

LIBRARIES

1624   **Fitch, J. A.** Some ancient Suffolk parochial libraries. PSIA 30, 1964/6, 44–87

1625   **Ferry, E. F.** Two East Suffolk public libraries. [Cratfield and Shotley]. SR 3, 1968, 202–06

RECORD OFFICES

1626   **Bury St. Edmunds and West Suffolk Record Office.** Summary guide. Bury St. Edmunds, 1951

1627   **Ipswich and East Suffolk Record Office.** Annual report of the Joint Archivist for 1952/3, 1953/4, 1954/5, 1955/6, 1970/72. Ipswich

1628   **Charman, D.** Ipswich and East Suffolk Record Office. Archives 4, 1959, 18–28

1629   **Ipswich and East Suffolk Record Office.** Archive news, no 1, Jan–June 1973, no 2, July–Dec 1973. *Cont. as* **Suffolk Record Office.** Archive news, no 3, Jan–June 1974–. Ipswich

PUBLIC UTILITIES
        See also Water resources, *above*, and individual localities, *below*

1630   **Eastern Electricity Board.** Report and statement of accounts for the period 1 Jan 1948 to 31 March 1949–

1631   **Eastern Electricity Board.** Eastern Electricity Magazine, 1948–. Ipswich

1632 **Eastern Gas Board.** Report and statement of accounts for the period 13 Jan 1949 to 31 March 1950

PLANNING AND DEVELOPMENT *See also* **298,** *and* individual localities

1633 Ordnance Survey. Area book of reference to the plans of the parishes ... in the county of Suffolk. 13v. 1882/5. O

1634 **Suffolk Preservation Society** [Founded 1929]. Annual reports, and News letters

1635 **Abercrombie, P.,** *and* **Kelly, S. A.** East Suffolk regional planning scheme: prepared for the East Suffolk Joint Regional Planning Committee. Liverpool, 1935

1636 **Butcher, R. W.** Land of Britain: Pts 72, 73. Suffolk (East and West). Land Utilisation Survey of Britain. 1941

1637 Suffolk planning survey: prepared for the East Suffolk County Council and the West Suffolk County Council Joint Planning Committee, by T. B. Oxenbury, County Planning Officer. Ipswich, 1946

1638 **East Suffolk County Council.** Planning Dept. An interim statement of the principles adopted ... in the preparation of a development plan for the county. Ipswich, 1950. [Typescript]

1639 **East Suffolk County Council.** Planning Dept. Preliminary report on the outline plan for East Suffolk. Ipswich, 1950. [Typescript]

1640 **East Suffolk County Council.** Planning Dept. County development plan, 1951. Report of survey (written analysis). Ipswich, 1951. [Typescript]

1641 **West Suffolk County Council.** Planning Dept. County Development plan, 1951. Report of survey (written analysis). Bury St. Edmunds, 1951. [Typescript]

1642 **East Suffolk County Council.** Planning Dept. County Development plan, 1951. Approved 1953. Written statement and maps for the county, Lowestoft, Beccles, Woodbridge, and 22 designation maps. Ipswich, 1953. [Typescript]

1643 **West Suffolk County Council.** Planning Dept. County development plan, 1951. Written statement. Bury St. Edmunds, 1955

1644 **East Suffolk County Council.** Planning Dept. County plan. Ipswich, 1956. 2v

1645 **East Suffolk County Council.** Planning Dept. County development plan. First quinquennial review. Report of survey. Ipswich, 1958

1646 **East Suffolk County Council.** Planning Dept. County Development plan. Amendment No 3. First quinquennial review, 1958. Approved 1961. Written statement and maps for county, Lowestoft, Beccles, Woodbridge, and Melton. Ipswich, 1958

1647 **West Suffolk County Council.** Planning Dept. Development control notes. Bury St. Edmunds, 1958

1648 **East Suffolk County Council.** Planning Dept. Planning for development: South-West Deben and villages around Ipswich. Factual survey and outline plan. Ipswich, 1959

1649 **East Suffolk County Council.** Planning Dept. County development plan: Amendment No 4, Ipswich periphery, 1960. Not approved. Written statement and maps of South-West Deben and 31 village envelope plans. Ipswich, 1960

1650 **East Suffolk County Council.** Planning Dept. Ipswich regional plan: Survey and analysis [draft report]. Ipswich, 1962

1651 **West Suffolk County Council.** Planning Dept. County development plan: First review 1962: report of survey, programme map, written statement. Bury St. Edmunds, 1962

1652 **East Suffolk County Council.** Planning Dept. Planning and development handbook. Ipswich, 1964. 2nd edn 1970

1653 **Ministry of Housing and Local Government.** South-east England. 1964

1654 **Ministry of Housing and Local Government.** South-east study, 1961–81. 1964

1655 **East Suffolk County Council.** Planning Dept. The Government's South-east study, 1961–81: a report by the County Planning Officer. Ipswich, 1964

1656 **West Suffolk County Council.** Planning Dept. Villages of outstanding importance. Bury St. Edmunds, 1964

1657 **East Suffolk County Council.** Planning Dept. County development plan: policy for the classification of settlements. Ipswich, [1965]. 2nd edn 1969

1658 **Labour Party Eastern Regional Council.** Economic Planning Committee. Eastern region social and economic survey. Ipswich, [1965]. NCL/N

1659 **Essex, West and East Suffolk County Councils.** Planning Depts. Dedham Vale. Pt 1. Survey report. 1966. Pt 2. Proposals. 1968. Chelmsford

1660 **East Anglia Economic Planning Council.** Growth and change – East Anglia. 1967

1661 **East Anglian Regional Studies Group.** Regional planning and East Anglia: report of the proceedings of the first annual conference ... Cambridge, 1967

1662 **East Suffolk County Council.** Planning Dept. Policy for conservation areas. Ipswich, 1967

1663 **South East Economic Planning Council.** A strategy for the South-east: a first report. 1967

1664 **West Suffolk County Council.** Planning Dept. Trees. Countryside Sub-committee report. Bury St. Edmunds, 1967

1665 **Conservative and Unionist Party.** Eastern Area. East of England: a Tory study. Cambridge, 1968

1666 **East Anglia Consultative Committee.** Planning Panel. East Anglia: a regional survey. Bury St. Edmunds, 1968

1667 **East Anglia Economic Planning Council.** East Anglia, a study: a first report of the East Anglia Economic Planning Council. 1968

1668 **West Suffolk County Council.** Planning Dept. Rural planning in West Suffolk, 1951–68. Bury St. Edmunds, 1968

1669 **West Suffolk County Council.** Planning Dept. Rural planning in West Suffolk: notes on the principles of rural planning and policy decisions adopted by the County Planning Committee. Bury St. Edmunds, Pt 1, 1968. Pt 2, 1971

1670 **Dept. of Economic Affairs.** Government reply to the East Anglia Economic Planning Council's East Anglia, a study. 1969

1671 **East Anglia Consultative Committee.** Planning Panel. East Anglia: a regional appraisal. Bury St. Edmunds, 1969

1672 **East Suffolk County Council.** Planning Dept. Policy for the classification of settlements: South-west Deben; policy statement and planning proposals. Ipswich, 1970

1673 **West Suffolk County Council.** Planning Dept. The future of the village. Bury St. Edmunds, 1971

1674 **East Anglia Regional Strategy Team.** Strategic choice for East Anglia. 1974

1675 **Suffolk County Council.** Planning Dept. Development plan scheme. [Ipswich], 1975

1676 **Suffolk County Council.** Planning Dept. Suffolk: the choice ahead. Ipswich, 1975

1677 **Department of the Environment.** East Anglia regional strategy. Government response to Strategic choice for East Anglia. 1976

1678 **Suffolk County Council.** Planning Dept. Suffolk: the next 15 years. Ipswich, 1976

1679 **Suffolk County Council.** Planning Dept. Suffolk county-structure plan. Written statement. Ipswich, 1977

1680 **Suffolk County Council.** Planning Dept. Suffolk county-structure plan. Appendices to report of survey. 14pts. Ipswich, [1977]

HOUSING *See* **4172, 6284, 6743–4, 6814, 6896**

LAW ENFORCEMENT

Medieval Period

1681 **Green, A.** Stewardship of the Liberty of the eight-and-a-half Hundreds. PSIA 30, 1964/6, 255–62

1682 **Bullen, R. F.** Mercy and judgement as seen in a Suffolk Assize roll, 24 Hen. III. E Ang NS 13, 1909/10, 314

1683 Justices of the Peace in Suffolk, 1361–1961. Catalogue of an exhibition arranged by the Ipswich and East Suffolk Record Office at the Magistrates Conference, Belstead House, 4 Nov 1961. Ipswich

1684 **Andrews, S.** *and* **Redstone, L. J.** Suffolk courts in English. PSIA 20, 1928/30, 199–213

1500–1800

1685 **Wayman, H. W. B.** Names and notes from the court book of the manor of Middleton Austins, co. Suffolk, 1694–1754. E Ang NS 13, 1909/10, 359–62

Local Government, Social Services, and Justice

19th and 20th Centuries

1686 Orders, rules, and regulations of the court of General Quarter Sessions of the Peace of the county of Suffolk. Bury St. Edmunds, 1826. 1830. O

1687 Returns ... showing the number of criminal offenders committed for trial or bailed for appearance at the assizes and sessions in each county, 1834–57. HC 1835–58

1688 **Phillips, J. S.,** *Ed.* Grand Juries of Suffolk, 1800–80, The Judges of Assize and the High Sheriffs of the county ... Bury St. Edmunds, 1882

Assize Sermons and Charges

1689 **Ward, S.** Sermon preached at a General Assizes held at Bury St. Edmunds, for the county of Suffolk. 1635. nl

1690 **Stephens, T.** Ad magistratum: three sermons preached before the Justices of Assizes, at Bury St. Edmunds ... Cambridge, 1661. Wing S 5456. SRO/B

1691 **Bohun, E.** Three charges at the General Quarter Sessions for the county of Suffolk, in the years 1691, 1692: to which is added the author's vindication from the calumnies and mistakes cast on him on account of his Geographical Dictionary. 1693. Wing B 3462. BL

1692 **Raymond, G.** Sermon preached at the Assizes at Bury St. Edmunds in Suffolk, March 26, 1716. 1716

1693 **Shelton, M.** A charge given to the grand-jury at the General Quarter sessions of the peace holden at St. Edmund-Bury in the county of Suffolk, 16 July 1716. 1716. O

1694 **Tweady, J.** Sermon preach'd at Bury St. Edmund's before Mr. Justice Wright, at the Assizes held there for the county of Suffolk, 16 March 1742. Ipswich, 1743. nl

1695 **Chedworth,** *Lord* **J.** Charge delivered to the Grand Jury at the General Quarter Sessions of the Peace for the county of Suffolk ... at Ipswich on Friday, 18 Jan 1793. Ipswich, 1793. nl

1696 **Mathew, G.** Sermon preached at Bury St. Edmund's before the Right Hon. Lord Chief Justice Alvanley, and Hon. Mr. Justice Grove, at the Assizes held there 5 Aug 1802. 1802. nl

1697 **Stewart, C. E.** Sermon preached at Bury St. Edmund's, before the Right Hon. Lord Chief Baron Macdonald, and Hon. Mr. Baron Hotham, at the Assizes held there 29 July 1803. Bury St. Edmunds, 1803. nl

1698 **Cobbold, S.** Sermon preached at the Assizes held at Bury St. Edmund's on Thursday, 30 March 1815, before the Hon. Mr. Justice Heath. Bury St. Edmunds, 1815. nl

1699 **Sandy, G.** Sermon preached at Bury St. Edmunds, at the Lent Assizes. 1846. nl

Police

1700 Resolution of the Justices of the Peace ... 6 Dec 1839 to adopt an Act for the establishment of county and district constables ... Bury St. Edmunds, 1839. O

1701 **Prescott, C.** Suffolk constabulary in the nineteenth century. PSIA 31, 1967/9, 1–46
1702 Reports of the inspectors of constabulary, 1858–1914. HC 1859–1916
1703 East Suffolk constabulary. 1866. nl
1704 East Suffolk police. Rifle shooting. 1914. nl
1705 History of the East Suffolk constabulary. Norfolk Life 12, April 1969. NCL/N
1706 **Staunton, G. S.** Report on police observation work in connection with raids by hostile aircraft and men-of-war on the county of East Suffolk. Ipswich, 1919
1707 Brief description of the West Suffolk constabulary. Bury St. Edmunds, 1952
1708 **Wheeler, J. D.** West Suffolk constabulary swords. SR 2, 1962, 167–9
1709 Official opening of the new Force and Divisional Headquarters [West Suffolk constabulary], Bury St. Edmunds, by Sir Charles Cunningham. Bury St. Edmunds, 1964. SRO/B
1710 **Suffolk Police.** Road accidents, 1968. SCL/L
1711 Constables' Country: the official magazine magazine of the Suffolk constabulary. v 1, no 1, Autumn 1967. Ipswich. Bi-annually

Penal Administration
1712 **Howard, J.** Account of the prisons and houses of correction in the Norfolk circuit [includes Suffolk]. 1789. O
1713 **Pearson, W. C.** Suffolk gaol calendar of the last century. E Ang NS 4, 1891/2, 113–14
1714 Account of all the gaols, houses of correction or penitentiaries, in the United Kingdom. HC 1819, 17
1715 Calendar of the prisoners for trial at the Lent Assizes, to be holden at Bury St. Edmund's ... on Saturday, 31 March 1821 ... Bury St. Edmunds, [1821]
1716 Gaols: reports and schedules transmitted to the Secretary of State, 1824–47. HC 1825–48
1717 Report of the select committee on gaols and houses of correction. HC 1835, 11
1718 Reports of the inspectors appointed to visit the different prisons of Great Britain. 1836. 1844–78. HC 1836–78
1719 Reports of the inspectors of prisons: reformatory and industrial schools. HC 1873, 31
1720 **M, A. E.** Stocks and whipping posts. EA Misc 1907, 60, 62, 67, 74

Crimes and Trials
1721 Murder!!! The trial at large of A.A. [Ann Arnold] for the wilful murder of her infant child ... at the Assizes held at Bury, March 26, 1813. Bury St. Edmunds, [1813]
1722 The genuine trial of Margery Beddingfield and R. Ringe, at Bury St. Edmunds, 21 March 1763, for petty treason and murder committed on John

Beddingfield, late of Sternfield ... farmer, late husband of the said Margery, and master of the said Ringe. 1763. SRO/B

1723 Confession of Richard Ringe, and Margery Beddingfield, who were condemned ... for the murder of Mr. John Beddingfield ... [1763]. BL

1724 L. *pseud.* Letter to Martin Thomas Cocksidge, Esq., being observations on the "Statement of facts", by John Benjafield, Esq. Bury St. Edmunds, 1813. SRO/B

1725 Trial of Roger Benstead the Elder and Roger Benstead the Younger, for the wilful murder of Thomas Briggs of Lakenheath ... at the Lent Assizes, 1792, holden at Bury St. Edmunds. Bury St. Edmunds, 1792

1726 [**Stebbing, G.**] Account of the case tried at the Suffolk Lent Assizes, 1779, of John Bothwick, Edward Barry, and fifteen other press men accused of the murder of Thomas Nicholls at the Green Man public house [Ipswich]. [1779?] MS

1727 Account of the late trial at the Assizes held at Bury St. Edmund's in Suffolk, on Friday, 21 March 1766 for the murder of Mary Booty; of which Eliz. Burroughs was convicted and executed April 4, 1766. 1766. nl

1728 Account of Robert Clarke, who was executed for uttering forged notes at Bury St. Edmunds, 8 April 1807. 1828

1729 Trial at large of Thomas Clarke, Thomas Carty, and John Deane, who were tried, convicted, and received sentence of death, for robbing Thomas Marsh, on the King's highway at Yoxford, of 187 dollars. At the Summer Assizes for the county of Suffolk ... Bury St. Edmunds, [1779?]. BL

1730 Account of the behaviour, confession, and last dying words, of Arundel Coke, Esq., and John Woodburne, labourer, who were executed at Bury St. Edmunds ... 31 March 1722, for the barbarous attempt on the life of E. Crispe ... [1722]. BL. 1760. SRO/B

1731 Exact and particular narrative of a ... murder attempted on the body of Edward Crispe, Esq., at St. Edmund's Bury ... by Arundel Coke ... and John Woodburne ... and an extract of an Act of Parliament relating to their case. 1722. SRO/B. 2nd edn 1722. BL

1732 Tryal and condemnation of Arundel Coke, alias Cooke, Esq., and of John Woodburne, labourer, for felony, in slitting the nose of Edward Crispe, gent ... at Bury St. Edmunds, Tuesday 13 March 1721 ... 1723

1733 **Oddie, E. M.** *pseud.* The slitting of Mr. Crispe's nose. 1940. SRO/B

1734 Account of the trial of W.C., for the murder of Maria Marten ... To which are added ... letters sent ... in answer to Corder's matrimonial advertisement. 1828. BL

1735 Authentic and faithful history of the mysterious murder of Maria Marten ... to which is added, the trial of William Corder ... with an account of his execution ... particulars relative to the village of Polstead ... the prison correspondence of Corder, etc. 1828. 1928. 1948 edn., *Ed.* by J. *and* N. 1849 Mackenzie by J Casts

1736 Trial, at length, of William Corder, convicted of the murder of Maria

Marten ... at Bury Assizes, on Thursday, 7 Aug 1828. Bury St. Edmunds, [1828?]. BL

1737 Trial of William Corder, at the Assizes, Bury St. Edmunds ... for the murder of Maria Marten, in the Red Barn, at Polstead: including the matrimonial advertisements ... 3rd edn 1828. BL

1738 **Hughes, G.** Sermon on the power of conscience, with an application to the recent trial and condemnation of W. Corder ... 1828. Bury St. Edmunds, [1828]. BL

1739 **Hyatt, C.** The sinner detected: a sermon preached ... on the occasion of the execution of W. Corder for the murder of M. Marten, including particulars of his life never before published. 1828. BL

1740 Address to my parishioners and neighbours on the subject of the murder lately committed at Polstead. By a Suffolk clergyman [i.e. John Whitmore?]. 1828. BL

1741 **Ford, J. C.** William Corder. E Ang NS 1, 1885/6, 295

1742 Maria Marten; or, The murder in the Red Barn: a traditional acting version here for the first time printed and published by the care of Mr. Montague Slater, Esquire. 1938. 1943

1743 **Gibbs, D.,** *and* **Maltby, H.** True story of Maria Marten. Ipswich, 1949

1744 **Burton, B. J.** Murder of Maria Marten, or, The Red Barn: a melodrama in three acts. 1964. SCL/L

1745 **McCormick, D.** Red Barn mystery: some new evidence on an old murder. 1967. SRO/B

1746 Second trial and capital conviction of Daniel Dawson for poisoning horses at Newmarket, in 1809 ... 1812

1747 Trial of John Dogharty and Matthew Reilly, at Bury St. Edmunds, 29 July 1809, for the wilful murder of Robert Howe. Ipswich, [1809]. SRO/B

1748 Trial of John Dowsing, for the wilful murder of Susan Dowsing, his wife. At the Summer Assizes held at Bury St. Edmunds, 30 July 1787. By W. Horne. Bury St. Edmunds, [1789]

1749 Authentick account of the life of Mr. Charles Drew, late of Long Melford ... tried and convicted at Bury Assizes for the murder of his father, Mr. Charles John Drew, late an Attorney-at-Law at Long Melford ... 1740

1750 Genuine trial of Charles Drew, at the assizes held at Bury St. Edmunds on Thursday, March 27, 1740, for the murder of his own father, to which is added an account of his behaviour, whilst under sentence of death. By a gentleman of Bury. 1740. SRO/I. 2nd edn 1747. SRO/B

1751 Life, behaviour, last dying words, and confession of Charles Drew, Esq., who was executed for shooting his own father. [1740]. O

1752 The Suffolk parricide: being the trial, life, transactions, and last dying words of Charles Drew of Long Melford ... who was executed at St. Edmund's-Bury on Wednesday, 9 April, for inhuman murder of his father ... By a gentleman of Long Melford. 1740

1753 The unnatural son: the whole tryal and condemnation of Charles Drew for the murder of his own father. [1740]. O

1754 Lines on the execution of Catherine Foster ... at Bury St. Edmunds ... for the wilful murder of John Foster, her husband. 1847. SRO/B

1755 Trial of Catherine Foster, for poisoning her husband. Bury St. Edmunds, 1847. SRO/B

1756 Voice from the gaol; or, The horrors of the condemned cell. Life, trial and sentence of Catherine Foster, who was tried at Bury, Saturday, 27 March for the wilful murder of John Foster, her husband, by administering arsenic to him. [1847?]. BL

1757 Voice from the gaol; or, The horrors of the condemned cell. Life, trial and sentence, and confession of Catherine Foster for the murder of her husband, three weeks after marriage ... [1847?]. BL

1758 Report of the trial, A. Gall ... versus F. K. Eagle ... at the summer Assizes at Bury St. Edmunds, Aug 3, 1833. Bury St. Edmunds. 2nd edn 1833. SRO/B

1759 Trial of William Gardiner (the Peasenhall case). *Ed.* by W. Henderson. 1934

1760 **Rowland, J.** Peasenhall mystery. 1962

1761 **White, R. J.** The women of Peasenhall. 1969

1762 Murders: the trial of Maurice Griffin for the wilful murder of Thomas MacMahon ... at Woodbridge ... 28 Aug 1813; also the trial of Mary Gibbs, for the wilful murder of her female bastard child by drowning, at Hollesley ... at the Assizes at Bury, March 25, 1814. Bury St. Edmunds, 1814

1763 Trials of Samuel Hammond, for the murder of Ann Avey; and Ann Gosling, for the murder of John Sage, at the Lent Assizes at Bury St. Edmunds, 25 March 1794. Newmarket, [1794]. SRO/B

1764 Trial of Thomas Harper, for shooting Thomas Briggs, of Lakenheath ... at the Lammas Assizes, holden at Bury St. Edmund's ... Lynn, [1788?]. BL

1765 Trial of John and Nathan Nichols (father and son), for the wilful murder of Sarah Nichols, daughter of the former ... at the Lent Assizes, 1794, holden at Bury St. Edmunds ... Bury St. Edmunds, 1794

1766 The remarkable trial, at large, of Wm Pizzy and Mary Codd, at the Assizes holden at Bury St. Edmund's on Thursday, 11 Aug 1808, for feloniously administering a certain noxious and destructive substance to Ann Cheney, with intent to produce a miscarriage. Ipswich, 1808. nl

1767 Authentic narrative of circumstances relative to the unfortunate youth Joshua Ranson, who, with W. Hilyard and H. Laws, was executed at Ipswich, on Saturday, 17 April 1819, for a robbery ... By Rev. James Payne. Ipswich, 1819

1768 Suffolk County Assizes ... 14 Aug 1813. Robinson, Clk. [Minister of Blyford] versus Jermyn, May, and Gooch [Trial for libel] Southwold, [1813]. BL

1769 Trials of Robert Rule who was convicted of robbing James Creasy on the highway in the parish of Long Melford, and Edward Green who was convicted of breaking into and robbing the house of Ann Amos, at Ufford ... Suffolk Summer Assizes, 1826. Ipswich, [1826]. BL

1770–79 *deleted*

1780 The Suffolk tragedy. The trial, confession, and execution of John and Eliz. Smith for the murder of their daughter, Mary Ann Smith. 1812. nl

1781   Brownrigg the Second; or, The cruel stepmother: the full particulars of the trial of John and Elizabeth Smith ... for the murder of Mary Ann Smith, ... to which is added the trial and execution of Edmund Thrower, for the murder of Thomas Carter and Elizabeth Carter. [1812?]

1782   Murder in Suffolk!! The trial of John and E. Smith for the wilful murder of M. A. Smith, their daughter ... [1812]. BL

1783   Suffolk Lent Assizes, 1788 ... case of the King against Sparks for an assault on Susanna, wife of Nathaniel Hillier, Esq. 1790. SRO/B

1784   Trial at large of James Steggles, for wilfully and maliciously shooting at Mr. William Macro of Barrow, at the Assizes held at Bury St. Edmunds, 18 March 1783

1785   Behaviour, confession and dying words of David Steward, who was executed, and hang'd in chains, on Rymer Heath, on Wednesday 3 April 1734, for poisoning his wife at Honington. Bury St. Edmunds, nd. nl

1786   Remarkable trial of Henry Steward, and Elizabeth Burroughs, for the wilful murder of Mary Booty, at the Assizes held at Bury St. Edmund's, Suffolk, on Friday, 21 March 1766. Bury St. Edmunds, 1806. SRO/B

1787   Murders in Suffolk!! Fairburn's edition of the trial of Edmund Thrower for the wilful murder of Thomas and Elizabeth Carter ... [1812]. SRO/B

1788   Trials for murder at the Suffolk Lent Assizes, 1812. The trial of E. Thrower for the wilful murder of T. Carter and E. Carter ... and also the trial of J. and E. Smith, for the murder of M. A. Smith, etc. Bury St. Edmunds, [1812]. BL

1789   Statement of facts: together with the trial of the printer ... of the County Chronicle [i.e. John Wheble] for a libel ... 22 Dec 1812. Bury St. Edmunds, [1813]. SRO/B

1790   Murder by poison. The trial at large of Eliz. Woolterton, for the wilful murder of Robert Sparkes, a child of six years old, who partook of a cake in which the prisoner had mixed arsenic, with intent to poison her uncle, Jifford Clarke, aged 82, at the Assizes held at Bury St. Edmund's July 22, 1815. Bury St. Edmunds, [1815] BL

Religion

CHURCH HISTORY

GENERAL

For the clergy, *see also* individual and family biography, *and* references under localities, *below*

1791 **Cox, J. C.** Ecclesiastical history. *In* VCH Suffolk 2, 1907, 1–52

1792 **Redstone, L. J.** History of Christianity in Suffolk. *In* East Suffolk county handbook of religious instruction. Ipswich, 1952. 1–58

1793 **Willis, J. C. N.** Founders and builders of the church in East Anglia, being notes concerning the patrons of the Canons' stalls in St. Edmundsbury cathedral. Ipswich, 1953. [Typescript]

1794 **Ipswich and East Suffolk Record Office.** Parish record survey ... in the county of East Suffolk and in the Archdeaconries of Ipswich and Suffolk in the Diocese of St. Edmundsbury and Ipswich. Ipswich, 1963. [Typescript]

PRE-REFORMATION CHURCH

See also individual localities, *especially* Bury St. Edmunds

General and Early

1795 **Fitch, W. S.** Suffolk monasteries. nd. 4v. MS

1796 **Cox, J. C.** Religious houses. *In* VCH Suffolk 2, 1907, 53–155

1797 **Gallyon, M.** Early church in Eastern England. Lavenham, 1973

1798 **Whitelock, D.** Pre-Viking church in East Anglia. *In* Anglo-Saxon England, v 1, 1972, 1–22

1799 **Bentham, J.** History and antiquities of the conventual and cathedral church of Ely, ... 1673–1771. Cambridge, 1771. 2nd edn 1812. Supplement 1817

1800 **Miller, E.** Abbey and bishopric of Ely: the social history of an ecclesiastical estate from the tenth century to the early fourteenth century. Cambridge, 1951. Rp 1969

1801 **Taylor, R. C.** Index monasticus; or, The abbeys and other monasteries, alien priories, friaries, colleges, collegiate churches, and hospitals ... formerly established in the diocese of Norwich and the ancient kingdom of East Anglia ... illustrated by maps of Suffolk ... and the arms of religious houses. 1821. Suffolk, 77–119

1802 **Grace, M.** Grey friars in East Anglia. [c.1934]. [Typescript]. NCL/N

1803 **Rigold, S. E.** Supposed see of Dunwich. JBAA 3rd Ser 24, 1961, 55–9

1804 **Redstone, V. B.** South Elmham deanery. PSIA 14, 1910/12, 323–31

1805 **Howlett, R.** Ancient see of Elmham. NA 18, 1914, 105–28

1806 **Hart, R.** Apostolical succession of the English clergy traced from the earliest times, and in the four dioceses of Canterbury, London, Norwich, and Ely continued to the year 1862. 1862

Religion

1807 **Jessopp, A.** Norwich. (Diocesan Histories). 1884
1808 **Landon, L.** Early archdeacons of Norwich diocese. PSIA 20, 1928/30, 11–35
1809 **Morley, C.** Catalogue of beneficed clergy of Suffolk, 1086–1550. PSIA 22, 1934/6, 29–85, index 321–33
1810 **Lunt, W. E.** Valuation of Norwich. Oxford, 1926
1811 **Hudson, W.** "Norwich taxation" of 1254. NA 17, 1906/07, 46–157
1812 **Gransden, A.** Some late-thirteenth century records of an ecclesiastical court in the archdeaconry of Sudbury. BIHR 32, 1959, 62–9
1813 **Manning, C. R.** First fruits, diocese of Norwich, *temp.* Henry VI and Edward IV. PSIA 7, 1889/91, 91–110
1814 **Redstone, L. J.** Suffolk limiters. PSIA 20, 1928/30, 36–42
1815 Dedications of Suffolk churches. N&Q 1st Ser 10, 1854, 45, 95; 4th Ser 3, 1869, 360, 414, 468
1816 **Olorenshaw, J. R.** Ancient church customs. E Ang NS 5, 1893/4, 175
       See also **5045, 6064, 6084, 8081**
1817 **Howard, J. J.** Seal and charters of the priory of Dodenes or Dodnach, Suffolk. PSA 4, 1857/9, 172, 211

14th and 15th Centuries
1818 **Scarfe, N.** Isolated churches and the Black Death. SR 1, 1957, 82–4
1819 **Welch, E.** Some Suffolk Lollards. PSIA 29, 1961/3, 154–65
1820 **Williams, J. F.** Ordination in the Norwich diocese during the fifteenth century. NA 31, 1957, 347–58
1821 Citations from the consistorial court of Norfolk. E Ang 1, 1858/63, 216–17
1822 **Jessopp, A.,** *Ed.* Visitations of the diocese of Norwich, A.D.1492–1532. Camden Soc NS 43, 1887. NCL/N

Religious Gilds
       See also church histories under individual localities, below, *and* **3638, 3748, 6041**
1823 **Bedell, A. J.** Suffolk gilds certificates. E Ang NS 2, 1887/8, 49–50
1824 **Redstone, V. B.** Chapels, chantries, and gilds in Suffolk. PSIA 12, 1904/06, 1–87
1825 **Westlake, H. F.** Origin, purposes, and development of parish gilds in England. PSIA 17, 1919/21, 163–74
1826 **Morley, C.** Check-list of the sacred buildings of Suffolk, to which are added gilds. PSIA 19, 1925/7, 168–211
1827 **Redstone, V. B.** Extracts from wills and other material showing the history of Suffolk churches, chantries, and gilds, being an appendix to the article in PSIA 12. PSIA 23, 1937/9, 50–78

REFORMATION
1828 **Stone, E. D.,** *Ed.* Norwich consistory court dispositions, 1499–1512 and 1518–1530. Rev. and arranged by B. Cozens-Hardy. Norwich, 1938. NRS 10

1829   Haslewood, F. Inventories of monasteries suppressed in 1536: Suffolk. PSIA 8, 1892/4, 83–116

1830   Registrum Vagum of Anthony Harison. Transcribed by T. F. Barton, 2 pts. Norwich, 1963. 1964. NRS 32, 33

1831   Church goods in Suffolk, *temp.* Edward VI. E Ang NS 1, 1885/6 – NS 6, 1895/6, *passim*

1832   Edwardian church goods confiscation. Citation to appear before the King's Commissioners A.D.1553: Bedingfield. E Ang NS 2, 1887/8, 346

1833   **Bullen, R. F.** Catalogue of beneficed clergy of Suffolk, 1551–1631 (with a few of earlier date). PSIA 22, 1934/6, 294–320, index 321–33

1834   **Baskerville, G.** Married clergy and pensioned religious in Norwich diocese, 1555. EHR 48, 1933, 43–64, 199–228

ELIZABETHAN AND EARLY STUART PERIOD

1835   **Redstone, V. B.** Records of the Sudbury archdeaconry. PSIA 11, 1901/03, 252–300

1836   **Pearson, W. C.** Archdeaconry of Suffolk. Mandates for induction, 1526–1629. E Ang NS 6, 1895/6; NS 8, 1899/1900; NS 9, 1901/02 *passim*

1837   **Calver, J.** Extracts from churchwardens' books [mainly 16th and 17th centuries]. E Ang 1, 1858/63; 2, 1864/6 *passim*

1838   **Green, A. J.** Popery as it was and is; the Suffolk martyrs ... from Foxe's Book of martyrs, etc. Sudbury, 1851

1839   **Layard, N. F.** Seventeen Suffolk martyrs. Ipswich, 1902

1840   **[Rand, P. H.]** Faithful unto death: the martyrs of East Anglia. [1937]. nl

1841   Mandate of the bishop of Norwich relating to schoolmasters and recusants, 1583. PSIA 2, 1854/9, 40

1842   Diocese of Norwich. Bishop Redman's visitation, 1597: Presentments in the archdeaconries of Norwich, Norfolk, and Suffolk. *Ed.* by J. F. Williams. Norwich, 1946. NRS 18

1843   Condition of the archdeaconries of Suffolk and Sudbury, 1603. PSIA 6, 1883/8, 361–400; 11, 1901/03, 1–46

1844   **Carter, E. H.** Norwich Subscription Books ... 1637–1800. 1937

1845   **Boorman, D. W.** Administrative and disciplinary problems of the Church on the eve of the Civil War, in the light of extant records of the dioceses of Norwich and Ely under Bishop Wren. B.Litt. thesis, Oxford, 1959

1846   **Shipps, K. W.** Lay patronage of East Anglian puritan clerics in pre-revolutionary England. Ph.D. thesis, Yale, 1971

1847   A magazine of scandall; or, A heape of wickednesse of two infamous ministers ... Thomas Fowkes of Earle Soham ... convicted by law for killing a man, and ... John Lowes of Brandeston, who hath been arraigned for witchcraft ... 1642. Wing M 248. BL

1848   **Ewen, C. L'Estrange.** Trial of John Lowes, clerk. 1937

1849   **White, J.** First century of scandalous, malignant priests ... 1643. Wing W 1777. BL

1850   Haslewood, F. Ministers of Suffolk ejected, 1643–4. PSIA 9, 1894/6, 307–09

1851   **Bullen, R. F.** Sequestrations in Suffolk. PSIA 19, 1925/7, 15–51, 141–67

1852   **Dow, L.** Sequestrations in Suffolk. PSIA 24, 1946/8, 125–8. *See also* **7863, 8118**

1853   **Holmes, C.** Suffolk committees for scandalous ministers, 1644–6. Ipswich, 1970. SRS 13

1854   The innocent in prison complayning; or, True relation of the proceedings of the committee at Ipswich ... against one Andrew Wyke, a witness of Jesus ... who was committed to prison, 3 June 1646 ... to which is annexed a relation of the imprisonment of John Dutten, who was violently surprised in his bed in the towne of Stradbrooke ... 1646

1855   An ordinance presented to the honourable House of Commons, by Mr. Bacon, a lawyer of Suffolke, and Mr. Taet ... pretended for preventing, growing and spreading of heresies. With some briefe observations thereupon. 1646. Wing B 355

1856   **Welch, E.** Commonwealth unions of benefices in Suffolk. SR 2, 1964, 213–16

1857   **Westup, W.,** *and* **Puckle, T.** Gentil-congregations no tithe-payers; or, Certain reasons wherein is clearly shewed what just ground there is for Gentiles conscientiously to make question of the lawfulness of their paying tithes, as they were presented unto the ... Justices of the Peace for the county of Suffolk, and members of the worshipful committee then sitting at the Grey-Hound in Ipswich. 1650. Wing W 1485

1858   "Hierophilus," *pseud.* Festered consciences new-launced: or, Tithe-paying defended against William Westup and Thomas Puckle ... Ipswich, 1650. Wing F 828. BL

1859   Hadleigh Deanery and its court, with two *Acta* books of the Deanery of Bocking. PSIA 15, 1913/15, 16–44

RESTORATION AND 18TH CENTURY   *See also* **354, 1531, 3152**

1860   East Anglian parishes assisted by briefs. E Ang NS 7, 1897/8, 145–7, 190; NS 8, 1899/1900, 322, 327–8; NS 13, 1909/10, 284–7, 290–91. *See also* **3645, 5242, 5260, 6118, 6134, 7370**

1861   **Grigson, F.** East Anglia institutions to benefices: Suffolk. E Ang NS 1, 1885/6, 105–07

1862   **Hutchinson, J. R.** Suffolk parish gleanings [17th century]. E Ang NS 10, 1903/04, 326–8

1863   **Dymond, D. P.** Suffolk and the Compton census of 1676. SR 3, 1966, 103–18

1864   Letter from a curate of Suffolk to a High Church member, concerning the D. of N. and *Mr.* W—le. 1712. nl

1865   **Williams, J. F.** Norwich diocesan faculty books, eighteenth century. NA 32, 1961, 353–61

1866   **Ecton, J.** Liber valorum et decimarum: being an account of the valuations and yearly tenths of all such ecclesiastical benefices of England and Wales, as now stand charged with the payment of first-fruits and tenths. 1711. Norwich diocese, 241–83. NCL/N

1867 Papers relating to Queen Ann's bounty, and to parliamentary grants for the augmentation of the maintenance of the poor clergy, 1703–1815. HC 1814/15, 12

1868 **Ecton, J.** State of the ... bounty of Queen Anne, for the augmentation of the maintenance of the poor clergy, 1704 to 1718. 1719. 2nd edn (to 1720), 1721. O

1869 **Ecton, J.** Thesaurus rerum ecclesiasticarum; an account of the valuations of ... benefices in the dioceses ... of England and Wales. 1742. 1754. 2nd edn. O

1870 **Lloyd, J.** Thesaurus ecclesiasticus. An improved edition of the Liber valorum et decimarum [of J. Ecton]. 1791. O

19TH AND 20TH CENTURIES *See also* **1531, 1538, 1546**

1871 Accounts of the population of certain benefices or parishes, with the capacities of their churches and chapels. HC 1818, 18. Suffolk, 298–305

1872 Return of the net annual revenue of ... ecclesiastical benefices ... on an average of three years ending 31 Dec 1831 ... of £250 and upwards. HC 1837, 41

1873 Report of the commissioners ... to inquire into the ecclesiastical revenues of England and Wales. HC 1835, 22

1874 Order in Council ratifying a scheme of the ecclesiastical commissioners, for augmenting the Archdeaconry of Sudbury. HC 1843, 22

1875 Abstract of ... return of every church rate ... within the last two years, in every parish. HC 1845, 41

1876 Return of all tithes commuted and apportioned under the Act 6 & 7 Will IV, c.71. HC 1847/8, 49; 1856, 46; 1887, 64

1877 **Wallace, D.** The tithe war. 1934. *See also* **1857–8, 2002**

1878 Clerical guide for the county of Suffolk, being a complete register of the several benefices, with their respective values ... and ... the names of the incumbents and patrons. Ipswich, [1848?]. BL

1879 **Gowing, R.,** *and* **Wright, H.** The Suffolk pulpit. *From* Suffolk Chronicle. No 1, 21 Nov 1857–no 153, 30 March 1861. Ipswich

1880 Return from each parish ... setting forth the gross amount expended during the last seven years for church purposes. HC 1859, 20

1881 Return of all glebe lands ... showing parishes ... and the estimated annual value. HC 1887, 64

1882 Royal Commission on ecclesiastical discipline. HC 1906, 23

1883 Re-arrangement of East Anglian diocese. Ely, Norwich, and St. Albans appeal for new dioceses for Essex and Suffolk. 1906

1884 Diocese of St. Edmundsbury and Ipswich: a retrospect, 1914–1927

1885 The Kingdom of God in a country diocese. Papers read and sermons preached at the 62nd Annual Church Congress, Ipswich, October 1927. Ipswich, 1927

1886 **Cranage, D. H. S.,** *Ed.* Thirteen-hundredth anniversary of the diocese of East Anglia. Official handbook. Norwich, 1930

1887   Form and order of the solemn thanksgiving for the 21st anniversary of the foundation of the diocese of St. Edmundsbury and Ipswich, 26 July 1935

1888   Survey of the ecclesiastical archives of the diocese of St. Edmundsbury and Ipswich [1952]. BL

1889   **St. Edmundsbury and Ipswich Diocese.** Jubilee year, 1964. Ipswich, 1964

1890   **St. Edmundsbury and Ipswich Diocese.** No secret plan [reorganisation of the clergy]. Ipswich, 1968

1891   **Fitch, J.** Churches of Suffolk: redundancy and a policy for conservation. Polstead, 1971

1892   **Fitch, J.** A curate's egg: the Ipswich deanery re-organization report considered. Brandon, 1972

1893   **Norwich Diocese.** Diocesan calendar and clergy list, 1856–. Norwich. NCL/N

1894   Norwich diocesan gazette, 1895–1953. *Cont. as* Norwich Churchman, 1960–

1895   **St. Edmundsbury and Ipswich Diocese.** Diocesan calendar and clergy list, 1915–. Ipswich

1896   **Briggs, G.** Diocesan arms: St. Edmundsbury and Ipswich. CA 7, 1963, 334–5

1897   **St. Edmundsbury and Ipswich Diocese.** Diocesan magazine for the county of Suffolk, 1914–57. News of the diocese, 1927–68. The church in Suffolk, 1968–. Ipswich

1898   Hoxne deanery magazine, Jan. 1909–June 1968; Hoxne deanery news, July 1968–April 1969

VISITATION ARTICLES, CHARGES, AND SERMONS
See also **1822, 1842,** *and* **2008–20**

	Suffolk archdeaconry.	Visitation articles.
1899		1618. STC 10340. O
1900		1625. STC 10341. O
1901		1633. STC 10342. O
1902		1636. STC 10343. O
1903		1637. STC 10343.5 O
1904		1638. STC 10344. O
1905		1639. STC 10345. O
1906		1640. STC 10346. O

	Sudbury archdeaconry.	Visitation articles.
1907		1624. STC 10337. O
1908		[1627]. STC 10338. O
1909		1636. STC 10338.5. O
1910		1639. STC 10339. O
1911		1663. Wing C 4085. O
1912		1665. SRO/I
1913		1672. Wing C 4085A O
1914		1700. Wing C 4085B O

1915   **Hutchinson, F.** Sermon preached at Beccles in Suffolk before the Right

Reverend ... John [Moore], Lord Bishop of Norwich, at ... his Lordship's primary visitation held there, 27 May 1692. 1692. Wing H 3830. BL

1916 **Warren, R.** Sermon preached to the clergy of the archdeaconry of Suffolk, at a visitation upon 11 April etc., 1746. Cambridge, 1746. nl

1917 **Canning, R.** Sermon preached at the ordinary visitation of the Right Reverend ... Thomas [Hayter], Lord Bishop of Norwich, in Ipswich, 17 June 1747. Ipswich, 1747. nl

1918 **Goodall, H.** Sermon preached to the clergy of the archdeaconry of Suffolk, at a visitation 28 April etc., 1748. Cambridge, 1748. nl

1919 Charge of the Right Reverend ... Philip [Yonge], Lord Bishop of Norwich, delivered to the clergy of his diocese, at his primary visitation, A.D. 1763. Norwich, 1763. nl

1920 Charge delivered to the clergy at the primary visitation of Lewis [Bagot], Lord Bishop of Norwich. Norwich, 1784. nl

1921 **Darby, S.** Sermon preached at the visitation of the Right Reverend Lewis [Bagot], Lord Bishop of Norwich, holden at Bury St. Edmunds ... 1784. BL

1922 **Knowles, T.** Letter to the Right Reverend ... Lewis [Bagot], Lord Bishop of Norwich: occasioned by his late visitation tour through the counties of Norfolk and Suffolk. 1784. nl

1923 **Rogers, G.** Sermon preached at the Archdeacon's visitation, 23 April 1790, in the parish church of St. Mary at Tower, Ipswich. Ipswich, [1790]. nl

1924 **Longe, J.** Sermon preached at the primary visitation of the Right Reverend ... Charles [Sutton], Lord Bishop of Norwich, holden at Ipswich, on Tuesday, 17 June 1794, for the deaneries of Ipswich, Samford, Colnes, and Claydon. Ipswich, 1794. nl

1925 Charge delivered to the clergy of the diocese of Norwich, at the primary visitation of that diocese in 1806, by Henry [Bathurst], Bishop of Norwich. Norwich, [1806]. nl

1926 **Glover, G.** Charge, delivered in May 1828, to the clergy and church-wardens of the Archdeaconry of Sudbury ... Norwich, [1828]. nl

1927 **Hervey,** *Lord* **A. C.** Sermon preached ... at the visitation of the ... Archdeacon of Sudbury. Bury St. Edmunds, [1840]. BL

1928 **Eyre, C. J. P.** Sermon at the visitation of the Archdeacon of Sudbury, 6 May 1845. Bury St. Edmunds, [1845]. BL

1929 **Hervey,** *Lord* **A. C.** Charge delivered to the clergy and churchwardens of the Archdeaconry of Sudbury, at his primary visitation in July 1862. Bury St. Edmunds, 1862. BL

1930 **Hervey,** *Lord* **A. C.** Charge delivered to the clergy and churchwardens of the Archdeaconry of Sudbury, at the general visitation in 1863. 1863

ROMAN CATHOLICISM

1931 Roman Catholic fugitives in Suffolk. E Ang 1, 1858/63, 129–30

1932 Popish recusants in Suffolk. E Ang NS 1, 1885/6, 345–6

1933 **C, J. L.** Refusal of Roman Catholics and others to take the Oath of Allegiance. Lists in East Anglia. E Ang NS 7, 1897/8, 285–8

1934   **Muskett, J. J.** Recantation of Anthony Yaxley of Over Rickingale, Suffolk (1525). E Ang NS 3, 1889/90, 380–81

1935   **Baines, W.** James Portus, a Suffolk recusant, 1651. E Ang NS 13, 1909/10, 65–6

1936   **Talbot, C.,** *Ed.* Decanatus Suff': recusants in Suffolk 1559. CRS 53, 1961, 108–11

1937   **Calthrop, M. M. C.,** *Ed.* Recusant roll no 1 (1592–3): Suffolk. CRS 18, 1916, 309–25

1938   **Bowler, H.,** *Ed.* Recusant roll no 2 (1593–4): Suffolk. CRS 57, 1965, 157–70

1939   **Bowler, H.,** *Ed.* Recusant roll no 3 (1594–5) and no 4 (1595–6): Suffolk. CRS 61, 1970, 88–95, 223–8

1940   **Rye, W.** Popish and sectary recusants in Suffolk, 1596. E Ang 2, 1864/6, 159–60, 176–85

1941   **Lacey, R.** Information against Monford Scott, and Catholics of Norfolk and Suffolk. CRS 5, 1908, 71–4

1942   Registry of the papists' estates within the division of Bury St. Edmunds. [1717]. O

1943   College of the Holy Apostles, of the Suffolk district. By a member of the Society of Jesus. Records of the English Province of the Soc of Jesus, 2, 1875, 393–613

1944   **Foley, H.** College of the Holy Apostles, of the Suffolk district. Records of the English Province of the Soc of Jesus, 5, 1879, 513–35

1945   **Congregation of Jesus and Mary.** Centenary souvenir of the English Province (1860–1960). Ipswich, [1960]

1946   **Northampton Diocese.** Catholic directory, 1937– NCL/N

NON-CONFORMITY

General   See also **1534–5**

1947   **Greenwood, H. D.** Origin and early history and Independency in Suffolk to 1688. B.Litt. thesis, Oxford, 1949

1948   **Harmer, T.** Nonconformity—Suffolk [c.1770]. MS

1949   **Harmer, T.** Historical and biographical accounts of the dissenting churches in the counties of Norfolk and Suffolk. MS of 1774, *ed.* by S. W. Rix. NRO

1950   [**Rix, S. W.?**] Memoranda relating to the history of Nonconformist churches in Norfolk and Suffolk. 2v. Ms. NCL/N

1951   **Redstone, V. B.** Records of protestant dissenters in Suffolk. Woodbridge, 1912

1952   **Duncan, J.,** *Ed.* Certificates of protestant dissenters 1801–12: to be used in conjunction with V. B. Redstone's Suffolk protestant dissenters. 1961. [Typescript]. SRO/B

1953   **Sydenham, G.** Early Nonconformist churches in Suffolk. SR 3, 1970, 293–6

1954   Conventicles in East Anglia, 1669. CHST 2, 1906, 282–5

1955   **Jewson, C. B.** Return of conventicles in Norwich diocese, 1669–. Lambeth MS. no 639. NA 33, 1965, 6–34

1956 Sloper, I. Christian churches the hope and joy of faithful ministers: a discourse, delivered at Needham Market, before the half-yearly Association of the Suffolk Independent Churches. Bungay, 2nd edn 1816. NCL/N

1957 Ray, J. M. Address, written at the request of the ministers of the Suffolk Independent Association ... recommending the observance of a day of special prayer, on Friday, 6 June, for a revival of personal religion ... Sudbury, 1828. NCL/N

1958 Binfield, J. C. G. Nonconformity in the eastern counties, 1840–85, with reference to its social background. Ph.D. thesis, Cambridge, 1965

1959 Duncan, J. Early Independents of Rede, Hargrave, Chevington, Ousden, Barrow, Lidgate, Wickhambrook, Chedburgh, etc. with many extracts from the Bury church book. 1961. [Typescript]. SRO/B

Baptist

1960 Klaiber, A. J. Story of the Suffolk Baptists, etc. [1931]

1961 "Octoginta" *pseud.* [i.e. C. T. Rust] Reminiscences of the four first Baptist churches in Suffolk. 1889. NCL/N

1962 Klaiber, A. J. Early Baptist movements in Suffolk. BQ 4, 1928/9, 116–20

1963 Hewett, M. F. A nineteenth-century revival in East Anglia. BQ 11, 1942/3, 233–6

1964 Short, K. R. M. Resolutions taken by Suffolk and Norfolk Old Association to sever ties with American Baptists connected with slavery. BQ 20, 1963/4, 256

1965 Toon, P. Two publications by Strict Baptists in Suffolk and Norfolk. BQ 21, 1965/6, 30, 32

1966 Norfolk and Suffolk Association of Baptist Churches. Circular letters ... 1814–20, 1822–4, 1836, 1839–41, 1845–7, 1849, 1851, 1883. NCL/N. 1839–41. BL

1967 Wright, G. Book of the decrees in the hand of the mediator: a sermon preached at the annual meeting of the Suffolk and Norfolk New Association of the Baptist churches ... June 1842. [1842]. BL

Congregational

1968 Sydenham, G. Source material for the history of Suffolk Congregationalism. SR 4, no 2, 1973, 41–52

1969 [Harmer, T.] Remarks on the ancient and present state of the Congregational churches of Norfolk and Suffolk. 1777. SRO/B

1970 Miscellaneous works of ... T.H. [T. Harmer], containing his letters and sermons, remarks on the ... state of the Congregational churches of Norfolk and Suffolk. 1823. BL

1971 Browne, J. History of Congregationalism, and memorials of the churches in Norfolk and Suffolk. 1877

1972 Hosken, T. J. History of Congregationalism, and memorials of the churches of our order in Suffolk. Ipswich, 1920

1973 Sydenham, G. Glimpses of Congregational church life in Suffolk during the 18th and 19th centuries. SR 3, 1968, 207–11

1974 **Bennett, J. H.** History of Congregationalism in Suffolk from 1870 to 1940. B.Litt. thesis, Oxford, 1953

1975 **Suffolk Congregational Union.** Report of the nineteenth annual meeting held at Sudbury ... 1877. Ipswich, [1877] NCL/N

1976 **Suffolk Congregational Union.** Among the byways of Suffolk. Ipswich, nd. SCL/L

1977 **Sydenham, G.** Australian Congregationalism's debt to Suffolk. SR 3, 1968, 250–52

1978 **Suffolk Congregational Union.** Suffolk Congregational Magazine, 1868–1870. Ipswich. NCL/N

Presbyterian

1979 **Redstone, V. B.** Presbyterian church government in Suffolk, 1643–1647. PSIA 13, 1907/09, 133–75

1980 Petition on the inhabitants of Suffolke, presented to the House of Peers [in favour of the Presbyterian government of the church]. 1646/7, Feb 16. Wing P 1805. BL-T

1981 November 5, 1645. The county of Suffolke divided into fourteene precincts for classicall Presbiteries, together with the names of the ministers ... 1647. Wing C 6573A. SRO/B

1982 Ordinance of Parliament, for the speedy dividing the severall counties into distinct classical Presbyteries. 1647/8, Jan 29. Wing E 2043. BL-T

Quaker

1983 The grounds and causes of our sufferings in Edmonds-Bury goal [sic] in Suffolk. From George Whithead, John Harwood, George Fox, George Rose, and Henry Marshall, Quakers. 1656, May 16. Wing W 1931, 1932. BL-T

1984 Apology for the people called Quakers, and an appeal to the inhabitants of Norfolk and Suffolk ... [By J.F., i.e. John Field]. 1699. Wing F 861. BL

1985 Sober reply, on behalf of the people called Quakers, to two petitions against them (the one of Norfolk, and the other from Bury in Suffolk), being some brief observations upon them. [By T. Ellwood]. 1699. Wing E 628. NCL/N

1986 **Stebbing, H.** Short and true account of a conference held at a Quaker's Meeting House in Suffolk with J. Middleton, ... Speaker. Together with some remarks thereupon. 1714. BL

1987 Account of the meeting houses, burial grounds, and other estates; and also of legacies and funds belonging to the Society of Friends in Suffolk quarterly meeting, 1852. Sudbury, 1852. Ipswich, 2nd edn 1868

1988 **Society of Friends.** Essex and Suffolk quarterly meeting. List of members. 1882. 1890

Unitarian

1989 **Godfrey, W. H.** Unitarian chapels of Ipswich and Bury St. Edmunds. Arch J 108, 1951, 121–6

1990 Suffolk Unitarian. No 9, Aug 1960–No 149, Nov 1972. Ipswich. [incomplete]. [Typescript]

Wesleyan Methodist

1991 **Nattrass, J. C.** Notes from the oldest register of the Great Yarmouth circuit [includes Lowestoft and Beccles]. Wesley Historical Soc Proc 3, 1901, 73–7

JUDAISM

1992 **Margoliouth, M.** Notes from a lecture on the historic vestiges of the Anglo-Hebrew in East Anglia. Arch J 26, 1869, 387–8

1993 **Margoliouth, M.** Vestiges of the historic Anglo-Hebrews in East Anglia. 1870

1994 **Davis, M. D.** Early Jews in East Anglia. E Ang NS 4, 1891/2, 321–2

1995 **Mander, R. P.** The Jew in medieval East Anglia. EAM 10, 1950, 162–5

RELIGIOUS SOCIETIES

1996 **Suffolk and Ipswich Association in Aid of the Church Missionary Society.** Reports. 1st, 1814; 14th, 1827; 18th, 1831. Ipswich

1997 **Suffolk Auxiliary Bible Society.** Interesting proceedings of the meetings of the Norfolk and Suffolk Auxiliary Bible Societies ... 1811–. BL

1998 **Suffolk Auxiliary Bible Society.** Reports. 1st, 1812; 4th, 1815; 8th, 1819; 14th–17th, 1825–8. Bury St. Edmunds

1999 **Suffolk Auxiliary Bible Society.** Fifth anniversary held ... 4 Oct 1816. Bury St. Edmunds. BL

2000 **Norwich Diocesan Church Building Association** [prospectus]. Norwich, 1836. NCL/N

2001 **Norwich Diocesan Church Defence Association.** Reports for the years 1872, 1881–4, 1890–1, with statements of accounts and lists of members. Norwich. NCL/N

RELIGIOUS CONTROVERSY

2002 A few proposals offered in humility, to ... the Parliament, ... holding forth a medium of essay for the removing of tythes, and establishing a maintenance for a godly ministry in the nation, ... presented to the Parliament by several well-affected people in the county of Suffolk ... 1659. Wing F 835. SRO/B

2003 **Hurrion, J.** Rights and duties of ministers. A sermon preached ... on the ... settlement of Mr. T. Milway in the pastoral care of a church of Christ in Ipswich. 1721. BL

2004 **Ray, J. M.** Christian liberty ... sermon preached at Stowmarket ... Dec 1, 1789, before the deputies from several Protestant Dissenting congregations in the county of Suffolk, assembled for the purpose of deliberating upon measures to be pursued for obtaining a repeal of the Corporation and Test Acts. [1789]. nl

2005 Anticipation; or, An account previous to the meeting of High-Churchmen in this county, of the business transacted there in opposition to the Dissenters, with speeches at length. [Ipswich?], 1790. BL

2006 Remarks on the temper of the present times, by a Clergyman of Suffolk. Addressed to the gentlemen, yeomanry, and common people. Ipswich, 1792

2007 **Hurn, W.** A farewell testimony, containing the substance of two discourses, preached in the parish church of Debenham, 13 Oct 1822, after public notice given ... to take leave of the people, and secede from the established church ... Woodbridge, 1823. BL

SERMONS

2008 **Gurnall, W.** The majistrates pourtraiture drawn from the Word, and preached in the sermon at Stowmarket ... upon 20 August 1656 ... before the election of Parliament men. [3 Oct], 1656. Wing G 2259. BL

2009 **Curtis, W.** The peace offering ... a sermon ... preach'd 25 June 1713 ... at St. Mary Tower in Ipswich, for the support of the charity schools there. 1713

2010 **C, J.** Sermon preached at Bury St. Edmunds ... before ... free and accepted Masons. Bury St. Edmunds, 1773. SRO/B

2011 **Black, J.** Political calumny refuted: addressed to the inhabitants of Woodbridge, containing an extract of a sermon preached at Butley ... 1793. Sermon preached at Otley ... on account of our naval victories ... Ipswich, [1800]. BL

2012 **Stewart, C. E.** Obedience to government, reverence to the constitution, and resistance to Bonaparte: a sermon. Bury St. Edmunds, 1803. SRO/B

2013 **Madge, T.** Importance of education to the poor stated, and the promotion of it recommended ... a sermon preached at the chapel ... Bury St. Edmunds, for the benefit of a charity school. Bury St. Edmunds, 1810. SRO/B

2014 Sermon ... to explain the objects and recommend the advantages of the Savings Bank established at Halesworth ... by the minister of a neighbouring parish [B. Philpot]. Halesworth, [1818]. BL

2015 **Hughes, T. S.** Sermon preached on ... 29 April 1826, at Bury Saint Edmund's, on behalf of the charity schools established in that town. 1827

2016 **Cobbold, R.** Sermon preached to the congregation of St. Mary Tower church, Ipswich ... to the members of the Seamen's Shipwreck Benevolent Society. Ipswich, [1829]. BL

2017 **Eyre, C. J. P.** Pure and undefiled religion. A sermon preached in aid of the Ipswich Seamen's Shipwreck Society. Ipswich, 1846. BL

2018 **Donaldson, J. W.** Farewell sermon, preached in St. James's church, Bury St. Edmunds. Bury St. Edmunds, 1855. SRO/B

2019 **Richardson, J.** Sermon on the blessings of the English Reformation, preached ... 1858. Bury St. Edmunds, 1858. SRO/B

2020 **Owen, H.** Sermon preached at the camp of the Brigade of Suffolk Rifle Volunteers, at Lowestoft on Sunday, 21 July 1867. Ipswich, 1867

Social History, Culture, and Recreation

GENERAL

2021 **Unwin, G.,** *and* **Kemp, D.** Social and economic history. *In* VCH Suffolk 1, 1911, 633–82

2022 **Morey, G. E.** East Anglian society in the fifteenth century: an historico-regional survey. Ph.D. thesis, London, 1951

2023 **Rollings, A. E.** Parents and children in the 18th century. SR 1, 1956, 15–18

2024 **Fussell, G. E.** Suffolk boyhood in the 1820's. SR 1, 1957, 84–7

2025 **Glyde, J.** Suffolk in the nineteenth century: physical, social, moral, religious, and industrial. [1856]

2026 **Emerson, P. H.** Pictures of East Anglian life, 1888. [Suffolk peasantry, 1–30; Suffolk fisherfolk, 31–40; Meteorological observations, Southwold 1885–6]. SCL/L

2027 **Suffolk Rural Community Council.** Annual reports 1937–. Ipswich

2028 **Suffolk Rural Community Council.** First thirty years, 1937–67: a short history of the Suffolk Rural Community Council. Ipswich, [1968]

2029 **Suffolk Rural Community Council.** Suffolk Rural Community Council, 1958. [Illustrated brochure to mark the 21st anniversary ...] Ipswich, 1958

2030 Suffolk – some social trends: a research project. Ipswich, 1968. Report by members of the Social Research team. Ipswich, 1970. [Sponsored by University of East Anglia, and Suffolk Rural Community Council]. [Typescript]

2031 **Blythe, R.** Akenfield: portrait of an English village [Charsfield and neighbouring villages]. 1969

2032 **Smedley, N.** Life and tradition in Suffolk and North-East Essex. 1976

FOLKLORE   *See also* **2316–17, 4484, 8068**

2033 The Suffolk miracle: or, a relation of a young man, who, a month after his death, appeared to his sweetheart, and carryed her behind him forty miles in two hours time, and was never seen but in the grave. [A ballad]. [1670?] and later edns. Wing S 6160–3. BL

2034 Suffolk garland: or, a collection of poems, songs, takes, ballads, ... relative to that county. [*Ed.* by J. Ford]. Ipswich, 1818

2035 **Rayson, G.** East Anglian folk lore. E Ang 2, 1864/6; 3, 1866/8; 4, 1869/70, *passim*

2036 **Glyde, J.,** *Ed.* New Suffolk garland: a miscellany of anecdotes, romantic ballads, . . . and statistical returns relating to the county of Suffolk . . . Ipswich, 1866

2037 **Gurdon,** *Lady* **E. C.** Folk-lore from south-east Suffolk. Folk-Lore 3, 1892, 558–60

2038 **Gurdon,** *Lady* **E. C.** County folk-lore. Printed extracts no 2. Suffolk. 1893

2039 **Groome, W. W.** Suffolk leechcraft. Folk-Lore 6, 1895, 117–27

2040 **Hartland, E. S.** Cleft ashes for infantile hernia [Needham]. Folk-Lore 7, 1896, 303–06

2041 **Gurdon,** *Lady* **E. C.** Suffolk tales and other stories. Fairy legends. Poems. Miscellaneous articles. 1897

2042 **Clodd, E.** Tom Tit Tot: an essay on savage philosophy in folk-tale. 1898

2043 **Fison, L. A.** Merry Suffolk: Master Archie and other tales, a book of folk-lore . . . with which is included "Tom Tit Tot" and sequel by Mrs. W. Thomas. 1899

2044 **James, M. H.** Cure for ague [Suffolk]. Folk-Lore 10, 1899, 365

2045 **Partridge, C.** Horse-shoe in a cover of scarlet – a Suffolk superstition. E Ang NS 9, 1901/02, 48

2046 **Anderson, R.,** *and* **Hadow, G. E.** Scraps of English folklore, 9 [Suffolk]. Folk-Lore 35, 1924, 346–60

2047 **Terry, M.** Scraps of English folklore, 12 [Suffolk]. Folk-Lore 37, 1926, 77–8

2048 **Moeran, E. J.,** *Ed.* Six Suffolk folk songs, collected and arranged with pianoforte accompaniment. [1931]

2049 **Harvey, A. S.** Ballads, songs, and rhymes of East Anglia. Norwich, 1936

2050 **Harvey, N.** Some Suffolk superstitions. Folk-Lore 54, 1943, 390–91

2051 **Coleman, S. J.,** *Ed.* Folklore of Suffolk. Douglas, Isle of Man, [1952]. [Typescript]

2052 **Coleman, S. J.** Traditional lore of East Anglia. Douglas, Isle of Man, 1961

2053 **Porter, E.** Folklore of East Anglia. 1974

WITCHCRAFT *See also* 3224

2054 **Bullen, R. F.** Suffolk witches in the time of Queen Elizabeth. E Ang NS 13, 1909/10, 181

2055 **Ewen, C. L'Estrange.** Witch hunting and witch trials. The indictment for witchcraft from the records of 1,373 assizes held for the Home Circuit, A.D.1559–1736. 1929

2056 **Nyndge, E.** A true and fearefull vexation of one Alexander Nyndge: being most horribly tormented with the devill . . . at Lyeringswoll [Herringswell] in Suffolk. 1615. STC 18753. BL

2057 Collection of . . . tracts relating to witchcraft in the counties of Kent . . . Suffolk . . . between the years 1618 and 1664. Rp verbatim from the original edns. 1838 etc. BL

2058   Signes and wonders from heaven ... and how 20 witches were executed in Suffolke this last assize ... 1645, [Aug 5]. Wing S 3777. BL-T

2059   **Stearne, J.** [of Lawshall] A confirmation and discovery of witchcraft ... together with the confession of many executed since May 1645 in the severall counties hereafter mentioned ... [1645]. Wing S 5364. BL. 1648. Wing S 5365. GU

2060   Lawes against witches and conjuration ... also the confession of Mother Lakeland of Ipswich, who was arraigned and condemned for a witch at Ipswich in Suffolk. 1645. Wing E 918. BL

2061   True relation of the araignment of eighteene witches, that were tried, convicted, and condemned at a sessions holden at St. Edmunds-Bury, in Suffolke ... and so were executed the 27 day of August, 1645, etc. 1645. Wing T 2928. BL-T

2062   True relation of the araignment of thirty witches at Chensford in Essex ... there being at this time a hundred more in severall prisons in Suffolke and Essex. 1645 BL

2063   **Hopkins, M.** Discovery of witches: in answer to severall queries, lately delivered to the Judges of Assize for the county of Norfolke ... 1647, [May 18]. Wing H 2751 BL-T. Rp verbatim from the original edn. 1837. 1931

2064   **Summers, A. J-M. A. M.** Discovery of witches. A study of Master Matthew Hopkins, commonly call'd Witch Finder Generall ... together with a reprint of "The discovery of witches" from the rare original of 1647. 1928

2065   Tryal of witches [Rose Cullender and Amy Duny] at the Assizes held at Bury St. Edmonds ... 10 March, 1664 ... 1682. Wing T 2240. 1716. 1838

2066   The wonder of Suffolk; being the true relation of one that reports he made a league with the devil for three years to do mischief. [Signed W. S. Harwich]. 1677. Wing S 208. SRO/B

2067   **Petto, S.** Faithful narrative of the fits which Mr. Tho. Spatchet, late of Dunwich and Cookly, was under by witchcraft. 1693. Wing P 1897. O

2068   **Hutchinson, F.** Historical essay concerning witchcraft ... 1718. BL

2069   **Pickford, J.** Witchcraft in Suffolk. N&Q 7th Ser 9, 1890, 425–6

2070   **Newman, L. F.** Notes on the history and practice of witchcraft in the eastern counties. Folk-Lore 57, 1946, 12–23

2071   **Merrifield, R.,** *and* **Smedley, N.** Two witch-bottles from Suffolk [Ipswich, Woodbridge]. PSIA 28, 1958/60, 97–100

2072   **Smedley, N.** *et al.* More Suffolk witch-bottles. PSIA 30, 1964/6, 88–93

GYPSIES   *See also* **6314**

2073   Anglo-Romani gleanings from East Anglian gypsies. GLSJ 3rd Ser 8, 1929, 105–34

2074   **Sampson, J.,** *Ed.* An East Anglian Romani vocabulary of 1798. GLSJ 3rd Ser 9, 1930, 97–146

2075   **Thompson, T. W.** Youngs, Gibsons, and their associates: an inquiry into the

origin of certain East Anglian and metropolitan gypsy families. GLSJ 3rd
Ser 24, 1945, 44–56

2076 **Thompson, T. W.** Youngs, Gibsons, and their associates: some migrant
faws and their East Anglian descendants. GLSJ 3rd Ser 25, 1946, 39–45

2077 **Evans, I. H. N.** Stray memories of British gypsies. GLSJ 3rd 35, 1956,
98–116

2078 **Winstedt, E. O.** Records of gypsies in the Eastern Counties. GLSJ 3rd Ser
40, 1961, 26–35

DIALECT   *See also* Place-names, *above, and* **5056, 5262**

2079 **Cullum,** *Sir* **J.** Some words and expressions used in this place [Hawsted],
and the neighbourhood. *In his* History and antiquities of Hawsted. 1784.
170–74

2080 **Moor, E.** Suffolk words and phrases; or, an attempt to collect the lingual
localisms of that county. Woodbridge, 1823. Rp 1970

2081 **Forby, R.** Vocabulary of East Anglia. An attempt to record the vulgar
tongue of . . . Norfolk and Suffolk . . . with proof of its antiquity from
etymology and authority. (Memoir of the author, by Dawson Turner) [*Ed.*
by G. Turner]. 2v. 1830. v 3 . . . by . . . W. T. Spurdens, 1858. Rp in 2v. 1970

2082 Local words in use among the labouring classes. *In* W. and H. Raynbird's
On the agriculture of Suffolk. 1849. 287–305

2083 **Baker, G. B.** Local proverbs. E Ang 1, 1858/63, 322

2084 **"Quill",** [*pseud.,* i.e. **J. I. Lushington**]. A Suffolk largess [verse, partly in
dialect]. 1865

2085 **Nall, J. G.** Etymological and comparative glossary of the dialect and
provincialisms of East Anglia, with illustrations derived from native authors.
In his Great Yarmouth and Lowestoft . . . 1866, 422–710

2086 Words used in Suffolk. E Ang 2, 1864/6, 327, 363

2087 **Whistlecraft, O.** Collection of Suffolk sayings, original tales, rhymes . . .
In Suffolk agriculture. *Ed.* by W. Raynbird. Bungay, 1867, 24–31

2088 Sea words and phrases along the Suffolk coast, Crabbe's Suffolk, and super-
superlative Suffolk. [By Edward FitzGerald]. E Ang 3, 1866/8, 347–63; 4,
1869/70, 109–18, 261–4

2089 Z. Of the derivation of some Suffolk words. E Ang 4, 1869/70, 107–08

2090 Notes of Suffolk words. N&Q 5th Ser 2, 1874, 326, 454

2091 **Skeat, W. W.,** *Ed.* English Dialect Society. Ser. B. Reprinted glossaries.
No 20. East Anglian words from Spurdens' Supplement to Forby, 1840. No 21.
Suffolk words from Cullum's History of Hawstead, 1813. 1879

2092 [**Spilling, J.**] Johnny's jaunt: a day in the life of a Suffolk couple. Norwich,
[1879]

2093 **Beazeley, A.,** *et al.* Suffolk phraseology. N&Q 6th Ser 3, 1881, 187, 336, 437

2094 Words in local use in Suffolk and Essex. E Ang NS 1, 1885/6, 84–6, 109

2095 **Layton, W. E.** "Silly Suffolk" E Ang NS 1, 1885/6, 262; NS 2, 1887/8, 303

2096 Ellis, H. D., *et al.* Gallicisms in East Suffolk. N&Q 7th Ser 8, 1889, 406, 517

2097 Fison, L. A. Brother Mike. An old Suffolk fairy tale. [1893]

2098 Zincke, F. B. Our East Anglian dialect. *In his* Wherstead: some materials for its history ... 2nd edn 1893, 241–81

2099 Rye, W. Glossary of words used in East Anglia, founded on that of Forby. English Dialect Society. 1895

2100 Cooper, E. R. "Black Toby". An old Suffolk tale. E Ang NS 6, 1895/6, 193–5

2101 Griffinhoofe, H. G., *and* R. R. Notes on origin of a Suffolk proverb. N&Q 8th Ser 9, 1896, 326, 437

2102 Fison, L. A., *and* Thomas, W. Suffolk folk tales. E Ang NS 7, 1897/8, 71–4, 102–03

2103 Green, W. C. Suffolk metrical story. Ant 35, 1899, 250

2104 Hughes, T. C., *et al.* Suffolk dialect word for a ladybird. N&Q 9th Ser 5, 1900, 48, 154, 274; 9th Ser 6, 1900, 255, 417

2105 Clare, J. B. Glossary of old-fashioned words. *In his* Wenhaston and Bulcamp, Suffolk. Halesworth, 1903. 63–119

2106 Fison, L. A. Spinning days and olden ways: a Suffolk story. [List of Suffolk words, 93–103] Ipswich, 1904

2107 Busby, W., *and* Wase, F. W. Hodge podge: or, A Suffolk medley. Halesworth, 1914. SCL/L

2108 Prose and poetry, by "Silly Suffolk", *pseud.* [i.e. C. Partridge]. Ipswich, 1925

2109 Kökeritz, H. Phonology of the Suffolk dialect: descriptive and historical. Uppsala, 1932

2110 Hohenstein, R. Intonation und Vokalqualität in den englischen Mundarten von Norfolk und Suffolk. Berlin, 1938. NCL/N

2111 Edmonds, P. "Owd Willum"; stories of Suffolk life. Diss, [1940]. SCL/L

2112 Partridge, C. Suffolk gossip, 1756–9. N&Q 194, 1949, 539–41

2113 Claxton, A. O. D. Suffolk dialect of the 20th century. Ipswich, 1954. 2nd edn 1960. 3rd edn 1968

2114 Orton, H., *and* Tilling, P. M., *Eds.* Survey of English dialects. (B) The basic materials. v 3, East Midland counties and East Anglia. Pts 1–3. Leeds, 1969

2115 Selten, B. Early East Anglian nicknames. (Scripta minora Regiae societatis humaniorum litterarum Lundensis, 1968/9: 3). Lund, 1969

HUMOUR

2116 East Anglian and his humour. Ipswich, [1966]

2117 More East Anglian humour. Ipswich, 1969

2118 East Anglia's humour. Ipswich, 1976

Social History, Culture, and Recreation

LITERARY ASSOCIATIONS *See also* Individual and family biography, *below*, and **2332, 2336, 3799–800**

2119 Prospectuses of works published by authors living in the county of Suffolk, or relating to that county. 1819–51. BL

2120 **Davy, D. E.** Athenae Suffolciensis: a catalogue of Suffolk authors and an account of their lives and a list of their meetings. BL. Add. MS 19,165–8. List of Suffolk authors' works giving details of when published, date, size, etc., with alphabetical index to authors. BL. Add. MS 19,169. Biographical notices of Suffolk writers. BL. Add. MS 19,170

2121 **Dutt, W. A.** Some literary associations of East Anglia. 1907

2122 **Moore, S.** Patrons of letters in Norfolk and Suffolk, c.1450. Publ. Modern Language Assoc. of America 27, 1912, 188–207; 28, 1913, 79–105

THEATRE *See also* **3759, 3985–8, 4404–08, 5161–3, 6773**

2123 **Bellamy, B. P.** Letter to the dramatic censor of the Suffolk Chronicle. Ipswich, [1813]. O

2124 **Eyre, H. R.** Materials for a history of Suffolk theatres. 6v. 1900. MSS etc.

2125 **Carver, J.** Norfolk and Suffolk Company of Comedians and the Fisher family ... Paper read before the Norwich Science Gossip Club 10 March 1909. Norwich, 1909. NCL/N

2126 **Burley, T. L. G.** Playhouses and players of East Anglia. Norwich, 1928

2127 **Norfolk Drama Committee.** East Anglian theatre: an exhibition devoted to the history of the players and playhouses of Norfolk and Suffolk. Castle Museum, Norwich, 3 May–3 June 1952. Norwich

PAGEANTS *See* **3990, 4410–13, 5013–15, 5235, 6181, 6184, 6290, 7087**

CELEBRATIONS *See* **3989, 4415–16, 6182–3, 6334, 6489–90, 6693, 7010**

CONCERTS *See* **6185–7**

ARTS *See also* Individual and family biography, *below*, and **3571, 5312, 7556**

2128 **Suffolk Fine Arts Association.** Catalogue of the first exhibition of the Suffolk Fine Arts Association at the Lecture Hall, Tower Street, Ipswich. Ipswich, 1850

2129 Loan exhibition of works by Gainsborough, Constable, and old Suffolk artists, at the Art Gallery, Ipswich. Ipswich, 1887

2130 **Suffolk Art and Aid Association.** Catalogue of the Bury St Edmunds Arts and Crafts exhibition ... and loan exhibition of pictures by Suffolk artists. Bury St. Edmunds, 1908. SRO/B

2131 Exhibition: The Smythes of Ipswich, 19 Nov–4 Dec 1964, Lowndes Lodge Gallery, London, S.W.1

2132 Newby, D. Guide to Suffolk art. Halesworth, 1966. Guide to East Anglian art. Halesworth, 1967–8 and later edns

2133 East Anglian art today: Royal Institute Gallery, London, 27 Jan–15 Feb 1969. Exhibition ... sponsored ... by the East Anglian Daily Times. Ipswich

2134 **Day, H. A. E.** East Anglian painters. 3v. Eastbourne, 1968/69

CRAFTS   *See also* **7556**

2135 Suffolk cooking, by George! [St. George's Church]. Bury St. Edmunds, 1963. More Suffolk cooking, by George! [St. George's Church]. Bury St. Edmunds, 1964

2136 Kirkley cook book: a collection of well-tried recipes, including some old Suffolk recipes contributed by members of the parish of St. Peter, Kirkley, Lowestoft ... Lowestoft, 1968

2137 **Jobson, A.** Household and country crafts. 1970

SPORTS

GENERAL   *See also* **4802, 4943**

2138 **Cuming, E. D.,** *Ed.* Sport ancient and modern. *In* VCH Suffolk 2, 1907, 357–84

2139 [**Symonds, B.**] Treatise on field diversions. By a Gentleman of Suffolk ... Norwich, 1776. 2nd edn 1823. 3rd edn 1825. entitled The Suffolk sportsman ... 1828

2140 Alphabetical list of certificates granted in the county of Suffolk ... [for the killing of game]. Ipswich, 1784

2141 **Eastern Sports Council.** First appraisal of major facilities and field games. Aug 1967. Bedford

ANGLING

2142 **Cooper, B.** Angling in Norfolk and Suffolk waters and sea-fishing around the coast. Norwich, [1958]. SCL/L

2143 **Shepherdson, A.** How to fish the Suffolk Stour. 1960

2144 **Gillespie, I.** The Wash to the Thames estuary. 1969

2145 **Wilson, J.** Fresh and saltwater fishing in Norfolk and Suffolk. Norwich, 1974. NCL/N

GOLF *See* **3572, 7212, 7388, 8057**

HUNTING, AND RACING   *See also* **6188–9,** *and* Newmarket, *below*

2146 Fixtures of the Suffolk Hunt. The Meet of the Suffolk Pack, 1851

2147 **Watson, J. Y.** Miscellaneous sketches [includes articles on Suffolk Hunt]. 1881

2148 **Greene, R.** Fox-hunting in Suffolk. ECM 2, 1901/02, 162–7

Social History, Culture, and Recreation

2149 **Josselyn, A.** Suffolk foxhounds. ECM, 2, 1901/02, 234–5
2150 **"Palafox", pseud.** Essex and Suffolk Hunt. 1924. 1929
2151 **F, M.** Southwold Hunt. CL 73, 1933, 138–41
2152 **Fawcett, W.** Essex and Suffolk Hunt. 1934
2153 **Greaves, R.** Eastern Harriers and Henham Harriers. [1953]
2154 **Greaves, R.** Eastern Harriers and Waveney Harriers. [1955]
2155 **Greaves, R.** Hunting in Suffolk. Oxford, [1957]
2156 **Greaves, R.** Hunting in Norfolk and Suffolk. [1959]
2157 **Greaves, R.** Hunting in Essex, Norfolk, and Suffolk. Tunbridge Wells, [1966]. [1967]
2158 Fox hunting in Essex, Norfolk, and Suffolk. Crowborough, [1967]. [1968]

YACHTING
2159 **Cowper, F.** Sailing tours: the yachtsman's guide to the cruising waters of the English coast. Pt 1, Coasts of Essex and Suffolk. 1892
2160 **Messum, S. V. S. C.** East coast rivers. Charts and sailing directions for the rivers ... Stour, Orwell, Deben, Ore, and Alde; together with general charts from the Thames to Southwold. 1903
2161 **Cooke, F. B.** London to Lowestoft: a cruising guide to the East coast. [1906]
2162 **Reynolds, H.** Coastwise-cross-seas: the tribulations and triumphs of a casual cruiser [Woodbridge, Lowestoft, Walberswick, Felixstowe]. 1921
2163 **Tripp, H. A.** Suffolk sea-borders. 1926. Rp 1972
2164 **Clarkson, A. T.** Short history of the Royal Norfolk and Suffolk Yacht Club, 1859–1909. Lowestoft, [1930]. SCL/L
2165 **Coote, J. H.** East coast rivers. 1956 and later edns. SCL/L
2166 Items of interest in the history of the Royal Norfolk and Suffolk Yacht Club. Lowestoft, [1960]. SCL/L
2167 **Hatt, E. M.** Sailing tours, Essex and Suffolk. 1963
2168 East Coast Yachtsman. v 1, no 1, Spring 1968–. Colchester
2169 **Eastern Sports Council.** Regional strategy for water recreation. [Bedford], 1971
2170 **Goodey, C.** Brown boats: the story of the Broads One-designs. Lowestoft, 1972. SCL/L
2171 **Hay, D.** East Anglia from the sea: Canvey Island to Great Yarmouth. 1972

CLUBS AND SOCIETIES
2172 **Elwes, (–).** A letter to Major-General Elwes ... occasioned by an advertisement signed by him, calling on the freeholders of Essex and Suffolk to form a True-blue club. Chelmsford, [1816?]. BL
2173 Suffolk societies: their aims and objects. SR 3, 1969, 297–303

COFFEE HOUSES *See* **4429, 6209–11**

FREEMASONRY   *See also* **2010**

2174   Watson, S. F. A bibliography of Freemasonry in Suffolk. 1971. [Typescript]

2175   **Parker, J. H.** Freemasonry in Suffolk in the 18th and early 19th centuries. SIMT, No 3913, 1927

2176   **Watson, S. F.** Two hundred years of Masonic jurisdiction in Suffolk, 1771–1971. 1971

2177   [**Neale, E.**] Stray leaves from a Freemason's note book, by a Suffolk rector. 1846. SRO/B

2178   Freemasons' calendar for Suffolk, 1885–1941. Suffolk Freemasons' year book, 1942–

2179   Transactions of the Suffolk Installed Masters' Lodge, No 3913. First Ser 1919–36. 2nd Ser 1949–

2180   **Sorrell, J. E. A.** The Suffolk adventure of a Norfolk Lodge [Unanimity no 102], 1814–23. NIMT 7, 1931

2181   **Lowther, G. M. J.** Suffolk Masonic venture – Suffolk Installed Masters' Lodge, No 3913. SIMT, No 3913, 1950

2182   Five Atholl Lodges in the Eastern counties [includes Doric Lodge, No 81, Woodbridge, and St. Luke's Lodge, No 225, Ipswich]. 1953

2183   **Griffiths, A.** Suffolk Installed Masters' Lodge in review. 1954

Architecture

GENERAL   *For* individual buildings and sites, *see under* Localities, *below*

2184 **Kirby, J. J.** Historical account of the twelve prints of monasteries, castles, antient churches, and monuments in the county of Suffolk, drawn by J.K. [Joshua Kirby], and published by him. Ipswich, 1748. [Bound set of prints and pamphlet. SRO/B]

2185 **Soane,** *Sir* **J.** Plans, elevations, and sections of buildings executed in the counties of Norfolk, Suffolk ... 1788. BL

2186 **Johnson, I.** Antiquities, consisting of architectural and monumental remains in the county of Suffolk. Woodbridge, 1820. 1821

2187 **Davy, H.** Series of etchings illustrative of the architectural antiquities of Suffolk, accompanied with an historical index. Southwold, 1827

2188 **Baggallay, F. T.** Use of flint in building, especially in the county of Suffolk. RIBAT NS 1, 1885, 105–24

2189 **Ministry of Housing and Local Government.** List of buildings of architectural or historic interest ... 4v. 1944. *passim.* NCL/N

2190 East Anglian buildings. [Catalogue of] an exhibition at the Castle Museum, Norwich, 26 May–26 Aug 1956. Norwich

2191 **Pevsner,** *Sir* **N. B. L.** Suffolk. [Buildings of England Ser.] Harmondsworth, 1961. 2nd edn 1974

2192 **Firman, R. J.,** *and* **P.** Geological approach to the study of medieval bricks (with special reference to East Anglia ...). Mercian Geologist 2, no 3, 1964

2193 **Girling, F. A.** Masons' marks. PSIA 30, 1964/6, 198–200

CASTLES, HALLS, AND MANOR HOUSES

2194 **Sparvel-Bayley, J. A.** Some Suffolk castles. E Ang NS 3, 1889/90, 329–34

2195 **Graham, R.** Norman castles in Suffolk. JAABI 2, 1931/2, 24–44

2196 **Kedney, R. J.** Castles in Suffolk. LA&LHS 1967/8, 33–6

2197 **Neale, J. P.** Views of seats in Suffolk. [From "Views of the seats of noblemen and gentlemen in England ..." 6v. 1818–23]

2198 **Davy, H.** Views of the seats of the noblemen and gentlemen in Suffolk. Pt first. [No more published] Southwold, 1827

2199 **Taylor, J. E.** Suffolk moated halls. Good Words, July 1893, 455–60

2200 **Gross, M.** Suffolk moated houses, with notes [Photographs c.1894–1901]. SRO/B

2201 **Durbridge, P. M.** Moated sites. LA&LHS 1966/7, 22–4

2202 **National Trust.** Houses and gardens open to the public in Eastern England. 1966–1969 ... in East Anglia. 1970 and later edns

OTHER SECULAR ARCHITECTURE

GENERAL

2203 **Farrer, E.** Some old houses in Suffolk [cuttings, photographs, index] 6v. [1905–29]

2204 **Oliver, B.** Old houses and village buildings in East Anglia ... [1912]

2205 **Girling, F. A.** Suffolk timber-framed houses. JBAA NS 34, 1929, 100–16

2206 **Morand, D.** Minor architecture of Suffolk: series one. 1929

2207 **Messent, C. J. W.** Old cottages and farm-houses of Suffolk. PSIA 22, 1934/6, 244–62

2208 **Welford, A.** Restoration of a sixteenth-century farm house in Suffolk. PSIA 24, 1946/8, 1–19

2209 **Chesterton, M.** Suffolk building: some critical considerations, etc. Ipswich, 1949

2210 **Hill, P. J.,** *and* **Penrose, D. G.** Medieval timber-framed houses in East Suffolk: an essay in classification. PSIA 30, 1964/6, 263–9

2211 **Penrose, D. G.,** *and* **Hill, P. J.** Suffolk timber houses. SR 3, no 2, 1965, 3–7

2212 **Colman, S.** West Suffolk inventories for 1665; some clues to house types. SR 3, 1968, 190–96

2213 **Eden, P. M. G.** Smaller post-medieval houses in Eastern England. *In* East Anglian studies. *Ed.* by L. M. Munby. Cambridge, 1968. 71–93

2214 **Eden, P. M. G.** Small houses in England, 1520–1820. 1969

2215 **Sandon, E.** View into the village. A study in Suffolk building. Lavenham, 1969

2216 **Penrose, D. G.** Some Suffolk buildings; compiled by teachers' working-parties. [1976]

2217 **Sandon, E.** Suffolk houses: a study of domestic architecture. Woodbridge, 1977

INNS

2218 **Edwards, E.** Old inns, etched by Edwin Edwards. First division – Eastern England. 1873

2219 **Matz, B. W.** Inns and taverns of "Pickwick", with some observations on their other associations. [1921]. BL

2220 **Thompson, L. P.** Old inns of Suffolk. Ipswich, [1946]

2221 **Luscombe, W. G.** Book of inns. No 5, East Anglia. 1947. SCL/L

2222 **Jones, V.** East Anglian pubs. 1965

2223 **Thompson, L. P.** Inns of the Suffolk coast. Hadleigh, 1969

2224 **Hedges, A. A. C.** Inns and inn-signs of Norfolk and Suffolk. Fenstanton, 1976

MILLS   *See also* 7240–41

2225   **Lummis, W. M.** Scrapbook on windmills and watermills, collected . . . for the Suffolk Preservation Society. 4v. [1928–9]. [Photographs and MSS]

2226   **Oldham, A. A.** Windmills (Broadland . . . Norfolk, Suffolk . . .) [Photographs and MSS]. 7v. nd. NCL/N

2227   **Woolford, A.** Windmills, with special reference to those in Suffolk. PSIA 20, 1928/30, 125–46

2228   **Kenney, G. A.** Notes on Suffolk windmills. 5v. [c.1930]. MS

2229   **Hopkins, R. T.,** *and* **Freese, S.** In search of English windmills. 1931

2230   **Society for the Protection of Ancient Buildings.** Reports. [Includes the Suffolk survey of post mills in 1926 and 1941; smock and tower mills in 1929 reports]

2231   **Wailes, R.** Suffolk windmills Pt 1. Post mills. NST 22, 1946, 41–63; Pt 2. Tower mills. NST 23, 1948, 37–54

2232   **Wailes, R.** Windmills in England; a study of their origin, development, and future. 1948

2233   **Jobson, A.** Some Suffolk windmills. CL 114, 1953, 1578–9

2234   **Wilton, H. E.** Records of windmills. SR 1, 1958, 151–3

2235   **Wailes, R.** Suffolk watermills. NST 37, 1967, 99–116

2236   **Freese, S.** Survey of Suffolk windmills. LA&LHS 1970/1, 14–16

2237   **Munnings, J.** Passing of the country miller and his mill: Rivers Stour and Waveney. LA&LHS 1970/1, 56–62

2238   **Flint, B.** Windmills of East Anglia. Ipswich, 1972

SPECIAL FEATURES
        See also 4435–40, 5057–8, 6253–5, 6302, 6848, 7098, 7914, 7966

2239   **Teasdel, R. D.,** *et al.* Ancient crosses of East Anglia. E Ang NS 1, 1885/6, 75–6

2240   **Girling, F. A.** Suffolk chimneys of the sixteenth century. PSIA 22, 1934/6, 104–07

2241   **Messent, C. J. W.** Market crosses of Suffolk. PSIA 23, 1937/9, 18–23

2242   **Messent, C. J. W.** Weather vanes of Suffolk. PSIA 23, 1937/9, 165–72, 224–9

2243   **Girling, F. A.** Pargetting in Suffolk. PSIA 23, 1937/9, 202–09

CHURCH ARCHITECTURE AND FURNISHINGS

GENERAL

2244   **Clarke, M. M.** Suffolk churches. 4v. nd. [MSS, photographs, drawings, cuttings]

2245   **Archaeological Institute of Great Britain and Ireland.** Ecclesiastical and architectural topography of England. Pt 7. Suffolk, by W. Caveler, *et al.* 1855

2246   **Freeman, E. A.** The Perpendicular of Somerset compared with that of East Anglia. Trans Somerset Arch and Nat Hist Soc 5, 1855, 1–28

2247 **Aldriche, J.** Ruined and decayed churches in the archdeaconry of Suffolk. E Ang 1, 1858/63, 340–41, 370–71

2248 **Gowers, W. R.** Architectural illustrations: No 1, Norman stoup, Blyford; Perpendicular piscina, Halesworth. Architectural notes: No 2, Lessons from rubble [Suffolk churches]. E Ang NS 3, 1889/90, 282–4; NS 5, 1893/4, 229–31

2249 **Clemence, J. L.** Ruined churches in Suffolk. E Ang NS 5, 1893/4, 154–5

2250 **Bryant, T. H.** Suffolk—county churches. v 1, Western division; v 2. Eastern division. 1912

2251 **Morley, C.** On traces of Saxon architecture yet remaining in the county of Suffolk. PSIA 18, 1922/4, 1–28

2252 **Messent, C. J. W.** Monastic remains of Norfolk and Suffolk. Norwich, 1934

2253 **Cautley, H. M.** Suffolk churches and their treasures. 1937. 2nd edn 1938. 3rd edn 1954. 4th edn 1975

2254 **Corke, J.**, *et al. Eds.* Suffolk churches: a pocket guide. Lavenham, 1976

2255 **Ough, C. J.** East Anglian church architecture in the fourteenth and fifteenth centuries, with special reference to the churches of the Stour valley. M.A. thesis, London, 1939

2256 **Ough, C. J.** Local style in church architecture in the Stour valley. Nottingham Medieval Studies 4, 1960, 81–104

BELLS
2257 **Sperling, J. H.** Suffolk bells. E Ang 1, 1858/63, 119–20, 161, 259, 416–17

2258 **Raven, J. J.** Inscriptions on church bells in Suffolk. E Ang 4, 1869/70, 133–6, 153–5; PSIA 5, 1876/86, 274–6

2259 **Lummis, W. M.** Collections of cuttings on Suffolk church bells ... [c. 1879–1904]

2260 **Raven, J. J.** Church bells of Suffolk ... with a complete list of the inscriptions on the bells, and historical notes. 1890

2261 **Hawkins, C. H.** Notes taken from a collection of inscriptions on ancient and interesting Suffolk church bells. [1938]. [Typescript]

2262 **Mander, R. P.** Medieval bell-founders of Norfolk and Suffolk. EAM 8, 1949, 665–70

BRASSES
2263 **Cotman, J. S.** Suffolk brasses ... Engravings of the most remarkable of the sepulchral brasses in Suffolk, etc. 1819. 42 plates. [only 38 in BL copy]

2264 **Cotman, J. S.** Engravings of sepulchral brasses in Norfolk and Suffolk ... 2v. 2nd edn 1839. [v 2 is in two parts, the second of which has a separate title-page, "Engravings of sepulchral brasses in Suffolk", and is dated 1838]

2265 Collection of brass rubbings in the possession of the Suffolk Institute of Archaeology. PSIA 10, 1898/1900, 237–49

2266 **Farrer, E.** List of monumental brasses remaining in the county of Suffolk, 1903. Norwich, 1903

2267 **Stephenson, M.** List of monumental brasses in the British Isles. 1926. Suffolk, 446–77

2268   **Griffin, R. H.** Cotman's Suffolk brasses, 1819 ... 1937

2269   Complete brass-rubbing guide to the figure brasses in the county of Suffolk. Norwich, 1972 and later edns. [Typescript]

2270   **MacCulloch, D. N. J.** Suffolk brasses; a study. Suffolk Fair 3, 1974, no 8, 18–20; no 9, 14–17; no 10, 28–30; no 11, 10–12

2271   **Blatchly, J. M.** Lost brasses of Suffolk, 1320–1420. TMBS 12, 1974, 21–45

2272   **Felgate, T. M.** Knights on Suffolk brasses. Ipswich. 1976

CHURCH PLATE

2273   **Hopper, E. C.,** *et al.* Church plate in Suffolk. PSIA 8, 1892/4, 275–33; 9, 1895/7, 1–76, 145–230, 279–306

2274   **Hopper, E. C.** Church plate in Suffolk. ECM 1, 1900/01, 122–7

2275   **Casley, H. C.** An Ipswich worker of Elizabethan church plate; and schedule of pre-Reformation or Elizabethan [Suffolk] plate with provincial worker's marks. PSIA 12, 1904/06, 158–83

2276   **Casley, H. C.** Suffolk workers of Elizabethan church plate. PSIA 13, 1907/09, 103–05

2277   **Jones, E. A.** Two pieces of old silver in Suffolk churches [Redgrave and Wenhaston]. Conn 110, 1942, 163

2278   **Suffolk Archdeaconry.** Exhibition of church treasures at Blythburgh church, 18–21 July 1961

2279   **Gilchrist, J.,** *et al.* Archdeaconry of Ipswich church treasures. 1965

2280   **Oman, C.** Church plate of West Suffolk. Conn 165, 1967, 105–07

FLOOR TILES   *See* 3823, 3897, 4471, 4947, 5419, 7038

FONTS   *See* 3851, 4638, 6086–7, 6346, 6904, 7612, 7775

LYCH GATES

2281   **Messent, C. J. W.** Lych gates and their churches in Eastern England. Blofield, 1970. Suffolk, 162–219

MONUMENTS   *See also* 2374, 2380

2282   **Weever, J.** Ancient funerall monuments ... Great Britaine and Ireland ... with the dissolved monasteries ... 1631. STC 25223. 2nd edn 1767. Diocese of Norwich, 457–583

2283   **Y., D. A. [D. E. Davy]** Summary catalogue of sepulchral memorials and remains of ancient art existing in parish churches: county of Suffolk [in Hundreds]. TG 1, 1846; 2, 1853, *passim*

2284   **Cuming, H. S.** Some knightly effigies in Suffolk churches. JBAA 33, 1877, 109–12

2285   **Linnell, C. L. S.** Suffolk church monuments. PSIA 27, 1955/7, 1–24

2286   **Baggs, A. P.** Sixteenth-century terra-cotta tombs in East Anglia. Arch J 125, 1968, 206–301

MURAL PAINTINGS

2287   Harris, H. A. Mediaeval mural paintings. PSIA 19, 1925/7, 286–303

2288   Harris, H. A. List of Suffolk churches associated with mural paintings. PSIA 19, 1925/7, 304–12

2289   Moore, W. H. Medieval church wall-paintings. LA&LHS 1969/70, 33–8

ROOD SCREENS

2290   Piggott, J. Rood-screens of East Anglia: Suffolk. E Ang 3, 1866/8, 316–17

2291   Henfrey, H. W., *and* Watling, H. East Anglian rood screens. JBAA 37, 1881, 135–40

2292   Strange, E. F. Painted rood screens of East Anglia. Architects' Mag 6, 1906, 105–06

2293   Lillie, W. W. Screenwork in the county of Suffolk. PSIA 20, 1928/30, 214–24, 255–64; 21, 1931/3, 179–202; 22, 1934/6, 120–26

2294   Constable, W. G. Some East Anglian rood-screen paintings. Conn 84, 1929, 141–7, 211–20, 290–94, 358–65

2295   [Cooper, J.] Church screens of East Anglia, with particular reference to Somerleyton. Oxford, [c.1969]. O

STAINED GLASS

2296   Birch, H. W. Remnants of old stained glass in the churches of S.E. Suffolk. E Ang NS 5, 1893/4, 257–8, 371–2

2297   Watling, H. Some old stained glass in Suffolk churches, with notes on rood screens. E Ang NS 13, 1909/10, 198–202

2298   Woodforde, C. Further notes on ancient glass in Norfolk and Suffolk. JMGP 5–6, 1933/7, 57–68

TOWERS

2299   Gage, J. Observations on the ecclesiastical round towers of Norfolk and Suffolk. Arch 23, 1831, 10–17

2300   C. Round-tower churches of Suffolk. E Ang 1, 1858/63, 108–10, 139, 165

2301   Roberts, E. On the round towers of churches in East Anglia. JBAA 21, 1865, 162–7

2302   Brock, E. P. L. Round towers of Norfolk and Suffolk. JBAA 37, 1881, 32–7

2303   Morley, C. Circular towers. PSIA 18, 1922/4, 144–55

2304   Haward, B. Medieval church towers of Suffolk, with photographs. RIBA thesis, Bartlett School of Architecture, London University, 1934

2305   Greenwood, G. B. Round towers in Norfolk, Suffolk, and Essex. ER 46, 1937, 162–3

2306   Messent, C. J. W. Round towers to English parish churches. Norwich, 1958. Suffolk, 250–333

OTHER FEATURES

2307   Sherlock, R. Chandeliers in Suffolk churches. PSIA 32, 1970/2, 255–68

2308 **Morley, C.** Old chests remaining in Suffolk churches. nd. [Typescript]. SRO/B

2309 **Redstone, V. B.** Suffolk church carving. JAABI 2, 1931/2, 145–7

2310 **Layard, N. F.** Some early crucifixes, with examples from Raydon, ... Ipswich ... Arch J 67, 1910, 91–7

2311 Acoustic pottery in Norfolk and Suffolk churches. E Ang NS 3, 1889/90, 45–8

2312 **Cautley, H. M.** Royal Arms and commandments in our churches [chiefly Suffolk]. Ipswich, 1934. Rp 1974

2313 **MacCulloch, D. [N. J.]** Royal arms in Suffolk churches [supplement to Cautley]. PSIA 32, 1970/72, 193–7, 279

2314 **Harris, H. A.** List of scratch dials on Suffolk churches. PSIA 23, 1937/9, 35–41

2315 **Sewell, J. W. S.** Scratch dials. PSIA 23, 1937/9, 116–27

2316 **Ellis, H. D.** The wodewose in East Anglian church decorations. PSIA 14, 1910/12, 287–93

2317 **Girling, F. A.** Wild men in church [wodewoses in Suffolk churches]. CL 123, 1958, 521

Biography, Genealogy, and Heraldry

COLLECTIVE BIOGRAPHY *See also* 1878

2318 **Fuller, T.** History of the worthies of England. 1662. Suffolk, 54–75. 1811, 2v. 1840, 3v. BL

2319 **Blome, R.** Alphabetical account of the nobility and gentrey which are (or lately were) related unto the several counties of England and Wales ... *In his* Britannia ... [Suffolk section contains about 400 names]. 1673. Wing B 3207. Rp 1892. 75 copies. BL

2320 List of medical men living in 1728, residing in Cambridge, Suffolk, and Norfolk. E Ang NS 2, 1887/8, 10–11

2321 Lives of eminent and remarkable characters, born or long resident in the counties of Essex, Suffolk, and Norfolk. 1820

2322 Cuttings from newspapers, etc., chiefly biographical; collected and arranged, with MS notes, by S. Tymms. [1820?–35?]. BL

2323 **Glyde, J.** ["Silverpen", *pseud.*] Suffolk worthies and persons of note in East Anglia. [From Suffolk Chronicle, 1858–60]

2324 Public men of Ipswich and East Suffolk: a series of personal sketches [by R. Gowing]. Rp from Suffolk Mercury. Ipswich, 1875

2325 **Stedman, A. E.** Index to family and personal histories relating to East Anglia in the indexes to archaeological papers, 1891–1907. E Ang NS 12, 1907/08, 53–4; NS 13, 1909/10, 87

2326 **Press, C. A. M.** Suffolk celebrities. Leeds, 1893

2327 [**Press, C. A. M.,** *and* **Gaskell, E.**] Norfolk, Suffolk, and Cambridgeshire leaders: social and political. Exeter, 1896

2328 **Langham, G. H.** Eminent East Anglians. 1904

2329 **Press, C. A. M.** Suffolk leaders: social and political. 1906

2330 **Pike, W. T.,** *and* **Hussey, F.** Norfolk and Suffolk in East Anglia: contemporary biographies. Brighton, 1911. Another edn. East Anglia in the twentieth century: contemporary biographies [Includes Newmarket, and East Anglians in London]. Brighton, 1912

2331 **Cox, H.** Norfolk, Suffolk, and Cambridgeshire. Cox's County Who's Who Series. 1912

2332 **Lingwood, H. R.** ["Rambler", *pseud.*] Suffolk novelists. EADT 1928–30

2333 **Baylis, E.,** *and* **Son, Ltd.** Who's who in Suffolk. Worcester, 1935

2334 **John O'Bosmere** [*pseud.* H. R. Lingwood]. Naturalists of Eastern England. EADT 1939–41

2335   **Smith-Dampier, J. L.** East Anglian worthies. Oxford, 1949

2336   **Cranbrook,** *Earl of.* Parnassian molehill. An anthology of Suffolk verse written between 1327 and 1864, with some account of the authors [153–255]. Ipswich, 1953. 500 copies

2337   Six Suffolk characters, 1500–1900: an exhibition held at Hill House, Aldeburgh, arranged by Ipswich and East Suffolk Record Office, 20–28 June, 1953. Ipswich, 1953. [Henry Tooley; Lady Elizabeth Brooke; Thomas Mills; Dudley North; Isaac Johnson; John Wood]

2338   **Morley, C.** Names of Suffolk naturalists, 1400–1900. TSNS 6, 1946/8, 175–99.

GENEALOGY AND HERALDRY

2339   **Ipswich and East Suffolk Record Office.** Short guide for genealogists. Ipswich, 1969

2340   **Suffolk Genealogical Society.** Newsletter, no 1, Jan 1975–. Lowestoft

2341   **Morley, C.** An attempt to muster Suffolk's medieval families of all degrees. 1951. [Typescript]

2342   **Mackerell, B.** Arms of all the High Sheriffs of Suffolk and Norfolk from the year 1154 down to this present time. [c.1738]. MS

2343   Visitation of Suffolke, made by William Hervey [in 1561] … With additions from … Jermyn, Davy, and other MSS, etc. *Ed.* by J. J. Howard. 2v. Lowestoft, 1866–76. [Extracted from the East Anglian. Publ. in pts. 1864–71]

2344   Visitations of Suffolk, made by Hervey … 1561, Cooke … 1577, and Raven … 1612, with notes and an appendix of additional Suffolk pedigrees. *Ed.* by W. C. Metcalfe. Exeter, 1882

2345   **Dashwood, G. H.,** *et al.* Visitation of Norfolk in the year 1563. Taken by W. Harvey, Clarenceux King of Arms. 2v. Norwich, 1878. 1895

2346   **Muskett, J. J.** An ancient notebook. William Tyllotson. [Suffolk armorials, 1594 and 1600]. E Ang NS 2, 1887/8, 177–9

2347   Tyllotson's MSS. E Ang NS 11, 1905/06, 352; NS 12, 1907/08, 16

2348   **Probert, W. G.** Arms and epitaphs in parish churches, chiefly in Suffolk and Essex, visited by William Tyllotson between 1594 and 1600. PSIA 19, 1925/7, 78–9

2349   **Lambarde, F.** Suffolk arms, c.1605. MGetH 5th Ser 6, 1926/8, 11–15

2350   Visitation of the county of Suffolk, begun 1664, and finished 1668. By Sir E. Bysshe. *Ed.* by W. H. Rylands. 1910. HS 61

2351   **White, C. H. E.,** *and* **Athill, C. H.** Index to the visitation of Norfolk made A.D. 1664. Ipswich, 1885. NCL/N

2352   **Blois, W.** The Blois MSS. 4v. MS. Indexed by E. Farrer. 1. Pedigrees of Suffolk families. 2. Additional pedigrees. 3. Church notes. 4. A Suffolk armory. PSIA 14, 1910/12, 147–226

2353   **Dow, L.** A Suffolk heraldic manuscript (by Fairfax, 1689). PSIA 25, 1949/51, 288–96

2354 **Dow, L.** Whereabouts of Suffolk 17th-century Suffolk heraldic MSS. N&Q 195, 1950, 567

2355 **Haslewood, F.** Ancient families of Suffolk [transcript of a MS of 'Antiquitates Suffolciences' by Sir Richard Gipps, d.1708]. PSIA 8, 1892/4, 121–214

2356 **Whayman, H. W.** Antient and modern nobility in Suffolk [transcript of the MS armorial by William Sharpe, c.1800] E Ang NS 7, 1897/8, *passim*. Index. E Ang NS 6, 1895/6, 251–5

2357 **Davy, D. E.** Arms of Suffolk families. MS. BL

2358 **Davy, D. E.** Genealogical histories of Suffolk families. MS. BL

2359 **Marsh, W.** Pedigrees of Suffolk families [alphabetical list of pedigrees in the Davy MS in BL]. E Ang 4, 1869/70; NS 1, 1885/6; NS 2, 1887/8; NS 3, 1889/90, *passim*

2360 **Gatfield, G.** Index to Davy's Suffolk collections. Gen NS 5, 1888, 117–28; NS 6, 1889, 56–63, 108–15, 139–45, 250–51

2361 **Darby, J. A.** Suffolk arms. 3v. 1825–7. MS

2362 **Jermyn, C., *and* G. B., *Eds.*** Heraldic insignia of Suffolk families. 26v. [c.1850]. SRO/B

2363 Jermyn's Armorial of Suffolk families. Herald and Genealogist 6, 1871, 89–90

2364 **Sperling, J. H.** Visitation of the monumental heraldry of Suffolk. E Ang 1, 1858/63, *passim*

2365 **King, T. W.** Collection of MSS in the College of Arms for the county of Suffolk. JBAA 21, 1865, 158–9

2366 **Farrer, E.** Suffolk churches: heraldic and genealogical. E Ang NS 3, 1889/90, 121–3, 144–6, 160–61, 197

2367 **Crisp, F. A., *Ed.*** Fragmenta genealogica. 13v. 1889–1909. New Series. 1v. 1910 [no more published]. BL. v 9, 10, & 13. SRO/I

2368 **Unwin, H. P. G., *et al.*** Information of Suffolk pedigrees. N&Q 8th Ser 2, 1892, 69, 118, 171

2369 **Howard, J. J., *and* Crisp, F. A.** *Eds.* Visitation of England and Wales. 35v. 1893–1921. 500 copies. BL

2370 **Cookson, E.** Indices nominum [from various sources]. [c.1895]. MS

2371 **Farrer, E.** Church heraldry of Suffolk [by Hundreds]. 12v. 1898–1912. MS

2372 **Partridge, C., *and* Radcliffe, J.** Location of Suffolk heraldic mss. N&Q 9th Ser 6, 1900, 509; 9th Ser 7, 1901, 175

2373 **Muskett, J. J.** Suffolk manorial families, being the county visitations and other pedigrees, ed. with extensive additions ... (v 3, *cont.* by F. Johnson). 3v. no more publ. Exeter, 1900 [1894]–1914

2374 **Partridge, C.** Heraldic headstones in East Anglian churchyards. E Ang NS 11, 1905/06, 31

2375 **Farrer, E.** Pedigrees and genealogical notes. 2v. [c.1920]. MS

2376 **Walker, T. A., *et al.*** Pedigrees and genealogical notes. 3v. [c.1930]. MS

2377 **Farrer, E.** Early Suffolk heraldry. PSIA, 21, 1931/3, 1–52

2378   Suffolk pedigrees. MGetH 5th Ser 9, 1935/7, *passim*
2379   **Campling, A.,** *Ed.* East Anglian pedigrees. 2v. 1939, 1945. HS 91, 97. *Also* NRS 13, 1940
2380   **Summers, P. G.** Funeral hatchments in Suffolk. PSIA 26, 1952–4, 208–13
2381   **De Freston, A.** The Freston quarterings. CA 4, 1956/7, 68–71
2382   **Corder, J.** A dictionary of Suffolk arms. Ipswich, 1965. SRS 7
2383   **Summers, P. [G.],** *and* **Corder, J.** *Eds.* Hatchments in Britain 2: Norfolk and Suffolk. 1976

SURNAMES   *See also* 5264

2384   S. Personal names in Suffolk Domesday. E Ang NS 3, 1889/90, 215
2385   **Partridge, C. S.** Suffolk surnames in 1340. E Ang NS 5, 1893/4, 225–9, 245–8, 259–61, 280–82, 307–08
2386   **Bowditch, N. I.** Suffolk surnames. Boston, Mass., 1857. 2nd edn 1858. 3rd edn 1861 [Settlers in Colonial America]
2387   **Woodward, B. B.** Surnames altered by common use in Suffolk and Norfolk. N&Q 2nd Ser 7, 1859, 526
2388   **Raven, J. J.** Local surnames. E Ang 1, 1858/63, 132–3
2389   **Charnock, R. S.** Suffolk surnames. E Ang 1, 1858/63, 163–5, 170–71
2390   **Barber, H.** Suffolk surnames. E Ang NS 4, 1891/2—NS 5, 1893/4, *passim*
2391   **McKinley, R.** Norfolk and Suffolk surnames in the Middle Ages. Leicester, 1975

REGISTERS, MARRIAGE LICENCES, AND MARRIAGE BONDS

2392   **Bullen, R. F.** Index to the parish registers of West Suffolk for 1630. [c.1939]. [Typescript]
2393   **Bullen, R. F.** Index to the parish registers of West Suffolk for the year 1696–7. [c.1936]. [Typescript]
2394   Crisp Collection. Cutting from Suffolk papers, 1855–68, 1874–9, with MS indexes to births, marriages, deaths, burials. 2v
2395   **Crisp, F. A.** *Ed.* List of parish registers and other genealogical works. 1897. 1898. 1899
2396   **Gooding, A. S.** Extracts from Suffolk parish registers. [Arranged by surname, with later index to parishes]. 1926. [Typescript]
2397   **Partridge, C.** Guide to Suffolk parish registers and churchyard inscriptions, with later additions by C. Partridge and the Ipswich Reference Library staff. [Key to genealogical section of the Suffolk Record Office and transcripts in private hands]. 1926. [Typescript]
2398   **Pearson, W. C.** Extracts from parish registers of Coddenham, Barham, and Henley. E Ang NS 4, 1891/2, 148–51
2399   **Plomer, H. R.** Suffolk parish registers. N&Q 7th Ser 10, 1890, 422, 502–03; 11, 1891, 42–3, 284

2400   **Dow, L.** Two sixteenth-century marriage settlements. PSIA 26, 1952/4, 144–7

2401   **Partridge, C.** Suffolk marriages [MS transcripts from parish registers]. 41v. nd

2402   **Pearson, W. C.** Marriage before justices in some Suffolk parishes. E Ang NS 4, 1891/2, 229–30

2403   **Cookson, E.** Transcripts of Suffolk parish registers. [c.1895]. MS

2404   **Phillimore, W. P. W.**, *et al.* Suffolk parish registers: marriages. 4v. 1910–31

2405   **Sperling, C. F. D.** Marriages in Sudbury and neighbourhood. [MS transcripts from parish registers]. 2v

2406   **Whitehead, L. H. H.** Marriages in the Hundreds of Babergh. 5v; Thedwastry. 2v; Thingoe. 2v; Lackford. 2v; Cosford. 1v; Risbridge. 4v. [MS transcripts from parish registers]. 16v

2407   **Boyd, P.** Marriage index—Suffolk. Men, 1500–1837. 20v. Women, 1500–1837. 20v. [c.1934]. [Typescript]

2408   **Rye, W.** Index to marriage licences granted by the Consistory Court of Norwich from 1563–1588. From a MS in the Public Library, Norwich. 1926. [Typescript]

2409   **Suffolk Archdeaconry.** Marriage licences from the official note-books of the archdeaconry of Suffolk deposited at the Ipswich Probate Court, 1613–1674. *Ed.* by F. A. Crisp. 1903. 100 copies

2410   **Suffolk Archdeaconry.** Marriage-licence bonds in the Suffolk Archdeaconry Registry at Ipswich, 1663–1750. *Ed.* by F. A. Crisp. 1900. 100 copies [The gap, 1687–1703/04, partly filled by transcript of marriage-licence bonds, 1673–99]

2411   **Sudbury Archdeaconry.** Allegations for marriage licences in the archdeaconry of Sudbury ... 1684–1839. *Ed.* by W. B. *and* G. G. B. Bannerman. 1918–21. 4v. HS 69–72

WILLS   *See also* **2441, 4446–8, 4681, 4820, 5581, 6292, 6965, 7048, 7115**

2412   **Bradfer Lawrence Collection.** Extracts of local wills from the Norwich Archdeaconry Court, Norfolk Archdeaconry Court, Prerogative Court of Canterbury, and Norwich Consistory Court, arranged A–Z by name. 7v. MS. NCL/N

2413   Index of wills proved in the Consistory Court of Norwich ... 1370–1550. *Ed.* by M. A. Farrow. 3pts. Norwich, 1943–5. NRS 16

2414   Calendar of wills relating to the county of Suffolk proved in the Prerogative Court of Canterbury between 1383 and 1604. *Comp.* by C. W. S. R. Cloke. *Ed.* by T. W. Oswald-Hicks. 1913. 100 copies. [English Monumental Inscriptions Society]

2415   **W[ayman], H. W. B.** Abstracts of Suffolk wills proved in the Prerogative Court of Canterbury, 1383–1604. REMI 2, 1913/14, 130–51

2416   **Suffolk Archdeaconry.** Calendar of wills [proved in the Court of the Archdeaconry of Suffolk] at Ipswich, 1444–1600. [*Ed.* by F. A. Crisp] 1895. 100 copies

2417 Calendar of early Suffolk wills—Ipswich Registry, 1444–1620. E Ang NS 1, 1885/6–NS 5, 1893/4, *passim*

2418 Index of wills proved in the Consistory Court of Norwich ... 1550–1603. *Ed.* by M. A. Farrow. Norwich, 1950. NRS 21

2419 Index of wills proved in the Consistory Court of Norwich ... 1604–1686. *Ed.* by M. A. Farrow, *and* T. F. Barton. Norwich, 1958. NRS 28

2420 Index of wills proved in the Consistory Court of Norwich ... 1687–1750. *Ed.* by T. F. Barton, *and* M. A. Farrow. Norwich, 1965. NRS 34

2421 **Suffolk Archdeaconry.** Calendar of wills at Ipswich, 1751–93. *Ed.* [from a MS by F. A. Crisp] by W. Gandy. 1923

2422 Index of wills proved in the Consistory Court of Norwich ... 1751–1818. *Ed.* by T. F. Barton, *et al.* Norwich, 1969. NRS 38

2423 **Tymms, S.,** *Ed.* Wills and inventories from the registers of the Commissary of Bury St. Edmunds and the Archdeacon of Sudbury. 1850. Camden Soc. 49

2424 **Redstone, V. B.** Calendar of pre-Reformation wills, testaments, probates, and administrations at the Probate Office, Bury St. Edmunds. PSIA 12, 1904/06, Appendix, dated 1907, separately paginated, 11+246

2425 **Partridge, C.** Tabular lists from Mr. Redstone's calendar of Bury wills. PSIA 13, 1907/09, 57–102

2426 **Redstone, V. B.** Early Suffolk wills. PSIA 15, 1913/15, 291–304

2427 **Schram, O. K.** Some early East Anglian wills. NA 22, 1926, 350–69

2428 **Mann, T. H.** Norfolk (including part of Suffolk) wills and administrations. 1930. [Typescript]

2429 **Mann, T. H.** Suffolk wills and administrations at Bury St. Edmunds and Ipswich. 1930. [Typescript]

2430 **Redstone, V. B.** Extracts from wills and other material showing the history of Suffolk churches, chantries, and guilds, being an appendix to the article— Calendar of pre-Reformation wills ... Bury St. Edmunds, in PSIA 12. PSIA 23, 1937/9. 50–78

INSCRIPTIONS

2431 **Marshall, G. W.** Lists of monumental inscriptions in the county of Suffolk. E Ang 1, 1858/63, 431–6

2432 **"Ipswichian",** *pseud.* Graveyards of Suffolk. From Ipswich Jour 21 March 1882–6 Oct 1883. 43pts. Ipswich

2433 **Haslewood, F.,** *Ed.* Monumental inscriptions in Ipswich and Suffolk churches and churchyards, 1883–1892. With an index by E. Cookson (1908). 20v. MS

2434 Suffolk monumental inscriptions in the city of Norwich. E Ang NS 2, 1887/8, 84–6, 101–03, 198–200

2435 **Edleston, R. H.,** *et al.* Monumental inscriptions from other counties relating to East Anglia. E Ang NS 2, 1887/8—NS 11, 1905/06, *passim*

2436 **Partridge, C. S.,** *et al.* Names on gravestones in Suffolk churchyards. E Ang NS 6, 1895/6, *passim*

2437 Index to monumental inscriptions in Suffolk churchyards. E Ang NS 7, 1897/8—NS 10, 1903/04, *passim*

2438 **Wayman, H. W. B.** Names on gravestones in Suffolk churchyards. E Ang NS 12, 1907/08, 144, 154, 211

2439 **Partridge, C.** List of Suffolk churchyard inscriptions in print up to 31 Dec 1907. E Ang NS 12, 1907/08, 217

2440 Monumental and churchyard inscriptions from parishes in the Hundred of Samford. REMI 1, 1911/12, 83–147; 2, 1913/14, 32–46

2441 **Oswald-Hicks, T. W.,** *Ed.* Register of English monumental inscriptions. 2v. 1912–13. 100 copies. Includes:- v 1, Orford, Aldham, Layham, Sweffling, Wantisden, and Samford Hundred. v 2, Belstead, Freston, Southwold Congregational chapel. List of transcripts of Suffolk monumental inscriptions, abstracts of Suffolk wills, P.C.C. 1383–1620. [English Monumental Inscriptions Soc]

2442 **Partridge, C.** Suffolk churchyard inscriptions, copied from the Darby transcription (made about 1825–34). Pt 1, Rp from PSIA 15, 1913/15; Pt 2, Rp from PSIA 17, 1920/22; Pt 3, Rp from PSIA 18, 1923/4; no more pub. Pt 4 in MS. 1913–23

2443 **Partridge, C.** Suffolk's "stone parish registers". ER 41, 1932, 33–6

2444 **Lawson, G. H.** Suffolk churchyard inscriptions. v 1, Blithing; v 2, Mutford and Lothingland; v 3, Wangford. 3v. nd. [Typescript]

SEALS   *See also* **4341–3, 4761, 5269, 7028, 7151, 7421, 7796, 8008, 8051**

2445 Sigilla antiqua Suffolciensia. BL Add. MS 21056

2446 **D.** Seal of Will. I de Bosco: a medieval seal set with an ancient gem. PSIA 4, 1864/74, 336–9

2447 **D[urrant], C. R.** Suffolk seals. E Ang NS 7, 1897/8, 161–2

PORTRAITS   *See also* **5535, 7724**

2448 Suffolk portraits. Mounted. 2v. nd

2449 **Farrer, E.** Suffolk portraits—East. 3v. nd. MSS and inserted photographs

2450 **Farrer, E.** Portraits in Suffolk houses, East … Index to the manuscript volume in the Ipswich (England) Public Library, etc. Boston, Mass., 1926

2451 **Farrer, E.** East Anglian portraits. nd. MSS and inserted photographs

2452 **Farrer, E.** Portraits in Suffolk houses—West. 1908

2453 **Farrer, E.** Suffolk portraits—West. Supplement. nd. MSS and inserted photographs

2454 **Farrer, E.** Catalogue of collection of Norfolk and Suffolk portraits, the gift of the late H.H. Prince Frederick Victor Duleep Singh … exhibited at the Guildhall, Thetford. 1927. NCL/N

2455 **Aldeburgh Festival Committee.** Portraits in East Anglia: catalogue. Aldeburgh 1955. SRO/B

2456 **Ipswich Borough Libraries.** Index to artists listed in Farrer's Portraits in Suffolk houses. Ipswich, 1971. [Typescript]

Individual and Family Biography, A–Z

Ablitt, N.	**2457**	The history, poems, writings, and miscellaneous correspondence. Ipswich, [c.1854]
Acheson Family	**2458**	**Acheson, A.** Outlying estates of ... the Earl of Gosford ... sale of the ... estates situate in the parishes of Brandeston, Kettleburgh, Framsden, Yarmouth, [1845] BI
Addison, H.	**2459**	Hawes, H. A Suffolk V.C. SR 3, 1968, 216–18
Agas, R.	**2460**	**MacCulloch, D.**[N. J.] Radulph Agas. PSIA 33, 1973/5, 275–84 DNB. *See also* **713, 4722**
Aikin, A. L.		*See* Barbauld, A. L.
Airy Family	**2461**	Airy of Playford. VE&W 7, 1899, 116–19
Alderson, Sir E. H.	**2462**	Selections from the charges and other detached papers of Baron Alderson: with an introductory notice of his life, by C. Alderson. 1858 DNB
Alexander Family	**2463**	**Pearson, W. C.** Extracts from parish registers. E Ang NS 7, 1897/8, 6–8
Alexander, M.	**2464**	Some account of the life and religious experience of Mary Alexander, late of Needham Market [Written by herself *Ed.* with a preface by W. A. Alexander]. York, 1811
Alexander, W. H. and S.	**2465**	Memorials of William H. Alexander and Sophia Alexander of Ipswich. 1867
Alington Family	**2466**	**Hervey,** *Lord* **A.** Horseheath and the Alingtons. PSIA 4, 1864/74, 111–22
Alis Family		*See* Ellis Family
Allenby Family	**2467**	Allenby of Felixstowe. VE&W 8, 1900, 17–19; Notes 7, 163–5
Allin, Sir T.		DNB. *See also* **936**
Almack, R.	**2468**	**Babington, C.** Obit. Richard Almack. PSIA 5, 1876/86, 1–4
Anderson, E. G.	**2469**	**Anderson, L. G.** Elizabeth Garrett Anderson, 1836–1917. 1939.
	2470	**Fancourt, M. St. J.** They dared to be doctors: Elizabeth Blackwell, Elizabeth Garrett Anderson. 1965. NCL/N.

2471 **Manton, J.** Elizabeth Garrett Anderson, 1965.
DNB

Angier Family   2472 **Partridge, C.** Angier family of Suffolk and Essex. E
Ang NS 12, 1907/08, 198–201

Appleton Family   2473 **Winthrop, R. C.,** *et al.* Appleton memoirs. Boston,
Mass., 1860–63

2474 Appleton family. Boston, Mass., 1866. 150 copies.

2475 A. J. Monumental memorials of the Appleton family.
Boston, Mass., 1867. 150 copies.

2476 **Appleton, W. S.,** *Ed.* Family letters from the
Bodleian Library: with notes by W. S. Appleton.
Cambridge, 1902. O

Appleton, S.   2477 **Jewett, I. A.,** *Ed.* Memorial of Samuel Appleton, of
Ipswich, Massachusetts. Boston, Mass., 1850. BL.
See also Isaac, M

Arnold, J.   2478 **Turner, D.** Memoir of Joseph Arnold, M.D. *In*
S. W. Rix's Fauconberge memorial. Ipswich, 1849.
68–79
DNB

Ashborne, J.   2479 **M, J. J.** A clerical mad-doctor of the seventeenth
century: Rev John Ashborne, of Norton-next Woolpit.
E Ang NS 1, 1885/6, 249–50

Ashton, A.   2480 **Ashton, A.** Fifty years' work in a Suffolk parish
[Uggeshall and Sotherton]. Lowestoft, 1936

Aungerville, R.   *See* Richard de Bury
Austin, C.   DNB
Bacon Family   2481 **Layton, W. E.** Bacon wills from Ipswich registry.
MGetH 2nd Ser 2, 1888, 284–6, 310–11, 334–6, 340–
343, 357–60, 377–8.

2482 **Pearson, W. C.,** *and* **Pink, W. D.** Bacons of Shrubland Hall. E Ang NS 4, 1891/2, 33–5, 49–54, 83–4

2483 **Pearson, W. C.** Suffolk marriage licences, Ipswich
Probate Registry, Bacon of Shrubland Hall. E Ang NS
5, 1893/4, 77–8

2484 **Ford, J.** Biographical notices of the family of Bacon
of Shrubland Hall in the parish of Coddenham. nd.
MS

2485 **Rye, W.** False pedigree and arms of the family of
Bacon of Suffolk, the ancestors of Sir Nicholas Bacon,
etc. Norwich, 1919. 100 copies

2486 **Palmer, W. L.** Bacon family of Helmingham and
Winston ... NEH&GR 90, 1936, 300–02

2487 Bacon as an East Anglian M.P. [Ipswich]. Baconiana
3rd Ser 8, 1910, 38–40. *See also* Gosnold Family

Bacon, Nath.   2488 **Westhorp, S.** Memoir of Nathaniel Bacon. *In* Bacon's
                           Annalls of Ipswich. 1884, 1–6.
                           DNB

Bacon, Sir Nich.   2489 **Tittler, R.** Nicholas Bacon: the making of a Tudor
                           statesman. 1976.
                           DNB, CBEL. *See also* **3497**

Baden-Powell   *See* Powell Family

Bailey Family   2490 Suffolk ancestry of Lord Glanusk. E Ang NS 8,
                           1899–1900, 48, 96, 112

Baker, P.   2491 **Appleton, W. S.** Ancestry of Priscilla Baker, who
                           lived 1674–1731, and was wife of Isaac Appleton, of
                           Ipswich. Cambridge, Mass., 1870. SRO/B

Bale, J.   DNB

Barbauld, A. L.   2492 **Le Breton, A. L.** Memoir of Mrs. Barbauld, includ-
                           ing letters and notices of her family and friends. 1874.

                      2493 **Clarke, S. M.** Bibliography of Mrs. Barbauld [Anna
                           Laetitia Aikin], together with a review of her life and
                           writings. Thesis, London School of Librarianship,
                           1949. [Typescript].
                           DNB. CBEL. *See also* **1329**

Barker Family   2494 Barker of Ipswich. VE&W 5, 1897, 25–7

Barlee, E.   2495 **Childers, C.** Life and death in Christ: a sermon
                           preached ... on the occasion of the death of the Rev.
                           Edmund Barlee, rector of Worlingworth ... 18 Sept
                           1853. Ipswich, 1853

Barlow Family   2496 Barlow of Sotterley. VE&W 11, 1903, 62–8; Notes 10,
                           5–8

Barnard Family   2497 Barnard of Withersfield. VE&W 19, 1917, 153–9;
                           Notes 7, 166–9

Barnardiston   2498 **Almack, R.** Kedington and the Barnardiston
Family   family. PSIA 4, 1864/74, 121–82
                      2499 Barnardiston of Sudbury. VE&W 8, 1900, 41–4;
                           Notes 7, 170–91. *See also* **891–5, 6300–01**

Barnardiston, A.   2500 **Shower, J.** Sermon upon the death of Mrs. A.
                           Barnardiston ... [with a prefatory memoir by S.
                           Fairclough]. 1682. Wing S 6390. 2nd edn 1691. BL

Barnardiston,   2501 Suffolk's tears: or elegies on that renowned knight,
Sir N.   Sir N. Barnardiston ... 1653. Wing S 6164. SRO/B

                      2502 **Fairclough, S.** The Saints worthiness and the worlds
                           worthlessness declared in a sermon preached at the
                           funerall of Sir Nathaniel Barnardiston. 1653. Wing
                           F 109A. SRO/B
                           DNB

Barnardiston, N. W. 2503 Major-General N. W. Barnardiston. PSIA 17, 1919/
                           1921, 86–7

Barne Family	2504	Barne of Sotterley. VE&W 7, 1899, 158–9; Notes 7, 121–9
Barrow Family	2505	**Round, J. H.** An early citizen squire [Barrow family of Barrow and London]. Ancestor 2, 1902, 58–61
Barton, B.	2506	Selection from the poems and letters of Bernard Barton ... [with a memoir of the author, signed E.F.G. i.e. Edward FitzGerald]. 1849. 1853
	2507	**Lucas, E. V.** Bernard Barton and his friends: a record of quiet lives. 1893.
	2508	Sale Catalogue. Furniture ... books ... prints and pictures ... of Bernard Barton. Woodbridge, 1849. BL DNB, CBEL
Bayfield, R.	2509	**Greene, J.** Richard Bayfield, monk of Bury: a biographical essay. Bury St. Edmunds, 1861. SRO/B DNB
Beale, M.	2510	**Cullum, G. G. M. G.** Mary Beale, artist. PSIA 16, 1916/18, 229–51
	2511	**Walsh, E.,** *and* **Jeffree, R.** 'The excellent Mrs Mary Beale'. Catalogue of exhibition 13 Oct–21 Dec 1975, Geffrye Museum, London. 1975. SRO/B DNB
Beare Family	2512	Beare of Bungay. VE&W 6, 1898, 39–40
Beaumont Family	2513	**Growse, F. S.** Beaumont family. E Ang 1, 1858/63, 73–4
	2514	**Muskett, J. J.** *et al.* Beaumont of Suffolk. E Ang NS 1, 1885/6, 110–11, 124, 130–31, 136, 151–2; NS 2, 1887/8, 191, 207, 322–3, 340; NS 4, 1891/2, 46–7, 62–3, 68–9, 127–8
Beaupré Family		*See* Bell Family
Beck, C.	2515	**Salmon, V.** Cave Beck, a seventeenth-century Ipswich schoolmaster. PSIA 33, 1973/5, 285–98. DNB
Bedingfield Family	2516	**Bedingfield, K.** Bedingfields of Oxburgh. 1912. BL
Bedingfield, Sir *H.*		DNB
Bedingfield, Sir *T.*		DNB
Bedingfield, Lady	2517	Lady Bedingfield of Darsham Hall. E Ang 2, 1864/6, 347–8
Beecroft, W. W.	2518	Little Welborne: a letter addressed to the children of the Wesleyan Sunday School, Lowestoft on the death of William Welborne Beecroft [6 Sept 1840] by a Sunday School Teacher. Norwich, [1840]. SCL/L
Bell Family	2519	**Josselyn, J. H.** Genealogical account of the descendants of Sir Robert Bell ... with a history of the

illustrious ancestry of his wife, Dorothy, co-heir of the ancient family of Beaupré. Ipswich, 1896

Bell, A. H.	2520	**Bell, A. H.** My own master. 1961. CBEL
Bell, N. pseud. [i.e. *S. Southwold*]	2521	**Bell, N.** My writing life. 1855. CBEL
Bence Family	2522	**Nayler, G.** Genealogy of the ancient family of Bence, etc., with additions to the present date (1882). [Genealogical table only]
	2523	**Whayman, H. W.** Bence of Aldeburgh and Orford. E Ang NS 6, 1895/6, 332
	2524	Bence of Suffolk. VE&W 21, 1921, 97–9. *See also* **7713**
Bennet Family	2525	Bennet of Rougham. VE&W 21, 1921, 136
Bennit, W.	2526	Some prison meditations of an humble heart ... [Written in the County Gaol, Ipswich]. 1668. Wing B1893. BL
	2527	**Bennit, W.** A collection of certain epistles and testimonies of divine consolation, experience, and doctrine [Written in the County Gaol, Ipswich]. 1685. Wing B1891
Berners Family	2528	**Warwick, M. A. S.** Some pictures from the past history of the Berners family. Ipswich, 1907. BL
Betham Family	2529	**Betham-Edwards, M. B.** Some notes on the Betham family. ECM 1, 1900/01, 190–05, 312–17
Betham, W.		DNB
Betham-Edwards, M. B.	2530	**Betham-Edwards, M. B.** Reminiscences. 1900
	2531	**Betham-Edwards, M. B.** Mid-Victorian memories. 1919. DNB, CBEL
Betts Family	2532	**Doughty, K. F.** The Betts of Wortham in Suffolk, 1480–1905. 1912
Bevan, A. B.	2533	Algernon Beckford Bevan. PSIA 18, 1922/4, 254
Bickers, G.	2534	**Bickers, G.** Interesting incidents connected with the life of George Bickers, originally a farmer's apprentice at Laxfield ... being an autobiography ... from 1809 to 1881 inclusive. Lowestoft, nd. SCL/L
Bickersteth, J.	2535	**B. J.,** *and* **Fearon, D. R.** Memoir of Mrs. John Bickersteth, with a sermon preached on the occasion of her death. 1830
Biddell Family	2536	Biddell of Playford. VE&W 3, 1895, 97–9
Bigg Family		*See* Ray Family
Bigod Family	2537	**Tasburgh, D.** The Bigods and their castle of Bungay. ECM 2, 1901 59–64

Birch, H. W. R.	2538	**Fitch, J. A.** A family affair, 1819–29 [correspondence between 1st Earl of Stradbroke and Rev. H. W. R. Birch in 1826]. SR 2, 1961, 99–118
Bird, J.	2539	**H[arral], T.** Selections from the poems of James Bird, with a brief memoir of his life. [1840]. BL DNB
Bland Family	2540	**Carlisle, N.** Collections for a history of the ancient family of Bland. 1826. 1900 with index by F. Bland
Blomfield Family Family	2541	**Pearson, W. C.** Extracts from parish registers: Stonham Aspal and Barking. E Ang NS 4, 1891/2, 81–3, 99–101, 115–19, 136–8
	2542	**Blomfield,** *Sir* **R. T.** A Suffolk family: being an account of the family of Blomfield in Suffolk. 1916. 100 copies
	2543	**Blomfield, E. V.** Account of the Blomfield families, with eleven pedigrees. 1950. 14 pts. [Typescript]. 30 copies
Blomfield, C. J.	2544	**Blomfield, A.** Memoir of Charles James Blomfield, D.D., Bishop of London, with selections from his correspondence. 1863. 2nd edn 1864. 2v
	2545	**Blomfield,** *Sir* **R.** Memoir of Charles James Blomfield, Bishop of London, 1828–56 [c.1935]. [Typescript] DNB
Bloomfield, R.	2546	**Storer, J.,** *and* **Greig, J.** Views in Suffolk, Norfolk and Northamptonshire: illustrative of the works of Robert Bloomfield, accompanied with descriptions, to which is annexed a memoir of the poet's life by E. W. Brayley. 1806. 1818
	2547	**Bloomfield, R.** Selections from the correspondence of Robert Bloomfield. *Ed.* by W. H. Hart. 1870. Rp 1968
	2548	Robert Bloomfield the Suffolk poet. PSIA 15, 1913/15, 45–62. [Honington]
	2549	**MacFarlane, C.** Life of Robert Bloomfield. Hitchin, 1916. SRO/B
	2550	**Cranbrook,** *Earl of, and* **Hadfield, J.** Some uncollected authors. 20. Bloomfield. Book Collector 8, 1959
	2551	**Hawes, H.** Robert Bloomfield. SR 3, No 1, 1965, 13–17
	2552	**Wickett, W.,** *and* **Duval, N.** The farmer's boy: the story of a Suffolk poet. Robert Bloomfield, his life and poems, 1766–1823. Lavenham, 1971

2553   Sale catalogue. Books ... furniture ... of Robert Bloomfield. Biggleswade, 1824. BL
DNB, CBEL

Bohun, E.

2554   **Bohun, E.** Diary and autobiography: with an introductory memoir, notes, and illustrations by S. W. Rix. Beccles, 1853. 12 copies
DNB. *See also* **1691**

Bois Family   *See* De Bois Family
Bokenham Family   *See* Buckenham Family
Bokenham, O.   DNB

Bolton Family

2555   Bolton of Suffolk. VE&W 19, 1917, 10–12; Notes 11, 55–60

Bonham Family

2556   **Kidston, G. J.** Bonhams of Wiltshire and Essex [with genealogical tables]. Devizes, 1948. BL

Borrow, G.

2557   **Dutt, W. A.** George Borrow in East Anglia. 1896 [Oulton]

2558   **Knapp, W. I.** Life, writings, and correspondence of George Borrow. 2v. 1899

2559   **Jenkins, H.** Life of George Borrow: compiled from unpublished official documents ... 1912

2560   **Borrow, G.** Letters to his mother, Ann Borrow, and other correspondents. 1913. 30 copies. BL

2561   **Borrow, G.** Letters to his wife, Mary Borrow. 1913. BL

2562   **Adams, M.** In the footsteps of Borrow and Fitzgerald. [1914]

2563   **Wise, T. J.** Bibliography of the writings in prose and verse of George Henry Borrow. 1914. Rp 1966

2564   **Hopkins, R. T.** George Borrow, lord of the open road ... [1922]. BL

2565   **Armstrong, M. D.** George Borrow. 1950

2566   **Bigland, E.** In the steps of George Borrow ... 1951

2567   **Meyers, R. R.** George Borrow. New York, [1966]
DNB, CBEL

Bostock, T.

2568   **Dow, L.** Note on Thomas Bostock (? of Hoxne). PSIA 25, 1949/51, 117–18

Botolph, Saint

2569   **Lingard, R.** St. Botolph's, Whitton, with Thurleston: the life and times of our patron saint, St. Botolph. Ipswich, 1962

2570   **Lingard, R.** St. Botolph: the story of this ·East Anglian saint. Ipswich, 1964. NCL/N.
See also **4337, 5441–3**
DNB

Bovile Family   *See* **6457**

Boyce, Boys Family		*See* De Bois Family
Bradstreet Family	2571	**French, E**. Genealogical research in England: Bradstreet of Gislingham, co. Suffolk. NEH&GR 65, 1911, 69–74
Brand Family	2572	**Brand, R. F**. Genealogy of the Canadian and American descendants of John Brand [1757/1841] and his wife, Margaret Head, both of Acton ... 1943. [Typescript]
Brand, J.	2573	**Dunne, C**. Report of the lunacy case of the late John Brand, Esq., of Sutton, Suffolk. 1831. nl
Brandon, **Duchess of Suffolk**		*See* Willoughby, C.
Brewse Family	2574	Brewse of Little Wenham. Frag Gen 8, 1902, 57–64
Brewster Family	2575	Brewster of Suffolk and Essex. VE&W 13, 1905, 17–23; Notes 10, 160–64
Brigges, M.	2576	B. B. Martin Brigges, rector of Brettenham. E Ang NS 2, 1888, 296–8
Bright Family	2577	**Bright, J. B**. Brights of Suffolk, England, represented in America by the descendants of Henry Bright, Jun., who came to New England in 1630 ... Boston, Mass., 1858
	2578	**Whitmore, W. H**. Family of Bright, of Suffolk. NEH&GR 13, 1859, 97–8
Bright, H.	2579	**Roe, F. G**. Henry Bright of the Norwich School. Walker's Quarterly no 1, Oct 1920
	2580	Henry Bright. SC 27 Sept 1873
	2581	Henry Bright, 1810–73. A catalogue of paintings and drawings in the collection of Norwich Castle Museum, 1973. Norwich. SCL/L DNB
Britten, B.	2582	**White, E. W**. Benjamin Britten: a sketch of his life and works. 1948. 1954. 1970
	2583	**Mitchell, D. C**., *and* **Keller, H**. *Eds*. Benjamin Britten: a commentary on his works from a group of specialists. 1952
	2584	**Boosey and Hawkes, Ltd**. Benjamin Britten: a complete catalogue of his published works. 1963. 1973
	2585	**Gishford, A**., *Ed*. Tribute to Benjamin Britten on his fiftieth birthday. 1963
	2586	**Holst, I**. Britten 1966. 2nd edn 1970
	2587	**Hurd, M**. Benjàmin Britten. [1966]. SCL/L
	2588	**Young, P. M**. Britten. 1966. SCL/L
	2589	**Kendall, A**. Benjamin Britten. 1973 *See also* **6698**

Broke, Sir *P. B. V.*	2590	**Brighton, J. G.** Admiral Sir P. B. V. Broke, Bart. A memoir chiefly from journals and letters ... 1866 DNB
Bromley Family	2591	Bromley of Wickhambrook. VE&W 5, 1897, 136–7; Notes 6, 45–6
Brooke Family	2592	Brooke of Sibton Park. VE&W 1, 1893, 73–5; Notes 2, 95. *See also* Wittewronge Family
Brooke, Lady *E.*	2593	**Parkhurst, N.** The faithful and diligent Christian described and exemplified: or, A sermon preached at the funeral of the Lady Elizabeth Brooke ... of Cockfield Hall in Yoxford ... 26 July 1683 ... to which is appended an account of the life and death of that eminent lady. 1684. Wing P 489 SRO/B DNB. *See also* **2337**
Broome, W.	2594	**Barlow, T. W.** Memoir of William Broome. Manchester, 1855. BL DNB
Browninge, T.	2595	**Partridge, C.** Elizabethan yeoman's will: Thomas Browninge of Higham. E Ang NS 8, 1899–1900, 382–4
Bryene, A. de		*See* De Bryene, A.
Buckenham Family	2596	**Maudsley, H.** To the glory of God ... [Pedigree of the family of Buckenham]. 1882. BL
	2597	**Maudsley, H.** Notes and extracts ... respecting the family of Bukenham or Bokenham of Norfolk and Suffolk from 1066 to ... 1883, and the places of that designation in the first named county. Pt 1 [All published]. 1884. 250 copies
Budd Family	2598	Budd of Suffolk. VE&W 10, 1902, 167–70.
Bunbury Family		*See* Hanmer, *Sir* T
Bunbury, Sir *C. J. F.*	2599	**Bunbury, F. J.** Memorials of Sir C. J. F. Bunbury, Bart. 8v. 1890–93
	2600	Life and letters and journals of Sir Charles J. F. Bunbury, Bart. *Ed.* by his wife Frances Joanna Bunbury. [1894]. 3v. Abridgement 1906
	2601	**Lyell, K. M.,** *Ed.* Life of Sir Charles J. F. Bunbury. 1906
Bunbury, Sir *H. E.*	2602	Memoir and literary remains of Lieutenant-General Sir Henry Edward Bunbury, Bart. *Ed.* by his son Sir C. F. J. Bunbury. 1868 DNB
Bunbury, H. W.	2603	**Thorner, H.** Henry William Bunbury, 1889. SRO/B
	2604	**Laver, J.** Henry William Bunbury: introduction. [1950]. [Typescript] DNB

Bunbury, Sir *T. C.*   2605   **Lawrence, J.** Memoir of the late Sir Thomas Charles Bunbury, Bart, of Great Barton, Suffolk. Ipswich, 1821. SRO/B. *See also* **941, 1501**

Bungay, Friar   2606   **Baker, G. B.** Friar Bungay. E Ang 3, 1866/8, 301–02. DNB. Emden to 1500, 1, 305

Bures Family   2607   **Burr, C. R.** Bures of Suffolk, England, and Burr of Massachussetts Bay Colony, New England. [*Ed.* by H. W. Hardon]. New York, 1926. 100 copies. BL *See also* **3516**

Burkitt, W.   2608   **Parkhurst, N.** Life of the Rev. W. Burkitt. 1704. 1780. BL

     2609   **McKeon, H.** Biographical sketch of W. Burkitt. *In his* Inquiry into the birth-place ... of W. Gurnall. Woodbridge, 1829 DNB

Burrell Family   2610   Burrell of Stoke Park, Ipswich (Baron Gwydyr). VE&W 12, 1904, 133–43; Notes 10, 108–14

Burrell, C.   2611   Suspension and deprivation of Christopher Burrell, parson of Great Wratting, 1638. E Ang NS 12, 1907/08, 33–4

     2612   **M, J. T.** Sons of Christopher Burrell, parson of Great Wratting. E Ang NS 12, 1907/08, 80

Burrough Family   2613   **Muskett, J. J.** A genealogical puzzle: memorial to Burrough in St. Margaret's, Ipswich. E Ang NS 9, 1901/02, 293–5

     2614   **Curtis, H.** Portraits by Gainsborough of the allied family of Burrough of Sudbury. N&Q 182, 1942, 2–6, 16–19

Burrows, Sir *J. C.*   DNB

Bury, E.   2615   Account of the life and death of Mrs. Elizabeth Bury ... together with her funeral sermon ... by the Rev. William Tong, and her elegy by the Rev. J. Watts. Bristol, 1720 DNB

Calamy, E.
1634–85   2616   Edmund Calamie, of Bury St. Edmunds. E Ang NS 3, 1889/90, 33–4 DNB

Calamy, E.
1671–1732   2617   **Calamy, E.** Historical account of my own life, with some reflections on the times I have lived in, 1671–1731. *Ed.* By J. T. Rutt. 2v. 1829 DNB, CBEL

Caley, R.   2618   **Caley, R.** Ipswich Jail and the Union: the second history of my life, since I have been lame, [Ipswich?], [1877?]

Call Family	2619	**Romanes, C. S.** Calls of Norfolk and Suffolk; their Paston connections and descendants. Edinburgh, 1920. 300 copies. SCL/L
Calthorpe Family	2620	**Calthrop, C. W. C.** Notes on the families of Calthorpe and Calthrop ... 1905. 3rd edn 1933
Candler, A.	2621	**Candler, A.** Poetical attempts by Ann Candler, a Suffolk cottager, with a short narrative of her life. Ipswich, 1803 DNB
Candler, M.	2622	Candler MSS—Matthias Candler, vicar of Coddenham. E Ang NS 1, 1885/6, 313–15
Capper Family		*See* Wittewronge Family
Capper, G.	2623	**Zincke, F. B.** Sermon ... preached ... after the funeral of the Rev. G. Capper. 1847. BL
Carnac, Rivett-		*See* Rivett-Carnac Family
Carthew Family	2624	Carthew of Woodbridge. VE&W 8, 1900, 6–7
Carthew, T.	2625	**Black, J.** Sermon occasioned by the death of the Rev. Thomas Carthew ... Woodbridge, [1791]. BL
	2626	Sale catalogue. Manor, livings, and several estates of ... Thomas Carthew. Woodbridge, 1791. BL
Casley, H. C.	2627	**Redstone, V. B.** H. C. Casley. PSIA 22, 1934/6, 342
Castleton Family	2628	Family of Castleton of Stuston Hall. E Ang 3, 1866/8, 249–50
	2629	**Orlorenshaw, J. R.** Extracts from parish registers. E Ang NS 5, 1893/4, 323; NS 6, 1895/6, 7
Catlin Family	2630	Catlin of Suffolk. VE&W 6, 1898, 32–3
	2631	**W, E. L.** Catlyn of Woolverston Hall. E Ang NS 9, 1901/02, 46–8
Cavendish Family	2632	**Ruggles, T.** Notices of the Manor of Cavendish in Suffolk and of the Cavendish family while possessed of that manor. Arch 11, 1794, 50–62
Cavendish, T.	2633	**Dyke, G.** Thomas Cavendish and the Roanoke voyage, 1585. SR 1, 1956 33–7
	2634	**Dyke, G.** The finance of a 16th-century navigator, Thomas Cavendish of Trimley ... MM 4, 1958, 108–15
	2635	The last voyage of Thomas Cavendish, 1591–1592: the autograph manuscript of his own account of the voyage. *Ed.* By D. B. Quinn. Chicago, 1975 DNB
Chambers, J.	2636	**Chambers, J.** Poetical works of James Chambers ... with the life of the author. Ipswich, 1820 [Earl Soham, Stradbroke]

2637   **Langdon, A.** Jemmy Chambers—itinerant poet. SR 2, 1959, 36–42

Chaplin, A.   2638   **Livett, R. G. C.** Goods of a Suffolk parson in the seventeenth century: Abraham Chaplin of Wetheringsett. E Ang NS 10, 1903/04, 33–6

Charlesworth, J.   2639   **Fitzgerald, J. P.** The quiet worker for good: a familiar sketch of the late John Charlesworth, B.D., formerly rector of Flowton ... 1865

Chaucer Family   2640   **Partridge, C. S.,** *et al.* Chaucer's connection with East Anglia. E Ang NS 5, 1893/4, 258, 319, 352

2641   **Redstone, V. B.** The Chaucer-Malyn family, Ipswich, PSIA 12, 1904/06, 184–99. CBEL. *See also* **3019**

Chedworth, 4th Baron   *See* Howe, J

Cheston, R.   2642   **Josselyn, J. H.** A Suffolk captain [Thomas Cheston] at the time of Queen Elizabeth. PSIA 11, 1901/03, 47–9

Chevallier Family   2643   **Chevallier, F. E. M.** Extracts from the Chevallier papers, 1728–42. [Chevallier of Aspall Hall, nr Debenham]. PSIA 16, 1916/18, 196–210

2644   Chevallier of Aspall. VE&W 20, 1919, 8–14; Notes 14, 130–32

2645   **Tye, W.** Chevallier family and their barley. SR 1, 1958, 198–201

Chickering Family   2646   **Chamberlain, G. W.** English ancestry of the Chickerings of New England. [Wrentham]. NEH&GR 60, 1915, 226–9

Churchyard, T.   2647   Thomas Churchyard, 1798–1865. History and exhibition catalogue, Nov 1965. [By S. Carter]. Norwich, 1965. NCL/N

2648   **Thomas, D.** [J. R.] Thomas Churchyard of Woodbridge. Chislehurst, [1966]

Clare Family   2649   **Round, J. H.** Family of Clare. Arch J 56, 1898, 221–31

2650   **Rye, W.** De Clares of Clare in Suffolk ... Gen NS 37, 1921, 169–73

2651   **Ward, J. C.** Estates of the Clare family, 1066–1317. [Thesis summary]. BIHR 37, 1964 114–17

2652   **Altschull, M.** A baronial family in medieval England: the Clares, 1217–1314. Baltimore, Md., 1965. SRO/B CP

Clare, Sister   *See* Warner, *Lady*

Clarkson, L.   2653   **Morton, A. L.** Laurence Clarkson, preacher of Suffolk. PSIA 26, 1952/4, 161–87

Clarkson, T. 2654 **Taylor, T.** Biographical sketch of Thomas Clarkson, M.A., with occasional brief strictures on the misrepresentations of him contained in the life of William Wilberforce ... 1839

2655 **Crummell, A.** The man, the hero, the Christian! An eulogium on the life and character of Thomas Clarkson. Delivered in New York, December 1846 ... New York, 1847. London, 1849

2656 **Elmes, J.** Thomas Clarkson: a monograph ... 1854

2657 **Griggs, E. L.** Thomas Clarkson, the friend of slaves. 1936
DNB, CBEL. *See also* **7114**

Clavering Family 2658 **[Morgan, G. B.]** Titular barony of Clavering. Its origin in, and right of inheritance by, the Norman house of Clavering ... [founders of Sibton Abbey]. 1891. BL

Clayton Family 2659 **Young, E.** Family of Clayton of Southolt, Bedfield, etc. E Ang NS 10, 1903/04, 204–07

Clodd, E. 2660 **Clodd, E.** Memories. 1916

2661 In memoriam, Edward Clodd, 1 July 1840—16 March 1930 ... [funeral service and spoken tributes]. [1930]. BL

2662 **McCabe, J.** Edward Clodd, a memoir. 1932.
DNB

Clopton Family 2663 **Erwin, L. L.** Ancestry of William Clopton of York county, Virginia. Rutland, Vt, 1939. nl. *See also* **6488**

Cobbold Family 2664 Cobbold of Ipswich. VE&W 20, 1919, 21–32; Notes 14, 142–6

Cobbold, E. 2665 **Cobbold, E.** Poems ... [with a memoir of the author by Laetitia Jermyn]. Ipswich, 1825
DNB

Coe Family 2666 **Bartlett, J. G.** Robert Coe, Puritan, his ancestors and descendants 1340–1910. With notices of the other Coe families. Boston, Mass., 1911

Coe, W. 2667 Diary of William Coe of Mildenhall, 1680–1729. E Ang NS 11, 1905/06: NS 12, 1907/08, *passim*

Coggeshall Family 2668 **Sterling, C. F. D.,** *et al.* Coggeshall family. E Ang NS 1, 1885/6, 221, 263; NS 5, 1893/4, 79, 142, 203–05; NS 7, 1897/8, 9; NS 12, 1907/08, 385; NS 13, 1909/10, 176

Coggeshall, H. 2669 **W[ayman], H. W. B.** Henry Coggeshall of Orford, inventor and mathematician. PSIA 18, 1922/4, 54–65

Coke Family 2670 Coke of Thorington. VE&W 8, 1900, 149–60; Notes 8, 108–16

Coke, A. 2671 **Steer, F. W.** Inventory of Arthur Coke of Bramfield,

1629. PSIA 25, 1949/51, 264–87

Colchester Family   2672   **Pearson, W. C.** Extracts from parish registers: Barking, Coddenham. E Ang NS 4, 1891/2, 195–8, 223

Cole Family   2673   **Cole, J. E.** Genealogy of the family of Cole, in the county of Devon, and those branches which settled in Suffolk ... 1867. BL

2674   **Crisp, F. A.** Cole family. Frag Gen 4, 1899, 17

2675   **Gray, G. J.** Index to the contents of the Cole manuscripts in the British Museum. Cambridge, 1912. SCL/B

Collings, J.   2676   Biographical sketch of Jesse Collings, M.P. Rp from Suffolk Times and Mercury, 15 Dec 1882. Ipswich, 1882

Colvile Family   2677   **Colvile,** *Sir* **C.,** *et al.* History of the Colvile family. 1896. 50 copies. nl

Conder, J.   2678   F, J. Suffolk biography. [Brief account of Mr. James Conder, of Ipswich. By J. F.]. [Ipswich?], [1820?] BL DNB

Constable, J.   2679   **Leslie, C. R.** Memoirs of the life of John Constable, R. A., composed chiefly of his letters. 1843 and var. edns

2680   **Holmes, C. J.** Constable and his influence on landscape painting. 2pts. 1902. BL

2681   **Lucas, E. V.** John Constable the painter. 1924

2682   **Leslie, P.,** *Ed.* Letters of John Constable to C. R. Leslie, R.A. ... 1826–37. 1931. BL

2683   **Shirley, A.** Constable as a portrait painter, and his early and middle periods. Burl 70, 1937, 267–80

2684   **Croft-Murray, E.** Drawings by John Constable at the British Museum. Burl 70, 1939, 295–6

2685   **Bunt, C. G. E.** John Constable, the father of modern landscape. Leigh-on-Sea, 1948. SCL/L

2686   **Beckett, R. B.** John Constable and the Fishers: the record of a friendship. 1952

2687   **Mayne, J.** Constable. Sketches. 1953

2688   **Reynolds, A. G.** Catalogue of the Constable collection: Victoria and Albert Museum. 1960. 2nd edn 1973

2689   John Constable's correspondence. *Ed.* by R. B. Beckett. v 1. The family at East Bergholt, 1807–1837. Ipswich, 1962. SRS 4

2690   v 2. Early friends and Maria Bicknell (Mrs. Constable). Ipswich, 1964. SRS 6

2691   v 3. Correspondence with C. R. Leslie, R.A. Ipswich, 1965. SRS 8

2692   v 4. Patrons, dealers, and fellow artists. Ipswich, 1966. SRS 10

2693   v 5. Various friends, with Charles Boner and the artist's children. Ipswich, 1967. SRS 11

2694   v 6. The Fishers. Ipswich, 1968. SRS 12

2695   John Constable's discourses. *Ed.* By R. B. Beckett. Ipswich, 1970. SRS 14

2696   John Constable: further documents and correspondence. Pt 1. Documents. *Ed.* by L. Parris and C. Shields. Pt 2. Correspondence. *Ed.* By I. Fleming-Williams. Ipswich, 1975. SRS 18

2697   **Reynolds, A. G.** Constable, the natural painter. 1965. 1970

2698   **Shields, C.,** *and* **Parris, L.** John Constable, 1776–1837. 1969

2699   **Taylor, B.** Constable: paintings, drawings, and watercolours. 1973. 2nd edn 1975

2700   **Day, J.** John Constable, R.A., 1776–1837; drawings, the golden age. Eastbourne, 1975
DNB. *See also* **2129**

Cooke Family   2701   **Hovendon, R.** Extracts from Cranbrook registers. MGetH, 2nd Ser 4, 1892, 173–4

Copinger Family   2702   **Copinger, W. A.,** *Ed.* History of the Copingers, or Coppingers, of the city of Cork, of Cloghan, etc. Manchester, 1882. 150 copies. 1884

Corbould Family   2703   **Round, J. H.** Corbould family. Gen NS 2, 1885, 94–5

    2704   **Poulter, G. C. B.** Corbould genealogy. Ipswich, 1935

Corder Family   2705   Corder of Claydon. VE&W 19, 1917, 134–6; Notes 14, 79–80

    2706   Corder of Ipswich. VE&W 19, 1917, 137–43; Notes 14, 79–80

Cornwallis Family   2707   A description to accompany the tables of descent of the Cornwallis family, blazoned by Louisa, Marchioness Cornwallis. [1845?]. nl

    2708   Cornwallis wills [16th century: Brome]. E Ang NS 10, 1903/04, 221–5

    2709   **Moriatry, G. A.** Early generations of Cornwallis of Brome. NEH&GR 110, 1956. 122–7

Cornwallis, Lady *J.*   2710   Private correspondence of Jane, Lady Cornwallis, 1613–1644. *Ed.* by Lord Braybrooke. 1842. 50 copies. SRO/B
DNB

Cornwallis, Sir *T.*   2711   **McGrath, P.,** *and* **Rowe, J.** Recusancy of Sir Thomas Cornwallis (Brome). PSIA 28, 1958/60, 226–71
DNB

Cornwell, E.   2712   **Jones, A. G. E.** Emerson Cornwell, Ipswich banker. N&Q 197, 1952, 406–08

Corsellis Family   2713   **Cullum, G. G. M. G.** Pedigree of the family of Corsellis, with abstracts from wills, parish registers ... Rp from MGetH. 1914. SRO/B

Cotton, J.   2714   **B[eart], J.** Funeral sermon on the death of John Cotton of Rattlesden ... who departed this life, 16 Nov 1710. Ipswich, 1775

Cowell, E. B.   2715   **Bendall, C.** Memoir of Edward Byles Cowell. Athenaeum, 14 Feb 1903

   2716   **Cowell, G.** Life and letters of Edward Byles Cowell. 1904

   2717   **Davids, T. W. R.** Memoir of Edwards Byles Cowell. Proc Brit Acad 1, 1903/04
DNB

Cowell, M. B.   2718   Rev Canon Maurice Byles Cowell (incumbent of the parish of Ashbocking). PSIA 17, 1919/21, 86

Cowley, A.   2719   **Taylor, J.** Anthony Cowley as school-master at Ipswich and Hadleigh. E Ang NS 3, 1889/90, 115–16

Crabb, J.   2720   **Sperling, C. F. D.** A Suffolk yeoman's goods, 1691 [John Crabb of Barking]. E Ang NS 5, 1893/4, 74

Crabbe, G.   2721   Poetical works of the Rev George Crabbe: with his letters and journals, and his life, by his son. 8v. 1834 and var. edns

   2722   Souvenir of the Crabbe celebration ... at ... Aldeburgh ... 1905. [*Ed.* by C. Ganz]. 1905

   2723   The commemoration of Crabbe, 1905. PSIA 12, 1904/06, 200–01

   2724   **Groves, J.** Crabbe as a botanist. PSIA 12, 1904/06, 223–32

   2725   **Huchon, R.** George Crabbe and his times, 1754–1832: a critical and biographical study. Trans by F. Clarke. 1907. Rp 1968

   2726   **Broadley, A. M.,** *and* **Jerrold, W.** The romance of an elderly poet ... revealed by his ten years' correspondence with Elizabeth Charter, 1815–25. 1913.

   2727   **Tennyson, C.** George Crabbe and Suffolk. Geographical Mag 16, 1943, 140–46

   2728   **Cranbrook,** *Earl of.* George Crabbe and Great Glemham. PSIA 25, 1949/51, 116–17

   2729   Biographical account of the Rev Geo. Crabbe. PSIA 26, 1952/4, 99–136

2730 **East Suffolk County Library**. George Crabbe, 1754–1832, bicentenary celebrations. Exhibition of works and manuscripts ... Aldeburgh. Ipswich, 1954

2731 **Blackburne, N.** The restless ocean: the story of George Crabbe, the Aldeburgh poet, 1754–1832. Lavenham, 1972
DNB, CBEL

Crane Family

2732 **Appleton, W. S.** Memorials of the Cranes of Chilton, with a pedigree of the family, and a life of the last representative. Cambridge, Mass., 1868

Cranworth, **Baron** *See* Gurdon Family

Craske Family

2733 **Symonds, W.,** *and* **Partridge, C.** West Suffolk families: Craske. E Ang NS 12, 1907/08, 128, 242–3

Cripps-Day Family

2734 Cripps-Day of Newmarket. VE&W 8, 1900, 50–51

Crisp Family

2735 **Crisp, F. A.,** *Ed.* Collections relating to the family of Crispe. 1882–97. 4v. 150 copies

2736 **Crisp, F. A.,** *Ed.* Collections relating to the family of Crispe. Further and final extracts ... from the records of the College of Arms. NS v 1. 1913. 100 copies. SRO/B

2737 Crisp of Bungay. VE&W 18, 1914, 204–05; Notes 13, 138

2738 Crisp of Southwold. VE&W 7, 1899, 97–104; Notes 7, 89–92

2739 Crisp of Suffolk. VE&W 13, 1905, 114–21; Notes 11, 30–31

Crowfoot Family

2740 Grant of arms to William John Crowfoot of Beccles, 1831 (with extracts ... from the parish registers of Sotterley, Henstead, Uggeshall, and Sotherton) MGetH NS 4, 1884, 40, 50–51

2741 Crowfoot of Beccles. VE&W 1, 1893, 26; Notes 1, 77–89

Crowley Family

2742 **Marshall, G. W.** Pedigree of the family of Crowley of Greenwich, co. Kent, and Barking, co. Suffolk. E Ang 3, 1866/8, 95–8

Cullum Family

2743 Cullum family. MGetH 2nd Ser 1, 1886—2nd Ser 5, 1894, *passim.* 4th Ser 3, 1910, 333–4

2744 Families of Cullum and Deane of the county of Suffolk. New England Register, July 1887. SRO/B

2745 Cullum of Hardwick House. VE&W 1, 1893, 171

2746 **Redstone, V. B.** Cullum letters. PSIA 14, 1910/1912, 280–85

2747 **Cullum, G. G. M. G.,** *Ed.* Genealogical notes relating to the family of Cullum ... 1928

See also Wittewronge Family

Cullum, Sir D.	2748	**Cullum, G. G. M. G.** Sir Dudley Cullum's school and college accounts 1668, and a college account of Sir John Cullum, 1752. E Ang NS 3, 1889/90, 217–19 DNB
Cullum, G. G. M. G.	2749	George Gery Milner Gibson Cullum. PSIA 17, 1919/21, 202
Cullum, Sir J.		DNB
Cullum, Sir T.	2750	The case of Sir Thomas Cullum ... the affronts ... offer'd him by Mr. Harris ... By an impartial hand. 1680. Wing C 1001. SRO/B DNB
Cunningham, F.	2751	**Hoare, E.** "The blessed hope"; a sermon on the occasion of the death of Mrs. Francis Cunningham. 1855. SCL/L
Curson, Sir R.	2752	**C, A. B.** Sir Robert Curzon, or Lord Curzon of Ipswich, E Ang NS 6, 1895/6, 78, 144, 160, 192
	2753	**Glyde, J.** Sir Robert Curson, otherwise Lord Curson. PSIA 9, 1895/7, 271–8
Cutler, B.	2754	**Glyde, J.,** *and* **Muskett, J. J.** Benjamin Cutler, Ipswich. E Ang NS 1, 1885/6, 166, 199–200
Cutler, R.	2755	Grant of arms to Robert Cutler of Ipswich (1612). MGetH 1, 1863, 228–9
Cutting, M.	2756	**Boddington, B.** Account of Margaret Cutting, a young woman now living at Wickham Market, who speaks readily and intelligibly, though she has lost her tongue. PTRS, 1742, 143–52. O
C'Ysterne, De		*See* De C'Ysterne
Dade Family	2757	**Watkins, E. A.,** *et al.* Dade family (Ipswich, Ubbeston, Dallinghoo, Chediston). MGetH 2nd Ser 1, 1886, *passim*
	2758	[**Howard, J. J.**]. Genealogical memoranda relating to the family of Dade of Suffolk. 1888. 50 copies
Dalton, T.	2759	**B, J. J.** The English home of Mr. Timothy Dalton, B.A., the teacher of the Church of Jesus Christ, in Hampton, N.E., from 1639 to 1661. Orange, N.J., [1898]
Dameron Family	2760	**Pearson, W. C.** Extracts from parish registers. E Ang NS 5, 1893/4, 189–90
	2761	**Snow, H. F.** Dameron-Damron genealogy: the descendants of Lawrence Dameron of Virginia [earlier of Henley, Suffolk]. Madison, Conn., nd. [Typescript]
Dandy Family	2762	Family of Dandy. E Ang 2, 1864/6, 164–6; NS 1, 1885/6, 283; NS 10, 1903/04, 143–4, 228
	2763	Dandy pedigree. PSIA 27, 1955/7, 133–53

Danforth, N.	2764	**Merriam, J. M.** Framingham to Framlingham. A greeting across the seas in memory of Nicholas Danforth and his descendants. Boston, Mass., 1931
	2765	**Booth, J.** Nicholas Danforth and his neighbours. Framlingham and Saxtead in the 17th century. Framingham, 1935. [Framingham Historical & Nat. Hist. Soc., Massachusetts]
	2766	**Booth, J.** Home of Nicholas Danforth in Framlingham, Suffolk, England in 1635. Framingham, 1954
Darwin, W. A.	2767	Rev W. A. Darwin. PSIA 17, 1919/21, 86
Davers Family		*See* 7204
Davy, D. E.		DNB *See also* 2343, 2357–60
Davy, H.	2768	**Denney, A. H.** Henry Davy, 1793–1865 [includes catalogue of his etched, lithographed, and engraved works]. PSIA 29, 1961/3, 78–90
	2769	Sale catalogue. Household furniture, books, prints, drawings and paintings, the property of Mr. Henry Davy, artist ... 16 April 1833 ... Ipswich. BL. DNB
Day Family		*See* Cripps-Day Family
Daye, J. d.1584	2770	**Oastler, C. A.** John Day, the Elizabethan printer. B.Litt. thesis, Oxford, 1965. Oxford Bibl Soc Occasional Publ 10. 1975. O DNB
Daye, J.	2771	**Muskett, J. J.** A country parson of 1627, John Daye of Little Thurlow. E Ang NS 10, 1903/04, 81–2
Deane Family		*See* Cullum Family
Debenham Family	2772	**Sweeting, W. D.,** *Ed.* Record of the family of Debenham of Suffolk. [1909]
	2773	**Debenham, F.** Debenham family tree. Cambridge, 1958
	2774	**Debenham, F.** Seven centuries of Debenhams. Cambridge, 1958
Debenham, G.	2775	**Haward, W. I.** Gilbert Debenham: a medieval rascal in real life. History NS 13, 1928/9, 300–14
De Bois Family	2776	De Bois, or Boyce. [Genealogical tables by R. Boyce]. 1927. [Typescript]. BL
	2777	**Boys, G. P.,** *Ed.* Three documented pedigrees ... of the family of Du Bois, Boys, Boyce, etc. 1939. SRO/B
De Bryene, A.	2778	Household book of Dame Alice de Bryene of Acton Hall, Suffolk, Sept 1412—Sept 1413. *Ed.* by V. B. Redstone. Ipswich, 1931
De Clare Family		*See* Clare Family

De C'Ysterne, R.	2779	**Jones, W. A. B.** Robert de C'Ysterne, a medieval cleric. SR 2, 1959, 29–31
De Grey Family	2780	**Crabbe, G.** The de Greys of Little Cornard. PSIA 6, 1883/8, 13–39
De la Pole Family	2781	**Napier, H. A.** Historical notices of the parishes of Swyncombe and Ewelme in the county of Oxford. [Refs De la Pole family]. Oxford, 1858. O
	2782	**Round, J. H.** Note on the De la Pole pedigree. Gen NS 3, 1886, 112
	2783	**Raven, J. J.** History of the De la Poles. PSIA 7, 1889/91, 51–6
	2784	**H, M. F.** An extinct Suffolk earldom. ECM 2, 1901/02, 259–63
	2785	**Harvey, A. S.,** *Ed.* Homeland of the De la Poles: Kingston-upon-Hull and Wingfield in Suffolk. Hull, 1934 CP. *See also* **5393**
De la Ramée, M. L.		*See* Ouida, *pseud*
Dennant, J.	2786	**Flower, J.** Brief notices of the life and ministerial labours of the Rev John Dennant, forty-four years pastor of the Independent Church of Halesworth, Suffolk: with the funeral sermon preached after his death. 1851. NCL/N
Denny Family	2787	**Denny, H. L.** Pedigrees of some East Anglian Dennys. Gen NS 38, 1921/2, 15–28; PSIA 19, 1925/7, 313–37
	2788	**Denny,** *Sir* **H. L. L.** Early Denny descents and armorial bearings. Burwash, 1944. BL
De Riveshall, Sir H.	2789	**M, T. T.** Sir Henry de Riveshall of Hepworth Manor. E Ang NS 6, 151–2, 164–6
De Vallibus Family	2790	De Vallibus family of Norfolk and Suffolk. *In* Hervey's Dictionary of Herveys. v 2. 1926
Devereux, E.	2791	**Muskett, J. J.** A clandestine marriage: Elizabeth Devereux, heiress of Butley Abbey. E Ang NS 3, 1889/90, 138–43
De Waldegrave		*See* Waldegrave
D'Ewes, Sir S.	2792	Extracts from the MS journals of Sir Simonds D'Ewes, with several letters to and from Sir Simonds and his friends. 1783
	2793	Autobiography and correspondence of Sir Simonds D'Ewes, Bt., during the reigns of James I and Charles I. *Ed.* by J. O. Hailiwell 2v. 1845. Typescript index by E. Bardswell. 1976
	2794	College life in the times of James I ... an unpublished diary of Sir Symonds D'Ewes ... [*Ed.* by J. H. Marsden]. 1851

2795 Journal of Sir Simonds D'Ewes. New Haven, 1942. BL.
DNB, CBEL. *See also* **6410**

Dewes, S., pseud.
[i.e. *J. St. C. Muriel*]

2796 **Dewes, S.,** *pseud.* Suffolk childhood. 1959

Donne, W. B.

2797 **Johnson, C. B.,** *Ed.* William Bodham Donne and his friends. 1905
DNB. *See also* **2875**

Doughty, C. M.

2798 **Fairley, B.** Charles M. Doughty, a critical study. 1927

2799 **Hogarth, D. G.** Life of Charles M. Doughty. 1928

2800 **Treneer, A.** Charles M. Doughty: a study of his prose and verse. 1935
DNB, CBEL

Dowsing Family

2801 **P.R.P.** Birthplace of Dowsing the Iconoclast—the Dowsings of Laxfield. E Ang 2, 1864/6, 359–62

2802 Dowsings of Stratford [St. Mary]. E Ang NS 1, 1885/8, 172

Dowsing, W.

2803 The will of William Dowsing, Parliamentary Visitor to the Suffolk churches, 1643–4. E Ang NS 1, 1885/6, 138

2804 [**Teasdel, R. H.**] A Suffolk field day: reminiscences of William Dowsing the iconoclast. NNA(GY) 1930, 9–12. NCL/N
DNB. *See also* **779–80**

Drake, N.

2805 Biographical memoir of Nathan Drake, M.D., of Hadleigh. Trans. Provincial Medical and Surgical Assoc. [c.1894]
DNB

Drury Family

2806 **Campling, A.,** *Ed.* History of the family of Drury in the counties of Suffolk and Norfolk from the Conquest ... 1937

2807 **Bald, R. C.** Donne and the Drurys. Cambridge, 1959

Drury, A.

2808 The true and p'fect inventory of all and singular the goods and chattales of the ladye Anne Druere late of Hargate als Hardwick in the county of Suff—weadoye, deceased—seene valued and prised the fifteenth daye of June 1624 ... by William Lucas [*et al.*] [Typescript]. SRO/B

Drury, E.

2809 **Salmon, V.** The other Elizabeth Drury: a tragic marriage in the family of John Donne's patron. PSIA 29, 1961/3, 198–207

Drury, Sir R.

2810 The true and perfect inventorye of all and singular the goodes rights creditts and chattals of Sir Robert Drury Knight, late while he lived of Hawstead in the county of Suff—deceased, seene valued and prised the sixteenth day of April, An Dmi. 1615, by Edward Bacon [*et al.*] [Typescript]. SRO/B. *See also* **5177**

Duleep Singh *See* Singh, *Prince* F. D. V.

Dunthorne Family 2811 **Farrer, E.** Dunthorne MSS (Dunthorne of Denning-ton). PSIA 20, 1928/30, 147–85

Duvall, J. 2812 **Dow, L.** John Duvall of Ipswich. HSLP 18, 1947, 98–9

Eachard, C. 2813 **Dow, L.** Christopher Eachard, Vicar of Cransford. PSIA 25, 1949/51, 306–07

Eadric 2814 **Morley, C.** Eadric of 'Laxfield', the King's falconer. HTM 1, 1923, 114–16

Eccleston, T. 2815 **Pearson, W. C.** Theodore Eccleston of Crowfield Hall. E Ang NS 12, 1907/08, 341–3

Eden Family 2816 **Sperling, C. F. D.** Ballingdon Hall and the Eden family. EAST NS 18, 1928, 169–71

Edgar Family 2817 **Edgar, E.** Ædes Edgarorum: a descriptive catalogue of the portraits at the Red House, in Suffolk, the seat of Mrs. M. G. Edgar. Ipswich, 1868. 30 copies

2818 Genealogical collections concerning the Scottish house of Edgar: with a memoir of James Edgar. *Ed.* by a Committee the Grampian Club. [Edgars of Clemham and Ipswich, 23–25] 1873. SRO/B

2819 Edgar family of the Red House, Ipswich, and their interest in a faculty pew in St. Margaret's church. E Ang NS 10, 1903/04, 118–20

Edge, H. J. F. 2820 **Edge, H. J. F.** Suffolk oak. Ipswich, 1954

Edmund, Saint 2821 **Strickland, A.** The royal Christian martyr: Saint Edmund, the last King of East Anglia. 1870. Rp with foreword by N. Scarfe. Southwold, 1969

2822 **Thompson, J. R.** Records of Saint Edmund of East Anglia, King and martyr. 1890. 1891

2823 **Mackinlay, J. B.** Saint Edmund, King and martyr: a history of his life and times . . . 1893

2824 **Clarke,** *Sir* **E.** The bones of St. Edmund. [Discussing the authenticity of the relics from the basilica of St. Sernin at Toulouse, brought to England in 1901]. Bury St. Edmunds, [1901]. BL

2825 **Hervey,** *Lord* **F.,** *Ed.* Corolla Sancti Eadmundi: the garland of Saint Edmund, King and martyr. 1907

2826 **Gould, I. C.** Greenstead and the course of St. Edmund's translation. EAST NS 10, 1907, 104–07

2827 **Floyd, J. A.** St. Edmund, King and martyr. nd. nl

2828 **Hervey,** *Lord* **F.,** *Ed.* History of King Eadmund the martyr and of the early years of his abbey. Oxford, 1929

2829 **Turner, J.** Saint Edmund: the champion. *In his* Shrouds of glory. 1958. 23–54

2830 **Eccles, A.** A critical edition of Lydgate's life of Saint Edmund, based on Harl. Ms 2278. PhD thesis, London, 1962

2831 **Richardson, L. B.** La vie Seint Aymon; the old French prose version of the life of St. Edmund, King of East Anglia. PhD thesis, Columbia, 1967

2832 **Whitelock, D.** Fact and fiction in the legend of St. Edmund. PSIA 31, 1967/70, 217–33

2833 **Scarfe, N.** The body of St. Edmund: an essay in necrobiography. PSIA 31, 1967/70, 303–17

2834 **Houghton, B.** Saint Edmund—King and martyr. Lavenham, 1970

2835 **Miller, J. I.** Literature to history: exploring a medieval saint's legend and its context. Rp from Monograph Ser 9, University of Tulsa, Dept of English. 1970. SRO/B
DNB. *See also* **4000, 5381–4**

Edwards Family 2836 Edwards of Framlingham. VE&W 1, 1893, 257–64; Notes 3, 87

Edwards, Betham- *See* Betham-Edwards

Eldred, J. 2837 **Scarfe, N.** John Eldred of Great Saxham. PSIA 25, 1949/51, 112–14. *See also* **7225**

Ellis Family 2838 **Ellis, W. S.** Notices of the Ellises of England, Scotland, and Ireland from the Conquest to the present time, including the families Alis, Fitz-Elys, Helles, etc. 4pts. 1857–66

Elliston, R. W. 2839 **Spencer-Cloke, C.** W. R. W. Elliston, comedian of Suffolk. E Ang NS 13, 1909/10, 16, 29
DNB

Elton Family 2840 **Cullum, G. G. M. G.** Family of Elton of Fornham All Saints. E Ang NS 3, 1889/90, 54–5; NS 4, 1891/2, 326–7

Elven, C. 2841 **Ridley, M. S.** "In memoriam", containing a brief sketch of the ministerial life and labours of the late Rev Cornelius Elven. Bury St. Edmunds, 2nd edn 1873 NCL/N

Elwes Family 2842 Genealogical notices relating to the Elwes family. 1867. nl

Elwes, J. 2843 **Topham, E.** Life of the late John Elwes, Esq. 1790. SRO/B

	2844	**Dixon, H. N.,** *Ed.* Reminiscences of an Essex country practitioner a century ago. John Elwes, the Suffolk miser. ER 25, 1916, 73–6, 150, 160 DNB *See also* under Stoke-by-Clare in White's History, gazetteer, and directory of Suffolk, 1844 and 1855
Emlyn, T.	2845	Memoirs of the life and writings of Mr. Thomas Emlyn ... 1746 DNB, CBEL
Ethelbert, Saint	2846	**James, M. R.** Two lives of St. Ethelbert, King and martyr. EHR 32, 1917, 241–4 DNB
Euston		*See* Trumpoor, W.
Evans, Lombe-		*See* Lombe-Evans Family
Ewen Family	2847	Ewen of Raydon Hall. VE&W 1, 1893, 127–8; Notes 2, 120–21
	2848	**Ewen, C. L'Estrange.** The families of Ewen of East Anglia ... 1928
Ewes, Sir S. D'		*See* D'Ewes, *Sir* S.
Fairclough Family	2849	**Partridge, C.** Fairclough family of Stowmarket. E Ang NS 11, 1905/06, 207–08
Fairfax, N.		DNB. *See also* 2353–4
Farmar, H.	2850	**Farmar, H.** Cottage in the forest. 1949
Farrer, E.	2851	**Stevenson, F. S.** In memoriam: Rev Edmund Farrer. PSIA 22, 1934/6, 228–9
Fauconberge, H.	2852	**Rix, S. W.** The Fauconberge memorial: an account of Henry Fauconberge, LL.D., of Beccles, and of the endowment provided by his will to encourage learning and the instruction of youth. Ipswich, 1849
Fawcett, M. G.	2853	**Fawcett, M. G.** What I remember. 1924
	2854	**Strachey, R.** Millicent Garrett Fawcett. 1931 DNB
Felbrigge, T.	2855	**Moriarty, G. A.** English connections of Thomas Felbrigge or Philbrick of Hampton, U.S.A. [Bures St. Mary]. NEH&GR 108, 1954, 252–8
Felix, Saint		DNB
Felton Family	2856	**Hervey,** *Lord* **A.** Playford and the Feltons. PSIA 4, 1864/74, 14–64
Felton, Lady E.	2857	**Browne, A. L.** Lady Elizabeth Felton and her daughters. PSIA 22, 1934/6, 170–77
Felton, M.	2858	Will of Mary Felton of Shotley, 1602. E Ang NS 3, 1889/90, 281–2
Fenn, J.	2859	**Fenn, J.** The Schoolmasters' legacy and family monitor ... Woodbridge, 1843

Firmin, T.   2860   Life of Mr. Thomas Firmin, late citizens of London: [by T. Nye] with a sermon ... preach'd on the occasion of his death ... 1698. Wing N 1508. 2nd edn 1791

              2861   **Cornish, J.** Life of Mr. Thomas Firmin, citizen of London. 1780
                     DNB

Fish, J.   2862   **Hopkins, W.** Funeral discourse delivered in the Independent Chapel, Southwold, on the occasion of the decease of Mr. John Fish, 14 Jan 1862. Beccles, 1862. NCL/N

Fiske Family   2863   **ffiske, H.** Fiske family papers. Norwich, 1902
Fitch, W. S.   2864   **Denney, A. H.** William Stevenson Fitch, 1792–1859. PSIA 28, 1958/60, 109–35
                     DNB. *See also* **502–3**

Fitz-Elys Family   *See* Ellis Family
FitzGerald, E.   2865   Letters and literary remains of Edward FitzGerald. *Ed.* by W. A. Wright. 3v. 1889. 7v. 1902–03

              2866   **Clodd, E.** Concerning a pilgrimage to the grave of Edward FitzGerald. 1894. 50 copies. BL

              2867   **Glyde, J.** Life of Edward FitzGerald. Introduction by E. Clodd. 1900

              2868   More letters of Edward FitzGerald. *Ed.* by W. A. Wright. 1901. BL

              2869   **Prideaux, W. F.** Notes for a bibliography of Edward FitzGerald. 1901

              2870   **Mosher, T. B.** Edward FitzGerald: an aftermath by F. H. Groome ... Portland, Me., 1902

              2871   **Wright, T.** Life of Edward FitzGerald. 2v. 1904

              2872   **Blyth, J.** Edward FitzGerald and "Posh", herring merchants, including a number of letters from Edward FitzGerald to Joseph Fletcher, or "Posh" ... 1908

              2873   Edward FitzGerald, 1809–1909. Centenary celebrations souvenir. Ipswich, 1909

              2874   Some new letters of Edward FitzGerald. *Ed.* by F. R. Barton. 1923

              2875   A FitzGerald friendship: being hitherto unpublished letters from Edward FitzGerald to William Bodham Donne. *Ed.* ... by N. C. Hannay. 1932

              2876   A FitzGerald medley. *Ed.* by C. Ganz. 1933
              2877   **Terhune, A. M.** Life of Edward FitzGerald ... 1947.
              2878   Letters of Edward FitzGerald. *Ed.* by J. M. Cohen. 1960

2879 **Hussey, F.** Old Fitz: Edward FitzGerald and East coast sailing. Ipswich, 1974
DNB, CBEL.
See also **2088, 2506–07, 2797, 2959, 3145**

Fitzroy, A. H. 2880 **Anson,** *Sir,* **W. R.** Autobiography and political
3rd Duke of correspondence of Augustus Henry, Third Duke of
Grafton Grafton: from hitherto unpublished documents in the possession of his family. 1898
DNB

Flatt Family 2881 Flatt of Blaxhall. VE&W 8, 1900, 34
Fletcher, J. ("Posh") *See* FitzGerald, E.
Flory Family 2882 Flory of Bramford. VE&W 1, 1893, 253
Folkard Family 2883 Family of Folkard. E Ang NS 2, 1887, 117–20; NS 5, 1893/4, 121

2884 **Folkard, A. C.** Monograph of the family of Folkard of Suffolk. 3v. [1890–6]

Fonnereau Family 2885 Fonnereau of Ipswich. VE&W 17, 1911, 161–4; Notes 13, 44

Ford, F. 2886 **Phillips, J. S.,** *et al.* Presentation to Mr. Francis Ford, editor of the Bury and Norwich Post, and Suffolk Herald. Bury St. Edmunds, 1883. SRO/B

Ford, J. 2887 Sale catalogue [of household furniture, effects, books, and MSS], 12–14 March 1850. Ipswich
DNB

Foster, H. 2888 Sketch of the life and work of Mr. Harry S. Foster. [M.P. for Lowestoft Division, 1892–1900]. np. nd.
SCL/L

Fox, W. J. 2889 **Garnett, R.** Life of W. J. Fox, public teacher and social reformer, 1786–1864. 1910
DNB

Freeman Family 2890 Freeman of Combs. VE&W 11, 1903, 48–50
2891 Freeman of Saxmundham. VE&W 9, 1901, 9–11
2892 Freeman of Suffolk. VE&W 10, 1902, 120–21
French Family 2893 French of Suffolk. VE&W 17, 1911, 196–8; Notes 13, 64

Frere Family 2894 Parentalia: pedigree of the family of Frere. 1843
2895 **Frere, H.,** *and* **A. H.,** *Eds.* Pedigree of the family of Frere, of Roydon in Norfolk, and Finningham in Suffolk. 1899

2896 **F[rere], J. G.** Frere of Suffolk and Norfolk from 1275–1965. Crowthorne, Berks, [1965]. SCL/L

Freston Family 2897 Freston of Mendham. Frag Gen 13, 1909, 49–54
Frost, G. 2898 George Frost, Feb 1744 to 28 June 1821. 150th

anniversary exhibition, Northgate Gallery, Ipswich. Ipswich, 1971

2899 Sale catalogue [including views of Ipswich and the neighbourhood], 7 June 1839. Ipswich
DNB

Fursey, Saint

2900 **Warren, F. E.** St. Fursey. PSIA 16, 1916/18, 252–77

2901 **Kenney, J. F.** Saint Fursey. *In his* Sources for the early history of Ireland: ecclesiastical. 1929. 500–03. Rp with addenda. Shannon, 1968
DNB. *See also* **4033**

Gage, J.   *See* Rokewode, J. G.

Gainsborough, T.

2902 **Thicknesse, P.** Sketch of the life and paintings of Thomas Gainsborough ... 1788

2903 **Fulcher, G. W.** Life of Thomas Gainsborough ... *Ed.* by his son [E. S. Fulcher]. 1856. 2nd edn 1856

2904 **Grosvenor Gallery, London.** Exhibition of the works of Thomas Gainsborough, R. A., with historical notes by F. G. Stephens. 1885

2905 **Armstrong,** *Sir* **W.** Thomas Gainsborough. 1894. 1905. 1906

2906 Thomas Gainsborough's mother. N&Q 8th Ser 9, 1896, 539; 8th Ser 10, 1896, 58, 105

2907 Gainsborough memorial, Sudbury, Suffolk. 1913. SRO/B

2908 **Whitley, W. T.** Thomas Gainsborough. 1915

2909 **Ipswich Corporation.** Bi-centenary memorial exhibition of Thomas Gainsborough ... 1927. [Catalogue compiled by W. Roberts]. Ipswich, 1927

2910 **Holmes, C.,** *and* **Turner, P. M.** Gainsborough: an exhibition, and discoveries at Ipswich. Burl 51, 1927, 45, 149–50, 239

2911 **Waterhouse, E. M.** Preliminary check list of portraits by Thomas Gainsborough. Walpole Soc. 33. Oxford, 1953. BL

2912 **Waterhouse, E. K.** Gainsborough. 1958

2913 **Gainsborough's House Society.** Gainsborough's House, Sudbury [Guide and catalogue] April 1961. Sudbury, 1961. 1965. SRO/B

2914 Letters of Thomas Gainsborough. *Ed.* by M. Woodall. 1963

2915 **Gainsborough's House Society.** Gainsborough's House: appeal. Chelmsford, 1964

2916 **Ripley, E.** Gainsborough: a biography. 1964

2917 **Leonard, J. N.** World of Gainsborough, 1727–88. New York, 1969

2918 **Williamson, G.** The ingenious Mr. Gainsborough, a biographical study. 1972

2919 **Worman, I.** Thomas Gainsborough: a biography, 1727–88. Lavenham, 1976
DNB. *See also* **2129, 7530**

Gardemau, B.   2920 **Fitch, J. A.** Balthazar Gardemau: a Huguenot squarson and his library. HSLP 20, 1968, 241–72. SRO/B

Gardiner, S.   2921 **Oswald, A.** Stephen Gardiner and Bury St. Edmunds. PSIA 26, 1952/4, 54–7
DNB, CBEL, Emden, 1501–40, 227. *See also* **3497**

Gardner, J.   2922 Will of John Gardner, Bury 1506. PSIA 1, 1848/53, 329–30

Gardner, T.   2923 **Vertue, F. H.** Family of Gardner, the historian of Dunwich. E Ang NS 3, 1889/90, 84–5

Garratt, S.   2924 **Garratt, E. R.** Life and personal recollections of Samuel Garratt, vicar of St. Margaret's, Ipswich, 1867–1895 ... Pt 1. Memoir, by his daughter, E. R. Garratt. Pt 2. Personal recollections by himself. *Ed.* by E. R. Garratt. 1908

Garrett Family   2925 Garrett of Leiston. VE&W 5, 1897, 139–44; Notes 6, 47–51

Gawdy Family   2926 **Royal Commission on Historical Manuscripts.** Ser 11, 10th Report, Append. 2. MSS of the Gawdy family, 1509–1675. 1885. NCL/N

2927 **Pink, W. D.,** *et al.* Gawdy of Crow's Hall [Debenham]. E Ang NS 4, 1891/2, 176, 189–90, 224

2928 **Millican, P.** Gawdys of Norfolk and Suffolk. NA 26, 1935/7, 335–90; 27, 1938/40, 31–93

Gayford, G.   2929 **Fussell, G. E.** George Gayford, 1800–188–, a farmer of the old school [Lackford and Harleston]. SR 1, 1957, 106–09

Gery Family   *See* Wittewronge Family
Gibson Family   *See* Milner-Gibson Family
Gibson, B.   2930 **Cullum, G. G. M. G.,** *and* **Muskett, J. J.** Barnaby Gibson of Suffolk. E Ang NS 3, 1889/90, 151, 199

Gilbert Family   2931 **Thompson, S. P.** Family and arms of Gilbert of Colchester. EAST 9, 1906, 197–211
See also Ray Family

Gillingwater, E.   2932 **Titlow, S.,** *and* **Curtis, C.** Gillingwater, the historian of Lowestoft. E Ang 4, 1869/70, 253–5, 276
DNB

Gipps, Sir R.   DNB. *See also* **2355**
Girling, A.   *See* Gyrlyng, A.
Glanfield Family   *See* Glanville Family

Glanusk Family		*See* Bailey Family
Glanville Family	2933	**Glanville-Richards, W. U. S.** Records of the Anglo-Norman house of Glanville from 1050 to 1880. 1882. BL
	2934	**Pearson, W. C.** Extracts from parish registers: family of Glanville or Glanfield. E Ang NS 5, 1893/4, 314–15
Glemham, E.	2935	The honourable actions of that most famous and valiant Englishman, Edward Glenham [Glemham], Esquire, latelie obtained against the Spaniards, and the Holy League, in foure sundrie fightes ... 1591. STC 11921. Rp 1820. BL DNB
Glenham, E.		*See* Glemham, E.
Glover Family	2936	Glover family of Frostenden. E Ang NS 5, 1893/4, 68
Glyde, J.	2937	John Glyde. EADT 15 June 1905. *See also* **506, 5600**
Goddard Family	2938	**Hollis, H.** The family memorial: an affectionate tribute to the memory of Mr. Daniel Poole Goddard, his beloved wife, and youngest daughter. [1846]
Godolphin, Mrs.	2939	**Evelyn, J.** Life of Mrs. Godolphin. *Ed.* by Samuel [Wilberforce], Lord Bishop of Oxford. 1847. 1938, *Ed.* by H. Simpson DNB
Godwin, W.	2940	**Paul, C. K.** William Godwin: his friends and contemporaries. 2v. 1876 DNB, CBEL
Golty Family		*See* Framlingham (*locality*). Danforth
Gooch Family	2941	**Johnson, F.** The Gooch pedigree. Ilketshall St. Margaret's. E Ang NS 4, 1891/2, 186–7
Gooch, Sir T.		DNB. *See also* **905–6**
Gooding Family		*See* Goodwin Family
Goodricke Family	2942	**Goodricke, C. A.,** *Ed.* History of the Goodricke family. 1885. BL
Goodwin Family	2943	**Jessopp, A.** The Goodwins of East Anglia. Norwich, 1889. NCL/N
	2944	Goodwins of Hartford, Connecticut, descendants of William and Ozias Goodwin. By various writers. 1891. Includes The Goodwins of East Anglia, by A. Jessopp. 1–74
	2945	**Pearson, W. C.** Extracts from parish registers: Stonham Parva, Westerfield, Great Blakenham. E Ang NS 4, 1891/2, 198–9
Gosford, Earl of		*See* Acheson Family
Gosnold Family	2946	**Lea, J. H.** Gosnold and Bacon. The ancestry of

Bartholomew Gosnold. Boston, Mass., 1904. Lib. of Congress.

2947 **Gookin, W. F.** Gosnold family. Rp from Virginia Mag. of Hist. and Biog. 57, 1949, 307–15

2948 **Gookin, W. F.** Family connections of Bartholomew Gosnold. NEH&GR 104, 1950, 27–36; 105, 1951, 5–22

2949 **Carney, D.** Origins of the Gosnold family. SR 3, no 1, 1965, 25–30

Gosnold, B.   2950 **Gookin, W. F.** Who was Bartholomew Gosnold? William and Mary Quarterly, 3rd Ser 6, 1949, 398–415

Grafton, 3rd Duke of   *See* Fitzroy, A. H., *3rd Duke of* Grafton

Gray.   2951 **Gray, S.,** *Ed.* Gray of Bradfield, a memoir. 1931. SRO/B

Green Family   2952 [Notice of the family of] Green of Worlingworth, Suffolk. Woodbridge, [1835?]. BL

Green, T.   2953 **Green, T.** Extracts from a diary of a lover of literature. Ipswich, 1810

2954 Memoir of T. Green ... of Ipswich, with a critique on his writings, and an account of his family and connections. [Signed J. F., i.e. Rev James Ford]. Ipswich, 1825. 100 copies
DNB

Grey, De   *See* De Grey Family

Grigg, W.   2955 Life and humorous adventures of W. G. [William Grigg] of Snarlton in Suffolk. Being a true history of many curious, memorable, and extraordinary exploits. Published from the original manuscript preserved in the Grub-street Vatican. By a Native of Grub-street. Pt 1. 1773. BL

Griggs Family   *See* Powell Family
Grimston, E.   DNB

Grimwade, E.   2956 In memoriam—Edward Grimwade, born 26 Aug 1812, died 25 Nov 1886. [Press notices and funeral sermon]. 1887

Groome Family   2957 Groome of Earl and Monk Soham. VE&W 5, 1897, 21–22; Notes 5, 177–9

Groome, R. H.   2958 **Groome, F. H.** Suffolk parson. Blackwood's Edinburgh Mag. 149, 1891, 309–32

2959 **Groome, F. H.** Two Suffolk friends [Being recollections of R. H. Groome and Edward FitzGerald]. Edinburgh, 1895
DNB. *See also* **2865–79**

Grubbe Family	2960	Grubbe of Southwold. VE&W 1, 1893, 27–32; Notes 1, 89–100
	2961	Genealogical memoranda relating to the Grubbe Family. 1893
Guild, G.	2962	**Cunningham, F.** Funeral sermon on the death of Mr. G. Guild ... Lowestoft, 1818. BL
Guinness, E. C. **1st Earl of Iveagh**	2963	**G, H. T.** Earl of Iveagh. PSIA 19, 1925/7, 365. [Elveden]
Gurdon Family	2964	.Gurdon of Assington and Grundisburgh (Baron Cranworth). VE&W 10, 1902, 89–97; 17, 1911, 121–123; Notes 9, 106–16. *See also* **751, 7535**
Gurdon, Lady *E. C.*	2965	Gurdon, *Lady* E. C. Memories and fancies. 1897
Gurdon, J.		DNB
Gurnall, W.	2966	**Burkitt, W.** The people's zeal provok't to an holy emulation, by the ... example of their dead minister; or, A seasonable memento to the parishioners of Lavenham ... a sermon preached to that people, soon after the interment of their Rev.... Minister, Mr. William Gurnall ... 1680. Wing B 5737 SRO/B
	2967	**Burkitt, W.** A sermon preached [to the parishioners of Lavenham] ... soon after the solemn interment of ... Wm Gurnall, who, aged 63, died Oct 12, 1679, and now at their request made publick. 1829
	2968	**McKeon, H.** Inquiry into the birth-place, parentage, life, and writings of the Rev William Gurnall, M.A., formerly rector of Lavenham, with a sketch of the life of Rev Wm. Burkitt. Woodbridge, 1829 DNB. *See also* **6396**
Gwydyr, **Baron**		*See* Burrell Family
Gyrlyng, A.	2969	**Rayson, G.** Old wills: Agnes Gyrlyng, of Fressingfield, 1521. E Ang 4, 1869/70, 47
Hake, T. G.	2970	**Hake, T. G.** Memoirs of eighty years. 1892. BL
Hakluyt, R.	2971	**Lillie, W. W.** Hakluyt of Wetheringsett. PSIA 22, 1934/6, 225–7 DNB
Hanmer, **Sir** *T.*	2972	**Hervey, T.** Letter ... to Sir T. Hanmer, Bart. [On his conduct towards Lady Hanmer, etc.]. [1741]. SRO/B
	2973	Correspondence of Sir T. H., Bart. with a memoir of his life. To which are added other relicks of a gentleman's [the Bunbury] family. *Ed.* by Sir H. Bunbury. 1838 DNB
Hannah, J.	2974	**Hannah, J.** Posthumous rhymes. [With an intro-

ductory memoir signed S.W.R[ix]. Beccles, 1854

Harmer Family 2975 **Fennemore, E. F.,** *and* **Harmer, H. J.** Biographical sketches of the Harmer family of Randwick, Gloucestershire, and Ipswich, Suffolk. 1921

Harris, J. 2976 **Harris, J.** Probation: a sheaf of memories. Thirty-four years' work in local police courts ... Lowestoft, 1937. SCL/L

Harvey, James 2977 **Harvey, A. J.** From Suffolk lad to London merchant: a sketch of the life of James Harvey. Bristol, 1900

Harvey, John 2978 **Harvey, B. S.** An eighteenth-century smuggler [John Harvey] PSIA 22, 1934/6, 153–4

Haslewood, F. 2979 **Haslewood, F. G.** Rev Francis Haslewood. PSIA 10, 1898/1900, 360–65

Hasted Family *See* Ray Family

Havens Family 2980 Havens family. Frag Gen 8, 1902, 70–71

Hawes, R. DNB

Hayles, W. 2981 **Golding, C.** Will of William Hayles the elder, of Sutton. E Ang 3, 1866/8, 293–5

Hayward, Sir J. 2982 **Scarfe, N.** Sir John Hayward [of Felixstowe], an Elizabethan historian. PSIA 25, 1949/51, 79–97 DNB, CBEL

Head, M. *See* Brand Family

Heigham Family 2983 Pedigree of the Heigham family ... of Wetherden, in the county of Suffolk. [Ed. by C. P. Heigham.] Lowestoft, 1876 *See also* Ray Family

Helles Family *See* Ellis Family

Henniker, A. 2984 **Henniker, F.** Arthur Henniker: a little book for his friends. 1912. SRO/B

Henslow, J. S. 2985 Biographical sketch of J.S.H. 1861. BL

2986 **Jenyns,** *afterwards* **Blomefield, L.** Memoir of the Rev John Stevens Henslow, M.A., etc., late rector of Hitcham and Professor of Botany in the University of Cambridge. 1862

2987 **Henslow, G.** A scientific Suffolk clergyman. ECM 1, 1900/01; 2, 1901/02, *passim*

2988 **Fussell, G. E.** Professor first, parson later. SR 3, 1968, 221–2 DNB

Hervey Family 2989 **Hervey,** *Lord* **A.** Family of Hervey. PSIA 2, 1852/1859, 291–427

2990 [**Hervey, S. H. A.**] Hervey, first Bishop of Ely, and some others of the same name, 1050–1500. Ipswich, 1923. SGB 19

	2991	**Hervey, S. H. A.** Dictionary of Herveys, of all classes, callings, counties, and spelling, from 1040–1500. Ipswich, 1924–9. 5v. SGB 20
	2992	**MacCarthy, M. J.** Fighting Fitzgerald and other papers. [Includes John, Lord Hervey; Frederick Hervey, 4th Earl of Bristol]. 1930
	2993	**Ponsonby, D. A.** Call a dog Hervey ... [1949]. *See also* **5420–37**
Hervey, Lord A. C.	2994	In memoriam: Arthur Charles Hervey ... Rp from Times, 1894. SRO/B
	2995	**Hervey, J. F. A.** Memoir of Lord Arthur Hervey, D.D., Bishop of Bath and Wells. np. 1896
Hervey, A. J. 3rd Earl of Bristol	2996	Augustus Hervey's journal: being an intimate account of the life of a captain in the Royal Navy ashore and afloat, 1746–1759. *Ed.* by D. Erskine. 1953 DNB
Hervey, Lord F.	2997	H[ervey], S. H. A. Lord Francis Hervey. PSIA 20, 1928/30, 318–19
Hervey, F. A., 4th Earl of Bristol	2998	**Childe-Pemberton, W. S.** The Earl Bishop: the life of Frederick Hervey, Bishop of Derry, Earl of Bristol ... 2v. 1925. SRO/B
	2999	**Fothergill, B.** The mitred earl: an eighteenth-century eccentric. 1974 DNB
Hervey, H.	3000	**Grey,** *Earl.* Hubert Hervey: student and imperialist —a memoir. 1899
Hervey, J., 1st Earl of Bristol	3001	Letter books of John Hervey, first Earl of Bristol, ... with Sir Thomas Hervey's letters during courtship ... 1651–1750. [*Ed.* by S. H. A. H(ervey)]. 3v. 1894. SGB 1
	3002	Diary of John Hervey, first Earl of Bristol. With extracts from his Book of Expenses, 1688 to 1742 ... [*Ed.* by S. H. A. H(ervey)]. 1894. SGB 2 DNB
Hervey, J. Baron Hervey of Ickworth *(1696–1743)*	3003	Some materials toward memoirs of the reign of King George II. *Ed.* by R. Sedgwick. 3v. 1931
	3004	Memoirs of the reign of George II from his accession to the death of Queen Caroline ... from the original MS at Ickworth. *Ed.* by J. W. Croker. 2v. 1848. 1855. 3v. 1884
	3005	Lord Hervey and his friends 1726–38. Based on letters from Holland House, Melbury, and Ickworth. *Ed.* by the Earl of Ilchester. 1950

3006 Lord Hervey's memoirs. *Ed.* by R. Sedgwick. 1952. SRO/B

3007 **Halsband, R.** Lord Hervey: eighteenth-century courtier. Oxford, 1973. BL
DNB, CBEL

Hervey, Lord J. 3008 **Gurdon,** *Sir* **W. B.** Lord John Hervey. PSIA 11,
(1841–1901) 1901/03, 149–51

Hervey, Lady M. 3009 Letters of Mary Lepel, Lady Hervey: with a memoir and illustrative notes. *Ed.* by J. W. Croker. 1821

3010 **Stuart, D. M.** Molly Lepel, Lady Hervey. 1936
DNB

Hervey, Sir N. 3011 **Hervey,** *Lord* **A.** Sir Nicholas Hervey, Knt. PSIA 3,
1860/63, 315–20

Hervey, T. 3012 Mr. Hervey's letter to the Rev Sir W. Bunbury, Bart. [A challenge]. [1753]. SRO/B
DNB

Hervey, Sir T. *See* Hervey, *Lord* J., 1st Earl of Bristol

Hervey, Hon W. 3013 Journals of the Hon. William Hervey, in North America and Europe, from 1755–1814 ... With memoir and notes. [*Ed.* by S. H. A. H(ervey)]. Bury St. Edmunds, 1906. SGB 14

Hervey, Lord W. 3014 **De B[illing], M.** Notice nécrologique sur Lord William Hervey. Paris, 1850. SRO/B

Heryng, J. 3015 **Tymms, S.** Will of John Heryng, 1419 [Bury St. Edmunds]. PSIA 1, 1858/53, 165–6

Hewett Family 3016 **Partridge, C. S.** Hewett or Hewitt of Suffolk. E Ang NS 5, 1893/4, 271

Hewitt, R. 3017 Memoirs and vicissitudes of the life of R.H. ... [of Wickham Market]. [1835]. BL

Heynes, S. 3018 Grant of arms by Robert Cooke, Clarenceux, to Simon Heynes of Mildenhall, co. Suffolk, gentleman, 1575. MGetH 1, 1868, 250–51

Heyrouns Family 3019 **Redstone, V. B.,** *and* **L. J.** Heyrouns of London. Speculum 12, 1937, 182–95. *See also* **2640–41**

Hitchman, Sir R. 3020 Extracts from the will of Sir R. Hitchman. Ipswich, [1820?] BL

3021 A copy of the will of Sir R. Hitchman. Framlingham, 1863. nl
DNB. *See also* **4978, 5015**

Holmes Family 3022 Holmes of Fressingfield. VE&W 19, 1917, 204–05; Notes 14, 126–7

Hooker Family 3023 **Geldart, A. M.** The Hookers in Norfolk and Suffolk. TNNS 13, 1929/34, 87–105

	3024	**Allan, M.** The Hookers of Kew, 1785–1911. 1967
Hooker, Sir J. D.	3025	**Huxley, L.** Life and letters of Sir Joseph Dalton Hooker. Based on materials collected and arranged by Lady Hooker. 2v. 1918
	3026	**Bower, F. O.** Joseph Dalton Hooker. 1919
	3027	**Turrill, W. B.** Joseph Dalton Hooker. [1963]. BL DNB, CBEL
Hooker, Sir W. J.	3028	**Allan, M.** Beer and botany: the Suffolk years of Sir William Jackson Hooker (1785–1865). TSNS 14, 1968/9, 175–81 DNB, CBEL
Hopton Family	3029	**Rutton, W. L.** Notes to the pedigree of Hopton of Suffolk and Somerset. MGetH Ser 3, 1900, 9–12, 49–53, 81–6
	3030	**Hopton, M.** Froma Canonica; or, The history of Canon Frome and the Hopton family . . . 1902. BL
Horne, C. S.	3031	**Selbie, W. B.,** *Ed.* Life of Charles Silvester Horne, M.A., M.P. [1920]
Horsfield, G. W.	3032	Letters from Whitton Lodge [Ipswich] from Mrs. Horsfield . . . to Mrs. Schiefflin of Geneva, New York, an American relation. 1947. nl
Howard Family	3033	**Howard, C.** *10th Duke* of Norfolk. Historical anecdotes of some of the Howard family. 1769. 1817
	3034	Analysis of the genealogical history of the family of Howard, with its connections. 1812. BL
	3035	**Howard, H.** Indications of memorials, monuments, paintings, and engravings of persons of the Howard family. Corby Castle. 2v. 1834–6. BL
	3036	**Causton, H. K. S.** The Howard papers, with a biographical pedigree and criticism. [1862]
	3037	**Brenan, G.,** *and* **Statham, E. P.** House of Howard. 2v. 1907. BL
	3038	**Richardson, E. M. E.** Lion and the rose: the great Howard story. Suffolk line, 1603–1917. 2v. [1922]. *See also* **5005–09**
Howard, J. *1st* **Duke of Norfolk**	3039	Household books of John, Duke of Norfolk, and Thomas, Earl of Surrey: temp. 1481–1490. *Ed.* by J. P. Collier. SRO/B. DNB
Howard, T. *4th* **Duke of Norfolk**	3040	**Williams, N. J.** Thomas Howard, fourth Duke of Norfolk. 1964
	3041	Funeral of Thomas Howard, Duke of Norfolk. [Framlingham]. E Ang 1, 1858/63, 15
	3042	**Mander, R. P.** Funeral of Thomas Howard, victor

of Flodden. EAM 8, 1948/9, 431–6
DNB

Howe, J.
4th Baron
Chedworth

3043 **Crompton, T.**, *Ed*. Letters from the late Lord Chedworth to the Rev Thomas Crompton. 1828
DNB

Hoxton Family

3044 **Reid, L. W.** The English ancestry of the Hoxtons of Maryland and Virginia. [Sotherton]. Virginia Mag of Hist and Biog 60, no 1, 1952

Hunnings Family

3045 **Foster,** *Sir* **W. E.** Pedigree of the families of Newcomen and Hunnings of co. Lincoln. Exeter, 1903. BL

3046 **Foster,** *Sir* **W. E.** Some notes on the families of Hunnings of South Lincolnshire, London, and Suffolk. Exeter, 1912. BL

Hunt Family

3047 Hunt of Culpho. VE&W 11, 1903, 105–09

Hurn, W.

3048 **Cooke, E.,** *and* **Rouse, E.** Brief memorials of William Hurn, late minister at the chapel, Woodbridge, formerly vicar of Debenham. 1831

3049 **Carey,** *Mrs., and* **Rouse, E.** Brief memorials of William Hurn, by his nieces. [With appendices by "Silverpen", *pseud*. (i.e. J. Glyde)]. 1878. nl. *See also* **2007**

3050 **Olorenshaw, J. R.** Rev William Hurn, vicar of Debenham, 1790–1823, and afterwards Baptist minister at Woodbridge. E Ang NS 10, 1903/04, 290

Hutchins, M. A.

3051 **Middleditch, T.** The youthful female missionary: a memoir of Mary Anne Hutchins . . . Compiled chiefly from her own correspondence by her father. 1840

Inchbald, E.

3052 **Boaden, J.,** *Ed*. Memoirs of Mrs Inchbald . . . 2v. 1833
DNB, CBEL

Ingelow, J.

3053 **Ingelow, J.** Some recollections of Jean Ingelow and her early friends. 1901. Rp Port Washington, N.Y., 1972

3054 **Peters, M.** Jean Ingelow: Victorian poetess. Ipswich, 1972
CBEL

Isaac, M.

3055 **Davis, W. G.** Ancestry of Mary Isaac, c.1549–1613, wife of Thomas Appleton of Little Waldingfield, co. Suffolk, and mother of Samuel Appleton of Ipswich, Massachusetts. Portland, Me., 1955. BL

Isaack Family

3056 **Cullum, G. G. M. G.** Isaack of Hitcham, co. Suffolk. MGetH 3rd Ser 3, 1900, 56–9, 76–80

Isham Family

3057 Isham family. E Ang NS 2, 1887/8, 141, 174, 192; NS 4, 1891/2, 250; NS 5, 1893/4, 151–2, 216–17

Iveagh, 1st Earl of

See Guinness, E. C.

Ives, J. 3058 **Turner, D.** Memoir [of John Ives], prefixed to 2nd edn. of Remarks upon the Garianonum of the Romans, by John Ives. Gt. Yarmouth, 1803

3059 **Scarfe, N.** John Ives, Suffolk Herald Extraordinary, 1751–76. PSIA 33, 1973/5, 299–309

3060 Sale catalogue. Library of J. Ives ... [London], [1777]. BL
DNB

Jackson Family 3061 **Cullum, G. G. M. G.** Jackson of Bury St. Edmunds. MGetH 3rd Ser 3, 1900, 56–9, 76–80

Jackson, C. 3062 Narrative of the sufferings and escape of C.J., late resident at Wexford, in Ireland. [Sudbury]. Cambridge, 3rd edn 1803

James Family 3063 **C, R. C.** Family of James, of London, Essex, Kent, Suffolk, and Surrey. E Ang 1, 1858/63, 330–31

James M. R. 3064 **James, M. R.** Eton and King's. Recollections mostly trivial, 1875–1925. 1926

3065 **Lubbock, S. G.** Memoir of Montague Rhodes James ... with a list of his writings by A. F. Scholfield. Cambridge, 1939

3066 **Gaselee, S.** Montague Rhodes James. Proc Brit Acad 22, 1936, 418–31
DNB, CBEL

Jancks *See* Tettrell, J.

Jarvis, K. 3067 **Jarvis, K.** Impressions of a parson's wife. [Great and Little Bealings]. 1951

3068 **Jarvis, K.** Nightingale in the sycamore. [Great and Little Bealings]. 1953. SRO/B

Jay Family 3069 **Jay, G. B.** *and* **Muskett, J. J.** Jay of Suffolk. E Ang NS 1, 1885/6, 15, 31–2, 77–8, 135

Jeaffreson Family 3070 Jeaffreson of Framlingham. VE&W 2, 1894, 52–3; Notes 4, 59–63

3071 **Jeaffreson, M. T.** Pedigree of the Jeaffreson family, with notes and memoirs. 1922. BL

Jeaffreson, C. 3072 A young squire of the seventeenth century: from the papers (1676–1686) of C.J. ... *Ed.* by J. C. Jeaffreson, etc. 2v. 1878

Jeaffreson, J. C. 3073 **Jeaffreson, J. C.** Book of recollections. 2v. 1894

Jennens Family 3074 **A, R.** Arms of Jennens. E Ang 4, 1869/70, 252

3075 **Jennens, W.** The Jennens case. Statement of facts in connection with the pedigree of W. Jennens ... with notes relating to the pedigree of the persons in possession of the estate of the deceased. [1874]. BL

3076 **Harrison, [W.** *and* **T.],** *and* **Willis, [G.]** *Eds.* The great Jennens case: being an epitome of the history of the Jennens family. Sheffield, 1879

Jenney Family   3077   Jenney of Knoddishall. E Ang NS 4, 1891/2, 224, 240

3078   **Jennings, H. W.,** *Ed.* Jenney family of Norfolk and Suffolk in England. 1965. [Typescript]. NCL/N

Jermy Family   *See* Jermyn Family

Jermyn Family   3079   Families of Jermyn and Jermy of Suffolk. E Ang 1, 1858/63, 58

3080   Jermyn of Halesworth. VE&W 3, 1895, 170–73; Notes 5, 57–8

3081   **Valdar, S.** Brief history of the Jermy family of Norfolk and Suffolk. 1958. [Typescript]. NCL/N. *See also* **6066, 7204**

Jermyn, G. B.   DNB. *See also* **2343, 2362–3**

Jermyn, H.   3082   [Statement respecting the affairs of H. Jermyn (of Sibton, Suffolk) and J.J., etc.]. MS notes [by D. E. Davy]. Halesworth, [1827?]. BL
DNB. *See also* **500**

Jermyn, Sir T.   3083   **Pink, W. D.** [Sir Thomas] Jermyn of Rushbrooke, M.P. for Bury St. Edmunds, 1621–44. E Ang NS 6, 1895/6, 159–60

Johnson Family   3084   Johnson of Aldborough. E Ang NS 3, 1889/90, 198, 214

Johnson, I.   3085   [**Lingwood, H. R.**] Isaac Johnson. EADT 5 and 12 May 1934. *See also* **2337**

Jones Family   3086   Jones of Pakenham. VE&W 1, 1893, 286–7

Jones, W.   3087   **Stevens, W.** Short account of the life and writings of the Rev W.J. [An extract from the edition of Jones's works, 1801]. [1801]. BL
DNB

Josselyn Family   3088   **Josselyn, J. H.** Genealogical history of the ancient family of Josselyn of Horksley, in the county of Essex. Ipswich, 1880. BL

3089   Josselyn of Ipswich. VE&W 2, 1894, 42–3; Notes 4, 32–49

3090   **Josselyn, J. H.** Genealogical record of Frederick Browne Bell, of Downham Market, Norfolk, and of George Josselyn, of Ipswich, traced back from the 20th to the 8th century. 1901. nl

3091   **Josselyn, J. H.** Genealogical memoranda relating to the family of Josselyn. 1903

Keble Family   3092   **Partridge, C. S.** Keble of Suffolk. E Ang NS 5, 1893/4, 248

	3093	**Muskett, J. J.** Keble arms in Tuddenham church. E Ang NS 11, 1905/06, 241
Keene, C. S.	3094	**Layard, G. S.** Life and letters of Charles Samuel Keene. 1892. 1893
	3095	**Hudson, D.** Charles Keene. 1947 DNB
Kemball Family	3096	**Partridge, C. S.** Kemball of Suffolk. E Ang NS 4, 1891/2, 276; NS 5, 1893/4, 210–11; NS 6, 1895/6, 366–7
Kemp Family	3097	**Hitchen-Kemp, F.** General history of the Kemp and Kempe families ... 1902. BL
Kerridge Family	3098	**Partridge, C. S.** Kerridge of Shelley Hall, Suffolk. E Ang NS 6, 1895/6, 89–91
Kettle Family	3099	**Kettle of Suffolk.** E Ang NS 6, 1895/6, 256, 352; NS 7, 1897/8, 63, 176; NS 8, 1899/1900, 111; NS 10, 1903/04, 63, 96
King, W.	3100	**Mercer, T. W.** Dr. William King and "The Co-operator," 1828–30. Manchester, 1922
	3101	**Pollard, S.** Dr. William King of Ipswich: a Co-operative pioneer. Co-operative College Papers 6, April 1959, 17–33. DNB
Kingsbury Family	3102	**Kingsbury of Suffolk.** E Ang NS 2, 1888/9, 287, 308
Kirby, J.	3103	**John Kirby, 1690–1763.** [Typescript]. SRO/B DNB
Kirby, W.	3104	**Freeman, J.** Life of the Rev William Kirby, M.A. ... rector of Barham. 1852 DNB
Kitchener Family	3105	**Kitchener of Suffolk.** VE&W 7, 1899, 1–16; Notes 6, 206–13. See also **6379**
Kitchin, G. W.		DNB
Knight, J.	3106	**Calvert, E. M.,** *and* **R. T. C.** Sergeant Surgeon: John Knight, Surgeon General 1664–80. 1939
Lane Family	3107	**Craig, A. T.** Pedigree of Lane of Campsea Ash. MGetH 5th Ser 2, 1916/17, 57
Lanseter, J.	3108	**Morton, A. L.** John Lanseter of Bury. PSIA 28, 1958/60, 29–53
Last, J.	3109	**Storr, F.** The Christian farmer, a memoir of Mr. John Last, of Otley, Suffolk. 1855
Latymer, E.	3110	**Wheatley, W.** History of Edward Latymer and his Foundation. Cambridge, 1936. Rev edn. 1953 DNB
Launce Family	3111	**Fella, T.** A memorable note wherein is conteyned the names in part of the cheefest kindred of Robert

Launce, late of Meetfield in the county of Suffolk: deceased. Collected ... by Thomas Fella of Hallisworth. 1902

Lawes Family   *See* Wittewronge Family

Layard, N. F.   3112 **Stevenson, F. S.** In memoriam: Miss Nina Frances Layard. PSIA 22, 1934/6, 228–9

Lebbard, W.   3113 **Dulley, M.** Old wills: Walter Lebbard of Worlingham, 1514. E Ang 3, 1866/8, 81–2

Lee Family   3114 **Suckling, F. H.** Lee Family of Lawshall. Gen NS 23, 1906, 137–43, 271–2

Leedes, E.   DNB

Legatt, R.   3115 Old wills: Richard Legatt of Dennington, 1485. E Ang 3, 1866/8, 33–4

Le Hemp Family   *See* Wittewronge Family

Leman Family   3116 **S, F. H.** Leman family of Suffolk. E Ang NS 11, 1905/06, 84–6

Lennox, Lady *S.*   3117 **Fox-Strangways, M.,** *and* **G.** Life and letters of Lady Sarah Lennox, 1745–1826 ... 1901. SRO/B

    3118 **Curtis, E. R.** Lady Sarah Lennox: an irrepressible Stuart, 1745–1826. 1947
        DNB

Lepel, M.   *See* Hervey, *Lady* M.

Lewkenor, Sir *E.*   3119 **Carter, B.** The wise king and learned judge, in a sermon lamenting the death of Sir Edward Lewkenor. [Cambridge], 1618. STC 4693. BL

    3120 **Oldmayne, T.** God's rebuke in taking from us Sir E. Lewkenor. 1619. STC 18805. O

    3121 **Oldmayne, T.** Life's brevitie and death's debility. Evidently declared in a sermon preached at the funerall of Sir E. Lewkenor. 1636. STC 18806. BL

Light, F.   3122 **Clodd, H. P.** Malaya's first British pioneer: the life of Francis Light ... 1948

    3123 **Tye, W.** Francis Light of Dallinghoo. SR 2, 1964, 232–9

Light, W.   3124 **Mayo, M. P.** Life and letters of Col. William Light. Adelaide, 1937
        DNB

Lillingstone Family   3125 Lillingstone of Ipswich. VE&W 9, 1901, 33–40

Lincolne, W.   3126 **Lincolne, W.** Collections and recollections of the late Mr. William Lincolne of Halesworth, Suffolk, with a sketch of the last hours of Mrs. Lincolne. By one of their sons. 1848

Lofft, C.   3127 Particulars relative to the life of Capel Lofft, Esq., communicated by himself. Monthly Mirror, June 1802. [Troston]

	3128	**Hawes, H.** Capel Lofft: some genealogical notes. SR 3, 1966, 86–90 DNB. *See also* **945**
Lombe-Evans Family	3129	Lombe-Evans of Suffolk. VE&W 19, 1917, 85–90; Notes 14, 42–9
Lovel Family	3130	**Pearson, W. C.** List of kinsfolk … of Richard Lovel of Needham Market … E Ang NS 4, 1891/2, 259–62
Lydgate, J.	3131	**Greene, J.** John Lydgate, monk of Bury. PSIA 10, 1898/1900, 7–18
	3132	**Schirmer, W. F.** John Lydgate: ein Kulturbild aus dem 15. Jahrhundert. Tübingen, 1952. 1961 English edn. trans. by A. E. Keep. SRO/B
	3133	**Pearsall, D. A.** John Lydgate. 1970 DNB, CBEL, Emden, to 1500, 2, 1185–6
Macro Family	3134	**Clarke,** *Sir* **E.** The last of the Macros. Rp from Bury Free Press, 29 April 1916. Bury St. Edmunds, 1916. SRO/B
Malet Family	3135	**Malet, A.** Notices of an English branch of the Malet family … 1885. BL
Malkin, B. H.		DNB
Malyn Family		*See* Chaucer Family
Manning, C. R.	3136	**Raven, J. J.** Canon C. R. Manning. PSIA 10, 1898/1900, 144–9
Manwood Family	3137	Manwood family. E Ang NS 6, 1895/6, 208, 320; NS 7, 1897/8, 48; NS 10, 1903/04, 31–2, 339; NS 11, 1905/06, 31, 240
Marshe, R.	3138	**Deedes, C.** Will of Robert Marshe of Bromeswell, 1526. E Ang NS 2, 1887/8, 233–4
Martin Family	3139	**Partridge, C. S.** Martin of Suffolk. E Ang NS 5, 1893/4, 87
Martin, T.	3140	[**Ives, J.**] Pastoral elegy on the death of Thomas Martin, Esq., F.S.A., of Palgrave in Suffolk. Great Yarmouth, 1772
	3141	**Fenn,** *Sir* **J.** Thomas Martin. MS. NRO DNB
Mason Family	3142	Mason of Ipswich. VE&W 15, 1908, 132–6; Notes 12, 31
Mason, F.	3143	**Wayman, H. W. B.** The Venerable Francis Mason, rector of Sudbourne-cum-Orford. A tercentenary memoir. PSIA 17, 1919/21, 151–62

3144   **Williams, J. F.** Francis Mason of Orford. PSIA 27, 1955/7, 54
       DNB

Matthews, T. R.   3145   **Wright, T.** Life of the Rev Timothy Richard Matthews, friend of Edward FitzGerald. 1934

Maurice, F. D.   3146   **Maurice,** *Sir* **J. F.** Life of Frederick Denison Maurice, chiefly told in his own letters. *Ed.* by his son, F. Maurice. 2v. 1884. BL
       DNB, CBEL

Maw, T.   3147   **Maw, L.** Tribute to the memory of Thomas Maw, by his widow, 1850

Meadowe, D.   3148   **Pearson, W. C.** Daniel Meadowe, sometime of Chattisham Hall. E Ang NS 5, 1893/4, 49–50

Meadows Family   3149   **Partridge, C. S.** Meadow of Suffolk. E Ang NS 5, 1893/4, 48

       3150   **Meadows, S. M. W.** Witnesham and the Meadows family. 1949–50. [Typescript]

       3151   **Sayer, F. D.** Meadows family of Witnesham and Norwich. 1971. [Typescript]. NCL/N

Meadows, J.   3152   **Taylor, E.** The Suffolk Bartholomeans: a memoir of the ministerial and domestic history of John Meadows, clk., A.M., ... ejected under the Act of Uniformity from the rectory of Ousden in Suffolk. 1840
       DNB

Melford, J.   *See* Reve, J.

Meller Family   3153   Meller of Suffolk. VE&W 7, 1899, 153–5; Notes 7, 119–20

Methold Family   3154   Methold of Hepworth House. VE&W 1, 1893, 145–147; Notes 3, 22

Middleton Family   3155   **Pearson, W. C.** Middletons of Crowfield Hall, afterwards of Shrubland Hall. E Ang NS 4, 1891/2, 77

       3156   **Cullum, G. G. M. G.** Myddleton family. MGetH 3rd Ser 2, 1898, 49, 66, 213, 261

Mighells Family   3157   **Lees, H. D. W.** Worthies of Lowestoft: Mighells family. LA&LHS 1969/70, 11–19

Mills, J.   3158   [**Mills, J.**]. From the plough tail to the college steps: being the first twenty-one years of the life of a Suffolk farmer's boy, an autobiography. 1885. BL

Milner-Gibson Family   3159   Milner-Gibson of Theberton. VE&W 1, 1893, 150–51

Milner-Gibson, T.   3160   [**Prémilly, J. de**]. Tablettes biographiques ... [Life of the Rt. Hon. Thomas Milner-Gibson]. Paris, 1884. SRO/B
       DNB

Minter Family	3161	Minter of Barham and Tuddenham. Frag Gen 10, 1904, 68–9
Mitford, J.	3162	**Houstoun, M. C.** Sylvanus Redivivus, the Rev. J. Mitford … 1889. 1891. SRO/B DNB
Moir, J. R.	3163	**M[aynard], G.** James Reid Moir. PSIA 24, 1946/8, 58–60
Monsey, M.	3164	Sketch of the life and character of the late Dr. Monsey. 1789. 2nd end 1790. BL DNB
Montchensi Family	3165	**Fowler, G. H.** Montchensi of Edwardstone and some kinsmen. MGetH 5th Ser 10, 1938, 1–10
Moody Family	3166	Pedigree: Moody of Suffolk and America. E Ang NS 2, 1887/8, 38–9
	3167	**Reed-Lewis, E., *Ed*.** Some genealogical notes regarding the Moodys of co. Suffolk, and America. Bedford, 1889. SRO/B
Moor Family	3168	Moor of Great Bealings. VE&W 5, 1897, 90–91; Notes 6, 8
Moore, H. G.	3169	The late Dr. Harry Gage Moore, Ipswich … a brief memoir … Ipswich, 1884
Morgan Family	3170	**Pearson, W. C.** Extracts from parish registers: Hemingstone, Henley, Barking, Gosbeck, and Westerfield. E Ang NS 7, 1897/8, 99–101, 235–8
Morrell, W.	3171	**Statham, M. P.** Journal of Wilberforce Morrell. SR 3, 1968, 219–20
Moult, M. M.	3172	**Moult, *afterwards* Page, M. M.** The escaped nun; the story of her life. East Bergholt, 1909. 1911
	3173	**Moult, *afterwards* Page, M. M.** Story of my life. 1909. BL
	3174	**Smith, S. F.** Escaped nun from East Bergholt. nd
Munnings, Sir A. J.	3175	**Munnings, *Sir* A. [J.]** An artist's life. 3v. 1950–52
	3176	**Pound, R.** The Englishman: a biography of Sir Alfred Munnings. 1962 DNB
Munnings, T.	3177	Thomas Munnings. E Ang NS 5, 1893/4, 175, 208
Muriel, J. St. C.		*See* Dewes, S., *pseud*.
Myddleton Family		*See* Middleton Family
Nashe, T.	3178	**Farrell, F. J.** Thomas Nashe, satirist. Beccles, 1914
	3179	**Tannenbaum, S. A.** Elizabethan bibliographies. No 21. Thomas Nashe. New York, 1941. Supplement, 1941–65, by R. C. Johnson. 1968. O DNB, CBEL

Naunton Family	3180	Steer, F. W. Naunton pedigree and family papers. PSIA 29, 1961/3, 34–66
Naunton, Sir *R.*	3181	Memoirs of Sir R. M. Naunton, author of the "Fragmenta Regalia", with some of his posthumous writings ... 1814
	3182	Arms of Sir Robert Naunton, of Letheringham. PSIA 10, 1898/1900, 380–81 DNB
Neale, E.	3183	Neale, E. Life-book of a labourer: or, The curate, with his trials, sorrows, checks, and triumphs. 1839. 2nd edn 1850 DNB
Neave, J. J.	3184	Leaves from the journal of Joseph James Neave. *Ed.* with notes by J. J. Green. [1911]
Nevill Family	3185	Nevill, E. Nevills of Long Melford. E Ang NS 10, 1903/04, 112, 128
	3186	Nevill, E. R. Nevills of Suffolk. Gen NS 31, 1914/1915, 141–53
Nicholas of Kenton	3187	Stevenson, F. S. Nicholas of Kenton. PSIA 13, 1907/09, 20–23
Nicholls, N.	3188	Letter [by T. J. Mathias] occasioned by the death of the Rev Norton Nicholls, LL.B., rector of Lound and Bradwell ... written privately to a friend. 1809 DNB
Norfolk, **Dukes** of		*See* Howard Family
North, R.	3189	Autobiography of the Hon. Roger North. *Ed.* by A. Jessopp. Norwich, 1887. NCL/N DNB, CBEL
Notcutt, W.	3190	Cornell, E. Sermon occasioned by the death of Mr William Notcutt, departed this life July 17th, 1756, aet 84. 1756
Nottidge, J. T.	3191	Reeve, J. W. Sermon preached on Sunday, Jan. 31st., 1847, on the occasion of the death of the Rev J. T. Nottidge. Ipswich, [1847]
	3192	Selection from the correspondence of the Rev J. T. Nottidge, with a prefatory sketch ... *Ed.* by C. Bridges. 1849
Nunn, L.	3193	Nunn, L. Musical recollections of more than half-a-century, 1826–1899. Ipswich, 1899
Oakes Family		*See* Ray Family
Offley Family	3194	Hunter, J. True account of the alienation and recovery of the estates of the Offleys of Norton, in 1754. 1841. SRO/B
Oliver, M.	3195	Appleton, W. S. Ancestry of Mary Oliver, who lived

1640–1698, and was wife of Samuel Appleton, of Ipswich. Cambridge, Mass., 1867. SRO/B

Ouida, pseud. [i.e. *M. L. de la Ramée*]

3196   Lee, E. Ouida: a memoir. 1914. SRO/B

3197   French, Y. Ouida: a study in ostentation. 1938

3918   Bigland, E. Ouida, the passionate Victorian. 1950

3199   Stirling, M. The fine and the wicked: the life and times of Ouida. 1957
DNB, CBEL

Overall, J.   DNB

Oxley-Parker Family   *See* Parker [later Oxley-Parker] Family

Packard, E.   3200   The late Mr. Edward Packard, born at Hasketon, 5 Jan 1819, died at Smallburgh, 27 Oct 1899 ... Rp from Ipswich Journal. Ipswich, 1900

Packard, Sir E.   3201   Packard, W. G. T., *Ed*. Sir Edward Packard, K.B., J.P. [Ipswich], [1936]

Page, B. W.   DNB

Page, M. M.   *See* Moult (*afterwards* Page, M. M.)

Paget, H. L.   3202   Paget, E. K. Henry Luke Paget, portrait and frame ... 1939

Pake, S.   3203   Grant of arms and crest to Samuel Pake of Bury St. Edmunds, 1723. MGetH 5th Ser 3, 1918/19, 1–2

Palgrave Family   3204   Palmer, C. J., *and* Tucker, S. I. *Eds*. Palgrave family memorials. Norwich, 1878. BL

3205   M, C. R. Palgrave family. E Ang NS 5, 1893/4, 112

Parker (later Oxley-Parker) Family   3206   Parker, O. D. Oxley-Parker family in Suffolk and Essex. 1925

Partridge Family   3207   Partridge family. E Ang NS 4, 1891/2—NS 11, 1905/06, *passim*

3208   Partridge of Acton, Sudbury, and Lavenham. PSIA 10, 1898/1900, 150–63

3209   Partridge, C. H. Pedigree and notes of the Partridge family, with some account of Wishanger Manor House, in Gloucestershire ... 250 years the family seat. Birmingham, 1903. nl. *See also* 3401

Partridge, A. & R.   3210   Partridge, C. A Suffolk yeoman's household goods and farming stock, 1789, 1794 [Arthur and Robert Partridge of Shelley Hall]. N&Q 192, 1947, 447–50, 558–60; 194, 1949, 1–4, 116–17, 269–70

Paske Family   3211   Gardner, C. Paskes of Creeting St. Peter. SR 4, no 2, 1973, 16–19

Pattison, W.   3212   Arnott, W. G. William Pattison, a mid-Victorian architect, 1805–78. [Woodbridge]. PSIA 28, 1958/60, 299–301

Peacock, F. C.	3213	Francis Charles Peacock. [Stowmarket]. PSIA 17, 1919/21, 149
Pearson, E.	3214	**Green, T.** Biographical memoir of the late E. Pearson, D.D. Ipswich, 1819. BL [Tattingstone]
	3215	Brief memoir of the life, writings, and correspondence of the Rev Edward Pearson ... 1845 DNB
Pearson, S.	3216	**Pearson, G.** Memoirs of the life and character of Mrs. Susanna Pearson. Ipswich, 1829
Penn Family	3217	**Coleman, J.** Pedigree and genealogical notes from wills, registers, and deeds of the highly distinguished family of Penn, of England and America. 1871
	3218	**Pound, A.** Penns of Pennsylvania and England. New York, 1932. BL
Penn, W.	3219	**Clarkson, T.** Memoirs of the private and public life of William Penn. 2v. 1813. 1849. BL DNB
Pepys Family	3220	**Pepys, W. C.** Genealogy of the Pepys family, 1273–1887. 1887. 2nd edn 1952. BL DNB, CBEL
Perry, J. & A.	3221	Journey of John and Anna Perry in 1789. FHSJ 16, 1919, 10–17
Peto, Sir *S. M.*	3222	Sir Morton Peto: a memorial sketch. 1893. SCL/L. [Somerleyton Hall]
	3223	**Chown, J. L.** Sir Samuel Morton Peto, Bart., M.P.: the man who built the Houses of Parliament. [1943]. SCL/L DNB
Pett, G.	3224	**Cotton, E.** A Suffolk legend illustrated [the story of Grace Pett, witch]. [c.1875]. nl
Philbrick, T.		*See* Felbrigge, T.
Pitman Family	3225	**Pitman, H. A.** Pitman of Woodbridge. BA 1, 1914/1920, 93–5
Playter Family	3226	**Wadley, T. P.** Family of Playter or Players of co. Suffolk. Gen NS 1, 1884, 45–9, 169–78, 243–56; NS 3, 1886, 117–18
Pole, de la, Family		*See* De la Pole Family
Poley Family	3227	**Hervey,** *Lord* A. Boxted Hall—family of Poley. PSIA 3, 1860/63, 358–74
Powell Family	3228	**Powell, E.,** *Ed.* Pedigree of the family of Powell sometime resident ... in co. Suffolk. 1891

	3229	**Powell, E.,** *Ed.* Some autograph letters of the Powell family reproduced in facsimile. 1901. SRO/B
	3230	**Powell, E.,** *Ed.* Pedigree of the families of Powell and Baden-Powell; also of Sparke of Hawstead, Griggs of Suffolk ... 1926
Powell, J.	3231	The New Westminster wedding; or, The rampant vicar, being a full relation of the late marriage of J-P-, clark, to Eliz. Hook, spinster ... nd
Poynings Family	3232	**Holland, T. A.** Poynings. Rp from Sussex Arch. Soc. Collections, 15, 1863. Lewes. nl
Pratt Family	3233	**W[hayman], H. W.** Family of Pratt of East Anglia. Wills proved at Norwich, Bury St. Edmunds, and Ipswich. E Ang NS 7, 1897/8, 294–5
Pretyman Family	3234	**Sweeting, W. D.,** *et al.* Pretyman family. E Ang NS 1, 1885/6, 209–11, 246–7
Punchard Family	3235	**Punchard, E. G.** Family of Punchard. E Ang NS 5, 1893/4, 104–07
	3236	**Punchard, E. G.** Punchard of Heaton-Punchardson; records of an unfortunate family. 3pts. 1894
	3237	Punchard of Suffolk. VE&W 3, 1895, 136; Notes 5, 36–40
Purchase, Sir B.	3238	**Jackson, R.** Coroner: the biography of Sir Bentley Purchase. 1963. BL
Pytches Family	3239	Pytches of Melton. VE&W 19, 1917, 208; Notes 14, 128–9
Quaplode Family	3240	**Clemence, J. L.** Quaplode family. E Ang NS 5, 1893/4, 336
Quyntyn, Sir W.	3241	**Haslewood, F.** Will of Sir Walter Quyntyn of Ipswich. PSIA 7, 1889/91, 111–12
Rainsford Family	3242	**Buckland, E. A.** Rainsford family. Worcester, 1933. BL
Ralling, J.		*See* Sharpin, E.
Ramée, M. D. de la		*See* Ouida, *pseud.*
Randall Family	3243	Randall of Orford. VE&W 3, 1895, 174–6
Ransome Family	3244	Ransome of Ipswich. VE&W 20, 1919, 107–23
Ransome, J. A.		DNB
Ransome, R.		DNB
Rant Family	3245	Rant of Yelverton and Mendham. Frag Gen 13, 1909, 43–8
Ratcliffe, G. T.	3246	**Ratcliffe, R.** George Thomas Ratcliffe, 1852–1898: a worker poet. SR 2, 1963, 175–83
Rattle Family	3247	**Rattle, T. W.** The Rattle family. Toronto, 1968. [Suffolk branches, 1–57]. nl

Raven, J. J.   DNB

Rawlinson Family   *See* Ray Family

Ray Family   3248   **Cullum, G. G. M. G.**, *et al.* Ray of Suffolk. E Ang NS 5, 1893/4, 352, 384

      3249   **Cullum, G. G. M. G.** Ray of Suffolk. MGetH 3rd Ser 3, 1900—3rd Ser 5, 1904, *passim*; 5th Ser. 7, 1929/31, 15–16

      3250   **Cullum, G. G. M. G.** Pedigree of Ray of Denston, Wickhambrook, and other places in Suffolk; together with Oakes, Rawlinson, Heigham, Hasted, etc., all of the said county. 1903. 100 copies

      3251   **Moriarty, C. A.** Ray-Gilbert-Bigg-Rowning[Suffolk families]. NEH&GR 104, 1950, 107–14

Rede Family   3252   Rede [Read, Reade] family (calendar of deeds, 1509–1772). Frag Gen 2, 1899, 1–18

Redstone, V. B.   3253   Vincent Burrough Redstone [Woodbridge]. PSIA 24, 1946/8, 61

      3254   **Scarfe, N.** Vincent Burrough Redstone, 1853–1941; Lilian Jane Redstone, 1885–1955. SRS 1, 1958, 7–13

Redwald, King   3255   **Ward, G.,** *and* **Engleheart, F. H. A.** When did King Redwald die? PSIA 26, 1952/4, 231–2; 27, 1955/7, 56–7
DNB. *See also* **7677**

Reeve, C.   DNB

Rendall, M. J.   3256   **Firth, N. D'E. E.** Rendall of Winchester: the life and witness of a teacher. 1954.
DNB

Rendlesham, Baron   *See* Thellusson Family

Reve, J.   3257   **Jenkins, T. B.** Abbot John Reve, alias Melford, and his arms. [Bury St. Edmunds]. CA 5, 1958, 52–4
Emden, 1501–1540, 394

Revett   *See* Rivett-Carnac Family

Reyce, R.   *See* Ryece, R.

Reymes Family   3258   **Raimes, A. L.** Family of Reymes of Wherstead. PSIA 23, 1937/9, 89–115; 27, 1955/7, 25–33

Reynolds Family   3259   Reynolds of Suffolk. VE&W 17, 1911, 172–6

Rhodes Family   3260   Rhodes of Dalham. VE&W 17, 1911, 165–8; Notes 13, 50

Rhodes, J.   3261   **Powell, E.** Accounts and diary of Rev John Rhodes, rector of Barton Mills, 1662–67. PSIA 15, 1913/15, 269–90

Rhudde Family   3262   **Dow, L.** Rhudde family. *In* R. B. Beckett's John Constable's discourses. Ipswich, 1970. 93–5. SRS 14

Richard de Bury		DNB, CBEL, Emden, to 1500, 1, 323–6
Richold Family	3263	**Richold, F. H.,** *and* **S. L.** Records of the Richold family, 1523–1913. Tonbridge, 1954. SRO/B
Rickards, S.	3264	**Hervey,** *Lord* **A. C.** Sermon ... preached ... after the funeral of ... S. Rickards, rector of Stowlangtoft. Bury St. Edmunds, [1865]. BL DNB
Riveshall, **Sir** *H. de*		*See* De Riveshall, *Sir* H.
Rivett-Carnac Family	3265	**Rivett-Carnac, J. H.** Family of Rivett-Carnac and its descent from Revett of Stowmarket and Brandeston Hall, Suffolk. Rougemont, 1909. O
Robert, **Saint**	3266	**Hill, H. C.,** *and* **Harris, H. A.** St. Robert of Bury St. Edmunds. PSIA 21, 1931/3, 98–107
Robinson, H. C.	3267	Diary, reminiscences, and correspondence of Henry Crabb Robinson ... *Selected* and *ed.* by T. Sadler. 3v. 1869. SRO/B DNB, CBEL
Rokewode, J. G.		DNB
Rolfh, R.	3268	Life of Richard Rolfh, the blind peasant of Lakenheath. Bury St. Edmunds, 1841. nl
Rope Family	3269	Rope of Suffolk. VE&W 2, 1894, 91–6. *See also* **4635**
Rope, G.	3270	**Rope, H. E. G.** George Rope of Blaxhall and Orford, 1814–1912. SR 2, 1959, 47–51
Roper Family	3271	**Elliott, E. K.** Roper family. E Ang NS 5, 1893/4, 125
Rose Family	3272	**M, T. T.** Family of Rose. E Ang NS 5, 1893/4, 255
Rose, H. J.	3273	**Snow, D. M. B.** Hugh James Rose, rector of Hadleigh. B.Litt. thesis, Oxford, 1960 DNB
Roser Family	3274	**Dow, L.** Roser family at Hacheston. PSIA 29, 1961/1963, 345–7
Round-Turner Family	3275	Round-Turner of Suffolk. VE&W 12, 1904, 1–6; Notes 10, 56–8
Rous Family	3276	**Green, E.** Monumental inscriptions to the family of Rous in Wangford church. Gen NS 19, 1902, 97–100 *See also* **899–901, 903**
Rous, H. J.	3277	**Bird, T. H.** Admiral Rous and the English turf, 1795–1877. 1939 DNB
Rous, J.	3278	Diary of John Rous, incumbent of Santon Downham, Suffolk, from 1625 to 1642. *Ed.* by M. A. E. Green. Camden Soc. 66. 1856 DNB

Rous, Sir J.	3279	Gatford, L. A true ... narrative ... of the death of Mr. W. Tyrel and the ... preservation of Sr. J. Rous ... published for the vindication of ... those persons honour from ... a ... libell entituled, Sad and lamentable news from Suffolk ... 1661. Wing G 339. BL
Rowning Family		*See* Ray Family
Roydon Family	3280	Royden, E. B. Three Roydon families. Edinburgh, 1924
Ruggle, G.		DNB
Rushbrooke Family	3281	Rushbrooke of Rushbrooke. VE&W 19, 1917, 9; Notes 13, 157
Rye Family	3282	Rye, W. Account of the family of Rye. 1876. BL
Rye, R.	3283	Bates, T. H. Rhyming will of Robert Rye. E Ang 3, 1866/8, 247–8
Ryece, R.	3284	Harlow, C. G. Robert Ryece of Preston, 1555–1638. PSIA 32. 1970/72, 43–70. *See also* 7126
Sabyn, W.	3285	Webb, J. G. William Sabyn of Ipswich: an early Tudor sea officer and merchant. MM 41, 1955, 209–21
Samuel, R.	3286	F, J. C. Suffolk martyrs: Robert Samuel. E Ang NS 1, 1885/6, 198
Sancroft Family	3287	Raven, J. J. The Sancrofts of Wingfield and Fressingfield. PSIA 7, 1889/91, 69–76
	3288	Boyce, C. Family of William Sancroft. PSIA 20, 1928/30, 117–22
Sancroft, W.	3289	Wagstaffe, T. A letter out of Suffolk ... to a friend in London, giving some account of the last sickness and death of Dr. William Sancroft, late Lord Bishop of Canterbury. 1694. Wing W 209. SRO/B
	3290	Familiar letters of Dr. William Sancroft to ... Sir H. North ... To which is prefixed some account of his life and character. 1757. SRO/B
	3291	D'Oyly, G. Life of William Sancroft, Archbishop of Canterbury. 2v. 1821. 2nd edn 1840 DNB, CBEL
Sanderson, M.	3292	Partridge, C. The Mistress of Queen Charlotte's dairy (Headstone in Acton churchyard—Mary Sanderson). E Ang NS 10, 1903/04, 211–12, 243
Sandys, F.	3293	Statham, M. P. Francis Sandys. SR 2, 1961, 119–20
Savage Family	3294	Dow, L. The Savage hatchment at Long Melford. PSIA 26, 1952/4, 214–19
Savage, J.	3295	Memoirs, containing some particulars of the life, family, and ancestors of John Savage, miller of St.

Mary Stoke, Ipswich, his little travels ... transcribed by him in the 70th and following years of his age and in the years of our Lord, 1793, '94, '95, '96. Ipswich, [1900]

3296 **Collett, H.,** *Ed.* Diaries of John Savage of Stoke, Ipswich, 1767–94, ... with biographical introduction. 1948. [Typescript].

Scott Family **3297** Lineage of Richard Scott, of Providence, U.S.A. [Glemsford]. E Ang 4, 1869/70, 29–31

Scott, J. B. **3298** An Englishman at home and abroad, 1792–1828 ... Being extracts from the diaries of J. B. Scott of Bungay, Suffolk. *Ed.* by E. Mann, *et al.* 1930

Scott, R. **3299** **Bowen, R. J.** Arms of Richard Scott. NEH&GR 96, 1942

Scrope, T. DNB

Seckford Family **3300** **Redstone, V. B.** Seckfords of Seckford Hall. PSIA 9, 1895/7, 359–69

3301 **Titcombe, J. C.** Illustrated Seckfordian history, ancient and modern A.D.1587–A.D.1900. Woodbridge, [1900]. *See also* **3701–02, 8018–24**

Seckford, T. **3302** **Redstone, V. B.** Portrait of Thos. Seckford, Master of Requests, Woodbridge. E Ang NS 4, 1891/2, 266 DNB

Seeger, T. **3303** **Toms, I.** The shining convert ... being memoirs of God's gracious dealings towards a poor illiterate husbandman, Thomas Seeger, of Kersey in Suffolk ... to which is added a sermon occasioned by his happy death. 1747. NCL/N

Sewell, M. **3304** **Bayly, M.** Life and letters of Mrs. Sewell. 1889. 1892 DNB

Sexton Family **3305** Sexton of Suffolk. VE&W 6, 1898, 21; Notes 6, 81

Sharpe Family **3306** **Bullen, R. F.** Sharpe family of Bury St. Edmunds. E Ang NS 13, 1909/10, 273–5, 298–301

Sharpin, E. **3307** An appeal to the public in general ... from Dr. Sharpin, and Mr. Steward, Surgeon of St. Edmunds Bury in Suffolk, with regard to their medical and chirurgical treatment of Mr. John Ralling. Bury St. Edmunds, 1764. SRO/B

3308 **Norford, W.** Letter to Dr. Sharpin, in answer to his appeal to the public, etc., concerning his medical treatment of Mr. John Ralling, apothecary, of Bury St. Edmunds in Suffolk. Bury St. Edmunds, 1764. SRO/B

3309   **Steward, T.** An appendix to the appeal, etc., containing some animadversions upon a pamphlet intitled, A letter to Dr. Sharpin, in answer to appeal to the public, etc. Bury St. Edmunds, 1764. SRO/B

Sheldrake Family   3310   Family of Sheldrake. E Ang NS 5, 1893/4, 35–7; NS 7, 1897/8, 64; NS 10, 1903/04, 63–4

Shelford, Sir W.   3311   **Shelford, A. E.** Life of Sir William Shelford ... 1909
DNB

Sheriffe Family   3312   Sheriffe of Henstead. VE&W 10, 1902, 140–41

Sherman Family   3313   Wills of the Shermans of Yaxley in Suffolk. NEH&GR 54, 1900, 62–9, 152–62

3314   **Sherman, T. T.** Shermans of Yaxley in Suffolk. NEH&GR 59, 1905, 397–400

Shewell, J. T.   3315   Memoir of the late John Talwin Shewell (collected and in part arranged by his ... wife), to which is appended notes on his Italian journey and fugitive poems. Ipswich, 1870

Shipp, J.   3316   Memoirs of the extraordinary military career of John Shipp, late a Lieutenant in His Majesty's 87th Regiment. Written by himself. 3v. 1829. 2nd edn 1830. 1843. 1890. 1897
DNB

Sicklemore Family   3317   Sicklemore of Bramford and Tuddenham. Frag Gen 10, 1904, 65–7

Singh,
   Prince F. D. V.   3318   Prince Frederick Duleep Singh. PSIA 19, 1925/7, 252–3. *See also* **2454**

Singleton, J.   3319   **Hendriks, F.** Joseph Singleton, artist, of Bury. N&Q 8th Ser 2, 1892, 249, 298–9

Skeels Family   3320   Skeels of Kirkley. VE&W 5, 1897, 19–20

Skinner Family   3321   Skinner of Ipswich. VE&W 10, 1902, 126–8

Skippon Family   3322   Skippon family. 1870. SRO/B

3323   Skippon family of Wrentham and Ketton. MGetH NS 1, 1874, 37–40

Smart, R.   3324   **Webb, J. [G.]** Richard Smart, a wealthy draper of 16th-century Ipswich. SR 1, 1958, 166–8

Smith Family   3325   **Cullum, G. G. M. G.** Smith of Cavendish, Bacton, and Thrandeston. MGetH 3rd Ser 1, 1896, 177–85

3326   **Muskett, J. J.** A churchly family: the Smiths of Stratford [St. Mary]. E Ang NS 3, 1889/90, 201–03, 220, 277–8, 390

3327   Smith of Thrandeston. E Ang NS 4, 1891/2, 15, 31, 360–62, 380

Smith, E. J. S.	3328	**Patterson, A. H.**, *et al.* E. J. Singleton Smith. [Lowestoft]. [1928]. [Typescript]. SCL/L
Smith, Lady P.	3329	In memoriam: Lady Smith (of Lowestoft) the veritable centenarian, who died on 3 Feb 1877, at the remarkable age of 104 years. 1877. SCL/L DNB
Smith, W.	3330	Smithiana: a collection of paper cuttings and other notes relating to William Smith, the actor of Bury. nd. SRO/B DNB
Soame Family	3331	Pedigree: Soame of Suffolk and London. E Ang NS 3, 1889/90, 210–11. *See also* **891, 893–5**
Southwold, S.		*See* Bell, N., *pseud.*
Spanton, W. S.	3332	A noted Burian [W. S. Spanton, artist and photographer in Abbeygate, Bury St. Edmunds]. [Typescript]. SRO/B
Sparke Family		*See* Powell Family
Sparrow Family	3333	**Glyde, J.** Sparrow family, Ipswich. E Ang NS 1, 1885/6, 150, 190–91
	3334	**Pearson, W. C.** Extracts from parish registers: Barking. E Ang NS 5, 1893/4, 46–7
Sparrow, R.	3335	**Turner, D.** Memoir of Robert Sparrow, of Worlingham. *In* S. W. Rix's Fauconberge memorial. Ipswich, 1849, 66–7
Spratt, M. A.	3336	**Wright, G.** . . . a sermon preached 27 Sept 1840, in the Baptist Meeting House, Fressingfield on the death of . . . Mary Ann Spratt. 1840. NCL/N
Spring Family	3337	**McClenaghan, B.** The Springs of Lavenham and the Suffolk cloth trade in the 15th and 16th centuries. Ipswich, 1924
Squirrel, M. E.	3338	**Norton, W. A.** The Suffolk case of real or supposed abstinence from food; together with the life of Mary Elizabeth Squirrell of Shottisham. Ipswich, [1852]. nl
	3339	The extraordinary case of fasting [by M. E. Squirrell] at Shottisham . . . , and twenty-one extraordinary cases of persons abstaining from food . . . from two to forty years, etc. 1852. BL
	3340	The Suffolk angel mystery: a marvellous case of superstition and credulity. Compiled . . . by kind permission of James Bendall. Ipswich, nd. nl
	3341	Autobiography of Elizabeth Squirrell . . . and selections from her writings; together with an examination and defence of her statements . . . by one of her watchers [Rev W. A. Norton]. Ipswich, 1853
Stanford Family	3342	Stanford of Ashbocking. VE&W 9, 1901, 90–96

Stannard, M.	3343	**Stannard, M.** Memoirs of a professional lady nurse. [Laxfield], 1873
Stanton, L. M.	3344	Short account of the life of Mrs. Lucy Ann Stanton. By her son. Halesworth, 1883. nl
Stanton, N.	3345	Will of Nicholas Stanton, minister of St. Margaret's, Ipswich. 1649. E Ang NS 8, 1899/1900, 193–5
Steel, J. J.	3346	Autobiography of John Jacques Steel of Walton, in the county of Suffolk. [1859]. Rp Exmouth, 1881. BL
Steffe, T.	3347	**Steffe, T.** Sermons ... with some extracts from his letters in an account of his life and character, ... by P. Doddridge. 1742. NCL/N
Steggall, J. H.	3348	John H. Steggall: a real history of a Suffolk man ... narrated by himself. [*Ed.* by ... R. Cobbold.] 1857. Enlarged edn, 1859
Stevenson Family	3349	Stevenson of Playford Mount. VE&W 12, 1904, 48–9
Steward, T.		*See* Sharpin, E.
Stiff Family	3350	**Phillimore, W. P. W.** Stiff family. Rp from Gloucestershire N&Q July 1884, etc. BL
	3351	**Phillimore, W. P. W.** Memorials of the family of Stiff, of Norton and Rougham, in the county of Suffolk. Stroud, 1885. BL
	3352	**Phillimore, W. P. W.** Collections relating to the family of Stiff ... Pt 1. Stroud, 1892. BL
	3353	**Phillimore, W. P. W.** Family of Stiff or Steff, Suffolk. MGetH 2nd Ser 4, 1892, 224
Stockton, O.	3354	The true dignity of St. Paul's elder, exemplified in the life of ... Mr. Owen Stockton ... preacher of God's Word at Colchester. To which is added his funeral sermon, by John Fairfax ... rector of Barking in Suffolk. 1681. Wing F 129. Rp 1826
	3355	**White, C. H. E.,** *et al.* Owen Stockton, sometime of Chattisham. E Ang NS 5, 1893/4, 21, 50–51, 326, 360; NS 12, 1907/08, 176
	3356	**Jones, W. A. B.** Owen Stockton, a seventeenth-century nonconforming minister. SR 1, 1958, 203–05
	3357	**Jewson, C. B.** Legacy of Owen Stockton, ejected minister at Ipswich to Caius College, Cambridge, 1680. BQ 23, 1969/70, 176 DNB
Stonham Family	3358	[**Stoneham, F. W.**] The arms of Stonham. [1932]. [Typescript]. SRO/B
Strickland, A.	3359	**Strickland, J. M.** Life of Agnes Strickland. Edinburgh, 1887
	3360	**Partridge, C.** Agnes Strickland, the historian.

Monumental inscription in Southwold church. E Ang NS 10, 1903/04, 291

3361 **Pope-Hennessy, U.** Agnes Strickland, biographer of the Queens of England, 1796–1874. 1940

3362 **Cooper, E. R.** Agnes Strickland and her birthplace. PSIA 24, 1946/8, 33–5
DNB, CBEL

Stubbin Family   3363 **Partridge, C. S.** Stubbin of Raydon and Higham. Extracts from the registers of the parish of Holton St. Mary. E Ang NS 4, 1891/2, 245; NS 5, 1893/4, 69–70

Stubbin, J.   3364 **Partridge, C.** Will of Josiah Stubbin of Offton, 1686. E Ang NS 10, 1903/04, 365–6

Style Family   3365 **Pearson, W. C.** Extracts from parish registers. E Ang NS 5, 1893/4, 274–7

Suckling Family   3366 Suckling of Barsham. VE&W 19, 1917, 195–8; Notes 14, 101–15

Suckling, A. I.   3367 **Gerish, W. B.** Rev A. Suckling, rector of Barsham. E Ang NS 5, 1893/4, 96
DNB

Suffolk, **Duchess of**   *See* Willoughby, C.

Sulyard Family   3368 **Murray, C. R. S.,** *et al.* Pedigree of the family of Sulyard of . . . Suffolk and Flemings, co. Essex. Gen 4, 1880, 226–34

3369 **Dimock, A.** Haughley Park and the Sulyards. PSIA 12, 1904/06, 88–96

Swann Family   3370 Swann of Great Ashfield. VE&W 1, 1893, 95–7; Notes 2, 99–105

Swinburne, A. J.   3371 **Swinburne, A. J.** Memories of a school inspector. Thirty-five years in Lancashire and Suffolk. Saxmundham [c.1912]. 2nd edn nd. *See also* **1605**

Talbot Family   3372 **W, D.** Talbot of Hintlesham. E Ang NS 5, 1893/4, 237, 256

Talmadge Family   3373 **Pearson, W. C.** Talmadges of Coddenham. E Ang NS 4, 1891/2, 73–5

3374 **Pearson, W. C.** Extracts from parish registers. E Ang NS 5, 1893/4, 140–42

Taylor Family   3375 **Taylor, I.,** *Ed.* The family pen: memorials, biographical and literary, of the Taylor family of Ongar. 2v. 1867

3376 **Taylor, H.,** *Ed.* Pedigree of the Taylors of Ongar. 1895

3377 **Armitage, D. M.** Taylors of Ongar: portrait of an English family of the eighteenth and nineteenth centuries. Drawn from family records of the great-great niece of Ann and Jane Taylor. Cambridge, 1939

3378 **Harris, G. E.** Contributions towards a bibliography of the Taylors of Ongar and Stanford Rivers. 1965. 350 copies. nl

3379 **Stewart, C. D.** The Taylors of Ongar: an analytical bio-bibliography. 2v. New York, 1975. SRO/B

Taylor, A. & J. 3380 Ann and Jane Taylor of Lavenham. ER 9, 1900, 1 DNB

Taylor, J. DNB

Taylor, R. 3381 **Stow, T. Q.** Memoirs of Rowland Taylor, Archdeacon of Exeter, rector of Hadleigh ... comprising an account of the rise of the Reformation in the counties of Norfolk and Suffolk. 1833

3382 **Must, J.** The martyr of Hadleigh, a dramatic poem founded on the martyrdom of Rowland Taylor. Sudbury, 1839

3383 **Religious Tract Society.** Dr. Rowland Taylor, the martyr. Hadleigh, 1929. 3rd edn. nl

3384 **Brown, W. J.** Dr. Rowland Taylor of Rothbury. Proc Soc of Antiquaries of Newcastle-on-Tyne, 5th Ser 1, 1951, 60–66

3385 **Brown, W. J.** Life of Rowland Taylor, LL.D., rector of Hadleigh in the deanery of Bocking. 1959 DNB. *See also* **5119**

Tettrell, J. 3386 **Statham, M. P.** Nuncupative will of Jone Tettrell, otherwise Jancks, of Acton, widow. SR 1, 1958, 192–3

Tharp Family 3387 **Day, J. W.** The squire of Newmarket. CL 113, 1953, 1066–7

Thellusson Family 3388 Thellusson of Suffolk (Baron Rendlesham). VE&W 14, 1906, 121–9; Notes 11, 107–11

Theobald Family 3389 Pedigree of Theobald of Barking Hall. E Ang NS 4, 1891/2, 158–9

Thicknesse, P. 3390 Letter from a parson [W. Myers?] to a Captain in Suffolk [P. Thicknesse?]. To which is annexed a specimen of the Captain's veracity, religious principles, party ... 1756. BL

3391 Memoirs and anecdotes of Philip Thicknesse, late Lieutenant Governor of Land Guard Fort ... 1788. SRO/B

3392 **Barnes, R. R.** Captain Philip Thicknesse [including an account of his "cottage" at Felixstowe]. GM 79, 1809, 1013–16

	3393	**Gosse, P.** Dr. Viper, the querulous life of Philip Thicknesse. 1952 DNB
Thomas, W. G. H.	3394	**Thomas, W. G. H.** Recollections of a Suffolk vicar. Ipswich, 1964
Thompson, Sir H.	3395	**Cope, Sir V. Z.** The versatile Victorian, being the life of Sir Henry Thompson, 1820–1904. 1951 DNB
Thompson, H.	3396	**Thompson, D.** Sophia's son: the story of a Suffolk parson, the Rev Henry Thompson, M.A., his life and times, 1841–1916. Lavenham, 1969
Thomson, J.	3397	Short biographical account of the late Mr. John Thomson, many years pastor of the Baptist church, Grundisburgh, Suffolk, comprising an account of the riots and persecutions attending the introduction of the gospel into Wickham Market, in the year 1810. Ipswich, nd. nl
Thorne Family	3398	**Pearson, W. C.** Extracts from parish registers. E Ang NS 5, 1893/4, 346–7
Thurlow, E.	3399	**Gore-Browne, R.** Chancellor Thurlow. 1953 DNB
Thurston Family	3400	Thurston of Little Wenham. Frag Gen 8, 1902, 68–9
Timperley Family	3401	Tymperley of Hintlesham and Partridge of Great Finborough. E Ang NS 6, 1895/6, 79; NS 12, 1907/08, 308
	3402	**Ryan, Sir G. H.,** *and* **Redstone, L. J.** Timperley of Hintlesham: a study of a Suffolk family ... 1931
Tollady, S.	3403	**Pumphrey, S. G.** The wreck of the "Kapunda": a short sketch of the life of Stephen Tollady [of Sudbury]. Leominster, [c.1888]. nl
Tollemache Family	3404	**G, J.** Tollemache family. E Ang NS 5, 1893/4, 255
	3405	**Roundell, C.** Tollemaches of Bentley and Helmingham. PSIA 12, 1904/06, 97–112
	3406	**Partridge, C.** Tollemache heraldry at Bentley Hall. E Ang NS 11, 1905/06, 31–2
	3407	**Tollemache, E. D. H.** Tollemaches of Helmingham and Ham. Ipswich, 1949
Tollemache, B.	3408	Career of a Second Lieutenant in the year 1914; in memory of ... Bevil Tollemache. 1915
Tollemache, L. A.	3409	**Tollemache, L. A.** Old and odd memories. 1908
	3410	**Tollemache, L. A.** Nuts and chestnuts. 1911
Toms, I.	3411	**Ray, T. M.** An old disciple: a sermon preached at Hadleigh in Suffolk, 15 Jan 1801, on the occasion of

the death of the Rev Isaac Toms. Sudbury, 1801. BL
See also **5119**

Tooley, H.	3412	**Webb, J. G.** Henry Tooley, merchant of early Tudor Ipswich. MA thesis London. 1953
	3413	**Webb, J. G.** Great Tooley of Ipswich: portrait of an early Tudor merchant. Ipswich, 1962. SRS additional publication. *See also* **2337**
Torlesse Family	3414	**Torlesse, F. H.** Bygone days. [A history of the family of Torlesse, with plates and genealogical tables]. 1914. BL
Tradescant Family	3415	**Allan, M.** The Tradescants: their plants, gardens, and museum, 1570–1662. 1964
Trimmer, S.	3416	Some account of the life and writings of Mrs. Trimmer, with original letters, and meditations and prayers, selected from her journal. 2v. 1814. 2nd edn 1816. 3rd edn 1825. DNB, CBEL
Trumpoor, W.	3417	Will of William Trumpoor, alias Euston [Sudbury]. PSIA 1, 1848/53, 267–8
Turner, J. E.	3418	**Turner, J. E.** Seven gardens for Catherine. 1968
	3419	**Turner, J. E.** Sometimes into England: a second volume of autobiography. 1970
Turner, Round-		*See* Round-Turner Family
Tusser, T.	3420	**Clark, C.,** *Ed.* Last will and testament of Thomas Tusser ... To which is added his metrical autobiography. Great Totham, 1846. BL DNB, CBEL. *See also* **1076–80**
Tyllotson, W.	3421	**Dow, L.** William Tyllotson, or Tylletson. PSIA 25, 1949/51, 295. *See also* **2346–8**
Tylney, Sir P.	3422	**Partridge, C.** Will of Sir Philip Tylney of Shelley Hall. N&Q 192, 1947, 297–300
Tymms, S.	3423	**Raven, J. J.** Samuel Tymms. E Ang NS 7, 1897/1898, 65–7 DNB
Tymperley Family		*See* Timperley Family
Tyrel, W.		*See* Rous, *Sir* J.
Tyrell, Sir J.	3424	**Sewell, W. H.** Memoirs of Sir James Tyrell (founder of chapel in Gipping, murderer of the princes in the Tower). PSIA 5, 1876–86, 125–80 DNB. *See also* **5078–9**
Upcher Family	3425	Upcher of Sudbury and Norfolk. VE&W 3, 1895, 25–8; Notes 4, 149–50

Vallibus, De		*See* De Vallibus Family
Valoynes Family	3426	**M, T. T.** Suffolk branch of the family of Valoynes. E Ang NS 5, 1893/4, 14
Ventris Family	3427	Ventris of Ipswich. Frag Gen 8, 65–7
Vince, S.		DNB
Wade Family	3428	Wade of Orford. VE&W 4, 1896, 137–40; Notes 5, 148–51
Walcott, T.	3429	**Whitley, W. T.** A Baptist governor for Carolina? (Thomas Walcott of Suffolk and Ireland). BQ 10, 1940/41, 319–22
Waldegrave Family	3430	**Probert, W. H. C.** Waldegraves of Bures. ER 41, 1932, 86–7
Waldegrave, Lady *M.*	3431	**Probert, W. H. C.** Lady Margery (Wentworth) Waldegrave of Smallbridge Manor, Bures. ER 38, 1929, 177–80
Waldegrave, Sir R. De	3432	**Roskell, J. S.** Sir Richard de Waldegrave of Bures St. Mary, Speaker in the Parliament of 1381–2. PSIA 27, 1955/7, 154–75 DNB
Waller Family	3433	Waller of Suffolk. VE&W 9, 1901, 177–80; Notes 9, 30–31
Walton, H.	3434	**Farrer, E.** Henry Walton, artist. Conn Nov 1909, 139–47
	3435	**Sutton, D.** Merits of a little-known artist. CL 1950, 225
Warbanks Family	3436	**Hill, E.** Warbanks at Cockfield, 1908. PSIA 13, 1907/09, 176–7
Ward Family	3437	**Partridge, C. S.** Ward of Old Newton, and Haughley. E Ang NS 5, 1893/4, 150–51, 158
Ward, B.	3438	**Butler, J. D.** Benjamin Ward. E Ang NS 5, 1893/1894, 127, 158–9
Ward, J.	3439	Jesse Ward, native of Ipswich and townsman of Croydon who founded "The Croydon Advertiser", 13 Feb 1869. Croydon, 1951
Ward, N.	3440	**Dean, J. W.** Memoir of the Rev Nathaniel Ward ... with notices of his family. Albany, 1868 DNB
Ward, S.	3441	Rev Samuel Ward of Ipswich. NEH&GR 37, 1883, 85–6 DNB
Warner Family	3442	**M, J. J.** Warner family of Suffolk. E Ang NS 1, 1885/6, 94–5
Warner, Sir *H.*	3443	**Tymms, S.** Will of Sir Henry Warner, Knt., of Wamhill Hall, Mildenhall, 1616. PSIA 1, 1848/53, 297–302

Warner, Lady	3444	Life of Lady Warner, of Parham in Suffolk; in religion called Sister Clare of Jesus. By a Catholic Gentleman [N.N., i.e., Edward Scarisbrike]. 1691. 2nd edn 1692. 3rd edn 1696. Wing C 574–6
Warner, Sir T.	3445	**Warner, R. S. A.** Sir Thomas Warner, pioneer of the West Indies. A chronicle of his family, etc. 1933. BL DNB
Warren, F. E.	3446	**Hervey, S. H. A.** Canon F. E. Warren. PSIA 20, 1928/30, 317–18
Watling, H.	3447	H. Watling. EADT 3 April 1908
Wayman Family	3448	**Whayman, H. W.** Wayman or Whayman of Suffolk, Norfolk, and Cambridgeshire. E Ang NS 6, 1895/6, 368; NS 7, 1897/8, 80, 112
	3449	**Bloom, J. H.** Wayman wills and administrations preserved in the Prerogative Court of Canterbury, 1383–1821. 1922
Webber Family	3450	Webber of Friston. VE&W 1896, 159–60
	3451	Webber of Hopton. VE&W 4, 1896, 158
Weightman Family		*See* Wightman Family
Wentworth Family	3452	**Rutton, W. L.** Wentworth of Nettlestead. E Ang NS 2, 1887/8, *passim*
	3453	**Rutton, W. L.** Three branches of the family of Wentworth ... 1891. 100 copies. SRO/B
Wenyeve Family	3454	**Betham, C. J.** Brettenham and the Wenyeve family. PSIA 9, 1895/7, 131–43
Wetherell Family	3455	**Peacock, M.** Wetherell of Suffolk. E Ang NS 5, 1893/4, 239, 256
Whatloke, G.	3456	Will of George Whatloke of Clare, 1539. PSIA 1, 1848/53, 187–90, 278–85
Whayman Family		*See* Wayman Family
Whetcroft Family	3457	**Muskett, J. J.** Suffolk wills from the Prerogative Court of Canterbury: Whetcroft of Suffolk. PSIA 6, 1883/8, 94–104
Whistlecraft, O.	3458	**Partridge, C.** Monumental inscription to Orlando Whistlecraft, "The Weather Prophet" of Suffolk. E Ang NS 10, 1903/04, 255
White, S.	3459	**Fussell. G. E.** Rev Stephen White, bee-keeper of Holton, c.1760. SR 1, 1958, 163–6
Whiteman Family		*See* Wightman Family
Wightman Family	3460	**I'Anson, A. B.** Records of the Wightman—Whiteman or Weightman—family. 1917. BL
Wilbye, J.	3461	**Wood,** *Sir* **J.** John Wilbye, 1574–1638. PSIA 23, 1937/9, 83–4 DNB

William of Hoo 3462 Letter-book of William of Hoo, Sacrist of Bury St. Edmunds, 1280–1294. *Ed.* by A. Gransden. Ipswich, 1963. SRS 5

Willoughby, C. 3463 Goff, *Lady* C. A woman of the Tudor Age [A biography of Catherine Willoughby, afterwards Brandon, Duchess of Suffolk]. 1930

Willoughby, Lady E. 3464 So much of the diary of Lady Willoughby as relates to her domestic history and the eventful period of the reign of Charles I. 2v. 1844–8. 1873

Wilson, D. 3465 Life of Daniel Wilson (written by himself) together with his writings and the testimony of his friends ... late pastor of the Baptist Church, Tunstall ... Woodbridge, 1844–8

Wingfield Family 3466 W, W. Memorial of the Wingfields. E Ang 1, 1858/1863, 327

3467 Dewing, E. M. Pedigree of Wingfield of Wingfield, Letheringham, Easton, etc. PSIA 7, 1889/91, 57–68

3468 Pearson, W. C. Extracts from parish registers. E Ang NS 5, 1893/4, 61–2

3469 Wingfield, M. E., *7th Viscount Powerscourt*. Muniments of the ancient Saxon family of Wingfield ... from the archives in the British Museum, etc. 1894. BL

3470 Wingfield, J. M., *Ed*. Some records of the Wingfield family. 1925. *See also* **6457**

Wingfield, Sir A. 3471 D, E. M. Sir Anthony Wingfield of Letheringham: his monumental brass. E Ang NS 2, 1887/8, 355–6 DNB

Winthrop Family 3472 Winthrop, R. C. Short account of the Winthrop family. Cambridge, 1887. SRO/B

3473 Muskett, J. J. Evidences of the Winthrops of Groton, co. Suffolk, England ... Being pt 1–4 of "Suffolk manorial families" ... issued with separate title page and table of contents, and a preface by R. C. Winthrop, Jun. [1897]. SRO/B

3474 Massachusetts Historical Society. Winthrop papers, 1498–1649. Boston, Mass., 1929–47. 500 copies

Winthrop, J. 3475 Winthrop, R. C. Life and letters of John Winthrop, Governor of the Massachusetts Bay Company at their emigration to New England, 1630. 2v. Boston, 1864–1867

3476 Twichell, J. H. John Winthrop, first Governor of Massachusetts Colony. New York, 1892. O

3477 Waters, T. F. Sketch of the life of John Winthrop

the Younger, founder of Ipswich, Massachusetts, in 1633. Ipswich, Mass., 1899. 2nd edn 1900. SRO/B

3478 **Robinson, G. W.** John Winthrop as Attorney: extracts from the Order Books of the Court of Wards and Liveries, 1627–9. Cambridge, Mass., 1930

3479 **Cowell, H. J.** John Winthrop ... the story of the life and work of John Winthrop of Groton, Suffolk ... and his wife, Margaret Winthrop. Colchester, 1949

3480 **Cowell, H. J.** John Winthrop (1588–1649) of Groton and Massachusetts. PSIA 25, 1949/51, 98–108 DNB, CBEL

Withipoll Family 3481 **Muskett, J. J.** Wythipoll family of Ipswich. Wills of Edmund and Frances Wythipoll. E Ang NS 10, 1903/ 1904, 85–9

3482 Pedigree of Wythipoll of Ipswich. E Ang NS 10, 1903/04, 302–04

3483 **Dunlop, J. R.** Pedigree of the Withipoll family of Somersetshire, Shropshire, Essex, and Suffolk. 1925

3484 **Moore-Smith, G. C.** Family of Withipoll with special reference to their manor of Christchurch, Ipswich ... 1936. Walthamstow Antiquarian Soc Official Publ. 34

Wittewronge Family 3485 **Cullum, G. G. M. G.** Pedigree of Wittewronge of Ghent in Flanders, ... together with those of their descendants Lawes, Capper, Brooke, Gery, Le Hemp, and Cullum. 1905. SRO/B

Wollaston Family 3486 **Waters, R. E. C.** Genealogical memoirs of the elder and extinct line of the Wollastons of Shenton and Finborough, their ancestors and connections ... 1877. 35 copies

3487 Wollaston of Bury. VE&W 18, 1914, 121–4; Notes 10, 82–9

3488 Wollaston of Suffolk. VE&W 12, 1904, 73–8; Notes 10, 82–9

Wollaston, W. 3489 **Hasted, H.** Reminiscences of Dr. Wollaston. PSIA1, 1848/53, 121–34

Wolsey Family 3490 **Casley, H. C.** The position in life of Wolsey's family. E Ang NS 2, 1887/8, 21–3, 33–6, 57–8, 74–5

3491 **Redstone, V. B.** Parentage of Cardinal Wolsey. PSIA 11, 1901/03, 77–80

3492 **Redstone, V. B.** Wulcy (Wolsey) of Suffolk. PSIA 16, 1916/18, 71–89

Wolsey, T. **Cardinal** 3493 History of the life and times of Cardinal Wolsey ... collected from antient records, manuscripts, and historians. 4v. 1742–4

3494 **Cavendish, G.** Life of Cardinal Wolsey ... 2v. 1825. 1827. 1852 and var. edns

3495 **Creighton, M.** Cardinal Wolsey. 1888. 1904

3496 **Pollard, A. F.** Wolsey. 1929

3497 **Thomson, G. S.** Three Suffolk figures—Thomas Wolsey, Stephen Gardiner, Nicholas Bacon: a study in social history. PSIA 25, 1949/51, 149–63

3498 **Wagner, A. R.** Arms of Thomas, Cardinal Wolsey. CA 3, 1954, 79, 162
DNB. Emden, to 1500, 3, 2077–80. C. Read. Bibl of British History, Tudor period, 2nd edn 1959.
See also **4777, 5890–95**

Wolton Family 3499 Wolton of Suffolk. VE&W 8, 1900, 127–8

Wood, J. 3500 Adventures, sufferings, and observations of James Wood ... 1840

Woolner, T. 3501 **Woolner, A.** Thomas Woolner, R. A., sculptor and poet: his life and letters. 1917
DNB

Wright, G. 3502 Memorials of George Wright, for forty-eight years pastor of the Baptist Church at Beccles. *Ed.* by S. K. Bland. 1875

Wright, W. A. DNB

Wrinch Family 3503 Wrinch of Erwarton. VE&W 8, 1900, 113–15

Wulcy Family *See* Wolsey Family

Wyncoll Family 3504 **Sier, L. C.** Wyncoll family. EAST NS 11, 1911, 236–45; NS 12, 1913, 1–13, 101–82

3505 **Wyncoll, C. E.** Wyncolls of Suffolk and Essex. Adapted from an account by L. C. Sier. [1912]

Wythipoll Family *See* Withipoll Family

Yelloly Family 3506 **Suckling, F. H. N.** A forgotten past ... 1898. BL

Yeo, E. H. 3507 **Gooding, W. J.** Outlines of a sermon preached at the Baptist Chapel, Halesworth, Suffolk, on ... 14 Oct 1860, upon the death of E. H. Yeo. Halesworth, 1860. NCL/N

Youell, G. 3508 **Youell, G.** Lower class. Seattle, Wash., 1938

Young, A. 3509 Autobiography of Arthur Young, with selections of his correspondence ... *Ed.* by M. B. Betham-Edwards. 1898

3510 **Defries, A.** Sheep and turnips: being the life and times of Arthur Young ... 1938
DNB, CBEL

Young, T. 3511 **Laing, D.** Biographical notices of Thomas Young, vicar of Stowmarket, Suffolk. Edinburgh, 1870
DNB

Localities

ACTON   *See also* 2572, 2607, 2778, 3208, 3292, 3386

3512   Acton parish history. SC 17.10.1930, Rp No 198
3513   **Leakey, A.** Restoration of the ancient parish church of Acton [an appeal]. 1883. O
3514   **Lambert, R. T.** Story of All Saints. church, Acton. Sudbury, 1950
3515   **Lambert, R. T.** Brief history of Acton church. Sudbury, 1955. nl
3516   **Ward, J. C.** Sir Robert de Bures. TMBS 10, 1963/8, 144–50

AKENHAM   *See also* 7938

3517   Akenham parish history. EADT 14.2.1934, Rp No 343
3518   **Birch, H. W.** Church notes: Akenham. E Ang NS 6, 1895/6, 69–70
3519   **Wilton, H. E.** Akenham and its church. Ipswich, 1958
3520   **Pearson, W. C.** Entries relating to the tithe customs in the parish of Akenham. E Ang NS 9, 1901/02, 75–6; NS 11, 1905/06, 37–8
3521   **Pearson, W. C.** Extracts from the registers of Akenham. E Ang NS 9, 1901/02, 43–6; NS 11, 1905/06, 51–4
3522   **Fletcher, R.** Akenham burial case. 1974

ALDEBURGH   *See also* Slaughden

DIRECTORY
3523   **Localads.** Aldeburgh, Leiston, Saxmundham, and districts directory, 1962/ 1963–. Needham Market, [1964–]

GUIDES AND VIEWS   *See also* 4890, 7321
3524   **[Ford, J.]** Aldborough described: being a full delineation of the fashionable ... watering place ... Ipswich, [1819?]
3525   Aldborough and its vicinity: an historical, antiquarian, and picturesque guide. Ipswich, 1844
3526   **[Clodd, E.]** Guide to Aldeburgh ... Aldeburgh, 1861. BL
3527   **Talbutt, J. F.** Guide to Aldeburgh, to which is added the history of Orford and Dunwich. Aldeburgh, 1880
3528   **Stebbings, A.** Visitors' guide book and directory to Aldeburgh. Lowestoft, [1887]. BL
3529   **Barrett, C. R. B.** Round Aldeburgh. 1892

3530 Jarrold's illustrated guide to Aldeburgh, including Southwold, Dunwich, Halesworth ... 5th edn 1894. 2pts. 1904

3531 **Hooper, J.** Illustrated handbook to Aldeburgh and neighbourhood. Norwich, [c.1900]. SRO/B

3532 Popular guide to Aldeburgh. Lowestoft, [1905] and later edns

3533 Notes on Aldeburgh. By a visitor. 1906

3534 **Young, C.** Illustrated guide to Aldeburgh-on-Sea. nd

3535 Ward Lock's pictorial and descriptive guide to Aldeburgh, Southwold, ... and the Suffolk coast. [1907] and later edns

3536 Official guide. [c.1927] and later edns

3537 **Aldeburgh Festival Committee.** Changing face of Aldeburgh: catalogue of an exhibition ... 16–27 June 1965. Aldeburgh, [1965]. [Typescript]

3538 **Burnet, E.** All sayles bearinge: an Aldeburgh notebook. Ipswich, [1968]

3539 **Blythe, R.,** *Ed.* Aldeburgh anthology. Aldeburgh, 1972

3540 Album of Aldeburgh views. [c.1890]. nl

GENERAL HISTORY *See also* 1283, 2523, 2721–31, 2865–79, 3084

3541 Historical collections for Aldeburgh in the county of Suffolk, 1086–1795. [*Ed.* by F. Capper-Brooke] nd. MS

3542 **Hele, N. F.** Notes or jottings about Aldeburgh, Suffolk. Relating to matters historical, antiquarian, ornithological, and entomological. Ipswich, 1870. 2nd edn. 1890

3543 **Redstone, V. B.** Aldeburgh. PSIA 12, 1904/06, 202–15

3544 Aldeburgh parish history. SC 13.7.1928, Rp No 80

3545 **Scarfe, N.** Growth of Aldeburgh. Felixstowe, 1951

3546 **Jobson, A.** Aldeburgh story. Lowestoft, 1954

3547 **Clodd, H. P.** Aldeburgh: the history of an ancient borough. Ipswich, 1959

3548 **Ganz, C.** Discovery of Roman remains at Aldeburgh, May 1907. PSIA 13, 1907/09, 24–32

3549 **Winn, A. T.** Aldeburgh Poll Tax, 1641. Colchester, 1926

3550 A signe from heaven; or, A fearefull and terrible noise heard in the ayre, at Aldbrow ... the 4 day of August ... 1642. Wing S 3776. BL-T

PARLIAMENTARY HISTORY *See also* 847

3551 **Smythe, S. W.** Former Aldeburgh elections [1571–1812]. ECM 1, 1900/01, 132–3; 2, 1901/02, 32–5

3552 **Bohun, W.** Collections of debates, reports, orders, and resolutions of the House of Commons, touching the right of electing members to serve in Parliament ... [includes Aldborough, Dunwich.] 1702. BL

3553 Poll book, 9 Oct 1812. Halesworth, 1812. SRO/B

HARBOUR AND FISHING *See also* 284

3554 Aldboro harbour, completed and drawn by William Scott [3 maps]. Ipswich, 1851. nl

3555 Aldborough harbour of refuge and improvement bill: Admiralty reports. HC 1852, 26

3556 **G, C.** Aldeburgh sprats. [6pp broadsheet]. Lowestoft, [1907]

3557 Eel industry at Aldeburgh. CL 25, 1909, 736–7

3558 **Welford, A.** Aldeburgh boats. MM 37, 1951, 168

LOCAL GOVERNMENT AND SOCIAL SERVICES

Municipal Government   See also **482, 1454, 1457**

3559 **Royal Commission on Historical Manuscripts.** Reports Ser 55 Var Coll. 4 ... Orford and Aldeburgh. 1907

3560 **Winn, A. T.,** *Ed.* Records of the borough of Aldeburgh. v 1. The Order Book, 1549–1631. v 2. Church. Hertford, 1926

3561 **Groome, J. H.** Appeal to the Freemen of the borough of Aldeburgh ... from a late decision of the bailiffs and capital burgesses of the same borough. 1812

3562 **Sweeting, R. D.** Report to the Local Government Board on the water supply of the borough of Aldeburgh-on-Sea. 1899

Education

3563 **Aldeburgh Lodge.** [School] Magazine, 1893–1937. [*Cont. as* Orwell Park, Nacton, Crespigny House, Eaton House]. nl

3564 **Orwell Park [School].** Class lists from 1870. nl

3565 **Convent of Our Lady of Perpetual Succour.** Boarding and day school ... Prospectus. Gloucester, [1937] BL

CHURCH OF ST. PETER AND ST. PAUL

3566 Story of Aldeburgh parish church. Gloucester, [1934]

3567 Aldeburgh parish church. [Ipswich], 1947. SRO/I. 1950. O

3568 Parish church of St. Peter and St. Paul, Aldeburgh, Suffolk, 1800–1951. [c.1951]

3569 **Blythe, R.** Parish church of St. Peter and St. Paul, Aldeburgh. Gloucester, 1957 and later edns

3570 **Godfrey, R. C. R.** Aldeburgh parish church. 1950

CULTURE AND RECREATION   *See also* **2582–9, 7275–9**

3571 **Aldeburgh Festival Committee.** Aldeburgh Festival of Music and the Arts. Programme book, 1948– Aldeburgh, 1948– SCL/L

3572 **Darwin, B.** Aldeburgh Golf Club: founded 1884. c.1933

BUILDINGS

3573 Suffolk bygone [stove at Aldeburgh]. Conn 56, 1920, 247

3574 Town and country Planning Act, 1947, section 30. Provisional list of buildings of architectural or historic interest ... Aldeburgh, nd. [Typescript]

3575 **Department of the Environment.** List of buildings of special architectural or historic interest: District of Suffolk Coastal (Aldeburgh area). 1974. [Typescript].

ALDERTON

3576 Alderton parish history. SC 10.4.1931, Rp No 223

ALDHAM   *See also* 2441

3577 Aldham parish history. SC 4.7.1930, Rp No 183
3578 **Partridge, C.** Churchyard inscriptions from Aldham. REMI 1, 1911/12, 35–7

ALDRINGHAM-CUM-THORPE

3579 Aldringham-cum-Thorpe parish history. EADT 18.4.1934, Rp No 350
3580 Origin of the Strict Baptist chapel, Aldringham, Suffolk, by a Sunday School teacher. [Signed Israel Nichols]. 1895. O

ALPHETON

3581 **Thompson, J. R.** Alpheton. [c.1900]. NCL/N
3582 Alpheton parish history. EADT 1.5.1935, Rp No 395
3583 **Holden, J. S.** Ancient camp, Alpheton. PSIA 14, 1910/12, 305–07

AMPTON   *See also* 576

3584 **P[age], A.** Topographical notices of the parishes of Ampton, Harkstead, and Livermere Parva, Suffolk. CTetG 7, 1842, 292–301
3585 Ampton parish history. SC 30.1.1931, Rp No 213
3586 Memoranda concerning the Boys' Hospital, founded by James Calthorpe, 1702. [By A. Page]. Ipswich, 1838
3587 **Page, A.** Ampton church. PSIA 1, 1848/53, 190–98
3588 [**Mills, C. J. H.**] Ampton church. 1950. [Typescript]. SRO/B
3589 **Wickham, W. A.** Parsons and patrons of Ampton. PSIA 18, 1922/4, 124–43
3590 **Marsham, R.,** *et al.* Brasses in Ampton church. PSA 2nd Ser 12, 1887/9, 369–74

ASHBOCKING   *See also* 2718, 3342

3591 **Morley, C.** Ashbocking. nd. [Typescript]
3592 Ash Bocking. PSIA 11, 1901/03, 228–46
3593 Ashbocking parish history. SC 1.3.1929, Rp No 113
3594 Corbet House [school]. Prospectus. [1929]
3595 Corbet House Review. v 1, No 5. Christmas 1928

3596   Birch, H. W. Church notes: Ashbocking. E Ang NS 5, 1893/4, 251–3

ASHBY

3597   Ashby parish history. EADT 25.9.1935, Rp No 411
3598   Long, C. M. A survey of the manor and church of Ashby. [c.1955]. SCL/L
3599   [Kirk, T.] St. Mary's church, Ashby. [Herringfleet], 1973. [Typescript]. SCL/L

ASHFIELD-CUM-THORPE
3600   Ashfield-cum-Thorpe parish history. EADT 13.3.1935. Rp No 390

ASHFIELD, GREAT   *See also* 3370

3601   Thompson, J. R. Ashfield Magna. [c.1900]. NCL/N
3602   Great Ashfield parish history. SC 15.11.1929, Rp No 150
3603   Ford, J. C. Tythe terrier of Ashfield Magna. E Ang NS 2, 1887/8, 334–6
3604   Hill, H. C. Great Ashfield cross. PSIA 20, 1928/30, 280–86

ASPALL

3605   Aspall parish history. SC 20.2.1914, Rp No 1
3606   Cornish, C. J. Aspall Hall. CL 4, 1898, 599–601
3607   Girling, F. A. Early sixteenth-century decorated bricks at Aspall Hall. PSIA 29, 1961/3, 342–4

ASSINGTON

3608   Assington parish history. SC 19.4.1929, Rp No 120
3609   Smith, D. E. Assington through the centuries. np, 1974. SRO/B
3610   Smith, D. E. The manor of Assington, Shimplingford, Stratton, and Serles in Cornard Parva. Assington, 1970. [Typescript]
3611   Gurdon, J. Co-operative farms at Assington. J. Royal Agric. Soc. of England 24, 1863, 4–6
3612   Assington church and Hall. PSIA 11, 1901/03, 220–24
3613   Wood, A. F., *and* Leonard, C. J. St. Edmund's church, Assington. Assington, 1950. [Typescript]
3614   Christian, J. A. Identifying the brasses at Assington, Suffolk. TMBS 11, 1975, 431–6

ATHELINGTON
3615   Athelington parish history. EADT 25.10.1933, Rp No 330

BABERGH HUNDRED   *See also* 693, 980, 2406

3616   Number of inhabited houses in the several parishes included within the hundred of Babergh ... with the amount of population, taken from the last census. HC 1842, 33

BACTON   *See also* 3325

3617   Bacton parish history. SC 18.1.1929, Rp No 107
3618   **Dodwell, B.** Some charters relating to the honour of Bacton. PRS NS 36, 1960, 147–66
3619   **Hemsworth, A. B.** Bacton church. PSIA 5, 1876/86, 185–94
3620   **Stannard, E. W.** St. Mary the Virgin, Bacton: a short guide. Bacton, 1968.

BADINGHAM

3621   **Redstone, V. B.** Badingham. PSIA 10, 1898/1900, 382–93
3622   Badingham parish history. SC 26.4.1929, Rp No 121
3623   Parish church of St. John the Baptist, Badingham. nd
3624   **Salmon, J.** Carving on the porch of Badingham church. PSIA 32, 1970/72, 88–90
3625   **Raven, J. J.** Rectory of Badingham ... in 1575 and 1631. E Ang NS 7, 1897/8, 321–2

BADLEY

3626   Badley parish history. EADT 7.1.1934, Rp No 342

BADWELL ASH

3627   Badwell Ash parish history. SC 15.6.1928, Rp No 76
3628   **Worth, J.,** *and* **Hunter,** *Dr.* Account of human bones filled with lead. Arch 4, 1777, 69–72
3629   **Winbolt, S. E.** Loom-weights from a kiln. Ant J 15, 1935, 474–5

BALLINGDON-CUM-BRUNDON   *See also* 1322, 2816

3630   Ballingdon-cum-Brundon parish history. EADT 13.4.1938
3631   **Moir, J. R.,** *and* **Hopwood, A. T.** Excavations at Brundon (1935–7). PPS NS 5, 1939, 1–32
3632   **Chancellor, F.** Ballingdon Hall. EAST NS 11, 1911, 57–8

BARDWELL   *See also* 716

3633   **Thompson, J. R.** Bardwell. [c.1900]. NCL/N

3634 Bardwell parish history. SC 21.8.1931, Rp No 242

3635 **Fyfe, A. D. C.** Parish church of S. Peter and S. Paul, Bardwell. 1967. SRO/B

3636 **Wilkinson, H.** 15th-century glass in Bardwell church. JMGP 5–6, 1933/7, 159–62

3637 **Dunlap, A. P.** Paintings on the walls of Bardwell church. PSIA 2, 1854/9, 41–50

3638 **Warren, F. E.** Gild of St. Peter in Bardwell (with churchwardens' accounts and Town wardens' accounts). PSIA 11, 1901/03, 18–145

3639 Bardwell churchwardens' accounts, 1588. SAAP, Pt 2, June 1847, 7–8

3640 **Warren, F. E.**, *Ed.* Registers of Bardwell, co. Suffolk, 1538 to 1650. 1893. 20 copies

3641 **Warren, F. E.** Parish registers of Bardwell. MGetH 2nd Ser 5, 1894, *passim*

BARHAM *See also* **2398, 2481–5, 3104, 3155, 3161**

3642 Barham parish history. SC 15.3.1929, Rp No 115

3643 **Paterson, T. T.** Studies on the Palaeolithic succession in England. No 1, The Barham sequence. PPS NS 3, 1937, 87–135

3644 **Birch, H. W.** Church notes: Barham. E Ang NS 6, 1895/6, 177–82

3645 **Pearson, W. C.** Collections on briefs made in the parish of Barham. E Ang NS 10, 1903/04, 194–5

3646 Shrubland Park. CL 10, 1901, 560–67

3647 **Wood, E.** Notes on the history of Shrubland. PSIA 17, 1919/21, 123–6

3648 **Hussey, C.** Shrubland Park. CL 114, 1953, 948–51, 1654–7, 1734–8

3649 **Dow, L.** Armorial shield at Shrubland Park. PSIA 27, 1955/7, 123–4

BARKING *See also* **2541, 2672, 2720, 2742, 3170, 3334, 3389**

3650 Barking history. SC 22.4.1927, Rp No 17

3651 Antique statue of bronze, discovered [near Barking Hall] in Suffolk and now in possession of the Earl of Ashburnham. Vet Mon 4, 1815, 11–15

3652 **Birch, H. W.** Church notes: Barking. E Ang NS 6, 1895/6, 292–8

3653 An appeal for the repair of Barking church, Suffolk. np, [c.1920]. nl

3654 **Lingwood, H. R.** St. Mary's church, Barking. Ipswich, 1954.

BARNARDISTON

3655 Barnardiston parish history. EADT 5.8.1936, Rp No 445

BARNBY

3656 Barnby parish history. EADT 11.11.1935, Rp No 418

3657   **East Suffolk County Council.** Planning Dept. Policy for the classification of settlements: policy statement and planning proposals. Barnby and North Cove. Ipswich, 1967

BARNHAM   *See also* **582**

3658   **Thompson, J. R.** Barnham [c.1900]. NCL/N
3659   Barnham parish history. EADT 26.6.1935, Rp No 401
3660   **Clarke, W. G.** Some Barnham palaeoliths. PPSEA 1, 1908/14, 300–03
3661   **O'Neil, B. H. St. J.** Beaker found at Barnham. Ant J 24, 1944, 147–8
3662   **Edwardson, A. R.** Bronze Age burial at Barnham. PSIA 27, 1955/7, 186–90
3663   **Pryke, W. W.** Barnham chapel. Lavenham, 1970

BARNINGHAM

3664   Barningham parish history. SC 28.10.1932, Rp No 289

BARROW   *See also* **1784, 1959, 2505**

3665   **Thompson, J. R.** Barrow. [c.1900]. NCL/N
3666   Barrow parish history. SC 13.3.1914, Rp No 4
3667   **Wright, J. R. M.** Growth of a village: a record of development in Barrow ... np, [1974]
3668   **Massey, M.** All Saints, Barrow: a short history. Bury St. Edmunds, 1970
3669   Parish magazine. Extant 1912–40; then as part of Deanery magazine to 1953; now The Stile, 1953–
3670   **Duncan, J.** Barrow Congregational church. 1964. [Typescript]. SRO/B

BARSHAM   *See also* **3366–7**

3671   **Suckling, F. H.** Some notes on Barsham Juxta Beccles ... (with pedigree of Etchingham). Gen NS 21, 1904– NS 23, 1906, *passim*. Rp Exeter, 1906
3672   Barsham parish history. SC 29.9.1929, Rp No 142
3673   Church of the Most Holy Trinity, Barsham. Beccles, 1929 and later edns

BARTON, GREAT   *See also* **2599–605**

3674   Great Barton parish history. SC 29.8.1930, Rp No 191
3675   **Jones, J.** Supposed vestiges of a pile-dwelling in Barton Mere, near Bury. QJISA 1, 1869, 31–6
3676   **Bunbury, H. E.** Silver coins of Edward the Confessor: Great Barton. PSIA 2, 1854/9, 276
3677   **Tymms, S.** Gold ear-ring bronze ring; and a lump of silver formed of coins of Edward the Confessor, found at Great Barton. PSA 4, 1857/9, 27

BARTON MILLS *See also* **576, 3261**

3678 Thompson, J. R. Barton Parva, Bertunna, or Barton Mills. 1901. NCL/N

3679 Barton Mills parish history. EADT 13.9.1933, Rp No 324

3680 **Fox, C.** Note on the excavation of a barrow [Beacon Hill]. Ant 4, 1924, 55–6

3681 **Cawdor,** *Earl, et al.* Beacon Hill barrow. PCAS 26, 1925, 19–65

3682 **Trotter, H. W. T.** The founder of the Davies charity, Barton Mills. SR 2, 1964, 267–71

3683 **Lacon, C. H.** St. Mary's church and the parish of Barton Mills. [c.1912]

3684 **Powell, E.** List of rectors with sundry documents relating to church matters at Barton Mills. PSIA 13, 1907/09, 178–90

3685 **Parker, J.** Reminiscences of the Baptist chapel, Barton Mills, 1803–1909, [and] a record of all those interred in the burial ground. *Ed.* with additions by J. Duncan. 1961. [Typescript]. SRO/B

BATTISFORD

3686 Battisford parish history. SC 2.12.1932, Rp No 293

3687 **Partridge, C.** Monumental inscriptions in Battisford churchyard. E Ang NS 11, 1905/06, 86–7

BAWDSEY *See also* **1033**

3688 Bawdsey parish history. SC 10.4.1931, Rp No 223

3689 **Wilson, D. M.** Anglo-Saxon playing piece for Bawdsey. PSIA 32, 1970/72, 38–42

3690 **Dyke, G.** Bawdsey church. SR 1, 1958, 160–62

3691 Accounts of the Roman castle at Bawdsey. GM 1st Ser 58, 1788, 1154–5

3692 Bawdsey Manor: the garden. CL 25, 1909, 628–9

BAYLHAM

3693 Baylham parish history. SC 5.12.1930, Rp No 205

3694 **Lingwood, E.** Neolithic flint implements found at Baylham. PSIA 7, 1889/91, 209–11

3695 **Watling, H.** Discovery of the remains of a Roman road in the parish of Baylham. JBAA 25, 1869, 387–8

3696 **West, S. E.** Roman road at Baylham mill. Ant J 36, 1956, 73–5

3697 **Birch, H. W.** Church notes: Baylham. E Ang NS 6, 1895/6, 369–72

BEALINGS, GREAT *See also* **3067–8, 3168, 3300–02**

3698 Great Bealings parish history. SC 30.3.1928, Rp No 65

3699 **Moor, E.** Bealings bells. An account of the mysterious ringing of bells at

Great Bealings, Suffolk, in 1834; and in other parts of England, etc. Woodbridge, 1841

3700 **Birch, H. W.** Church notes: Great Bealings. E Ang NS 13, 1909/10, 261–4
3701 T. Seckford Hall. CL 27, 1910, 90–95
3702 Short history of Seckford Hall and the Seckford family. [1966]

BEALINGS, LITTLE   *See also* 3067–8

3703 Little Bealings parish history. EADT 17.1.1934, Rp No 340
3704 **Beck, J.** Anglo-Saxon sword-knife, or *scramura-seax* [from] Little Bealings. PSA 2nd Ser 10, 1883/5, 17–18
3705 **Pearce, J. W. E.,** *and* **Redstone, V. B.** Suffolk find of Roman coins. PSIA 22, 1934/6, 150–52
3706 **Birch, H. W.** Church notes: Little Bealings. E Ang NS 13, 1909/10, 279–80

BECCLES

DIRECTORIES AND ALMANACS
3707 **Stebbings, A.** Directory of Beccles, 1887–. Lowestoft. BL
3708 **Kelly's** directory of ... Beccles. *See* Lowestoft: Directories
3709 **Localads.** Beccles, Bungay, Loddon directory, 1962/63–. Needham Market
3710 Beccles illustrated almanack and cash diary for 1890–1903. Beccles. SRO/B. 1896. SCL/L

GUIDES
3711 **Glyde, J.** Johnson's guide to Beccles, and handbook of information to visitors. Beccles, 1870. BTH
3712 **Jordan, A. W.** Illustrated guide to Beccles: a full and comprehensive history of the town. Beccles, [1894]. NCL/N
3713 Official guide. 1901 and later edns

GENERAL HISTORY   *See also* 2740–41
3714 **Charnock, R. S.,** *and* **Spurdens, W. T.** On the etymology of Beccles. PSIA 4, 1864/74, 90–93
3715 Beccles parish history. 2 pts. SC 4.10.1929; 11.10.1929. Rp Nos 144, 145
3716 A proper newe sonet declaring the lamentation of Beccles, Suffolke, which was in the great winde upon S. Andrewes eue last most pittifully burned with fire, to the losse by estimation of twentie thousande pound and upwards, and to the number of foure score dwelling houses. 1586. [A ballad, signed: T.D., i.e. Thomas Deloney]. STC 6564. BL
3717 **Goodwyn, E. A.** Beccles and Bungay Georgian miscellany. Beccles, [1969]
3718 **Goodwyn, E. A.** A century of a Suffolk town: Beccles, 1760–1860. Pt 1. 1760–1815. Ipswich, [1968]

3719   Goodwyn, E. A. A Suffolk town in mid-Victorian England: Beccles in the 1860's. Beccles, [1965]

3720   Goodwyn, E. A. Beccles past. Ipswich, [1973]

3721   Goodwyn, E. A. Small town jubilee: Beccles in 1897. Ipswich, 1975

3722   Goodwyn, E. A. Beccles matters. Beccles, [1976]. [Typescript]

3723   Snowden, F. L. Ploughshares into swords: the history of G. Company (Beccles) 1st Suffolk Battn., Home Guard. Beccles, 1945. BTH

ECONOMIC HISTORY   *See also* **1336, 1351, 1393**

3724   Clowes, W. B. Family business, 1803–1953. [1953]

3725   Clowes, W., *and* Sons. 150th anniversary celebrations: souvenir programme. June 1953. SCL/L

LOCAL GOVERNMENT   *See also* **1454–5**

3726   Catalogue of muniments belonging to the corporation of Beccles. Beccles, 1916. BTH

3727   Rix, W. S. Beccles collections. 35v. MSS, etc. BTH

3728   General report to the King in council from the honourable Board of Commissioners on the Public Records. [Includes Beccles, Dunwich, and Southwold]. 1837

3729   **Royal Commission on Historical Manuscripts.** Reports Ser 55. Var Coll. 7 ... Corporations of Beccles, Dunwich, Southwold ... 1914

3730   Ulph, E. C. A Suffolk manorial water-leet. SR 1, 1958, 149–51

3731   Account of the receipts and disbursments of E. C. Sharpin, Treasurer of the Beccles Division ... from Midsummer 1847 to Midsummer 1848. Beccles, [1848]. BL

3732   Ashby, W. J. Extracts from the Beccles overseers' accounts, 1637–45. E Ang NS 2, 1887/8, 402–03

3733   Beccles Corporation. Account of the corporation of Beccles Fen ... with a translation of their charter ... Norwich, 1807. Beccles, 1826

3734   Byelaws for the borough administration ... Beccles, 1841. 1843. BTH

3735   Byelaws ... relating to Beccles Common. Beccles, 1933. BTH

3736   Abstract of Treasurer's account, 1836–7; 1838–9; 1841–2; 1844–5. Beccles, 1837–45. O

3737   Bretton, R. Civic arms: Beccles. CA 5, 1958/9, 108

Poor Relief, Charities, Public Health, Education   *See also* **2852**

3738   **Beccles Medical Dispensary.** State of the charity from 24 June 1826 to 25 June 1827. Beccles. [1827]. BL

3739   **Beccles Medical Dispensary.** State of the charity from 1836–7; 1837–8; 1838–9; 1839–40; 1841–2; 1842–3: 1843–4: 1844–5: 1845–6. Beccles, 1837–46. O

3740   **Beccles Medical Dispensary.** Rules, to which is subjoined the report of the proceedings for the year ending 24 July 1840. Beccles, 1840. O

3741 Petition to the Mayor, Aldermen, and Councillors of the Beccles corporation from 7 local doctors re "Child health". Beccles, 1905. BTH

3742 **Ulph, E. C.** *and* **McCarthy, A. M.** Sir John Leman school, Beccles, 1631–1969. Beccles, 1970

Planning and Development   See also **1642, 1646**

3743 **East Suffolk County Council.** Planning Dept. Factual survey and outline plan for the borough of Beccles. Ipswich, 1950. 1951 with amendments. [Typescript]. SCL/L

3744 **East Suffolk County Council.** Planning Dept. Beccles, with part of Wainford Rural District: survey and appraisal. Ipswich, 1966

3745 **East Suffolk County Council.** Planning Dept. Beccles with part of Wainford Rural District. Draft town map review, 1967. Draft town centre map, 1967. Ipswich, 1967

3746 **East Suffolk County Council.** Planning Dept. Beccles, with part of Wainford Rural District: town map, written statement. Ipswich, 1967

3747 **East Suffolk County Council.** Planning Dept. County development plan. Amendment No 8. Beccles and parts of Wainford Rural District, 1968. Approved 1972. Written statement and town map. Ipswich, 1968. 1972. SCL/L

RELIGION AND CHURCHES

General

3748 **Guild of the Holy Ghost, Beccles.** E Ang 3, 1866/8, 52–4; 91–2; 116–18; 119–21

3749 **Pond, C. C.,** *and* **Ulph, E. C.** Memorial to Beccles martyrs, 1556–1956: to commemorate the quater-centenary service at the Martyrs' Memorial Chapel, Beccles, 16 May 1956. Beccles, 1956. BTH

Church of St. Michael

3750 **Davy, H.** Set of etchings illustrative of Beccles church and other Suffolk antiquities, with a descriptive index. Norwich, 1818

3751 Parish church of St. Michael, Beccles. Beccles, 1929 and later edns

3752 Beccles parish church: a brief sketch of its history from the earliest times. [c.1950]

3753 **Ashby, W. J.** Beccles churchwardens' accounts. E Ang NS 2, 1887/8, *passim*

3754 MS notes inserted in a copy of King Edward VI's first Prayer Book, in the church library at Beccles. PCAS 1, 1859, 67–9

3755 Parish magazine. Extant 1952

Nonconformity   See also **1991, 3502**

3756 **Rix, S. W.** Brief records of the Independent church at Beccles, Suffolk, including biographical notices of its ministers, etc. 1837

3757 **Rix, S. W.** Nonconformity, the development of a principle: an historical sketch for a Bicentenary Commemoration (1852). A brief summary of the growth of nonconformity in Beccles from the Independent church in that town in 1652 to the Commemoration in 1852. Beccles, 1852. SCL/L

3758 Proceedings at the celebration of the twenty-fifth anniversary [17 Feb 1859] of the pastorate of the Rev. John Flower, over the Congregational church, Beccles. [Rp from "Beccles and Bungay Weekly News"]. NCL/N

THEATRE

3759 **Vertue, F. H.** Norfolk and Suffolk school of comedy—Beccles. E Ang NS 2, 1887/8, 90–91

SOCIETIES

3760 **Beccles Museum.** Announcement of the formation of a society for the study of natural history, signed W. J. Crowfoot. Beccles, 1839. O

3761 **Youngman, A. W.** Some notes on Apollo Lodge, No 305, Beccles, 1794–1844. SIMT, No 3913 1930

BUILDINGS

3762 **Tymms, S.** Roos Hall. PSIA 4, 1864 74, 94–8

3763 **Philips, J.** Beccles, no 14, Northgate [early harbour wall?]. PSIA 30, 1964/6, 285

3764 **Department of the Environment.** List of buildings of special architectural or historic interest: borough of Beccles, East Suffolk. 1971. [Typescript]

BEDFIELD   *See also* **2659**

3765 Bedfield parish history. EADT 21.6.1933, Rp No 315

BEDINGFIELD

3766 Bedingfield parish history. SC 9.3.1928, Rp No 62

3767 **Millard, J. W.** Destruction of parish vermin in the sixteenth century at Bedingfield. E Ang NS 2, 1887/8, 328–9

3768 Registers of St. Mary's, Bedingfield, Suffolk, 1538–1935. *Ed.* by A. L. Bedingfield. 1936. [Typescript]

BELSTEAD   *See also* **2441**

3769 Belstead parish history. SC 26.6.1931, Rp No 234

3770 **Birch, H. W.** Church notes: Belstead. E Ang NS 7, 1897/9, 241–4; 266–8

3771 Views of Hill House, Belstead, taken by W. Vick, Ipswich, 1887. 2v

BELTON

3772 Belton parish history. EADT 23.9.1936, Rp No 450

3773 **East Suffolk County Council.** Planning Dept. Outline plan for Belton. Ipswich, 1964. SCL/L

3774 **East Suffolk County Council.** Planning Dept. Belton: policy statement and planning proposals. Ipswich, 1964

BENACRE   *See also* **8099**

3775 Benacre parish history. EADT 1.4.1936, Rp No 432

3776 **L[oder], R.** Large hoard of silver coins found at Benacre. GM 1st Ser 56, 1786, 472–3

BENHALL

3777 Benhall parish history. EADT 23.11.1932, Rp No 292

3778 **Chappell, W.** Bronze fifteenth-century purse-mounting found at Benhall. PSA 2nd Ser 4, 1867/70, 74

3779 **Aldred, H. W.** History of the manor of Benhall ... 1887

BENTLEY   *See also* **3404–6**

3780 Bentley parish history. SC 24.12.1930, Rp No 208

3781 **Birch, H. W.** Church notes: Bentley. E Ang NS 7, 1897/8, 220–21

BEYTON

3782 Beyton parish history. SC 5.6.1931, Rp No 231

BILDESTON

3783 **Growse, F. S.** Materials for a history of the parish of Bildeston ... with pedigrees and genealogical notices ... compiled in the year 1859, revised and brought up to date in 1891. 1892. 25 copies

3784 Bildeston parish history. SC 10.6.1927, Rp No 24

3785 **Ray, V. S. P.** Short history of Bildeston. Bildeston, 1951

3786 **Nelson, S.** Medieval and later finds from near Bildeston church. PSIA 33, 1973/5, 315–18

3787 **Kaye, R.** Church of St. Mary Magdalene, Bildeston. 1972

BLACKBOURNE HUNDRED

3788 **Powell, E., *Ed*.** A Suffolk hundred in the year 1283. The assessment of the Hundred of Blackbourne for a tax of one-thirtieth and a return showing the land tenure there. Cambridge, 1910

3789 **Colman, S., *Ed*.** Hearth Tax returns for the Hundred of Blackbourne, 1662. PSIA 32, 1970/02, 168–92

BLAKENHAM, GREAT   *See also* 2945

3790   Great Blakenham parish history. SC 14.3.1930, Rp No 167
3791   **Birch, H. W.** Church notes: Blakenham Magna. E Ang NS 6, 1895/6, 102–04
3792   **Prime, R. G.** Great Blakenham Baptist chapel, 1873–1973. Great Blakenham, 1973

BLAKENHAM, LITTLE

3793   Little Blakenham parish history. SC 14.3.1930, Rp No 167
3794   **Birch, H. W.** Church notes: Blakenham Parva. E Ang NS 6, 1895/6, 104–05

BLAXHALL   *See also* 2881, 3270

3795   Blaxhall parish history. SC 4.4.1930, Rp No 170

BLUNDESTON

3796   Blundeston parish history. SC 3.1.1930, Rp No 157
3797   **Steward,** *Mrs.* Views of Blundeston. 1855. SCL/L
3798   **Mayes, I.** History of Blundeston school, 1726–1976. Somerleyton, 1976
3799   Charles Dickens and Blundeston. Lowestoft, 1928
3800   **Blundeston Dickens Centenary Festival Committee.** Blundeston Charles Dickens centenary festival, 1870–1970. Blundeston, 1970
3801   **W.** Monumental inscriptions at Blundeston. E Ang 4, 1869/70, 199–201, 207–09, 225–6

BLYFORD   *See also* 2248

3802   Blyford parish history. EADT 19.10.1932, Rp No 288
3803   **Noot, J. F.** Blyford church. PSIA 8, 1892/4, 427–8

BLYTH RURAL DISTRICT

3804   Official guide. 1949 and later edns
3805   Town and Country Planning Act, 1947, Section 30. Provisional list of buildings of architectural or historic interest for consideration ... Rural district of Blyth. Dec 1948. List of buildings of special architectural or historic interest. Rural district of Blyth. 25 Oct 1951. 7 Dec 1966. 24 July 1970. 8 Oct 1970. 16 Jan 1973. [Typescript]

BLYTHBURGH   *See also* 7322

3806   **Raven, J. J.** Blythburgh. PSIA 4, 1864/74, 225–43
3807   Blythburgh parish history. SC 26.8.1927, Rp No 35

3808 **Waller, J. G.** Table-book found at Blythburgh. PSA 2nd Ser 19, 1901/03, 40–42

3809 **Mason, C.** Blythburgh and its church. Reliquary NS 12, 1906, 217–28

3810 **Becker, M. J.** Blythburgh: an essay on the village and its church. Halesworth, 1935

3811 **Andrews, F. C.** Blythburgh and Bulcamp. Rp from Leiston Observer. Leiston, [1937]

3812 Bygone Blythburgh exhibition in aid of Bells for Blythburgh Fund, Ipswich Art Gallery, 28 Oct–3 Nov 1946. [Ipswich], [1946]

3813 **Royal Commission on historical manuscripts.** Ser 13. 10th Report, Appendix 4 ... Manuscripts of the Rev. T. S. Hill ... relating to the Priory of Blythburgh ... 1885. Rp 1906

3814 **Hartshorne, A.** Blythborough church. Arch J 44, 1887, 1–14

3815 **Oakes, T. H. R.** Blythburgh church, priory, and Holy Rood chapel. PSIA 8, 1892/4, 422–7

3816 History of Blythborough church. Colchester, 1896. nl

3817 Blythburgh and Walberswick churches: appeal for £2,000. Ipswich, 1901. nl

3818 [**Thompson, A. D.**] Pocket guide to the church of Holy Trinity, Blythburgh. 1922 and var. edns. to 1969, Rev. and rewritten by O.K.C., i.e. Mrs O. K. Collett

3819 **Johnston, P. M.** Blythburgh church, Holy Trinity. JBAA NS 34, 1929, 96–9

3820 **Fowler, J.** Account of a window in Blythburgh church. PSA 2nd Ser 8, 1879/81, 136–42

3821 **Woodforde, C.** Fifteenth-century glass in Blythburgh church. PSIA 21, 1931/3, 232–9

3822 **Gowers,** *Sir* **W. R.** Flint-work inscription on Blythburgh church. PSIA 11, 1901/03, 51–8

3823 **Harley, L. S.** Medieval floor-tiles from Blythburgh priory. PSIA 32, 1970/72, 276–9

3824 Extracts from the old churchwardens' accounts of Blythburgh. E Ang NS 2, 1887/8, 180–81

3825 Parish magazine. Jan. 1929–

BLYTHING HUNDRED   *See also* **695, 2444, 7817**

3826 **Parr, R. T. L.** Two townships in Blything Hundred. PSIA 25, 1949/51, 297–303

3827 To the Hon. the House of Commons ... the humble petition of the gentry, etc., within the Hundred of Blything, Suffolk [against repealing the Corn Laws]. [Halesworth], [1840?]. BL

3828 General statement of the accounts of the Blything Hundred Savings Bank, 1822, 1823, 1824, 1825, 1826, 1829, 1832. Halesworth, [1825–32]. BL

3829 **White, R. G.** A friendly address to the poor of the Hundred of Blything. Ipswich, 1746. BL

3830 Account of the general receipts and expenditure of the corporation of Blything [for the maintenance ... of the poor] ... from Easter 1810 to Easter 1817. [Halesworth?], 1827. BL

3831 Report of the committee ... of the Guardians of the Poor, within the Hundred of Blything ... to enquire into, and examine the state of the corporation. Halesworth, [1817]. BL

3832 Instructions to the overseers of the Hundred of Blything ... Halesworth. 1818. BL

3833 Bye-laws ... for the better governing of the corporation of Guardians of the Poor, in the Hundred of Blything ... Halesworth, 1818. 1828. BL

3834 To the Hundred of Blything. [An address on the subject of the Poor-Law assessment. By J. Jermyn?]. [Southwold?], [1812?]. BL

3835 Pro & con, or Hundred arguments, for a new Act, and against it. The second edition. [An address "To the Hundred of Blything". By J. Jermyn?] Southwold, [1821?]. BL

3836 General abstract of the receipts and disbursements of the corporation ... for the year ending Easter 1822, 1826, 1828, 1829, 1830, 1834. Halesworth, [1822–34]. BL

3837 List of directors and acting guardians, etc., 1825–26, 1828–29. Halesworth, [1825. 1828]. BL

3838 Bye-laws ... relating to the binding-out poor apprentices by the Guardians of the Poor, in the Hundred of Blything ... Halesworth, 1829. BL

3839 **White, J. M.** Some remarks on the statute law affecting parish apprentices. [Contains list of directors and acting guardians of the Blything Hundred]. Halesworth, 1829

3840 Report of a mission from the Blything Union to ascertain the probable employment of the agricultural labourer and his family in the manufacturing districts. [Signed by H. B. Bence and John Long]. 1835. BL

3841 Official account of the parochial charities and public trust funds belonging to each parish in the Blything Union. [*Ed.* with an introduction by S. Clissold]. Halesworth, 1838

3842 Blything Union. [Resolutions of the weekly meeting held 27 Jan 1845. Signed Harry White, clerk]. 1845. O

3843 Rules of an Association for the protection of property and punishment of offenders ... in the Hundred of Blything and parishes adjacent. Halesworth, [1830?]. BL

BOSMERE AND CLAYDON HUNDRED

3844 Bye-laws, rules, orders, and instructions for the better government and support of the poor, in the Hundred of Bosmere and Claydon ... [By W. Butler]. 1813. BL

3845 Rules, orders, and instructions for the better government and support of the poor, in the Hundred of Bosmere and Claydon. Ipswich, 1824. nl

BOTESDALE

3846 **Localads.** Diss and districts, including Botesdale, Eye, Harleston, etc. 1967 directory. Needham Market, 1968

3847 Botesdale parish history. EADT 5.5.1937, Rp No 470

3848 The Suffolk wonder, or the pleasant, facetious, and merry dwarf of Bottesdale, Christopher Bullock, watch and clockmaker; being in height three feet six inches . . . and no less than seven feet round his body. np, 1755. Soc of Antiquaries

3849 **Turner, J.** St. Botolph's chapel, Botesdale. E Ang NS 1, 1885/6, 78

BOULGE   *See also* 2865–79

3850 Boulge parish history. SC 8.3.1929, Rp No 114

3851 **Fowler, J. T.** Supposed Tournay font at Boulge, Suffolk. Ant J 3, 1923, 154–5.

BOXFORD

3852 Boxford parish history. SC 24.2.1928, Rp No 60

3853 [**Kingsbury, W. B.**] Short history of Boxford parish and its church of St. Mary. Colchester, 1962. SRO/B

3854 **Tugman, R.** History and development of Boxford. Boxford, [1972]

3855 **Mead, J.,** *Ed.* Boxford from old photographs. Boxford, 1974

3856 **Owles, E. [J.],** *and* **Smedley, N.** Two Belgic cemeteries at Boxford. PSIA 31, 1967/9, 88–104

3857 **Wells, C.** Cremated bones [found in Belgic cemeteries at Boxford]. PSIA 31, 1967/9, 104–07

3858 **Corrie, G. E.** On the parish accounts of Boxford, 1529–96. PCAS 1, 1850, 265–72

3859 **Tymms, S.** Boxford church. PSIA 3, 1860/63, 291–5

3860 St. Mary's church, Boxford. Cambridge, [1955]. SRO/B

3861 **Warman, J. P.** Churchwardens' accounts of a Suffolk parish in the sixteenth century, with extracts. E Ang NS 13, 1909/10, 337–40, 362–6

BOXTED   *See also* 3227

3862 Boxted parish history, 2 pts. SC 28.8.1936. 4.9.1936, Rp Nos 447, 448

BOYTON   *See also* 713

3863 Boyton parish history. 20.5.1932, Rp No 271

3864 Gold torque found at Boyton. Arch 26, 1836, 471

3865 **W.** Extracts from parish registers. E Ang 4, 1869/70, 217–20

BRADFIELD COMBUST   *See also* 2951

3866   Bradfield Combust parish history. SC 27.1.1933, Rp No 299

3867   **Duncan, J.** Bradfield Combust Methodist chapel. 1964. [Typescript]. SRO/B

3868   Out in the open: Bradfield Methodist church, 1867–1967. Bradfield, 1967. SRO/B

BRADFIELD ST. CLARE

3869   **Feltoe, C. L.** Bradfield St. Clare. PSIA 9, 1895/7, 323–9

3870   Bradfield St. Clare parish history. SC 10.1.1934, Rp No 339

3871   **Haslewood, F.** Parish register of Bradfield St. Clare, 1541–95. PSIA 9, 1895/7, 311–22

BRADFIELD ST. GEORGE

3872   Bradfield St. George parish history. EADT 20.3.1935, Rp No 391

3873   **Baker, M.,** *and* **Oxborrow, G.** Roman road at Bradfield St. George. PSIA 33, 1973/5, 311–13

3874   **Duncan, J.** First Baptist chapel at Bradfield St. George. 1965. [Typescript]. SRO/B

3875   **Duncan, J.** History of Bradfield St. George Baptist chapel. 1965. [Typescript]. SRO/B

BRADLEY, GREAT

3876   Great Bradley parish history. EADT 15.4.1936, Rp No 433

3877   **Johnson, A.** Church of St. Mary the Virgin, Great Bradley. 1973. [Typescript]

BRADLEY, LITTLE   *See also* 7732

3878   Little Bradley parish history. EADT 3.6.1936, Rp No 439

BRADWELL

3879   Bradwell parish history. EADT 18.8.1937

3880   Extracts from the award of the Commissioners … for inclosing lands in the parishes of Bradwell, Belton, and Fritton. 1814. nl,

BRAISEWORTH   *See also* 4862

3881   Braiseworth parish history. EADT 20.12.1933, Rp No 336

BRAMFIELD   *See also* 2671

3882   Bramfield parish history. SC 5.10.1928, Rp No 92

3883 Bramfield St. Andrew. PSIA 4, 1864–74, 454–6

3884 **Smith, M. E. O.** Bramfield church and village through the centuries. Halesworth, 1945 and later edns

3885 Parish registers of Bramfield. MGetH 2nd Ser 3–4, 1890/02, *passim*

3886 Regestrie booke off Bramefeide off all christnyngs weddyngs and buryings ... 1539–96 and 1693–1889. *Ed.* by T. S. Hill. 1894

BRAMFORD *See also* **629, 2882, 3317**

3887 Bramford parish history. SC 25.1.1929, Rp No 108

3888 **Moir, J. R.** Flint implements: Bramford. Ant 9, 239–43

3889 **Moir, J. R.** Fractured flints of the Eocene 'bull-head' bed at Coe's Pit, Bramford. PPSEA 1, 1908/14, 397–404

3890 **Birch, H. W.** Church notes: Bramford. E Ang NS 12, 1907/08, 364–7; NS 13, 1909/10, 8–9

3891 Pilgrim's guide to the parish church of St. Mary the Virgin, Bramford. Ramsgate, [1966]. SCL/I

BRAMPTON *See also* **447**

3892 Brampton parish history. EADT 16.5.1934, Rp No 354

3893 **Rye, N.** Brampton, Suffolk. Brampton, 1977. SCL/L

BRANDESTON *See also* **1847–8, 2458, 3265**

3894 Brandeston parish history. SC 28.2.1930, Rp No 165

3895 **Brandeston Hall History Society.** Survey of the parish of Brandeston. [1971]

3896 **Ferris, J.** Parish church of All Saints, Brandeston. nd

3897 **Rivett-Carnac, J. H.** Some 'glazing quarries' in Brandeston church. ECM 1, 1900/01, 183–90

BRANDON *See also* **613, 1240–41**

3898 **Localads.** Brandon and district directory. 1967/8–. Needham Market, [1968–]. NCL/N

3899 **Clarke, W. G.** Guide to the town of Brandon and the oldest industry in Britain. Thetford, 1908

3900 Official guide. [1936] and later edns

3901 Brandon parish history. SC 24.5.1929, Rp No 124

3902 **Skertchly, S. B. J.** On the survival of the Neolithic period at Brandon. RBA 1879, 400–01

3903 **Myers, C. S.** Account of some skulls discovered at Brandon [Romano-British]. JRAI 26, 1897, 113–28

3904 **Lethbridge, T. C.,** *and* **O'Reilly, M. M.** Samian bowl found ... near Brandon. PCAS 32, 1930/31, 61–2

3905 **Franks, A. W.** Description of two British urns and a rare stone object found near Brandon. PSA 2nd Ser 5, 1870/73, 270–75, 289

3906 **Morley, C.** Norse camp at Brandon. SBVC 10, 1928/9, 264–6

3907 To the humane and benevolent. The humble petition of the sufferers by fire, at Brandon. [Brandon], [1789]. BL

3908 **Munday, J. T.** Brandon manor rolls of the 1380's. Lakenheath, 1972

3909 **Harrison, J. P.** British flint-workers at Brandon. RBA 1880, 626–7

3910 **Lovett, E.** Gun-flint manufactory at Brandon, with reference to ... flint working in prehistoric times. Proc. Soc. of Antiquaries of Scotland 21, 1886/7, 206–12

3911 **Phillips, M.** Two industries connected with flint at Ling Heath, near Brandon. PSA 2nd Ser 23, 1909/11, 102

3912 **Lovett, E.** Gun-flint industry of Brandon. 1913

3913 **Clarke, R. R.** Flint-knapping industry at Brandon. Ant 9, 1935, 38–56

3914 Official opening of new bridge at Brandon: the bridge and its origins. Bury St. Edmunds, 1954

3915 [**Green, H. T.**] Brief history of the parish churches of Brandon Ferry, Santon Downham, Wangford ... Ramsgate, 1958 and later edns

3916 Parish magazine. 1897–

BRANTHAM *See also* **1358, 4022**

3917 Brantham parish history. EADT 28.12.1923, Rp No 296

3918 Rare urn from Suffolk (Brantham). Ant J 5, 1925, 73–4

3919 Brantham urn. CAGB 2, 1959, 5

3920 **Birch, H. W.** Church notes: Brantham. E Ang NS 8, 1899/1900, 143

3921 **Gooch, J. W.,** *and* **Smith, A. L.** St. Michael the Archangel, Brantham. Saffron Walden, [1971]

3922 **Gilmour, R. A.** Beaker and Bronze Age burials at Brantham Hall. PSIA 33, 1973/5, 116–30

BREDFIELD *See also* **2865–79**

3923 Bredfield parish history. SC 8.3.1929, Rp No 114

3924 **Borrett, A. H. V.** Bredfield. np, 1975

BRENT ELEIGH

3925 Brent Eleigh parish history. SC 8.8.1930, Rp No 188

3926 St. Mary the Virgin, Brent Eleigh: a short history and guide. Gloucester, [1961]

BRETTENHAM *See also* **2576, 3454**

3927 Brettenham parish history. SC 11.12.1931, Rp No 254

3928 **Betham, C. J.** Brettenham. PSIA 7, 1889/91, 251–2

3929 **Hill, H. C.** Combretonium and Brettenham. PSIA 19, 1925/7, 227–32

3930 **Old Buckenham Hall School** (formerly South Lodge [Lowestoft] School). South Lodge School magazine, c.1900–14, 1923–34; Old Buckenham Hall School magazine, 1952, 1954, 1957–62. O.B.H., 1962–. [At Brettenham since 1956]

3931 **Evans, G.** Hatchment in Brettenham church. CA 1, 1950/51, 61–2

BRICETT, GREAT

3932 Great Bricett parish history. SC 26.10.1928, Rp No 95

3933 **Fairweather, F. H.** Excavations on the side of the Augustinian alien priory of Great Bricett. PSIA 19, 1925/7, 99–109

3934 **Dickinson, P. G. M.** Brief notes on the discoveries at Great Bricett priory. SR 1, 1956, 41–4

BRIGHTWELL

3935 Brightwell parish history. SC 20.1.1933, Rp No 298

3936 **Moir, J. R.** Excavation of two tumuli on Brightwell Heath. IFCJ 6, 1921, 1–14

3937 **Birch, H. W.** Church notes: Brightwell. E Ang NS 13, 1909/10, 326–8

BROCKFORD   *See* Wetheringsett-cum-Brockford

BROCKLEY

3938 Brockley parish history. EADT 30.1.1935, Rp No 385

BROME   *See also* 2707–11

3939 Brome parish history. SC 3.2.1928, Rp No 57

3940 **Smith, L. T.,** *Ed.* A common-place book of the fifteenth century, containing a religious play and poetry, legal forms, and local accounts. Printed from the original manuscript at Brome Hall, Suffolk, by Lady C. Kerrison. 1886

3941 **Bateman-Hanbury, A. R.** Brome Hall. PSIA 14, 1910/12, 227–37

3942 **West, S. E.** Brome, Suffolk: excavation of a moated site. 1967. JBAA 3rd Ser 33, 1970, 89–121

3943 **[Elvin, E. F. C.]** Short guide to the memorials in Brome church, Suffolk, with notices of the memorials now lost ... remarks about Brome families and their estates. Diss, 1938

BROMESWELL   *See also* 3138

3944 Bromeswell parish history. SC 1.4.1932, Rp No 266

BRUISYARD

3945   Bruisyard parish history. SC 20.11.1931, Rp No 252
3946   Haslewood, F. Monastery at Bruisyard. PSIA 7, 1889/91, 320–23
3947   **Wayman, H. W. B.** Church notes: Bruisyard. E Ang NS 12, 1907/08, 162–4

BRUNDISH

3948   Brundish parish history. SC 22.11.1929, Rp No 151
3949   **Raven, J. J.** The Solemn League and Covenant made and subscribed at Brundish, 1942. E Ang NS 6, 1895/6, 338
3950   **Raven, J. J.** Brundish church. E Ang NS 3, 1889/90, 186–7
3951   **Raven, J. J.** Foundation deed of Brundish chantry. E Ang NS 9, 1901/02, 33–6
3952   Parish registers of Brundish, Suffolk. [*Ed.* by F. A. Crisp]. 1885. 30 copies

BRUNDON   *See* Ballingdon-cum-Brundon

BUCKLESHAM

3953   Bucklesham parish history. EADT 28.2.1934, Rp No 345

BULCAMP   *See also* 3811, 7859–60

3954   **Parr, R. T. L.** The battle of Bulcamp [A.D.654]. nd. [Typescript]. SRO/B
3955   Rules, orders, and regulations for the better government of the poor, in the Poor's House at Bulcamp. Ipswich, 1767. BL

BUNGAY

DIRECTORIES AND ALMANACS
3956   **Localads.** Beccles, Bungay, Loddon directory, 1962/63–. Needham Market
3957   Raynor's Bungay almanack. Bungay. Extant 1889–90. nl

GUIDES
3958   Official guide. 1919 and later edns

GENERAL AND ECONOMIC HISTORY   *See also* 1083, 1336–9, 2512, 2606, 2737, 3298
3959   **Raven, J. J.** Stray notes on the churches and town of Bungay. E Ang NS 2, 1887/8, 5–6
3960   Bungay parish history. 2 pts. SC 21.5.1929, 7.6.1929, Rp Nos 126, 127
3961   **Mann, E.** Old Bungay. 1934
3962   **Workers' Educational Association:** Bungay Branch. Bungay translations and transcriptions from six original manuscripts illustrating aspects of Bungay's local history between 1269 and 1786. Bungay, 1975
3963   **Braun, H.** Scarborough and Bungay. YAJ 33, 1936/8, 287–9

213

3964 **Clarke, R. R.** Anglo-Saxon burials at Bungay. PSIA 25, 1949/51, 304–06
3965 **Fleming, A.** A strange and terrible wunder wrought very late in the parish
church of Bongay ... the fourth of this August ... 1577, in a great
tempest ... with the appearance of an horrible shaped thing ... [1577]. STC
11050. Rp 1820
3966 **Baker, G. B.** Coins found at Bungay [Roman and medieval Scottish]. E
Ang 3, 1866/8, 90
3967 **Spencer, H. E. P.** Thirteenth-century steelyard weight from Bungay. PSIA
23, 1937/9, 175–6

LOCAL GOVERNMENT AND SOCIAL SERVICES
3968 Annual report of the Medical Officer of Health ... for the Bungay Urban
District Council for the year 1915. Bungay, [1916]. BL
3969 **Scott, J. B.** Bungay Grammar School. Bungay, 1858. SRO/B
3970 **Cane, L. B.** Bungay Grammar School. EAM 4, 1938/9, 456–66
3971 **Houghton, R. R.** Bungay Grammar School, 1565–1965. Bungay, [1965]
3972 **East Suffolk County Council.** Planning Dept. Conservation in Bungay:
townscape appraisal and policy statement. Ipswich, 1970
3973 **East Suffolk County Council.** Planning Dept. Bungay: policy statement and
planning proposals. Ipswich, 1971
3974 **Waveney District Council.** Planning Dept. Bungay: outstanding conservation area. Lowestoft, [1976]. SCL/L

RELIGION AND CHURCHES *See also* **3749**
3975 **Raven, J. J.** Deed of transfer to the Bungay nuns of a mother and her son,
with their dwelling-house, *temp.* Edw. I. E Ang NS 10, 1903/04, 221
3976 **Raven, J. J.** Ecclesiastical remains of Bungay. PSIA 4, 1864/74, 65–77
3977 Church of St. Mary, Bungay. nd. SCL/L
3978 **Wood, J.** Notes on St. Mary's church, Bungay. [c.1926]. MS
3979 **[Mann, E.]** Church of St. Mary, Bungay. [c.1935]. O
3980 **Lummis, W. M.** Churches of Bungay. [Based on "The church of St. Mary,
Bungay" and other works by E. Mann]. Gloucester, 1950 and later edns
3981 **Fleming, I.** Churches of Holy Trinity and St. Mary, Bungay. Southwold,
1972. NCL/N
3982 **Woodward, B. B.** Notices of the Reformation and the Great Rebellion ...
from the churchwardens' account book of St. Mary's parish, Bungay. PSA 4,
1853/9, 68, 155–8
3983 **Baker, G. B.** Extracts from churchwardens' books: Bungay St. Mary.
E Ang 3, 1866/8, 19–21, 43, 198–200
3984 **Baker, G. B.** Church bells of St. Mary's, Bungay. E Ang 3, 1866/8, 28–9.

CULTURE AND RECREATION

3985 Song of "Old Bungay": as sung at the theatre, by Mr. Fisher. [By S. Ashby?]. Bungay, [1816?]. BL

3986 Address spoken by Mr. C. Fisher at the opening of the new theatre, Bungay, on Thursday, 28 Feb 1828. Bungay, 1828. nl

3987 **Partridge, C. S.** Suffolk ballad: the pleasant history of the King and Lord Bigod of Bungay. E Ang NS 6, 1895/6, 56–9

3988 **Parr, R. T. L.** Who wrote the Bungay ballad? nd. [Typescript]. SRO/B

3989 Bungay Reform Festival, 27 June 1832. Printed at the Town Pump ... in the midst of 2,500 persons ... met to celebrate the passing of the Reform Bill, with the first printing press set up by the late Mr. Charles Brightly. By J. R. and C. Childs. Bungay, 1832. NCL/N

3990 **Kemp, J. O.** Historical scenes from ancient Bungay reproduced in the Castle ruins, 24 June 1908. Bungay, 1908. NCL/N

3991 **Baker, G. B.** Church ale-games, and interludes (Bungay). E Ang 1, 1858/63, 291–2, 304, 334–6

THE CASTLE *See also* **2537**

3992 **Raven, J. J.** Recent excavations at Bungay castle. PSIA 7, 1889/91, 212–13

3993 **Braun, H.** Bungay castle. PSIA 22, 1934/6, 109–19, 201–23. 334

3994 **Braun, H.** Bungay castle: historical notes and account of the excavations. 2nd edn. nd

3995 **Dunning, G.** Pottery from the mortar layer, Bungay castle. PSIA 22, 1934/6, 334–8

3996 **Braun, H.** The keep of Bungay castle. JBAA 3rd Ser 1, 1937, 157–67

3997 **Cane, H.** Bungay castle guide. Norwich, [1965]. SCL/L

3998 **Kedney, R. J.** Tower keep at Bungay. LA&LHS 1970/71, 17–20

BUNGAY URBAN DISTRICT

3999 **Department of the Environment.** List of buildings of special architectural or historic interest: Urban district of Bungay, East Suffolk. 1972. [Typescript]

BURES ST. MARY *See also* **2855, 3430–32**

4000 **Jervis, W. H. E. R.** Coronation of St. Edmund, King and martyr, at Bures St. Mary, 25 Dec A.D. 855; with a short description of Chapel Barn, the village, and Smallbridge Hall. Colchester, 1899

4001 Bures St. Mary parish history. SC 1.7.1927, Rp No 27

4002 **Probert, W. G. C.** Some notes on the history of Bures. ER 38, 1929, 125–9

4003 Ancient chapel of Bures. PSIA 15, 1913/15, 218–24

4004 Church of St. Mary the Virgin, Bures. Ramsgate, 1956 and later edns

BURGATE

4005   Burgate parish history. SC 27.6.1930, Rp No 182
4006   **Farrer, E.** Burgate Hall charters. PSIA 19, 1926/7, 352–4
4007   **Hill, P. O.** Echoes from the past life of Burgate, Suffolk. Ipswich, [1932]
4008   **Manning, C. R.** Burgate church. PSIA 1, 1848/53, 208–17
4009   **Appleyard, B.** Burgate: recent history in an ancient church. Eye, [1931] SRO/B
4010   Brief account of Burgate church. nd

BURGH

4011   **Raven, J. J.** Burgh, near Woodbridge. PSIA 9, 1895/7, 332–7
4012   Burgh parish history. SC 13.3.1931, Rp No 219
4013   **Woodbridge Field Club.** Excavations at Castle Field, Burgh, 1900–1901. [Woodbridge], [1901]
4014   **Birch, H. W.** Church notes: Burgh. E Ang NS 13, 1909/10, 313–14
4015   **Schofield, R. W.** Guide to Burgh church. Ipswich, 1970

BURGH CASTLE   *See also* **1276, 2900–01**

4016   Burgh Castle parish history. SC 25.10.1929, Rp No 147
4017   **Ives, J.** Remarks upon the Garianonum of the Romans: the site and remains fixed and described. 1774. [*Ed.* by Dawson Turner, with memoir of John Ives] Great Yarmouth, 1803
4018   **Turner, D.** Objects found in the Roman station of Burgh, near Yarmouth, and other antiquities of Burgh. PSA 1, 1843/9, 43
4019   **Smith, C. R.** Romano-British urn found at Burgh Castle. PSA 2, 1849/53, 171
4020   **Boileau, J. P.** Romano-British urn found at Burgh Castle. NA 3, 1849/52, 415–16
4021   **Boileau, J. P.** Saxon silver coin found at Burgh Castle. NA 6, 1859/63, 38–41
4022   **Philp, B. J.** Anglo-Saxon animal brooches from Burgh Castle and Brantham. PSIA 27, 1955/7, 191–3
4023   **Harrod, H.** Excavations at Burgh Castle. PSA 3, 1849/56, 227–30
4024   **Boileau, J. P.** Sceatta found at Burgh Castle. NA 5, 1855/8, 233–5
4025   **Harrod, H.** Excavations made at Burgh Castle between 1850 and 1855. NA 5, 1855/8, 146–60
4026   **Taylor, E. S.** Inscriptions at Burgh Castle. E Ang 1, 1858/63, 72
4027   **Raven, J. J.** Garianonum and the Count of the Saxon Shore. PSIA 6, 1883/8, 345–9
4028   **Gerish, W. B.,** *Ed.* Garianonum: Burgh Castle ... some materials for a history of. MSS, cuttings, etc. 1890–92 SCL/L

4029 **Gerish, W. B.** East Anglian crosses: Burgh Castle. E Ang NS 5, 1893/4, 191

4030 [**Venables, G.**] Burgh Castle, Cnobheresburg, or Garianonum. Gt. Yarmouth, [1897]

4031 **Redstone, V. B.** Burgh Castle. PSIA 11, 1901/03, 308–14

4032 **Dutt, W. A.** Recent discoveries at Burgh Castle. Antiquary 55, 1909, 210–13

4033 **Dahl, L. H.** The Roman camp and the Irish saint at Burgh Castle: with local history. 1913

4034 **Raven, J. J.** Burgh Castle. Great Yarmouth, nd. SCL/L

4035 Burgh Castle. Lowestoft, 1922

4036 **Dahl, L. H.** Burgh Castle: ... account of the ... Roman walls, also of the church ... Great Yarmouth, [1927]

4037 **Rumbelow, P. E.** Burgh Castle. 1928. [Typescript]. NCL/N

4038 **Morris, A. J.** Saxon Shore fort at Burgh Castle. PSIA 24, 1946/8, 100–20

4039 **Ministry of Works.** Burgh Castle. 1948 and later edns

4040 **Morris, A. J.,** *and* **Hawkes, C. F. C.** Fort of the Saxon Shore at Burgh Castle. Arch J 106, 1949, 66–9

4041 **Henig, M.** An intaglio from Burgh Castle. PSIA 33, 1973/5, 313–15

4042 Parish church of St. Peter and St. Paul, Burgh Castle. 3rd edn 1966, and later edns

4043 **Bately, J.** Short historical notes of Burgh water frolic, showing how it originated ... revived in the present year. Great Yarmouth, 1889. SCL/L

BURSTALL

4044 Burstall parish history. SC 27.5.1932, Rp No 272

4045 **Birch, H. W.** Church notes: Burstall. E Ang NS 13, 1909/10, 67–8

4046 [**Clayton, J. H.**]. St. Mary's church, Burstall. Ipswich, 1972

4047 **Partridge, C.** Monumental inscriptions in Burstall churchyard. E Ang NS 12, 1907/08, 174–5

BURY ST. EDMUNDS

DIRECTORIES AND ALMANACS   *See also* 51

4048 Kelly's directory of Bury St. Edmunds and neighbourhood ... 1930 and later edns

4049 **Regency Publicity Service.** Bury St. Edmunds book: the reference guide and directory of the commercial, business, and community activities of the borough, 1966–67 and later edns. Folkestone

4050 Wilkins' Bury St. Edmunds almanack 1889. Bury St. Edmunds. SRO/B

4051 Pawsey's St. Edmunds almanac and diary, 1948 and later edns. Bury St. Edmunds. SRO/B

4052 **Localads.** "St. Edmunds" almanac and diary, 1962–3 and later edns. Needham Market, [1962–]

GUIDES

4053 Guide to the town, abbey, and antiquities of Bury St. Edmunds; with brief notices of the villages and country seats within a circuit of eight miles. Ipswich, 1821. Bury St. Edmunds, 2nd edn 1836, and later edns to 1868. SRO/B

4054 Bury St. Edmund's illustrated in twelve etchings, by J. G. Strutt. 1821

4055 Description of Bury St. Edmund's and its environs within the distance of ten miles. Ipswich, 1825. BL

4056 Concise description of Bury St. Edmund's and its environs, within the distance of ten miles. 1827

4057 Guide to Bury. Bury St. Edmunds, 1833. SRO/B

4058 Guide to the town, abbey, and antiquities of Bury St. Edmunds, with a list of numerous benefactors ... Bury St. Edmunds, 1836. 2nd edn 1864

4059 A visit to Bury St. Edmund's; or, An old-fashioned week in the nineteenth century. Cambridge, 1845. BL

4060 **Tymms, S.** Handbook to Bury St. Edmund's ... 1854 to 9th edn. 1916. 5th edn. onwards include additions by J. P. Thompson. SRO/B and BL

4061 Guide to the town and antiquities of Bury St. Edmunds, with a classified list of trades and professions. Bury St. Edmunds, 1867. SRO/B

4062 Plain guide to the main objects of interest in Bury St. Edmunds. Bury St. Edmunds, 1867

4063 Stranger's illustrated guide to Bury St. Edmund's, Suffolk, with a sketch of its history. Bury St. Edmunds, 1871. SRO/B

4064 Twelve months' pleasure: commerce, and doings in "Dull Bury". 1884. SRO/B

4065 **Grieve, P.** Short walks from Bury St. Edmunds. Bury St. Edmunds, 1887. nl

4066 Guide to Bury St. Edmunds. Bury St. Edmunds, 1905. SRO/B

4067 Bury St. Edmund's and district illustrated (Bury and Norwich Post illustrated handbook to Bury St. Edmund's and district) Bury St. Edmunds, [1906]. SRO/B. [1907]. O

4068 Bury St. Edmunds guide. Bury St. Edmunds, 1906. SRO/B

4069 Guide to Bury St. Edmunds. Cheltenham, 1906

4070 **Astley, H. J. D.** Bury St. Edmund's; notes and impressions. 1907

4071 **Dutt, W. A.** Bury St. Edmunds, Suffolk, with its surroundings. (Homeland Assoc. Handbooks, No. 56.) Bury St. Edmunds, 1907. 2nd edn 1908. 3rd edn 1909–10

4072 **Willoughby, L.** Bury St. Edmunds. Conn 17, 1907, 246–55

4073 Official guide. 1921 and later edns

4074 Guide to the main objects of interest in Bury St. Edmund's. Bury St. Edmund's, [1930?]. BL

4075   Bury St. Edmunds: places of interest. SC 2.12.1938

4076   **Vale, E.** City of Bury St. Edmunds. (Trust House Local Information Sheets, No 20). 1938. SRO/B. 1947. SRO/I

4077   Bury St. Edmunds: for U.S. Armed Forces in U.K. [c.1944]

4078   **Addison, W. W.** Bury St. Edmunds. [Travel Assoc.] 1947. SRO/B

4079   **Bury St. Edmunds and District Citizens' Association.** What to see in Bury St. Edmunds. Bury St. Edmunds, [c.1949]

4080   **Maltby, H. J. M.** Bury St. Edmunds: short guide to places of interest. Bury St. Edmunds, [1950]. 1953

Views

4081   Bury St. Edmunds. [16 views]. Bury St. Edmunds, [c.1890]. nl

4082   **Bury St. Edmunds Corporation.** John Green collection of prints of Bury St. Edmunds ... Bury St. Edmunds, 1934. SRO/B

GENERAL AND POLITICAL HISTORY

See also **787, 795, 805, 3061, 3108, 3203, 3319, 3332, 3487**

4083   **Powell, J. G.** Bury Abbey manuscript collection [notes on Jermyn's Suffolk collections in BL. Add. MS 8193]. MS

4084   **Redstone, L. J.** Exhibition of records of the borough of Bury St. Edmunds. nd. [Typescript]. SRO/B

4085   **Hawkins, W.** Corolla varia, etc. Cambridge, 1634. [Describes Bury St. Edmunds and the procession of the Bull]. STC 12964. BL

4086   **Barker, H. R.,** *Ed.* List of the dates of all the principal events connected ... with the history of Bury St. Edmunds from A.D.637 to 1919. Bury St. Edmunds, 1919. nl

4087   **Barker, H. R.,** *Ed.* List of the dates of all the principal events connected ... with the history of Bury St. Edmunds from A.D.637 to 1931. Bury St. Edmunds, 1931. SRO/B

4088   **Barker, H. R.,** *Ed.* Bury St. Edmunds: dates of historical and interesting events from A.D.633 to 1950. Bury St. Edmunds, 1951

4089   Notes concerning Bury St. Edmund in com. Suffolk, extracted out of the ... Earl of Oxford's library by Mr. Wanley. 17—. O

4090   Description of the ancient and present state of the town and abbey of Bury St. Edmund's ... Bury St. Edmund's, 1768. 2nd edn. by Sir J. Cullum, 1771. SRO/I. 3rd edn. by G. Ashby, 1782. BL

4091   **Yates, R.** An intended history of Bury St. Edmunds. GM 1st Ser 73, 1803, 492–3; 1st Ser 75, 1805, 917–18

4092   **Gillingwater, E.** Historical and descriptive account of St. Edmund's Bury ... the abbey, etc. St. Edmunds-Bury, 1804. 2nd edn 1811

4093   Bury St. Edmunds: its origin, history, antiquities, and environs. Bury St. Edmunds, 1845. 1852

4094   **Hills, G. M.** Antiquities of Bury St. Edmunds. JBAA 21, 1865, 32–56, 104–40

4095   **Barker, H. R.** History of, and guide to Bury St. Edmund's etc. Bury St. Edmund's, 1885

4096   Memorials of the past, relating to Bury St. Edmund's and West Suffolk. Rp from the "Bury and Norwich Post". Pts 1 to 3. (All published] Bury St. Edmund's, 1889–90. 100 copies

4097   **Catling, S.** History of Bury St. Edmunds from 855 to 1892. Bury St. Edmunds, 1892. 2nd edn 1900

4098   **Clarke,** *Sir* **E.** The Haberdon. Rp from the "Bury Free Press", 3 Feb 1902. SRO/B

4099   **Astley, H. J. D.** Bury St. Edmund's: notes and impressions. Antiquary 43, 1907, 210–16, 258–64

4100   **Spanton, W. S.** Bury St. Edmund's, its history and antiquities. Cheltenham, [1933]

4101   **Auston, E.** Historic St. Edmundsbury. Dovercourt, 1946. O

4102   **Maltby, H. J. M.** Haberdon earthworks. 1950. [Typescript]. SRO/B

4103   **Maltby, H. J. M.** Bury St. Edmunds. Arch J 108, 1951, 160–62

4104   **Maltby, H. J. M.** Early history of Bury St. Edmunds. 1952. [Typescript]. nl

4105   **Statham, M. P.** Ancient Bury St. Edmunds. Municipal Rev 34, 1963, 241–5

4106   **Keith, A.** Bury St. Edmunds cranial fragment. Jour of Anat. and Physiology 47, 1912/13, 73–9

4107   **Edwardson, A. R.** Excavations at Gainsborough Road, Bury St. Edmunds. PSIA 27, 1955/7, 89–95

4108   **West, S. E.** Excavation of the town defences at Tayfen Road, Bury St. Edmunds, 1968. PSIA 32, 1970/72, 17–24.

4109   **Hasted, H.** Lead plate inscribed in Anglo-Saxon. PSIA 1, 1848/53, 308–09

4110   **Wright, T.** Leaden tablet or book cover with an Anglo-Saxon inscription, found at Bury St. Edmund's. PSA 2, 1849/56, 104/05

4111   **Round, J. H.** The first charter of St. Edmund's Bury, Suffolk [temp. Stephen]. American Hist. Rev. 2, 1897, 688–90

4112   **Hartshorne, C. H.** Visits of Edward I to Bury St. Edmund's and Thetford. PSIA 1, 1848/53, 91–7

4113   **Lobel, M. D.** Detailed account of the 1327 rising at Bury St. Edmund's and the subsequent trial. PSIA 21, 1931/3, 215–31

4114   **Lobel, M. D.** Some additions to André Réville's account of events at Bury St. Edmund's following the revolt of 1381. PSIA 21, 1931/3, 208–14

4115   **Statham, M. P.** Bury St. Edmunds in 1433–4. SR 4, no 2, 1973, 7–15

4116   Woefull and lamentable wast and spoile done by a suddaine fire in S. Edmonds-bury in Suffolke, on Munday the tenth of April 1608. 1608. STC 4181. Rp Ipswich, 1845. 12 copies. SCO/B

4117   Charter for incorporating the burgh of Bury St. Edmunds, newly and carefully translated, by an inhabitant. Bury St. Edmunds, 1810. SRO/B

4118   Old plan of Bury. E Ang NS 1, 1885/6, 48, 184

4119   **Smith, J. T.** Origin of the town plan. Arch J 108, 1951, 162–4

PARLIAMENTARY HISTORY   *See also* **847, 3083**

4120   The case of Saint Edmund's Bury. The Hon. Carr Hervey and Aubrie Porter, sitting members, against Jermyn Davers and Gilbert Affleck, petitioners. 1680. Wing C 980A. BL

4121   The fair candidate ... [An address to] ... the corporation of St. Edmund's Bury, in Suffolk. By an English gentleman. Bury St. Edmunds, 1730. BL

4122   Poll for members of Parliament ... taken ... the 13th and 14th days of Dec 1832 ... 1832. SRO/B

4123   Account of the proceedings at the election for members for the borough of Bury St. Edmunds, 13 and 14 Dec 1832 ... Bury St. Edmunds, 1833

4124   Poll for members of Parliament to represent the borough of Bury St. Edmunds ... 24 and 25 July 1837. Bury St. Edmunds, 1837. SRO/B

4125   Poll of the borough election of Bury St. Edmunds taken 29 June 1841. Bury St. Edmunds, 1841. SRO/B

4126   Poll book, 1852. NCL/N

4127   Report of Select Committee on petition [Bury St. Edmunds], with minutes of proceedings. HC 1852/3, 8

4128   Poll for the borough of Bury St. Edmunds ... taken 28 March 1857. Bury St. Edmunds, 1857. SRO/B

4129   **Bury St. Edmunds Corporation.** Bury St. Edmunds election: minutes of evidence taken before the select committee ... with the proceedings of the committee. 1857. SRO/B. HC 1857, 5

ECONOMIC HISTORY AND COMMUNICATIONS
See also **1197, 1292, 1294, 1335, 1354, 1393**

4130   Maltby, H. J. M. Bury St. Edmunds as a farming centre. 1953. [Typescript]. SRO/B

4131   Tymms, S. Mortgage of messuage, 1435: Bury. PSIA 2, 1854/9, 277

4132   Grant of messuage in Bury St. Edmund's [?14th century]. PSIA 3, 1860/63, 311–14

4133   Johnson, J. G. St. Nicholas tokens [Bury]. PSIA 2, 1854/9, 95

4134   Golding, C. Mints of Bury. Arch J 26, 1869, 384–7

4135   Jones, A. G. E. Early banking in Bury St. Edmund's. N&Q 199, 1954, 169–73, 209–12, 265–6

4136   [Suttle, W. V.] Lloyds Bank, Bury St. Edmunds. 1953. [Typescript]. SRO/B

4137   Spanton, R. P. Bury St. Edmunds Permanent Benefit Building Society: the first hundred years 1866 to 1966. Bury St. Edmunds, [1966]. SRO/B

4138   Raven, J. J. Bury bell founders. E Ang 1, 1858/63, 112–13

4139   Bevis, T. A. Bury St. Edmunds bellfounders. Bells and Bellringing 1, May 1966. SRO/B

4140   History of Robert Boby Ltd. 1963. [Typescript]. SRO/B

4141   Gainsford, W. R. Good ale: a famous brewery [Greene King]. Town and Country News, 8 April 1927, 18–21. SRO/B

4142   Greene King and Sons, Ltd. Greene King: a brief history, 1799–1974. Bury St. Edmunds, 1974. SRO/B

4143 **R, W.** A Bury fairing. Bury St. Edmunds, 1851

4144 **Ford, J. C.** Bury Fair in the past. Rp from the Bury and Norwich Post. Bury St. Edmunds, 1871. nl

4145 **Maltby, H. J. M.** The old Bury Fair. Bury St. Edmunds, nd. SRO/B

4146 **Dickinson, R. E.** Markets and market areas of Bury St. Edmunds. Sociological Rev. 22, 1930, 292–308. SRO/B

4147 **Statham, M. P.** Bury fairs. Bury St. Edmunds, [1973]. [Typescript]. SRO/B

4148 **Wilton, H. E.** Postmaster Decks of Bury St. Edmunds. E Ang Postal Hist. Study Circle Bull. 18, 1966, 4–7

4149 **Driver, G.** Postal history of Bury St. Edmunds from 1637 to the present day. E Ang Postal Hist. Study Circle Bull. 18, 1966, 7–21

LOCAL GOVERNMENT, SOCIAL SERVICES, AND JUSTICE

Municipal Government   See also **1454–5**

4150 **Royal Commission on Historical Manuscripts.** Ser 37, Fourteenth report, Appendix 8 ... Corporation of Bury St. Edmunds ... 1895

4151 **Lobel, M. D.** Borough of Bury St. Edmunds. A study in the government and development of a monastic town. Oxford, 1935

4152 **Davis, H. W. C.** The commune of Bury St. Edmunds, 1264. EHR 24, 1909, 313–17

4153 **Davis, H. W. C.** The liberties of Bury St. Edmunds. EHR 24, 1909, 417–31

4154 **Redstone, L. J.** The liberty of St. Edmund. PSIA 15, 1913/15, 200–11. *See also* **1444**

4155 **Lobel, M. D.** List of aldermen and bailiffs of Bury St. Edmunds from the twelfth to the sixteenth century. PSIA 22, 1934/6, 17–28

4156 **Redstone, V. B.** St. Edmund's Bury and town rental for 1295. PSIA 13, 1907/09, 191–222

4157 **Ford, J. C.** Aldermen and mayors of Bury St. Edmunds from 1302 [to 1896]. MS. SRO/B

4158 **[Dallas, R. C.]** Letters addressed to the aldermen of Bury St. Edmunds ... 1795. Bury St. Edmunds, 1795. SRO/B

4159 **Symonds, W.** Booke of Subscriptions, 1663–1705 [Record of oaths taken by members and officers of corporation of Bury]. PSIA 13, 1907/09, 44–56

4160 State of the poll for the election of three paving commissioners for the town of Bury St. Edmunds, 4 June 1832. Bury St. Edmunds, 1832. SRO/B

4161 Proceedings at the election of two burgesses for the borough of Bury St. Edmund's, and the poll, taken ... 6, 8, and 9 Jan 1835. Candidates, the Right Hon Earl Jermyn, the Right Hon Lord C. Fitzroy, Charles Fox Bunbury, Esq. Bury St. Edmunds, [1835]

4162 Poll for the election of the new Town Council for the borough of Bury St. Edmunds ... Bury St. Edmunds, [1835?]. SRO/B

4163 Poll at the election of two burgesses ... 31 July 1847. Bury St. Edmunds, 1847. SRO/B

4164 Statham, M. P., *Ed*. Freemen of Bury St. Edmunds, 1652–1835. [Typescript]. SRO/B

4165 **Bury St. Edmunds Corporation.** Accounts of receipts and payments of the Town Council of Bury St. Edmunds, 9 Nov 1841, 31 Aug 1843. Bury St. Edmunds, 1843. SRO/B

4166 **Bury St. Edmunds Corporation.** Accounts and newspaper cuttings, 1886–1900. SRO/B

4167 **Bury St. Edmunds Corporation.** Borough Treasurer's Dept. Abstract of accounts, 1919/21, 1922/4, 1925/6, 1931/2, 1937/8–. Bury St. Edmunds. 1920–. SRO/B. Incomplete

4168 **Bury St. Edmunds Corporation.** Year book of general information for the use of the Town Council, 1891/92, 1896/97, 1933/34–. Bury St. Edmunds, 1891–. BL. 1933–. SRO/B. Incomplete

4169 **Bury St. Edmunds Corporation.** Minutes of council and committees, 1958–. Bury St. Edmunds. SRO/B

4170 **Bury St. Edmunds Corporation.** Annual report on the sanitary condition of the borough of Bury St. Edmunds, for the year 1892, 1895, 1897, 1903/05, 1907/09. Bury St. Edmunds, 1893–1910. BL

4171 **Bury St. Edmunds Corporation.** Annual reports of the Medical Officer of Health, 1931, 1938, 1950/61. Bury St. Edmunds. SRO/B

4172 **Bury St. Edmunds Corporation.** Housing Committee. Tenants' handbook. 2nd ed 1963. SRO/B

4173 **Payne, L. E. H.** Borough fire brigade. Bury St. Edmunds, 1952. [Typescript]. SRO/B

4174 **Cooke, H. M. A.** Bury St. Edmunds corporation insignia and plate. nd. SRO/B

4175 **Champness, Thurlow, and Son.** Inventory ... consisting of certain articles of the corporation plate. 1951. [Typescript]. SRO/B

4176 Arms of Bury St. Edmund's. N&Q 4th Ser 3, 1869, 384

4177 **Bretton, R.** Civic arms: Bury St. Edmunds's. CA 8, 1964/5, 19–20

4178 **Bury St. Edmunds Corporation.** Armorial bearings of Bury St. Edmunds: blazon and description. Bury St. Edmunds, [1967]. SRO/B

4179 **Statham, M.** The maces of the Bury St. Edmunds corporation. Bury St. Edmunds, 1974. SRO/B

4180 **Bury St. Edmunds Corporation.** Civic news, 1962–. Bury St. Edmunds. 1962–. SRO/B

Poor Relief

4181 **[Bullen, H.]** Letter to the Guardians of the Poor of the burgh of Bury St. Edmunds ... and remarks on the duty of a Guardian. 1778. SRO/B

4182 **[Pate, J.]** To the author of a letter to the Guardians of the Poor of Bury St. Edmunds. Bury St. Edmunds, 1778. SRO/B

4183 **Ford, J. C.** Bury St. Edmunds workhouse A.D.1747–1878. Bury St. Edmunds, 1878

Charities   See also **1542**

4184 Account of the charitable donations in the borough of Bury St. Edmund's, delivered in according to the 27th George III. Bury St. Edmund's, [1788]. BL

4185 **Charity Commission.** Memorandum relating to the original charity of John Sutton. 1914. SRO/B

4186 **Sandford, J. H.** History of the foundation of the Guildhall Feoffment Trust. Bury St. Edmunds, 1931. SRO/B

4187 Guildhall Feoffment scheme. Bury St. Edmunds, 1865

4188 Guildhall Feoffment charity. A translation of the will of John Smyth, the founder of the Guildhall Feoffment. Bury St. Edmunds, nd. SRO/B

4189 Guildhall Feoffment charity: records ... deposited in the Muniment Room, Bury St. Edmunds, 12th-century—1939. Bury St. Edmunds, 1940. SRO/B

4190 **Sandford, J. H.** Notes on the Feoffees' earliest minute book. [Rp from Bury Free Press, 10 March 1934]. Bury St. Edmunds, 1934. SRO/B

4191 Guildhall Feoffment charity estates as contained in the decree of 22 July 1771. Indenture and schedule. [Bury St. Edmunds], 1772. 37 copies. BL

4192 Guildhall Feoffment charity estates, 10 Aug 1810. Bury St. Edmunds, 1811. SRO/B

4193 Guildhall Feoffment charity. Clerk's list of applicants for gifts. nd. SRO/B

4194 Guildhall Feoffment charity. Speech of Mr. Pemberton in the Rolls' Court ... and the judgment ... 13 April 1836, in the cause Attorney-General versus Cullum and others. [Alleged mishandling of the charity]. Bury St. Edmunds, 1836. SRO/B

4195 Guildhall Feoffment charity. Report of the Finance Committee of the Town Council of Bury St. Edmund's, upon the charity. Bury St. Edmund's, 1839. SRO/B

4196 Guildhall Feoffment charity. Report of Master Lynch in the causes, Attorney-General v. Cullum, Le Grice, as confirmed by Vice-Chancellor Knight Bruce on 24 March 1842, as to the management of the property and the application of the income. Bury St. Edmunds, [1842]. SRO/B

4197 Guildhall Feoffment charity. Epitome of the receipts and payments ... 1844/5, 1847/8. SRO/B

4198 First, second, and third reports of a committee of inhabitants on the charities of the town of Bury. Bury St. Edmunds, 1831. SRO/B

Public Health   See also **1558–60, 3306–9, 4346–50**

4199 **Hartley, D.** Some reasons why the practice of inoculation ought to be introduced into the town of Bury at present. Bury St. Edmunds, 1733. SRO/B

4200 I have perused a pamphlet entitled, "Some reasons why the practice of inoculation ought to be introduced into the town of Bury at present." etc. [A reply to that pamphlet, by Dr. Warren?]. [Bury St. Edmunds], [1733]. BL

4201 [**White, –.**]. State of the Bury Dispensary. Bury St. Edmunds, 1790. SRO/B

4202 **Tymms, S.** Notes towards a medical history of Bury. PSIA 1, 1848/53, 33–49

4203 **Bury St. Edmund and District Junior Chamber of Commerce.** Report of community survey in the borough of Bury St. Edmunds. Bury St. Edmunds, 1969. SRO/B

Education   See also **2013, 2015**

4204 Maximam partem ex Indice Rhetorico Farnabii deprompta: ... in Usum Scholae Regiae Grammaticalis apud S. Edmundi Burgum. [By E. Leedes, Junior]. 1717. nl

4205 **Randall, J.** *Ed.* Nomina quorundam e primariis olim Regiae Grammaticalis Scholae Buriae Sti. Edmundi, inter Icenos celeberrimae carminibus illustrata. 1719. SRO/B

4206 Catechesis Ecclesiae Anglicanae ... in usum Scholae Regis Edwardi eius nominis Sexti in Burgo Sancti Edmundi. [By E. Leedes, Junior]. 1729. SRO/I. 1747. SRO/B

4207 **Hill,** *Mrs.* Bury Grammar school charity plays, 1783–4. PSIA 2, 1854/9, 223

4208 State of the accounts of the charity schools in Bury St. Edmund's for the year 1788. Bury St. Edmund's, 1788. BL

4209 **Downing, D. J.** Guildhall Feoffment Junior Mixed School, Bury St. Edmunds, Suffolk, 1843–1965: a case study in administration. Bury St. Edmunds, [c.1966]. [Typescript]. SRO/B

4210 **Holt, A.** Development of secondary education in Bury St. Edmunds from 1902 to the present day. Bury St. Edmunds, [c.1969]. [Typescript]. SRO/B

4211 **Kendall, H. E.** Bury St. Edmunds school designs. 1847. SRO/B

4212 King Edward VI's school, 1849. Cambridge, 1849. BL

4213 **Wratislaw, A. H.** Discovery of the statutes of King Edward VI's Grammar school at Bury St. Edmunds. Arch J 26, 1869, 389–93

4214 **Redstone, L. J.** King Edward VI Free Grammar school, Bury St. Edmunds, 1550–1950. 1950. [Typescript]

4215 **Elliott, R. W.** Story of King Edward VI school, Bury St. Edmunds. Bury St. Edmunds, [1963]

4216 Record of the tercentenary of the foundation of King Edward VIth's Free Grammar school, Bury St. Edmunds, on Friday, 2 August 1850 ... 3 pts. Bury St. Edmund's, 1850

4217 Biographical list of boys educated at King Edward VI Free Grammar school, Bury St. Edmunds, from 1550 to 1900. [*Ed.* by S. H. A. Hervey]. Bury St. Edmunds, 1908. SGB 13

4218 King Edward VI's school. Bury St. Edmund's Grammar school list, 1900–1925. Bury St. Edmunds, 1930. BL

4219 King Edward VI's school. [Meeting to decide on the form of a War Memorial, together with the Roll of Honour, June 1919]. 1919. SRO/B

4220 **Bury St. Edmunds Corporation.** Catalogue of the exhibition of the works of Henry William Bunbury [1750–1811]: ancient manuscripts and records of the King Edward VIth school. Bury St. Edmunds, 1950

4221 **Bartholomew, A. T.,** *and* **Gordon, C.** On the library at King Edward VI school at Bury St. Edmunds. Lib 3rd Ser 1, 1910, 1–27, 329–31

4222 King Edward VI's school. The Burian, 1895–1940. Bury St. Edmunds, 1895–1940. SRO/B

4223 **Raven, J. J.** A reminiscence of Bury school. E Ang NS 7, 1897/8, 127

Museums and Libraries   See also 4421

4224 **Jennings, J.** Moyes Hall: the new museum at Bury St. Edmund's. PSIA 10, 1898/1900, 233–6

4225 **Barker, H. R.** Short account of Moyes Hall, Bury St. Edmund's, and its contents. Bury St. Edmund's, 1906. [c.1938]. 1948

4226 **Maltby, H. J. M.** Moyse's Hall: a history of the building and the museum. Arch J 108, 1951, 165–7

4227 **Maltby, H. J. M.** Moyse's Hall Museum: its history, description, and collections. Bury St. Edmunds, 1954

4228 **Maltby, H. J. M.** New museum at Bury St. Edmunds. MJ 1954, 121–3

4229 **Edwardson, A. R.** Moyse's Hall Museum, and a short guide to places of interest. Bury St. Edmunds, 1960. *See also* **481, 648**

4230 Laws for the regulation of the Suffolk Public Library, Bury St. Edmund's ... instituted 1790, ... and a catalogue of the books. Bury St. Edmund's, 1791. SRO/I. 1792. 1793. SRO/B

4231 Laws for the regulation of the new Public Library, established in Bury St. Edmunds, 5 Feb 1795; together with a list of subscribers and a catalogue of the books. Bury St. Edmunds. 1802. SRO/B

4232 Catalogue of the books in the united Public Libraries. Bury St. Edmunds, 1822

4233 Foundation of the Bury St. Edmunds Library. Lib 6, 1894, 404

4234 Bury St. Edmunds Library. Lib 7, 1895, 406

4235 **Maltby, H. J. M.** Cullum Library. Bury St. Edmunds. [c.1951]. [Typescript]. SRO/B

4236 **Hepworth, P.** Cullum Library. EAM 14, 1954/5, 338–44

4237 Bury St. Edmunds Public Library. Summing-up, 1955–60. [Typescript]

4238 Bury St. Edmunds Public Library. Ten years later, 1955–65. [Typescript]

Planning and Development

4239 **West Suffolk County Council.** Planning Dept. Factual survey and outline plan for the Borough of Bury St. Edmunds. Bury St. Edmunds, 1951. [Typescript]

4240 **Bury St. Edmunds Corporation.** The question, and the answer. [Opportunities for industrialists]. Bury St. Edmunds, 1956. SRO/B

4241 **Bury St. Edmunds Corporation.** Bury St. Edmunds: opportunity for industry. Bury St. Edmunds [1958]. SRO/B

4242 **Bury St. Edmunds Corporation.** Central area re-development proposals. Report of sub-committee of the Development Committee, appointed Nov 1959. 1960. SRO/B

4243 Report on the Corn Exchange, Abbeygate Street, Bury St. Edmunds, prepared for the Borough Council by the architects Tayler and Green ... Aug
1961. 1961. [Typescript]. SRO/B

4244 **West Suffolk County Council.** Planning Dept. Bury St. Edmunds town
map. First review, 1962. Programme map, report of survey, written statement. Bury St. Edmunds, 1962

4245 **Crowe, S., and Associates.** Bury St. Edmunds cathedral close: landscape
report. 1964. [Typescript]. SRO/B

4246 **West Suffolk County Council.** Highways Dept. Bury traffic 1965: abridged
edition of the traffic survey carried out in Bury St. Edmunds during
September 1965. Bury St. Edmunds, 1966. SRO/B

4247 **West Suffolk County Council.** Planning Dept. Bury St. Edmunds: re-
development proposals for part of the town centre. Bury St. Edmunds, 1966

4248 **Bury St. Edmunds Corporation.** Bury St. Edmunds and town expansion.
Bury St. Edmunds, 1969. SRO/B

4249 **Bury St. Edmunds Corporation.** Bury St. Edmunds: "town expansion and
you". Bury St. Edmunds, 1970. SRO/B

4250 **West Suffolk County Council.** Planning Dept. Bury St. Edmunds: Brackland area scheme. Bury St. Edmunds, 1970

4251 **Suffolk Preservation Society.** Bury St. Edmunds town centre study. 1971

4252 **West Suffolk County Council.** Planning Dept. Bury St. Edmunds town
map: comprehensive development amendments. Bury St. Edmunds, 1971

4253 **West Suffolk County Council.** Planning Dept. Bury St. Edmunds: town
development, 1972 (Hillyer Parker). Bury St. Edmunds, 1972

Prisons and Police   See also **772, 1542, 1715, 1983**

4254 **Howard, J.** Account of the principal lazarettos in Europe. 1789. [Gaol at
Bury St. Edmunds, 156]

4255 Plan for a new gaol at Bury St. Edmunds. GM 1st Ser 71, 1801, 697–8

4256 **Neild, J.** Gaols at Bury St. Edmund's and Sudbury. GM 1st Ser 74, 1804,
800–01

4257 **Neild, J.** Gaols of Bury St. Edmund. GM 1st Ser 75, 1805, 1091–2, 1093–5

4258 Rules, orders, and regulations to be observed and enforced in the gaol and
house of correction for the Liberty of Bury St. Edmunds ... approved ...
22 July 1805. Bury St. Edmunds, 1805. SRO/B

4259 **Orridge, J.** Description of the gaol at Bury St. Edmunds. To which is
added designs for a prison, made ... for the Emperor of Russia. 1819. SRO/B

4260 **Lobel, M. D.** Gaol of Bury St. Edmunds. PSIA 21, 1931/3, 203–07

4261 **Wheeler, J. D.** Borough of Bury St. Edmunds constabulary, 1836–57. SR 2,
1963, 194–7

4262 **[Statham, M.]** Bury St. Edmunds magistrates. Bury St. Edmunds, 1974.
SRO/B. [Typescript]

RELIGION AND CHURCHES

General   See also **2921–2, 3266**

4263   Apportionment of the rent charges, in lieu of tithes, in the parishes of St. Mary and St. James. 1845. SRO/B

4264   Martin's church notes: Bury St. Edmund's. E Ang NS 1, 1885/6, 79

4265   **G, St. C.** Matters ecclesiastical at Bury St. Edmund's in the seventeenth century. E Ang NS 6, 1895/6, 129–31

THE ABBEY   *See also* **705, 2509, 3131–3, 3257, 3462, 5220**

Chronicles, Cartularies, Charters, and Administrative Documents

4266   **Jocelinus de Brakelonda.** Chronica Jocelini de Brakelonda, de rebus gestis Samsonis Abbatis Monasterii Sancti Edmundi. *Ed.* by J. G. Rokewode [formerly J. Gage]. Camden Soc 13, 1840

4267   **Jocelinus de Brakelonda.** Monastic and social life in the twelfth century, as exemplified in the Chronicles of Jocelin of Brakelond ... from A.D. 1173 to 1202. Trans. with notes ... by T. E. Tomlins ... 1844. 2nd edn 1849

4268   **Hervey,** *Lord* **F.** Relics of S. Edmund: a fragment belonging to the history of the abbey of Bury St. Edmunds. Bury St. Edmunds, 1886. SRO/B

4269   **Arnold, T.,** *Ed.* Memorials of St. Edmund's abbey. 3v. 1890–96

4270   **Barber, R. W.** Abbot Samson from the chronicle of Jocelin of Brackland. 1903

4271   **Jocelinus de Brakelonda.** Chronicle of Jocelin of Brakelond: a picture of monastic life in the days of Abbot Samson. *Ed.* by Sir E. Clarke. 1903. 3rd edn 1907

4272   **Reichel, O. J.** Joceline de Brakelond and the *servicium debitum*. DAR 36, 1906, 123–6

4273   **Clarke,** *Sir* **E.** Bury chroniclers of the thirteenth century. Rp from the Bury Free Press. Bury St. Edmunds, 1905

4274   **Redstone, L. J.** "First minister's account" of the possessions of the abbey of St. Edmund. PSIA 13, 1907/09, 311–66

4275   **Jocelinus de Brakelonda.** Chronicle of Jocelin of Brakelond ... *Ed.* by L. C. Jane. 1925

4276   Pinchbeck register (of the abbey of S. Edmund, compiled by Walter ... of Pinchbeck), etc. *Ed.* by Lord Francis Hervey. 2v. Brighton, 1925

4277   **Koenig, C.** Englisches Klosterleben im 12 Jahrhundert auf Grund der Chronik des Jocelinus de Brakelonda. Jena, 1928

4278   Feudal documents from the abbey of Bury St. Edmunds. *Ed.* by D. C. Douglas. 1932

4279   **Fisher, J. L.** The Harlow cartulary. EAST NS 22, 1936/40, 238–72

4280   **Galbraith, V. H.** The St. Edmundsbury chronicle, 1296–1301. EHR 58, 1943, 51–78

4281   **Jocelinus de Brakelonda.** Chronicle of Jocelin of Brakelond, concerning the acts of Samson, Abbot of the monastery of St. Edmund. *Ed.* by H. E. Butler. 1949

4282   Kalendar of Abbot Samson of Bury St. Edmunds and related documents. *Ed.* ... by R. H. C. Davis. Camden 3rd Ser 84. 1954

4283   **Gransden, A.** A critical edition of the Bury St. Edmunds chronicle in Arundel MS. 30 (College of Arms). PhD thesis, London, 1957

4284   **Gransden, A.** The "Chronica Buriensis" and the abbey of St. Benet of Hulme. BIHR 36, 1963, 77–82

4285   **Gransden, A.,** *Ed.* Chronicle of Bury St. Edmunds, 1212–1301. 1964

4286   **Thomson, R. M.** Chronicle of the election of Hugh, Abbot of Bury St. Edmunds and later Bishop of Ely. Oxford, 1974

4287   **Goodwin, C. W.** Ancient charters in the possession of the corporation of Kings Lynn (relating to Bury St. Edmund's abbey). NA 4, 1852/4, 93–117

4288   **Redstone, L. J.** Report of the Hon. Archivist on charters of Cnut and Hardecnut to St. Edmund. 1950. [Typescript]

4289   **Douglas, D. C.** Charter of enfeoffment under William the Conqueror [made by the abbot of Bury St. Edmunds]. EHR 42, 1927, 245–7

4290   **Way, A.** Indenture for making a pastoral staff for William Curteys, abbot of St. Edmund's. PSIA 1, 1848/53, 160–65

4291   **Douglas, D. C.** Fragments of an Anglo-Saxon survey from Bury St. Edmunds. EHR 43, 1928, 376–83

4292   **Ritchie, C.** Black Death at St. Edmund's abbey. PSIA 27, 1955/7, 47–50

4293   **Gransden, A.** Reply of a fourteenth-century abbot of Bury St. Edmunds to a man's petition to be a recluse. EHR 75, 1960, 464–7

4294   **Ord, C.** An account of the entertainment of King Henry VI at the abbey of Bury St. Edmunds. Arch 15, 1806, 65–71

4295   **Gage, J.** Letters from King Henry VI to the Abbot of St. Edmundsbury and to the aldermen and bailiffs of the town for the suppression of the Lollards. Arch 23, 1831, 339–43

Other Manuscripts, Library, and Scriptorium

4296   **James, M. R.** Bury St. Edmunds manuscripts. EHR 41, 1926, 251–60

4297   **James, M. R.** Description of the ancient manuscripts in the Ipswich Public Library. PSIA 22, 1934/6, 86–103

4298   **Cooke, H. M. A.** *Ed.* Notes on the manuscript psalter and calendar formerly belonging to the abbey of St. Edmund. nd. [Typescript]. SRO/B

4299   **Dewick, E. S.** On a MS psalter belonging to the abbey of Bury St. Edmunds. Arch 54, pt 2, 1895, 399–410

4300   **Cooke, H. M. A.** Valuable Bury St. Edmunds relics: an old manuscript psalter. Rp from Bury Free Press, 14 March 1936. Bury St. Edmunds, 1936. SRO/B

4301   **Parker, E.** Twelfth-century cycle of New Testament drawings from Bury St. Edmunds abbey. PSIA 31, 1967/9, 263–302

4302   **James, M. R.** On the abbey of St. Edmund at Bury. 1. The library. 2. The church. Cambridge Antiq Soc Publ 28. Cambridge, 1895

4303   **Savage, E. A.** Early monastic libraries ... with an account of the *Registrum Librorum Angliae* and of the *Catalogus Scriptorum Ecclesiae* of John Boston of the abbey of Bury St. Edmunds. Rp from Edinburgh Bibl Soc Publ 14, 1928

4304   **Parker, E.** Scriptorium of Bury St. Edmunds in the twelfth century. 1965. Ph.D. thesis, London, 1965

Historical Studies

4305   **Battely, J.** Antiquitates Rutupinae et Antiquitates S. Edmundi Burgi ad Annum 1272 perductae. [*Ed.* by O. Battely, with an appendix, and list of abbots from 1279, by Sir J. Burrough]. 1711. 2nd edn 1745

4306   **Yates, R.** An illustration of the monastic history and antiquities of the town and abbey of St. Edmund's Bury, with views of the most considerable monasterial remains by ... W. Yates. 2v. 1805. 2nd edn 1843, supplementary sheets only

4307   **Jessopp, A.** Studies by a recluse in cloister, town, and country. [Includes From century to century at St. Edmund's abbey, 66–89]. 1893

4308   **Barker, H. R.,** *Ed.* Guide to the abbey of St. Edmundsbury. Bury St. Edmunds, [1913]. SRO/B

4309   **Galbraith, V. H.** The East Anglian see and the abbey of Bury St. Edmunds. EHR 40, 1925, 222–8

4310   **[Teasdel, R. H.]** The abbey at Bury: episodes in its history. NNA(GY) 1929, 17–20. NCL/N

4311   **Goodwin, A.** Abbey of St. Edmundsbury. Gladstone memorial prize essay, 1926. Oxford, 1931

4312   Bury St. Edmunds: the abbey. Pts 1 and 2. SC 14.10.1938, 21.10.1938

4313   **Webling, A. F.** Abbey of St. Edmundsbury: an address to young people who came on the Pilgrimage of Youth. Bury St. Edmunds, [c.1949]. SRO/B

4314   **Whittingham, A. B.** Bury St. Edmunds abbey: official guide of the Ministry of Works. 1971

4315   **Davis, R. H. C.** Monks of St. Edmund, 1021–1148. History NS 40, 1955/6, 227–39

4316   **Scarfe, N.** A monk named Jocelin ... Edinburgh, 1976

4317   **Graham, R.** A papal visitation of Bury St. Edmunds and Winchester in 1234. EHR 27, 1912, 728–39

4318   **Galbraith, V. H.** The death of a champion [The consequence of a suit concerning Semer and Groton, which belonged to St. Edmund's abbey, 1287]. *In* Studies in medieval history presented to F. M. Powicke. *Ed.* by R. W. Hunt *et al.* Oxford, 1948, 283–95

Architecture

4319   **King, E.** Remarks on the abbey church of Bury St. Edmunds. Arch 3, 1775, 311–14

4320 **Morant, A. W.** On the abbey of Bury St. Edmunds. PSIA 4, 1864/74, 376–404

4321 **Dewing, E. M.** St. Edmund's Bury—the abbey church and monastery. 1886

4322 **Whittingham, A. B.** Plan, design, and development of the church and monastic buildings. Arch J 108, 1951, 168–87

4323 Bury St. Edmund's abbey excavations: report and statement by ... S. H. A. Hervey. Bury St. Edmunds. [Photostat]. SRO/B

4324 **M[altby], H. J. M.** Excavations of the abbey ruins, Bury St. Edmunds. PSIA 24, 1946/8, 256–7

4325 **Bury St. Edmunds and District Citizens' Assoc.** Minutes of a meeting ... 2 Sept 1948 [to discuss the possibilities of the excavation of the abbey of St. Edmund]. 1948. [Typescript]. SRO/B

4326 Bury St. Edmunds: some account of the abbey gatehouse, St. Edmund's Bury. Rp from the Arch. Antiq. v3. nd. SRO/B

4327 **W[alford], W. S.** On the heraldry within the abbey gate at Bury St. Edmunds as evidence for its date. PSIA 2, 1854/9, 90–94

4328 **Gage, J.** Historical notices of the great bell tower of the abbey church of St. Edmundsbury. Arch 23, 1831, 327–33

4329 Restoration of the Norman tower: proposals. [Bury St. Edmunds], [1840]. BL

4330 **Cottingham, L. N.** Report ... on the present state of the Norman tower ... and the necessary repairs thereof. [Bury St. Edmunds], [1842]. SRO/B

4331 Restoration of the Norman tower ... [Proposals and a list of subscriptions]. [Bury St. Edmunds], [1843]. BL

4332 Restoration of the Norman tower ... [Proceedings of the committee, letter of appeal, and list of subscribers]. [Bury St. Edmunds], [1845]. BL

4333 Historical and architectural notice of the gate-tower of the ancient cemetery of St. Edmund, known as the Norman tower, St. Edmund's Bury. [By S. Tymms], 1846. SRO/B

4334 Restoration of the Norman tower [Report of the committee upon the completion of the work of restoration]. [Bury St. Edmunds], [1849]. BL

4335 **Drewett, P. L.,** *and* **Stuart, I. W.** Excavations in the Norman gate tower, Bury St. Edmunds abbey. PSIA 33, 1973/5, 241–52

4336 **Gilyard-Beer, R.** Eastern arm of the abbey church at Bury St. Edmunds. PSIA 31, 1967/9, 256–62

Relics, Inscriptions, Tombs, Heraldry, and Small Objects

4337 Relics of St. Botolph at St. Edmund's abbey, Bury. E Ang NS 4, 1891/2, 160, 319, 336

4338 Discovery of five stone coffins with human remains on the site of the old abbey at Bury St. Edmund's. Antiquary 39, 1903, 36–7

4339 **Clayton, C. E. A.** Tombs of abbots of Bury St. Edmunds. N&Q 9th Ser 11, 1903, 106–07

4340 **Redstone, L. J.** Arms of the last abbot. 1944. [Typescript]. SRO/B

4341 **King, E.** An account of the great seal of Ranulph, Earl of Chester; and of two inscriptions found in the ruins of St. Edmund Bury abbey. Arch 4, 1777, 119–31

4342 Seal of the abbey of St. Edmundsbury in Suffolk and the shrine of St. Edmund. Vet M 2, 1789, Plate 7

4343 **Ouvry, F.** Bury abbey seal. PSIA 2, 1854/9, 188–9

4344 **Hoving, T. P. F.** Bury St. Edmunds cross [Ivory cross, c.1150, made for abbot Samson]. Metropolitan Museum of Art Bull June 1964, 317–40. New York. O

4345 **Serjeantson, M. M.** Mabilia of St. Edmundsbury. From Embroidery, the Jour of the Embroiders' Guild, Sept 1939. SRO/B

Medieval Hospitals

4346 **Rowe, M. J.** Notes on the medieval hospitals of Bury St. Edmunds. nd. [Typescript]. SRO/B

4347 **Rowe, M. J.** Medieval hospitals of Bury St. Edmunds. Rp from Medical History 2, 1958, 253–63

4348 **Harris, H. A.** Site of St. Peter's Hospital chapel, Bury St. Edmund's. PSIA 17, 1919/21, 199

4349 **Bevan, B.** Foundation deed of S. Saviour's Hospital, Bury St. Edmund's. PSIA 6, 1883/8, 296–301

4350 **Burdon, R.** St. Saviour's Hospital, Bury St. Edmunds. PSIA 19, 1925/7, 255–85

St. James's Church (Cathedral)   See also **1793, 4382**

4351 Bury St. Edmunds: St. James parish. SC 30.9.1938

4352 **Deck, P.** Answer to a second letter, addressed to the hearers of a sermon preached ... at St. James' church ... Bury St. Edmunds. 1788. SRO/B

4353 Scheme of the Cathedral Commissioners for England, being the constitution and the statutes for the government of the cathedral church of St. James, Bury St. Edmunds. [1935]

4354 **Bevan, B.** Brief records of St. James' church, Bury St. Edmunds. Bury St. Edmunds, 1878. 60 copies

4355 **Cullum, G. G. M. G.** Wednesday lectures at St. James' church, Bury St. Edmund's, A.D. 1685. E Ang NS 3, 1889/90, 188–90

4356 **Fairbairns, W. H.** Notes on cathedrals: St. Edmundsbury. [c.1920]. SRO/B

4357 **Ditchfield, P. H.** Church of St. James, Bury St. Edmunds. JBAA NS 34, 1929, 71–8

4358 **Parker, E. J.** St. Edmundsbury cathedral. Bury St. Edmunds, 3rd edn 1934. 4th edn 1940

4359 **Bower, S. E. D.** The cathedral, Bury St. Edmunds: a report. 1943. SRO/B

4360 St. Edmundsbury cathedral development, 1948–49. Rp from Report of the Diocesan Board of Finance, 1949. Bury St. Edmunds. SRO/B

4361 St. Edmundsbury cathedral: summary of accounts ... 1949 and 1953. Bury St. Edmunds, 1949, 1953. SRO/B

4362 Notes on the cathedral, Bury St. Edmunds (for the use of visitors). Bury St. Edmunds, [c.1950]. SRO/B

4363 **Bower, S. E. D.** The cathedral church of St. James, Bury St. Edmunds: the scheme of enlargement. Ipswich, 1953. SRO/B

4364 **White, J. L.** Short history of the cathedral of St. James the Greater, Bury St. Edmunds. Bury St. Edmunds, 1954. Later edns. by M. R. Pirani. SRO/B

4365 A Suffolk story: the mother church of the county ... its place in Britain's history. nd

4366 Order of service for the blessing of the porch and library by the Lord Archbishop of Canterbury on Tuesday, 19 July 1960, ... St. James' cathedral. Bury St. Edmunds, 1960. SRO/B

4367 Order of service for the dedication of the memorial in the cloister and the presentation of the memorial bay to the cathedral ... to the memory of George, 3rd Earl of Stradbroke ... Sunday, 7 May 1961, ... St. James' cathedral. Bury St. Edmunds, 1961. SRO/B

4368 **Waddington, J. A. H.** Pictorial history of St. Edmundsbury cathedral: the cathedral church of St. James, Bury St. Edmunds. 1961 and later edns

4369 **Pepin, D.** Let's explore St. Edmundsbury cathedral. [Bury St. Edmunds], 1969. SRO/B

4370 Hallowing of the new quire and crossing, 29 Sept 1970 [Bury St. Edmunds]. SRO/B

4371 Bury St. Edmunds: St. James' church: history of the organ. [Typescript]. SRO/B

4372 **Oxley, H.** St. Edmundsbury cathedral organ. [Bury St. Edmunds], 1970. SRO/B

4373 **B, B.** Ancient painted glass in S. James' church, Bury St. Edmunds. E Ang NS 6, 1895/6, 41-2

4374 **Bevan, B.** Scheme for the painted glass proposed for the side windows of the aisles of St. James' church. Bury St. Edmunds, 1919

4375 St. James parish magazine, 1882-1959; Cathedral news, 1959-

St. Mary's Church

4376 **Tymms, S.** Architectural and historical account of the church of St. Mary, Bury St. Edmunds. Bury St. Edmunds, 1854

4377 **Gray, H. B.** History of the church of St. Mary's in Bury St. Edmunds. 1920

4378 **Sandford, J. H.** Church of St. Mary, Bury St. Edmunds. JBAA NS 34, 1929, 66-70

4379 **Sandford, J. H.** Description of St. Mary's church, Bury St. Edmunds. Gloucester, [c.1931] and later edns. SRO/B

4380 Bury St. Edmunds: St. Mary's church. EADT 31.8.1938

4381 St. Mary's church, Bury St. Edmunds: some questions answered. nd. nl

4382 **Whittingham, A. B.,** *and* **Godfrey, W. H.** St. Mary's church: St. James' cathedral; the Unitarian chapel. Arch J 108, 1951, 187-90

4383 Restoration appeal [St. Mary's]. Bury St. Edmunds, 1963. SRO/B

4384 **Tolhurst, J. B.** Hammer-beam figures of the nave roof of St. Mary's church, Bury St. Edmunds. JBAA 3rd Ser 25, 1962, 66–70

4385 **Ashley, H.** Exhibition of photographs of the fifteenth-century carvings in the nave and aisle roofs of St. Mary's church, Bury St. Edmunds. 1964. [Typescript]. O

4386 **Wells, C.** Fifteenth-century woodcarvings in St. Mary's church, Bury St. Edmunds. Rp from Medical History 9, 1965. SRO/B

4387 **Statham, M. P.** St. Mary's church, Bury St. Edmunds. Ipswich, 1968. 2nd edn 1971

4388 St. Mary's parish magazine, c.1880–1966; Tower and Spire (with St. John's), 1966–70; The Bridge, 1971–

Bells

4389 **Rogers, J. C. T.**, *et al.* Bells at Bury St. Edmunds. N&Q 6th Ser 1, 1880, 193, 303; 2, 1880, 97–8

4390 **Flitton, A. R.** Bells of Bury St. Edmunds and the district: an account of the weight, inscriptions, etc. Bury St. Edmunds, 1908. SRO/B

Roman Catholicism

4391 Copy of a letter [dated 30 Nov 1688] out of the country to one in London, discovering a conspiracy of the Roman Catholicks at St. Edmunds-bury in Suffolk. SRO/B

4392 **Rowe, J.** Story of Catholic Bury St. Edmunds. Bury St. Edmunds, 1959. SRO/B

Nonconformity See also **1959, 1983, 1985, 1989, 2616–17**

General

4393 **Duncan, J.** Origins of the Free church in Bury St. Edmunds. 2v. 1955. [Typescript]. SRO/B

4394 **Duncan, J.** History of the Free churches in Bury, 1955–70. [Typescript]. SRO/B

Individual Congregations

4395 **G[etley], T. A. H.** Garland Street Baptist church, Bury St. Edmunds, centenary, 1834–1934. Bury St. Edmunds, 1934. SRO/B

4396 **Duncan, J.** History of the Baptist church in Bury St. Edmunds: the first 80 years. 1963. [Typescript]. SRO/B

4397 Bury St. Edmund's church covenants. CHST 2, 1906, 332–6

4398 **Peel, A.** Congregational martyrs at Bury St. Edmunds: how many? CHST 15, 1946, 64–7

4399 **Grieve, A. J.**, *and* **Jones, W. M.** These three hundred years: being the story of Congregational work and witness in Bury St. Edmunds, 1646–1946. 1946. SRO/B

4400 **Duncan, J.** History of the Congregational church in Bury St. Edmunds: its first 150 years. [c.1960]. SRO/B

4401 **Duncan, J.** Copy of the early Congregational record, 1646–1801, of Bury St. Edmunds. 1961. SRO/B

4402 **Duncan, J.** Methodists in Bury St. Edmunds and district: Bury St. Edmunds circuit. 1963. Supplements 1964, 1967. SRO/B

4403 **Duncan, J.** History of Presbyterians in Bury St. Edmunds. 1961. [Typescript]. SRO/B

THEATRES *See also* **3330**

4404 **Statham, M.** Plays and playhouses in Bury St. Edmunds. 1970. [Typescript]. SRO/B

4405 **Rosenfeld, S. W.** Wilkins and the Bury St. Edmunds theatre. Theatre Notebook 13, 1958, 20–25. SRO/B

4406 **Wood, O. I.,** *and* **Mackintosh, J.** Theatre Royal, Bury St. Edmunds. Tabs 23, 1965, 6–14. SRO/B

4407 **Statham, M.** Theatre Royal, Bury St. Edmunds: an outline history. Bury St. Edmunds, 1965. [Typescript]. SRO/B

4408 **Statham, M.** Theatre Royal, Bury St. Edmunds: a short history of dramatic entertainment in Bury St. Edmunds. Bury St. Edmunds, 1967. SRO/B

4409 What's on, Bury St. Edmunds. v 1, no 1 Aug 1964–v 6, no 10, May 1970. Penge. SRO/B. Incomplete

PAGEANTS AND FESTIVALS

4410 Bury St. Edmunds pageant, 1907. [Rp from the Bury Free Press]. Bury St. Edmunds, 1907. SRO/B

4411 **Parker, L. N.** Bury St. Edmunds pageant, 8–13 July 1907. 2nd edn, with musical score. Bury St. Edmunds, 1907. O

4412 Bury St. Edmunds folk play, 8–13 July 1907. ER 16, 1907, 142–6

4413 Bury St. Edmunds: pageant of Magna Carta, 10–20 June 1959. Bury St. Edmunds, 1959. SCL/L

4414 Son et Lumière: Abbey Gardens, Bury St. Edmunds, 31 August–26 Sept 1964. Bury St. Edmunds, 1964. SRO/B

4415 St. Edmund year festival: programme . . . April–Nov 1970. Bury St. Edmunds, 1970. SRO/B

4416 **Harling, D.,** *Ed.* St. Edmund year festival, 1970. Bury St. Edmunds, 1970. SRO/B

ASSOCIATIONS

4417 **Independent Order of Oddfellows.** Story of a great record of social achievement, 1842–1942, of the Bury St. Edmunds District. Bury St. Edmunds, 1947. SRO/B

4418 Bury St. Edmund's Oddfellows' calendar in connection with the four Bury Lodges . . . (1894–6). 3 pts. Bury St. Edmunds, [1893–5]. BL

4419 [**Bullen, H.**] Rules and orders for the Provident Society of St. Edmund. Bury St. Edmunds, [1788]. SRO/B

4420 **Robertson, C.** History of the Bury St. Edmunds Clerical Society. Bury St. Edmunds, 1955. SRO/B

4421 Bury St. Edmunds Athenaeum: annual report 1890/1, 1894/5. Bury St. Edmunds, 1891, 1895. SRO/B. *See also* **445, 472, 4428**

Freemasonry

4422 **Burdon, J. R.** Freemasonry in Bury St. Edmunds. SIMT Lodge, No 3913, 1934

4423 **Burdon, J. R.** Freemasonry in Bury St. Edmunds. 1954

BUILDINGS

4424 Report on the buildings of architectural and historical interest prepared for the corporation of Bury St. Edmunds by the Society for the Protection of Ancient Buildings. Nov 1947. [Typescript]. SRO/B

4425 Town and Country Planning Act, 1947, section 30. Provisional list of buildings of special architectural or historic interest . . . Borough of Bury St. Edmunds. May 1949. [Typescript]. SRO/B

4426 **Corder, J. S.** Architectural remains found in Abbeygate Street, Bury St. Edmunds. PSIA 7, 1889/91, 124–8

4427 **Bury St. Edmunds and West Suffolk Record Office.** "Angel Corner", 8, Angel Hill, Bury St. Edmunds. Bury St. Edmunds, 1964. [Typescript]

4428 **Statham, M. P.** Bury St. Edmunds: the Athenaeum. Bury St. Edmunds, 1965. SRO/B. *See also* **4421**

4429 Coffee-house in Bury St. Edmunds. Antiquary 16, 1887, 72–3

4430 **Tymms, S.** Cupola House, Bury St. Edmunds. PSIA 3, 1860/63, 375–85

4431 **Maltby, H. J. M.** Cupola House, the Athenaeum, and some Georgian houses in Bury St. Edmund's. Arch J 108, 1951, 167–8

4432 **Hurrell, H. M.** Ancient House, Eastgate Street, Bury St. Edmunds. Bury St. Edmunds, nd. SRO/B

4433 **Statham, M.** Guildhall, Bury St. Edmunds. PSIA 31, 1967/9, 117–57

4434 Suffolk Hotel, Bury St. Edmunds. (Tales of old inns, no 59). nd

4435 **Bidwell, J.** Early print of the market cross of Bury St. Edmunds. PSA 2, 1849/53, 261

4436 **Longland, S.** Bury St. Edmunds cross. Conn 172, 1969, 163–73

4437 **Scarfe, N.** The Bury St. Edmunds cross. PSIA 33, 1973/5, 75–85

4438 **Tymms, S.** Some lead crosses found at Bury St. Edmunds. PSA 3, 1853/6, 165–7

4439 **Tymms, S.** Medieval lead crosses, Bury St. Edmunds. PSIA 2, 1854/9, 215–17

4440 **Waterton, E.** Lead cross and lead seal found at Bury St. Edmund's. PSA 2nd Ser 2, 1861/4, 301–02

4441 **Corder, J. S.** Bury corner posts. PSIA 16, 1916/18, 187–95

REGISTERS, WILLS, AND INSCRIPTIONS   *See also* **2423–4, 2429–30, 3015**

4442   Bury St. Edmunds: St. James parish registers. Baptisms, 1558–1800. Burials, 1562–1800. Marriages, 1562–1800. 3v. Bury St. Edmunds, 1915–16. SGB 17

4443   St. Mary's, Bury St. Edmunds. Copy of register for 1538 to 1579. [1935]. MS. SRO/B

4444   **Powell, E.** Extracts from parish registers: St. Mary's, Bury St. Edmunds. E Ang NS 4, 1891/2, 110–11

4445   **Symonds, W.** Burials of pre-reformation clergy at St. Mary's church, Bury St. Edmunds. 1538–74. E Ang NS 12, 1907/08, 65–6

4446   **Crossfield, T.** Bury will index, 1660–1802. nd. MS. SRO/B

4447   **Hervey,** *Lord* **J.** Early wills relating to Bury. PSIA 7, 1889/91, 217–25

4448   **Bullen, R. F.** Index to Bury wills in the Prerogative Court of Canterbury, 1383–1604. E Ang NS 13, 1909/10, 116–21

4449   **Haslewood, F.** Monumental inscriptions at Bury St. Edmunds in the abbey burying ground. Inscriptions in the church of St. Mary and St. James ... with index. 6 v. 1887. [Typescript]

4450   **Barker, H. R.** Monumental inscriptions in the Baptist burial ground (Lower Baxter Street) ... and ... in the churchyard adjoining the Congregational church (Whiting Street), Bury St. Edmunds. 1917. MS. SRO/B

BUTLEY   *See also* **713, 2791, 7611**

4451   Butley parish history. SC 16.9.1927, Rp No 38

4452   **Snell, A.,** *Ed.* Handbook and guide to the parishes of Butley, Chillesford, and Wantisden in the county of Suffolk, 1325–1950. Winchester, 1950

4453   **Gray, H. St. G.** Earthwork near Butley. PSIA 14, 1910/12, 69–90

4454   Register or Chronicle of Butley Priory, Suffolk, 1510–35. *Ed.* by A. G. Dickens *et al.* Winchester, 1951

4455   **Day, R. J.** Butley Priory in the Hundred of Loes. PSIA 4, 1864/74, 405–13

4456   Excursion of the Archaeological Society to Butley Abbey and Orford castle. Rp from Ipswich Jour 13 July 1872

4457   **White, H. G. E.** Unpublished fourteenth-century rent roll of the Priory of Butley, Suffolk, with singular liturgical, legal, and other matter. E Ang NS 11, 1905/06, *passim*

4458   **Mann, J. C.** Butley Priory. CL 73, 1933, 308–14

4459   **Myres, J. N. L.,** *et al.* Butley Priory. Arch J 90, 1933, 177–281

4460   **Myres, J. N. L.** Notes on the history of Butley Priory. *In* Oxford essays in medieval history presented to H. E. Salter. Oxford, 1934. 190–206

4461   **Barker, A. V.** The future of Butley Priory. CA 1, 1950/51, 223–4

4462   **Sinclair, K. V.** Another MS belonging to Butley Priory. N&Q 207, 1962, 408–10

4463   **Scarfe, N.** An Elizabethan note on Tangham Manor. SR 1, 1957, 104–05

BUXHALL   *See also* 7138

4464 **Copinger, W. A.** History of the parish of Buxhall in the county of Suffolk. 1902

4465 Buxhall parish history. SC 7.2.1930, Rp No 162

4466 **Kendall, C. N.** St. Mary's church, Buxhall. Buxhall, 1972

BUXLOE   *See* Knodishall-cum-Buxloe

CAMPSEY ASH   *See also* 3107, 4795

4467 Campsea Ash. CL 18, 1905, 54–62

4468 Campsea Ash parish history. SC 6.12.1929, Rp No 153

4469 Resolutions of the Vestry of Campsey-Ash on a circular statement received from the Lord Lieutenant of Suffolk as chairman of the county magistrates, and on the introduction of a labour rate. Woodbridge, [1830]. BL

4470 **Sherlock, D.** Excavation at Campsea Ash priory, 1970. PSIA 32, 1970/72, 121–39

4471 **Keen, L.** Medieval floor-tiles from Campsea Ash Priory. PSIA 32, 1970/72, 140–51

4472 Psalter formerly belonging to Campsea Ash nunnery and now preserved in the library of Shipdham church, c.1300. NA 10, 1884/7, 390

4473 Parish magazine, 1909–12

4474 **Haslewood, F.** Parish registers of Campsea-Ashe: licence to eat flesh on fast days, and other entries. E Ang NS 2, 1887/8, 363

CAPEL ST. MARY

4475 Capel St. Mary parish history. EADT 21.2.1935, Rp No 382

4476 **Pickess, J.** Fragmentary history of Capel St. Mary from early times to present day. 1948. [Typescript]

4477 **East Suffolk County Council.** Planning Dept. Capel St. Mary: factual survey and outline plan. Ipswich, 1963

4478 **East Suffolk County Council.** Planning Dept. Capel St. Mary: review of densities. Ipswich, 1966

4479 **Birch, H. W.** Church notes: Capel St. Mary, E Ang NS 8, 1899/1900, 247–8

4480 **Pickess, J.** History of Capel St. Mary Congregational chapel. 1946. [Typescript]

4481 Extracts from the register of Capel S. Mary. E Ang NS 5, 1893/4, 114–16

CARLFORD HUNDRED   *See* Colneis and Carlford Hundreds

CARLTON   *See* Kelsale-cum-Carlton

CARLTON COLVILLE

4482   Carlton Colville parish history. EADT 11.3.1936, Rp No 430

4483   Carlton Colville, Oulton, and Kirtley ... inclosure. State of claims. [A notice of the hearing of objections]. Great Yarmouth, 1801. BL

4484   E. East Anglian folk-lore: "fairy loaf" in Carlton Colville. E Ang 3, 1886/8, 45

4485   **Chambers, C.** Carlton Colville emigrants, 1836. E Ang NS 10, 1903/04, 278–281

4486   **Thomas, F.** St. Peter's, Carlton Colville. Carlton Colville, 1976. SCL/L

CAVENDISH   *See also* **2632, 3325**

4487   Cavendish parish history. SC 21.10.1927, Rp No 42

4488   **Barnard, J. D.** Bygone Cavendish. Sudbury, 1951

4489   **Atkinson, T. D.** On the manor of Overhall in the parish of Cavendish. PCAS 9, 1896/8, 280–81

4490   Cavendish church [with Davy's notes of 1805]. PSIA 8, 1892/4, 263–73

4491   **Fow, C. S.** St. Mary's church, Cavendish. nd. nl

4492   **Hope, W. H. St. J.** St. Mary's church, Cavendish. [c.1915]. [c.1964]. nl

4493   **Grieve, A. J.** Cavendish church. CHST 15, 1946, 7–17 SRO/B

4494   **Grieve, A. J.** Cavendish: further notes. CHST 15, 1946, 73–4 SRO/B

4495   Old house of Overhall. PSIA 8, 1892/4, 261–3

4496   Registers of Cavendish church. *Ed.* by O. G. Knapp. 1939. BL

CAVENHAM

4497   Cavenham parish history. SC 4.9.1931, Rp No 244

4498   **Briscoe, T.** A squat ground axe from Cavenham. PSIA 33, 1973/5, 310–11

4499   **Layard, N. F.** Bronze crowns and a bronze head-dress from a Roman site at Cavenham Heath. Ant J 5, 1925, 258–65

4500   **P, C.** Another yeoman brass, Cavenham church. E Ang NS 10, 1903/04, 3

4501   **Green, H. T.** Brass of John Thurston at Cavenham. PSIA 19, 1925/7, 354

CHARSFIELD   *See also* **2031**

4502   Charsfield parish history. SC 1.5.1931, Rp No 226

4503   Notes and letters inserted in the Dunthorne MS. Historia Caresfeld. [Typescript]. nd

CHATTISHAM   *See also* **3148, 3355–7**

4504   **W, H. A.** Field names, Chattisham. E Ang NS 4, 1891/2, 246

4505   Chattisham parish history. SC 24.7.1931, Rp No 238

4506   W, H. A. Village customs: Chattisham and Copdock. E Ang NS 5, 1893/4, 272

4507   G, J. Chattisham Place: owners and occupiers, 1650–1850. E Ang NS 10, 1903/04, 356

4508   **Partridge, C.** Chattisham Place: owners and occupiers, 1650–1850. E Ang NS 11, 1905/06, 255

4509   W, H. A. Extracts from parish registers: Chattisham. E Ang NS 5, 1893/4, 90–91

4510   Monumental inscriptions on stones in Chattisham church. E Ang NS 5, 1893/4, 19–20; NS 6, 1895/6, 143

CHEDBURGH   *See also* 1959

4511   Chedburgh parish history. EADT 13.5.1936, Rp No 437

CHEDISTON   *See also* 2757–8

4512   Chediston parish history. EADT 24.4.1935, Rp No 394

4513   Hovell's Manor, Chediston. E Ang NS 8, 1899/1900, 16, 18

4514   **Raven, J. J.** Chediston church. E Ang NS 6, 1895/6, 111–12

4515   **Farrer, E.** Calendar of deeds of the Chediston estate. 1929. MS

4516   Registers of Chediston, Suffolk (1653–1924). Transcribed by F. C. Lambert. 1924. [Typescript] BL. *Ed.* by A. S. Gooding. SRO/I

CHELMONDISTON

4517   Chelmondiston parish history. SC 22.5.1931, Rp No 229

4518   **Birch, H. W.** Church notes: Chelmondiston. E Ang NS 8, 1899/1900, 42–4

CHELSWORTH

4519   A[usten, *Sir*], H. E. History of Chelsworth, in Suffolk. Hadleigh, 1850

4520   Chelsworth parish history. SC 29.6.1928, Rp No 78

4521   **Pocklington, G. R.** Chelsworth: the story of a little Suffolk village. Bury St. Edmunds, 1956

4522   **Austen,** *Sir* **H. E.** Mural paintings, Chelsworth church. PSIA 1, 1848/53, 146–7

CHEVINGTON   *See also* 1959

4523   Chevington parish history. SC 15.1.1932, Rp No 258

4524   **Tymms, S.** Chevington church. PSIA 2, 1854/9, 434–8

4525   Parish registers of Chevington, co. Suffolk, 1559 to 1812. *Ed.* by W. Brigg. Leeds, 1915. BL

CHILLESFORD   *See also* **4452**

4526   Chillesford parish history. SC 24.6.1932, Rp No 275

4527   **Owles, E. J.,** *and* **Smedley, N.** Collared urn of the early Middle Bronze Age from Chillesford. PSIA 31, 1967/70, 108–10

4528   Parish registers of Chillesford, Suffolk. *Ed.* by F. A. Crisp. 1886. 100 copies

CHILTON   *See also* **2732, 7579–80**

4529   Chilton parish history. EADT 22.11.1933, Rp No 333

4530   **Bent, J. T.** The tombs at Chilton. Antiquary 5, 1882, 59–60

CHIMNEY MILLS   *See* Culford

CLARE

GENERAL HISTORIES AND DESCRIPTIONS

4531   **Dickinson, P. G. M.** Clare in Suffolk, and the twenty-four villages of its rural district. Clare, 1952

4532   **Dickinson, P. G. M.** Historic Clare and its rural district. Clare, 1952

4533   **Thornton, G. A.** A study in the history of Clare, Suffolk: with special reference to its development as a borough. TRHS 4th Ser 11, 1928, 83–115

4534   **Thornton, G. A.** History of Clare, Suffolk, with special reference to its development as a borough during the Middle Ages, and its importance as a centre of the woollen industry in the fifteenth to seventeenth centuries. [Thesis summary] BIHR 6, 1928/9, 31–3

4535   **Thornton, G. A.** History of Clare, Suffolk. Cambridge, 1928. 1930

4536   **Thornton, G. A.** Short history of Clare, Suffolk. Colchester, 1946. 1963 rev edn

Medieval History   *See also* **2649–52, 3456**

4537   **Ware, S.** Battle-axe heads found near Clare. Arch 31, 1846, 496–7

4538   **Ault, W. O.,** *Ed.* Court rolls of the abbey of Ramsey, and of the Honor of Clare. New Haven, Conn., 1928. BL

4539   **Ward, J. C.** Honour of Clare in Suffolk in the early Middle Ages. PSIA 30, 1964/6, 94–111

Post-Medieval History

4540   Clare parish history. SC 30.9.1927, Rp No 40

4541   **Thornton, G. A.** Chancery case illustrating life in Clare at the end of the sixteenth century. PSIA 19, 1925/7, 72–7

Economic History

4542   **Armstead, J. B.** Cloth manufactory at Clare. E Ang 1, 1858/63, 80–81

Localities: Clare

LOCAL GOVERNMENT AND SOCIAL SERVICES

4543 **Armstead, J. B.** Some account of the court leet of the borough of Clare, with extracts from the verdicts of the headboroughs [1612–1782]. PSIA 2, 1854/9, 103–12

4544 **Armstead, J. B.** Town criers of Clare. E Ang 1, 1864, 384–6

4545 **Clare Middle School** [formerly Clare Secondary School]. Magazine, 1956/ 1970, SRO/B

RELIGION AND CHURCHES

Clare Priory

4546 **Jarvis, H.** Clare Priory. PSIA 6, 1883/8, 73–84

4547 Clare Priory. PSIA 14, 1910/12, 108–09

4548 **Webb, G.** Clare Priory and Clare village. CL 60, 1926, 208–15

4549 **Dickinson, P. G. M.** The Augustinians return to Clare, 1248–1538–1953. 1954

4550 **Barnardiston, K. W.** Clare Priory: seven centuries of a Suffolk house. *Ed.* by N. Scarfe. Cambridge, [1962]

4551 Clare Priory, by one of the friars. Clare, c.1970

Church of SS Peter and Paul

4552 **Armstead, J. B.** The ruined state of Clare church. E Ang 2, 1864/6, 27

4553 Clare church. PSIA 8, 1892/4, 222–38

4554 **Hope, W. H. St. J.** Clare church. 1915. SRO/B

4555 Church of SS Peter and Paul, Clare. Ramsgate, 3rd edn [1961]

4556 Short history of St. Peter and St. Paul, Clare. Gloucester, [1968]. O

4557 **Armstead, J. B.** Bells at Clare. E Ang 1, 1858/63, 28–9

Nonconformity

4558 Proceedings and penalties under the Conventicle Act at Clare [1683]. E Ang NS 9, 1901/02, 183–5

4559 **Duncan, J.** History of Clare Congregational church. 1968. [Typescript]. SRO/B

Clare Reliquary and Pectoral Cross

4560 **Coleman, J. C.,** *and* **Jenner, S.** Gold reliquary found at Clare. E Ang 3, 1866/8, 44–5

4561 **Way, A.** Gold pectoral cross found at Clare castle. Arch J 25, 1868, 60–71

4562 Clare reliquary (gold pectoral cross) presented to the British Museum. Ant J 16, 1936, 321–2

4563 **Tonnochy, A. B.** Clare reliquary. BMQ 11, 1936/7, 1

FREEMASONRY

4564   **Thornton, H.** History of Royal Clarence Lodge, No 1823, Clare, 1879–1929. 1929

BUILDINGS

4565   Chapel House, Clare. PSIA 8, 1892/4, 239–40

4566   **Tymms, S.** Clare castle. PSIA 1, 1848/53, 61–6

4567   **Knocker, G. M.** Clare castle excavations, 1955. PSIA 28, 1958/60, 136–52

4568   **Almack, R.** Sign of the White Swan. PSIA 1, 1848/53, 50–52

4569   **W[alford], W. S.** Carving in front of the White Swan, Clare. PSIA 1, 1848/1853, 67–73, 145

HERALDRY

4570   Heraldic notes taken at Clare in the reign of Queen Elizabeth. TG 2, 1853, 398–402

REGISTERS

4571   **Armstead, J. B.** Clare parish registers. E Ang 1, 1858/63, 42–3

CLARE RURAL DISTRICT

4572   Official guide. [c.1960] and later edns

4573   Annual report of the Medical Officer of Health, 1896–8, 1901–05, 1908–09. Clare. [1897–1910] BL

CLAYDON   *See also* **695, 2705**

4574   Claydon parish history. SC 14.4.1933, Rp No 307

4575   **White, C. H. E.** Ancient steelyard weight (*temp.* 13th century) found at Claydon. PSIA 6, 1883/8, 131–5

4576   **Birch, H. W.** Church notes: Claydon. E Ang NS 6, 1895/6, 213–15; NS 13, 1909/10, 171–3

4577   **Partridge, C. S.,** *et al.* Mockbeggar's Hall, Claydon. E Ang NS 4, 1891/2, 335, 352, 367–8, 383–4

4578   **Hills, W. P.** Claydon and Mockbeggar's Hall. PSIA 23, 1937/9, 6–17

4579   **Pearson, W. C.** Extracts from the parish registers ... E Ang NS 11, 1905/06, 100–03

CLOPTON

4580   Clopton parish history. SC 13.3.1931, Rp No 219

CLOVESHOE   *See* Mildenhall

COCKFIELD   *See also* **3436**

4581   **Babington, C.** Materials for a history of Cockfield. PSIA 5, 1876/86, 195–252

4582   Cockfield parish history. SC 13.1.1928, Rp No 54

4583   **Hart, C.** An early charter of Adam of Cockfield, 1100–1118. EHR 72, 1957, 466–9

4584   St. Peter's church, Cockfield. [Typescript]. nd. nl

4585   **Duncan, J.** History of Cockfield Congregational church. 1969. [Typescript]. SRO/B

CODDENHAM   *See also* **2398, 2484, 2622, 2672, 3155, 3373**

4586   **Martin, F.,** *and* **E.** Sketches of Coddenham, with description of church. Ipswich, [1886]

4587   Coddenham parish history. SC 8.7.1927, Rp No 28

4588   **Lummis, W. M.** Material for a history of Coddenham. 1933. [Typescript]

4589   **Gage, J.** A letter accompanying a Roman speculum. Arch 27, 1838, 359–60

4590   **Smedley, N.** Two bellarmine bottles from Coddenham. PSIA 26, 1952/4, 229–30

4591   **Lummis, G. M.** Parish of Coddenham: surveyor's accounts, 1773–80. E Ang NS 3, 1889/90, 376

4592   **Birch, H. W.** Church notes: Coddenham. E Ang NS 6, 1895/6, 33–7

4593   **Lummis, G. M.** Collections upon briefs, Coddenham. E Ang NS 6, 1895/6, 131–3

4594   St. Mary the Virgin, Coddenham. PSIA 17, 1919/21, 127–34

4595   **Lummis, G. M.** Stone coffins in Coddenham church. E Ang NS 5, 1893/4, 134

4596   **Corder, J. S.** "Live and Let Live" [former inn], Coddenham. PSIA 16, 1916/18, 65–6

COLNEIS AND CARLFORD HUNDREDS   *See also* **693, 695, 1507, 4902**

4597   Rules, orders, and regulations for the better government of the poor in the House of Industry for the Hundreds of Colneis and Carlford. Ipswich, 1759. BL

COMBS   *See also* **2890, 7138**

4598   Combs parish history. EADT 21.6.1939, Rp No 12

4599   **Florance, H. K.** Combs church and parish. Ramsgate, nd

4600   **Watling, H.** Painted glass in Suffolk churches: Combs. E Ang NS 5, 1893/4, 344–6

CONEY WESTON

4601   Coney Weston parish history. EADT 29.5.1935, Rp No 398

COOKLEY

4602   Cookley parish history. EADT 18.10.1933, Rp No 329

4603   **Lewis, R. W. M.** Unrecorded brass at Cookley. TMBS 8, 1943/51, 370

COPDOCK

4604   Copdock parish history. SC 11.9.1931, Rp No 245

4605   **Birch, H. W.** Church notes: Copdock. E Ang NS 7, 1897/8, 273–4

4606   **D, C. R.** Decorated vane: Copdock church. E Ang NS 7, 1897/8, 312

4607   **Birch, H. W.** A legend of Copdock Hall. E Ang NS 6, 1895/6, 25–6

CORNARD, GREAT   *See also* 7579–80

4608   Great Cornard parish history. SC 17.4.1931, Rp No 224

4609   **Oliver, V.** Great Cornard. [c.1950]. [Typescript]. SRO/B

CORNARD, LITTLE   *See also* 2780, 3610

4610   Little Cornard parish history. SC 8.5.1931, Rp No 227

4611   **Hewitt, H. D.** Prehistoric human remains at Little Cornard. PPSEA 1, 1908/1914, 297–300

4612   **Deedes, C.** Old documents belonging to the parish of Little Cornard. E Ang NS 1, 1885/6, *passim*

4613   **Deedes, C.** Little Cornard parish accounts. E Ang NS 3, 1889/90, 73–7

4614   **Cooper, P. H. M.** Some notes on the history of the church of All Saints and the ancient parish of Cornard Parva. Cornard, 1972

CORTON

4615   **Gerish, W. B.,** *Ed.* Corton, some materials for the history of. 1890–92. MSS, cuttings, etc. SCL/L

4616   **Gerish, W. B.** Materials towards a history of Corton. E Ang NS 4, 1891/2, 177–81, 193–5

4617   Corton parish history. EADT 26.5.1937, Rp No 472

4618   **Harrod, H.** Flint implement found on Corton beach. PSA 2nd Ser 3, 1864/7, 19

4619   Corton, Hopton, and Gorleston inclosure: extracts from the award of the Commissioners ... 3 pts. Great Yarmouth, [1813]. BL

4620   **Allen, C. A. B.** Short history of Corton church. [1953]. SCL/L

4621   **Gerish, W. B.** Carved stone pinnacle or gable cross found in Corton church. E Ang NS 4, 1891/2, 151–2; NS 5, 1893/4, 175

COSFORD RURAL DISTRICT   *See also* **2406**

4622 Official guide. [c.1959] and later edns
4623 Annual report of the Medical Officer of Health, 1896, 1901–04, 1907–09, 1912, 1959–. Sudbury, [1897–]. BL

COTTON

4624 Cotton parish history. SC 21.6.1929, Rp No 1929
4625 Brief account of Cotton church. SAAP Pt 2. June 1847, 1–3

COVEHITHE   *See also* **276–7, 7322, 8099**

4626 **Browne, J.** History and antiquities of Covehithe. Lowestoft, 1874. 1922
4627 Covehithe parish history. EADT 15.8.1934, Rp No 364
4628 **Raven, J. J.** Bronze strigil found at Covehithe. PSIA 8, 1892/4, 215–18
4629 St. Andrew's church, Covehithe. nd

COWLINGE

4630 Cowlinge parish history. 2 pts. EADT 4.9.1936, 11.9.1936, Rp Nos 409, 410
4631 **Johnson, A.** Brief guide to the church of St. Margaret of Antioch, Cowlinge. [1969]
4632 **Duncan, J.** History of Cowlinge Congregational church. 1969. [Typescript]. SRO/B

CRANSFORD   *See also* **2813**

4633 Cransford parish history. EADT 14.11.1934, Rp No 375
4634 **Rope, H. E. G.** The manor of Cransford Hall. SR 2, 1962, 137–8
4635 **Rope, H. E. G.** Cransford and the Rope family. SR 2, 1962, 133–6

CRATFIELD   *See also* **1625, 5393**

4636 Cratfield: a transcript of the accounts of the parish, from A.D.1490 to A.D.1642, with notes by the late Rev. William Holland ... With a brief memoir of the author, by his widow. *Ed.* ... by J. J. Raven. [1895]
4637 Cratfield parish history. SC 18.5.1928, Rp No 72
4638 **Bedell, A. J.** Cratfield church: the font. PSIA 15, 1913/15, 229–37

CREETING ST. MARY

4639 Creeting St. Mary parish history. EADT 27.7.1932, 12.10.1932, Rp No 279
4640 [**Lingwood, H. R.**] St. Mary's church, Creeting. Martlesham, [1958]

CREETING ST. PETER   *See also* 3211

4641   Creeting St. Peter parish history. SC 14.10.1932, Rp No 287
4642   Creeting St. Peter church. [c.1969]
4643   **Harris, H. A.** Creeting St. Peter: wall-painting. PSIA 18, 1922/4, 77

CRETINGHAM

4644   Cretingham parish history. SC 14.2.1930, Rp No 163

CROWFIELD   *See also* 2815

4645   Crowfield parish history. SC 10.6.1932, Rp No 273
4646   **Birch, H. W.** Church notes: Crowfield. E Ang NS 5, 1893/4, 340–41

CULFORD

4647   **Roumieu, J. J.** Past and present: the three villages of Culford, Ingham, and Timworth. Bury St. Edmunds, 1892
4648   Culford parish history. EADT 3.10.1934, Rp No 370
4649   **Skinner, J. W.,** *et al.* Culford School, 1881–1951. Bury St. Edmunds, 1951. SRO/B
4650   Culford School (formerly East Anglian School for Boys). East Anglian School Record, 1895–1934; Culfordian, 1935–
4651   **Tymms, S.** Mural paintings discovered in Culford old church. PSA 3, 1849/56, 250
4652   Parish registers of Culford, co. Suffolk. Baptisms, marriages, burials, 1560–1778. *Ed.* by W. Brigg. Leeds, 1909

CULPHO   *See also* 3047

4653   Culpho parish history. EADT 22.12.1937, Rp No 492
4654   **Birch, H. W.** Church notes: Culpho. E Ang NS 6, 1895/6, 358
4655   Parish registers of Culpho, Suffolk. *Ed.* by F. A. Crisp. 1886. 100 copies

DALHAM   *See also* 3260

4656   Dalham parish history. EADT 19.9.1934, Rp No 368
4657   **Hussey, C.** Dalham Hall. CL 54, 1923, 280–85
4658   Short descriptive history of the Dalham Hall estate from A.D.1086 to A.D.1901. Bury St. Edmunds, [1901?]. SRO/B
4659   Dalham parish registers. nd. [Typescript]. SRO/B

DALLINGHOO   *See also* 2757–8, 3122–3

4660   Dallinghoo parish history. SC 22.1.1932, Rp No 259

DARMSDEN

4661   Darmsden parish history. EADT 9.2.1938

4662   **Moir, J. R.** Series of pre-Palaeolithic implements from Darmsden. PPSEA 2, 1914/18, 210–12

4663   **Birch, H. W.** Church notes: Darmsden. E Ang NS 6, 1895/6, 310–11

DARSHAM   *See also* **2517**

4664   Darsham parish history. SC 1.8.1930, Rp No 187

DEBACH

4665   Debach parish history. EADT 17.3.1937, Rp No 465

4666   How the parish of Debach borrowed £400 and refused to pay it all back. [By R. Thomas]. 1879

DEBENHAM   *See also* **1279, 2643–5, 2926–8, 3048–50**

4667   **Fitch, W. S.** Collections towards a history of Debenham, Suffolk, collated from the MSS of Sam.Dove, Esq., (late of that parish) and other authentic sources. 1845

4668   **Morley, C.** Debenham: the market, fair, church, halls, and other antiquities. Ipswich, 1922

4669   Debenham parish history. SC 12.8.1927, Rp No 33

4670   **Cornish, J. G.** Reminiscences of country life. 1939

4671   **Heywood, P.,** *Ed.* Short history of Debenham. Debenham, 1975

4672   **East Suffolk County Council.** Planning Dept. Debenham: policy statement and planning proposals. Ipswich, 1972

4673   S. Mary, Debenham. CB New Issue 5, 1884, 56–60

4674   **Hocking, J. H.** Debenham church: proposed restoration. 2nd edn [1884]. nl

4675   **Redstone, V. B.** Debenham church. PSIA 20, 1928/30, 110–12

4676   Short guide to the parish church of St. Mary, Debenham. Ipswich, [c.1962]

4677   Brief history of the Congregational church, Debenham. nd

4678   Debenham: its halls and manor. PSIA 12, 1904/06, 218–22

4679   **Owles, E. J.** Medieval moated farmstead at Debenham. PSIA 31, 1967/9, 160–71

4680   **Harris, H. A.** Wall-paintings at Debenham. PSIA 23, 1937/9, 181–2

4681   **Fitch, W. S.** Sepulchral memorials in the church, churchyard, and the Dissenting chapel of Debenham, with extracts from ancient wills. 1847. MS

4682   **Sperling, J. H.** Inscription from a coffin plate at Debenham. E Ang 1, 1858/63, 149–50

4683   **Bacon, H. F.** Monumental inscriptions: Debenham church. E Ang NS 1, 1885/6, 55–7

DEBEN RURAL DISTRICT *See also* **4920–21, 8038–41**

4684 Official guide. 1951 and later edns

DENHAM, nr Bury St. Edmunds

4685 Denham St. Mary parish history. SC 3.1.1936, Rp No 422
4686 Extracts from the registers of Denham, in the Hundred of Risbridge. E Ang NS 4, 1891/2, 230–33
4687 Denham parish registers, 1539–1850: with historical notes and notices. [Preface signed, S. H. A. H(ervey)]. Bury St. Edmunds, 1904. SGB 8

DENHAM, nr Eye

4688 Denham parish history. SC 29.3.1935, Rp No 392

DENNINGTON *See also* **811, 2811, 3115**

4689 **Raven, J. J.** Dennington notes. PSIA 7, 1889/91, 120–23
4690 Dennington parish history. SC 3.6.1927, Rp No 23
4691 **Raven, J. J.** Extracts from the parish book of Dennington. E Ang NS 3, 1889/90, 273–4
4692 **Raven, J. J.** List of subscriptions to the engagement of 1651 from Dennington. NEH&GR 44, 1890, 365–6
4693 **Key, T. E.** Dennington church. PSIA 8, 1892/4, 65–75
4694 **Raven, J. J.** Dennington church notes. PSIA 10, 1898/1900, 231–2
4695 Church of St. Mary the Virgin, Dennington. [Appeal for restoration fund]. 1949. nl
4696 **Ricketts, C. M.** Church of St. Mary the Virgin, Dennington. Saffron Walden, 1949
4697 St. Mary's church, Dennington: notes about the church. [1966]. [Typescript].
4698 **Haslewood, F.** Sand writing-table at Dennington. PSIA 8, 1892/4, 76
4699 **Haslewood, F.** Monumental inscriptions in Dennington church. List of the rectors. PSIA 8, 1892/4, 77–82

DENSTON *See also* **3248–51**

4700 Davy's Suffolk collections: notes on Denston [with extracts from the parish registers]. PSIA 6, 1883/8, 437–55
4701 Denston parish history. SC 16.8.1929, Rp No 137
4702 **Haslewood, F.** Parish records of Denston. PSIA 6, 1883/8, 425–32
4703 **Fleming, I. J. R.** Denston parish accounts. SR 1, 1958, 187–9
4704 **Fleming, I. J. R.** Denston parish records. SR 2, 1959, 17–19
4705 **Fleming, I. J. R.** A sidelight on the "health service" in the nineteenth century [Denston]. SR 2, 1959, 19–20

4706 **Cooke, W.** The college or chantry of Denston. 1898
4707 **Haslewood, F.** Collegiate church of Denston. PSIA 6, 1883/8, 401–06
4708 **Fleming, I. J. R.** St. Nicholas' church, Denston. Bury St. Edmunds, 1957. Haverhill, 1964. SRO/B
4709 **Haslewood, F.** Denston Hall. PSIA 6, 1883/8, 433–6
4710 **Haslewood, F.** Monumental inscriptions in the parish of Denston. PSIA 6, 1883/8, 407–24

DEPDEN

4711 Depden parish history. EADT 20.11.1935, Rp No 417
4712 **Cullum, G. G. M. G.** Extracts from the registers of Depden. E Ang NS 4, 1891/2, 209–12

DRINKSTONE

4713 Drinkstone parish history. SC 24.4.1931, Rp No 225
4714 **Sharratt, N.** Church guide: All Saints, Drinkstone. Kettleburgh, 1972
4715 **Duncan, J.** Drinkstone Methodist chapel. 1964. [Typescript]. SRO/B
4716 **Powys, A. R.** An old cottage saved: how derelict cottages at Drinkstone, in Suffolk, were brought into use again. 1921
4717 **Cresswell, G. G. B.** Drinkstone parish registers. E Ang NS 5, 1893/4, 327–331, 366–7, 375–8
4718 **Cresswell, G. G. B.** Inscription and coats of arms formerly in the windows of Drinkstone church. E Ang NS 6, 1895/6, 5–7

DUNNINGWORTH   *See also* Tunstall

4719 Dunningworth parish history. SC 28.8.1931, Rp No 243

DUNWICH

COAST EROSION   *See also* **277,** *and* Southwold *and* Walberswick, *below*
4720 **Seward, M.** All Saints' church, Dunwich. A series of sketches illustrating the progress of coast erosion between 1880 and the final destruction of the church in November 1919. Cambridge, 1920. NCL/N
4721 The passing of All Saints' church, Dunwich. Photographs by F. Jenkins of two engravings, 1750 and 1785, and 22 photographs 1880–1920. Southwold, [c.1920]. SCL/L

HISTORY   *See also* **680, 3527, 3530, 6574, 7321–2**
4722 Exact facsimile of the folding plan [by Ralph Agas] of the ancient city of Dunwich, 1587, with its rivers and antiquities. nd. nl
4723 **Gardner, T.** Historical account of Dunwich, ... Blithburgh, ... [and] Southwold, with remarks on some places contiguous thereto. 1754. *See also* **2923**

4724 **Bird, J.** Dunwich: a tale of the splendid city. In four cantos. 1828.

4725 **Watling, H.** History of Dunwich, ancient and modern. Compiled from most of our historians. Beccles, 1853

4726 **Chester, G. J.** Note on a large number of antiquities found at Dunwich. Arch J 15, 1858, 154–5

4727 **Abbot, S. F.,** *Ed.* History of the ancient city of Dunwich. Lowestoft, 2nd edn. [1883]

4728 **Raven, J. J.** Dunwich. PSIA 7, 1889/91, 237–40

4729 **Gowers,** *Sir* **W. R.** Stow's notes on Dunwich. E Ang NS 5, 1893/4, 324–6

4730 **Smythe, S. W.** City of the dead. ECM 2, 1901/02, 282–6

4731 **Wase, F. W.** History of the ancient city of Dunwich. Halesworth, 1905. 2nd edn. 1907

4732 **Andrews, F. C.** Dunwich from the time of Sigebert, King of East Angles. From Leiston Observer. Leiston, nd

4733 **Andrews, F. C.** Through the ages: Dunwich and Southwold. From Leiston Observer. Leiston, nd

4734 Olde Dunwich. The ancient capital of East Anglia. Lowestoft, [1925?]. SCL/L

4735 Dunwich. Lowestoft, 1927

4736 Dunwich parish history. SC 2.12.1927, Rp No 48

4737 **Cooper, E. R.** Memories of bygone Dunwich. Southwold, 1931. 2nd edn 1948. 3rd edn 1967

4738 **Allan, V.** Dunwich tapestry. Ipswich, [1939]

4739 **Gay, N. S.** Glorious Dunwich. Its story throughout the ages ... Ipswich, [1947]

4740 **Jobson, A.** Dunwich story. [Southwold], 1951 and later edns

4741 **Carter, J. I.,** *and* **Bacon, S. R.** Ancient Dunwich: Suffolk's lost city. np, 1975

4742 **Spencer, H. E. P.** Excavation of Temple Hill, Dunwich. PSIA 22, 1934/6, 198–200

4743 **West, S. E.** Excavation of Dunwich town defences, 1970. PSIA 32, 1970, 25–33

4744 **Scarfe, N.** Note on the historical record of Dunwich's defences. PSIA 32, 1970/72, 34–7

4745 **Hancox, E. R. H.** Finds of medieval cut halfpence and farthings at Dunwich. BNJ 1st Ser 5, 1909, 123–34

PARLIAMENTARY HISTORY *See also* **847, 3552**

4746 **Willis, B.** Ancient indenture relating to a burgess in Parliament [Dunwich, 3 Ed. IV]. Arch 1, 1770, 204

4747 Case of the burrough of Dunwich in Suffolk, upon the election of members to serve in the Convention appointed to meet the 22 January 1689. [1690]. Wing C 1022. BL

ECONOMIC HISTORY

4748 **Parsons, H. A.** Dunwich mint. BNJ 1st Ser 9, 1913, 119–28

4749 Letter from Edw. Lord Zouch, to the mayors, jurats, etc., of the Cinque Ports, recommending collections to be made for the repair of the ancient haven of Dunwich, Southwold, and Walberswick ... 19 June 1619. 1619. STC 5323a.2. Soc of Antiquaries

4750 Letter from the Privy Council to the Judges on the Circuit, requiring them to give public and strict command for the speedy paying in of all monies collected for the repair of the haven of Dunwich, Southwold, and Walberswick ... 12 July 1620. 1620. STC 7754.4. Soc of Antiquaries

4751 **Cooper, E. R.** Dunwich Iceland ships. MM 25, 1939, 170–77

THE MUNICIPALITY *See also* **482, 1454, 1457, 1542, 1588**

4752 **Royal Commission on Historical Manuscripts.** Reports Ser 55, Var. Coll. 7 ... Corporations of Beccles, Dunwich, Southwold ... 1914

4753 **Cooper, E. R.** Dunwich charter of King John, of 1215. PSIA 23, 1937/9, 230–35

4754 **Hope, W. H. St. J.** Insignia of the borough of Dunwich. PSIA 8, 1892/4, 118–19

RELIGION AND CHURCHES *See also* **1803**

4755 **Norris, N. E. S.** First and second reports on excavations at Grey Friars monastery, Dunwich. PSIA 22, 1934/6, 287–93. Third report. PSIA 23, 1937/9, 210–18

4756 **Haslewood, F.** Monuments in the churchyard of All Saints, Dunwich. PSIA 7, 1889/91, 253–4

4757 Four fragments of brasses (including one of Thomas Cooper, from Dunwich). NA 13, 1895/7, 359–60

4758 **Lewis, R. W. M. A.** Dunwich brass. TMBS 8, 1943/51, 203–04

4759 Register book of St. Peter's, Dunwich. E Ang 2, 1864/6, 129

4760 Inscription in St. Julian's church, Dunwich. TMBS 7, 1934/42, 364–5

4761 **Gurney, H.** Observations on the seal of Ethilwold, bishop of Dunwich, lately discovered at Eye in Suffolk. Arch 20, 1824, 479–83

EARL SOHAM *See also* **1847, 2636–7, 2957**

4762 Earl Soham parish history. SC 20.4.1928, Rp No 68

4763 **Beaumont, G. F.** Custom roll of the manor of Soham Earl. E Ang NS 2, 1887/8, *passim*

4764 **Fussell, G. E.** Earl Soham fair in George III's reign. SR 8, 1956, 3–5

EARL STONHAM

4765 Earl Stonham parish history. SC 17.6.1927, Rp No 25

4766 **Raven, J. J.** Earl Stonham and the Ship Money. E Ang NS 6, 1895/6, 337–8

4767 **Rahbula, E. A. R.** Earl Stonham church. Arch J 108, 1951, 156–7

4768 Rowell, F. St. Mary-the-Virgin, Earl Stonham. 1962. 1967. 1975

EAST BERGHOLT   *See also* **2679–700, 3172–4**
4769 **Grace, F. R.** Population of East Bergholt, 1653–1836: an analysis of the parish registers. SR 3, 1970, 260–72
4770 **East, W.** The saving of Flatford Mill, with the Miller's House and Willy Lott's Cottage, their lands and waters, for a national possession in memory of John Constable. Ipswich, 1928
4771 **Hynard, A.** Birthplace of John Constable, R.A. [c.1948]
4772 Bits about Bergholt, by a villager [*i.e.* George Nelson Godwin]. 1874
4773 East Bergholt parish history. EADT 3.4.1914, Rp No 7
4774 **Paterson, T. F.** East Bergholt ... giving some account of early times ... the parish records and charities ... Cambridge, 1923
4775 **East Suffolk County Council.** Planning Dept. East Bergholt: policy statement and planning proposals. Ipswich, 1968
4776 **Birch, H. W.** Church notes: East Bergholt. E Ang NS 12, 1907/08, 309–11, 333–8, 343–4
4777 **Tyrrell-Green, E.** The constructive genius of Cardinal Wolsey: benefactions to Suffolk—East Bergholt church and tower. ER 47, 1938, 140–43
4778 Parish church of St. Mary-the-Virgin, East Bergholt. Ipswich, nd
4779 **Hynard, A.** Church of St. Mary-the-Virgin, East Bergholt. [c.1947]
4780 **Sewell, W. H.** East Bergholt church: lettering on the leaves of the West door. E Ang NS 4, 1891/2, 311–12
4781 **Thompson, R. W.** Bells of East Bergholt. CL 106, 1949, 484–7

EASTON   *See also* **3467**
4782 Easton parish history. SC 30.5.1930, Rp No 178
4783 **Packard, J.** Easton, Suffolk; the fields and field-names. 1972. SCL/L
4784 **Welch, H.** All Saints' church, Easton. 1964. 2nd edn 1965. [Typescript]
4785 **Duncan, H. N.** Easton: All Saints' church. 1968
4786 **Duncan, H. N.,** *and* **Packard, J.** Easton All Saints church: church and churchyard inscriptions. [1972]

EDWARDSTONE   *See also* **3165**
4787 **Bird, A. B.** Short guide to Edwardstone. 1970
4788 Edwardstone parish history. SC 20.2.1931, Rp No 216
4789 Edwardstone, its church and priory. PSIA 15, 1913/15, 87–99

ELLOUGH
4790 Ellough parish history. EADT 10.7.1935, Rp No 403
4791 Parish registers of Ellough, Suffolk [*Ed.* by F. A. Crisp]. 1886. 50 copies

4792   Monumental inscriptions in the church and churchyard of Ellough, Suffolk. [*Ed.* by F. A. Crisp]. 1889. 50 copies

ELMSETT

4793   Elmsett parish history. SC 12.4.1929, Rp No 119

4794   **Birch, H. W.** Church notes: Elmsett. E Ang NS 7, 1897/8, 167–71

ELMSWELL

4795   **[Nichols, J.]**. Collections towards the history and antiquities of Elmeswell and Campsey Ash in the county of Suffolk. 1790. Bibliotheca topographica Britannica, no 52

4796   Elmswell parish history. SC 21.2.1930, Rp No 164

4797   **Duncan, J.** Elmswell Methodist chapel. 1964. SRO/B

ELVEDEN   *See also* **604, 2963**

4798   Elveden parish history. SC 24.7.1936, Rp No 444

4799   **Carson, R. A. G.,** *and* **Brailsford, J. W.** Elveden treasure trove. NC 6th Ser 14, 1954, 204–08

4800   **Briscoe, G.** Elveden silver coin hoard. PSIA 27, 1955/7, 120–22

4801   **Martelli, G.** The Elveden enterprise. A story of the second agricultural revolution. 1952

4802   **Turner, T. W.** Memoirs of a gamekeeper. [Elveden 1868–1953]. 1954

4803   Church of SS. Andrew and Patrick, Elveden. 1907. nl

ERISWELL   *See also* **582**

4804   Eriswell parish history. SC 30.6.1933, Rp No 316

4805   **Munday, J. T.** Topography of medieval Eriswell. PSIA 30, 1964/6, 201–09

4806   **Munday, J. T.** Eriswell—the layout of a Fen village. SR 3, 1968, 197–201

4807   **Munday, J. T.** Eriswell land utilisation, 1652–1818. [Typescript]. SRO/B

4808   **Donnan, W. H.** History of Eriswell. Bury St. Edmunds, 1956

4809   **Munday, J. T.** Eriswell-cum-Chamberlains. Soham, 1966

4810   **Munday, J. T.** Eriswell notebook. [Typescript]. 1967

4811   **Dymond, D. P.** Excavation of a prehistoric site at Upper Chamberlain's farm, Eriswell. PSIA 33, 1973/5, 1–18

4812   **Briscoe, G.,** *and* **Furness, A.** Hoard of Bronze Age weapons from Eriswell. Ant J 35, 1955, 218–19

4813   **Munday, J. T.** Prelude to a chapter on medieval Eriswell. 1963. [Typescript]

4814   **Munday, J. T.** Early medieval Eriswell. rev edn 1965. [Typescript]. SRO/B

4815   **Munday, J. T.** Twenty-four more Eriswell documents, 1250–1340. 1967. [Typescript]. SRO/B

4816   **Munday, J. T.** Eriswell-cum-Coclesworth: chronicle of Eriswell. Pt 1, until 1340. Lakenheath, 1969. [Typescript]. O

4817   **Munday, J. T.** Eriswell—justice in a mediaeval West Suffolk community. SR 3, 1968, 238–46

4818   **Munday, J. T.** Eriswell court-leet orders, 1629–1794. [1964]. [Typescript]. SRO/B

4819   **Duleep Singh,** *Prince* F.[V.] Short account of Eriswell, and the chapel of St. Lawrence. E Ang NS 2, 1887/8, 220–23

4820   **Munday, J. T.** Twelve Eriswell wills; 1500–45. 1965. [Typescript]. SRO/B

ERISWELL, LITTLE

4821   **Hutchinson, P.** Anglo-Saxon cemetery at Little Eriswell. PCAS 59, 1966, 1–32

ERWARTON   *See also* **3503, 7056**

4822   Erwarton parish history. SC 29.4.1927, Rp No 18

4823   **Birch, H. W.** Church notes: Erwarton. E Ang NS 8, 1899/1900, 104–08

EUSTON   *See also* **2880**

4824   Euston parish history. EADT 28.8.1935, Rp No 408

4825   Short history of Euston. Thetford, 1940. SRO/B

4826   **Machin, J.** An uncommon case of a distempered skin [the son of a labourer at Euston]. PTRS 424, 1732, 299–301

4827   **Davies, E. N.** Euston church guide. nd. nl

4828   **Oswald, A.** Euston Hall. CL 121, 1957, 58–61, 102–05, 148–51

4829   **Dunlop, I.** The Frenchness of Euston Hall, Suffolk. Conn 163, 1966, 142–7

4830   **[Barber, R.]** Euston Hall: a guidebook to the home of the 11th Duke of Grafton. Ipswich, [1975]. SCL/L

EXNING   *See also* **1475**

4831   **Foster, J. E.** History of Exning. PCAS 9, 1896/8, 342–6

4832   **Dibden, T. F.** Some account of the church and parish of Exning: "Horae Exningianae". [c.1850]. nl

4833   Exning parish history. EADT 2.12.1936, Rp No 456

4834   **[Edmundson, E. J.]** Village and church of Exning. Ramsgate, [1960]. 2nd edn [1961]

4835   **Smith, C. R.** Roman coins: Exning. PSIA 2, 1854/9, 222

4836   **Johnston, D. E.** Roman well at Exning. PCAS 52, 1958/9, 11–20

4837   Exning church. British Mag 1832, 221–30

4838   **Sydney, W.** Exning church. E Ang NS 2, 1887/8, 234–6

4839   **Child, K.** Story of St. Agnes' church, Exning. Gloucester, [1967]. SRO/B

4840   **Clark, J. F.** Pyx found at Exning. PSIA 1, 1848/53, 157–9

EYE

GUIDES

4841   Official guide. 1947 and later edns

GENERAL HISTORY   *See also* **857**

4842   **Maclear, G. F.** Peeps at Eye in olden times. Eye, 1862

4843   Eye parish history. SC 20.3.1914, Rp No 5

4844   **Short, M. E.** Historical reminiscences of Eye. Eye, 1922

4845   **Kerrison, E.** Set of small toilet implements of bronze, found in an urn at Eye. PSA 3, 1849/56, 186–7

4846   **Bolton, E. D.** Anglo-Saxon urn, Eye. PSIA 2, 1854/9, 214, 218

4847   **Leaf, E.** History of Eye, 1066–1602, with special reference to the growth of the borough in the reign of Elizabeth. M.A. thesis, Leeds, 1935

THE MUNICIPALITY   *See also* **482, 1454–5, 1542**

4848   **Royal Commission on Historical Manuscripts.** Ser 13. Tenth report, appendix 4, Comprising ... Eye. 1885. re-issue 1906

4849   **L.** Mandate of the Duke of Suffolk to the bailiffs of Eye [18 Edw. IV]. E Ang 4, 1869/70, 21

4850   **Deye, W.** To the right honourable the Knights, citizens, and burgesses of the Commons House ... the humble petition of William Deye, gentleman, one of the principal burgesses of ... Eye [difficulties in serving a writ upon Simon Dormer, a popish schoolmaster, formerly of Eye]. [1626]. STC 6798.6. nl

4851   **Carthew, G. A.** Armorial insignia of the borough of Eye. PSIA 6, 1883/8, 85–7

4852   **Manning, C. R.** Additional particulars of the grant of arms to the borough of Eye. PSIA 7, 1889/91, 33–50

4853   **East Suffolk County Council.** Planning Dept. Eye: policy statement and planning proposals. Ipswich, 1967

4854   **East Suffolk County Council.** Planning Dept. Conservation in Eye: appraisal of the quality and character of its townscape. Ipswich, 1969

PRIORY AND CHURCHES

4855   **Fairweather, F. H.** Excavations on the site of the priory church and monastery of St. Peter, Eye. Ant J 7, 1927, 299–312

4856   **Redstone, V. B.** Eye priory and church. nd. [Typescript]

4857   **Creed, H.** Church of St. Peter and St. Paul, Eye. PSIA 2, 1854/9, 125–148

4858   Short history of SS. Peter and Paul, Eye. Ramsgate, 1962. O
4859   Guide to the parish church of Eye. Eye, 1969. nl
4860   **Cuming, H. S.** Portrait of Henry VI in Eye church. JBAA 36, 1880, 432–4
4861   **Corder, J. S.** Ancient helmets in Eye church. PSIA 15, 1913/15, 1–2
4862   Parish magazine, from mid-1880's, followed by Deanery Magazine of the North Hartismere Rural Deanery to 1856 ... Parish news sheet for SS. Peter and Paul, Eye, and St. Mary, Braiseworth, Nov 1966–
4863   **Cason, W.** Brief history of the Baptist church, Eye, for the first fifty years. [1860]. NCL/N

THE CASTLE
4864   **Creed, H.** Castle and honor of Eye. PSIA 2, 1854/9, 117–24
4865   **Manning, C. R.** Eye Castle. PSIA 5, 1876/86, 102–14
4866   **Harris, H. A.** Eye castle. PSIA 1910/12, 249–58

BUILDINGS
4867   White Lion, Eye. Tales of old inns, No 48a. nd. nl
4868   **Department of the Environment.** List of buildings of special architectural or historic interest: borough of Eye, East Suffolk. 1971. [Typescript]

REGISTER
4869   **Schofield, B.** Register of Eye priory. BMQ 11–12, 1937/8, 9–10

EYKE

4870   History of Eyke. nd. [Typescript]
4871   Eyke parish history. SC 22.2.1929, Rp No 112

FAKENHAM, GREAT   *See also* **607**

4872   Great Fakenham parish history. EADT 29.1.1936, Rp No 425
4873   **Grimes, W. F.** Round barrow at Fakenham Magna. *In* Excavations on defence sites, 1939–45. 1960, 247

FALKENHAM

4874   Falkenham parish history. SC 7.3.1930, Rp No 166
4875   S. Ethelbert's church, Falkenham. Ipswich, 1961. SRO/B

FARNHAM

4876   Farnham parish history. EADT 15.11.1933, Rp No 332

FELIXSTOWE

DIRECTORIES *See also* **5453–7**

4877 Directory of Felixstowe, 1901. Felixstowe, 1901. nl

4878 Directory of Felixstowe, Walton, and Trimley for 1909 and later edns. to 1934, 8th edn. Felixstowe, 1909–34. *Incorp. in* Kelly's directory of Felixstowe, 1936 and later ends 1936–

4879 New directory of Felixstowe, 1932

4880 **Regency Publicity Services, Ltd.** The Felixstowe book, 1967–8: a classified directory of businesses, trades, professions, and voluntary organisations. Folkestone [1967]

GUIDES *See also* **2162, 5471, 5481, 5484, 5491, 5508, 7321**

4881 Harwich guide … Likewise a description of Landguard-Fort, Felixstow, Walton, Trimley, Shotley, etc. Ipswich, 1808

4882 [**Goodwin, H.**] Letters from Felixstow, by "Humble Gumble". 1854. nl

4883 **Badham, C. D.** An August at Felixstow. Ipswich, [1857]

4884 **"Hospes"**, *pseud.* Guide to Felixstow. Ipswich, 1857. nl

4885 Guide to Felixstowe and its neighbourhood. Ipswich, [c.1872]. [c.1878]

4886 **B[umstead], G.** Pearls of eloquence and love for Felixstowe and its neighbourhood. Diss, 1883

4887 **Taylor, J. E.** Illustrated guide to Felixstowe and neighbourhood. Including a trip down the Orwell to Harwich. 1888. 6th edn 1897

4888 **Taylor, J. E.** Story of Felixstowe cliffs. Ipswich, [1891]

4889 **Taylor, J. E.,** *and* **Hollingsworth, A. G. H.** Guide to Felixstowe: with short descriptions of Ipswich, Harwich, and other places in the neighbourhood. Ipswich, 1898

4890 Ward Lock's pictorial and descriptive guide to Felixstowe, … Aldeburgh, and Southwold … [1901] and later edns

4891 **Redstone, V. B.** Felixstowe, its highways and byways. Ipswich and the Orwell. Ipswich, [c.1906]

4892 **Lingwood, L.** Illustrated official handbook to Felixstowe and neighbourhood. Norwich, [1906]

4893 Official guide. 1920 and later edns

4894 Residential attractions of Felixstowe. [1929]

4895 **"Breckland"**, *pseud.* Felixstowe as a touring centre for East Anglia. Ipswich, [c.1930]

4896 **Fawkes, F.A.,** *Ed.* Handbook of Felixstowe amusements and sports. 1932–9

4897 **Wall, S. D.** Felixstowe and district, from articles in the Felixstowe Times, 1933–47, with additional information based on the researches of W. G. Arnott of Woodbridge. 1947. [Typescript]

GENERAL HISTORY *See also* **621, 2467, 2982**

4898 Felixstowe parish history. 2 pts. SC 6.2.1931, 13.2.1931, Rp Nos 214, 215

4899 **Wallis, L.** Felixstowe in days gone by: a short and interesting history of Felixstowe in olden days. [c.1932]

4900 **Thompson, L. P.** Old Felixstowe: its mystery and romance. Ipswich, 1945. 2nd edn 1946

4901 **Jobson, A.** Felixstowe story. Lowestoft, 1956. 1968

4902 **Felixstowe Archaeological Movement.** Journal, *cont. as* Archaeology in Colneis, 1960–. Felixstowe

4903 **Evans, J.** Account of a bronze hoard from Felixstowe. PSA 2nd Ser 11, 1885/7, 8–12

4904 **Moore, E. St. F.** Roman and other articles found at Felixstowe. PSA 2nd Ser 11, 1885/7, 12–14

4905 **Collingwood, R. G.** Samian bowl by Pervincus from Felixstowe. Ant J 4, 1924, 154–5

4906 **Myers, W.** Catalogue of Roman coins found at Felixstowe. nd. MS

4907 **Redstone, V. B.** 'Angulus Anglie', a corner of Anglia [medieval history of Felixstowe area]. PSIA 23, 1937/9, 155–64

4908 **Crowfoot, G. M.** Medieval tablet-woven braid from a buckle found at Felixstowe. PSIA 25, 1949/51, 202–04

4909 **Corker, C.,** *Ed.* In and around Victorian Felixstowe. [Photographs]. Felixstowe, 1972

DOCKS *See also* 1416

4910 **Felixstowe Dock and Railway Co.** Felixstowe Dock and Railway Company, 1875+1975. [Felixstowe], 1975

4911 Felixstowe Railway and Dock Company: rates, tolls ... 1886

4912 **Felixstowe Dock and Railway Co.** Port of Felixstowe: official handbook, 1964–. [from 1967–68, Port of Felixstowe: the year book of the Felixstowe Dock and Railway Company] Cheltenham, 1964–

FINANCE AND HEALTH

4913 **Partridge, C.** Felixstowe parish officers and accounts. nd. MS

4914 **Griffiths, A.** The Bartlett Convalescent Home, Felixstowe. 1926

PLANNING AND DEVELOPMENT

4915 **East Suffolk County Council.** Planning Dept. Factual survey and outline plan of Felixstowe Ipswich, 1953. [Typescript]

4916 **East Suffolk County Council.** Planning Dept. County development plan: Amendment No 1, Felixstowe, 1954. [Approved 1956]. Written statement and maps of Felixstowe ... Ipswich, 1954. [Typescript]

4917 **East Suffolk County Council.** Planning Dept. Felixstowe Ferry: factual survey and outline plan. Ipswich, 1962

4918 **East Suffolk County Council.** Planning Dept. Felixstowe town map: report of survey and analysis. Ipswich, 1963

4919 **East Suffolk County Council.** Planning Dept. Felixstowe, with parts of Deben Rural District: report of survey. Appraisal. Ipswich, 1968

4920   **East Suffolk County Council.** Planning Dept. Felixstowe, with parts of Deben Rural District: draft town-map review, and draft town-centre map Ipswich, 1969

4921   **East Suffolk County Council.** Planning Dept. County development plan. Amendment No 7. Felixstowe, and parts of Deben Rural District, 1970. [Approved 1972]. Written statement and town map. Ipswich, 1970

RELIGION AND CHURCHES

4922   **Fawkes, F. A.** Sunday excursions: a handbook of religious Felixstowe. [c.1924]

4923   Parish church of S. John the Baptist, Felixstowe. Jubilee 1895–1945. [1945]

4924   Felixstowe parish church year-book, 1953

4925   Parish church of St. Peter and St. Paul, Felixstowe. Ramsgate, [1963]. 1968

4926   **[Taylor, R.]** Short guide to Felixstowe parish church, 1394–1972. Felixstowe, 1972. [Typescript]

4927   Parish magazine, 1894–

FREEMASONRY

4928   **Paternoster, F. M.** History of Felix Lodge, No 2371, Felixstowe, 1890–1950. 1950

BUILDINGS

4929   Town and Country Planning Act, 1944, section 42. Provisional list of buildings of architectural or historic interest for consideration ... Felixstowe. 1947. [Typescript]

LANDGUARD FORT

4930   Account of ... sinking wells at ... Harwich and Landguard Fort for supplying those dock-yards and garrisons with fresh water. 1797. O

4931   Report on Landguard Fort. HC 1892, 133, 34

4932   **Leslie, J. H.** History of Landguard Fort, in Suffolk. 1898

FELSHAM

4933   Felsham parish history. SC 13.11.1931, Rp No 251

4934   **Tilley, *Sir* T.** Notes for the history of Felsham. Felsham, 1951. [Typescript]

FINBOROUGH, GREAT   *See also* **3401, 3486**

4935   Great Finborough parish history. SC 23.12.1932, Rp No 295

FINBOROUGH, LITTLE

4936   Little Finborough parish history. EADT 9.6.1937, Rp No 473

FINNINGHAM   *See also* 2894–6

4937   Finningham parish history, Pts 1 and 2. SC 17.2.1933, 24.2.1933, Rp Nos 301, 302

FLEMPTON

4938   Flempton parish history. SC 10.7.1931, Rp No 236

FLIXTON, nr Bungay

4939   **Toms, A. A.** Records of Flixton. 1915

4940   Flixton parish history. SC 26.7.1929, Rp No 134

4941   **Ridgard, J. M.** Social and economic history of Flixton in South Elmham, Suffolk, 1300–1600. M.A. thesis, Leicester, 1970

4942   **Salvin, A.** Tower of Flixton church, and a curious interment found there. Arch J 14, 1857, 360–62

4943   **Brice, A. A.** Letter addressed to Alexander Adair, Esq., of Flixton Hall. [shooting rights]. Norwich, 1803. SRO/B

FLIXTON, nr Lowestoft

4944   Flixton parish history, EADT 1.2.1939

4945   **Oliver, J.** Flixton church. E Ang 1, 1858/63, 22

4946   **Harris, P.** Flixton church. LA&LHS 1966/7, 18–21

4947   **West, S. E.** A medieval floor-tile from Flixton St. Andrew. PSIA 32, 1970/72, 201

FLOWTON   *See also* 2639

4948   Flowton parish history. SC 15.7.1932, Rp No 277

4949   **[Wodderspoon, J.]** Extracts from the parish paper of Flowton, Suffolk, relative to assessments made on that parish during the Civil War ... *temp.* 1643. [Ipswich], [1831?]

4950   **Birch, H. W.** Church notes: Flowton. E Ang NS 7, 1897/8, 106–07

FORDLEY   *See* Middleton-cum-Fordley

FORNHAM   *See also* 2840

4951   Fornham All Saints, St. Genevieve, St. Martin parish histories. SC 19.7.1929, Rp No 133

4952   Battle of Fornham [and] Fornham St. Genevieve. nd. [Typescript]. SRO/B

4953   **Edwardson, A. R.** Fornham sword [12th-century]. PSIA 32, 1970/72, 87

4954   **Layard, N. F.** Alabaster figures from the church of Fornham All Saints. PSA 2nd Ser 22, 1907/09, 502–03

FOXHALL   *See also* **629**

4955   Foxhall parish history. EADT 28.2.1934, Rp No 345

FRAMLINGHAM

GUIDES   *See also* **5491**

4956   The town and castle of Framlingham in Suffolk described. Ipswich, 1820

4957   **Green, R.** Strangers' guide to the town of Framlingham, its church, and castle; with short memoirs of the possessors . . . of the domain . . . Framlingham, [1853]

4958   **Green, R.** Guide to the town of Framlingham, its church, and castle. 2nd edn 1865. 3rd edn Framlingham, [1878]. 4th edn Framlingham, [1895]. 5th edn 1913

4959   **Adams, O. F.** Our English parent towns: Framlingham. NEH&GR 57, 1903, 193–8

4960   Guide to Framlingham. Framlingham, [c.1930]. nl

4961   Framlingham. [Photographs, with a short description of the town]. [1951]. BL

4962   Framlingham: a typical East Anglian town. [1951]

4963   **Booth, J.** Guide to Framlingham. Framlingham, 1954. rev. edn 1958

4964   **Sitwell, O. R.** Guide to Framlingham. Framlingham, 1970

4965   **Bridges, J.** Framlingham, portrait of a Suffolk town. Long Melford, 1975

HISTORY   *See also* **2764–6, 2836, 3033–42, 3070–73**

4966   **Hawes, R.** History of Framlingham, in the county of Suffolk, including . . . notices of the Masters and Fellows of Pembroke-Hall in Cambridge . . . begun . . . by R. Hawes. [*Ed.*] with . . . additions and notes by R. Loder. Woodbridge, 1798. 250 copies

4967   **Clay, E.** History and description of Framlingham . . . interspersed with explanatory notes, poetical extracts, and translations to the Latin inscriptions. Halesworth, [1800]

4968   **Green, R.** History, topography, and antiquities of Framlingham and Saxted . . . With biographical sketches. 1934 and later edns

4969   Framlingham parish history. SC 24.6.1927, Rp No 26

4970   **Booth, J.** Framlingham. The history of its castle, its church, and its college, etc. [1931]

4971   Framlingham Committee. To the electors of the Eastern Division of the county of Suffolk in the interest of Mr. Shawe. Framlingham, [1832]. BL

AGRICULTURE

4972   Framlingham Horticultural Society. Rules, prizes proposed, etc. Framlingham. [1833]. BL

4973   Farmers' Club, Framlingham. Annual reports, 1st—12th, 1841–52. Framlingham. nl

4974 Jubilee book of the Framlingham Live-Stock Association and Framlingham Egg Society, 1953. nl

SAVINGS BANK

4975 Rules and regulations of Framlingham Savings Bank. Woodbridge, 1824

4976 Framlingham Savings Bank. Report of the general annual meeting ... 1825/7. Framlingham. BL

4977 General statement of the funds of the Framlingham Savings Bank, 20 Nov 1837. BL

CHARITIES

4978 Ordinance for settling and confirming the manors of Framlingham and Saxsted, in the county of Suffolk, and the lands, tenements, and hereditaments thereunto belonging, devised by Sir Robert Hitcham, Knt. and late serjeant-at-law, to certain charitable uses. 1654. nl

EDUCATION

4979 Framlingham Union School for boys and girls. Rules ... for the government of the institution. Framlingham, [1835?]. BL

4980 Framlingham Union School ... Annual report, 30 May 1843. Framlingham. BL

4981 **Booth, J., *Ed*.** Framlingham College. The first sixty years. Ipswich, 1925

4982 Bye-laws of the Albert Middle-Class College in Suffolk, erected at Framlingham. May 1885. Saxmundham, 1885

4983 Framlingham College register. 1907. BL

4984 Framlingham College register. *Ed*. by J. Booth. Ipswich, 1926. 3rd edn 1949. 4th edn 1968

4985 **Causebrooke, A.** College chapel echoes. 1942

4986 Framlingham College: proposed new buildings and war memorial [inviting contributions]. Ipswich, 1946. SRO/B

4987 **Society of Old Framlinghamians.** Jubilee commemoration booklet, 1900–1950. Ipswich, 1950

4988 Framlingham College. Centenary programme, 1864–1964. Framlingham, 1964

4989 Framlingham College. The Framlinghamian, no 1, April 1889–

LIBRARY

4990 Framlingham District Lending Library. A catalogue of books ... Framling-ham, 1833. BL

PLANNING AND DEVELOPMENT

4991 **East Suffolk County Council.** Planning Dept. Framlingham: factual survey and outline plan. Ipswich. 1959

4992 **East Suffolk County Council.** Planning Dept. Conservation in Framlingham: and appraisal of the quality and character of its townscape. Ipswich, 1972

4993 **East Suffolk County Council.** Planning Dept. Framlingham: policy statement and planning proposals. Ipswich, 1972

RELIGION

General

4994 District Committee of the Society for Promoting Christian Knowledge. Reports for the years 1827–8. Framlingham. BL

4995 The history and mystery of the Holy War at F. [Verses in reference to a newspaper controversy arising out of a local Anti-Trinitarian course of lectures]. Woodbridge, [1830?]. BL

4996 Rules and regulations of the Church of England Tract Society, instituted at Framlingham, 1838. Framlingham. BL

4997 Framlingham Tracts. By F. Storr. Nos 3–4. 1840. BL

Church of St. Michael

4998 **Gowing, T. S.** Framlingham church. PSIA 3, 1860/3, 340–51

4999 Framlingham church. JBAA NS 34, 1928/9, 79–81

5000 **Jones, P. T.** Church of St. Michael, Framlingham, Gloucester, 1936. 2nd edn 1939. O

5001 Church of St. Michael, Framlingham. Saxmundham, [1950]. SCL/L 2nd edn 1958. SRO/B

5002 **Bulstrode, M. W.** Church of St. Michael, Framlingham. Framlingham, [1960]. 6th edn 1967

5003 Correspondence, etc., respecting a proposed gallery in Framlingham church, 1831–2. Framlingham. BL

5004 Framlingham [inviting contributions to the church-tower fund, August 1952]. Ipswich. SRO/B

5005 **Howard, P.** Excavation of the vaults in the chancel of Framlingham church. PSA 1, 1843/49, 14

5006 **Edwards, G. O.** Howard monument in the south aisle of Framlingham church. PSIA 3, 1860/3, 352–7

5007 **Dow, L.** Howard tombs at Framlingham. *In* Aldeburgh Festival programme book, 1957. Aldeburgh, 1957. 16–17

5008 **Stone, L.,** *and* **Colvin, H.** Howard tombs at Framlingham. Arch J 122, 1965, 159–71

5009 **Ganz, C.** Norfolk helmet in Framlingham church. PSIA 13, 1907/09, 227–32

5010 Framlingham and Saxtead parish magazine, 1949–

Roman Catholicism

5011 **Booth, J.** Prisoners of Framlingham. [1930]. [Catholic Truth Soc.]

Nonconformity

5012 **Amey, A.** The Old Meeting, Framlingham. Trans. Unitarian Hist. Soc. 1, 1916/18, 88–92

PAGEANTS

5013 Framlingham Castle historical pageant ... 8–11 July 1931. Official souvenir programme and book of the pageant. Ipswich, 1931

5014 **Hudson, J.,** *and* **A.** Framlingham Castle: an historical pageant, 8–11 July 1931. Book of words. 1931.

5015 Framlingham pageant, 1936: Sir Robert Hitcham's tercentenary celebrations. Elizabethan masque. 16–18 July 1936. Ipswich, 1936. nl

FREEMASONRY

5016 **Thomas, C. E.** An epitome of the fortunes of Fidelity Lodge, No 555, Framlingham, from 1848 to 1948. 1948

THE CASTLE

5017 History of Framlingham castle. By Dr. Sampson, 1663, printed in Leland's Collectanea, 1, Pt 2, 681–4. 1770

5018 **Bird, J.** Framlingham: a narrative of the castle. In four cantos. 1831

5019 **Phipson, R. M.** Framlingham castle. PSIA 3, 1860/3, 386–93

5020 **Ministry of Works.** Framlingham castle. 1938 and later edns

5021 **Brown, R. A.** Framlingham castle and Bigod, 1154–1216. PSIA 25, 1949/51, 127–48

5022 **Reynolds, P. K. B.** Framlingham castle. Arch J 108, 1951, 151–3

5023 **Knocker, G. M.** Excavations at Framlingham castle. PSIA 27, 1955/7, 65–88

5024 **Coad, J. G.** Recent excavations within Framlingham castle. PSIA 32, 1970/72, 152–63

5025 **Renn, D.** Defending Framlingham castle. PSIA 33, 1973/5, 58–67

INNS

5026 The Crown at Framlingham. Tales of old inns, No 33. nd. nl

5027 **Stannard, P. J.** Inns of Framlingham, past and present. Framlingham & Dist. Local Hist. & Preservation Soc. 1959. [Typescript]

PARISH REGISTER

5028 **Raven, J. J.** Framlingham parish reigster, 1622: "pothokes" for the neck. E Ang NS 5, 1893/4, 112, 128

FRAMSDEN   *See also* **2458**

5029 Framsden parish history. SC 3.5.1929, Rp No 122

5030 **Partridge, C.** Sale catalogue of a Suffolk farm, 1795 [Framsden Hall]. N&Q 196, 1951, 156–9

FRECKENHAM

5031 **White, C. H. E.** Parish of Freckenham. E Ang NS 12, 1907/08; NS 13, 1909/10, *passim*

5032 **Morley, C.** Freckenham, Suffolk: notes and theories on the village and its unrecorded castle. PSIA 17, 1919/21, 182–92

5033 **Callard, E.** Manor of Freckenham: an ancient corner of East Anglia. 1924

5034 Freckenham parish history. EADT 2.10.1935, Rp No 412

5035 **Mattingly, H.** Freckenham hoard of Roman coins. NC 6th Ser 13, 1953, 19–73

5036 **Montagu, H.** Find of ancient British gold coins [of the Iceni, at Freckenham]. NC 3rd Ser 6, 1886, 23–37

5037 **Montagu, H.** Gold coins of the Iceni recently discovered at Freckenham. PSA 2nd Ser 12, 1887/9, 83–4

5038 St. Andrew's, Freckenham: list of rectors and vicars. E Ang NS 13, 1909/10, 71–4

5039 Extracts from the parish registers. E Ang NS 12, 1907/08, 299

FRESSINGFIELD   *See also* **2969, 3022, 3287, 3336**

5040 Fressingfield parish history. SC 1.6.1928, Rp No 74

5041 **Raven, J. J.** Fressingfield advowson. E Ang NS 8, 1899/1900, 195

5042 **Bedingfield, J.,** *and* **Simpson, R. J.** Fressingfield church. PSIA 3, 1860/63, 321–30

5043 **Raven-Hart, W. R.** Church of SS. Peter and Paul, Fressingfield. Harleston, 1912. nl

5044 **Raven, J. J.** Fressingfield porch and pews. PSIA 8, 1892/4, 31–5

5045 **Raven, J. J.** Parish house for church ales and other "drynkynggs" at Fressingfield. E Ang NS 6, 1895/6, 49–50

5046 Fox and Goose at Fressingfield. Tales of old inns, No 25. [1927]

5047 **Raven, J. J.** Families in Fressingfield, England, 1836, wishing to emigrate to America. NEH&GR 49, 1845, 337–8

5048 **Raven, J. J.** Extracts from parish registers. E Ang NS 1, 1885/6, 224–5

5049 **Raven, J. J.** Parish register entries in the Commonwealth period. E Ang NS 9, 1901/02, 84

5050 **Raven, J. J.** The cover of the oldest Fressingfield register. E Ang NS 10, 1903/04, 333

FRESTON   *See also* **2441**

5051 Freston parish history. SC 5.2.1937, Rp No 462

5052 **Owles, E. J.,** *et al.* Hoard of Constantinian coins from Freston. NC 7th Ser 12, 1972, 145–57

5053 **Birch, H. W.** Church notes: Freston. E Ang NS 8, 1899/1900, 68–70

5054 Life in a Suffolk village. *Ed.* by C. R. Durrant from Freston parish magazine, 1886–1908. [Freston]. BL

5055 Parish magazine, 1887–1905. 19 v

5056 **Durrant, C. R.** Local dialect ... in the parish of Freston. E Ang NS 5, 1893/4, 129–31, 155

5057 **Tymms, S.** Freston tower. PSIA 2, 1854/9, 270–71

5058 **Durrant, C. R.** Freston tower. PSIA 13, 1907/09, 382–8

FRISTON   *See also* Hazelwood, *and* **3450**

5059 Friston parish history. SC 18.8.1933, Rp No 321

FRITTON

5060 Fritton parish history. SC 2.1.1931, Rp No 209

5061 **Cheshire, C. J.** Fritton. *In* Field excursions in Eastern England. *Ed.* by V. C. Keyte. 1970. 154–59

5062 St. Edmund's church, Fritton. Gt. Yarmouth, [c.1900]

5063 Fritton St. Edmund parish church. St. Christopher. [Appeal for restoration of wall painting]. 1969. nl

FROSTENDEN   *See also* **2936**

5064 Frostenden parish history. EADT 5.12.1934, Rp No 379

5065 **Morley, C.** Roman mill-stone at Frostenden. PSIA 25, 1949/51, 110

5066 **Bruce, J.** Deed purporting to bear the signature of Anne of Cleves appointing Philip Chewte bailiff of the manor of 'Frossenden' in Suffolk. PSA 4, 1853/9, 265

5067 **Morley, C.,** *and* **Cooper, E. R.** Sea port of Frostenden. PSIA 18, 1922/4, 167–79

5068 **Gowers, W. R.** Architectural notes, No 3. An Early English ornament at Frostenden. E Ang NS 5, 1893/4, 241–3

5069 Parish registers of Frostenden, Suffolk. [*Ed.* by F. A. Crisp]. 1887

GAZELEY

5070 **Butler, G. H.** History of a parish [Gazeley]. Bury St. Edmunds, [1910]

5071 Gazeley parish history. EADT 9.1.1935, Rp No 383

5072 **Petersen, F.** Excavation of an Early Bronze Age cemetery at Pin Farm, Gazeley. PSIA 33, 1973/5, 19–46

5073 Gazeley parish register. *Ed.* by W. D. Peckham. 1961. [Typescript]. SRO/B

GEDDING

5074 Olorenshaw, J. R. Notes on Gedding, county of Suffolk. Norwich, 1905. SRO/B

5075 Olorenshaw, J. R. Gedding. E Ang NS 11, 1905/06, *passim*

5076 Gedding parish history. SC 17.8.1928, Rp No 85

GIPPING   *See also* **3424**

5077 Gipping parish history. EADT 6.3.1935, Rp No 389

5078 King, H. W. The Tyrell badge. EAST 3, 1865, 198–203

5079 Sewell, W. H. Sir James Tyrell's chapel at Gipping. Arch J 28, 1871, 23–33

5080 Turner, P. J. Chapel of St. Nicholas, Gipping. PSIA 20, 1928/30, 270–79

GIPPING RURAL DISTRICT   *See also* **7467–9**

5081 Official guide. 1950 and later edns

GISLEHAM

5082 Gisleham parish history. EADT 9.10.1935, Rp No 413

5083 Gisleham and Pakefield inclosure. A state of the claims delivered to the Commissioners. Great Yarmouth, [1798]. BL

GISLINGHAM,   *See also* **2571**

5084 Gislingham parish history. EADT 14.6.1933, Rp No 314

5085 Elliott, R. J. Brief history of Gislingham. SR 3, 1970, 286–92

5086 Mid-Suffolk District Council. Gislingham draft village plan. Needham Market, 1975. [Typescript]. SCL/L

5087 P, T. A. Inscriptions found in Gislingham church. PSIA 20, 1928/30, 110

GLEMHAM

5088 Account of Glemham Magna and Glemham Parva, including a description of Glemham Hall. Ipswich, 1812. nl

GLEMHAM, GREAT

5089 Great Glemham parish history. EADT 24.8.1932, Rp No 282

GLEMHAM, LITTLE

5090 Little Glemham parish history. SC 17.2.1928, Rp No 59

5091 Royal Commission on Historical Manuscripts. Reports Ser 55, Var. Coll. 4 ... Orford and Aldeburgh ... Glemham Hall. 1906

5092 **Raven, J. J.** Bishop Wren and his candidates for confirmation at Little Glemham in 1636. E Ang NS 7, 1897/8, 129–31

5093 **Gunnis, R.** Monument by William Hubbard at Little Glemham church. CL 120, 1956, 480

5094 T. Glemham Hall. CL 27, 1910, 18–26

5095 Brief history of Glemham Hall. [c.1969]

GLEMSFORD   *See also* 447

5096 Glemsford parish history. SC 9.11.1928, Rp No 97

5097 **Richold, F. H.** Glemsford: a short history. 1946. [Typescript]. SRO/B

5098 **Glass, K. W.** Short history of Glemsford, Suffolk. Ipswich, [1962]. [Typescript]

5099 **Deeks, R.** Glorious Glemsford. Glemsford, 1977. SRO/B

5100 **Glemsford Urban District Council.** Annual report of the Medical Officer of Health, 1897–1916. BL

5101 **Duncan, J.** Glemsford: early non-conformist work … 1965. [Typescript]. SRO/B

GOSBECK   *See also* 3170

5102 Gosbeck parish history. SC 10.6.1932, Rp No 273

5103 **Birch, H. W.** Church notes: Gosbeck. E Ang NS 5, 1893/4, 313–14

GROTON   *See also* 3472–4, 4318

5104 **Bird, A. B.** Groton, Suffolk: a short guide. Groton, 1951 and later edns

5105 Groton parish history. SC 20.3.1931, Rp No 220

5106 **Hardy, E.** Life on a Suffolk manor in the 16th and 17th-centuries. SR 3, 1968, 225–37

GRUNDISBURGH   *See also* 2964, 3397

5107 Grundisburgh parish history. SC 20.1.1928, Rp No 55

5108 **East Suffolk County Council.** Planning Dept. Grundisburgh: policy statement, planning proposals, and conservation area appraisal. Ipswich, 1972

5109 **Birch, H. W.** Church notes: Grundisburgh. E Ang NS 13, 1909/10, 210–12, 244–6

5110 **Redstone, V. B.** Grundisburgh church and a house there. PSIA 16, 1916/8, 67–8

5111 [**Thursfield, J. A.**] Grundisburgh church. [1957]. O

5112 Grundisburgh church. 1961

5113 **Schofield, R. W.** Church of St. Mary, Grundisburgh. Ipswich, 1967

5114 Notes on the history of Bastes or Basts, commonly called Weir Farm House, in Grundisburgh. 1923

GUNTON

5115 Gunton parish history. EADT 26.5.1937, Rp No 472

5116 Gunton St. Peter, Lowestoft: a short guide and history. Gloucester, 1961 and later edns. SCL/L

5117 **Hedges, A. A. C.** The Gunton story. Gunton, 1977. SCL/L

HACHESTON *See also* 3274

5118 Hacheston parish history. SC 10.1.1930, Rp No 158

HADLEIGH *See also* 1859, 2719, 2805, 3273, 3381–5, 5453, 5455

5119 Description of Hadleigh in the county of Suffolk, and the adjoining villages; with some account of Dr. Rowland Taylor, the Rev. John Boyse, and the Rev. Isaac Toms, etc. Ipswich, 1815

5120 Brief description of the town of Hadleigh, in Suffolk; ... with some account of the most eminent persons connected with it. [By E. Levien]. Hadleigh, 1853. BL

5121 **Pigot, H.** Hadleigh: the town, the church, and the great men who have been born in, or connected with the parish. PSIA 3, 1860/63, 1–289. Rp Lowestoft, 1860

5122 **Pigot, H.** Guide to the town, church, and chief objects of interest in Hadleigh. Hadleigh, 1866. 2nd edn 1874. 3rd edn, an abridgement, 1890

5123 Official guide. 3rd edn. nd. 6th edn 1960 and later edns

5124 Hadleigh. PSIA 11, 1901/03, 209–15

5125 Hadleigh parish history. SC 29.7.1927, Rp No 31

5126 **Tipping, H. A.** Hadleigh. CL 66, 1929, 256–62

5127 **Jones, W. A. B.** Hadleigh through the ages ... Ipswich, 1977

5128 **Corbishley, M. J.** Interim report on prehistoric excavations at Ivy Tree Farm, Hadleigh. PSIA 33, 1973/5, 109–15

5129 **Beeton, E. G.** Life in a seventeenth-century weaving town as illustrated by Hadleigh's 'Book of the Sessions of the Peace, 1619–24'. HTM 8, 1925, 162–5

5130 **Hervey,** *Lord* **J.** Extent of Hadleigh manor, 1305. PSIA 11, 1901/03, 152–72

5131 **Niblet, J. D. T.** Transcript of survey of manor of Hadleigh, made March 1305. From Harleian and Davy MSS in BL. 1857. MS

5132 **Hadleigh Urban District Council.** Annual report of the Medical Officer of Health, on the health and sanitary condition of the district during the twelve months ending 31 Dec 1895 (MS), 1897, 1898, 1901, 1902, 1904, 1905, 1908, 1909, 1947–. Hadleigh. BL

5133 **Howard, J. J.** Grant of arms to Hadleigh in 1618, and an aulnage seal found there. PSA 2nd Ser 1, 1859/61, 227–8

5134   Grant of arms to the town of Hadleigh. PSIA 3, 1860/3, 311–13

5135   **West Suffolk County Council.** Planning Dept. Factual survey and outline plan for the Urban District of Hadleigh. Bury St. Edmunds, 1965. SRO/B

5136   **West Suffolk County Council.** Planning Dept. Hadleigh town map. Programme map, written statement. Bury St. Edmunds, 1968

5137   **West Suffolk County Council.** Planning Dept. Hadleigh: conservation area no 1. Town centre. Bury St. Edmunds, 1968. SRO/B

5138   **Eastern Federation of Amenity Societies.** Hadleigh: a townscape analysis. [1969?]. [Typescript]. SRO/B

5139   **Snow, D. M. B.** Hadleigh church, Suffolk, as illustrating English church life from the Reformation to the nineteenth century. nd. MS

5140   **Downes, E. A.** Hadleigh and the centenary commemoration of the Oxford Movement. Hadleigh, 1933. nl

5141   **Carter, F. E.** Church of the Blessed Virgin Mary, Hadleigh. Hadleigh, 1934 and later edns

5142   **Niblett, J. D. T.** Inventories of the furniture and goods of Hadleigh church, both before and after the Reformation, and a document relating to Topfield manor, Hadleigh (36 Hen III). PSA 4, 1857/9, 143–4

5143   **Spooner, E.** Almshouse chapel, Hadleigh, and the will of Archdeacon Pykenham. PSIA 7, 1889/91, 378–80

5144   **Sydenham, G.** Story of Congregationalism in Hadleigh and district. Hadleigh, 1967

5145   **Sydenham, G.** Hadleigh Congregational Sunday School bi-centenary anniversary, 1969: a brief history. 1969. [Typescript]

5146   **Garman, A. S.** History of Lodge of Virtue and Silence, No 332, Hadleigh, 1811–1961. 1961

HALESWORTH   *See also* **1393, 2014, 2248, 2786, 3079–81, 3111, 3126, 3507, 3530**

5147   **Stebbings, A.** Directory to Halesworth, and almanac for 1887. BL

5148   Gale's Almanack, 1952. Halesworth, Southwold, and surrounding district

5149   **Localads.** Halesworth and Southwold directory, 1963–4–. Needham Market

5150   Official guide. 1937 and later edns

5151   **Lambert, F. C.,** *Ed.* Records of Halesworth, with particulars of St. Mary's church, etc., the manors, old buildings, charities, etc., and list of rectors from 1308. Halesworth, 1906. 2nd edn 1913. 3rd edn 1934

5152   Halesworth parish history. 2 pts. SC 23.8.1929, 30.8.1929, Rp Nos 138, 139

5153   **Moore, J. C.** Bronze Age axes from Halesworth and district. PSIA 24, 1946/8, 121–4

5154   Halesworth Review and Council News, Nov 1932–Feb 1935 BL

5155   **Newby, J. W.** Story of Halesworth Patrick Stead Hospital. Halesworth, 1964

5156   **East Suffolk County Council.** Planning Dept. Halesworth: factual survey and outline plan. Ipswich, 1962

5157 **East Suffolk County Council.** Planning Dept. Halesworth, with Holton: policy statement and planning proposals. Ipswich, 1970

5158 Halesworth church. PSIA 4, 1864/74, 444–7

5159 **Northeast, P.** Church of St. Mary, Halesworth. 1966 and later edns

5160 **Newby, J. W.,** *Ed.* History of Independency in Halesworth and district Halesworth, 1936. SCL/L

5161 Halesworth Dunciad: a satire on pedantry addressed to the censor of the stage [J. Dennant]. [By J. Hugman]. Halesworth, 1808. BL

5162 Halesworth Review, 14 Sept—14 Oct 1808. [A notice of the various pamphlets published at Halesworth ... reporting plays by J. Jermyn]. Halesworth, [1808]. BL

5163 Halesworth theatre tracts, 1808. [17 pamphlets dealing with the visit of the Players to Halesworth]. Halesworth, 1808

5164 **Payne, G.** Carved beam or panel on a house at Halesworth. PSA 2nd Ser 11, 1885/7, 307–08

5165 **Haslewood, F.** Monumental inscriptions in Halesworth church and church-yard. PSIA 9, 1895/7, 234–55

HALESWORTH URBAN DISTRICT

5166 Town and Country Planning Act, 1944, section 42. Provisional list of buildings of architectural or historic interest ... Halesworth Urban District. 1947. [Typescript]

5167 **Department of the Environment.** List of buildings of special architectural or historic interest: Urban district of Halesworth, East Suffolk. 1972. [Typescript]

HARDWICK   *See also* **2743–50, 2808, 5223–4**

5168 Hardwick parish history. EADT 24.11.1937

5169 **Redstone, L. J.** Plans of the Hardwick estate. [Typescript]. SRO/B

5170 Customs of Hardwick. PSIA 1, 1848/53, 177–86

5171 **Tymms, S.** Hardwick House. PSIA 2, 1854/9, 24–33

5172 **Donaldson, J. W.** Etruscan tomb at Hardwick House. PSIA 2, 1854/9, 34–9

5173 Hardwick House. Country Mag 1890, 25–7. SRO/B

5174 **Redstone, L. J.** Hardwick House. PSIA 14, 1910/12, 267–74

5175 Picture at Hardwick House of a window formerly in the abbey of Bury St. Edmunds. The 'Ichotypicon Buriense' of Spelman. PSIA 14, 1910/12, 275–9

5176 **Farrer, E.** Hardwick Manor House, and its evolution. 1928

5177 Inventory taken [at Hardwick House] ... after the decease of Sir Robert Drury in 1615. nd. [Typescript]. SRO/B

HARGRAVE   *See also* **1959**

5178 Hargrave parish history. SC 10.4.1914, Rp No 8

HARKSTEAD *See also* 3584

5179 Harkstead parish history. SC 8.1.1932, Rp No 257
5180 **Birch, H. W.** Church notes: Harkstead. E Ang NS 8, 1899/1900, 115–16
5181 **Tymms, S.** Harkstead church, 1565 [Letter from Earl of Leicester to Archbishop Parker]. PSIA 2, 1854/9, 217

HARLESTON

5182 Harleston parish history. SC 16.1.1931, Rp No 211

HARTEST

5183 Hartest parish history. EADT 9.5.1934, Rp No 353

HARTISMERE RURAL DISTRICT *See also* 763

5184 Official guide. 1950 and later edns
5185 Town and Country Planning Act, 1947, Section 30. Provisional list of buildings of architectural or historic interest for consideration, ... Rural district of Hartismere. April 1950. List of buildings of special architectural or historic interest, Rural district of Hartismere. 29 July 1955. [Typescript]

HASKETON *See also* 3200

5186 **Wait, F. W.** Hasketon, near Woodbridge, Suffolk: various notes. Ipswich, 1927. O
5187 Hasketon parish history. EADT 1.2.1933, Rp No 300
5188 Warrant for collecting the land tax for the parish of Hasketon in the county of Suffolk, for the year 1713–14. BL
5189 **Birch, H. W.** Church notes: Hasketon. E Ang NS 13, 1909/10, 295–7

HAUGHLEY *See also* 3369, 3437

5190 Haughley parish history. SC 9.9.1927, Rp No 37
5191 **MacCullough, N. J. H.** Account of the parishes of Haughley and Wetherden. [c.1967]. [Typescript and MS]
5192 **Muskett, J. J.** Dead lanes—Gallows places. The Fallows Field of Haughley. E Ang NS 3, 1889/90, 165–6, 215
5193 **Soil Association.** The Haughley experiment: the first twenty-five years, 1938–62. 1962. *See also* 1048
5194 Haughley and Wetherden Consistory Court. Electoral roll case, rectors of Haughley and Wetherden. Newspaper cuttings, 1935–49
5195 **MacCullough, N. J. H.** Churchwardens' accounts of St. Mary-the-Virgin, Haughley, 1664–83. SR 3, 1970, 273–85

5196 Redstone, V. B. Haughley Castle and its Park. PSIA 11, 1901/03, 301–07

5197 Insall, D. W., *and* Scarfe, N. Correspondence on Haughley Park. CL 129, 521, 771, 1037

HAVERHILL *See also* 1385

5198 Regency Publicity Service. Haverhill Regency town book and information guide to the commercial, business, and community activities of the borough and surrounding area, 1969–70. Folkestone, 1969

5199 Webb, J. Haverhill, a descriptive poem; and other poems. 1810

5200 Official guide. 1921 and later edns

5201 Official guide and industrial review. Carshalton, 1968

5202 Product Services Ltd. Haverhill: a survey, 1974. Haverhill, 1975. SRO/B

5203 Clay, C. Haverhill. PSIA 4, 1864/74, 99–106

5204 Haverhill parish history. 2 pts. SC 15.4.1932, 22.4.1932, Rp Nos 267, 268

5205 Webb, B. Extracts from a Suffolk note-book ['A book of dismal happenings', Haverhill, 1826–38]. ER 54, 1945, 99

5206 Haverhill Urban Sanitary District. Annual report of the Medical Officer of Health, 1892, 1894. *Cont. as* Haverhill Urban District. Annual report of the Medical Officer of Health, 1895–98, 1901–05, 1907–09. BL. 1969–72. SRO/B

5207 West Suffolk County Council. Planning Dept. Factual survey and outline plan for the Urban District of Haverhill. Bury St. Edmunds, [1956]

5208 The future of Haverhill. Joint technical report by West Suffolk County Council Planning Dept., Greater London Council, and Ministry of Housing and Local Government. Bury St. Edmunds, 1961

5209 West Suffolk County Council. Planning Dept. Haverhill town map, First review, 1963. Programme map, report of survey, written statement. Bury St. Edmunds, 1963

5210 West Suffolk County Council. Planning Dept. People in Haverhill: a report on the population in 1966. Bury St. Edmunds, 1968. SRO/B

5211 Seeley, I. H. Planned extension of county towns [includes Haverhill]. 1968. SRO/B

5212 West Suffolk County Council. Planning Dept. Haverhill: master plan. Bury St. Edmunds, 1971

5213 Unwin, F. D. West End Congregational church: the story of a century, 1836–1936. Haverhill, 1936. nl

5214 Haverhill Methodist church: Diamond Jubilee, 1874–1934: souvenir booklet. Haverhill, 1934. nl

5215 Haverhill Methodist church: events in the 25 years' ministry of the Rev. W. Rose, 1926–51. Haverhill, 1951. nl

HAWKEDON

5216 **Franks, A. W.** Amphora and two figures found at Hawkedon, Jan. 1880. PSIA 6, 1883/8, 10–12

5217 **[Rotherham, W.]** Historical notices of Hawkedon. 1887. SRO/B

5218 Hawkedon parish history. EADT 26.7.1933, Rp No 319

5219 **Painter, K. S.** Roman bronze helmet from Hawkedon. PSIA 31, 1967/9, 57–63; BMQ 33, 1968, 121–30

5220 **G.** Grant of lands at Pridinton in Hawkedon, Suffolk, from Richard FitzGilbert, Earl of Clare, to the abbey of St. Edmund. CTetG 1, 1834, 388–9

5221 Parish church of Hawkedon. [c.1940]. [Typescript]. nl

5222 **Haslewood, F.** Thurston Hall and Swan Hall, Hawkedon. PSIA 8, 1892/4, 258–9

HAWSTEAD   *See also* **2079, 2810, 3230**

5223 **Cullum,** *Sir* **J.** History and antiquities of Hawsted [and Hardwick] in the county of Suffolk. 1784. Bibliotheca topographica Britannica, no 23. 1790 [a re-issue]

5224 **Cullum,** *Sir* **J.** History and antiquities of Hawsted, and Hardwick, in the county of Suffolk. 2nd edn with additions by Sir T. G. Cullum 1813. 230 copies

5225 Hawstead parish history. SC 1.5.1914, Rp No 10

5226 **Tymms, S.** Hawsted church; Hawsted Rectory House; Hawsted Place. PSIA 2, 1854/9, 1–24

5227 **Mercer, L.** Hawstead church, PSIA 7, 1889/91, 324–9

5228 **Mercer, L.** Rectors of Hawstead. PSIA 7, 1889/91, 334–6

HAZELWOOD   *See also* Friston

5229 Hazelwood parish history. EADT 9.11.1938

HELMINGHAM   *See also* **2486, 3404–7**

5230 Helmingham parish history. SC 6.5.1927, Rp No 19

5231 **Cardew, G.** Leaden ampulla and brass quadrant, both found at Helmingham. PSA and Ser 2, 1861/4, 420

5232 **Cardew, G.** Sepulchral remains found at Helmingham. Arch J 21, 1864, 172–4

5233 **Cardew, G.** Discovery of human skeletons and ancient remains at Helmingham. JBAA 21, 1865, 267–73

5234 **Vincent, J. A. C.** Queen Elizabeth at Helmingham. Exeter, 1900. 50 copies. SRO/B

5235 Helmingham Pageant, 28 June–1 July 1933. Ipswich, 1933

5236 **Cornish, C. J.** Helmingham Hall. CL 4, 1898, 720–24

5237   **Roundell, C.** Helmingham Hall at the close of the nineteenth century. PSIA 12, 1904/06, 113–28
5238   **Oswald, A.** Helmingham Hall. CL 120, 1956, *passim*
5239   **Waterhouse, E. K.** The collection of pictures in Helmingham Hall, Suffolk. [1958]. 150 copies

HEMINGSTONE   *See also* **3170**

5240   Hemingstone parish history, SC 9.1.1931, Rp No 210
5241   **Birch, H. W.** Church notes: Hemingstone. E Ang NS 5, 1893/4, 353–6
5242   **Pearson, W. C.** Collections on briefs made in the parish of Hemingstone. E Ang NS 4, 1891/2, 105–06
5243   **Pearson, W. C.** Old communion cloth at Hemingstone. E Ang NS 4, 1891/2, 145–6

HEMLEY   *See also* **7802**

5244   Hemley parish history. SC 18.12.1936, Rp No 457

HENGRAVE

5245   **Gage, J.** [*afterwards* **Rokewode, J. G.**] History and antiquities of Hengrave, in Suffolk. 1822
5246   Hengrave parish history. SC 12.12.1930, Rp No 206
5247   **Tymms, S.** Hengrave Hall. PSIA 1, 1848/53, 331–9
5248   **G[age], H. R.** Hengrave Hall, Suffolk. 1870
5249   **Leyland, J.** Hengrave Hall. CL 2, 1897, 624–6
5250   **Willoughby, L.** Hengrave Hall and its art treasures. Conn 16, 1906, 85–92, 175–82
5251   **T.** Hengrave Hall. CL 27, 1910, 558–67
5252   **Wood,** *Sir* **J.** Hengrave Hall. JBAA NS 34, 1928/9, 60–65
5253   **Woodforde, C.** Stained and painted glass in Hengrave Hall. PSIA 22, 1934/6, 1–16, 243
5254   **Convent of the Assumption.** Hengrave Hall. 1958 [c.1970]. nl

HENHAM   *See also* **2153**

5255   Henham parish history. EADT 8.6.1938
5256   **Barber, A. V.** Henham Hall. 1953. [Typescript]
5257   **B, W. H.** Will of William Mekilfelde, Esq., of Henham, 1439. CTetG 5, 1838, 12–18

HENLEY   *See also* **2398, 2760–61, 3170**

5258   Henley parish history. EADT 27.12.1933, Rp No 337

5259   **Birch, H. W.** Church notes: Henley. E Ang NS 6, 1895/6, 10–13

5260   **Pearson, W. C.** Collection on briefs made in the parish of Henley. E Ang NS 4, 1891/2, 42

5261   **Pearson, W. C.** Extracts from the churchwardens' and overseers' accounts of the parish of Henley, commencing 1602. E Ang NS 4, 1891/2, 92–4

5262   **Pearson, W. C.** Local dialect [in the parish of Henley]. E Ang NS 5, 1893/4, 152–4

5263   **Pearson, W. C.** Extracts from the registers of Henley. E Ang NS 4, 1891/2, 20–23

5264   **Pearson, W. C.** Surnames in parish registers: Henley. E Ang NS 4, 1891/2, 56–60

HENSTEAD   *See also* **2740, 3312, 8099**

5265   Henstead parish history. EADT 19.2.1936, Rp No 428

5266   **Hollis, T. K.** St. Mary's church, Henstead. nd

5267   Extracts from parish registers: Henstead. E Ang 4, 1869/70, 107–08

HEPWORTH   *See also* **2789, 3154**

5268   Hepworth parish history. EADT 1.8.1934, Rp No 362

5269   **Corder, J. S.** Old bronze seal recently found in Hepworth. PSIA 15, 1913/15, 253–4

5270   **Corbett, W. J.,** *and* **Methold, T. T.** Rise and devolution of the manors in Hepworth. PSIA 10, 1898/1900, 19–48, 125–43

5271   **Radice, A. A. H.** Some notes on St. Peter's church, Hepworth. 1968. [Typescript]. NCL/N

5272   **Methold, T. T.** Parish of Hepworth and its rectors. PSIA 8, 1892/4, 380–407

5273   **Methold, T. T.** Hepworth and its rectors. PSIA 18, 1922/4, 66–9

5274   **Methold, T. T.** Early registers of Hepworth. E Ang NS 5, 1893/4, 23–4

HERRINGFLEET

5275   Herringfleet parish history. SC 28.11.1930, Rp No 204

5276   **Haverfield, F. J.** Roman bronze vessel found ... at Herringfleet. PSA 2nd Ser 16, 1895/7, 237–40

5277   **Wynne, W. A. S.,** *et al.* St. Olave's priory and Herringfleet parish (Wynne diaries). 1904–15. 15 v. [Typescript]. NCL/GY

5278   **Wynne, W. A. S.** St. Olave's priory and bridge, Herringfleet, Suffolk. Norwich, 1914

5279   **Kent, E. A.** St. Olave's priory. JBAA NS 31, 1925/6, 110–13

5280   **Davis, K. R.** St. Olave's priory, Herringfleet, Suffolk. Ministry of Works. 1949 and later edns. SCL/L

5281   [**Long, C. M.**, *et al.*] Story of St. Margaret's church and the parish of Herringfleet. Somerleyton, 1966. [Typescript]. SCL/L

5282   **Fowler, J.** Representation of the moon in the east window of Herringfleet church. PSA 2nd Ser 6, 1875/6, 459–61

5283   Village hall for St. Olave's. RIBAJ 3rd Ser 56, 1949, 536

5284   **Suffolk Preservation Society.** St. Olave's windpump. [Appeal]. nd. nl

HERRINGSWELL   *See also* 2056

5285   Herringswell parish history. EADT 11.7.1934, Rp Np 360

5286   **Davies, I.** Story of Herringswell. 1951. [Typescript]. SRO/B

5287   **Livett, R. G. C.** Some fourteenth-century documents relating to Herringswell. E Áng NS 10, 1903/04; NS 11, 1905/06, *passim*

5288   Herringswell church. Q JSIA 1, 1869, 44–5

HESSETT

5289   **Cooke, W.** Materials for a history of Hessett. PSIA 4, 1864/74, 301–32; 5, 1875/86, 1–103

5290   Hessett parish history. 2 pts. SC 25.4.1930, 2.5.1930, Rp Nos 173, 174

5291   **Cooke, W.** Description of a painted linen corporas case and of an object of knitted material kept in an old parish chest at Hessett. PSA 2nd Ser 4, 1867/70, 86–7

5292   Ancient burse and veil preserved at Hessett church. Eccl 29, 1868, 86–9

5293   **Piggott, J.** Relics at Hessett church. E Ang 4, 1869/70, 8–10

5294   **Andrew, S.** Pyx veil or sindon at Hessett. JAABI 1, 1930/1, 121–7

5295   **Townshend, C. H.** Entries in the parish register of Hesset. NEH&GR 38, 1884, 342–3

5296   **Townshend, C. H.** Gleanings from parish registers of Hessett and vicinity. NEH&GR 52, 1898, 42–4

HEVENINGHAM

5297   Heveningham parish history. SC 15.8.1930, Rp No 189

5298   **B, O.** Heveningham Hall. CL 23, 1908, 594–603

5299   **Tipping, H. A.** Heveningham Hall. CL 58, 1925, 432–40, 472–9, 508–15

5300   **Musgrave, C.** Heveningham—a great unified interior. Conn 139, 1957, 71–5

5301   Heveningham Hall: a brief history and guide. 1967 and later edns

5302   **Cornforth, J.** The future of Heveningham Hall. CL 146, 1969, 670–73

HIGHAM, nr. Bury St. Edmunds

5303   Higham parish history. EADT 22.6.1938

5304   **Marr, J. E.** An implement from Higham. PPSEA 4, 1922/4, 163–4

HIGHAM, nr. East Bergholt   *See also* **2595**

5305   Higham parish history. SC 23.11.1928. Rp. No 99

5306   **Benton, G. M.** Domestic wall-paintings at Higham. Ant J 10, 1930, 255–6

HINDERCLAY

5307   Hinderclay parish history. EADT 13.2.1935, Rp No 387

5308   Parish magazine, 1903–07. 17 nos. SRO/B

HINTLESHAM   *See also* **3372, 3401–2**

5309   Hintlesham parish history. SC 2.3.1928, Rp No 61

5310   **Birch, H. W.** Church notes: Hintlesham. E Ang NS 13, 1909/10, 82–6

5311   **Eeles, F. C.** Description of Hintlesham church. [c.1930]

5312   **Hintlesham Festival Trust.** Programmes of the Hintlesham Summer Festival. 13th, 1963; 15th, 1965; 20th, 1970.

5313   **Corder, J. S.** Hintlesham Hall. PSIA 14, 1910/12, 294–304

5314   Visit to Hintlesham Hall. PSIA 14, 1910/12, 308–09

5315   **Oswald, A.** Hintlesham Hall. CL 64, 1928, 232–8

5316   **Corder, J. S.** Hintlesham Hall. JBAA NS 34, 1928/9, 87–95

5317   **Partridge, C.** Monumental inscriptions in Hintlesham churchyard. E Ang NS 11, 1905/06, 229–31, 252–4

HITCHAM   *See also* **2985–8, 3056**

5318   Hitcham parish history. SC 12.10.1928, Rp No 93

5319   **Hill, H. C.** Roman finds at Hitcham and near Easthow Hill. PSIA 19, 1925/7, 93–4

5320   **Henslow, J. S.** Accounts of receipts and disbursements for parish objects during the years 1843–6, 1848–52, 1854–5, 1857–8 [Hitcham]

5321   **Henslow, J. S.** Allotment reports for 1855–88. [Hitcham]

5322   **Henslow, J. S.** Appendix to Hitcham allotment report for 1857. [Hadleigh?], [1858]. BL

HOLBROOK

5323   Holbrook parish history. SC 16.12.1927, Rp No 50

5324   **Lewin, E.** Articles on Holbrook [from parish magazine]. nd

5325   Royal Hospital School. Manchester, [1933?]. SRO/B

5326   **MacLeod, N.** History of the Royal Hospital School. MM 35, 1949, 182–202

5327   Chapel of the Royal Hospital School. RIBAJ 3rd Ser 42, 1935, 1044–7

5328   **East Suffolk County Council.** Planning Dept. Holbrook: policy statement and planning proposals. Ipswich, 1968

5329   **Birch, H. W.** Church notes; Holbrook. E Ang NS 8, 1899/1900, 116–18

5330 **Phipson, R. M.** Small effigy found in Holbrook church. Arch J 21, 1864, 89–90

5331 **Phipson, R. M.** On a heart burial at Holbrook church. JBAA 21, 1865, 140–44

HOLLESLEY *See also* **1762**

5332 Hollesley and Shingle Street parish histories. SC 30.9.1932, Rp No 286

5333 **Cobb, R. T.** Shingle Street, a brief geographical introduction. *In* Annual Report of the Field Studies Council, 1956–7. nl

5334 **Nichols, F. M.** Description of a court-roll of the manor of Hollesley, with the arms of Stanhope. PSA 2nd Ser 3, 1864/7, 260–64

5335 Colonia: the Colonial College magazine. v 1, no 1.—v 7, no 3, Dec 1889– Dec 1902. Woodbridge, 1889–1902. BL

5336 **East Suffolk County Council.** Planning Dept. Hollesley: policy statement and planning proposals. Draft. Ipswich, 1970. Final proposals. 1971

5337 Particulars of the advowson of the rectory of Hollesley. [1831?]. BL

5338 **D[urrant], C. R.**, *et al.* Matrix of an early brass at Hollesley church. E Ang NS 4, 1891/2, 238, 254–5, 272

5339 **Field, J. E.** Matrix of a brass at Hollesley. E Ang NS 5, 1893/4, 116–17

5340 **Blatchly, J. M.** Mid-14th century indents at Hollesley and Westleton. TMBS 12, 1974, 47–9

5341 Parish registers of Hollesley ... *Ed.* by W. B. Bannerman. 1920. BL

HOLTON, nr. Hadleigh *See also* **3363, 3459**

5342 Holton parish history. SC 16.12.1932, Rp No 294

5343 The state and principal rules of the charity school at Holton in Suffolk. Ipswich, 1759. Rp in E Ang NS 12, 1907/09, 300–04

5344 **Birch, H. W.** Church notes: Holton St. Mary. E Ang NS 12, 1907/08, 197–8, 312

5345 **Partridge, C.** Holton St. Mary and Stratford St. Mary church notes. E Ang NS 12, 1907/08, 312–13

HOLTON, nr. Halesworth *See also* **5157**

5346 Holton parish history. SC 16.9.1932, Rp No 284

5347 Registers of Holton, Suffolk [1538–1924]. [Transcribed by A. S. Gooding]. 1924. [Typescript]

HOMERSFIELD

5348 Homersfield parish history. EADT 15.3.1933, Rp No 304

5349 **Smedley, N.,** *and* **Owles, E. J.** Some Suffolk kilns: 1. Romano-British pottery kiln at Homersfield. PSIA 28, 1958/60, 168–84

5350 Smedley, N., *and* Owles, E. J. A face-mould from the Romano-British kiln site at Homersfield. PSIA 30, 1964/6, 210–12

5351 Homersfield parish book, 1684–1744. Transcribed by A. Welford. 1949. MS

HONINGTON See also 1785, 2546–53

5352 Honington parish history. SC 18.9.1931, Rp No 246

5353 Fell, C. I. Late Bronze Age urnfield and grooved-ware occupation at Honington. PCAS 45, 1951/2, 30–43

5354 Duncan, J. Honington Methodist church. 1964. [Typescript]. SRO/B

HOO

5355 Hoo parish history. EADT 19.7.1933, Rp No 318

HOPTON, nr. Thetford See also 3451

5356 Hopton parish history. SC 17.6.1932, Rp No 274

5357 Wren, J. History of All Saints church, Hopton. 1972. nl

HOPTON, nr Lowestoft

5358 Hopton parish history. SC 7.2.1936, Rp No 426

5359 East Suffolk County Council. Planning Dept. Hopton-on-Sea: policy statement and planning proposals. Ipswich, 1968. SCL/L

5360 Orde, J. The old church at Hopton. Great Yarmouth, 1897. nl

5361 Parish church of St. Margaret, Hopton-on-Sea: centenary. Great Yarmouth, 1966

HORHAM

5362 Horham parish history. SC 8.11.1929, Rp No 149

HORRINGER (HORNINGSHEATH)

5363 Hervey, M. W. Annals of a Suffolk village: being historical notes on the parish of Horringer. Cambridge, 1930

5364 Horringer parish history. SC 26.2.1932, Rp No 262

5365 Ward, Z. History of Horringer and Ickworth, np, 1975

5366 Tymms, S. Horringer church. PSIA 2, 1854/9, 430–34

5367 Macrae, P. Church of St. Leonard, Horringer. nd. [Typescript]

5368 Horringer parish registers: baptisms marriages, and burials with appendices and biographical notes, 1558–1850. [Preface signed S.H.A.H(ervey)]. Woodbridge, 1900. SGB 4

HOXNE, Hundred of *See also* **787, 982, 7262**

5369 Loyal Association of the Hundreds of Hoxne and Hartsmere for preserving liberty and property, against republicans and levellers. A letter addressed to the inhabitants of Great Britain, shewing them the dangerous tendency of libellous publications, and guarding them against being imposed upon by the false representations such writings contain. Ipswich, [1793]. BL

5370 Resolutions and petition [to the House of Commons on the distressed state of agriculture]. Fressingfield, 1816. O

5371 **Bishop, W. E.** Views of churches in the Hundred of Hoxne, Suffolk. Harleston, 1833

HOXNE *See also* **604, 2568, 2821–35**

5372 Hoxne parish history. SC 30.12.1927, Rp No 52

5373 **Frere, J.** Account of flint weapons discovered at Hoxne. Arch 13, 1800, 204–05

5374 **Chester, G. J.** Flint implements found at Hoxne. Arch J 17, 1860, 169–70

5375 **Reid, C.,** *and* **Ridley, H. N.** Further notes on the Arctic and palaeolithic deposits at Hoxne. RBA 1895, 679–80

5376 **Evans, J.,** *et al.* The relation of palaeolithic man to the glacial epoch [Hoxne]. RBA 1896, 400–16

5377 **Moir, J. R.** Silted-up lake of Hoxne and its contained flint implements. PPSEA 5, 1925–8, 137–65

5378 **West, R. G.,** *and* **McBurney, C. M. B.** Quaternary deposits at Hoxne and their archaeology. PPS NS 20, 1954, 131–54

5379 **Henniker,** *Lord.* Saxon knife, a spear-head, pryck spurs, and stirrups, etc., found at Hoxne. PSA 2nd Ser 8, 1879/81, 80

5380 **Low, C. W.** Iron Anglo-Saxon brooch supposed to have been found at Hoxne. PSIA 14, 1910/12, 1–5

5381 **Mahon,** *Lord, and* **Lemon, R.** Iron point found in an oak at Hoxne believed to be that to which King Edmund was bound for his martyrdom. PSA 1, 1843/9, 279, 286–7

5382 **P, A.** King Edmund and Hoxne. E Ang NS 1, 1885/6, 15–16

5383 **Sewell, W. H.** The Edmund oak. E Ang NS 5, 1893/4, 351–2

5384 **Maling, S.** Where King Edmund was slain. ECM 2, 1901/02, 105–11

5385 Story of Hoxne school. nd. [Typescript]

5386 Church of St. Peter and St. Paul, Hoxne. [1963]. 1968

5387 **Manning, C. R.** Font at Hoxne church. E Ang NS 1, 1885/6, 329–30

5388 Mutilated brass inscription found in a pond at Hoxne. TMBS 8, 1943/51, 147, 384

HUNDON

5389 Hundon parish history. EADT 3.7.1935, Rp No 402

5390 **Strudwick, J.** Account of some Saxon coins found at Honedon (Hundon), nr. Clare, 1687. BNJ 28, 1955/7, 180–82

5391 **Duncan, J.** History of Hundon Congregational church, 1968. [Typescript]. SRO/B

HUNSTON

5392 Hunston parish history. EADT 25.8.1933, Rp No 322

HUNTINGFIELD

5393 **[Swinburne, A. J.]** Notes and gatherings for a history of Huntingfield, and its owners [also on Cratfield and the De la Pole family] 20 v. MS. nd

5394 Huntingfield parish history. SC 5.9.1930, Rp No 192

5395 **Bickley, J.** Huntingfield and its church of St. Mary. Halesworth, 1959 and later edns

5396 **Holland, W.,** *and* **Woodward, B. B.** Some early accounts of the church-wardens and inventory of church furniture at Huntingfield. PSA 2nd Ser 1, 1859/61, 116–19

ICKLINGHAM

5397 Icklingham parish history. SC 20.6.1930, Rp No 181

5398 **Sturge, W. A.** Chronology of the Stone Age [Icklingham] PPSEA 1, 1908/14, 43–105

5399 **Smith, R.** Striated flints of neolithic appearance found at Icklingham. PSA 2nd Ser 23, 1909/11, 238–49

5400 **Kraay, C. M.** Early Christian object from Icklingham. Ant J 22, 1942, 219–20

5401 **Rokewode, J. G.** Silver dish from Mileham, Norfolk, and other vessels from Icklingham. Arch 29, 1842, 389–90

5402 **Fell, C. I.,** *et al.* Enamelled bronze fragment from Icklingham Heath. PCAS 42, 1948/9, 129–30

5403 **Briscoe, G.** Bronze Age burials at Hoo Hill, Icklingham. PCAS 48, 1954/5, 6–9

5404 **Liversidge, J.** Bronze bowl and other vessels from Icklingham. PCAS 55, 1961/2, 6–7

5405 **Bunbury, H. E.** Roman stations at and near Icklingham. PSIA 1, 1848/53, 250–52

5406 **Warren, J.** Roman fibulae, Icklingham. PSIA 3, 1860/63, 402–03

5407 **Prigg, H.** Roman house at Icklingham. JBAA 34, 1878, 12–15

5408 **Liversidge, J.** New hoard of Romano-British pewter from Icklingham. PCAS 52, 1958/9, 6–10

5409 **Prigg, H.** Hoard of Roman silver coins [from Icklingham]. PSIA 4, 1864/74, 282–6

5410 **Hill, G. F.** Two hoards of Roman coins ... 2. Silver coins of the late fourth century from Icklingham. NC 4th Ser 8, 1908, 208–21

5411 **Mattingley, H.,** *and* **Pearce, J. W. E.** Hoards of Roman coins [including that from Icklingham]. NC 5th Ser 9, 1929, 319–27

5412 **Pearce, J. W. E.** Notes on the Terling and other silver hoards found in Britain. NC 5th Ser 13, 1933, 178–9

5413 **Mattingley, H.** Three hoards of barbarous Roman coins [including one from Icklingham]. NC 5th Ser 14, 1934, 255–68

5414 **Pearce, J. W. E.** New hoard of siliquae from Icklingham. NC 5th Ser 16, 1936, 257–61

5415 **Pearce, J. W. E.** Icklingham II redivivus. NC 5th Ser 18, 1938, 59–61

5416 **Prigg, H.** Icklingham papers. Manors, churches, town-lands, and antiquities of Icklingham, together with text and translation of Berners' Baronial accounts, 1342–3 ... With notes and additions by V. B. Redstone. Woodbridge, 1901

5417 **Singh,** *Prince* **F. D.**[V] All Saints' church, Icklingham. E Ang NS 5, 1893/4, 370–71

5418 Icklingham All Saints. nd. [Typescript]. nl

5419 **Keen, L.,** *and* **Thackray, D.** Fourteenth-century mosaic tile pavement with line-impressed decoration from Icklingham. PSIA 33, 1973/5, 153–67

ICKWORTH *See also* **1274, 2989–3014, 5365**

5420 **Hervey, A. F. T.,** *Marchioness of Bristol.* History of Ickworth. Ipswich, nd. SRO/B

5421 **Hervey, S. H. A.** Ickworth. PSIA 11, 1901/03, 65–8

5422 Ickworth parish history. EADT 7.7.1937

5423 **Covell, T.** Ickworth survey boocke. Año 1665 (Surveyed, and layed downe in a mapp, by Thomas Covell). [A facsimile of the original MS. The preface signed J.H., i.e. Lord J. W. N. Hervey] Ipswich, 1893

5424 **Hervey,** *Lord* **A.** Ickworth church. PSIA 2, 1852/9, 428–9

5425 **Hervey, A. F. T.,** *Marchioness of Bristol.* A fresco at Ickworth church. PSIA 14, 1910/12, 57–8

5426 **Kendrick,** *Sir* **T. D.** St. Cuthbert's pectoral cross, and the Wilton and Ixworth crosses. Ant J 17, 1937, 283–93

5427 **Hervey,** *Lord* **A.** Ickworth Manor House. PSIA 1, 1848/53, 29–32

5428 Ickworth Park. CL 18, 1905, 870–77

5429 **Tipping, H. A.** Ickworth Park. CL 58, 1925, 668–75, 698–705

5430 Ickworth House [A descriptive pamphlet]. [1953]. BL

5431 **Hussey, C.** Ickworth Park. CL 117, 1955, 678–81

5432 History and treasures of Ickworth, Bury St. Edmunds, Suffolk, a property of the National Trust. [1957] and later edns

5433 **Lines, R. C.** Ickworth. Conn 141, 1958, 69–73

5434 **Willoughby, L.** Marquess of Bristol's collection at Ickworth. Conn 14, 1906, 203–10; 15, 1906, 3–10, 84–90

5435 **Gore, St. J.** Pictures at Ickworth. CL 136, 1964, 1508–13

5436 **Binney, M.** From the sentimental to the sublime: exhibition of neoclassical drawings at Ickworth. CL 145, 1969, 1360–61

5437 **Joy, E. T.** Furniture in the east wing at Ickworth. Conn 177, 1971, 77–85

5438 Ickworth parish registers. Baptisms, marriages, and burials, 1566 to 1890. [Ed. by S.H.A.H(ervey)]. Wells, 1894. SGB 3

IKEN

5439 Iken parish history. SC 17.7.1931, Rp No 237

5440 **Davis, A.** Iken, its church and manor. 1931. SRO/B

5441 **Stevenson, F. S.** St. Botolph and Iken. PSIA 18, 1922/4, 29–52

5442 **Whitley, W. T.** Botulph's Yeean-Ho. JBAA NS 36, 1930, 233–8

5443 **Smith, L. P.** Story of St. Botolph. [c. 1950]. [Typescript]

ILKETSHALL ST. ANDREW

5444 Ilketshall St. Andrew parish history. SC 17.7.1936, Rp No 443

ILKETSHALL ST. JOHN

5445 Ilketshall St. John parish history. SC 26.6.1936, Rp No 441

5446 **Baker, G. B.** Fourteenth-century ring brooch found at Ilketshall St. John. PSA 4, 1857/9, 294

ILKETSHALL ST. LAWRENCE

5447 Ilketshall St. Lawrence parish history. SC 14.8.1936, Rp No 446

ILKETSHALL ST. MARGARET   *See also* 2941

5448 Ilketshall St. Margaret parish history. SC 27.11.1936, Rp No 455

5449 **Easton, J. G.** Earliest parish register of Ilketshall St. Margaret. E Ang NS 4, 1891/2, 161–7

INGHAM   *See also* 4547

5450 Ingham parish history. SC 25.12.1931, Rp No 256

5451 **Prigg, H.** Roman-British cemetery at Ingham. PSIA 1883/8, 41–54

5452 Parish register of Ingham, Co. Suffolk. Baptisms 1538 to 1804. Marriages, 1539 to 1787. Burials, 1538 to 1811. *Ed.* by W. Brigg. Leeds, 1909

IPSWICH

DIRECTORIES

5453 Steven's directory of Ipswich and neighbourhood, with Felixstowe, Walton, Hadleigh, Needham Market, Stowmarket, Woodbridge, etc. 1881. 1885. 1894. SRO/I. 1889. O

5454 Jarrold's directory of Ipswich, together with Felixstowe, Walton, Harwich ... 1890

5455 Jewell's Ipswich directory, together with Felixstowe, Hadleigh, Stowmarket, Walton, Woodbridge. Ipswich, 1898

5456 Kelly's directory of Ipswich [and neighbourhood], 1899–1900 and later edns. BL. 1900–. SRO/I Incomplete

5457 **Town and Country Directories.** Ipswich and district trades' directory. Edinburgh, 1919–32. Incomplete

5458 **Kingsway Publicity Ltd.** Kingsway householder's trades, services, and supplies directory for Ipswich. 1960

5459 **Localads.** Ipswich and district directory: classified trades and professions. Needham Market, [1961]. [1963]. nl

5460 **Priest's Publications.** Ipswich and district classified directory of trades, professions, etc. Snettisham, 1965. 1966

5461 **Regency Publicity Service.** Ipswich and district book of businesses, trades, and professions (with separate section for Woodbridge). Folkestone, 1966

5462 **Regency Publicity Service.** Ipswich book: the reference book of the resources of the area; local supplies and services; the community associations and voluntary organisations. 3rd edn Folkestone, 1969

ALMANACS

5463 Clark. 1634. A new almanack and prognostication for this year ... calculated for the town of Ipswich, etc. [Cambridge], [1634]. STC 430. BL

5464 Staines' almanack. Ipswich, 1865

5465 Pawsey and Hayes' almanack and companion for Ipswich and Suffolk. Ipswich, 1890

5466 Suitall almanack, diary, and directory of Ipswich traders, with local information. Ipswich, 1893–

5467 Old Dredge's annual calendar. Ipswich, 1896

5468 Harrison's Ipswich almanac and companion. [Ipswich], 1899. 1900

GUIDES *See also* 4889, 4891

5469 **Wodderspoon, J.** New guide to Ipswich containing notices of its ancient and modern history, antiquities, buildings, institutions, social and commercial condition. Ipswich, 1842

5470 Cowell's Ipswich handbook, containing a short account of the history, antiquities, public buildings ... of the ancient borough of Ipswich. Ipswich, [1848]

5471 Hunt's descriptive handbook of Ipswich, the river Orwell, ... and Felixstow. Ipswich, [1864]

5472 Glyde's guide to Ipswich, its public buildings, objects of interest. Ipswich, [1869]

5473 Watson's visitor's and general guide to Ipswich. Ipswich, [1869]

5474 **Taylor, J. E.**, *Ed*. Descriptive handbook of Ipswich and the neighbourhood ... with an account of the botany, geology, archaeology, etc. of the district. Ipswich, [1873]. 1875. 1883

5475 Watson's guide to Ipswich, etc., with album of 20 beautiful views ... Ipswich, [c.1882]

5476 King's guide to the footpaths of Ipswich. Ipswich, [1885]

5477 Pawsey and Hayes' illustrated guide to Ipswich and the neighbourhood ... with an account of the botany, geology, archaeology, etc., of the district ... originally written by J. E. Taylor. Ipswich, 1890. 1892. 1895

5478 Watson's guide to Ipswich, Harwich, and Dovercourt. Ipswich, 1890

5479 Robinson, Son and Pike's descriptive account of Ipswich. Brighton, [c.1892]

5480 **Barrett, C. R. B.** Round Ipswich. 1893

5481 Harrison's guide to Ipswich and neighbourhood. Together with the river Orwell ... and Felixstowe. Ipswich, 1900. [c.1909]. Another edn, with addendum, Ipswich worthies, by W. R. Elliston, issued for the British Medical Association, Ipswich meeting, 1900

5482 Burrow's official guide to Ipswich. Cheltenham, [c.1905]

5483 Trades Union Congress, Ipswich 1909. Souvenir issued by the Ipswich and District Trades and Labour Council. Ipswich, [1909]

5484 **Woolnough, F.**, *Ed*. Guide to Ipswich and neighbourhood, together with the river Orwell ... and Felixstowe ... Ipswich, [c.1909]. [c.1913]

5485 Official guide. [c.1911] and later edns

5486 **Walton, F.**, *pseud*. [i.e. F. Woolnough]. Guide to Ipswich and neighbourhood. Ipswich, 1921

5487 Harrison's official handbook and guide to the county borough of Ipswich, issued for the National Union of Railwaymen, annual general meeting, Ipswich ... 1931. Ipswich, 1931

5488 **Benjamin, G.** Residential attractions of Ipswich and district, an illustrated guide. Gloucester, [1936]. O

5489 Harrison's official handbook and guide to the county borough of Ipswich. Ipswich, [c.1937]

5490 **Ipswich Corporation.** County borough of Ipswich. "Stay-at-home Holidays" 1944: Programme. Ipswich, 1944

5491 Ward Lock's pictorial guide to Ipswich, Woodbridge, Framlingham, Felixstowe. [1950] and later edns. BL

5492 [**Rotheroe, J. W.**]. Discovering Ipswich. [Woodbridge], 1964

5493 **Pawsey, J. T.** Ipswich. Ipswich. 1970

Views and Photographs   See also **959**

5494 [Eight views of Ipswich and its neighbourhood]. [Ipswich], [1844?]. BL

5495 Picturesque antiquities of Ipswich. A selection from the remains of ancient edifices existing in that town, drawn by F. Russel and etched by W. Hagreen. The antiquarian and architectural descriptions by John Wodderspoon. Ipswich, 1845. Also copy containing original monochrome wash-drawings and first proofs

5496 **Hanbury, D.** One day from the diary of a stag. [Plates by E. R. Smyth of a stag hunt around and through the streets of Ipswich]. Ipswich, [1846?]. 1847

5497 Pawsey, *Mrs.* Publisher. Six views in Ipswich. Ipswich, [1853]

5498 **Burrows, R.** [Photographs of Ipswich and neighbourhood]. 1858

5499 **Rock and Co.** Views of Ipswich [Six engravings]. 1861

5500 **Pococke, E.** Views of old Ipswich, being hand-painted illustrations of old buildings in Ipswich. [c.1870]

5501 Young Ipswich. 16 views of the town, etc. Ipswich, [c.1880]

5502 **Rock and Co.** Royal cabinet album of Ipswich. Recollections of Ipswich [views dated 1864–81]. [c.1882]

5503 **Charles, Reynolds and Co.** Album of Ipswich, Harwich, and Dovercourt views. [c.1882]

5504 **Taylor, J. E.** In and about ancient Ipswich: illustrating the origin and growth of an old English historic town. Norwich, 1888. 75 copies imperial quarto. 350 copies demy-quarto

5505 **Glyde, J.** Illustrations of old Ipswich. With architectural description of each subject and such historical notices as illustrate the manners and customs of previous ages in the old borough, etc. Ipswich, 1889

5506 Gems of Ipswich: a collection of permanent photographs with descriptive text. Ipswich, 1890

5507 **Rock and Co.** Royal Ipswich cabinet album. [c.1892]

5508 Smiths, Suitall. Publishers. Collotypes of Ipswich and Felixstowe ... new views. Ipswich, [c.1892]

5509 **Vick, W.** Ipswich past and present, with notes and descriptions. 2 v. Ipswich, 1890–94. [Photographs]

5510 **Vick, W.** Photographs of Ipswich in 1894. Ipswich, 1894

5511 Frost's drawings of Ipswich and sketches in Suffolk. With memoir and portrait of George Frost, and short descriptive notes on the principal plates, by Frank Brown. Ipswich, 1895. 105 copies

5512 **Gilbert, E. W.** Portfolio of old Ipswich: a set of 11 views from the original copper plates, 1830. Ipswich, 1901

5513 **Watling, H.** Old houses, etc., in Ipswich. Ipswich, 1902

5514 Aerial views of Ipswich (38 photographs). [c.1920–30]

5515 **Serjeant, W. R.** *Ed.* Ipswich remembered in Victorian and Edwardian photographs. Ipswich, 1975

GENERAL AND POLITICAL HISTORY

General   See also **2817–19, 6021**

5516   **Redstone, V. B.** Ipswich borough (corporation) records. Rp from EADT. No 1–20. [Based on Extracts from the borough records, 1279–1820—no more published]. Ipswich, [1926–38]

5517   Principal charters, which have been granted to the corporation of Ipswich ... translated [by R. Canning]. 1754

5518   Ipswich charters. [Correspondence (MS) between John Glyde and Hardy and Page, concerning the history of the charters. Bound with a pamphlet, Charters given to the Ipswich museum, by W. H. Booth, copied and translated by J. H., i.e. Lord J. W. N. Hervey]. Ipswich, nd

5519   Ancient and modern perambulations: and extracts from charters, trials, and other records relative to the liberties of Ipswich, by land and water, intended as a companion to the maps of those jurisdictions. Ipswich, 1815

5520   **Clarke, G. R.** History and description of the town and borough of Ipswich, including the villages and country seats in its vicinity ... Ipswich, 1830 Grangerized copies. (1) by Rev. J. Ford. 1 v. (2) by H. R. Eyre. 5 v. with typescript index

5521   **Ford, J.** Notes on Ipswich. 3 v. [c.1849]. MS

5522   **Wodderspoon, J.** Memorials of the ancient town of Ipswich, in the county of Suffolk. Ipswich, 1850. Grangerized copies. 2 v. & 3 v. Index. [c.1910)

5523   **Fitch, W. S.** Notitia towards a history of the borough of Ipswich. 1852. v 1. MS. No further volumes

5524   British Archaeological Association at Ipswich, 1864. JBAA 21, 1865

5525   "Antiquarius", *pseud.* Ipswich of the olden time: some pictures of the past. EADT 1883

5526   **Bacon, N.** Annalls of Ipswiche, the lawes, customes, and govern^mt of the same. Collected out of ye records, bookes, and writings of that towne ... 1654. *Ed.* by W. H. Richardson ... with a memoir by S. Westhorp. Ipswich, 1884

5527   **Farrar, R. H.** Index to Annalls of Ipswiche, by Nathaniell Bacon ... *Ed.* by E. M. Till. 1935. [Typescript]. Name index by C. Partridge

5528   **Glyde, J.,** *Ed.* Materials for a history of Ipswich, 12v. [c.1890]. MS notes, illus., cuttings—each volume devoted to one parish

5529   British Association for the Advancement of Science. [Programme of] the sixty-fifth annual meeting [at Ipswich]. 11 Sept 1895

5530   **Glyde, J.,** *Ed.* Memoranda relating to Ipswich. [c. 1898]. MSS and printed material

5531   **Glyde, J.,** *Ed.* Ipswich charters [c.1900]. MS and cuttings

5532   **Glyde, J.,** *Ed.* Notes on Ipswich history and customs. [c.1900]. MS

5533   **Glyde, J.,** *Ed.* Various MSS relating to Ipswich. [c.1900]

5534   **Woolnough, F.** Index of Ipswich events. [c.1910]. MS

5535   **Farrer, E.** Suffolk portraits—Ipswich. MSS and inserted photographs. [c.1920]

5536 **Lingwood, H. R.** ["Rambler", *pseud.*]. Worthies of Ipswich [58 persons]. EADT 1931–9. *See* **5481**

5537 Ipswich: echoes of the past. EADT 18.10.1939

5538 **Thompson, L. P.** Tales of old Ipswich. Ipswich, [c.1947]

5539 **Redstone, L. J.** Ipswich through the ages. Ipswich, 1948. 1969

5540 **Redstone, L. J.** Ipswich. Arch J 108, 1951, 133–5

5541 **Dodd, W. A.** School History of Ipswich. [Ipswich], 1951

5542 Catalogue of an exhibition ... illustrating the government and life of Ipswich, 1250–1950. Ipswich borough libraries. 9–16 June 1951. [Typescript]

5543 **Royal Archaeological Institute of Great Britain and Ireland.** Programme of summer meeting 1951, at Ipswich, 16–20 July. SRO/B

5544 Ipswich through the ages exhibition [catalogue]. Ipswich Historical Association jubilee celebration, 1956

5545 **Clegg, M. E.** Some finds from the "Ipswich through the ages" exhibition. SR 1, 1956, 44–5

Prehistory See also **577, 580, 583–4, 598–9, 606, 617, 624–5, 635**

5546 **Moir, J. R.** Antiquity of man in Ipswich. INHSJ 1, Pt 1, 1925, 1–6

5547 **Taylor, *Dr.*** Results of some excavations in the streets of Ipswich. PSIA 6, 1883/8, 341–2

5548 **Moir, J. R.** Occurrence of a human skeleton in a glacial deposit at Ipswich. PPSEA 1, 1908/14, 194–202

5549 **Keith, A.** Discovery of the Ipswich skeleton. PPSEA 1, 1908/14, 203–09

5550 **Moir, J. R.** Discovery of a flint 'workshop-floor' in Ipswich. PPSEA 1, 1908/14, 475–9; IFCJ 4, 1913, 7–12

5551 **Layard, N. F.** Animal remains from the railway cutting at Ipswich. PSIA 14, 1910/12, 59–68

5552 **Layard, N. F.** Report on discoveries in Ipswich and the neighbourhood. PSIA 15, 1913/15, 84–6, 226–7

5553 Discovery of human remains near Ipswich. JBAA NS 21, 1915, 377–8

5554 **Layard, N. F.** Discoveries made by residents in Ipswich and the neighbourhood, 1916. PSIA 16, 1916/18, 68–70

5555 **Smith, R. A.** Rare flint implement from Ipswich. PSA 2nd Ser 30, 1918, 160–65

5556 **Layard, N. F.** Stoke bone-bed, Ipswich. PPSEA 3, 1918/22, 210–19

5557 **Moir, J. R.** Four flint implements [from Ipswich]. Ant J 18, 1938, 258–61

5558 **Ditchfield, P. H.** Report of the congress at Ipswich, 1928. JBAA NS 34, 1929, 3–54

5559 **Layard, N. F.** Discoveries of palaeolithic implements in Ipswich. JRAI 33, 1903, 41–3; 34, 1904, 306–10; 36, 1906, 233–6. RBA 1905, 725–6; 1907, 693–4

5560 **Layard, N. F.** Account of a palaeolithic site in Ipswich. PCAS 11, 1907, 493–502

5561 Boswell, P. G. H., *and* Moir, J. R. Pleistocene deposits and their contained palaeolithic flint implements at Foxhall Road, Ipswich. JRAI 53, 1923, 229–62

5562 Moir, J. R. Early neolithic 'floor' discovered at Ipswich. Man 20, 1920, 84–7

5563 Brailsford, J. W. Hoard of early Iron Age gold torcs from Ipswich. PSIA 31, 1967/9, 158–9

5564 Owles, E. J. Ipswich gold torcs. Ant 43, 1969, 208–12

5565 Owles, E. J. Sixth gold torc from Ipswich. PSIA 32, 1970/72, 87–8

5566 Brailsford, J. W., *and* Stapley, J. E. Ipswich torcs. PPS NS 38, 1972, 219–34

Roman

5567 Moir, J. R. Buried shafts at Ipswich [Roman burial pits]. PSIA 22, 1934/6, 141–9

Anglo-Saxon

5568 Layard, N. F. Anglo-Saxon cemetery in Ipswich. Man 6, 1906, 158–9. Arch 60, pt 2, 1907, 325–52. RBA 1907, 694–5

5569 Layard, N. F., *and* Smith, R. A. Discovery at Ipswich of an Anglo-Saxon cemetery of considerable extent. PSA 2nd Ser 21, 1905/07, 241–7, 403

5570 Layard, N. F. Anglo-Saxon cemetery, Hadleigh Road, Ipswich. PSIA 13, 1907/09, 1–19

5571 Layard, N. F. Points of special interest in the Anglo-Saxon discoveries in Ipswich. PSIA 16, 1916/18, 278–80

5572 Hurst, J. G. Stamford-ware pitcher from Ipswich. PSIA 28, 1958/60, 297–8

5573 Ozanne, A. Context and date of the Anglian cemetery at Ipswich. PSIA 29, 1961/3, 208–12

5574 West, S. E. Excavations at Cox Lane [1958] and at the town defences, Shire Hall Yard. PSIA 29, 1961/3, 233–303

5575 Dunning, G. C. Imported pottery found at Cox Lane and Shire Hall Yard excavations, Ipswich. PSIA 29, 1961/3, 279–86

5576 Charman, D. Documentary evidence on the history of the Ipswich rampart and ditch. PSIA 29, 1961/3, 301–03

5577 Smedley, N., *and* Owles, E. J. Some Suffolk kilns. 4. Saxon kilns in Cox Lane, Ipswich. PSIA 29, 1961/3, 304–35

5578 Smedley, N., *and* Owles, E. J. Sherd of Ipswich ware with face-mask decoration. PSIA 31, 1967/9, 84–7

Medieval   See also **2640–41**

5579 Powell, E. Taxation of Ipswich for the Welsh war in 1282. PSIA 12, 1904/06, 137–57

5580 Martin, G. H. Early Court Rolls of the borough of Ipswich. Leicester, 1954

5581 Martin, G. H., *Ed.* Ipswich recognizance rolls, 1294–1327. Ipswich, 1973. SRS 16. [A calendar of deeds and wills enrolled in the borough court]

5582 **Martin, G. H.** The borough and the merchant community of Ipswich, 1317–1422. D.Phil. thesis, Oxford, 1955

5583 **Martin, G. H.** Records of the borough of Ipswich to 1422. SAJ 1, 1956, 87–93

5584 Domus Day of Gippeswiche. *In* Black book of the Admiralty. Appendix, pt 2, v 2, 1–241. *Ed.* by Sir Travers Twiss. Rolls Ser 55, v 2. 1873

5585 **White, C. H. E.** Ipswich 'Domesday' books and especially concerning Percyvale's Great Domesday book, and that part of the 'Liber sextus' containing the taxes paid to the King's Grace by every town in Suffolk. PSIA 6, 1883/8, 195–219

5586 **Percyvale, R.** Great Domesday book of Ipswich, Liber Sextus, with an introduction ... by C. H. E. White. Ipswich, 1885. 250 copies. *See also* 712

5587 Rhyming chronicle of the kings of England [William I to Edward IV] from the Ipswich Great Domesday. E Ang NS 1, 1885/6, 38–41

Early Modern   See also 768, 773, 935, 937, 2752, 3324, 3493–8

5588 **Fitch, W. S.,** *Ed.* Rental of the manor of Christchurch, Ipswich, 38th Henry VIII. [c.1860]. MS

5589 **Goodwyn, H.** Wikess Ufford (Wykes Ufford). The rental of the same made by Henry Goodwyn from copies of the old rentals ... in the sixth year of King Edward VI, 1552. Transcribed by W. S. Fitch. [c.1860]. MS

5590 "**Alpha**" *pseud.* Queen Elizabeth at Ipswich and Christchurch Mansion. E Ang NS 4, 1891/2, 251

5591 **Webb, J.** [G] Ipswich deposition books, 1572–1607. SR 2, 1959, 22–6

5592 **Redstone, V. B.** Dutch and Huguenot settlements at Ipswich. HSLP 12, 1921, 183–204

5593 **Jones, A. G. E.** The Great Plague in Ipswich, 1665–6. PSIA 28, 1958/60, 75–89

5594 A full and true account of the barbarous rebellion and rising of the Lord Dunbarton's regiment, at Ipswich in Suffolk, with their pretences of declaring for the late King James. 1689. Wing F 2301. BL

5595 **Jones, A. G. E.** Ipswich in 1689. N&Q 208, 1963, 43–50

5596 **Jones, A. G. E.** Ipswich and New England. SR 3, 1966, 71–82

Eighteenth Century   See also 944

5597 **Corder, J. S.** Extracts from the diary of Sir James Thornhill, 1711 [dealing mainly with Ipswich and vicinity]. PSIA 13, 1907/09, 33–43

5598 **C, W.** [W. **Coward**?]. Hydro-sideron; or, A treatise of ferruginous-waters, especially the Ipswich-Spaw; being an excellent spring of that nature there lately discovered ... N.B. To this Ipswich-Spaw adjoins a very convenient cold-bath. 1717

Nineteenth Century

5599 East Anglian Daily Times Special Supplement: Ipswich, its history and progress, 1830–1930. Ipswich, 1930

5600 **Glyde, J.** Moral, social, and religious condition of Ipswich in the middle of the nineteenth century, with a sketch of its history, rise, and progress. Ipswich, 1850. Rp with an introduction by A. F. J. Brown. Wakefield, 1971

5601 **Purland, T.** A pylgrymage to Yppswyche, beynge Master Naso Hys deazel. 1850. MS

Twentieth Century

5602 Ipswich and District Trades Council, 1885–1967: a short history. Ipswich, 1969. [Typescript]

5603 Ipswich and the Great War, 1914–18. Unveiling of the Christchurch Park memorial . . . Programme of the proceedings with list of 1,481 names recorded on the memorial. Saturday, 3 May 1924. Ipswich

5604 **Ratcliffe, R.** History of the working-class movement in Ipswich to the end of the nineteenth century, 1900–18, 1918–26, 1926–35. 4 v. 1953. [Typescript]

5605 Who's who in Ipswich. 1959

5606 **Cross, R. L.** Ipswich looks ahead. Ipswich, 1963

5607 **Cross, R. L.** Ipswich profile. Ipswich, 1964. 1967. 1971

PARLIAMENTARY HISTORY *See also* **847, 857, 2487**
Elections

5608 **Glyde, J.,** *Ed.* Materials for a Parliamentary history of Ipswich. [c.1890]. MSS, cuttings, broadsheets

5609 **Glyde, J.,** *Ed.* Members of Parliament for the borough of Ipswich from 1298. [c.1900]. MS

5610 Instructions to the representatives of Ipswich. GM 1st Ser 26, 1756, 545–6

5611 **Sansom, J.** Payments to members of Parliament for Ipswich, 1448–1680. N&Q 2nd Ser 4, 1857, 273

5612 **Luders, A.** Reports of the proceedings in committees of the House of Commons, upon controverted elections, heard and determined during the present Parliament [1784–6]. 3 v. 1785–90. Ipswich in chapter 2

5613 Collection of political broadsides relating to Ipswich elections, 1818–20

5614 **Thorndike, J.,** *and* **Sparrow, J. E.** Letter to the free burgesses of Ipswich, in vindication of the conduct of the returning officers during the late contest for members to serve in Parliament for that borough. By the bailiffs. Ipswich, 1820

5615 Report of the select committee on bribery at elections. HC 1835, 8. Ipswich, 74–91

5616 Report from the select committee on the Ipswich borough election report; together with the minutes of evidence taken before them. Ordered . . . 22 July 1835. HC 1835, 9. [Includes MSS collected by W. S. Fitch]

5617 **Knapp, J. W.,** *and* **Ombler, E.** Cases of controverted elections in the twelfth Parliament of the United Kingdom ... 1837. Includes Ipswich

5618 Minutes of evidence taken before the select committee on the Ipswich borough election petition, with the proceedings of the committee. Ordered 28 Feb 1838. HC 1837/8, 10

5619 Minutes of the proceedings and evidence taken before the select committee on the Ipswich election petition. Ordered 26 April 1842. HC 1842, 7

5620 Minutes of the proceedings and evidence taken before the select committee on the Ipswich election petition. Ordered 1 Aug 1842. HC 1842, 7

5621 Tommy Teagle's political pipelights, 1875–9

5622 Trial of the Ipswich election petition against the return of Mr H. W. West and Mr Jesse Collings, 8 March–1 April 1886, as reported in the EADT. Ipswich. 1886

Poll Books

5623 Poll for members ... 1741. O

5624 Supplement to the poll ... 8 May 1741

5625 Poll ... 1754

5626 Poll ... 16 March 1768

5627 Poll ... 9 Sept 1780. SRO/B

5628 Poll ... 3 April 1784. O

5629 Poll ... 25 June 1784. nl

5630 Poll ... 18 June 1790

5631 Poll ... 29 Oct 1806

5632 Poll ... 5–6 May 1807

5633 Poll ... 16–20, and 22 June 1818

5634 Poll ... 7–11 and 13 March 1820. [2 edns]

5635 Poll ... 12–17 June 1826. Polls 1 and 2

5636 Poll ... 2–4 May 1831

5637 Poll ... 11–12 Dec 1832

5638 Poll ... 6–7 Jan 1835

5639 Poll ... 18–19 June 1835

5640 Register of persons entitled to vote ... from 1 Dec 1836 inclusive, to 1 Nov 1837, first in respect of property, ... secondly as freemen of the said borough. Ipswich, 1836

5641 Poll ... 13 July 1839

5642 Poll ... 2 July 1841

5643 Poll ... 16 Aug 1842

5644 Poll ... 30 July 1847. [2 edns]

5645 Poll ... 7 July 1852, etc. BL

5646 Poll ... 8 July 1852

5647 Poll ... 28 March 1857

5648 Poll ... 30 April 1859. [2 edns]
5649 Poll ... 13 July 1865
5650 Poll ... 19 Nov 1868

ECONOMIC HISTORY AND COMMUNICATIONS
General   See also **1282, 1393, 1413, 1430, 3100–3101, 3285, 5582**

5651 Scopes, T. H. Aspects of the economic history of the borough of Ipswich in the reign of Elizabeth. Thesis. 1949–50. [Typescript]
5652 Haslewood, F. Ipswich a mart for general traffic [papers from the Burleigh MSS of 1573 and 1578]. PSIA 7, 1889/91, 288–98
5653 [Gouldsmith, R.]. Some considerations on trade and manufactories, address'd to the inhabitants of the town of Ipswich. 1725
5654 Ipswich Local Committee of the Conference on Christian Politics, Economics, and Citizenship. Ipswich: a survey of the town. Ipswich, 1924
5655 [Cook, R. H.] Ipswich, the industrial capital of East Anglia. Issued by the Ipswich Industrial Development Association ... Ipswich, 1932. Revised edns. issued as Souvenirs of the Royal Show, 1934; Ancient Order of Foresters' High Court, 1937
5656 Harris, C. D. Ipswich, England. Ec Geog 18, 1942, 1–12
5657 Ipswich Junior Chamber of Commerce and Shipping. Ipswich: a town in profile. Ipswich, 1971

Apprenticeship
5658 Ipswich records. Apprentice indentures at Ipswich, etc., 1596–1651. [c.1900]. MSS
5659 Hutchinson, M. B. Ipswich apprentice books. N&Q 10th Ser 1, 1904, 41–2, 111
5660 Webb, J. [G] Apprenticeships in the maritime occupations at Ipswich, 1590–1651. MM 46, 1960, 29–34

Port   See also **959, 1307–21, 1334, 5736–9**
5661 Redstone, V. B. List of Ipswich vessels, 1621–32, 1636, 1646–7, extracted from records at the Town Hall. nd. [Typescript]
5662 Day, H. J. R., *Ed.* Port of Ipswich. Register of all vessels from 1000 tons register and upwards that have entered the dock from 1842–1937. 2 v. and index. 1900–37. MS
5663 Ipswich Dock, a grandfather's tale, A.D. 1920. Rp from EADT March 6, 1875. Ipswich, 1875. nl
5664 Redstone, V. B. Ipswich port books. PSIA 14, 1910/12, 238–42
5665 Cobbold, J. M. Gates of adventure. Ipswich: port of East Anglia. Geographical Mag 9, 1939, 101–10
5666 Jones, A. G. E. Port of Ipswich. SR 3, 1968, 247–9

5667   Plan of the proposed improvements of the river Orwell from Ipswich to Freston Reach, 20 Sept 1804

5668   Act for improving and rendering more commodious the port of Ipswich ... 45 Geo III, 1805

5669   **Starr, A. J.** Study of the function of Ipswich as a centre of East Anglia and its development as a port since 1805. M.Sc.(Econ.) thesis, London, 1939

5670   **Hare, J.** Ipswich wet dock: embankment near Downham Reach recommended. Ipswich, 1836. BL

5671   **Palmer, H. R.** Report on the proposed improvements in the port of Ipswich. [1836]

5672   **Hare, J.** Proposed plan of a wet dock at the port of Ipswich, 1837. 1837

5673   [Ipswich wet dock]. Report of the committee appointed at a public meeting of the inhabitants of Ipswich ... 4 Nov 1836. Ipswich, 1837

5674   Ipswich Dock Commission and the construction of the wet dock, 1837–1842: a display of documents, maps, and photographs at the Town Hall, Ipswich, 13–23 April 1971. Ipswich, 1971

5674   Ipswich Dock Commissioners. Copies of the contract and specification for the works ordered at a general meeting of the commissioners, held on Friday, 14 Sept 1838. Ipswich, [1838]

5676   **Hurwood, G.** Port of Ipswich. Report upon proposed channels from 'Round Ooze' to 'Cliff Reach', 20 Dec 1845. Ipswich, [1845]

5677   **Hurwood, G.** On the river Orwell and the port of Ipswich. From Minutes of the Proceedings of the Institution of Civil Engineers, v 20. Session 1860–61

5678   **Titchmarsh, E.,** *Ed.* Ipswich Dock Commission. Scrap-book, 1869–94

5679   **Bateman, J. F.** Port of Ipswich Report and plan. 3 Oct 1872. Additional appendices to the report ... on the proposed new lock entrance and improvements in the river Orwell. Ipswich 8 May 1875

5680   Opening of the new lock entrance ... Wednesday, 27 July 1881. Rp from EADT.

5681   Ipswich Dock Commission. Port information and the tide table at the dock, 1945-. Ipswich. Incomplete

5682   Ipswich Dock Commission. Port of Ipswich Bulletin, no 1, July 1963-

5683   Journal of Commerce and Shipping Telegraph. [Surveys of the port of Ipswich]. 8 Jan 1965; 14 Jan 1966

5684   Port of Ipswich: a brief introduction to the port facilities. Ipswich, 1969

5685   Ipswich Dock Commission. Shipping statistics, 1969-

Markets and Fairs
5686   **Cross, R. L.** Ipswich markets and fairs. Ipswich, 1965

Coins and Tokens
5687   **Evans, J.** Discovery of Anglo-Saxon coins at Ipswich. NC NS 4, 1864, 28–33

5688 **Francis, R. S.** Saxon coins found at Ipswich. E Ang 2, 1864/6, 8; JBAA 21, 1865, 190–93

5689 **Dolley, R. H. M.** Coins found at Cox Lane and Shirehall Yard excavations. PSIA 29, 1961/3, 286–91

5690 **Fitch, W. S.** Ipswich and its early mints. SAAP Pt 3, Nov 1848, 1–10

5691 **Sadler, J. C.** History of the Ipswich mint and its Saxon and Norman moneyers. Ipswich, 1976

5692 Ipswich tokens. SAAP Pt 3, Nov 1848. 10–12

5693 **Cranbrook,** *Earl of.* A rare Ipswich token. PSIA 27, 1955/7, 54

Banking
5694 **Jones, A. G. E.** Early banking in Ipswich. N&Q 196, 1951, 402–05; 197, 1952, 86. *See also* **2712**

Bellfounders
5695 **Bevis, T. A.** Ipswich bellfounders. Hadlow, Kent, [1966]

Brewing   See also **2664–5**
5696 **Walton, F.,** *pseud.* [i.e. **F. Woolnough**]. Souvenir of the bi-centenary of the Cliff Brewery, Ipswich. Cobbold and Co., 1723–1923. Containing a selection of ancient and historical inns attached to the Cliff Brewery. [Ipswich], 1923

5697 **Jacobson, M.** Cliff Brewery, 1723–1973. Ipswich, 1973

Building Societies
5698 Rules of the Orwell Building Society. [Ipswich], 1876

5699 Jubilee of the Ipswich and Suffolk Freehold Land Society, 1849–99. Ipswich, 1899

5700 1849–1949: centenary brochure of the Ipswich and Suffolk Permanent Benefit Building Society [Freehold Land Society]. Ipswich, [1949]

5701 Freehold Land Society's estate in the Borough of Ipswich ... 98¾ acres. Ipswich, [c.1850]

5702 One hundred years of service, 1850–1950. A brief history of the Ipswich Permanent Benefit Building Society. Ipswich, [1950]

Coachbuilding
5703 Bennett and Sons, merchant coach- and harness-makers and exporters. Special export catalogue for 1886. [Ipswich], [1885]

5704 **Botwood, W. T.,** *and* **S. E.** Ipswich carriage works. Carriage designs. [Ipswich], [c.1894]

Engineering   See also **3244**
5705 **Ipswich Engineering Society.** Transactions, v 1–9, 1899/1900–1907/08. Ipswich

5706 **Newby, A. E.,** *et al. Eds.* History of engineering in Ipswich. By the Ipswich Engineering Society on the occasion of their Jubilee, 1899–1949. Ipswich, 1950

5707 **Morrison, R. D. McD.,** *Ed.* History of engineering in Ipswich. By the Ipswich Engineering Society on the occasion of its 75th anniversary, 1899–1974. Ipswich, 1974

5708 Sketch of the Society for Mental Improvement at Ransome's foundry, Ipswich: its rise and progress. Established 1836. Ipswich, 1842

5709 **Ransome, J. A.** Implements of agriculture. 1843. 1884

5710 **Ransome, J. R.,** *and* **A.,** *and* **May, C.** [Catalogue of agricultural implements and machines]. Ipswich, 1848. BL

5711 **May, C.** On the application of chilled cast iron to the pivots of astronomical instruments. *In* British Assoc. for the Advancement of Science report of the 21st meeting at Ipswich, 1851. 1851

5712 **May, C.** On railway chairs and compressed wood fastenings. *In* British Assoc. for the Advancement of Science report of the 21st meeting at Ipswich, 1851. 1851

5713 **Ransome, J. E.** Ploughs and ploughing: a lecture delivered at the Royal Agricultural College, Cirencester. Edinburgh, 1865

5714 **Ransome** *and* **Rapier.** The tramway nuisance and its true remedy. An address to local authorities ... [1879]

5715 **Ransome** *and* **Rapier, Ltd.** The "Stoney" sluice, with Stokes' patent improvements, and its application to works for water storage and control. 4th edn [c.1908]

5716 **Ransomes, Sims,** *and* **Jefferies.** Description of the Orwell works, Ipswich. From Proceedings of the Institution of Mechanical Engineers, Cambridge meeting, 1913. With additional notes and illustrations. [Ipswich], [1913]

5717 **Ransomes** *and* **Rapier, Ltd.** Ransomes and Rapier's annual, 1921–3, 1925–6. Ipswich

5718 **Ransomes, Sims,** *and* **Jefferies, Ltd.** Orwell works magazine, v 1–9, 1931–1940. Bi-monthly. [First 5 issues of v 1 entitled The Dot and Dash magazine]. Ipswich

5719 **Ransomes, Sims,** *and* **Jefferies, Ltd.** Ransome's 'royal records'; a century-and-a-half in the service of agriculture, 1789–1939. Ipswich, 1939

5720 Ransomes and the Second World War, 1939–45. Ipswich, 1946

5721 **Lewis, R. S.** Eighty years of enterprise, 1869–1949, being the intimate story of the Waterside works of Ransomes and Rapier Limited of Ipswich, England. Ipswich, [1951]

5722 **Ransomes, Sims,** *and* **Jefferies, Ltd.** Wherever the sun shines: 175 years of progress ... Ipswich, [1964]

5723 Ransomes yesterday—today—tomorrow. Ipswich, 1967

5724 **Beaumont, A.** Ransomes' steam engines; an illustrated history. Newton Abbot, 1972

5725 **Grace, D. R.,** *and* **Phillips, D. C.** Ransomes of Ipswich: a history of the firm and a guide to its records. Reading, 1975

5726 Description of the works and productions of E. R. and F. Turner, Limited,

St. Peter's and Greyfriars works, Ipswich. Rp with additions from "Machinery Market". 1898

Printing

5727 **Duff, E. G.** English provincial printers, stationers, and bookbinders to 1557. Lecture 4, on printing at Ipswich and elsewhere. Cambridge, 1912

5728 **Watson, S. F.** History of printing and publishing in Ipswich. PSIA 24, 1946/8, 182–227. Also typescript copy, with photographs

5729 **Watson, S. F.** An Ipswich book of 1534. Ipswich, 1948

5730 **Oldham, J. B.** Bibliographical note: an Ipswich master-stationer's tiff with his journeyman. Rp from the Cambridge Bibliographical Soc Monographs 2, 1958, 381–4

5731 **Ireland, G.** The press in the Buttermarket [W. S. Cowell Ltd.]: a camera study. Ipswich, 1960

Services and Retail Trade

5732 **Garrod, Turner, and Son.** Chartered auctioneers and estate agents: a short history of the firm on the occasion of the bicentenary of its foundation in 1770. Ipswich, 1970

5733 Through sixty years. A record of progress and achievement, prepared on the occasion of the diamond jubilee of the Ipswich Industrial Co-operative Society, Ltd., 1868–1928. Ipswich, 1928

5734 1868–1968: a century of service, the success story of the Ipswich Co-operative Society. Ipswich, [1968]

5735 **Melville, F. J.** Then and now: a dynasty of stamp kings [Whitfield King and Company, Ipswich]. Ipswich, [c.1938]

Shipbuilding

5736 **Jones, A. G. E.** Shipbuilding in Ipswich, 1700–1750. MM 43, 1957, 294–305; 1750–1800. MM 58, 1972, 183–93

Whaling

5737 **Jones, A. G. E.** Whaling trade of Ipswich, 1786–1793. MM 40, 1954, 297–303

5738 **Moffat, H. W.** Whaling trade of Ipswich. MM 41, 1955, 62

Wool and Cloth

5739 **Martin, G. H.** Shipments of wool from Ipswich to Calais, 1399–1402. JTH 2, 1955, 177–81

5740 **Coke, E.** Reports of Sir Edward Coke, in thirteen parts. New edn. by J. H. Thomas and J. F. Fraser. 6 v. 1826. The case of the tailors, etc., of Ipswich ... [their trade monopoly]. v6, 101–04

5741 French Protestant refugees at Ipswich in connection with the linen industry during the seventeenth century. E Ang NS 2, 1887/8, 374–9, 398–400

5742 Linen manufacturing at Ipswich and the French Protestant refugees [1686]. E Ang NS 12, 1907/08, 21–2

Postal History

5743 **Ipswich Philatelic Society.** Silver jubilee handbook, *ed.* by Gladys Driver. [Ipswich postal history, 16th-century to 1970]. Ipswich, 1970. NCL/N

MUNICIPAL GOVERNMENT, SOCIAL SERVICES, AND JUSTICE
Municipal Administration   See also **482, 1454–5, 5580–86**

5744 **Royal Commission on Historical Manuscripts.** Ser 8, 1. 9th Report, Pt 1 ... Corporation of Ipswich. 1883. Rp 1895

5745 **Jeaffreson, J. C.** Manuscripts of the corporation of Ipswich, co. Suffolk. (Offprint of section of appendix to 9th Report of the Royal Commission on Historical Manuscripts). 1883

5746 **Glyde, J.,** *Ed.* Materials for a history of municipal Ipswich. 2 v. [c.1900]. Cuttings, illustrations, MSS

5747 **Layton, W. E.** Notices from the Great Court and Assembly Books of the borough of Ipswich. E Ang NS 1, 1885/6—NS 8, 1899/1900, *passim*

5748 [Manor of Stoke (Ipswich). Copies of terriers, extracts from court rolls, etc. c.1540–1651]. [c.1900]. MS

5749 **B[ooty], E. J.** High Stewards of Ipswich, 1557–1949. Ipswich, 1949. [Typescript]

5750 **Hutchison, J. R.** Administration of the borough of Ipswich under Elizabeth I and James I. 1952. Dissertation. [Typescript]

5751 Ipswich municipal memoranda, *temp.* 16th century. "Remembrances for the bailiffs to be doon". E Ang NS 4, 1891/2, 268–9

5752 Collection of letters, petitions, documents, and material relating to Ipswich, chiefly of the period Geo. II and Geo. III. 2 v. MSS

5753 **Ipswich Corporation.** Oaths of office of the chief magistrates, subordinate officers, and free burgesses ... [Ipswich], 1794

5754 Remarks on the expediency of applying to Parliament for a bill to incorporate the several parishes of the borough of Ipswich. Ipswich, 1815

5755 Statistics relating to Ipswich and Suffolk, c.1830–65 [Expenditure, population, deaths from small-pox, state of crime, etc.]. MS

5756 **Grimsey, B. P.** Borough of Ipswich, Members of the council in and since 1835, in alphabetical order. Ipswich, 1892. Also proof copy which includes the mayors of Ipswich 1835–41, *cont as* cuttings from EADT carrying the history from 1875–7

5757 **Vick, W.** Mayors of Ipswich from 1835–1890. Ipswich. [mainly photographs]

5758 **Ipswich Corporation.** Schedule of properties belonging to the Mayor, Aldermen, and Burgesses of the borough of Ipswich. Prepared 31 Dec 1892; Roderick Donald Fraser, Mayor. Ipswich, 1892

5759 **Ipswich Corporation.** Schedule of properties belonging, or leased, to the Mayor, Aldermen, and Burgesses of the borough of Ipswich. Prepared 31 Dec 1892. Revised and brought up to date, 29 Sept 1923; Alfred Sizer, Mayor. Ipswich, 1923

5760 **Ipswich Corporation**. Proceedings at meetings of the Town Council, 1868–1947. (verbatim reports). Ipswich

5761 **Ipswich Corporation**. Reports to Council and Council meetings. Ipswich, 1947–

5762 **Ipswich Corporation**. Municipal year book. Ipswich, 1900–

Ipswich Corporation. Byelaws and regulations:–

5763 1859 Building of new streets

5764 Cleansing of footways and pavements; removal of refuse; cleansing of privies, ashpits, and cesspools

5765 Prevention of nuisances arising from snow, filth, dust, ashes, and rubbish, and the keeping of animals

5766 Regulation of slaughterhouses

5767 1877 Management ... of the public baths

5768 1884 Hackney carriages [and 1948, 1950, 1957]

5769 1890 Cattle market

5770 1901 Dairies, cowsheds, and milkshops

5771 Good rule and government of the borough, [and 1913 (disturbances in schools), 1927, 1935 (wireless, loudspeakers, gramophones), 1950]

5772 1902 Common lodging-houses

5773 1903 Government of the borough lunatic asylum

5774 Tramways, [and 1904]

5775 1904 Posts, wires, tubes over, along, or across streets

5776 1905 Pleasure grounds

5777 1907 Employment of children and the engagement of young persons in street trading, [and 1948]

5778 1912 Registries for female domestic servants

5779 1917 Regulations made by the Ipswich Port Sanitary Authority for removal to hospital of persons brought ... by ship, who are infected with a dangerous infectious disorder

5780 1923 Slaughterhouses

5781 1924 Offensive trades

5782 1925 New streets and buildings

5783 1926 Conduct of persons using sanitary conveniences

5784 1928 Hoardings and advertisements

5785 1929 Nursing homes

5786 1939 Building byelaws, [and 1953]

5787 1948 Personal weighing machines

5788 1949 Regulation of employment exchanges

5789 Management of the mortuary and post-mortem room

5790 Securing cleanliness of hairdresser's and barber's premises, and of instruments, towels, and materials used

5791 1950 Sale of coal and coke
5792 Recreation grounds and public walks
5793 Handling, wrapping, and delivery of food, and sale of food in the open air
5794 Prevention of nuisances
5795 1967 Public libraries
5796 **Ipswich Corporation.** Ipswich information, no 1, Sept–Oct 1964–no 76, April 1977. [with occasional supplements]. [Discontinued]
5797 **Ipswich Corporation.** Meet your Town Hall: programme of events, 9–22 Nov 1970

Municipal Elections
5798 Collection of papers relating to the election of bailiffs of Ipswich, Sept 1754. [Ipswich], [1754]
5799 **Burrow, J.** Reports of cases argued and adjudged in the court of King's Bench [1756–72]. 5 v. 4th edn 1790. Rex *v.* Richardson, 31 Geo. II [election of portmen of Ipswich]. v 1, 517–41
5800 Report upon the proposed municipal boundary and division into wards of the borough of Ipswich. Municipal corporations boundaries (England and Wales) Royal Commission. Reports Pt 2. HC 1837, 27
5801 **Ipswich Corporation.** County borough of Ipswich. Local Government Act, 1933, section 25. Petition for an alteration in the number and boundaries of the wards of the county borough of Ipswich ... Feb 1952 [Typescript]

Municipal Poll-Books, Burgess Rolls, Registers of Electors
5802 Poll for bailiffs ... 8 Sept 1754
5803 Poll for bailiffs ... 8 Sept 1768
5804 Poll for bailiffs ... 8 Sept 1781 SRO/B
5805 Poll for bailiffs and town clerk ... 8 Sept 1790
5806 Poll for bailiffs ... 8 Sept 1803. nl
5807 Poll for bailiffs and town clerk ... 8 Sept 1806
5808 Poll for the clerk to the commissioners for paving and lighting ... 18 Feb 1817
5809 Poll for the collectorship of the duties on coals ... 15 April 1823
5810 Poll for bailiffs and town clerk ... 8 Sept 1823
5811 Poll for the collectorship of the rates and assessments ... 14 Oct 1823
5812 Poll for bailiffs and town clerk ... 8 Sept 1825
5813 Poll for the recorder ... 11 March 1831
5814 Burgess roll for the borough of Ipswich. 1835
5815 Burgess roll, 1840–3, 1848, 1850, 1871, 1873, 1875, 1876–7, 1877–87/8. Annually 1888–1919. From 1890 entitled Burgess roll—register of electors
5816 Copy of the burgess roll or ward lists of the borough of Ipswich ... for the third or middle ward ... 22 Oct 1861

5817 Ipswich parliamentary borough register of electors. Spring 1920. Spring and autumn 1921–7. Annually 1928–39. May 1945. Oct 1945. 1946–

Municipal Insignia, Heraldry, and Plate   See also **1470**

5818 **Grimsey, B. P.** Armorial insignia of the borough of Ipswich. PSIA 6, 1883/8, 456

5819 Grant of arms to the town of Ipswich, 1561. MGetH 2nd Ser 2, 1888, 343–4

5820 **Cross, R. L.** Ipswich corporation civic regalia. Ipswich, [1964]

5821 **R, H. R.** Burghmote horn of corporation of Ipswich. N&Q 176, 1939, 373–4

Freemen

5822 Freemen of the borough of Ipswich, admitted in, and since, the year 1722–[1885] MS

5823 **Grimsey, B. P.** Freemen of the borough of Ipswich complete to the end of open voting, 1889. [Containing Pts 1 and 2, and cuttings from the EADT 1889, continuing the history]. [Ipswich], [1889?]

5824 **Grimsey, B. P.** Freemen of the borough of Ipswich. Pt 1. [Ipswich], [1892]

5825 **Hutchinson, J. R.** Ipswich freemen. E Ang NS 10, 1903/04, 375–6

Municipal Finance

5826 Extracts from the early Chamberlains' accounts of the borough of Ipswich. E Ang NS 1, 1885/6, 119–21

5827 **Fitch, W. S.** Accounts of the Chamberlains of the borough of Ipswich for the year 1555. [1851?]

5828 **Chamberlain, H.,** *Ed.* Ipswich 200 years ago: showing the extent and rateable value of the town at that period. Being a correct copy of an assessment made in the year 1689. Ipswich, [1889]

5829 **L, E.** Letter to the freemen of Ipswich, upon the revenues of that ancient borough: containing a view of their present state, with some suggestions for amending and improving their application. Ipswich, 1821. 2nd edn 1821

5830 **Ipswich Corporation.** Abstract of the Treasurer's accounts, 1841/2–1853/4. Incomplete

5831 **Ipswich Corporation.** Abstract of the accounts of the Treasurer of the borough of Ipswich, 1854/5–. Ipswich

5832 **"Ratepayer",** *pseud.* How the corporation of Ipswich lends our municipal funds on mortgage. Ipswich, [1904]

5833 **Collins, A.** [Report relating to the financing of the corporation of Ipswich on capital account, 13 April 1926]. 1926

5834 **Ipswich Corporation.** Abstract of loans, 1947/9. Ipswich

5835 **Ipswich Corporation.** Financial statistics, 1948/9–. Ipswich. Incomplete

5836 **Ipswich Corporation.** Civic restaurants accounts, 1949, 1950. Ipswich

Poor Relief

5837 **Webb, J. [G],** *Ed.* Poor relief in Elizabethan Ipswich. Ipswich, 1966. SRS 9

5838   **Vagrant Mendicity Society**, Ipswich. Resolutions taken for the suppression of mendicity in Ipswich. [c.1810]. SRO/B

5839   Report of the committee appointed to enquire into the present state of the poor, and the workhouses, in Ipswich ... Ipswich, 1822

5840   **Fonnereau, W. C.** Remarks and suggestions relative to the management of the poor in Ipswich. Ipswich, 1833

5841   Ordering of parish workhouses in the eighteenth and nineteenth centuries. [St. Margaret's and St. Clement's, Ipswich]. E Ang NS 10, 1903/04, 145–7

5842   Correct account of the circumstances which took place at the destruction of part of St. Clement's workhouse, Ipswich ... 16 Dec 1835. Ipswich, [1835]. BL

5843   **Ipswich Union.** Parish of St. Margaret. Account shewing the amount at which the various properties are assessed to the poor's rate ... Nov 1848. Ipswich, 1848

5844   **Ipswich Union.** Parish of St. Margaret. Statement of the assessment of the various properties in the said parish. Ipswich, 1852

5845   **Ipswich Union.** Parish of St. Matthew. Statement shewing the amounts at which the various properties are assessed, according the poor rate made 22 Nov 1861. Ipswich, 1861

5846   **Ipswich Union.** Statement of accounts of the above union for the half-year ending Michaelmas, 1862, with a list of persons receiving out-door relief, charged to the parishes of the union. Ipswich, 1862

5847   **Ipswich Union.** Parish of St. Mary Stoke. Statement shewing the amounts at which the various properties are assessed, according to the poor rate made 5 May 1864. Ipswich, 1864

5848   **Ipswich Union.** Statements (for each parish) showing the amounts at which the various properties are assessed according to the poor rate made 23 Nov 1876. Ipswich, [1876]

5849   **Ipswich Union.** Statement of the accounts of the above union ... with a list of persons receiving out-door relief. Half-year ending Michaelmas, 1883–half-year ending Michaelmas, 1895. Ipswich. Incomplete

5850   Ipswich and its workhouses: a sketch in commemoration of the opening of the new Ipswich workhouse, on Wednesday, 10 May 1899 ... Ipswich, 1899

5851   Girls' Industrial Home, St. Matthew's Street, Ipswich. Annual reports, 1862–1864, 1867, 1869. Ipswich

5852   Seventh report of the Ipswich Social Settlement, 1903. 9th report, 1905, 15th report, 1911. Ipswich

5853   **Ipswich Labour Party.** Labour members of, and candidates for the Ipswich Board of Guardians, from the earliest known records to the coming into operation of the Public Health Act (1929). [Typescript]

Charities   See also **1542, 3412–13, 5837**

5854   **Canning, R.** Account of the gifts and legacies that have been given and bequeathed to charitable uses in the town of Ipswich, with some account of the present state and management, and some proposals for the future regulation of these. Ipswich, 1747. 2nd edn 1819, with abstracts of charters and Acts of Parliament relating to the improvement of the town, together with some account of the various public institutions, charity schools, benevolent societies, etc. By W. Edge

5855 Scheme for the administration of Benjamin Brame's Ipswich charities and the application of the income thereof ... 1862

5856 Brame's Charity, Ipswich. Statement of accounts, 1901–07. Ipswich

5857 **Ipswich Municipal Charities Trustees.** Short account of the municipal charities of the borough of Ipswich. Ipswich, 1878. [MS revisions dated 1901]

5858 **"Radical"**, *pseud.* Our Ipswich charities and what has been done with them. Carefully revised and reprinted from the "Ipswich Free Press". Ipswich, [c.1883]

5859 **Charity Commissioners.** Charities of Ipswich: public enquiry, 8 Feb 1894. [Newspaper cuttings reporting the proceedings]

5860 **Ipswich Municipal Charities.** Almshouses: financial statements, 1901. 1904/07. [Ipswich]

5861 **Ipswich Municipal Charities.** Statement of accounts, 1901–1907. [Ipswich]

Public Health   See also **1561–4, 1570**
5862 **Austin, H.** Report on the present sanitary condition of the town of Ipswich, and the means to be adopted for its improvement ... Ipswich, 1848

5863 **Ranger, W.** Report to the General Board of Health on a preliminary inquiry into the sewerage, drainage, supply of water, and the sanitary condition of the inhabitants of the borough of Ipswich. 1856

5864 **Ipswich Corporation.** Borough of Ipswich. Public Health Act, 1848, Towns Improvement Clauses Act, 1847, and Town Police Clauses Act, 1847, as far as they are applied to the borough of Ipswich by the Public Health Supplemental Act, 1857. Ipswich, 1857

5865 **Ipswich Corporation.** Annual reports on the sanitary condition of the borough and port of Ipswich ... 1874–1906. Annual reports of the Medical Officer of Health and School Medical Officer, 1907–. Ipswich

5866 **Elliston, W. A.** Address upon modern researches in sanitation ... Friday, 9 July 1886. Ipswich, 1886

5867 **Ipswich Borough Asylum.** Annual reports, 1906, 1911/12, 1920/38, 1944/8 [Mental Hospital from 1911]. Ipswich

5868 **Ipswich Corporation. Public Health Committee.** Better health, v 1, no 1, July 1928– v 5, no 12, Dec 1932. Ipswich

5869 **Ipswich Corporation.** National Health Service Act, 1946. A guide to the health services provided by the local health authority, Ipswich group hospitals management committee, Suffolk mental hospitals management committee, executive council for the borough of Ipswich. [Ipswich], [c.1948]

5870 **Ipswich Corporation.** National health service executive council. Reports, 1954– Ipswich. Incomplete. [Typescript]

5871 **Ipswich Corporation.** To help you: a guide to health and welfare services and organisations in Ipswich. Ipswich, 1968

5872 Gyppeswyke magazine, for clubs and associations carried on for the welfare of others. Jan 1892, no 2

5873 **Ipswich Blind Society.** Reports and balance sheets, 1914 (Ipswich and Suffolk Institution ... for ... the Blind, 40th report]; 1919, 1928/9, 1930/33, 1936/8. Ipswich

5874 **Ipswich Blind Society.** Crackers, the annual of the Ipswich Blind Society, 1938–69. Ipswich. Incomplete

5875 Accounts books of Christ's hospital, Ipswich. E Ang NS 1, 1885/6, 336–9

5876 **East Anglian Daily Times.** King Edward memorial sanitorium, Ipswich, in 1912. Ipswich, 1912

5877 **Chamberlain, N. A.,** *Ed*. St. Clement's rendezvous: St. Clement's hospital, Ipswich, 1870–1970 ... Centenary celebration. Ipswich, 1970

5878 Ipswich for the disabled. Ipswich, 1970

5879 **Grimsey, B. P.** Longevity in Ipswich. List of persons who have died ... between 1 Jan 1868 and 1 Jan 1889 ... 85 years and upwards. Ipswich, 1890

Emergency Services   See also **1575–7**

5880 **Ipswich Corporation.** The Warble. Official magazine of the Ipswich A.R.P. services [later the Civil Defence Services], Dec 1939–March 1945, and the victory souvenir, 1939–45. Ipswich

5881 **Ipswich Fire Services.** A.F.S. Ipswich [magazine]. 4 nos. Oct 1939–March 1940. Ipswich.

5882 **'2222'** A magazine for the Ipswich Fire Services. April 1940–Oct 1941. Ipswich

Education   See also **2515, 2719, 3490–98, 6133**
Ipswich School and Wolsey's College
5883 **Layard, N. F.** Brief sketch of the history of Ipswich School, 1477–1851. Ipswich, 1901

5884 **Gray, I. E.,** *and* **Potter, W. E.** Ipswich School, 1400–1950. Ipswich, 1950

5885 **Gray, I. E.** Ipswich School before 1800. N&Q 12th Ser 12, 1923, 230, 275, 355, 396

5886 **Wolsey, T.** Rudimenta Grammatices et Docendi methodus, non tam Scholae Gypswichianae ... [London], 1529. STC 25945. IS

5887 **Leman, J.** To the high court of Parliament. A petition to restore the school at Ipswich to its original location. 1624. STC 15453.3. Soc of Antiquaries

5888 Catechesis Ecclesiae Anglicanae, Una cum precibus aliquot Selectis in Usum Scholae, Regis Henrici Ejus Nominus Octavi, in Burgo Gippovicensi. Ipswich, 1722. IS

5889 Epigrammatum et Poematum Sacrorum et Psalmorum Delectus in Usum Scholarum Gippovici. Ipswich, 1722. IS

5890 **Grove, J.** Two dialogues in the Elysian Fields, between Cardinal Wolsey and Cardinal Ximenes, . . . to which are added historical accounts of Wolsey's two colleges, and the town of Ipswich. 1761

5891   **S, C.** Letter from Cardinal Wolsey to Count Beaumont, respecting stone for building his colleges at Ipswich and Oxford. CTetG 1, 1834, 241–2

5892   **Dillon,** *Viscount.* Portrait of Henry VIII on the charter to Wolsey's college at Ipswich. Middlesex and Herts. N&Q 1, 1895, 37–9

5893   **Partridge, C. S.,** *and* **Radcliffe, J.** Arms of Ipswich Grammar School. N&Q 8th Ser 10, 1896, 51, 266

5894   **Layard, N. F.** Remarks on Wolsey's college and the priory of St. Peter and St. Paul, Ipswich. Arch J. 56, 1899, 211–15

5895   **Caine, C.** Cardinal Wolsey's college, Ipswich. JBAA NS 20, 1914, 91–106, 225–41

5896   **Morfey, W. M.** Ipswich School, 4 July 1851 [Visit of Albert, Prince Consort] Ipswich, 1951. IS

5897   Sermons on the Lord's Prayer preached in the church of St. Mary-le-Tower, Ipswich, by the Rev S. J. Rigaud, M. A., Headmaster, 1852. IS

5898   Borough of Ipswich. Report of the Grammar School committee, presented at a special meeting of the Town Council, and ordered to be printed, 19 May 1856. [Ipswich], 1856

5899   Growth in grace and knowledge: a farewell sermon preached 20 Dec 1857 in the chapel of Ipswich Grammar School by S. J. Rigaud, D.D., Headmaster. Ipswich, 1857. IS

5900   Ipswich School. Testimonials laid before the Corporation of Ipswich in favour of the Rev. H. A. Holden, M.A., and now Head Master of the above School. Ipswich, 1858. IS

5901   **Holden, H. A.** Plain statement of the circumstances attending my resignation of the head-mastership of Ipswich Grammar School. Ipswich, 1883

5902   Ipswich School lists, with calendar and prize exercises: 1853, 1854, June 1859, Dec 1859, with Prolusiones: 1860, 1861, 1862. Lists, 1883, 1885, 1888, then called Blue book, 1895, 1897–1905. School lists, annually, 1951–. Ipswich. IS

5903   **Morfey, W. M.,** *Ed.* Alphabetical list of Ipswichians known to have been educated at the school . . . to . . . 1857. Ipswich, 1976. 70 copies

5904   Old Ipswichian Club. Lists of members, 1899, 1902, 1906, [1953–72 in Old Ipswichian Magazine], 1974, 1976. Ipswich. IS

5905   Old Ipswichian Club. Officers for 1906–07. Ipswich, 1907. O

5906   List of old Ipswichians who are known to have served in His Majesty's Forces during the Great War. Ipswich, 1920. IS

5907   **Fiske, E. J. W.,** *Ed.* List of old Ipswichians who served in His Majesty's Forces during the World War, 1939–45. Ipswich, 1948. IS

5908   Visit of HRH the Duke of Edinburgh to Ipswich School, 1 May 1956. Ipswich, 1956. IS

5909   Visit of HRH the Duke of Edinburgh to Ipswich School, 14 June 1973. Ipswich, 1973. IS

5910 Ipswich School [formerly Ipswich Grammar School, Queen Elizabeth's Grammar School]. Elizabethan, v 1–3, 1852–68; Ipswich School Magazine, v 4–18, 1874–1937; Ipswichian, v 19–27, 1938–67, unnumbered annually 1968–. The Old Ipswichian, annually, 1953–. Ipswich School Record, 1967–1973, bi-annually. IS

Other Schools

5911 Ipswich district national schools in the parish of St. Matthew. First report, 1848

5912 Anglesea College Quarterly Magazine, Ipswich, 1876–8. 2 v. Ipswich

5913 Ipswich charity school. Abstract of the rules and orders for the management and direction of the charity school, of Grey Coat Boys and Blue Coat Girls, instituted in ... 1709 ... Ipswich [c.1810]. rev. edn 1826, by M. Edgar *et al*

5914 **Stone, H.** Ipswich charity schools of Grey Coat Boys and Blue Coat Girls, 1709–1809. PSIA 25, 1949/51, 172–92

5915 **Cobbold, T.** Sermon for the schools of Greycoat Boys and Bluecoat Girls. Ipswich, 1809

5916 Ipswich charity schools. Revision of rules. Ipswich, 1881

5917 **Congregation of Jesus and Mary.** Centenary souvenir of the English province (1860–1960). Ipswich, 1960. [Deals, in part, with Ipswich Convent School]

5918 Ipswich dormitory and school of industry. 2nd annual report, 20 Oct 1853. Ipswich, 1853

5919 **Rowntree, C. B.** Friends' schools at Ipswich (1790–1800). FHSJ 25, 1938, 50–59

5920 **Johnston, L.** Friends' school in Ipswich, 1790–1800. SR 1, 1957, 70–76

5921 Ipswich Higher Grade School magazine. Extant 1894–7. nl

5922 Pageant of education: Ipswich High School, 1878–1928. Ipswich, 1928. nl

5923 Ipswich High School. School News, 1885–. [except 1940–5]

5924 The Ipswich Modern, being the magazine of the Middle School for Boys, Ipswich. Midsummer 1895–Easter 1906. 3 v

5925 Northgate Grammar School for Boys [formerly Municipal Secondary School for Boys] Magazine, 1908–68. Northgate News, 1969–. Northgate Year Book, 1969–

5926 Northgate Old Boys' Magazine, 1950–65, followed by a Year Book, merged with Northgate Year Book, 1969–

5927 Northgate School for Girls [formerly Municipal Secondary School for Girls] Green Book [school magazine], 1932–62. Imprint, 1971–

5928 Northgate Grammar School for Girls, Ipswich. Jubilee Magazine [1906–56]. Summer, 1956

5929 **Westripp, W.,** *and* **Bonner, S. T.** A century of service. St. Matthew's, schools, Ipswich, 1847–1947. [Ipswich], [1947]

5930 **Ipswich Corporation.** Education Committee. Educational census, 1911.

Appendix to report [dated 8 Jan 1912] of the Attendance Sub-committee. [Ipswich], 1912

5931 **Ipswich Corporation.** Education Committee. Scholarships, bursaries, and exhibitions. Ipswich, 1912

5932 **Ipswich Corporation.** Education Committee. Memorandum on the problems connected with the programme of educational development for the period, 1930–33. Ipswich, 1929. Programme for the period, 1930–33. Ipswich, 1930

5933 **Ipswich Corporation.** Education Committee. Re-organisation of secondary education ... Comprehensive secondary schools for the 11–16 year age-range followed by separate post-16 provision. Ipswich, 1966. [Typescript]

5934 **Ipswich Corporation.** Education Committee. Scheme for further education and proposals for county colleges. Ipswich, 1948

5935 **Ipswich Corporation.** Youth Advisory Committee. Ipswich youth organizations. 1945

5936 **Ministry of Education.** General area survey of youth service in the county borough of Ipswich held during the Spring term, 1949. 1949

5937 **Ipswich Corporation.** Advisory Committee for Informal Further Education. Youth and adult organisations, 1950, 1951/2–. Ipswich

5938 **Ipswich Corporation.** Education Committee. What to do in Ipswich: spare-time activities for men and women, 1946/47 – 1949/50. Ipswich

5939 **March, L.** Education shop. A report on a social experiment [in Ipswich]. [1966]

Museums See also **633, 680**

5940 **Henslow, J. S.** Address delivered in the Ipswich museum 9 March 1848. Ipswich, 1848

5941 Statement of donations received for the liquidation of the debts of the Ipswich museum and how they have been expended, 20 May 1853. Ipswich, 1853. nl

5942 Catalogue of the temporary museum at the Ipswich congress of the British Archaeological Association, 1864. JBAA 21, 1865, 343–9

5943 **Ipswich Corporation.** Guide to the Ipswich museum. Ipswich, 1871

5944 **Woolnough, F.** Guide to the Ipswich museum. Ipswich, 1895. [c.1920]

5945 **Woolnough, F.** History of the Ipswich museum. MJ 8, 1908, 191–200

5946 **Ipswich Corporation.** Annual reports [of Museum], 1888–. *See also* Libraries.

5947 Christchurch Park for the people. Ipswich, 1892

5948 **Corder, J. S.** Christchurch, or Withepole House: a brief memorial. Ipswich, 1893. Grangerized edn. by H. R. Eyre

5949 **Woolnough, F.** Short history of the mansion and estate of Christchurch, Ipswich. Ipswich, 1899. 3rd edn 1904. 4th edn 1908. 5th edn 1913

5950 The 'Motto' inscriptions at Christchurch Mansion ... Ipswich. E Ang NS 13, 1909/10, 385–6

5951 **Maynard, G.** Christchurch Mansion, Ipswich. JBAA NS 34, 1929, 55–9

5952 **Ipswich Corporation.** Annual reports of the museum and art gallery, 1931/2–

5953 Christchurch Mansion, Ipswich. Souvenir and guide. [Ipswich], 1932 and later edns

5954 **Oswald, A.** Christchurch Mansion, Ipswich. CL 116, 1954, 496–9, 572–5, 644–7

5955 Christchurch Mansion, Ipswich: a brief history and guide. Ipswich, 1964
See also **2885, 3481–4**

Libraries See also **4297**

5956 **Westhorp, S.** On the library of the town of Ipswich. JBAA 21, 1865, 65–75

5957 Ipswich library. Lib 4, 1892, 130; 6, 1894, 89

5958 **Ogle, H.** An old town library. Library Assistant 4, 1904, 141–5

5959 **Jones, T. E.** Ipswich libraries and book clubs. Rp from Book Auction Records, 11, 1913/14

5960 **Ipswich Corporation.** Numerical catalogue of the books in the town library under the public grammar-school, Ipswich [compiled by the Rev. J. King]. Ipswich, 1799

5961 [**Hammelmann, H. A.**]. An ancient public library. Times Literary Suppl 1950, 524

5962 **Hepworth, P.** Old town library, Ipswich. EAM 14, 1954/5, 455–60

5963 **Walker, H.,** *Ed.* Ipswich Institute, 1824–1924, an historical sketch. [Ipswich], [1924]

5964 **Ipswich Mechanics Institution.** Rules and orders of the Ipswich Mechanics Institution for the promotion of useful knowledge among the working classes. Established 4 Jan 1825. Ipswich

5965 **Ipswich Institute.** (formerly Ipswich Mechanics Institution). Annual report and statement of accounts, 1835–1936. [Reports from 1919 contain lists of books]. Incomplete

5966 **Ipswich Institute.** Catalogue of the library, 1839–1913. Incomplete

5967 **Sulley, C.** Penny readings in Ipswich and elsewhere [includes history of Ipswich Mechanics Institution, with readers, accounts, etc.]. 1861. BL. 3rd ed 1864. nl

5968 **Ipswich Working Men's College.** [Established 1864]. Classified catalogue of the library. Ipswich, 1874

5969 Laws for the regulation of the Ipswich public library, instituted 1791: with a list of the subscribers, and a catalogue of the books. MS annotations and additions. Ipswich, 1791

5970 Public library, Ancient House, Old Buttermarket, Ipswich. Catalogue 1851, 1861, 1874. Supplements 1878, 1884. Ipswich

5971 **Ipswich Corporation.** Free library, High Street: catalogue of books in reference department, 1906, compiled by Henry Ogle, librarian and clerk. Ipswich, 1906

5972 **Ipswich Corporation.** Museum and Victoria free library, Schools of science and art committee. Annual report and statement of accounts, 1888–94 [1893 missing]

5973 **Ipswich Corporation.** Museum and Victoria free library, and Science, art, and technical schools committee report ... 1895

5974 **Ipswich Corporation.** Museum, Victoria free library, and Technical instruction committee. Annual report and statement of accounts, 1897/8–1902/03

5975 **Ipswich Corporation.** Museum and free library committee. Annual report. 1903/04–1911/12. [Library report separately, 1905/06, 1906/07, 1909/10, 1911/12]

5976 **Ipswich Corporation.** Museum, art gallery, and free library committee. Free library report, 1912/13–1923/4

5977 **Ipswich Corporation.** County borough of Ipswich. Public libraries. Report of the committee, 1924/5

5978 **Ipswich Corporation.** Ipswich public library. A year's work, 1925/6–1931/2

5979 **Ipswich Corporation.** County borough of Ipswich. Public libraries. Annual report, 1932/3–1938/9; 1945/6–1963/4. [After 1964 reports as off-prints from the Council agenda]

5980 **Ipswich Corporation.** Ipswich Library Journal, nos 1–46, 1925–39

5981 Ipswich borough libraries: the wealth of the reference library. An exhibition 1–6 Jan 1951. [Typescript]

5982 **Hancock, G.** History of the Stoke branch library – opened 1908, closed 1966. Extracted from EADT. [c.1969]. MS

Public Utilities

5983 **Glyde, J.,** *Ed.* History of gas lighting in Ipswich, c.1900. MS

5984 Ipswich Gas Light Co. Hundred years of public service: an epitome of a century's progress (1821–1921). [Ipswich], [1921]

5985 **Ayton, F.** Ipswich corporation electric light and power supply: conditions under which the corporation are prepared to supply ... rules for wiring. Ipswich, 1906

5986 **Ipswich Corporation.** Electricity supply and Transport depts. Reports, 1907–47. Ipswich. Incomplete. [1945 includes general survey of the war years]

5987 **Ipswich Corporation.** Electricity supply dept. Souvenir of the opening of new showrooms at Electric House, 2 Feb 1933. Ipswich, 1933

5988 **Ipswich Corporation.** Electric supply and Transport dept. Souvenir of the construction of Cliff Quay generating station by the county borough council, June 1945–31 March 1948, when the partly-constructed station became vested in the British Electricity Authority. Ipswich, [1948]

5989 **Ipswich Corporation.** Electricity supply dept. Report and accounts, 1948. Ipswich, 1948

5990 Cliff Quay generating station, 1950. Ipswich, 1950

5991 **Markham, R.** Public transport in Ipswich, 1880–1970. Ipswich, 1970

5992 **East Anglian Daily Times.** County borough of Ipswich, its growth and progress: a souvenir [to commemorate the installation of electric tramways]. Ipswich, [1903]

5993 **Ipswich Corporation.** Transport dept: report and accounts, 1948–. Ipswich

5994 **Storey, J. B.** 1970–75: A traffic and transport plan for Ipswich. Ipswich, [1969?]

5995 **Buckham, E.** Borough of Ipswich. Report of information obtained from other towns on the opening of roads for water and gas supply. Ipswich, 1895

5996 **Oldham, C. W. S.** Whitton pumping station, Ipswich corporation waterworks 1914

5997 **Ipswich Corporation.** Water Acts, 1945 and 1948. Regrouping of the following water undertakings: Ipswich ... Felixstowe ... Stowmarket ... Woodbridge...Deben...Gipping...Samford; map, reports and recommendations, and draft order. Ipswich, 1964

5998 **Ipswich Corporation.** Water accounts, 1949–52. Water undertaking 1953–. Ipswich. Incomplete

5999 **Ipswich Corporation.** Water undertaking. Corporation water area: report on resources. By P. Hothersall, Sept 1967. Ipswich, 1967

Planning and Development   See also **1648–50**

6000 Competition for property of the borough of Ipswich. TPR 4, 1913, 62–3

6001 Ipswich garden suburb. TPR 4, 1913, 180–81

6002 **Ipswich Corporation.** Plan for Ipswich, compiled by the Housing and Town Planning committee ... 1945–6. Ipswich, 1946. [Typescript]

6003 **Communist Party** [of Ipswich]. The new Ipswich. Plan for the development of the town, with comments on the official proposals. Ipswich, [1946]. [Typescript]

6004 **Ipswich Corporation.** Town and Country Planning Act, 1947. County borough of Ipswich. Development plan: Written statement [1951]. Written analysis [1951]. Ipswich, 1951. 1954. [Typescript]

6005 Winning design and finalists of the two-stage Ipswich Civic Centre competition. Architects' Jour 129, 1959, 369–83

6006 **Ipswich Corporation.** Town and Country Planning Act, 1947. Development plan. Report of survey. Written analysis, and written statement. Ipswich, 1959. Amendment no 1. [1960]

6007 **Ipswich Corporation.** Town and Country Planning Act, 1962. Development plan. Written statement. Ipswich, [1962] Amendment no 1, [1963]

6008 **Bosman, M. A.** Ipswich to-morrow. [c.1962]

6009 **P.I.C.** [Property Investments Consolidation]. Proposals for Ipswich Greyfriars re-development. Prepared by Skipper and Corless, Norwich. Norwich, [c.1962]

6010 **Vincent, L. G.,** *and* **Gorbing, R.** County borough of Ipswich: a planning study for town development. A report to the Ministry of Housing and Local Government on the practical and financial implications of town expansion. 1964. [Typescript]

6011 **Shankland, Cox, and Associates.** Expansion of Ipswich: designation proposals, consultants' study of the town in its sub-region; a report to the Minister of Housing and Local Government. 1966

6012 **East Suffolk County Council.** Planning Dept. The Shankland–Cox report on Ipswich expansion: report by the County Planning Officer. Ipswich, 1966

6013 **East Suffolk County Council.** Planning Dept. Shankland–Cox supplementary report: report by the County Planning Officer. Ipswich, 1967

6014 **Grove, D.** Expansion of Ipswich. Town Planning Institute Jour 52, 1966, 424

6015 **Ministry of Housing and Local Government.** New Towns Act, 1965: draft Ipswich New Town (Designation) Order, explanatory memorandum. 1968. [Typescript]

6016 **Shankland, Cox, and Associates.** Ipswich draft basic plan: consultants' proposals for the expanded town: a report to the Minister of Housing and Local Government and Ipswich County Borough Council. 1968

6017 **Shankland, Cox, and Associates.** Expansion of Ipswich: comparative costs: a supplementary report to the Minister of Housing and Local Government. 1968

6018 **East Suffolk County Council.** Planning Dept. Proposed expansion of Ipswich. Report of the chairman of the County Planning Committee. Ipswich, 1968

6019 **East Suffolk County Council** *and* **Ipswich Corporation.** Planning Depts. Ipswich fringe area: interim planning statement. Ipswich, 1970

6020 **East Suffolk County Council** *and* **Ipswich Corporation.** Planning Depts. Structure plan for the Ipswich Sub-region. 15 v. Ipswich, 1973

6021 **Scole Committee.** Ipswich: the archaeological implications of development. 1973. SCL/L

Jurisdiction, Trials, and Maintenance of the Peace
    See also **1726, 2526–7, 2618**
6022 **Cross, R. L.** Justice in Ipswich, 1200–1968. Ipswich, 1968

6023 Petition for the summer assizes to be held at Ipswich. GM 1st Ser 19, 1749, 99–100

6024 General regulations for the government of the new goal [*sic*] at Ipswich, for the county of Suffolk, etc. Ipswich, [1791]. BL

6025 **Cubitt, W.** Description of the tread-mill invented by Mr William Cubitt, of Ipswich, for the employment of prisoners. 1822

6026 Ipswich borough police. East Anglia Life, 13, Jan. 1970

RELIGION AND CHURCHES
General   See also **1996, 3357, 3441**
6027 Reformers in Ipswich during Queen Mary's reign. E Ang NS 8, 1899/1900, 225

6028 Queen Elizabeth and the Ipswich clergy. E Ang NS 12, 1907/08, 34

6029 Newes from Ipswich: discovering certaine late detestable practices of some domineering Lordly Prelates, to undermine the established doctrine and discipline of our church ... by Matthew White [William Prynne]. Printed at Ipswich [on title page, but proved to have been printed in Edinburgh. 2nd edn (2 variants) and 3rd edn printed in London], 1636. STC 20469, 20469.3, 20469.7. 1641 edn by Matthew White, printed at Ipswich. Wing W 1797

6030 Absolution of Ipswich ministers, 1636. E Ang NS 12, 1907/08, 17–18

6031 **Layton, W. E.** Ecclesiastical disturbances in Ipswich during the reign of Charles I. E Ang NS 2, 1887/8, *passim.* Also bound MS copy

6032 Suppression of ecclesiastical disorders at Ipswich [1638]. E Ang NS 12, 1907/08, 46

6033 **Pollard, K. G.** Sir Stephen Glynne's Ipswich church notes, 1832 and 1844. PSIA 32, 1970/72, 71–9

6034 **Welsby, P. A.** Church and people in Victorian Ipswich. Church Quarterly Review, April–June, 1963

6035 Ipswich Envelope Series [of religious tracts]. Nos 1 and 2. [no more published]. Ipswich, [1864]. BL

6036 The Ipswich Series [of religious tracts]. 12 pts. Stirling, [1902]. BL

6037 Official programme of the sixty-second annual Church Congress, Ipswich, 1927 ... Illustrated guide to the Church Congress and Church Congress exhibition held in Ipswich 1–7 Oct 1927, with historical and descriptive notes on Ipswich and the diocese, compiled by Guy Maynard. 1927

6038 **Raven, J. J.** Some old church bells in Ipswich. PSIA 7, 1889/91, 369–71

6039 **Layard, N. F.** Some English paxes, including an example recently found in Ipswich. Arch J 61, 1904, 120–30

6040 **Gowing, R.,** *and* **Wright, H.** The Ipswich pulpit. 24 pts from Suffolk Chronicle. 1857. Ipswich

Gilds

6041 **Fitch, W. S.** Notices of the Corpus Christi Guild, Ipswich. PSIA 2, 1854/9, 151–63

Religious Houses

6042 **Layard, N. F.** Underground Ipswich [Blackfriars excavations]. EADT 28 Sept 1898

6043 **Layard, N. F.** Original researches on the sites of religious houses in Ipswich. Arch J 56, 1899, 232–8; PSIA 10, 1898/1900, 183–8

6044 **Redstone, V. B.** Carmelites of Ipswich. PSIA 10, 1898/1900, 189–95

6045 Seal of Christ Church priory. E Ang NS 1, 1885/6, 184

6046 **Wodderspoon, J.** Grey and White Friars, Ipswich. SAAP Pt 3, Nov 1848, 13–20

6047 **Grimsey, B. P.** Grey Friars monastery, Ipswich. PSIA 9, 1895/7, 373–8

6048 **Zimmerman, B.** White Friars at Ipswich. PSIA 10, 1898/1900, 196–204

6049 Priory of the Holy Trinity. Two rentals of the priory of the Holy Trinity in Ipswich ... temp Henry III and Edward I. *Ed.* by W. P. Hunt. Ipswich, 1847

6050 **Haslewood, F.** Our Lady of Ipswich. PSIA 10, 1898/1900, 53–5

6051 **Parker, J. J.** Our Lady of Ipswich. Ipswich, c.1965

6052 **Cheney, C. R.** A visitation of St. Peter's priory, Ipswich. EHR 47, 1932, 268–72

Churches   See also **2310**

6053 **'Ecclesiologist',** *pseud*. [i.e. **C. H. E. White**]. History and description of the churches of Ipswich, with some account of their antiquities: St. Margaret's, St. Helen's, St. Matthew's, St. Clement's, St. Mary-at-the-Quay. *In* Ipswich Jour 11 April 1882–18 Dec 1883

All Saints'

6054 **Caine, C.** All Saints' parish, Ipswich. A record of thirty years' work ... 1902. Ipswich, [1910]

6055 All Saints' parish magazine, 1888–

St. Andrew's

6056 St. Andrew's magazine, 1936–. *Now* St. Andrew's Church Messenger

St. Augustine's

6057 [**Evans, T. G.**] St. Augustine of Hippo, Ipswich, 1927–52: twenty-five years of Christian witness. Ipswich, [1952]

St. Bartholomew's

6058 [**Powell, C. T. G.**] Fifty years of the Catholic revival in an Ipswich parish 1895 to 1945. Ipswich, [1945]

6059 St. Bartholomew's parish magazine, 1895–

St. Clement's   See also **6053**

6060 St. Clement's parish history. SC 18.6.1936, Rp No 474

6061 Parish of St. Clement, Ipswich. Perambulation ... 14 May 1902, describing the boundary marks [ascertained and performed 7 May 1807]. Ipswich, [1902]

6062 **Birch, H. W.** Church notes: St. Clement's, Ipswich. E Ang NS 9, 1901/02, 39–41, 53–6, 68–70

6063 Church of St. Clement, Ipswich. Ramsgate, [1965]. SCL/L

6064 **Haslewood, F.** "The mock of the church"—St. Clement's, Ipswich. E Ang NS 1, 1885/6, 260

6065 Report of the committee for the restoration of the parish church of Saint Clement, Ipswich. Treasurer's account and list of donations, Dec 1860

6066 Licence to eat flesh during Lent granted to Sir Isaac Jermy, Knt., Lady Jermy, and others of St. Clement's Ipswich. E Ang NS 3, 1889/90, 67–8

6067 Extracts from the churchwardens' books of St. Clement's, Ipswich, A.D. 1594–1652. E Ang NS 3, 1889/90, 203–06, 289–91, 355–7; NS 4, 1891/2, 4–7

6068 Report of the parochial societies of St. Clement's and St. Helen's, Ipswich, for the year 1865. Ipswich, 1866

St. Edmund's

6069 **Budden, W.,** *et al.* Church of St. Edmund-a-Pountney, Ipswich. E Ang NS 1, 1885/6, 150, 168, 183–4, 203–05, 231–2, 270–71

St. Helen's See also **6053, 6270**

6070 **Birch, H. W.** Church notes: St. Helen, Ipswich. E Ang NS 9, 1901/02, 127–131

6071 **Wood, J.** Historical and other notes regarding the church and parish of St. Helen, Ipswich. [1915–c.1921] MS

6072 Church of St. Helen, Ipswich. Ramsgate, [1965]. SCL/L

6073 **Casley, H. C.** Ruinated tower in St. Helen's, Ipswich. E Ang NS 2, 1887/8, 108

St. John-the-Baptist's

6074 St. John-the-Baptist parish history. EADT 29.3.1939

6075 **Hinde, H. W.,** *et al.* St. John-the-Baptist church, Ipswich: Jubilee, 1899–1949. [Ipswich], [1949]

St. Lawrence's See also **6263**

6076 St. Lawrence parish history. EADT 26.1.1938

6077 **Grimsey, B. P.** Monograph on the parish of St. Lawrence, Ipswich. Ipswich, 1887–8

6078 [**Smith, G. V. V.**] St. Lawrence of the past. Ipswich, 1888

6079 **Birch, H. W.** Church notes: St. Lawrence, Ipswich. E Ang NS 9, 1901/02, 149–52, 166–9, 185–7

6080 **Pope, G.** Brief outline of the history of St. Lawrence church, Ipswich. Ipswich, 1932

St. Margaret's See also **2819, 2924, 3345, 6053, 6091, 6264, 6271**

6081 **White, C. H. E.** Materials for a history of St. Margaret's, Ipswich. Includes property assessments and "History and description . . . of St. Margaret . . . with an account of the priory of the Holy Trinity or Christ Church". nd. nl

6082 **Birch, H. W.** Church notes: St. Margaret's, Ipswich. E Ang NS 9, 1901/02, 187–8, 202–05, 213–16, 231–4

6083 **Batterby, T.** St. Margaret's, Ipswich. [Ipswich], [1959]

6084 **Proctor, F.,** *et al.* "The mock of the church", St. Margaret's, Ipswich. E Ang NS 1, 1885/6, 279–80

6085 **Hooper, J.,** *et al.* Inscription in St. Margaret's, Ipswich. N&Q 10th Ser 1, 1904, 368, 431–2 *See also* **2613**

6086 **White, C. H. E.** Inscription on font in St. Margaret's church, Ipswich. N&Q 6th Ser 3, 1881, 488–9

6087 **White, C. H. E.,** *and* **Fryer, A. C.** Font at St. Margaret's church, Ipswich: a description and correspondence. Antiquary 55, 1909, 7–12, 79–80

6088 St. Margaret's parish magazine, July/Dec 1938–Jan/Feb 1941

St. Mary's-at-the-Elms

6089 **Birch, H. W.** Church notes: St. Mary-at-Elms, Ipswich. E Ang NS 9, 1901/02, 253–4, 265–9

6090 **[Adams, M.]** Some notes on the church of St. Mary-at-the-Elms, Ipswich. Ipswich, 1905

6091 **Dow, L.** Ipswich churches: St. Mary Elms, St. Mary-at-Quay, St. Peter's, St. Margaret's. Arch J 108, 1951, 139–40

6092 St. Mary-at-the-Elms parish magazine. Pre 1914-. *Now* Weekly Bulletin

St. Mary's-at-the-Quay *See also* **6053, 6091**

6093 **Birch, H. W.** Church notes: St. Mary-at-Quay, Ipswich. E Ang NS 9, 1901/02, 291–2, 305–08, 314–16

6094 St. Mary-at-the-Quay, Ipswich. [Appeal by the Friends of Friendless Churches]. nd

6095 **Benton, G. M.** Flemish brass of Thomas Pownder at St. Mary Quay, Ipswich. TMBS 8, 1943/51, 347–8

6096 St. Mary Quay parish magazine, Sept 1924–

St. Mary's-at-Stoke

6097 **Grimsey, B. P.** Monograph on the parish of St. Mary Stoke, Ipswich. Rp from Ipswich Journal. Ipswich, 1885–7

6098 St. Mary-at-Stoke parish history. EADT 11.1.1939

6099 **Birch, H. W.** Church notes: St. Mary-at-Stoke, Ipswich. E Ang NS 9, 1901/02, 336–9

6100 Church of St. Mary-at-Stoke, Ipswich. [The parish of St. Mary Stoke]. [Ipswich], [1969]

6101 St. Mary Stoke parish magazine. Nov 1948–. *Now* Contact. [Incomplete]

St. Mary's-le-Tower

6102 St. Mary-le-Tower parish history. EADT 16.3.1938

6103 **Birch, H. W.** Church notes: St. Mary-at-the-Tower, Ipswich. E Ang NS 10, 1903/04, 7–10, 29–31, 38–42

6104 **Streeten, A. H.** Short history of the church of St. Mary-le-Tower, Ipswich. Gloucester, [c.1931], and later edns to 1952

6105 **Morfey, W. M.** Story of St. Mary-le-Tower church, Ipswich. Gloucester, 1963 and later edns

6106 **Layton, W. E.** "Taske Book" of St. Mary at the Tower, Ipswich, and James I. E Ang NS 1, 1885/6, 217–21

6107 St. Mary at the Tower. Extracts from the account books of the churchwardens [1604/5–1732]. 2 v. MS

6108 **Layton, W. E.** Curious extracts from the churchwardens' order and appointment book, St. Mary-le-Tower. E Ang NS 1, 1885/6, 189

6109 **S, J. H.,** *and* **Casley, H. C.** Brass in the church of St. Mary-le-Tower, Ipswich. Antiquary 8, 1883, 135, 242–3

6110 Heraldic monumental brasses, replacement of. St. Mary Tower, Ipswich. E Ang NS 8, 1899/1900, 205

St. Matthew's See also **6053, 6272–3**

6111 St. Matthew's parish history. SC 21.5.1936, Rp No 471

6112 The church and its ministrations in St. Matthew's, Ipswich. A summary of the stated services and occasional offices ... together with the various good works in which ... parishioners are associated ... Ipswich, 1861

6113 **Haslewood, F.** St. Matthew's parish, Ipswich. Miscellanea, extracted from various sources. [c.1890] MS

6114 **Haslewood, F.** St. Matthew's church, Ipswich [with Davy's notes on the church, 1824]. PSIA 7, 1889/91, 129–208

6115 **Birch, H. W.** Church notes: St. Matthew's, Ipswich. E Ang NS 9, 1901/02, 360–63, 379–82

6116 **Morfey, W. M.** St. Matthew's church, Ipswich. A short history and guide. [Ipswich], 1930

6117 Extracts from the churchwardens' books of accounts, St. Matthew's, Ipswich. A.D. 1574–1676. E Ang NS 4, 1891/2, *passim*

6118 **Haslewood, F.** Church briefs at St. Matthew's Ipswich. E Ang NS 4, 1891/2, 141–3, 174–5

6119 **Haslewood, F.** Monumental inscriptions in the parish of St. Matthew's, Ipswich. Ipswich, 1884

6120 St. Matthew's parish magazine, 1870–1952. [Incomplete]

6121 St. Matthew's parish year book, 1 Jan 1931, ... list of parish charities. [Ipswich], 1931

St. Michael's

6122 **West, A. G.** St. Michael's church. Jubilee year souvenir booklet: some interesting facts. Ipswich, 1929

St. Nicholas's See also **6265, 6274–5**

6123 **Drummond, H. P.** Church of St. Nicholas, Ipswich. SAAP Pt 3, Nov. 1848, 21–8

6124 **Grimsey, B. P.** Monograph on the parish of St. Nicholas, Ipswich. Ipswich, 1889–91

6125 **Birch, H. W.** Church notes: St. Nicholas, Ipswich. E Ang NS 10, 1903/04, 52–56, 71–3

6126 **Dufty, A. R.** St. Nicholas church, Ipswich. Arch J 108, 1951, 136–7

6127 **Glass, K.** Church and parish of St. Nicholas, Ipswich: a brief history. Ramsgate, [1965] and later edns

6128 **Galbraith, K. J.** Early sculpture at St. Nicholas church, Ipswich. PSIA 31, 1967–9, 172–84

6129 **Galbraith, K. J.** Further thoughts on the boar at St. Nicholas' church, Ipswich. PSIA 33, 1973/5, 68–74

6130 **Cookson, E.,** *Ed.* Registers of St. Nicholas, Ipswich. 1897

6131 St. Nicholas ... parish magazine, 1895–. *Now* Newsletter

St. Peter's *See also* **5890–95, 6091, 6266**

6132 **Birch, H. W.** Church notes: St. Peter's, Ipswich. E Ang NS 12, 1907/08, 115–19

6133 [**B, A. W.**] Saint Peter's church and Wolsey's gate, Ipswich. [Ipswich], [1927]. [c.1938]

6134 Briefs—St. Peter's parish, Ipswich, 1666–1706. E Ang NS 1, 1885/6, 144–6

6135 Old printed papers in parish chest at St. Peter's church, Ipswich. E Ang NS 1, 1885/6, 298–302

6136 St. Peter's parish magazine. Extant 1889–94

St. Stephen's *See also* **6267**

6137 **Birch, H. W.** Church notes: St. Stephen's, Ipswich. E Ang NS 12, 1907/08, 129–34

6138 Notes on St. Stephen's church, Ipswich, collected by Henry Cade when churchwarden in 1913–14. MS, also some copies of parish magazine, 1914–16

6139 **Birch, H. W.,** *and* **Casley, H. C.** Correspondence on the discovery of a niche at St. Stephen's church, Ipswich. Antiquary 5, 1882, 231; 9, 1884, 94–5

6140 Extracts from the earliest books of churchwardens' accounts, etc., St. Stephen's, Ipswich. E Ang NS 1, 1885/6, 175–9

Roman Catholicism

6141 St. Pancras Catholic church, Ipswich, 1861–1961. Centenary souvenir and guide. Ipswich, 1961

Nonconformity
General

6142 Observations relating to pastoral authority occasioned by some recent proceedings among Methodists and Dissenters of Ipswich. Ipswich, 1836

6143 Free Churchman. Organ of the Ipswich and Sudbury and Districts Free Church Councils. Jan 1939–June 1940. Ipswich

Individual Congregations

6144 **Garrard, A. E.** History of "Bethesda" [With sermon preached by the Rev. H. J. Galley]. Ipswich, [1924]

6145 **Smith, F. G.** The Bethesda story: a history of Bethesda Baptist church, Ipswich, 1829–1963. Ipswich, 1963

6146 **Everett, S. J.** History of the Baptist church at Stoke Green, Ipswich, compiled from authentic sources. Ipswich, 1871. NCL/N

6147 Introducing Stoke Green Baptist church, Maidenhall, 1757–1957. A guide to 200 years of witness. [Ipswich], [1957]. [Typescript]

6148 [**Smith, R. A.,** *Ed.*] 1842–1942. The centenary historical record of Turret Green Baptist church, Ipswich, and preliminary programme of commemoration gatherings, 25–27 Oct 1942. Ipswich

6149 [Rees-Tyrer, S.] These hundred years! The story of California chapel, 1854–1954 [St. John's Congregational church]. Ipswich, 1954

6150 Manual of Tacket Street Congregational church, Ipswich, 1900 . . . founded 12 Oct 1686. Ipswich, 1900. *See also* **6276**

6151 **Ritson, T. N.,** *Ed.* Story of a century: history of Wesleyan Methodism in the Ipswich circuit. [c.1908]

6152 [**Warren, W. D.**]. Museum Street Methodist church, Ipswich: A century of witness and service, 1861–1961. Felixstowe, [1961]

6153 **Ipswich Sunday School Union.** 73rd annual report, as presented at Museum Street Wesleyan church, on Thursday, 11 April 1929. [Draft copy]. Ipswich, 1929

6154 **Presbyterian Church of England, Ipswich.** [Activities, 1885]. [Ipswich], 1885

6155 **Godfrey, W. H.** Unitarian chapel, Ipswich. Arch J 108, 1951, 137–8. *See also* **1989**

6156 **Hewett, A. P.** Story of an old meeting house. A short history of St. Nicholas old meeting house, now called the Unitarian meeting house, Friars Street, Ipswich. Ipswich, 1956. 2nd edn 1959

6157 **Pert, K. G.** Reflections on an old meeting house. Ipswich, 1976

Judaism

6158 **Davis, M. D.** Medieval Jews of Ipswich. E Ang NS 3, 1889/90, 89–93, 105–106, 123–7

6159 **Abrahams, B. L.** Condition of the Jews of England at the time of their expulsion in 1290. Appendix relating to the Jews of . . . Ipswich . . . Jewish Historical Society of England. Transactions, Session 2, 1894/5, 85–105

6160 **Gollancz, H.** A ramble in East Anglia. Appendix 1. Endorsements to title deeds of the Ipswich Jewish cemetery in 1764. 2. Texts of indentures. 3. Jewish cemetery at St. Clement's, Ipswich. Jewish Historical Society of England. Transactions, Session 2, 1894/5, 106–140

CULTURE AND RECREATION *See also* **2953–4**
Theatres

6161 Bishop Bale's "Kynge John" at Ipswich. E Ang NS 1, 1885/6, 197–8, 245

6162 **Eyre, H. R.** *Ed.* Drama and theatres in Ipswich from the year 1296 to 1890. 7 v. MS. [c.1890]

6163 **Chambers, E. K.** Players at Ipswich [accounts from the borough archives, 1553–4 to 1624–5]. Malone Society's Collections 2, pt 3, 1931

6164 **Lingwood, H. R.** Ipswich playhouses. Chapters of local theatrical history. Ipswich, 1936. Rp from EADT

6165 **Eyre, H. R.** *Ed.* Things theatrical in Ipswich. 1895. MS

6166 Theatre, Ipswich. Playbills, prints, portraits, etc., 1797–1832. [A collection with notes by W. H. Booth]

6167 **Bellamy, B. P.** Letter to the dramatic censor of the Suffolk Chronicle. Ipswich, [1813]. BL

6168 Playbills of the Theatre Royal, 1833–8, 1859–90. 8 v

6169   **Eyre, H. R.** *Ed.* Interesting matter relating to the scenery, decoration, etc., of the Theatre Royal, Tacket Street, Ipswich. [c.1895]. MS

6170   **Rosenfeld, S.[W]** An Ipswich theatre book. A study of Eyre's Interesting matter relating to ... the Theatre Royal. Theatre Notebook 13, 4, Summer, 1959

6171   Lyceum Theatre, Ipswich. Playbills, 1934–Oct 1935

6172   Ipswich Arts Theatre. Cuttings, programmes, etc.

6173   Ipswich Arts Theatre. Index of plays produced ... from 1947–. MS

6174   Ipswich Arts Theatre Guild. Proscenium, v 1, no 1, Dec 1950–v. 3, no 4, 1954. [Quarterly]

Pageants and Celebrations

6175   **Ipswich Corporation.** Proclamation of King Edward VII. An account of the ceremony at Ipswich 25 Jan 1901. William F. Paul, Mayor. [1901]. 97 copies

6176   **Ipswich Corporation.** Coronation of Edward VII. Official souvenir programme of public rejoicings at Ipswich, Aug 1902. Ipswich, 1902

6177   **Ipswich Corporation.** Coronation of King George V. Official souvenir programme of public rejoicings at Ipswich, June 1911. Ipswich, 1911

6178   **Ipswich Corporation.** Peace celebrations. Official programme of public rejoicings at Ipswich, 19 July 1919. Ipswich, 1919

6179   Wolsey pageant, Ipswich, 23–28 June 1930. Souvenir programme. Also cuttings. 4 v

6180   Ipswich Blind Society. Tudor pageant "To kill the Queen" by L. R. McColvin, 17–20 June 1931. [Press cuttings 11.3.1931–29.6.1931]

6181   Ipswich High School. Historical pageant of Ipswich, 25–26 June 1935

6182   **Ipswich Corporation.** Ipswich coronation celebrations [George VI]. Official programme. Ipswich, [1937]

6183   **Ipswich Corporation.** Programme of the Victory Celebrations, Saturday, 8 June 1946

6184   Ipswich pageant, 9–16 June 1951. Programme and cuttings

Concerts

6185   **Ipswich Chamber Music Society.** Concert programmes. 1926/7–1933/4. Incomplete

6186   **Ipswich Corporation.** Library Committee. Programmes of organ recitals. 1st Ser 1927/8—4th Ser 1930/1

6187   **Ipswich Corporation.** Library Committee. Ipswich municipal concerts. Programmes. 6th Ser 1927/8–10th Ser 1932/3. 2 v

Races

6188   **Glyde, J.,** *Ed.* Materials for a history of Ipswich Races from 1751. Cuttings, posters, etc. [c.1900]

6189   Handbills of Ipswich Races, 1805–55, and one relating to the Essex and Suffolk Hunt Steeplechases, 1861

Associations

6190 **Pye, J. T.** History of the British Legion Club, Ltd., Old Manor House, Ipswich. 1918–1940. [Typescript]

6191 **Ipswich Conservative Party.** The Ipswich Elector, May 1937. Contact [Bimonthly], 1955–60. [all published—incomplete]

6192 **Ipswich Fine Art Club.** Exhibition catalogues: 1875–97 (bound volume), 1898–1969. Incomplete. [After 1924 renamed Ipswich Art Club]

6193 **Ipswich Art Club.** Centenary exhibition of the Ipswich Art Club: catalogue of paintings, drawings, and sculptures representing 100 years of the Art Club's work, 1874–1974. Ipswich, 1975

6194 **Girls' Friendly Society.** G.F.S. records, 1893–1925. Scrapbook

6195 **Institution of Mechanical Engineers.** Ipswich meeting, 1926. Proceedings no 4, 1926. Ipswich summer meeting, June 1926

6196 Forward: the Ipswich Labour Monthly, Oct 1938–Sept 1939

6197 Report of the committee of the Ipswich Ladies' Bible Association, with an address to the collectors, drawn up . . . by . . . J. T. N[ottidge] Ipswich, [1827]. BL

6198 Ipswich Liberal, July and August 1925

6199 **Ipswich Literary Society.** Minutes and procedure of meetings, 1896–1915. 3 v. MSS

6200 Ipswich Parliament. Names of members and constituencies represented, Oct. 1910

6201 **Ipswich Philosophical Society.** Laws, regulations, and catalogue of the library, March 1852

6202 **Rotary Club of Ipswich.** Rotula, Jan 1929–Dec 1934 (monthly). [Rotaria, from Jan–Sept 1929]

6203 **Rampling, A. R.** History of the Ipswich and district Provincial Grand Lodge, Royal Antediluvian Order of Buffaloes, Grand Lodge of England. Ipswich, [c.1956]. [Typescript]

6204 Ipswich Science Gossip Society, 1873. Rules and by-laws and list of members. [founded 1869]

6205 **Ipswich Scientific Film Society.** Journal and proceedings, Dec 1946

6206 **Ipswich Scientific Society.** Handbook, 1910

6207 **Working Men's College,** Ipswich. Thirty-second annual report . . . 28 Nov 1894. Ipswich, 1895

6208 What's on, Ipswich. v 1, no 1, July 1960–v 8, no 8, 1968. Penge

Coffee Houses

6209 **Jones, A. G. E.** Coffee houses and Ipswich. N&Q 197, 1952, 246–9, 322–3; 198, 1953, 440

6210 **Cardew-Rendle, H. C.** Coffee houses and Ipswich. N&Q 198, 1953, 406–07

6211 **Jones, A. G. E.** Early coffee houses in Ipswich. SR 2, 1961, 126–30

Freemasonry   See also **2182**

6212   Serious address to the members of the House of Commons, and gentlemen residing in the counties of Suffolk, Norfolk, and Essex [concerning the Samaritan Club, accused of running the town of Ipswich]. 1790

6213   **Brookhouse, J. C.** Good Samaritans or Ark Masons in politics [Ipswich parliamentary election, 1790]. Ars Quatuor Coronatorum 24, 1911, 81–106

6214   **Davies, R. O.** History of Prudence Preceptory, No 16, Ipswich, 1810–1912 … [Appendix—History of Royal Plantagenet Preceptory, No 80, Ipswich, 1864 until moved to Great Yarmouth in 1888]. Colchester, 1914

6215   **Williment, G. J.** Lodge of Perfect Friendship, No 376, Ipswich. Centenary address and history.. Ipswich, 1924

6216   **Sadd, A. H.,** *and* **Martin, L. J.** Minute books of British Union Lodge, No 114, Ipswich. Pt 1, 1762 to 1874. Ipswich, 1932

6217   **Pierce, J. E.** Ipswich Lodges and their homes of recent times. SIMT, No 3913, 1936

6218   **Bloomfield, S. T.** History of Corinthian Lodge, No 3093, Ipswich, 1905–55. Ipswich, 1955

6219   **Watson, S. F.** History of British Union Lodge, No 114, Ipswich, 1762–1962. Ipswich, 1962

6220   **Clarke, J. C.** History of Lodge Prince of Wales, No 959, Ipswich, 1863–1963. [Ipswich], 1963

6221   **Watson, S. F.** History of Victoria Chapter of S. P. Rose Croix of H.R.D.M., No 22, Ipswich, 1867–1967. Ipswich, 1967

6222   **Cousins, J. C.** History of Gippeswyk Lodge, No 4254, Ipswich, 1921–71. [Ipswich], 1971

6223   **Skippen, R. B.** History of St. Luke's Royal Arch Chapter, No 225, Ipswich, 1821–1972. Ipswich, 1972

BUILDINGS AND TOPOGRAPHY   *See also* **6021**
Buildings   For Christchurch Mansion, *see* **5948–55**

6224   **Corder, J. S.** Timber-framed buildings of Ipswich and their pargetting. PSIA 7, 1889/91, 371–7

6225   **Corder, J. S.** Ye olde corner postes of Ipswiche: with illustrations in photo-lithography from original sketches. Ipswich, 1890

6226   **Roe, F.** Some historic Ipswich woodwork. Conn 91, 1933, 20–27

6227   Ancient buildings and the Museum committee. An example from Ipswich. MJ 39, 1939, 57–60

6228   **Ipswich Corporation.** Museum Committee [Memorandum on the remaining ancient buildings in Ipswich, which it is desirable to preserve]. 1945

6229   Town and Country Planning Act, 1944, section 42. Provisional list of buildings of architectural or historic interest for consideration … Ipswich, 1946. [Typescript]

6230   Town and Country Planning Act, 1947, section 30. Buildings of special architectural or historic interest. Ipswich, 1951. [Typescript]

6231 **McDowell, R. W.** Domestic architecture of Ipswich. Arch J 108, 1951, 142–8

6232 **Woolnough, F.** Ye Ancient House att Ipswich. Ipswich, 1905 and later edns to 1957

6233 **Redstone, V. B.** The Ancient House, or Sparrowe House, Ipswich. Ipswich, 1912. *See also* **3333**

6234 The Ancient House, Ipswich. Ipswich, 1957. *See also* **5970**

6235 **Grimsey, B. P.** Lord Curson's House: the Bishop's Palace, Ipswich. PSIA 7, 1889/91, 255–6, 381–2

6236 Episcopal Palace at Ipswich. E Ang NS 7, 1897/8, 239

6237 The Chantry, Ipswich, 1509–1972. Ipswich, 1973

6238 **G[lyde], J.** Old Custom House, Ipswich. E Ang NS 1, 1885/6, 123, 135

6239 **Haslewood, F.** Elizabeth House, Upper Brook St., Ipswich. PSIA 7, 1889/91, 366–7

6240 **Phipson, R. M.** Sparrowe's House, Ipswich. PSIA 2, 1854/9, 164–7

6241 **Cross, R. L.** The living past – a Victorian heritage: the origins, building, use and renewal of the Town Hall and Corn Exchange, Cornhill, Ipswich. Ipswich, 1975

Inns

6242 **White, C. H. E.** Old inns and taverns of Ipswich, their memories and associations. PSIA 6, 1883/8, 136–83. Grangerized copy

6243 Great White Horse at Ipswich. Tales of old inns, no 11. nd

Districts, Walls, Streets and Street Names

6244 Hieroglyphical list of inhabitants in Tavern, Westgate, and St. Matthew's streets, Ipswich. Ipswich. 1st sheet, 1 Jan 1846. nl

6245 Borough of Ipswich: names of streets, lanes, courts, etc. Revised and corrected up to Jan 1875. Ipswich, [1875]

6246 **Vertue, F. H.,** *et al.* Ipswich localities. E Ang NS 1, 1885/6, 196, 215–16, 232, 248, 263; NS 2, 1887/8, 169

6247 **Ford, J. C.,** *et al.* "Hog Lane" as a place name in Ipswich and Bury. E Ang NS 2, 1887/8, 388

6248 **G[lyde], J.,** *and* **Casley, H. C.** The North Gate, Ipswich. E Ang NS 1, 1885/6, 79, 111–12

6249 Pykenham House, Northgate, Ipswich. [16 photographs c.1912]

6250 **McDowell, R. W.** Pykenham's Gateway, Ipswich. Arch J 108, 1951, 140–41

6251 **Owles, E. [J.]** The West gate of Ipswich. PSIA 32, 1970/72, 164–7

Bridges and Crosses

6252 **G[lyde], J.** St. Peter's bridge, Ipswich. E Ang NS 1, 1885/6, 77

6253 **White, G. H. E.** The 'Stoneing Cross' of Dowsing's Journal. An inquiry into the meaning and application of the term, with some remarks on the ancient stone crosses of Ipswich. PSIA 6, 1883/8, 1–8, 88–93

6254   Casley, H. C. The 'Stoney Cross' at Ipswich. E Ang NS 1, 1885/6, 330–33

6255   Manning, C. R. Old Ipswich town cross. E Ang NS 1, 1885/6, 364–5

Open Spaces

6256   Coyte, W. B. Hortus Botanicus Gippovicensis; or, A systematical enumeration of the plants cultivated in Dr. Coyte's Botanic Garden at Ipswich ... to which is added an investigation of the natural produce of some grass-lands in High Suffolk. Ipswich, 1796

6257   Wilton, H. E. Coyte's gardens, Ipswich. SR 1, 1958, 201–03

6258   St. Margaret's Green, Ipswich ... based on research by D. Charman. Ipswich, 1963

Natural Environment

6259   Clarke, W. B. Sketch of the flora of the neighbourhood of Ipswich. Magazine of Natural History, NS 1840

6260   **Ipswich and District Field Club.** Journal, v 1, 1908–v 6, 1921. [all published]

6261   **Ipswich and District Natural History Society.** Journal, v 1, pts 1–4, 1925, 1930, 1932, 1935 [all published]. Programmes, 1924–70, [incomplete]. Ipswich

REGISTERS, WILLS   *See also* **2409–10, 2416–17, 2421, 2429, 2481, 2483, 3233, 3241**

6262   Marriage and obituary notices extracted from the Ipswich Magazine, Feb 1799–Feb 1800. [*Ed.* by F. A. Crisp]. 1888

6263   Transcript of the parish registers of St. Lawrence, Ipswich, 1539–1812. nd. [Typescript]

6264   Early register books of St. Margaret's, Ipswich. E Ang NS 10, 1903/04, 147–51, 173–9, 190–3, 201–04

6265   Registers of St. Nicholas, Ipswich, co. Suffolk. Baptisms, 1539–1709. Burials, 1551–1710. Marriages, 1539–1710. *Ed.* by E. Cookson. 1897

6266   Parish registers of St. Peter's, Ipswich [Baptism, 1657–1700; burials, 1658–1700; marriages, 1662–1702]. [*Ed.* by F. A. Crisp]. 1897. 50 copies

6267   Extracts from the register books of St. Stephen's, Ipswich. E Ang NS 2, 1887/8, 290–92

INSCRIPTIONS   *See also* **2433**. For Ipswich genealogies, not cross-referenced here, *see* Individual and Family Biography, *above*

6268   **Baldrey, R.** Sepulchral memorials of Ipswich. 1824. MS.

6269   **Haslewood, F.,** *Ed.* Inscriptions on the monuments and other memorials in the cemetery, Ipswich. 24 v. Index. 3 v. 1883. MSS

6270   **Wollaston, D. O.** Inscriptions on the monuments and tombs in St. Helen's church and yard, Ipswich. [Ipswich?], 1882. Lithographed MSS

6271   **Wollaston, D. O.** Inscriptions on the monuments and tombs in St. Margaret's church and yard, Ipswich. [Ipswich?], 1881. Lithographed MSS

6272   **Wollaston, D. O.** Inscriptions on the monuments and tombs in St. Matthew's church and yard, Ipswich. [Ipswich?], [1883]. Lithographed MSS

6273   Monumental inscriptions in the parish church of Saint Matthew's Ipswich ... *Ed.* by ... F. H[aslewood]. Ipswich, 1884. Grangerized edn

6274   **Wollaston, D. O.** Inscriptions on the monuments and tombs in St. Nicholas church and yard, Ipswich. [Ipswich?], 1882. Lithographed MSS

6275   **Okasha, E.** Some lost Anglo-Saxon inscriptions from St. Nicholas church, Ipswich. PSIA 32, 1970/72, 80–84

6276   Account of the graves in the burying-ground belonging to the Meeting House in Tacket Street. According to a plan of the ground, first taken in 1756, by W. B. Filled up and numbered in 1802, by Chas. Atkinson. [MS additions to 1853]. *In* Crisp's Frag Gen v 13

IXWORTH   *See also* **654**

6277   Ixworth parish history. SC 27.9.1929, Rp No 143

6278   **Warren, J.** Antiquities found at Ixworth. PSIA 1, 1848/53, 74–8

6279   Ornamental metal disc found at Ixworth. Reliquary NS 13, 1907, 133–4

6280   **Warren, J.** Saxon gold buckle found in Suffolk [?near Ixworth]. PSA 2, 1849/53, 216

6281   **Warren, J.** Bronze fibula, Ixworth [Anglo-Saxon?]. PSIA 2, 1854/59, 275

6282   **Warren, J.** Saxon remains found near Ixworth. PSIA 3, 1860/63, 296–8

6283   **Warren, J.** Roman road near Ixworth ... PSIA 2, 1854/59, 221

6284   Housing of the Working Classes Act, 1890. Reports of Lord Francis Hervey, M.P., and Col. Frederic Pocklington, upon inquiries held by them on 15 June 1891, and 9 Oct 1891, respectively, as to the housing of the working classes in the parish of Ixworth. Ipswich, [1891]. BL

6285   **Ixworth Secondary School.** Mosaic [school magazine], 1958–66

6286   **Tymms, S.** Ixworth church notes. PSIA 1, 1848/53, 98–102

6287   **Cartwright, R. N.** Remains of Ixworth priory. PSIA 1, 1848/53, 87–8

6288   **Rowe, J.** Ixworth abbey, Bury St. Edmunds, Suffolk: a short history and a simple guide. Bury St. Edmunds, 1964. SRO/B

6289   **Duncan, J.** Ixworth Methodist chapel. 1964. [Typescript.]. SRO/B

6290   Pageant of Ixworth abbey, Bury St. Edmunds, 16–17 June 1921. [Text of pageant and photographic record]. O

6291   **Colman, S.** A Wealden house at Ixworth. PSIA 29, 1961/3, 336–41

6292   **Tymms, S.** Wills and extracts from wills relating to Ixworth and Ixworth Thorpe. PSIA 1, 1848/53, 103–120

IXWORTH THORPE

6293   Ixworth Thorpe parish history. EADT 29.4.1936, Rp No 435

KEDINGTON   *See also* **2498–503, 3322–3**

6294   Kedington parish history. SC 4.11.1927, Rp No 44

6295 Fell, C. I., *et al.* Amphora from Kedington. PCAS 42, 1948/9, 129

6296 Kedington: a short account of the church. 1914. SRO/B

6297 **Turnbull, W. H.** Church of SS. Peter and Paul, Kedington. nd

6298 **Turnbull, W. H.** St. Peter and Paul, Kedington: a notable church in East Anglia. JBAA NS 36, 1930, 291–317

6299 Church of SS. Peter and Paul, Kedington. *By* W. H. Turnbull. 1930. 1934. 1950. Rev. edn., Ketton through the centuries: an account of the architecture and history of the church ... by W. H. Turnbull, 1961. Another edn. by P. M. Harbottle, Ipswich 1963

6300 Barnardiston vault. Letters and photographs relating to the Barnardiston vault at Kedington church. 1905. SRO/B

6301 Barnardiston vaults in Kedington church. PSIA 16, 1916/18, 44–8

6302 **Hill, H. C.** Kedington cross. PSIA 20, 1928/30, 287–9

KELSALE-CUM-CARLTON

6303 Kelsale-cum-Carlton parish history. 2 pts. SC 11.4.1930, 18.4.1930, Rp Nos 171, 172

6304 **Gooding, J.** Small bronze head found at Kelsale. PSA 2, 1849/53, 101

6305 **Gooding, J.** Musquetoon found at Kelsale. PSA 2, 1849/53, 144

6306 **Partridge, C.** Kelsale deed of 1549. E Ang NS 10, 1903/04, 216–220

6307 **Cullum, G. G. M. G.** Kelsale church notes. E Ang NS 4, 1891/2, 247–50

6308 **Irving-Davies, G.** Kelsale church. PSIA 8, 1892/4, 36–7

6309 **Holland, C. G.** Kelsale guildhall. PSIA 30, 1964/6, 129/48

6310 Parish registers of Kelsale, Suffolk. [*Ed.* by F. A. Crisp]. 1887. 50 copies

6311 Parish registers of Carlton, Suffolk. [*Ed.* by F. A. Crisp]. 1886. 50 copies

KENTFORD

6312 Kentford parish history. EADT 13.6.1934, Rp No 357

6313 **Lord, J. W.** St. Mary's, Kentford. 1932

6314 **Evans, I. H. N.** The 'Boy's grave', near Kentford. GLSJ 3rd Ser 33, 1954, 156–8

KENTON   *See also* **3187**

6315 Kenton parish history. EADT 27.9.1933, Rp No 326

KERSEY   *See also* **3303**

6316 Kersey: the priory and the church. PSIA 11, 1901/03, 216–19

6317 Kersey parish history. SC 23.12.1927, Rp No 51

6318 Priory of Austin Canons at Kersey. SAAP Pt 1, Oct 1846, 1–8

6319 Pocket guide to St. Mary's church, Kersey. Hadleigh, 1948 and later edns

KESGRAVE

6320   Kesgrave parish history. EADT 24.3.1937, 26.3.1937, Rp No 466

6321   Origin of the name Kesgrave. E Ang 1, 1858/63, 6, 14

6322   Official guide. 1969 and later edns

6323   **Lummis, W. M.** Parish of Kesgrave and All Saints parish church: extracts from Davy's Suffolk collections, v 10. MS

6324   **Lummis, W. M.** Short guide to church and parish, Kesgrave. Ipswich, 1937

6325   All Saints'. The church magazine, later the parish magazine, Jan 1928–

KESSINGLAND

6326   **Caine, E.** Kessingland ... brief facts for the use of visitors. [1910]. NCL/N

6327   **Dutt, W. A.** Guide to Kessingland. Kessingland, [1911]. SCL/L

6328   **Cherry, P.** Kessingland and its characters. [Lowestoft], 1971. SCL/L

6329   Kessingland parish history. SC 19.9.1930, Rp No 194

6330   **East Suffolk County Council.** Planning Dept. Kessingland village and coast: policy statement and planning proposals. Ipswich. Draft, 1970. Final proposals, 1971

6331   **Chitty, C.** Story of St. Edmund's parish church and the village of Kessingland. v 1—Edward VI. 1951. [Typescript]

6332   Parish church of St. Edmund, Kessingland: a short history of the church and parish. Ramsgate, 1966. 1970. NCL/N

6333   **Chitty, C.** Kessingland and Walberswick church towers. PSIA 25, 1949/51, 164–71

6334   Kessingland festival week: souvenir brochure, 23–29 June 1968. Kessingland, 1968. SCL/L

KETTLEBASTON

6335   Kettlebaston parish history. SC 23.10.1931, Rp No 249

6336   **Hart, W. H.** Rent-roll of the manor of Kettlebaston, 1 Edw. IV. PSA 2nd Ser. 1, 1859/61, 99

6337   **Taylor, M. R.** Kettlebaston alabasters. PSIA 30. 1964/6, 252–4

6338   **Butler, H. C.** Kettlebaston alabasters. PSIA 32, 1970/72, 202

6339   **Beck, J.** Latten roundel of arms found at Kettlebaston. PSA 2nd Ser 12, 1887/9, 415

KETTLEBURGH   *See also* **2458**

6340   Kettleburgh parish history. SC 3.7.1931, Rp No 235

6341   **O'Connor, B.** Two groups of prehistoric pottery from Kettleburgh. PSIA 33, 1973/5, 231–40

6342   [Order of assessment, made by the Directors of the Poor for the Hundreds of Loes and Wilford, in the parish of K.]. Woodbridge, [1831]. BL

6343 Kettleburgh Penny Clothing Club, 1837 ... Rules. Framlingham, [1837]. BL
6344 **Welford, A.** Kettleburgh parish church. PSIA 26, 1952/4, 59–60
6345 **Fawcett, J. R. L. R.** St. Andrew's, Kettleburgh. nd
6346 **Bond, T.** Kettleburgh font. E Ang NS 3, 1889/90, 173–5; NS 4, 1891/2, 169

KIRKLEY *See* Lowestoft

KIRTON

6347 Kirton parish history. SC 7.3.1930, Rp No 166
6348 **Birch, H. W.** Church notes: Kirton. E Ang NS 13, 1909/10, 349–50
6349 Kirton parish church. [c.1960]. nl

KNETTISHALL

6350 Knettishall parish history. EADT 8.5.1935, Rp No 396

KNODISHALL-CUM-BUXLOE *See also* **3077**

6351 Knodishall-cum-Buxloe parish history. EADT 4.10.1933, Rp No 327
6352 **Nichols, I.** 60 years in Suffolk ... 1943. [Typescript]
6353 **Watson, J. A.** Brief notes on St. Lawrence church, Knodishall. Leiston, 1948
6354 Register of the parish church of Knodishall, co. Suffolk, 1566–1705. *Ed.* by A. T. Winn. 1909

LACKFORD *See also* **1475–6, 2406, 2929**

6355 Lackford parish history. SC 25.12.1931, Rp No 256
6356 **Barker, H. R.** Anglo-Saxon urns found near Lackford. PSIA 16, 1916/18, 181–2
6357 **Lethbridge, T. C.** Cemetery at Lackford, Suffolk: report of the excavation of a cemetery of the pagan Anglo-Saxon period in 1947. Cambridge Antiquarian Soc Quarto Publ NS 6. Cambridge, 1951

LAKENHEATH *See also* **1119, 1725, 1764, 3268,** *and* Undley, *below*

6358 Lakenheath parish history. SC 14.6.1929, Rp No 128
6359 **Briscoe, G.,** *Ed.* History of Lakenheath, Suffolk. Compiled by members of the W.I. Lakenheath, 1951. NCL/N
6360 Skull and ancient pottery found at Lakenheath. JBAA NS 27, 1921, 227
6361 **Briscoe, G.** Face-urn from Lakenheath. PSIA 27, 1955/7, 176–7
6362 **Briscoe, G.** Combined Beaker and Iron Age sites at Lakenheath. PCAS 42, 1948/9, 92–111
6363 **Briscoe, G.** Giant Beaker and rusticated ware from Lakenheath, and reproduction of ornament. PCAS 53, 1959/60, 1–7

6364 Gell, A. S. R. Early Iron Age site at Lakenheath. PCAS 42, 1948/9, 112–16

6365 Crompton, G., *and* Taylor, C. C. Earthwork enclosures on Lakenheath Warren, West Suffolk. PSIA 32, 1970/72, 113–20

6366 Allen, J. R. An S-shaped fibula of late-Celtic design from Lakenheath. Reliquary NS 13, 1907, 62–3

6367 Newton, W. F. Bronze socketed celt with loop found near Lakenheath. PSA 2nd Ser 1, 1859/61, 105–06

6368 Briscoe, G. Roman site at Lakenheath. PCAS 41, 1943/7, 67–70

6369 Fell, C. I., *and* Briscoe, G. Recently discovered Romano-British site near Lakenheath. PCAS 45, 1951/2, 66–8

6370 Briscoe, G. Romano-British settlement at Lakenheath. PSIA 26, 1952/4, 69–84

6371 Briscoe, T. Anglo-Saxon S-shaped brooch in England, with special reference to one from Lakenheath. PCAS 61, 1968, 45–54

6372 Munday, J. T. Lakenheath records, 1–8. Lakenheath, 1969–72. [Typescript]. NCL/N

6373 Munday, J. T. Lakenheath Manor of Clare Fee, 1086–1331. Lakenheath, 1970

6374 Munday, J. T. Two Suffolk parishes in the Middle Ages now partly covered by Lakenheath Airbase. Lakenheath, 1973. SRO/B

6375 Briscoe, G., *et al.* Icenian coin hoard from Lakenheath. BNJ 29, 1959/60, 215–19

6376 Munday, J. T. The economy of old Lakenheath. Lakenheath, 1969 [Typescript]

6377 Short description of, and guide to, St. Mary's church, Lakenheath. Cambridge, [1951]. O

6378 Munday, J. T. St. Mary's, Lakenheath. Ramsgate, 1971. nl

6379 Partridge, C. Lord Kitchener's ancestors in Lakenheath churchyard. E Ang NS 10, 1903/04, 14–15

6380 Parish magazine, c.1933–, *now* Parish church news, from 1970–

6381 Duncan, J. Early Methodist history in Lakenheath and around. 1967. [Typescript]. SRO/B

LANGHAM

6382 Langham parish history. EADT 11.10. 1933, Rp No 328

LAVENHAM

GUIDES

6383 Scott, T. Visitor's guide to Lavenham and its church. Bury St. Edmunds, 1897. 1903

6384 Official guide. 2nd edn [c.1950] and later edns

6385 **Lenox-Conyngham, G. H.** Lavenham church and town. Sudbury, [1927]. 1929 and later edns

6386 **Whitehead, L. H. H.** Lavenham: its antiquities. Lavenham, [1927]. SCL/L

6387 **Ranson, F. L.,** *and* **Whitehead, L. H. H.** Lavenham, past and present. Lavenham, [1931]

6388 **Ranson, F. L.** Lavenham. Ipswich, 1937 and later edns

6389 **Thompson, H. D.** A night in Lavenham. 1947. nl

GENERAL AND ECONOMIC HISTORY *See also* **3208, 3337, 3380**

6390 Lavenham parish history. SC 15.7.1927, Rp No 29

6391 **[Teasdel, R. H.]** History and antiquities of Lavenham and Long Melford. NNA(GY) 1932, 20–23. NCL/N

6392 **Deacon, G.** Lavenham deed, 1591. PSIA 2, 1854/9, 212

6393 **Deacon, G.** Silver penny of Cuthred, Lavenham. PSIA 2, 1854/9, 211

6394 **Babington, C.** Account of Roman silver coins found at Lavenham, in June 1874. PSIA 4, 1864/74, 414–16; NC NS 15, 1875, 140–43

LOCAL GOVERNMENT AND SOCIAL SERVICES

6395 **McKeon, H.** Inquiry into the principal charities left to the poor in the parish of Lavenham ... Being part the first of a history of that ancient town, in preparation. 1826

6396 **McKeon, H.** Inquiry into the rights of the poor, of the parish of Lavenham, in Suffolk ... to which are added, biographical sketches of ... H. Steward, ... R. Ryece ... W. Gurnall, etc. 1829

6397 **Insall, D. W.** Lavenham: past—present—future. [Report prepared] for the County of West Suffolk and the Rural District of Cosford. Bury St. Edmunds, 1961. [1964]

6398 **West Suffolk County Council.** Planning Dept. Lavenham: buildings of architectural and historic interest. Bury St. Edmunds, 1961

6399 **West Suffolk County Council.** Planning Dept. Lavenham: conservation and village plan. Bury St. Edmunds, 1972

CHURCH OF SS. PETER AND PAUL *See also* **2966–8**

6400 **[Ribbans, R.,** *Ed.*]. Lavenham church, a poem. Ipswich, 1822

6401 **Dewing, E. M.** Lavenham church and parish. PSIA 6, 1883/8, 105–30, 225–35

6402 **Caroe, W. D.** Lavenham: the church and its builders. 1910. SRO/B

6403 **Howard, F. E.** Lavenham parish church, Suffolk. Report on the condition of the roofs and other woodwork. 1925

6404 **L, H.,** *and* **W, H.** Notes on the restorations at Lavenham. PSIA 15, 1913/15, 82–3

6405 Saving Lavenham church. Rp from EADT 11 July 1930

6406 **Page, M. F.** Church of SS. Peter and Paul, Lavenham. Gloucester, 1952 and later edns

6407   Specimens of Gothic ornaments selected from the parish church of Lavenham in Suffolk, on forty plates. [By Isaac Taylor]. 1796

6408   **Malden, H. C.** Lavenham church tower. PSIA 9, 1895/7, 370–72

6409   **Cooper, G. A. D.** Bells of the church of St. Peter and St. Paul, Lavenham. Lavenham, 1965. SRO/B

6410   Monumental brasses to the infant son of Sir Simonds D'Ewes in Lavenham church. E Ang NS 8, 1899/1900, 49–50

6411   **Benton, G. M.** Notes on a brass at Lavenham church. EAST NS 13, 1913/14, 309–10; NS 15, 1918/20, 156

6412   **R, E. G.** Latin verses on a tombstone at Lavenham church. E Ang 1, 1858/63, 332–3, 362

6413   **Duncan, J.** Lavenham Methodist chapel. 1964. [Typescript]. SRO/B

BUILDINGS

6414   **Corder, J. S.** Guildhall of Corpus Christi, Lavenham. PSIA 7, 1889/91, 113–118

6415   **National Trust.** Guildhall, Lavenham. nd. nl

6416   **Gardiner, R.** Guildhall, Lavenham. 1975. SCL/L

6417   **Lavenham Preservation Committee.** The Lavenham appeal, made jointly by the Lavenham Preservation Committee and the Trustees of the Guildhall group of buildings. [Committee formed Aug 1944]. SRO/B

6418   Lavenham, 11 November 1918. Bury St. Edmunds, 1918. SRO/B

6419   **[McCausland-White, R.]** Festival exhibition at the Phoenix Gallery, Lavenham: souvenir catalogue. 1952. SRO/B

6420   **Trust Houses, Ltd.** Swan Hotel at Lavenham. 1952 and later edns

LAWSHALL   *See also* **722, 3114**

6421   Lawshall parish history. EADT 12.6.1935, Rp No 400

6422   **Saunders, H. W.** Bailiff's roll of the manor of Lawshall, 1393–4. PSIA 14, 1910/12, 111–46

6423   **Baillie, E.** Letter to the parishioners of Lawshall, telling them why he left them and became a Catholic. 1858. nl

LAXFIELD   *See also* **2534, 2801, 2803–4, 2814, 3343**

6424   Laxfield parish history. SC 4.5.1928, Rp No 70

6425   **Hayes, M. R.** Some aspects of the growth and life of the agricultural village of Laxfield in Suffolk. [c.1970]

6426   **Marchant, R. A.** Manors of Laxfield [History of Laxfield. Pamphlet no 1]. Halesworth, nd

6427   All Saints' church, Laxfield. [Typescript]

6428   **P, G. R.** Extracts from the parish registers of Laxfield. E Ang 2, 1864/66, 256–8

LAYHAM   *See also* **2441**

6429   Layham parish history. SC 14.12.1928, Rp No 102
6430   **Partridge, C.** Churchyard inscriptions from Layham, 1901. REMI 1, 1911/12, 35–46

LEAVENHEATH

6431   Leavenheath parish history. EADT 30.3.1938

LEISTON   *See also* **974, 1613–17, 2925, 6574**

6432   Official guide. 1935 and later edns.
6433   Leiston parish history. SC 10.8.1928, Rp No 84
6434   **Schofield, B.** Wreck rolls of Leiston abbey. *In* Studies presented to Sir Hilary Jenkinson. *Ed.* by J. C. Davies. Oxford, 1957. 361–71
6435   **Leiston Grammar School** (formerly Leiston Secondary School). The Leistonian, c.1922–
6436   **East Suffolk County Council.** Planning Dept. Leiston and Aldeburgh: factual survey and outline plan. Ipswich. 1961. Amendment report. Ipswich, 1962
6437   **Whitehead, R. A.** Garretts of Leiston. 1964
6438   **Davy, D. E.** Short account of Leiston abbey. With descriptive and illustrative verses [by B. Barton *and* W. Fletcher. *Ed.* by J. Bird]. 1823
6439   Leiston abbey ruins. Lowestoft, 1922. SCL/L
6440   **Wrightson, R. G.** Leiston abbey. Leiston, 1930. nl
6441   Guide to St. Mary's abbey, Leiston. Leiston, [c.1930]
6442   **Fryer, F. A.** Leiston abbey. EAM 12, 1953, 139–42
6443   **Welsby, P. A.** Guide to St. Mary's abbey, Leiston. Leiston, 1953
6444   Leiston abbey. Leiston, [1962]
6445   St. Mary's abbey, Leiston: the Retreat House and Conference Centre of the diocese of St. Edmundsbury and Ipswich. Ipswich, [1962] NCL/N
6446   **Ministry of Public Building and Works.** Leiston abbey, Suffolk. 1966
6447   Parish church of St. Margaret's, Leiston. Ramsgate, [1962]. O
6448   Parish magazine. Extant 1951
6449   Quakers of Leiston: a story of Friends and their meeting house. Saxmundham, [1960]

LEISTON-CUM-SIZEWELL URBAN DISTRICT

6450   Town and Country Planning Act, 1947, Section 30. Provisional list of buildings of architectural or historic interest for consideration, ... Leiston-cum-Sizewell Urban district, June 1947. List of buildings of special architectural or historic interest, Urban district of Leiston-cum-Sizewell, 13 March 1951. [Typescript]

LETHERINGHAM   *See also* 3180–82, 3466–71

6451   Letheringham parish history. SC 8.6.1928, Rp No 75

6452   **Edwards, H. F. O.** A shield from Letheringham. TMBS 11, Pt 1, 1969/71, 37

6453   **Farrer, E.** Letheringham abbey. PSIA 20, 1928/30, 9–10

6454   **Welch, H.** Brief history of St. Mary's, Letheringham, and All Saints, Easton. Woodbridge, [1963]. NCL/N

6455   **Welch, H.** St. Mary's church, Letheringham. Nelson, 1967. nl

6456   **Dickinson, P. G. M.** St. Mary's church, Letheringham. Letheringham, 1970. nl

6457   **Blatchly, J.[M.]** Lost and mutilated memorials of the Bovile and Wingfield families at Letheringham. PSIA 33, 1973/5, 168–94

6458   Transcripts of the parish registers of Letheringham ... A.D. 1588–1758 and 1812, and of all the sepulchral inscriptions and arms now and formerly within its church and churchyard, with notes on some of the persons named ... and an account of the said parish, its rectory, church, dissolved priory, etc. *Ed.* by P. C. Rushen. 1901. 50 copies

LEVINGTON   *See also* 1120

6459   Levington parish history. SC 12.2.1932, Rp No 260

6460   Registers of Levington, 1562–1787. *Ed.* by E. Cookson. nd. [Typescript]

LIDGATE   *See also* 1959

6461   Lidgate parish history. EADT 4.3.1936, Rp No 429

LINDSEY

6462   Lindsey parish history. SC 13.4.1932, Rp No 270

6463   **Smith, M.** Short history of St. James' chapel, Lindsey. 1952. [Typescript]. SRO/B

6464   Lindsey castle and chapel. PSIA 13, 1907/09, 243–51

LINSTEAD MAGNA

6465   Linstead Magna parish history. EADT 27.4.1938

LINSTEAD PARVA

6466   Linstead Parva parish history. EADT 22.5.1935, Rp No 397

LIVERMERE

6467   **Munday, J. T.** A misplaced Suffolk vill. SR 4, no 2, 1973, 20–23

6468 **Rodwell, J.** Tumuli at the Seven Hills, Livermere. Anthropologia 1, 1873/5, 70–71 [Supplement]

LIVERMERE, GREAT

6469 Great Livermere parish history. SC 14.11.1930, Rp No 202

LIVERMERE, LITTLE   *See also* 3584

6470 Little Livermere parish history. SC 14.11.1930, Rp No 202
6471 **Dow, L.** Livermere Parva: a missing hatchment found. PSIA 30, 1964/6, 272–4

LOES AND WILFORD HUNDREDS   *See also* 447, 7161

6472 **Hawes, R.** History of Loes Hundred. MS
6473 Rules and orders for regulating the meetings and proceedings of the directors and acting guardians of the poor ... of the Hundreds of Loes and Wilford. Woodbridge, 1792. BL
6474 Report of the Committee ... of the owners and occupiers of lands within the incorporated Hundreds of Loes and Wilford ... to investigate the receipts and expenditure for the support of the poor ... for the preceding twenty-four years. Woodbridge, 1825. BL
6475 List of the directors and acting guardians of the poor within the Hundreds of Loes and Wilford, with their months of attendance at the House of Industry for the years 1825 and 1826. Woodbridge, [1825]. [1826]. Bl

LONG MELFORD

HISTORY   *See also* 1541, 1749–53, 3185–6
6476 **Ford, J.** Melford surveyed: an account of the ancient and present state of that village; its church, hospital, and halls, with notices of monuments, sculpture, paintings, and biography. 2 v. [c.1840]. MS
6477 **Deedes, C.** Dr. Bisbie's manuscript collections for Long Melford [with extracts]. PSIA 7, 1889/91, 78–90
6478 **Parker,** *Sir* **W.** History of Long Melford. 1873
6479 **Parker,** *Sir* **W.** Additional notes ... 1874–89. *Ed.* by T. Howlett. 1971. [Typescript]. SRO/B
6480 **Adams, E. E.** Accounts and records of Long Melford, Suffolk. [Long Melford], 1896. SRO/B
6481 Long Melford parish history. SC 26.6.1914, Rp No 15; SC 7.12.1928, Rp No 101
6482 **Oswald, A.** Long Melford. CL 82, 1937, 168–73
6483 **Ambrose, E.** Melford memories. Long Melford, 1972
6484 **Almack, R.** Roman urns and glass, Melford. PSIA 2, 1854/9, 96
6485 **Holden, J. S.** Ancient Roman settlement at Long Melford. PSIA 15, 1913/15, 267–8

6486   Elliot, C. R. Roman finds at Rodbridge, near Long Melford. PSIA 25, 1949/51, 307

6487   Smedley, N. Roman Long Melford. PSIA 28, 1958/60, 272–89

6488   Almack, R. Melford conveyance (Clopton family, etc.) 1499. PSIA 2, 1854/9, 95

6489   Cuttings from Suffolk and Essex Free Press: royal visit to Long Melford. 1865

6490   Royal visit to Melford: series of 25 photographs of Melford Hall and its neighbourhood, November 1865. Bury St. Edmunds, 1865

HOSPITAL

6491   Report of the Charity Commissioner respecting Melford Hospital, founded by Sir W. Cordell, Kt, 1573. Long Melford, [1836]. SRO/B

6492   A, R. Melford Hospital: letter of Elizabeth Darcy, Countess Rivers. E Ang 3, 1866/8, 33

CHURCH OF THE HOLY TRINITY   *See also* 3294

6493   Francis, B. Church of the Holy Trinity, Melford, Suffolk. 1825. nl

6494   Almack, R. Some account of Melford church. PSIA 2, 1854/9, 73–83

6495   Conder, E. L. Church of the Holy Trinity, Long Melford, Suffolk. 1887

6496   Whitehead, L. H. H. Holy Trinity, Long Melford. [Lavenham], [1928]. 2nd edn 1930

6497   Ince, G. J. B., *Ed.* Church of the Holy Trinity, Long Melford. Ipswich, [1935]. rev. edn 1937. SRO/B

6498   Evans, J. Long Melford church. Arch J 108, 1951, 194–6

6499   Simpson, F. S. W. Church of the Holy Trinity, Long Melford: the fifteenth-century ideal. Gloucester, 1957. 1961. SRO/B

6500   Blunden, E. The great church of the Holy Trinity, Long Melford. Ipswich, 1965 and later edns

6501   Adams, E. E. The tower: church of the Holy Trinity, Long Melford. Long Melford, 1936. SRO/B

6502   Baily, C. Painted glass in the windows in Long Melford. Proc. of the evening meetings of the London and Middlesex Archaeology Soc. 1871, 8–23. SRO/B

6503   Piggot, J. Glass at Long Melford. EAST 5, 1873, 243–5

6504   Parker, *Sir* W. Long Melford: handbook to the ancient painted glass in the church of Holy Trinity. Ipswich, 1888

6505   Le Couteur, J. D. Long Melford church, and its portrait glass, a medieval portrait gallery. JMGP 2, 1927/8, 74–7

6506   Whitehead, L. H. H. Glass in Long Melford church. PSIA 21, 1931/3, 172–3

6507   Woodforde, C. Medieval stained glass of Long Melford church. JBAA 3rd Ser 3, 1938

6508   Ord, C. Description of a carving in the church at Long Melford. Arch 12, 1796, 93–5

6509   B, B. Steeple-board at Long Melford. E Ang NS 1, 1885/6, 322

6510 **Stevenson, F. S.** Symbolism in Long Melford church. PSIA 21, 1931/3, 171–2
6511 **Woodforde, C.** Two unusual subjects in Long Melford church. PSIA 21, 1931/3, 63–6
6512 Parish magazine, extant 1870, *now* The Parish Letter

NONCONFORMITY
6513 **Duncan, J.** Non-conformists of Long Melford, with notes on Glemsford. 1968. [Typescript]. SRO/B

BUILDINGS
6514 **Tymms, S.** Kentwell Hall, Melford. PSIA 2, 1854/9, 59–72
6515 Kentwell Hall. CL 12, 1903, 464–71
6516 **De Serre, J.** Chair from Kentwell Hall. CL 65, 1929, 312
6517 **Tymms, S.** Melford Hall. PSIA 2, 1854/9, 50–59
6518 **Parker, *Sir* W.** Melford Hall, past and present, and its owners. Sudbury, nd
6519 Melford Hall. CL 10, 1901, 496–503
6520 **Oswald, A.** Melford Hall. CL 82, 1937, 116–21, 142–7
6521 Melford Hall, Suffolk, 1552: the home of Sir Richard William Hyde Parker, Bt. [c.1956]. nl
6522 **Hyde Parker, *Lady*.** Melford Hall, official guide: the historic Suffolk home of the Hyde Parker family. Derby, [1957]. 1968
6523 Melford Hall: official guide. 1958
6524 **Country Life.** Melford Hall, Suffolk. 1961
6525 **Lees-Milne, J.** Melford Hall, Suffolk: a property of the National Trust. 1961 and later edns
6526 **O, A. S.** The furniture at Melford Hall. CL 82, 1937, 394–5
6527 **Tymms, S.** Melford Place. PSIA 2, 1854/9, 84–8
6528 **Trust Houses Ltd.** The Bull at Long Melford, Suffolk. nd. Tales of old inns, no 27
6529 **Christy, R. M.** The Bull Inn at Long Melford. [1928]. BL

LOTHINGLAND *See also* 814, 1587–9, 1592, 6590–91, 6738, 6740, 6745

6530 Official guide. 1950 and later edns. SCL/L
6531 [Ives, J.] Proposals for printing The history and antiquities of the Hundred of Lothingland in the county of Suffolk. 1771. BL
6532 **Chambers, J.** Stone Age and Lake Lothing. Norwich, 1911. SCL/L
6533 **Druery, J. H.** Twenty-four views displaying the beauties of Yarmouth and its environs, extending from Caister Castle to Lowestoft lighthouse ... by J. Lambert ... with a concise description ... and an historical notice of Yarmouth by J.H.D. Great Yarmouth, [1821–2]. BL
6534 **Druery, J. H.** Graphic illustrations of Great Yarmouth and its environs ...

[24 plates] engraved ... by J. Lambert ... With a descriptive index by J.H.D. Great Yarmouth, 1822. BL

6535 **Druery, J. H.** Historical and topographical notices of Great Yarmouth ... and its environs, including the parishes and hamlets of the Half Hundred of Lothingland in Suffolk. 1826. SCL/L

6536 Hundred Rolls and extracts therefrom ... with a translation by ... Lord John Hervey. County of Suffolk. Lothingland. [*Ed.* by F. H. (i.e. Lord Francis Hervey)] Ipswich, 1902

6537 **Redstone, V. B.** Island of Lothingland, 1584. PSIA 20, 1928/30, 1–8

6538 **Lothingland Rural District Council.** Minutes, Feb 1966–. SCL/L

6539 **Lothingland Rural District Council.** Annual report of the Medical Officer of Health for the year 1934–. Lowestoft, 1935–. BL. 1955–. SCL/L

6540 **Lothingland Secondary Modern School,** Lound. Magazine. [c.1966–]

6541 **East Suffolk County Council.** Planning Dept. North-east Lothingland: factual survey and outline plan. Ipswich, 1955. SCL/L

6542 Town and County Planning Act, 1947, Section 30. Provisional list of buildings of architectural or historic interest for consideration ... Rural district of Lothingland. Aug 1949. List of buildings of special architectural or historic interest. Rural district of Lothingland. 27 Nov 1954. [Typescript]

LOUND   *See also* **3188, 6540**

6543 Lound parish history. EADT 6.11.1935, Rp No 416

6544 **Green, M.** Antiquities found at Lound. GM 1st Ser 58, 1788, 593

6545 St. John-the-Baptist, Lound. King's Lynn, nd. nl

6546 Church of St. John-the-Baptist, Lound. Lowestoft, 1960. SCL/L

LOWESTOFT   *See also* **3328–9**

DIRECTORIES

6547 Mathieson's Yarmouth and Lowestoft directory for 1867–8. Lowestoft. BL

6548 Cook's directory of Lowestoft and Kirkley ...1883. Lowestoft. SCL/L

6549 Huke's Lowestoft and Kirkley directory, 1892, 1896, 1898. Lowestoft. SCL/L

6550 Kelly's directory of Lowestoft and Kirkley, with Beccles and neighbourhood ... for 1899–1900, and later edns. BL. 1902–. SCL/L

6551 **Regency Publicity Service.** Lowestoft and district book: a classified directory of business, trades, professions, and voluntary organisations, 1968/9, and later edns. Folkestone. SCL/L

ALMANACS

6552 **Crisp, G. S.** Lowestoft companion to the almanacs, 1862. Lowestoft. SCL/L

6553 Lowestoft almanack and companion, 1883–. Lowestoft. BL

6554 O'Driscoll, J. R. Illustrated commercial, nautical, and household almanack, diary, and annual, 1899, 1900, 1901. Lowestoft. SCL/L

6555 Great Yarmouth and Lowestoft annual, 1904. Great Yarmouth. SCL/L

6556 Lowestoft home almanac, 1928, 1929. Lowestoft. SCL/L

GUIDES *See also* 272, 374, 7318

6557 **Baker, J.** Guide through the neighbourhoods of Yarmouth and Lowestoft. Great Yarmouth, [c.1810]. O

6558 Lowestoft guide: containing a descriptive account of Lowestoft and its environs. By a Lady. Great Yarmouth, 1812. SCL/L

6559 New handbook of Lowestoft and its environs; compiled from Gillingwater's History, Suckling's Antiquities, and other sources. Lowestoft, 1849. SCL/L

6560 Illustrated hand-book to Lowestoft, with details of the new route to Denmark, by the author of 'The Eastern counties illustrated guide'. [1851]. O

6561 Hand-book to Lowestoft. [1853]. [1854]. SCL/L

6562 Illustrated guide-book to Lowestoft and its neighbourhood; historical and descriptive. 3rd edn. rev. and enlarged 1854. SCL/L

6563 **Colman, T.** Historical and topographical handbook of Lowestoft and its neighbourhood; with maps ... Lowestoft, 1858

6564 Chapman's illustrated handbook of Lowestoft and its neighbourhood. Lowestoft, 1852. 1862. SRO/I. new edn. 1866. BL. new edn. 1871. SCL/L

6565 **Wright, H.** Hand book to Lowestoft and it neighbourhood. Lowestoft, 1868. SLC/L. 1875. O.

6566 **Salmon, J.** Lowestoft and its environs. Descriptive of natural scenery, historical, and general. Lowestoft, 1869. SCL/L

6567 **Stebbings, A.** Guide-book to Lowestoft and its vicinity. [Lowestoft], [1873]. BL

6568 **Stebbings, A.** Visitors' guide-book to Lowestoft, etc. Lowestoft, [1875]. BL [1887]. O

6569 **Stebbings, A.** Visitors' penny guide to Lowestoft. Lowestoft, [1878]. [1887]. BL

6570 Complete guide to Lowestoft. Lowestoft, [c.1880]. SCL/L

6571 Jarrold's guide to Lowestoft and Southwold. [c.1887]. SCL/L

6572 **Stebbings, F.** Illustrated guide to Lowestoft ... and the 'Broads' of Norfolk and Suffolk. Lowestoft, [1891]. BL. 1894. O.

6573 Flood's popular guide to Lowestoft. Lowestoft, [1895]. O. [1902] and later edns. SCL/L

6574 Illustrated guide to Lowestoft, including Dunwich, Leiston ... Southwold ... 2 pts. 10th edn. [1897]. BL

6575 **Murton, A. E.** O'Driscoll and Dotesio's new Illustrated visitors' guide book to Lowestoft and its environs. Lowestoft, [1898]. SCL/L

6576 Ward Lock's pictorial and descriptive guide to Lowestoft, with excursions to Norwich, the Broads, Yarmouth, etc. [1900] and later edns. SCL/L

6577   Lowestoft, illustrated, its past and present with some anticipations of the future. Horwich, Lancs., [c.1900]. SCL/L

6578   **Hooper, J.** Jarrold's illustrated guide to Lowestoft and neightbourhood. [c.1902]. SCL/L

6579   Lowestoft, Suffolk: Queen of the East coast. Lowestoft, [1904]. SRO/I. [1906]. O

6580   **Westgate, T. W.** Illustrated handbook to Lowestoft and district. Norwich, [1904]. SCL/L. [1908]. O

6581   Lowestoft, Suffolk. An ideal holiday haunt, etc. [Lowestoft], [1908]. BL

6582   "Borough" guide to Lowestoft. Cheltenham, [1909]. SCL/L [1919]. BL

6583   Official guide. Lowestoft. 1910 and later edns. SCL/L

6584   **Biggs, G. H. W.** Notes on Lowestoft in connection with the visit of the Institution of Municipal and County Engineers, 22 June, 1912. SCL/L

6585   **Robinson, F., & Co.** Guide to Lowestoft and its environs ... Lowestoft, [c.1914]. SCL/L

6586   **Stephen, G. A.** Jarrold's illustrated guide to Lowestoft and neighbourhood. Norwich, 1928. 2nd edn 1934. SCL/L

6587   **Lowestoft Corporation**. Entertainment and Publicity Dept. Tourism in Lowestoft. Lowestoft, [1968]. SCL/L

Views

6588   **Rock and Co.** Views of Lowestoft. 1850–. Various edns. SCL/L

6589   **Trery, H. C.** Sketches in Lowestoft. 1852. SCL/L

HISTORY   *See also* **308, 520, 788, 841, 947, 2582–9, 2872, 2888, 2962, 2976, 3157, 3178–9, 3222–3, 3320, 3328–9**

6590   **Gillingwater, E.** Historical account of the ancient town of Lowestoft ... to which is added some ... remarks on the adjoining parishes and a general account of the island of Lothingland. [1790]. Grangerized copy. 3 v. SCL/L
See also **2932, 6593**

6591   **Suckling, A. I.** History and antiquities of Lowestoft, and part of the Hundred of Lothingland ... Extracted from his History and antiquities of the county of Suffolk 2, 1848, 1–114. SCL/L

6592   **Suckling, A. I.** History and antiquities of the town of Lowestoft. Extracted from his History and antiquities of the county of Suffolk 2, 1848, 59–114, with litho frontispiece. Great Yarmouth, 1862. 4 copies. nl

6593   **Gillingwater, E.** Gillingwater's history of Lowestoft. A reprint: with a chapter on more recent events, by A. E. Murton. Lowestoft, 1897

6594   **Longe, F. D.** Lowestoft in olden times. Lowestoft, [1899]. 2nd edn 1905. SCL/L

6595   **Chambers, C. G.** Earlier days. [1913]. SRO/B

6596   Lowestoft: souvenir of the conference of the National Union of Teachers, Easter 1914. SCL/L

6597   **Chambers, C. G.** Lowestoft and the Scottish crown. Lowestoft, [1920]

6598 **Chambers, C. G.** Corner of Suffolk. Notes concerning Lowestoft and the Hundred of Mutford and Lothingland. Lowestoft, 1926. SCL/L

6599 **Munnings, J.** Lowestoft through the centuries: a lantern lecture delivered on 31 March 1927, to the Lowestoft and District Literary and Scientific Society. [Typescript]. SCL/L

6600 Lowestoft parish history. 2 pts. EADT 5.1.1938, 12.1.1938

6601 Kirkley parish history. EADT 1.3.1939

6602 **Steward, A. V.** Lowestoft: town against the sea. Norwich, [1950]

6603 **Beamish, J.** Lowestoft reminiscences. Lowestoft, 1952

6604 **Powell, M. L.** Lowestoft through the ages. Lowestoft, [1952]

6605 **Steward, A. V.** Lowestoft before 1900: some notes on an exhibition held at the Art Centre, Lowestoft, 3–14 July 1959. SR 2, 1959, 51–3

6606 **Murton, A. E.** Lowestoft in the nineteenth century: the history of a hundred years. Lowestoft, 1901. Rp from Lowestoft Journal, 5 Jan 1901. SCL/L

6607 **Davies, K. M.,** *and* **Muddeman, L. R.** Development of Lowestoft since 1800. [1975]. [Typescript]

6608 **Nicholson, R. B.** Some recollections of Lowestoft during fifty years, 1873–1925: a lecture delivered on 5 March 1925 to the Lowestoft and District Literary and Scientific Society. [Typescript]. SCL/L

6609 **Chambers, C. G.** Lowestoft to-day [1913]. SRO/B

6610 Bombardment of Lowestoft, Tuesday, 25 April 1916. Lowestoft, [1916]

6611 **Jenkins, F.** Port war: Lowestoft, 1939–1945. Ipswich, [1946]

6612 **Goodey, C.,** *and* **Rose, J.** HMS Europa: the story of the Royal Naval Patrol Service. Lowestoft, 1977. SCL/L

6613 **Cheeseman, J.** Lowestoft: a study in urban continuity with particular reference to post–1946 development. 1969. [Typescript]. SCL/L

6614 **Rose, J.** Lowestoft then and now: a walk in the past. Lowestoft, 1973. [Typescript]

6615 **Lees, H. D. W.** Evidence of the use of stocks and other means of apprehension in Lowestoft. SR 2, 1959, 42–4

REGISTER OF ELECTORS
6616 Register of electors: Lowestoft division, 1931/2–. SCL/L

ECONOMIC HISTORY AND COMMUNICATIONS *See also* **1381, 1390, 1402 1423, 1430, 1433**
6617 **Woolner, A. H.** Economic geography of the development and present position of Lowestoft as a port and holiday resort. M.Sc. (Econ.) thesis, London, 1956. [Typescript]. SCL/L

6618 **Lowestoft Incorporated Chamber of Commerce**. Report of the council and statement of accounts, 1924–33. SCL/L

6619 **Lowestoft Incorporated Chamber of Commerce**. Official handbook: a detailed account of the industrial activities and civic life of the borough of Lowestoft. Lowestoft, [c.1928]. SCL/L

6620 Survey of the port and industries of Lowestoft. Lowestoft Journal Supplements, 23 Oct 1959; 18 Feb 1966. SCL/L

6621 **Lowestoft Corporation.** Industrial sites. Lowestoft, 1968. SCL/L

FISHERIES *See also* **955–6, 1168–71**

6622 The case of the towns of Great Yarmouth and Laystoft (in relation to the Bill for making Billingsgate a free market for fish), as prayed in their several petitions to the Commons of England in Parliament assembled. [1695?] Wing C 1169. BL

6623 Fisheries exhibition … Public Hall, Lowestoft, 2–7 Aug 1886. Official catalogue. SCL/L

6624 Fishery guide for 1890, containing a history of all the vessels belonging to and sailing from the ports of Yarmouth and Lowestoft. Great Yarmouth, [1889]. BL

6625 Yachting and fisheries exhibition, London, 1897. Lowestoft exhibits and exhibitors, local committees, officials, and illustrated souvenir. Lowestoft, [1897]. SCL/L

6626 **Chambers, C. G.** Fishing industry. [1913]. SRO/B

6627 Lowestoft, the foremost fishing port. Cheltenham, [c.1928]. SCL/L

6628 Flood's list of fishing vessels registered at the port of Lowestoft. 1929, 1933, 1935, 1937. Lowestoft. SCL/L

6629 **Lowestoft Fishing-vessel Owners' Association.** Fishing port of Lowestoft. Cheltenham, [1955] and later edns. BL

6630 **Ministry of Agriculture, Fisheries, and Food.** Marine fisheries research. [Brief description of the work being done in the Ministry's laboratories at Lowestoft]. Lowestoft, 1970. SCL/L

6631 **King, D. L.** From steam to stern: a history of the Colne Group, Lowestoft. Lowestoft, 1975. [Typescript]. SCL/L

PORT, LIGHTHOUSES, AND LIFEBOATS *See also* **279, 288, 1196, 1340–53 2161–2**

6632 Report of Admiralty on the Lowestoft Harbour Improvement Bill. HC 1854, 37

6633 Rules and regulations of Lowestoft harbour and fish-markets, with tables of dues, rates, and charges, and bye-laws in force, 1 Oct 1874. Lowestoft, 1880. SCL/L

6634 Opening of the new dock at Lowestoft: programme and MS. account of proceedings. Lowestoft, 1883. SCL/L

6635 **Queen's Bench Division.** Mutual admissions between Her Majesty's Attorney-General, informant, and Richard Henry Reeve, defendant [Lowestoft foreshore]. 1885. SCL/L

6636 Changing Lowestoft bridge: a notable event. Lowestoft, 1897. SCL/L

6637 **Willis, J. B.** Making of Lowestoft harbour: a lecture delivered on 16 March 1928 to the Lowestoft and District Literary and Scientific Society. [Typescript]. SCL/L

6638 **Port of Lowestoft Research Society.** Newsletter, no 1, Feb 1965–. SCL/L

6639 **Lowestoft and East Suffolk Marine Society.** Cottage museum, Sparrow's Nest, Lowestoft. [1970]. SCL/L

6640 **Chaplin, W. R.** History of the Lowestoft lighthouse. nd. [Typescript]. SCL/L

6641 **Mitchley, J.** Story of the Lowestoft lifeboats. Pt 1. 1801–1876. Lowestoft, 1974. SCL/L

6642 **Moore, R. W.** On service: the story of the Lowestoft lifeboats. Lowestoft, 1977. SCL/L

TOKENS

6643 **W.** Lowestoft tokens. E Ang 1, 1858/63, 5–6, 15

COACHBUILDING

6644 **Eastern Coach Works Ltd.,** Lowestoft. Brief history and survey of the Company's progress since the year 1912. [Lowestoft], 1969. [Typescript]. SCL/L

LOWESTOFT CHINA

6645 **"A Collector."** Lowestoft china. E Ang 2, 1864/6, 109

6646 Specimens from Lowestoft china factory. Arch J 26, 1869, 401–02

6647 **Casley, H. C.** Lowestoft china factory. PSIA 11, 1901/03, 339–69

6648 **Smith, A. M.** Old Lowestoft china [Extracts from Lowestoft Journal, 12 Dec 1902]. Lowestoft, 3rd edn 1912. SCL/L

6649 **Solon, L.** Lowestoft porcelain factory and the Chinese porcelain made for the European market during the eighteenth century. Burl 2, 1903, 271–8

6650 Recent discovery of Lowestoft moulds. Conn 5, 1903, 268–70

6651 **Hodgson, W.** English Lowestoft china. Conn 7, 1903, 99–102

6652 **Sachs, E. T.** The real Lowestoft. Conn 8, 1904, 237–42; 9, 1904, 16–22

6653 **Spelman, W. W. R.** Lowestoft china. Norwich, 1905

6654 **Crisp, F. A.** Catalogue of Lowestoft china in the possession of Frederick Arthur Crisp. 1907

6655 **Crisp, F. A.** Lowestoft china factory, and the moulds found there in December 1902. 1907

6656 **Hallam, W. W.** Lowestoft china. Lowestoft, 1914. SCL/L

6657 **Roe, F. G.** Aldreds of Lowestoft. Conn 66, 1923, 100–01

6658 **Kiddell, A. J. B.** Inscribed and dated Lowestoft porcelain. EPCT 3, 1931, 7–54

6659 **Murton, A. E.** Lowestoft china; compiled from various sources. Lowestoft, 1932

6660 **Powell, M. L.** Lowestoft china. Lowestoft, 1934. SCL/L

6661 Exhibition of valuable collection of old Lowestoft china. Kindly lent by S. F. Brown, Esq., at 11, The Bridge, Lowestoft. [c.1935]. SCL/L

6662 **Hyde, J. A. L.** Oriental Lowestoft. With special reference to the trade with China and the porcelain decorated for the American market. New York, [1936]. SCL/L

6663 **Kiddell, A. J. B.** Lowestoft china. Conn 100, 1937, 130–36, 182–7

6664 **Kiddell, A. J. B.** Richard Powles (1764–1808), Lowestoft painter. ECCT 2, 1939, 112–14

6665 **Hughes, G. B.** Lowestoft porcelain. CL 109(1), 1951, 801–03

6666 **Hunting, D. M.** Early Lowestoft. ECCT 3, 1951, 71–82

6667 **Hyde, J. A. L.** Oriental Lowestoft, Chinese export porcelain, porcelaine de la Cie des Indes ... Newport, R.I., 2nd edn 1954. 3rd edn 1964. SCL/L

6668 **Godden, G. A.** Lowestoft figures. Connoisseur year book, 1957, 72–5

6669 Lowestoft china bi-centenary, 1757–1957. Exhibition catalogue. Wolsey Art Gallery, Christchurch Mansion, Ipswich. 1957

6670 Lowestoft porcelain: an exhibition to commemorate the two hundredth anniversary of the founding of the Lowestoft factory, 27 July–5 Oct 1957. Catalogue. Worthing, 1957. SCL/L

6671 **Turner, N. P.** 'Lowestoft'. *In* Saturday Book, 18, *ed.* by J. Hadfield. 1958, 69–77

6672 **Turner, N. P.** Lowestoft porcelain. Estates Gazette 185, 1963, 769–75

6673 **Goodey, C.** Links with Lowestoft china? LA&LHS 1967/8, 22–4

6674 **Levine, G. J.** Inscribed Lowestoft porcelain. Brundall, Norwich, [1968]

6675 **Godden, G. A.** Illustrated guide to Lowestoft porcelain. 1969

6676 **Howell, J.** Transfer-printed Lowestoft porcelain. ECCT 7, 1970, 210–19

6677 **Danks, P.** The Lowestoft site. ECCT 7, 1970, 220–21

6678 **Smith, S.** Lowestoft porcelain in Norwich Castle Museum. v 1. Blue and white and excavated material. [Norwich], 1975

Lowestoft China—Sale Catalogues

6679 Spelman, Lowestoft. Collection of porcelain of William Rix Seago, 1873. SCL/L

6680 Spelman, Lowestoft. Two collections of the Rev. Roger Lee and T. T. Freeman, 1873. SCL/L

6681 Spelman, Lowestoft. Collection of B. M. Bradbeer, 1873. SCL/L

6682 Catchpole and Richards, Lowestoft. Collection of A. Merrington Smith, 1927. SCL/L

6683 Sotheby and Co. London. 1935 (Crisp). nl. 1948 (Colman); 1959 (Denney); 1961 (Hunting); 1962; 1963, 1964 (Arnold); 1964; 1965 (Allman); 1966 (2); 1969 (Caldwell); 1970; 1973 (Middleton). SCL/L

SHIPBUILDING *See also* **932, 955–6**
6684 Chambers Chronicle: the works magazine of John Chambers Ltd., shipbuilders and engineers, Oulton Broad, Lowestoft. v 1, no 1, June 1919–no 10, Dec 1920. SCL/L

6685 [**Richards, L. E.**]. Eighty years of shipbuilding and designing: sailing vessels in 1876, steam 1899, diesel 1928: Richards Ironworks Ltd., Lowestoft. Lowestoft, [1956]. SCL/L

6686 **Goodey, C.** The first hundred years: the story of Richards shipbuilders. Ipswich, 1976

POSTAL HISTORY

6687 **Lees, H. D. W.** Story of the post office in Lowestoft and its many moves. SR 3, no 2, 1965, 8–10

6688 **Lees, H. D. W.** Some account of postmasters and post offices in Lowestoft. East Anglia Postal Hist Study Circle Bull 37, Sept 1971, 21–7

6689 **Mylius, W. A. J.** Telegraph repeater station, Lowestoft. 1938. [Typescript]. SCL/L

LOCAL GOVERNMENT AND SOCIAL SERVICES
Municipal administration

6690 **Lowestoft Corporation.** Council minutes and committee reports, v 1, 1885/ 1886–. SCL/L

6691 **Lowestoft Corporation.** Calendar, 1913–. SCL/L. Incomplete

6692 **Lowestoft Corporation.** Byelaws relating to Lowestoft, 1887–1968. SCL/L

6693 **Lowestoft Corporation.** Jubilee celebrations, 2–6 July 1935. SCL/L
Lowestoft Corporation. Presentation of the Honorary Freedom of the Borough:–

6694 Howard Hollingsworth, Esq. C.B.E., J.P., Friday, 9 Nov 1928. SCL/L

6695 Alderman Alfred George Notley, J.P. and Alderman Arnall Brame Capps, J.P., Wednesday, 4 Sept 1935. SCL/L

6696 Frederick Spashett, Esq. J.P., Wednesday, 13 Jan 1943. SCL/L

6697 Major Selwyn Wollaston Humphrey, O.B.E., T.D., J.P., Monday, 3 Jan 1949 SCL/L

6698 Benjamin Britten, Esq., Saturday, 28 July 1951. SCL/L

6699 Alderman John William Woodrow, J.P., Saturday, 16 March 1963. SCL/L

6700 Francis B. Nunney, Esq., Saturday, 4 Dec 1965. SCL/L

6701 Alderman Jeannie Mary Mann, M.B.E., J.P., Saturday, 7 March 1970. SCL/L

Finance

6702 **Lowestoft Corporation.** Borough Treasurer's Dept. Abstract of accounts, 1901–. SCL/L

Charities See also **1551**

6703 Lowestoft church and town estate and amalgamated poor and almshouse charities. 1888. SCL/L

Public Health   See also **1571**

6704   Lowestoft Dispensary. Report, August 1837. [Lowestoft]. O

6705   Lees. H. D. W. Asiatic cholera epidemic at Lowestoft, 1848–9. SR 1, 1958, 153–6

6706   Hawkshaw, *Sir* **J.** Lowestoft South drainage. Report 13 July 1886. Lowestoft, [1886]. SCL/L

6707   Lowestoft Corporation. Health Dept. Annual report of the Medical Officer of Health, 1888–. SCL/L. Incomplete

Education

6708   Lowestoft Coporation. School Board. Report of the work and proceedings of the Lowestoft School Board for the three years ended 31 July 1899. Lowestoft, [1899]. SCL/L

6709   Lowestoft Corporation. Education Dept. Reports of the Education committee, 1903–. SCL/L

6710   Lowestoft Corporation. Education Dept. Annual reports of the School Medical Officer, 1911–. SCL/L. Incomplete

6711   St. Mary's Convent, Kirkley Cliff, Lowestoft . . . Illustrated souvenir and prospectus. Gloucester, [1938]. BL

6712   Lowestoft Education Week, 29 June–6 July 1947. [Historical and educational survey]. Lowestoft. SCL/L

6713   East Suffolk County Council. Education in Lowestoft, 1945–: a factual survey presented on the occasion of the offical opening of the new Education Office premises in Clapham Road, 1962. Lowestoft, 1962. SCL/L

6714   Lowestoft Corporation. Education Dept. Report . . . on the implementation of secondary re-organisation. Lowestoft, 1967. SCL/L

6715   Lowestoft Corporation. Education Dept. Comprehensive re-organisation. Lowestoft, [1969].SCL/L

6716   Denes High School [formerly Lowestoft Municipal Secondary School, later Lowestoft Grammar School]. Lowestoftian, 1914/43, 1947/69. Perspective, 1970–. SCL/L. Incomplete.

6717   Kirkley High School [formerly Alderman Woodrow School]. The Cresset, July 1962–1967. *Cont. as* The Kirkley Runner, 1968–. SCL/L

6718   Lowestoft Corporation. Educational Dept. Youth Service handbook, 1966–. SCL/L

Libraries

6719   Catalogue [and rules] of the Lowestoft parochial library. Lowestoft, 1857. SCL/L

6720   Note on Lowestoft library. Lib 3, 1891, 24, 156

6721   Rules, bye-laws, and catalogue of the Lowestoft Public Library and Reading Rooms [established October 1870] Lowestoft, 1893. SCL/L

6722   Catalogue of the Lending and Reference Departments of the Lowestoft Public Library. Lowestoft, 1906. 1914. 1920. SCL/L

6723 Opening of the new Central Library, Lowestoft, 8 May 1975. SCL/L

Public Utilities   See also **1430**

6724 **Lees, H. D. W.** Paving and lighting of Lowestoft in the early nineteenth century. LA&LHS 1970/71, 40–51

6725 Lowestoft tramways. [1903]. [cuttings and photographs]. SCL/L

6726 **Lowestoft Corporation.** Transport Dept. Accounts, 1948–. SCL/L. Incomplete

6727 **Boon, J. M.** Lowestoft Water and Gas Company: a hundred years of service, 1853–1953. Lowestoft, [1953]. SCL/L

Planning and Development   See also **1642, 1646**

6728 **Lowestoft Corporation.** Planning Dept. Report of the main factors to be considered in the preparation of the preliminary planning scheme. Lowestoft, 1942. [Typescript]. SCL/L

6729 **East Suffolk County Council.** Planning Dept. Borough of Lowestoft factual survey, by T. B. Oxenbury and G. A. M. Gentry. Ipswich, 1948. [Typescript]. SCL/L

6730 **East Suffolk County Council.** Planning Dept. Outline plan for Lowestoft; an interim report. Ipswich, 1949. [Typescript]. SCL/L

6731 **Lowestoft Corporation.** Interim report on the outline development plan for the borough of Lowestoft. Lowestoft, 1949. [Typescript]. SCL/L

6732 **East Suffolk County Council.** Planning Dept. Outline plan for Lowestoft, by T. B. Oxenbury and G. A. M. Gentry. Ipswich, [1950]. [Typescript]

6733 **East Suffolk County Council.** Planning Dept. Whapload Road Comprehensive development area. Ipswich, 1959

6734 Lowestoft amenity improvement schemes, prepared by Taylor and Green, architects. Lowestoft, [1960]. SCL/L

6735 **East Suffolk County Council.** Planning Dept. Lowestoft central area; survey and appraisal. Ipswich, 1964. SCL/L

6736 **East Suffolk County Council.** Planning Dept. County development plan. Amendment no 4. Lowestoft Beach area comprehensive development area. Written statement and maps. Ipswich, 1964. Approved 1966. SCL/L

6737 **East Suffolk County Council.** Planning Dept. Lowestoft central area draft plan. Ipswich, 1965. SCL/L

6738 **East Suffolk County Council.** Planning Dept. Lowestoft with parts of Lothingland Rural District; draft town-map review and written statement. Ipswich, 1966

6739 **East Suffolk County Council.** Planning Dept. Lowestoft town centre map. Ipswich, 1967. SCL/L

6740 **East Suffolk County Council.** Planning Dept. County development plan. Amendment no 6. Lowestoft with parts of Lothingland. Written statement and town map. Ipswich, 1967. Approved 1971. SCL/L

6741 **East Suffolk County Council.** Planning Dept. Lowestoft interim planning statement. Ipswich, 1973. SCL/L

6742 Great Yarmouth-Lowestoft area: land-use transportation study. Summary report—Lowestoft. [1974]. SCL/L

Housing

6743 **Lowestoft Corporation.** Housing Dept. Municipal tenants' handbook, etc. Gloucester, [1955] and later edns. SCL/L

6744 **Lowestoft Corporation.** Housing Dept. St. Peter's Court: official opening ceremony. Lowestoft, [1968]. SCL/L

CHURCHES

6745 **Clemence, J. L.** Lectures on the churches of Lowestoft and Lothingland, 1858 and 1860. Lowestoft. [Typescript]. SCL/L

Christ Church

6746 Christ Church, Lowestoft. Centenary celebrations ... 9–16 Feb 1969. SCL/L

St. John's

6747 St. John's church annual reports, 1866–1908. SCL/L

6748 St. John's parish magazine, 1880–1969. 70 v. SCL/L. Incomplete

St. Margaret's

6749 **Clemence, J. L.** Lowestoft church. Lowestoft, 1879. SCL/L

6750 **Clemence, J. L.** Lowestoft church. JBAA 36, 1880, 34–9

6751 **Youngman, W.,** *and* **Maddison, W.** The parish church (St. Margaret's). Lowestoft, [c.1890]. SCL/L

6752 Church of St. Margaret. Parish of Lowestoft: St. Margaret. Lowestoft, 1932

6753 **Lees, H. D. W.** Chronicles of a Suffolk parish church: Lowestoft, St. Margaret. Lowestoft, 1949

6754 St. Margaret's church: the restoration of 1950. Lowestoft, 1951. SCL/L

6755 Church of St. Margaret, Lowestoft. Gloucester, [1952]. [1956]. [1966]. SCL/L

6756 [**Hazell, K. S.**] Saint Margaret's: the parish church of Lowestoft. Lowestoft, 1961. SCL/L

6757 Lowestoft magazine. NS Sept 1872–Dec 1883. *Cont. as* Lowestoft parish magazine. Jan 1884–March 1970. *Cont. as* The Lowestoft Group: the newspaper of St. Margaret's, St. John's, Kirkley St. Peter's. April 1970–. SCL/L. Incomplete

St. Peter's

6758 Kirkley parish magazine. 1884–1915. SCL/L. Incomplete

NONCONFORMITY

Individual Congregations

6759 **Thomas, A. V.** Centenary souvenir of the London Road Baptist church, Lowestoft (1813–1913). Lowestoft, 1913. SCL/L

6760 **Kerridge, W. E.** Short history of the London Road Baptist church, Lowestoft, 1813–1963. Lowestoft, 1963 SCL/L

6761 London Road Congregational church, Lowestoft. Centenary souvenir [of church building opened Sept 1852]. Lowestoft, 1952. SCL/L

6762 **Watts, S. M.** London Road Congregational church, Lowestoft: ter-centenary souvenir [of founding of church in 1665]. Lowestoft, 1965. SCL/L

6763 Lowestoft Sailors' and Fishermen's Bethel. 51st annual report, 1901. Diamond Jubilee celebration ... and 60th annual report, 1909. Lowestoft. SCL/L

6764 South Cliff Congregational church, 1885–1945. Souvenir handbook. Lowestoft, 1945. SCL/L

6765 History of Wesleyan Methodism in the town of Lowestoft, Suffolk: by the author of "Little Welborne", etc. Great Yarmouth, 1843. SCL/L. *See also* **1991, 2518**

6766 Wesley at Lowestoft. E Ang 3, 1866/8, 363

6767 Wesley's journal—first visit to Lowestoft. E Ang 4, 1869/70, 119–20

ASSOCIATIONS   *See also* **520, 2164, 2166**

6768 Report of the committee of the Lowestoft Branch Bible Society made ... on the fourth anniversary [and on the 5th, 8th, 10th, 11th, and 12th]. Lowestoft, 1815–23. BL

6769 Address to the subscribers ... to the Church Missionary Association ... at Lowestoft, read at the annual meeting ... 30 Aug 1825. Lowestoft, [1825]. BL

6770 Proposal for forming a Lowestoft division of the Society for Promoting Christian Knowledge. Lowestoft, [184?]. O

6771 Children's Missionary Magazine, 1844. *Ed.* by J. M. Randall, Assistant Curate of Lowestoft. SCL/L

6772 **Lowestoft and District Literary and Scientific Association.** Annual reports, 1918–32, 1934–. SCL/L

6773 Theatre Royal magazine, no 1, Feb 1960–no 9, Sept 1960. Lowestoft

Freemasonry

6774 **Knocker, G. S.** Digest of lecture on Lodge of Unity, no 71, Lowestoft. SIMT no 3913, 1919. nl

6775 **Storm, R. E.** History of Stradbroke Lodge, no 3291, Lowestoft, 1908–32 Lowestoft, 1932. nl

6776 **Sorrell, J. E. A.** Records of Lodge of Unity, no 71, Lowestoft, 1747–1936. Lowestoft, 1937. SCL/L

6777 **Knocker, G. S.** Lodge of Unity, no 71, Lowestoft: bicentenary celebration and short history, 1947. Lowestoft, 1947. nl

6778   **Croft, J. W.** Jubilee and history, Stradbroke Lodge, no 3291, Lowestoft, 1908–1958. Lowestoft, 1958. nl

6779   **Croft, J. W.** Golden jubilee book of statistics, Orient Lodge, no 4085, Lowestoft, 1920–70. Lowestoft, 1970. SCL/L

6780   **Slatcher, J. H.** St. Margaret's Lodge, no 1452 [Lowestoft] Centenary, 1873–1973. [Lowestoft], 1973. SCL/L

STREETS AND BUILDINGS

6781   **Westwood, W. J.** List of streets in the ecclesiastical parishes of the Church of England, in the borough of Lowestoft. Lowestoft, 1965. [Typescript]. SCL/L

6782   Town and Country Planning Act, 1944, section 42. Provisional list of buildings of architectural or historic interest for consideration . . . Borough of Lowestoft. Jan 1947. [Typescript]. SCL/L

6783   Town and Country Planning Act, 1947, section 30. List of buildings of special architectural or historic interest . . . Borough of Lowestoft, 13 Dec 1949. [Typescript]. SCL/L

6784   **Lees, H. D. W.** Town under the cliff. LA&LHS 1967/8, 5–11

6785   **Lees, H. D. W.** Almshouses and the Cocoa Tree Tavern in High Street, Lowestoft. SR 2, 1959/63, 85–7

6786   **Lees, H. D. W.** The passing of Day's Yard, Lowestoft. SR 2, 1959/63, 20–22

6787   **Lees. H. D. W.** Martin's Score, Lowestoft. SR 2, 1959/63, 163–6

6788   **Bunn, I.** *and* **Burgess, M.** Haunted Lowestoft. Lowestoft, 1975. SCL/L

NATURAL ENVIRONMENT

6789   **Carruthers, J. N.** Note on the geology of the Lowestoft area. Lowestoft, 1928. SCL/L

6790   **Miller, S. H.** Reduction of meteorological observations at Lowestoft from 1879–98. 1900. SCL/L

6791   **Lowestoft Corporation.** Monthly report of the meteorological observer, 1951–. SCL/L

6792   **Rhodes, L. A.** Record of phenomenal tides, 1936–53. [c.1954]. MS. SCL/L

REGISTERS

6793   Parish registers of Lowestoft . . . [1561–1720. Transcribed by J. P. Steel and F. D. Longe, and reprinted from the Lowestoft Parish Magazine, 1895–8]. Lowestoft, [1899]. [Typescript index by H. D. W. Lees and M. Chamberlain. v 1. 1895. Lowestoft, 1974]. SCL/L

6794   Index to the parish registers of Lowestoft, 1561–1610, by J. P. Steel. MS. SCL/L

6795   Index to the parish registers of Lowestoft: Christenings, 1561–1650, by J. P. Steel. MS. SCL/L

6796   Index to the parish registers of Lowestoft: Marriages, 1561–1610 [women only], by J. P. Steel. MS. SCL/L

6797 Parish registers of Lowestoft, Suffolk: Marriages, 1650–1850. Baptisms and burials, 1724–50. *Ed.* by F. A. Crisp. 1901. 50 copies

6798 Parish registers of Lowestoft, Suffolk: Marriages, 1752–1812. Baptisms, 1709–1711, 1751–1812. Burials, 1751–1812. *Ed.* by F. A. Crisp. 1904. 50 copies.

6799 Births, deaths, and marriages index at Lowestoft, 1879–86, as reported in the Lowestoft Journal. SCL/L

INSCRIPTIONS
6800 [**Clemence, J. L.**] St. Margaret's church, Lowestoft: inscriptions. [1898]. MS. SCL/L

MARKET WESTON

6801 Market Weston parish history. EADT 20.7.1932, Rp No 278
6802 **Newham, H. B.** Market Weston. 1951. [Typescript]. SRO/B

MARLESFORD

6803 Marlesford parish history. SC 30.10.1931, Rp No 250

MARTLESHAM

6804 Martlesham parish history. SC 14.10.1927, Rp No 41
6805 **Maynard, G.,** *and* **Spencer, H. E. P.** Report on the removal of a tumulus on Martlesham Heath. PSIA 24, 1946/8, 36–57
6806 **Kinsey, G.** Martlesham Heath: the story of the Royal Air Force Station, 1917–73. Lavenham, 1975
6807 **Birch, H. W.** Church notes: Martlesham. E Ang NS 13, 1909/10, 356–59
6808 Martlesham church, 1911, with parish register for 1910. [c.1911]. nl
6809 **Lingwood, H. R.** Martlesham church. Ipswich, 1951. 1963
6810 **Lingwood, H. R.** Rectors of Martlesham. PSIA 25, 1949/51, 193–201
6811 **Anderson, R. C.** Martlesham Lion, MM 23, 1937, 237

MELFORD RURAL DISTRICT

6812 Official guide. 1950 and later edns
6813 **Melford Rural District Council.** Annual report of the Medical Officer of Health for 1894–. Sudbury. BL
6814 **Melford Rural District Council.** Council tenant's handbook ... Gloucester, [1952]. BL

MELLIS

6815 **C, R.** Etymology of Mellis. E Ang 1, 1858/63, 318
6816 Mellis parish history. EADT 10.5.1933, Rp No 310

6817   **Creed, H.** Extracts from the accompts of the churchwardens of Mellis, A.D.1611–45. PSIA 1, 1848/53, 79–83

6818   **Creed, H.** Extracts from the registers of Mellis. PSIA 1, 1848/53, 286–96

MELLS   *See also* Wenhaston

6819   Mells parish history. EADT 17.8.1938

6820   **Gowers, W. R.** Chapel of St. Margaret, Mells; the ruin and its history. PSIA 8, 1892/4, 334–79

6821   **Gowers, W. R.** Ruined chapel of Mells. E Ang NS 5, 1893/4, 214–16

MELTON   *See also* **1573, 1646, 3239, 8037, 8056**

6822   Melton parish history. 2 pts. EADT 24.2.1937, 3.3.1937, Rp Nos 463, 464

6823   Rules and orders: Melton house of industry. 1791

6824   Report of the committee appointed to inquire into the actual estate of the house of industry at Melton . . . delivered . . . 15 Feb 1791. Woodbridge, [1791]

6825   Proposed rules and regulations for the government of the Pauper Lunatic Asylum erected at Malton. Bury St. Edmunds, [1803?]. BL

6826   Extract from the proceedings of the general quarterly meeting of visiting justices of the Suffolk Lunatic Asylum, 6 April, 1841. Woodbridge, 1841. O

6827   **Redstone, V. B.** Melton old gaol. PSIA 15, 1913/15, 65–73

6828   Short history of the churches of St. Andrew and St. Etheldreda, Melton. Ramsgate, [1961]

6829   Melton Grange [Hotel], Woodbridge, Suffolk. Woodbridge, 1931. nl

MENDHAM   *See also* **2897, 3245**

6830   **Turner, S.** Mendham. E Ang 2, 1864/6, 322

6831   Mendham parish history. SC 27.11.1931, Rp No 253

6832   **Fitch, W. S.** Inventory of furniture at Mendham Hall, 1548. PSIA 2, 1854/9, 242–7

MENDLESHAM

6833   Mendlesham parish history. SC 20.5.1927, Rp No 21

6834   **Royal Commission on Historical Manuscripts.** Ser 4, Fifth report, Pt 1. Parish . . . of Mendlesham. By J. C. Jeaffreson. 1876. 593–96.

6835   **Tye, W.** Brewing day in the nineties [Mendlesham]. SR 1, 1958, 156–60

6836   **Mayfield, A.** Short description of St. Mary's church, Medlesham, Suffolk, its history, architecture, and antiquities. [Norwich], 1910. SRO/B

6837   St. Mary-the-Virgin, Mendlesham. Ipswich, 3rd edn 1971. nl

6838 **Mayfield, A.** Account of the arms and armour in Mendlesham church, Suffolk. [Norwich], 1910. SRO/B

6839 **Redstone, V. B.** Two earliest registers of the parish of Mendlesham, in the county of Suffolk, for the years 1558–1661. [Typescript]. 1915

6840 **Partridge, C.** Monumental inscriptions in Mendlesham churchyard. E Ang NS 12, 1907/08, 250–51

METFIELD   *See also* 3111

6841 Metfield parish history. EADT 26.9.1934, Rp No 369

6842 Church of St. John-the-Baptist, Metfield. nd. nl

6843 **Bower, N. H.** Extracts from Metfield churchwardens' account-books, etc. PSIA 23, 1937/9, 128–47

METTINGHAM

6844 Mettingham parish history. SC 16.11.1928, Rp No 98

6845 **Manning, C. R.** Extracts from the ancient accounts of Mettingham college. Arch J 6, 1849, 62–8

6846 **Manning, C. R.** Mettingham castle and college. PSIA 4, 1864/74, 77–89

6847 **Redstone, V. B.** Mettingham college and castle, 1562. PSIA 11, 1901/03, 315–319

6848 **Gray, B. B.** Wayside crosses, Mettingham. E Ang 3, 1866/8, 32

MICKFIELD

6849 Mickfield parish history. EADT 31.1.1934, Rp No 341

MIDDLETON-CUM-FORDLEY   *See also* 1685

6850 Middleton-cum-Fordley parish history. SC 30.11.1928, Rp No 100.

6851 **Cochran, H. S.** Our village: a companion to notes on Middleton. 1949. SRO/B

6852 **Cochran, H. S.** Notes on Middleton church and parish. [Ipswich], 1946. 1954. nl

MILDEN

6853 Milden parish history. EADT 27.2.1935, Rp No 388

MILDENHALL

DIRECTORIES AND GUIDES

6854 **Localads.** Mildenhall and district direetory. 1966/7–. Needham Market [1966–]

6855 Official guide. 1950 and later edns

HISTORY   *See also* 2667, 3018, 3443

6856   **Prescott, K.** Mildenhall, a poem. Cambridge, 1771. BL

6857   **Gedge, J. D.** Mildenhall. PSIA 4, 1864/74, 340–56

6858   **Simpson, A. E.,** *Ed.* History of Mildenhall and its celebrities of the past. Midenhall, 1892. 2nd edn 1893. 3rd edn 1901. 4th edn 1915

6859   Mildenhall parish history. 2 pts. SC 28.6.1929, 5.7.1929., Rp Nos 130, 131

6860   **Rees, H. G. St. M.** Short history of the parish and church of Mildenhall. Gloucester, [1951] and later edns

Prehistory

6861   **Marr, J. E.** Excavation at High Lodge, Mildenhall in 1920: report on the geology. PPSEA 3, 1918/22, 353–67

6862   **Moir, J. R.** Description of the humanly-fashioned flints found during excavations at High Lodge, Mildenhall. PPSEA 3, 1918/22, 367–72

6863   **Smith, R. A.** Summary of previous flint finds [at High lodge, Mildenhall]. PPSEA 3, 1918/22, 373–9

6864   **Clark, J. G. D.,** *et al.* Excavations at the Neolithic site at Hurst Fen, Mildenhall, 1954, 1957, and 1958. PPS NS 26, 1960, 202–45

6865   **Clark, J. G. D.** Report on a late Bronze Age site in Mildenhall Fen. Ant J 16, 1936, 29–50

6866   **Kelley, T. C.** Series of late Middle Bronze Age sites, Wilde Street, Mildenhall. PSIA 31, 1967/9, 47–54

Roman

6867   **Bunbury, H.** Roman and British antiquities discovered at Mildenhall. Arch 25, 1834, 609–12

6868   **Pearce, J. W. E.** *Siliquae* from a find at Mildenhall. NC 6th Ser 2, 1942, 105–06

6869   **Brailsford, J. W.** Mildenhall treasure. PSIA 24, 1946/8, 252–3

6870   **British Museum.** Mildenhall treasure: a provisional handbook. 1947 and later edns

6871   **Lethbridge, T. C.** Treasure trove in England [Mildenhall treasure]. Classical Jour. [Chicago] 42, 1947, 282–6

6872   **Brailsford, J. W.** Where was the Mildenhall treasure made? ANL 1, 1948, 7–8

6873   **Maryon, H.** Mildenhall treasure; some technical problems. Man 48, 1948, 25–47

6874   **Dohrn, T.** Spätantikes Siber aus Britannien [Mildenhall treasure]. Mitteilungen des deutschen archäologischen Instituts, 2, 1949, 67–139. BL

6875   **Brailsford, J. W.** Mildenhall treasure. BMQ 15, 1952, 69–71

6876   **Robertson, A. S.** Roman coin hoard from Mildenhall. NC 6th Ser 14, 1954. 40–52

6877   **Hartley, K. F.** Amphora stamp found near Mildenhall. Ant J 38, 1958, 91–2

6878 **Coles, J. M.,** *and* **Trump, B. V.** Rapier and its scabbard from West Row [near Mildenhall]. PCAS 60, 1967, 1–5

Anglo-Saxon   See also **674**
6879 **Prigg, H.** Tumuli of Warren Hill, Mildenhall. PSIA 4, 1864/74, 287–99
6880 **Prigg, H.** Anglo-Saxon graves, Warren Hill, Mildenhall. PSIA 6, 1883/8, 57–72
6881 **Manning, C. R.** Cloveshoe in Mildenhall. E Ang NS 2, 1887/8, 69–70, 112–14
6882 **Raven, J. J.** Mildenhall and the metropolis. E Ang NS 5, 1893/4, 222
6883 **Harris, H. A.,** *et al.* Cloveshoe. PSIA 18, 1922/4, 77–8, 91–122
6884 **Reaney, P. H.** Cloveshoe and Mildenhall. PSIA 26, 1952/4, 220–24

BANKING
6885 **Angerstein, J. J. W.** Proposal for forming the Mildenhall savings bank. With extracts from the Bury Herald. Bury St. Edmunds, 1840. O
6886 **Angerstein, J. J. W.** Appeal to the nobility and gentry, etc., of Suffolk, in behalf of the depositors in the Mildenhall savings bank. [Bury St. Edmunds], 1840. BL
6887 **Angerstein. J. J. W.** Letters in behalf of the depositors in the Mildenhall savings bank, being a fragment of the Bury Herald. [Bury St. Edmunds], [1840]. BL

CHURCHES
6888 **Tymms, S.** Mildenhall church. PSIA 1, 1848/53, 269–77
6889 **Wilkinson, L.** Church of St. Mary-the-Virgin, Mildenhall. Mildenhall, 1938
6890 **Munday, J. T.** Lost figure from Mildenhall. TMBS 11, pt 1, 1969/71, 31
6891 **Waller, J. G.** On the roof of the church of St. Andrew, Mildenhall. Arch 54, pt 2, 1895, 255–66
6892 **[Sawbridge, P. F.].** Roof carving in Mildenhall church. Oxford, 1938. SRO/B

NONCONFORMITY
6893 **Duncan, J.** History of West Row (Mildenhall) Baptist chapel. 1965. [Typescript]. SRO/B
6894 **Fincham, B.** Short history of the Methodist church, Holywell Row, Mildenhall ... formerly a Quaker Meeting House. 1949. SRO/B

MILDENHALL RURAL DISTRICT

6895 **Mildenhall Rural Sanitary Authority.** Fourth to twenty-first annual reports of the Medical Officer of Helath, 1892–. [incomplete]. Mildenhall. BL
6896 **Mildenhall Rural District Council.** Tenants' handbook. Mildenhall, 1963. SRO/B

MONEWDEN

6897 Monewden parish history. SC 19.2.1932, Rp No 261

MONKS ELEIGH

6898 Monks Eleigh parish history. SC 11.5.1928, Rp No 71

6899 **Northcote, A. F.** Notes on the history of Monks Eleigh. Ipswich, 1930

6900 Rules and regulations relating to Monks Eleigh fire-engine. Hadleigh, 1846

6901 **Anderson, A.** Former timber spire of Monks Eleigh church. PSIA 31, 1967/9, 201–06

MONK SOHAM   *See also* **2957**

6902 Monk Soham parish history. SC 29.1.1937, Rp No 461

6903 **Partridge, C.** Tithe customs of Monk Soham, in 1617. E Ang NS 10, 1903/04, 245–8

6904 **Morley, C.** Font at Monks' Soham. PSIA 17, 1919/21, 13–20

6905 Registers of the parish of Monks' Soham, in the county of Suffolk. *Ed.* by C. Morley. 1920. 150 copies

MOULTON

6906 Moulton parish history. SC 21.11.1930, Rp No 203

6907 **Watkins, A. A.** Moulton pack-horse bridge. PSIA 21, 1931/3, 110–19

6908 **Mortlock, E.** The Court of Chancery or the Charity Commission: which is supreme? ... the case of the Moulton charities. 1869. nl

6909 Parish church of St. Peter and St. Paul, Moulton: a brief history and guide. [c.1962]. nl

MOULTON RURAL DISTRICT

6910 **Moulton Rural District.** Annual report of the Medical Officer of Health, 1896–1909 [incomplete]. Newmarket. BL

MUTFORD

6911 Mutford parish history. SC 9.8.1935, Rp No 406

6912 **Creed, H. K.** The stones in Mutford Wood. PSIA 4, 1864/74, 244

MUTFORD AND LOTHINGLAND   *See also* **827, 2444, 6598, 7817**

6913 **Knight, Frank, and Rutley.** Lordships of the manors of the Half Hundreds of Mutford and Lothingland ... a detailed introduction, history [by D. Charman] and particulars of sale. [1971]

6914 Rules for a Society for rescuing persons in danger of shipwreck, within the Hundreds of Mutford and Lothingland, Blithing, and Wanford [*sic*]. Great Yarmouth, [1806]. BL

6915 **Mutford and Lothingland Labourer's Friend Society.** Subscribers for the year 1839. Lowestoft, [1839]. O

6916 Byelaws of the Guardians of the Poor in Mutford and Lothingland. Lowestoft, 1836. nl

6917 To the directors and acting guardians of the poor of the Hundreds of East and West Flegg, Mutford and Lothingland [an order appointing Robert Rising of Horsey auditor of the Hundreds]. 10 March 1845. O

6918 To the guardians of the poor of the Blofield and Erpingham unions, Hundreds of Mutford and Lothingland [ordering the setting-up of the East Norfolk audit circuit]. 11 March 1845. O

6919 **Worthington, W. C.** Numerical table of the out-cases attended by Mr. W. C. Worthington at the Mutford and Lothingland General Dispensary, from August 1822 to August 1837. [1837]. O

6920 **Mutford and Lothingland,** General Dispensary. State of the charity from 27 Aug 1827 to 26 Aug 1828. Lowestoft, [1828]. BL

6921 **Mutford and Lothingland,** General Dispensary and Infirmary. Rules, orders, and regulations. 1841. O

6922 **Mutford and Lothingland Rural District Council.** Report of the Medical Officer of Health for 1911–33 [1915 missing]. Lowestoft. BL

NACTON

6923 Nacton parish history. SC 28.12.1928, Rp No 104

6924 **Warsop, D.** Social aspects of Nacton Workhouse in its early years. SR 4, no 2, 1973, 25–40.

NAUGHTON

6925 Naughton parish history. SC 27.4.1928, Rp No 69

NAYLAND

6926 **Slade, S.,** *and* **Syrett, M.** History of Nayland. 1913–19. [Typescript]

6927 Nayland-with-Wissington parish history. SC 3.8.1928, Rp No 83

6928 **Fitch, J. A.** Nayland parochial library: a catalogue and historical note. Halesworth, nd. [Typescript]. nl

6929 **Layard, N. F.** Nayland figure-stone. PSIA 15, 1913/15, 3–8

6930 **Shorrocks, D. M. M.** John Abell's bridge, Nayland. ER 61, 1952, 225–32

6931 **Langdon, A.** Bell bridge, Nayland—its history and records. SR 2, 1959, 10–13

6932 St. James' church, Nayland. From Dr. Slade's "Notes of Nayland history." [1970]

6933 **Smith, H. C.** Fifteenth-century painted panels from the rood-screen of Nayland church. Ant J 3, 1923, 345–6

6934 **Blomfield, C. J.** Some notes on Alston Court . . . Architectural Rev 21, 1907, 244–56

6935 **Hussey, C.** Alston Court in Nayland. CL 56, 1924, 100–06

NEDGING

6936 Nedging parish history. SC 27.4.1928, Rp No 69

NEEDHAM MARKET *See also* **2464, 3130, 5453**

6937 **Platten, E. W.** Rambles round and jottings about Needham Market, with special reference to its historical features and antiquarian remains. Stowmarket, 1925

6938 Needham Market parish history, 2 pts. SC 11.3.1932, 18.3.1932, Rp Nos 263, 264

6939 **Platten, E. W.** Short history of Needham Market. Needham Market, [c.1935]

6940 **Allen, J. R.** Bronze bowl found at Needham Market. Reliquary NS 6, 1900, 242–50

6941 Needham Market Pavement Subscription lists, reports and balance sheets, 1876–93. Ipswich

6942 **Society of Friends.** At a meeting of sundry Friends from the counties of Essex ... Proposal for establishing a school at Needham Market for the county of Essex. 1783

6943 **East Suffolk County Council.** Planning Dept. Conservation in Needham Market: townscape appraisal and policy statement. Ipswich, 1970

6944 **East Suffolk County Council.** Planning Dept. Needham Market: policy statement and planning proposals. Ipswich, Draft 1970. Final proposals 1971

6945 **Birch, H. W.** Church notes: Needham Market. E Ang NS 6, 1895/6, 309–10

6946 **Lingwood, E. T.** Needham Market church. PSIA 17, 1919/21, 136–41

6947 [**Lingwood, H. R.**]. Story of Needham Market church. Needham Market, [1957]. 1960

6948 **Sewell, W. H.** Chapel of St. John-the-Baptist, Needham Market. PSIA 4, 1864/74, 245–56

6949 Records in connection with St. John's church, Needham Market, taken from the parish book, and other documents. Ipswich, 1893

NETTLESTEAD *See also* 3452–3

6950 Nettlestead parish history. SC 19.8.1927, Rp No 34

6951 **Birch, H. W.** Church notes: Nettlestead. E Ang NS 6, 1895/6, 153–6

NEWBOURNE *See also* **7802**

6952 Newbourne parish history. SC 14.10.1927, Rp No 41

6953 **Welford, A.** Graffiti at Newbourne church. PSIA 24, 1946/8, 255–6

6954 **Dow, L.** Carved heraldic panels at Newbourne Hall. PSIA 30, 1964/6, 270–71

NEWMARKET

DIRECTORIES AND GUIDES

6955 E.C. Supplies Co. Newmarket and district annual and directory, etc. Newmarket, 1932– BL

6956 Official guide. 1922 and later edns

GENERAL, POLITICAL, SOCIAL AND ECONOMIC HISTORY

See also 663, 774–5, 801, 806, 815, 1383–4, 1393, 1400, 2330, 2734, 3387

6957 **Hore, J. P.** History of Newmarket and the annals of the turf with memoirs and biographical notices ... 3 v. [v 1 Newmarket], [v 2–3 London], 1885–6

6958 Newmarket parish history. EADT 27.10.1937, 3.11.1937

6959 **Lyle, R. C.** Royal Newmarket. 1945

6960 **Slater, J.** Newmarket; home of horse racing: a pictorial study. Lavenham, 1968

6961 **Kerrich, T.** Account of an urn found in the Beacon Hills, Newmarket Heath. Arch 18, 1817, 436

6962 **May, P.** A fifteenth-century market court [1399–1413]. Newmarket, 1976

6963 **May, P.,** *Ed.* Court rolls of Newmarket in Suffolk, 1408–10. Newmarket, 1973

6964 **May, P.** Newmarket 500 years ago. PSIA 33, 1973/5, 253–74

6965 **May, P.** Twenty Newmarket wills, 1439–97: a glimpse of fifteenth-century Newmarket. Newmarket, 1974

6966 **May, P.** Newmarket inventories, 1662–1715. Newmarket, 1976

6967 **May, P.** High Street and market: Newmarket and its beginnings. [Newmarket], 1975

6968 To keepers of the liberties of England by authority of Parliament to all parsons, Justices of the Peace and other officers, greeting [Letters patent, ordering collections to be made for the relief of sufferers by the fire at Newmarket, 11 Aug 1651]. 1653. BL-T

6969 **S, J.** Letter from a gentleman at New-market, giving a full and true account of the dreadful fire that began there on Thursday the 22d of this instant March, etc., 1683. Wing S 70. BL

6970 **Cole, J.** A full and more particular account the late fire, with several losses at Newmarket. 1683. Wing C 5023. BL

6971 To the House of Commons ... the petition of the noblemen and other persons ... of the town and neighbourhood of Newmarket [that the projected Elsenham-Norwich railway should run through Wickhambrook with a branch to Newmarket, so as not to disturb the horses]. [c.1840]. O

6972 **Newmarket Co-operative Society.** Newmarket's Co-operative jubilee history, 1899–1949. By W. H. Brown. Newmarket, 1949. Bl

PUBLIC HEALTH, PLANNING AND DEVELOPMENT

6973 **Newmarket Rural Sanitary District.** Annual report of the Medical Officer of Health. 1892, 1894. [Newmarket]. BL

6974 **Newmarket Urban Sanitary District.** Annual report of the Medical Officer of Health. 1895. *Cont.as* Urban District of Newmarket. Annual report of the Medical Officer of Health. 1896–1908 [incomplete]. BL

6975 **West Suffolk County Council.** Planning Dept. Factual survey and outline plan for the Urban District of Newmarket. Bury St. Edmunds, 1953. [Typescript]

6976 **West Suffolk County Council.** Planning Dept. Newmarket. Report on Rookery and Wellington Street (Hillyer Parker). Bury St. Edmunds, 1959

6977 **West Suffolk County Council.** Planning Dept. Newmarket. Re-development of Rookery and Wellington Street central area. Bury St. Edmunds, 1960

6978 **West Suffolk County Council.** Planning Dept. Newmarket town map: comprehensive development area report. Bury St. Edmunds, 1966. SRO/B

CHURCHES

6979 All Saints church. Yearbook, 1946

6980 **Prankerd, J.** Story of St. Mary's church, Newmarket. Gloucester, 1932, 2nd edn. by H. C. Eves [1947]. 3rd edn [1955]. 4th edn. by D. M. B. Ellis [1969].

6981 **May, P.** St. Mary's church: a guide and history. Gloucester, 1972. SRO/B

6982 Parish magazine. 1872–1910; 1946–

NONCONFORMITY

6983 **Duncan, J.** Congregational church at Newmarket. [196–?]. [Typescript]. SRO/B

RACING HISTORY *See also* **1746**

6984 **Muir, J. B.** Olde New-Markitt calendar of matches, results, and programs from 1619 to 1719. 1892. BL

6985 Newmarket; or, An essay on the Turf. Containing, among other grave and weighty matters, a parallel ... between Newmarket Races and the Olympic Games. [By P. Parsons]. 2 v. 1771. BL

6986 Newmarket first Spring meeting begins 20 April 1772 [Programme of the Races]. [Newmarket]. BL

6987 Newmarket third October, or Houghton meeting, 1801 [List of entries]. Newmarket, 1801. BL

6988 **Black, R.** The Jockey Club and its founders. 1891. BL

6989 **Siltzer, F.** Newmarket: its sport and personalities. 1923

6990 **Orchard, V. R.** Tattersalls. Two hundred years of sporting history. 1953 BL

6991 **Mortimer, R.** The Jockey Club. 1958. BL

6992 **Laird, D.** National Stud, Newmarket. 1967. SRO/B

6993 **Onslow, R.** The Heath and the turf. 1971

6994 **Wright, A. P. M.** Horse-racing. *In* VCH Cambridgeshire and the Isle of Ely 5, 1973, 279–87

NEWTON

6995 Newton parish history. SC 29.11.1929, Rp No 152

6996 Church of All Saints, Newton-by-Sudbury. [c. 1970]. [Typescript]. nl

6997 **Manning, C. R.** Sepulchral monument at Newton-by-Sudbury. PSIA 9, 1895/7, 262–70

6998 Parish magazine, 1971–

6999 **Benton, G. M.** Domestic wall-paintings, dated 1623, at Newton. Ant J 21, 1941, 68–72

NORTH COVE *See also* **3657**

7000 North Cove parish history. EADT 20.5.1936, Rp No 438

7001 Extracts from the parish register of North Cove. E Ang 2, 1864/6, 317

NORTON *See also* **2479, 3194, 3350–53**

7002 Norton parish history. SC 23.3.1928, Rp No 64

7003 **Tymms, S.** Norton church. PSIA 2, 1854/9, 288–90

7004 **Tymms, S.** Little Haugh Hall, Norton. PSIA, 2, 1854/9, 279–87

7005 **Scarfe, N.** Little Haugh Hall. CL 123, 1958, 1238–41

NOWTON

7006 Nowton parish history. EADT 17.4.1935, Rp No 393

7007 **Longworth, I. H.** Two gold bracelets from Nowton, Bury St. Edmunds. PSIA 32, 1970/72, 271

OAKLEY

7008 Oakley parish history. EADT 11.4.1934, Rp No 349

7009 **Elvin, C. F. C.** Account of the Oakleys, Suffolk. With a compiler's vagaries about some of the inhabitants there whose names have been found in various records dating from early times, etc. Oakley, 1936–42. 54 copies

7010 Poetic description of the festivities at Oakley Park, 27 Sept 1832. By an oyster from home, unaccustomed to roam, etc. [i.e. R. H. Cobbold]. Ipswich, 1832. BL

7011 T. Oakley Park. CL 23, 1908, 18–26

OCCOLD

7012 Occold parish history. SC 6.6.1930, Rp No 179

OFFTON *See also* **3364**

7013 Offton parish history. SC 28.3.1930, Rp No 169

OLD NEWTON   *See also* **3437**

7014   Old Newton parish history. EADT 11.11.1932, Rp No 290

7015   **Low, C. W.** Account of the discovery of Roman remains at Old Newton. PSIA 13, 1907/09, 255–8

7016   Monumental inscriptions in Old Newton church. E Ang NS 4, 1891/2, 332–3, 343; NS 5, 1893/4, 221–2

ONEHOUSE

7017   Onehouse parish history. SC 16.1.1931, Rp No 211

ORFORD   *See also* **283, 286, 293, 970, 2522–4, 2668–9, 3144, 3243, 3270, 3428, 3527**

GENERAL, POLITICAL, AND ECONOMIC HISTORY

7018   **Andrews, F. C.** Orford; historical notes. Rp from Leiston Observer. nd

7019   **Whayman, H. W.** Field names of Orford. E Ang NS 6, 1895/6, 133

7020   **Redstone, V. B.** Orford. Ipswich, nd

7021   **Redstone, V. B.** Orford and its castle. PSIA 10, 1898/1900, 205–30

7022   Orford and its castle. Lowestoft, 1922. SCL/L

7023   Orford parish history. SC 13.5.1927, Rp No 20

7024   **Rope, H. E. G.** Some Orford memories. SR 2, 1961, 77–81

7025   **Roberts, R. A.** "Oreford-nigh-the-seas". The church and parish of St. Bartholomew, Orford, and the mother church of All Saints, Sudbourne, with the Austin Friars in Orford, and other particulars: historical sketches by the Rector's Warden [i.e. R. A. Roberts]. Bungay, 1935

7026   **Roberts, R. A.** "Oreford-nigh-the-seas". The church and parish of St. Bartholomew, Orford, reprinted from Historical sketches by the late R. A. Roberts. Orford, 1958. 1960. 1965

7027   **Royal Commission on Historical Manuscripts.** Reports Ser 55. Var. Coll. 4. ... Orford and Aldeburgh. 1907 *See also* 482

7028   **Wayman, H. W. B.** Seal of the dissolved corporation of Orford. E Ang NS 13, 1909/10, 225–6

7029   Petitioners' case of the corporation of Orford in Suffolk [concerning the extent of the franchise in that borough]. [1695?]. Wing P1863. BL

7030   **Roberts, R. A.** The borough business of a Suffolk town (Orford), 1559–1660. TRHS 4th Ser 14, 1931, 95–120 *See also* **1454, 1457, 1470, 1542**

7031   Regulations and tables of dues payable at Orford Quay. nd

CHURCH OF ST. BARTHOLOMEW

7032   Historical notes relating to the church and castle of Orford, with a list of the rectors of Orford and a list of the chaplains of the chantry in Orford church. nd

7033   **Dow, L.** Orford church in 1706. PSIA 26, 1952/4, 225–8

7034   St. Bartholomew, Orford. CB New Issue 16, 1895, 39–41

7035   **Rahbula, E. A. R.** St. Bartholomew's church, Orford. Arch J 108, 1951, 148–50

7036   **Fairweather, F. H.** Excavations in the ruined choir of the church of St. Bartholomew, Orford. Ant J 14, 1934, 170–76

7037   **Rigold, S. E.** A face carved on a capital in Orford church. PSIA 32, 1970/72, 90–91

7038   **Keen, L.,** *and* **Sherlock, D.** Medieval floor-tiles from Orford and Sudbourne. PSIA 32, 1970/2, 198–200

THE CASTLE   *See also* **4456**

7039   **Hartshorne, C. H.** Upon the present state of Orford castle . . . with some conjectures as to the probable uses to which parts of the building were assigned. Arch 29, 1842, 60–69

7040   **T, R.** Orford castle. Sharpe's London Mag 1847, 195–9

7041   Survey of Orford castle, 1600. PSIA 11, 1901/03, 50

7042   **Balding, B. J.,** *and* **Turner, P.** Orford castle: its history and structure. [1927]

7043   Orford Castle: an appeal. 1928

7044   **Roberts, R. A.** Orford castle. JBAA NS 34, 1928/9, 82–6

7045   **Roberts, R. A.** Story of Orford castle, told briefly by the Claviger of the Orford Town Trust [R. A. Roberts]. Ipswich, [1930] and later edns

7046   **Brown, R. A.** Orford castle, Suffolk. Ministry of Public Buildings and Works. 1964

MARRIAGE LICENCES, WILLS, AND INSCRIPTIONS

7047   **Whayman. H. W.** Orford marriage licences, from the official note books of the Archdeaconry of Suffolk, deposited at Ipswich Probate Court, 1613–74. E Ang NS 10, 1903/04, 312–13

7048   **W[ayman], H. W. B.,** *Ed.* Suffolk wills (Orford) proved in the Prerogative Court of Canterbury between 1383 and 1800. English Monumental Inscriptions Society, 1915

7049   **Wayman, H. W. B.** Monumental inscriptions in the church of St. Bartholomew, at Orford. E Ang NS 13, 1909/10, 66–7 193–6, 265

7050   Monumental inscriptions remaining in the church of St. Bartholomew at Orford in the county of Suffolk, 1911. *Ed.* H. W. B. W[ayman]. English Monumental Inscriptions Society, 1911. 100 copies

7051   **W[ayman], H. W. B.** Monumental inscriptions remaining in the church of St. Bartholomew at Orford, 1911. REMI 1, 1911/12, 1–30. *See also* **2441**

ORWELL

7052   **Marsden, R. G.** The mythical town of Orwell. EHR 21, 1906, 93–8

7053   **Wylie, J. H.** Town of Orwell. EHR 21, 1906, 723–4

OTLEY *See also* **3109**

7054 Otley parish history. SC 6.7.1928, Rp No 79
7055 **Owles, E. J.** Roman road at Otley. PSIA 31, 1967/9, 185–7
7056 **Hussey, C.** Two Suffolk Halls: Otley Hall and Erwarton Hall. CL 65, 1929, 152–9

OULTON *See also* **2557–67**

7057 Oulton, Lowestoft. 1922. SCL/L
7058 Oulton parish history. EADT 23.12.1936, Rp No 458
7059 Oulton parish church. Historical notes. [By W. H. Plumtree], [Oulton], [1946?]. [Typescript]. BL
7060 **Furlong, H. B.** Parish church of Saint Michael, Oulton. Lowestoft, 1958
7061 **Boutell, C.** Brass in Oulton church. NA 1, 1846/7, 355

OULTON BROAD

7062 **Chambers, C. G.** Oulton Broad and Mutford bridge. Lowestoft, [1904]. SCL/L
7063 **Cox, S., *Ed.*** "Borough" guide to Oulton Broad. Cheltenham, [1910]. NCL/N
7064 **Lowestoft Corporation.** Oulton Broad: a centre for recreational facilities. [Booklet issued for] visit by the Minister of Sport, 6 June 1967. Lowestoft, 1967. SCL/L

OUSDEN *See also* **1959, 3152**

7065 Ousden parish history. EADT 10.6.1036, Rp No 440

PAKEFIELD

7066 **Clemence, J. L.** Some field names in the parish of Pakefield. E Ang NS 5, 1893/4, 220–21
7067 Pakefield parish history. EADT 24.12.1925, Rp No 421
7068 **[Hunt, B. P. W. S.].** Pakefield, together with a brief description of its ancient church. Lowestoft, 4th edn [1935]. SCL/L
7069 Vanished village: Pakefield of yesterday and to-day. Lowestoft, 1936. SCL/L
7070 **[Hunt, B. P. W. S.]** Pakefield: the church and village. Lowestoft, 5th edn [1938]
7071 **[Hunt, B. P. W. S.]** Pakefield: 1939–45 [being an appendix to Pakefield: the church and the village. 5th edn 1938]. Lowestoft, [1945]. SCL/L
7072 **Hunt, B. P. W. S.** Flinten history, being the story of Pakefield and its church. Lowestoft, 7th edn 1953. SCL/L
7073 Pakefield life-boat [Subscription list]. Lowestoft, [1839]. O

7074 [Hunt, B. P. W. S.] All Saints', Pakefield: a brief description of this ancient church. Lowestoft, [1930]. SCL/L

7075 All Saints' and St. Margaret's church: re-dedication by the Bishop of Norwich. Sunday, 29 Jan 1950. SCL/L

7076 Parish church of All Saints and St. Margaret, Pakefield. Year book, 1958. SCL/L

7077 Brass in Pakefield church. E Ang 2, 1864/6, 321, 324

PAKENHAM   *See also* 3086

7078 Pakenham parish history. SC 13.12.1929, Rp No 154

7079 **Jones, C. W.** Pakenham. PSIA 10, 1898/1900, 169–75

7080 **Warren, J.** Fibula and bracelet, Pakenham. PSIA 3, 1860/3, 403

7081 **Brown, J. W.**, *et al.* Excavations at Grimstone End, Pakenham. PSIA 26, 1952/4, 189–207

7082 **Smedley, N.,** *and* **Owles, E. J.** Some Suffolk kilns: 2, Two kilns making colour-coated ware at Grimstone End, Pakenham. PSIA 28, 1958/60, 203–25. 3, Small kiln at Grimstone End, Pakenham. PSIA 29, 1961/3, 67–72

7083 **Hartshorne, C. H.** Pakenham church. PSIA 1, 1848/53, 89–90

7084 St. Mary's church, Pakenham. nd. nl

7085 **Jones, C. W.** Vicars of Pakenham. PSIA 8, 1892/4, 408–12

7086 **Duncan, J.** Early days of Methodism in Pakenham. 1964. [Typescript]. SRO/B

7087 Souvenir of the Pakenham pageant . . . [includes history of Pakenham]. 1965. SRO/B

7088 **Bryant, J.** Story of Pakenham mill. *Ed.* by G. Wood. 1964. NCL/N

7089 Parish registers of Pakenham, Suffolk. [*Ed.* by F. A. Crisp]. 1888. 50 copies

PALGRAVE   *See also* 2492–3, 3139–41

7090 **Manning, C. R.** Field-names, etc., Palgrave. E Ang NS 3, 1889/90, 236–8

7091 Palgrave parish history. SC 25.3.1932, Rp No 265

7092 **Manning, C. R.** Gold pendant found at Palgrave [Saxon?]. PSIA 2, 1854/9, 88–9. Arch J 9, 1852, 107

7093 **Palgrave Union Benefit Club.** Rules and tables . . . with the amendments . . . agreed upon . . . 1847. Diss, 1848. BL

7094 **Manning, C. R.** Register of Palgrave. E Ang NS 3, 1889/90, 270–71

PARHAM   *See also* 3444

7095 Parham parish history. SC 5.8.1927, Rp No 32

7096 **L, T. N. D.** Parham Old Hall. CL 10, 1901, 264–5

7097 **T.** Parham Old Hall. CL 25, 1909, 702–07

7098   **James, A.** Old paintings in a village house at Parham. CL 124, 1958, 650–51, 844–5, 1184–7

7099   **Linnell, C. S. L.** Incised slab at Parham. TMBS 10, 1963/8, 7–8

7100   **Wilson, C. P. H.** Incised slab at Parham, Suffolk. TMBS 11, 1973, 319–20

PEASENHALL   *See also* 1759–61

7101   Peasenhall parish history. SC 13.6.1930, Rp No 180

7102   **Suffolk Coastal District Council.** Planning Dept. Peasenhall and Sibton: appraisal and policy statement. [Woodbridge]. Draft, Sept 1975 [Approved Jan 1976].

PETTAUGH

7103   Pettaugh parish history. SC 15.2.1929, Rp No 111

7104   **Birch, H. W.** Church notes: Pettaugh. E Ang NS 5, 1893/4, 273–4

7105   Collections upon briefs: Pettaugh. E Ang NS 8, 1899/1900, 318–19, 328–31, 348–50

7106   **Pearson, W. C.** Extracts fron the registers of Pettaugh. E Ang NS 8, 1899/1900, 358–60; NS 11, 1905/06, 138–9

PETTISTREE   *See also* 7949

7107   Pettistree parish history. SC 27.3.1931, Rp No 221

PLAYFORD   *See also* 2461, 2536, 2856, 3349

7108   **Biddell, M.** Materials towards a history of Playford. 1883–4

7109   Playford parish history. SC 16.3.1928, Rp No 63

7110   **Biddell, A.** Roman urn: Playford. PSIA 3, 1860/63, 398

7111   **Airy, A.** Playford church. 1956

7112   **Biddell, M.** Playford parish papers. [Contains letters dated 1883 and 1884 printed by F. A. Crisp]

7113   **Benton, C. M.** Vicissitudes of the brass of Sir George Felbrigg, 1400, Playford. TMBS 8, 1943/51, 319–21

7114   **Biddell, H.** Thomas Clarkson and Playford Hall. 1912. MS

7115   **Ipswich Probate Court.** Playford will list, 1444–1800. MS

PLOMESGATE HUNDRED   *See also* 982

7116   Plomesgate Union. Comparative expenditure in relief of the poor, for one year before, and one year since, the formation of the Union. Framlingham, [1837]. BL

POLSTEAD   *See also* **1734–45**

7117   Polstead parish history. SC 13.4.1928, Rp No 67

7118   **Scates, D. A.,** *and* **M.** Polstead school, 1876–1976. Polstead, 1976

7119   Polstead church. PSIA 11, 1901/03, 220–24

7120   **Harley, L. S.** Polstead church and parish. Ipswich, 1951. 2nd edn Gloucester, 1955. 3rd edn 1965

7121   **Benton, G. M.** Sixteenth-century wall-painting at Polstead Hall. Ant J 21, 1941, 72–3

7122   Polstead Hall: souvenir brochure. [c.1950]. nl

POSLINGFORD

7123   Poslingford parish history. SC 4.1.1929, Rp No 105

7124   **Wilson, D. M.** Poslingford ring. BMQ 20, 1956, 90–92

7125   **Jarvis, H.** Poslingford church [with Davy's notes, 1831.] PSIA 8, 1892/4, 241–56

PRESTON   *See also* **3284**

7126   Preston parish history. EADT 20.8.1932, Rp No 281

RAMSHOLT

7127   Ramsholt parish history. SC 29.4.1932, Rp No 269

RATTLESDEN   *See also* **2714, 7847**

7128   **Olorenshaw, J. R.** Rattlesden papers. E Ang NS 5, 1893/4, 28–9

7129   **Olorenshaw, J. R.,** *Ed*. Notes on the history of the church and parish of Rattlesden, in the county of Suffolk ... parish registers from 1558 to 1758, and an index of the marriages. [Rattlesden], 1900. 200 copies

7130   **Lasko, P. E.** The 'Rattlesden' St. John [bronze gilt figure c.1180]. PSIA 32, 1970/72, 269–71

7131   **Bartlett, J. G.** New England colonists from Rattlesden, co. Suffolk, England. NEH&GR 57, 1903, 331–2

7132   **Olorenshaw, J. R.** Particulars of service in the manor of Rattlesden, from an extent of 1277. E Ang NS 10, 1903/04; NS 11, 1905/06, *passim*

7133   Rattlesden parish history. EADT 8.5.1914, Rp No 11

7134   **Olorenshaw, J. R.,** *Ed*. Notes on the church of St. Nicholas, Rattlesden. Coventry, 1910. SRO/B

7135   **Thompson, B. T.** Rattlesden church. Elmswell, 1967. 1969, by P. Northeast

7136   **O[lorenshaw], J. R.** Nonconformity in Suffolk [Rattlesden, 1672]. E Ang NS 11, 1905/06, 271

7137   **Duncan, J.** Origin of the Free Churches in Rattlesden. 5 v. 1957. [Typescript]. SRO/B

7138 **Duncan, J.** Early Independents at Rattlesden and Combs, Buxhall, and other places—with many extracts from the Bury Church Book. 1961. [Typescript]. SRO/B

7139 **Hitchcock, H. T.** Rattlesden Baptist church, 1813–1963. [1963]. [Photocopy]. SRO/B

RAYDON   *See also* **2310, 2847, 3363**

7140 Raydon parish history. SC 3.4.1931, Rp No 222
7141 **Dunningham, P.** Raydon . . . an illustrated local survey. 1958. [Typescript]
7142 **Birch, H. W.** Church notes: Raydon. E Ang NS 12, 1907/08, 231–3

REDE   *See also* **1959**

7143 Rede parish history. SC 2.6.1933, Rp No 313
7144 Rede church [Appeal for restoration of tower]. [1958]. nl

REDGRAVE   *See also* **685, 2277**

7145 Redgrave parish history. SC 22.8.1930, Rp No 190
7146 **Dodd, K. M.** History of the manor of Redgrave in the county of Suffolk, 1538–1700. Ph.D. thesis, Chicago, 1958
7147 **[Todd, J. K.]** Historical notes about Redgrave village. Redgrave, [c.1976]
7148 **[Todd, J. K.]** History of Redgrave church. 1968. 1970. 1973. [Typescript]
7149 **Farrer, E.** Ancient deed box [at Redgrave Hall]. PSIA 18, 1922/4, 235–8
7150 **Farrer, E.** Redgrave Hall muniments. 1924. MS
7151 **Farrer. E.** Armorial seals on the charters in the muniment room at Redgrave Hall and Keswick Hall. 1926. MS
7152 **[Farrer, E.]** Redgrave Hall of the 16th century. MSS, newspaper cuttings, and articles from EADT, 1928
7153 **Sandeen, E. R.** Building of Redgrave Hall, 1545–54. PSIA 29, 1961/3, 1–33

REDISHAM, GREAT

7154 Great Redisham parish history. EADT 28.7.1937

REDLINGFIELD

7155 Redlingfield parish history. SC 23.5.1930, Rp No 177

RENDHAM

7156 Rendham parish history. SC 29.5.1931, Rp No 230

RENDLESHAM

7157 Rendlesham parish history. SC 28.10.1927, Rp No 43

7158 Ashton, P. Rendlesham, a brief history and guide. 1975

7159 Bruce-Mitford, R. L. S. Saxon Rendlesham. PSIA 24, 1946/8, 228–51

7160 Arnott, W. G. Early medieval occupation site at Rendlesham. PSIA 25, 1949/51, 308

7161 Letter to the churchwardens and overseers of the parish of Rendlesham on a Bill for repealing Acts relative to the incorporation of the Hundreds of Loes and Wilford. Woodbridge, 1825. BL

REYDON   *See also* 1606, 7369, 7832

7162 Reydon parish history. SC 28.9.1928, Rp No 91

7163 Our parish: past and present. Catalogue of an exhibition at the parish church of St. Margaret, Reydon, 16–19 July 1963. [Typescript]. SM

7164 Reydon inclosure. State of claims [delivered to the Commissioners]. Great Yarmouth, [1798]. BL

7165 Welford, A. Reydon parish church. PSIA 26, 1952/4, 58

7166 Reydon and Wangford parish magazine, 1887–1949, *cont. as* Reydon parish magazine, 1950–

RICKINGHALL

7167 Rickinghall Inferior and Superior parish histories. SC 3.10.1930, Rp No 196

7168 Tuck, –. Rickinghall; compiled from notes and records by B. Brown. [c.1952]. [Typescript]. SRO/B

7169 Flowerdew, A. K. Rickinghall in the county of Suffolk. Rickinghall, [1953]. SRO/B

7170 Farrer, E. Rickinghall surveys. 1929. MS

RINGSFIELD

7171 Ringsfield parish history. EADT 28.12.1934, Rp No 381

7172 Ringsfield and its church. 1949. nl

7173 Ringsfield church, Suffolk, 1450–1950, fifth centenary: broadcast service. [1950]

7174 Shelford, –. A book of the rectory of Ringsfield, 1603. nd [Typescript]

RINGSHALL

7175 Ringshall parish history. EADT 24.5.1933, Rp No 312

7176 Growse, F. S. Curious fresco in Ringshall church. E Ang 1, 1858/63, 77, 110

RISBRIDGE RURAL DISTRICT   *See also* 2406

7177   **Risbridge Rural Sanitary District**. Annual report of the Medical Officer of Health, 1892, 1894. Clare. BL

RISBY

7178   Risby parish history. SC 18.7.1930, Rp No 185

7179   **Webling, A. F.** Risby. Leicester, 1945

7180   Contents of a barrow in Risby and Barrow parishes. GM 1st Ser 54, 1784, 85–6

7181   **Gedge, J. D.,** *and* **Greenwell,** *Canon.* Examination of Suffolk tumuli: Risby. QJSIA 1, 1869, 37–40

7182   **Hewitt, H. D.** Some flint-chipping sites at Risby. PPSEA 3, 1918–22, 67–72

7183   **Edwardson, A. R.** Further excavations on tumuli at Risby, 1959. PSIA 28, 1958/60, 153–60

7184   **Legg, F. T.** Parish church of St. Giles, Risby. Bury St. Edmunds, [1972]

7185   **Rouse, E. C.** Wall-paintings in Risby church. PSIA 26, 1952/4, 27–34

RISHANGLES

7186   Rishangles parish history. SC 12.6.1931, Rp No 232

ROUGHAM   *See also* 2525, 3350–53

7187   Rougham parish history. SC 16.5.1930, Rp No 176

7188   **Henslow, J. S.** Account of the Roman antiquities found at Rougham, near Bury St. Edmunds, 15 September 1843. Bury St. Edmunds, 1843. SRO/B

7189   **Henslow, J. S.** Roman tumulus, Eastlow Hill, Rougham. Rp from Bury Post. [Bury St. Edmunds], [1844]. BL

7190   **Bablington, C.,** *and* **Henslow, J. S.** Roman antiquities found in Rougham in 1843 and 1844. PSIA 4, 1864/74, 257–81

7191   **Henslow, G.** Romans at Rougham. ECM 1, 1901, 195–203

7192   Romano-British lamp found at Rougham. Reliquary NS 8, 1902, 127–30

7193   Church of St. Mary, Rougham. Ipswich, 1965. SCL/L. 1968. SRO/B

RUMBURGH

7194   **Raven, J. J.** Rumburgh. PSIA 9, 1895/7, 256–61

7195   Rumburgh parish history. SC 9.8.1929, Rp No 136

7196   **Redstone, V. B.** Site of Rumburgh priory. PSIA 14, 1910/12, 319–22

7197   **Cane, L. B.** Rumburgh priory church. PSIA 22, 1934/6, 155–69

RUSHBROOKE   *See also* **3083, 3281**

7198   Rushbrooke parish history. SC 26.9.1930, Rp No 195

7199   **Turner,** *Canon.* Rushbrooke church. PSIA 7, 1889/91, 332–3

7200   **Davy, H. I.,** *and* **D. E.** Rushbrooke church notes: rectors, monuments, and extracts from parish registers. PSIA 7, 1889/91, 336–62

7201   **Bennett, J. W.** Rushbrooke church. Bury St. Edmunds, 1969. 1971. nl

7202   **Haslewood, F.** Rushbrooke Hall. PSIA 7, 1889/91, 329–32

7203   Rushbrooke Hall. CL 14, 1903, 524–51

7204   Rushbrook parish registers, 1567–1850, with Jermyn and Davers annals. [Preface signed: S.H.A.H. (ervey)]. Woodbridge, 1903. SGB 6

RUSHMERE, nr Ipswich

7205   **Chevallier, T.** Rushmere St. Andrew: our village past and present. 1930. MS

7206   Rushmere St. Andrew parish history. EADT 6.12.1933, Rp No 335

7207   **Tye, W.** Rushmere St. Andrew, the parish with a difference. SR 2, 1961, 91–8

7208   Rushmere bricks. SR 2, 1963, 184–7

7209   **Tye, W.** St. Andrew's church, Rushmere. SR 2, 1964, 260–66

7210   **Fraser, J.** Rushmere 800 + : a commemorative brochure on the occasion of the re-hallowing . . . of the parish church of St. Andrew, Rushmere, 30 June 1968. Ipswich, 1968

7211   Outlook [parish magazine], Jan 1941–

7212   Rushmere Golf Club. Official handbook. Var. edns

RUSHMERE, nr Lowestoft

7213   Rushmere parish history. EADT 8.9.1937, Rp No 482

ST. OLAVES   *See* Herringfleet

SAMFORD HUNDRED   *See also* **694–695, 2440–41**

7214   **Partridge, C.** Suffolk rural population a hundred years ago [Samford Hundred]. ER 53, 1944, 126–7

7215   **Partridge, C.** Churchyard inscriptions from parishes in the Hundred of Samford. English Monumental Inscriptions Soc 1912. SRO/B

SAMFORD RURAL DISTRICT

7216   Official guide. 1950 and later edns

SANTON DOWNHAM *See also* 613, 3278

7217 **Parker, J.** Santon Downham forest walk [Walks in Thetford Forest, no 2]. nd
7218 Santon Downham parish history. EADT 24.7.1935, Rp No 404
7219 **Smith, R. A.** Hoard of metal found at Santon Downham [Roman]. PCAS 13, 1908/09, 146–63
7220 **Evans, J.** Hoard of ancient British coins found at Santon Downham. NC NS 9, 1869, 319–26. Arch J 27, 1870, 92–8
7221 Santon Downham: the parish church. [1966]. [Typescript]. SRO/B

SAPISTON

7222 Sapiston parish history. EADT 31.8.1932, Rp No 283

SAXHAM, GREAT *See also* 2837

7223 Great Saxham parish history. SC 27.2.1914, Rp No 2
7224 **Scarfe, N.** Great Saxham Hall. PSIA 26, 1952/4, 230–31
7225 **Jones, G. A.** John Eldred. TMBS 8, 1943/51, 56–60

SAXHAM, LITTLE

7226 Little Saxham. PSIA 11, 1901/03, 68–71
7227 Little Saxham parish history. SC 27.3.1914, Rp No 6
7228 Little Saxham parish registers: Baptisms, marriages, and burials, with appendices, biographies, etc. 1559 to 1850. [Preface signed S.H.A.H(ervey)]. Woodbridge, 1901. SGB 5

SAXMUNDHAM *See also* 1115, 2891

7229 Official guide. 1956 and later edns
7230 Saxmundham parish history. 2 pts. EADT 6.1.1937, 13.1.1937, Rp Nos 459, 460
7231 **Saxmundham and Wickham Market Horticultural Society.** Annual reports, 1837–44. Saxmundham. BL
7232 Prospectus for enlarging and improving the Corn and Cattle Market, in the town of Saxmundham, etc. Saxmundham, [1836]. BL
7233 **Oldershaw, A. W.** Experiments on arable crops at Saxmundham. Rp from J of Roy Agric Soc of England 102, 1941
7234 Parish church of St. John-the-Baptist, Saxmundham. Gloucester, [1936]. 1967. O
7235 Parish magazine Jan 1887–Dec 1966: Saxmundham Review Jan 1967–
7236 Town and Country Planning Act, 1947, section 30. Provisional list of buildings of architectural or historic interest for consideration. Saxmundham, nd. [Typescript]

7237 **Department of the Environment.** List of buildings of special architectural or historic interest: District of Suffolk Coastal (Saxmundham area). 1975. [Typescript]

SAXSTEAD   *See also* **4968, 4978, 5010**

7238 Saxstead parish history. EADT 13.1.1933, Rp No 297
7239 **Owles, E. [J]** Roman road at Saxstead. PSIA 32, 1970/2, 272–3
7240 **Wailes, R.** Saxstead Green mill. Arch J 108, 1951, 154–6
7241 **Ministry of Works.** Saxstead Green mill. By R. Wailes. [1960] and later edns

SEMER   *See also* **4318**

7242 Semer parish history. SC 20.7.1928, Rp No 81

SHADINGFIELD   *See also* **8099**

7243 Shadingfield parish history. EADT 6.6.1934, Rp No 356
7244 **Hollis, T. K.** Church of St. John-the-Baptist, Shadingfield. nd

SHELLAND

7245 Shelland parish history. EADT 7.3.1934, Rp No 346
7246 **Hill, H. C.** Church plate, Shelland. PSIA 19, 1925/7, 355–6

SHELLEY   *See also* **3098, 3210, 3422**

7247 **Partridge, C.** Notes on the history of the parish of Shelley. nd. MS
7248 Shelley parish history. SC 21.3.1930, Rp No 168

SHIMPLING

7249 Shimpling parish history. EADT 28.3.1934, Rp No 348

SHINGLE STREET   *See* Hollesley

SHIPMEADOW

7250 **Chambers, W. J.,** *Ed.* Extracts and notes relating to Shipmeadow, co. Suffolk. 1920. MS. SCL/L
7251 **Chambers, W. J.,** *Ed.* A few facts about Shipmeadow, co. Suffolk. [c.1920]. MS. SCL/L
7252 Shipmeadow parish history. EADT 22.4.1936, Rp.No 434
7253 **Mann, E.** Shipmeadow Union House. Extract from the diary of an inmate of Shipmeadow Union House, from 1837 to April 1850. PSIA 23, 1937/9, 42–9
7254 Parish registers of Shipmeadow, co. Suffolk. *Ed.* by W. J. Chambers. 1920. SCL/L

SHOTLEY   *See also* 949, 1625, 2858, 4881

7255 Shotley parish history. SC 12.8.1932, Rp No 280

7256 **Birch, H. W.** Church notes: Shotley. E Ang NS 8, 1899/1900, 22–3

7257 Shotley parish registers, 1571 to 1850, with all tombstone inscriptions in church and churchyard Shotley parish records. With illustrations, maps and pedigrees. [*Ed.* by S. H. A. Hervey]. 2 v. Bury St. Edmunds, 1911–12. SGB 16

SHOTTISHAM   *See also* 3338–41

7258 Shottisham parish history. SC 29.4.1932, Rp No 269

SIBTON   *See also* 2592, 2658, 3082, 7102

7259 Sibton parish history. SC 7.9.1928, Rp No 88

7260 **Attmere, A. A.** Worth a mention: recollections of my boyhood in the rambling parish of Sibton, Suffolk. Norwich, [1971]. SCL/L

7261 Report of the Orphans' Home, Sibton, Yoxford, Suffolk. First, second, third, fifth, ninth, 1869–. Saxmundham. BL. First report. SRO/I

7262 **Manning, C. R.** Note on MSS: register of Sibton abbey, Edward III; Subsidy roll of Hoxne hundred, 17 Car. II. Arch J 26, 1869, 406

7263 **Hope, W. H. St. J.** Sibton abbey. PSIA 8, 1892/4, 54–60

7264 **Brown, R. A.** Early charters of Sibton abbey. PRS NS 36, 1960, 65–76

7265 **Denney, A. H.** Sibton abbey estates: selected documents, 1325–1509. Ipswich, 1960. SRS 2.

7266 **Moore, J. L. M.** Sibton church. PSIA 8, 1892/4, 60–64

SIZEWELL   *See* Leiston

SLAUGHDEN   *See also* Aldeburgh

7267 **Smith, C. H. H.** Slaughden story. Leiston, 1964. SCL/L.

SNAPE

7268 Snape parish history. SC 21.10.1928, Rp No 90

7269 **Davidson, S.** Discovery in … 1862 of antiquities on Snape Common. PSA 2nd Ser 2, 1861/4, 177–82

7270 **Scarth, H. M.** Excavations of Anglo-Saxon burials at Snape. Arch J 20, 1863, 188–91

7271 **Francis, F.** Excavations of Anglo-Saxon burials at Snape. Arch J 20, 1863, 373–4

7272 **West, S. E.,** *and* **Owles, E.** [J.] Anglo-Saxon cremation burials from Snape. PSIA 33, 1973/5, 47–57

7273 **Bruce-Mitford, R. L. S.** Snape boat grave. PSIA 26, 1952/4, 1–26

7274 **Irving, R. A.** Snape: the short history of a Suffolk village. Ipswich, 1948. 2nd edn. Framlingham, 1966

7275 **Simper, R.** Over Snape bridge: the story of Snape Maltings. Ipswich, [1967]

7276 **Pipe, J.** Port on the Alde: Snape and the maltings. Snape, [1976]. NCL/N

7277 Maltings Concert Hall and Opera House, Snape: a brief illustrated description. 1966. SCL/L

7278 **Sugden, D.** Snape Concert Hall. Arup Jour 1, no 4, June 1967

7279 **Aldeburgh Festival Committee.** Appeal for £112,000 to complete the re-building of Snape Maltings Concert Hall and Opera House. [1969]. SCL/L

SOMERLEYTON *See also* **2295, 3222–3, 7318**

7280 [**Halpin, J.**] Somerleyton: an illustrated guide. Norwich, 1975. SCL/L

7281 **Brooks, E. C.** Somerleyton: a thousand years of village history. Somerleyton, [1977]. SCL/L

7282 Bronze hoard from Suffolk [Somerleyton]. Ant J 8, 1928, 236–7

7283 [**Butler, A.,** *and* **A.**] History of the brickfields, Somerleyton. Somerleyton, 1974. 2nd ed 1976. [Typescript]. SCL/L

7284 **B[ean], C. W.** Brief history of the manor of Somerleyton and Somerleyton church in pamphlet form, as compiled from various sources. 1903. SCL/L

7285 Particulars of Somerleyton estate and church. nd. SCL/L

7286 **Brooks, E. C.** Church of St. Mary, Somerleyton, its benefactors and environment. [1970]. O

7287 **Long, C. M.** Somerleyton Hall. 1954. SCL/L

7288 Somerleyton Hall, Suffolk home of Lord and Lady Somerleyton. Norwich, 1969. SCL/L

SOMERSHAM

7289 Somersham parish history. SC 28.3.1930, Rp No 169

7290 **Birch, H. W.** Church notes: Somersham. E Ang NS 6, 1895/6, 156–7

SOMERTON

7291 Somerton parish history. EADT 17.10.1934, Rp No 372

7292 **Rotherham, W.,** *Ed.* Parish registers of Somerton, in the county of Suffolk. 4 v. Somerton, 1879–84. nl

SOTHERTON *See also* **2480, 2740, 3044**

7293 Sotherton parish history. EADT 28.10.1936, Rp No 453

SOTTERLEY   *See also* **2496, 2504, 2740, 8099**

7294   Sotterley parish history. EADT 12.9.1934, Rp No 367

7295   **Hollis, T. K.** St. Margaret's church, Sotterley. Southwold, nd

7296   Sotterley, with Willingham and Shadingfield parish magazine, *extant* 1948–60, *cont. as* The Sheaf 1963–.

7297   Monumental inscriptions at Sotterley church. E Ang 4, 1869/70, 289–91

SOUTH COVE

7298   South Cove parish history. EADT 25.7.1934, Rp No 361

SOUTH ELMHAM ALL SAINTS-CUM-ST. NICHOLAS   *See also* **1588**

7299   South Elmham All Saints-cum-St. Nicholas parish history. EADT 1.9.1933. Rp No 323

SOUTH ELMHAM ST. CROSS   *See also* **1588, 1804–05**

7300   South Elmham St. Cross parish history. SC 10.10.1930, Rp No 197

7301   **Woodward, B. B.** The old minster, South Elmham. PSIA 4, 1864/74, 1–7

7302   **Harrod, H.** On the site of the bishopric at Elmham. PSIA 4, 1864/74, 7–13

7303   **Raven, J. J.** The 'old minster', South Elmham. PSIA 10, 1898/1900, 1–6

7304   **Middlethwaite, J. T.** The old minster at South Elmham classified and described. PSIA 16, 1916/18, 29–35

7305   **Stevenson, F. S.** Present state of the Elmham controversy. PSIA 19, 1925/7, 110–16

7306   **Smedley, N.,** *and* **Owles, E. J.** Excavations at the old minster, South Elmham. PSIA 32, 1970, 1–16

SOUTH ELMHAM ST. JAMES   *See also* **1588**

7307   South Elmham St. James parish history. EADT 29.3.1933, Rp No 306

7308   **Turner, S. B.** Discovery of mural paintings in the church of St. James, South Elmham. Arch J 7, 1850, 297–8

SOUTH ELMHAM ST. MARGARET   *See also* **1588**

7309   South Elmham St. Margaret parish history. SC 24.10.1930, Rp No 199

SOUTH ELMHAM ST. MICHAEL   *See also* **1588**

7310   South Elmham St. Michael parish history. EADT 2.8.1933, Rp No 320

SOUTH ELMHAM ST. PETER   *See also* **1588**

7311   South Elmham St. Peter parish history. EADT 10.10.1934, Rp No 371

7312 Farrer, E. St. Peter's Hall, South Elmham. PSIA 20, 1928/30, 48–72

7313 Cane, L. B. St. Peter's Hall, South Elmham. nd. [Typescript]

SOUTHOLT *See also* 2659

7314 Southolt parish history. EADT 23.1.1935, Rp No 384

SOUTHWOLD

GUIDES *See also* 734, 3530, 3535, 4890, 6571, 6574

7315 [Wodderspoon, J.] Southwold and its vicinity, etc. Ipswich, 1844. BL

7316 **Stebbings, A.** Visitors' guide book to Southwold (and its vicinity). Lowestoft, [1887]. BL

7317 **Barrett, C. R. B.** Round Southwold. 1892. 1894. Grangerized copy

7318 Illustrated guide to Southwold, including Lowestoft, Somerleyton. 7th edn [1897]. BL

7319 **Lingwood, L.** *Ed.* Jarrold's illustrated guide to Southwold and neighbourhood. Norwich, 1904

7320 **Cooper, E. R.** Southwold, the official publication of the corporation. 1905 and later edns

7321 Ward Lock's pictorial and descriptive guide to Southwold, Dunwich, Aldeburgh, Felixstowe, and the Suffolk coast. 3rd edn [1907] and later edns

7322 **Jenkins, F.** Pictorial and descriptive guide to Southwold, Walberswick, Dunwich, Blythburgh, and Covehithe. Southwold, [1908]. O

7323 "Borough" pocket guide to Southwold. Cheltenham, [1919]. BL

7324 Official guide. 1929 and later edns

7325 Southwold: a guide which includes 'Bygone Sowl' by E. R. Cooper, and nature study notes by D. W. Collings. Southwold, 1932. O

7326 16 views of Southwold and neighbourhood, publ. by Francis Pipe. Southwold, nd

GENERAL AND ECONOMIC HISTORY *See also* 1247–8, 1420–24, 2026, 2738, 2960–61, 3359–62

7327 Catalogue of books and documents belonging to the corporation of Southwold, 1 Sept 1869. 1871

7328 An interesting history and topographical description of Southwold and its vicinity. Halesworth, 1817

7329 **Wake, R.** Southwold and its vicinity, ancient and modern. Great Yarmouth, 1839. 2nd edn London, 1842

7330 Southwold parish history. SC 2.9.1927, Rp No 36

7331 **Becker, M. J.** *Ed.* Story of Southwold. Southwold, 1948

7332 Southwold: a survey made by the boys of Eversley School. Southwold, [1970]. SCL/L

7333 **Bottomley, A. F.** Short history of the borough of Southwold. Southwold, 1974

7334 **Carter, J. I.,** *and* **Bacon, S. R.** Southwold, Suffolk: the fortified anchorage of Sole Bay. np. 1976. SCL/L

7335 **Gooding, J.** Brass coin of Constantius I found at Southwold. PSA 2, 1849/53, 184

7336 **Grubb, J. E.** Vestiges of Roman colonization discovered in the neighbourhood of Southwold. PSIA 7, 1889/91, 303–10

7337 **M, J.** Southwold in the sixteenth century. E Ang 3, 1866/8, 49–51, 62–3, 71–3

7338 **Becker, M. J.** Sutherland House and Sole Bay. Southwold, [c.1945]. SCL/L

7339 **Mackesy, P. J.** Southwold guns. Southwold, 1950. 2nd edn 1965. SCL/L

7340 **X.,** The Southwold horses. CL 26, 1910, 871–4

7341 **Johnson, F. H. C.** Southwold fair. Folk-Lore 63, 1952, 36

MARITIME HISTORY AND HARBOUR *See also* **276, 938–9, 1300, 1304, 2160,** Dunwich, *above, and* Walberswick, *below*

7342 Battle of Sole Bay, May 28, 1672. Tercentenary commemoration week programme. Southwold, 1972. nl

7343 Southwold petition (on fishing). GM 1st Ser 20, 1750, 294–5

7344 Articles made and agreed to by a Friendly Society of Sailors, etc., at Southwold in Suffolk, 6 Nov 1792. Ipswich, 1794. nl. 8 Jan 1805, Halesworth 1805. LSE. 5 March 1834, Southwold, 1834, LSE

7345 Account of the melancholy accident which happened to a Southwold fishing boat near the Hasborough Sand ... 11 Oct 1823. Bungay, 1823. BL

7346 Southwold harbour. Abstract of the Treasurer's account for the year ending the 30th June 1836 [to the year ending 30 June 1844]. Southwold, [1836–44] BL

7347 Report [of F. W. Ellis] on Southwold harbour, submitted at a special meeting of the commissioners held 27 June 1839. Southwold, 1839

7348 Letter addressed to ... the Earl of Stradbroke as to the expediency of improving the harbour of Southwold by means of the river Blyth. Halesworth, 1840

7349 **Walker, J.** Report made 25 Aug 1841 to the Commissioners of the Southwold harbour on the state of the harbour, bar, and river ... Halesworth, 1841. SM

7350 **Maggs, J.** Handbook to the port and shipping at Southwold. Halesworth, 1842

7351 **Calver, E. K.** Proposals for improvement of Southwold harbour. Beccles, 1844

7352 Report of William Teasdel to the commissioners of Southwold harbour, 5 July 1856

7353 **Cooper, E. R.** Story of a hundred years' fight with the sea. Southwold, 1905

7354 **Cooper, E. R.** Brief history of Southwold haven, illustrated from the corporation records, pages of Gardner and Wake, and from other sources. Southwold, 1907. NCL/N

7355 **Cooper, E. R.** Southwold old harbour: a collection of ... photographs. 1907. SCL/L

7356 Southwold life-boat [Resolution of the managing committee in reference to the support of the "Life Boat Fund"]. [Southwold], [1847]. BL

7357 **Cooper, E. R.** Seventy years' work of the Southwold lifeboats [from 1840 to 1912]. Southwold, 1912. nl

LOCAL GOVERNMENT AND SOCIAL SERVICES
The Municipality See also **1454–5, 1470, 1542**

7358 Extracts from the report of the Select Committee of the House of Commons ... on the privileges and private property of the Freemen of cities and boroughs in England and Wales. With the proceedings of the Committee and minutes of evidence as far as the same relate to the borough of Southwold. Southwold, 1840. BL

7359 **Royal Commission on Historical Manuscripts.** Reports Ser 55. Var. Coll. 7 ... Corporations of Beccles, Dunwich, Southwold ... 1914

7360 **Southwold Corporation.** Agenda for the council meeting on 1 July 1958, and minutes of meetings of the council and committees. Southwold, 1958–. BL

7361 **Southwold Corporation.** Municipal year book, 1960/61–. Southwold, 1960–. SCL/L

7362 **Southwold Corporation.** Epitome of accounts ... for the year ended 31 March 1959–. Southwold, 1959–. BL

Public Health

7363 Rules and regulations of the Southwold institution for the relief and assistance of the necessitous sick, lying-in, and infirm poor. Southwold, 1838. nl

7364 **Southwold Corporation.** Annual report on the health of the borough for the year 1954–, by ... Medical Officer of Health. Southwold, 1954–. [Typescript]

Education

7365 St. Felix School, Southwold, 1897–1923. [*Ed.* by E. Watson *and* B. C. Brown]. [1924]. SCL/L

7366 Saint Felix School, Southwold, 1897–1972. Frinton-on-Sea, 1975. SCL/L

7367 Cloister, St. Felix School, Southwold. RIBA J 3rd Ser 42, 1935, 317–19

Planning and Development

7368 **East Suffolk County Council.** Planning Dept. Factual survey of the borough of Southwold, by T. B. Oxenbury. Ipswich, [1948]. [Typescript]. SCL/L

7369 **East Suffolk County Council.** Planning Dept. Southwold and Reydon: factual survey and outline plan. Ipswich, 1961

CHURCH OF ST. EDMUND
7370 **M, G. W.** The Southwold brief. E Ang 3, 1866/8, 103
7371 Southwold St Edmund. PSIA 4, 1864/74, 450–53

7372 **Phipson, R. M.** Southwold church. JBAA 36, 1880, 201–05

7373 **Grubbe,** *Captain.* Southwold church. PSIA 8, 1892/4, 413–16

7374 Southwold parish church: its history and interesting features. Southwold, 1912

7375 Southwold parish church (the chapel of St. Edmund): guide and history. 1930

7376 **Muir, D. E.** Historical guide to Southwold parish church. Southwold, 1950 and later edns

7377 Parish magazine, 1868–1924, *cont. as* Southwold magazine. SM

7378 **Gooding, J.** Paintings on the roof of Southwold church. PSA 2, 1849/56, 170–71

7379 **Blackburne, E. L.** Some account of the ancient painted decorations existing in Southwold church. Civil Engineer and Architects' Jour 1860, 22–3

7380 **M, J.** Inscriptions on bells: Southwold. E Ang 3, 1866/8, 224

ROMAN CATHOLICISM

7381 Church of the Sacred Heart, Southwold. Consecration programme, 7 June 1956. SCL/L

BUILDINGS

7382 **Department of the Environment.** List of buildings of special architectural or historic interest: borough of Southwold, East Suffolk. 1971. [Typescript]

7383 Panel painting found in a cottage at Southwold. NA 8, 1871/8, 326

7384 Crown Hotel, Southwold. nd

7385 **Adnams & Co. Ltd.** Signposts to Adnams: where to find good beer and how to get there. Southwold, [1966]. SCL/L

NATURAL ENVIRONMENT   *See also* 2026, 2151

7386 **Bradfield, W.** Popular essay on bathing, with remarks on scrofula, and on the salubrity of Southwold. Halesworth, 1840. SCL/L

7387 **Herbert, A. C.** Southwold: a memoir on its climatology. Bromley, 1898

7388 Southwold Golf Club. Official handbook. nd

INSCRIPTIONS   *See also* 2441, 3360

7389 **Gooding, D. R.** Monumental inscriptions remaining in the churchyard at the parish church of St. Edmund, Southwold. REMI 2, 1913/14, 104–14

7390 **Gooding, D. R.** Monumental inscriptions from the graveyard of the Congregational church, Southwold. REMI 2, 1913/14, 46–7

SPEXHALL

7391 Spexhall parish history. EADT 16.9.1936, Rp No 449

7392 Spexhall and Wissett parish magazine, c.1930–1970, *now* News Letter

SPROUGHTON

7393   Sproughton parish history. SC 27.2.1931, Rp No 217

7394   L[arkin], L. B. Grant of Sprouton [*sic*] by Robert de Blancheville to the canons of Ipswich. CTetG 4, 1837, 242–3

7395   Read, C. H. Bronze Age dagger blade from Sproughton. PSA 2nd Ser 22, 1907/09, 86–8

7396   Birch, H. W. Church notes: Sproughton. E Ang NS 13, 1909/10, 136–41

7397   Wells, E. A. All Saints' church, Sproughton. Ramsgate, 1964 and later edns

STANNINGFIELD

7398   Stanningfield parish history. SC 12.9.1930, Rp No 193

7399   Wake, T. St. Nicholas church, Stanningfield. 1970

7400   Long, E. T. Stanningfield Doom. Burl 70, 1937, 128

7401   Parish magazine, 1922–67, *cont. as* Parish Newsletter, May, 1967–

7402   Tymms, S. Coldham Hall in Stanningfield, and Stanningfield church. PSIA 3, 1860/63, 301–10

7403   Parish registers of Stanningfield, Suffolk: index, 4 v. in 1 v. 1897–8. [v 1. Baptisms, marriages, burials, 1561–1702. v 2. Baptisms, 1703–91; marriages, 1703–52; burials, 1703–91. v 3. Marriages, 1753–1812; v 4. Baptisms, burials, 1792–1812]. SRO/B

STANSFIELD

7404   Stansfield parish history. SC 27.3.1936, Rp No 431

7405   Little, J. R. Stansfield parish notices. PSIA 10, 1898/1900, 345–59

7406   Colman, G., *and* S. Thirteenth-century aisled house: Purton Green Farm, Stansfield. PSIA 30, 1964/6, 149–65

STANSTEAD

7407   Stanstead parish history. EADT 27.6.1934. Rp No 358

7408   Atkinson, B. F. C. Fragment of Nicholas Trevet on the mass [in Stanstead church]. PSIA 23, 1937/9, 179–80

STANTON

7409   Stanton parish history. 2 pts. EADT 25.4.1934, 2.5.1934, Rp Nos 351, 352

7410   Maynard, G., *and* Brown, B. Roman settlement at Stanton Chair [Chare], near Ixworth. PSIA 22, 1934/6, 339–41

7411   Dymond, D. [P.] Parish churches of Stanton, Suffolk. Stowmarket, 1977

STERNFIELD

7412   Sternfield parish history. EADT 22.3.1933, Rp No 305

7413   **Fayle-Parr, W.** Parish church of St. Mary Magdalene, Sternfield: reflections by the rector. 1961

STOKE ASH   *See also* **654, 657–8**

7414   Stoke Ash parish history. SC 9.5.1930, Rp No 175

7415   **Sewell, W. H.** On the parish and parish church of All Saints, Stoke Ash. PSIA 4, 1864/74, 417–43

7416   **Raven, J. J.** Marriages of "foreigners" at Stoke Ash. E Ang NS 9, 1901/02, 102–05

STOKE-BY-CLARE   *See also* **714, 1541, 2842–4**

7417   **Payne, A.** Story of Stoke-by-Clare. [c.1928]. [Typescript]

7418   Stoke-by-Clare parish history. SC 18.10.1929, Rp No 146

7419   **Hope, W. H. St. J.** Inventories of the college of Stoke-by-Clare taken in 1534 and 1547–8. PSIA 17, 1919/21, 21–77

7420   **Rose, H.** Stoke-by-Clare parish church: a few brief notes. 1950 and later edns. [Typescript]

7421   **Farrer, E.** Seal of the priory of Stoke-by-Clare. PSIA 20, 1928/30, 265–9; 21, 1931/3, 166–9

STOKE-BY-NAYLAND   *See also* **2460**

7422   **Torlesse, C. M.,** *Ed.* Some account of Stoke-by-Nayland, Suffolk. 1877. 90 copies

7423   Stoke-by-Nayland parish history. SC 9.12.1927, Rp No 49

7424   **Torlesse, C. M.** Stoke-by-Nayland church. PSIA 4, 1864/74, 183–207

7425   Church of St. Mary-the-Virgin, Stoke-by-Nayland. Hadleigh, [c.1956]

7426   **Engleheart, F. [H. A.]** Church of St. Mary-the-Virgin, Stoke-by-Nayland. Gloucester, [1964]. 1971

7427   **Jarrett, B.** Catholic registers of Rev. James Dominic Darbyshire, O.P., at ... Stoke-by-Nayland, Suffolk, 1728 ... CRS 25, 1925, 247–52

7428   **Tipping, H. A.** Gifford's Hall in Stoke-by-Nayland. CL 54, 1923, 488–95, 524–31

7429   **Bagenhall, H.** Gifford's Hall: notes written for a visit of the Suffolk Institute of Archaeology, 1947. [Typescript]. SRO/B

7430   **Clifton-Taylor, A.,** *and* **Graham, A.** Gifford's Hall. Conn 154, 1963, 209–15

7431   **Spittle, D.** Gifford's Hall, Stoke-by-Nayland. PSIA 30, 1964/6, 183–7

7432   **Evans, H. F. O.** Peyton slabs at Stoke-by-Nayland. TMBS 10, 1963/8, 13–15

7433   **Blatchly, J. M.** The Peyton indents at Stoke-by-Nayland. TMBS 11, 1973, 382

7434 **Partridge, C.** Heraldry at Stoke-by-Nayland vicarage. E Ang NS 10, 1903/04, 259–60

7435 Inscriptions in Stoke-by-Nayland churchyard, Suffolk. [*Ed.* by C. M. Torlesse], 1877. nl

STONHAM ASPAL *See also* 2541

7436 Stonham Aspal parish history. SC 6.3.1914, Rp No 3

7437 History of Stonham Aspal. Rp from Stonham Aspal School Magazine, 1954–9

7438 **Smedley, N.,** *et al.* Romano-British bath house at Stonham Aspal. PSIA 30, 1964/6, 221–51

7439 Church of St. Mary and St. Lambert, Stonham Aspal. Based on notes by T. O. Wonnacott. [c.1960]. nl

7440 **Watling, H.** Ancient painted glass at Stonham Aspal. E Ang NS 6, 1895/6, 45–6

7441 **Penrose, D.,** *and* **Hall, P.** Houses of Stonham Aspal. SR 4, no 1, 1971, 8–45

7442 **Charman, D.** Ubbeston Hall in Stonham Aspal. SR 4, no 1, 1971, 46–52

7443 **Pearson, W. C.** Earliest register of Stonham Aspal. E Ang NS 7, 1897/8, 75–7, 93–5

STONHAM, LITTLE *See also* 2945

7444 Little Stonham parish history. SC 25.7.1930, Rp No 186

7445 **Watling, H.** Roman remains at Stonham. JBAA 24, 1868, 184–6

7446 **Shrubbs, R. S.** Short history of St. Mary's church, Stonham Parva. [c.1962]

STOVEN

7447 Stoven parish history. EADT 5.7.1934, Rp No 359

STOWLANGTOFT *See also* 3264

7448 Stowlangtoft parish history. SC 25.5.1928, Rp No 73

STOWMARKET

DIRECTORIES AND GUIDES *See also* 5453, 5455

7449 Newby's Stowmarket annual guide and directory. 1942 and later edns. Stowmarket

7450 **Localads.** Stowmarket, Needham Market, and mid-Suffolk directory. 1965 and later edns. Needham Market, 1965–

7451 **Regency Publicity Service.** The Stowmarket book: the directory and reference guide to the commercial, business, and community activities of the area, 1970–71. Folkestone, 1970

7452 Howard, G. F. "Borough" guide to Stowmarket, etc. Cheltenham, [1919]. BL.

7453 Official guide. Croydon, 1965

7454 **Stowmarket Town Council and Stowmarket and District Chamber of Trade**. Stowmarket town guide and directory. Stowmarket, 1977

GENERAL, POLITICAL, SOCIAL, AND ECONOMIC HISTORY *See also* **942, 1334, 1619–23, 2849, 3213, 3265, 3511**

7455 **Hollingsworth, A. G. H.** History of Stowmarket, the ancient county town of Suffolk, with notices of the Hundred of Stow. Ipswich, 1844

7456 **Glyde, J.** Materials for a history of Stowmarket. nd. MSS and cuttings

7457 **"Octoginta"**, *pseud.* [i.e. **C. T. Rust**] Two more chapters in the history of Stowmarket (Supplementary to Hollingsworth's History ... 1844). [Rp from EADT 1888–9] Stowmarket, 1905

7458 Stowmarket parish history. SC 12.6.1914, 19.6.1914. Rp No 14

7459 **Wilkes, H. E.** Notes on the history of Stowmarket. 3 v. [c.1930]. MS

7460 **Black, D.** Stowmarket past and present. Stowmarket, 1946

7461 **Fancourt, St. J. F. M.** Discovery of prehistoric implements at Danecroft Stowmarket. PSIA 13, 1907/09, 113–32

7462 Account of proceedings at a meeting at Stowmarket, 30 Nov 1795 [for a petition against "an Act ... against treasonable and seditious practices and attempts"]. [Stowmarket?], [1795]. BL

7463 **Ince, R. J.** Care of the poor in the parish of Stowmarket, 1780–1830. 1967. [Typescript]

7464 **Driver, G.** Stowmarket postal history. East Anglia Postal History Study Circle Bull. 34, Dec 1970, 17–19

Planning and Development

7465 **East Suffolk County Council**. Planning Dept. Factual survey and outline plan of Stowmarket. Ipswich, 1954. [Typescript]

7466 **East Suffolk County Council**. Planning Dept. County development plan, Amendment no 2. Stowmarket. Approved 1957. Written statement and maps. Ipswich, 1957

7467 **East Suffolk County Council**. Planning Dept. Stowmarket, with parts of Gipping Rural District: report of survey, and appraisal. Ipswich, 1968

7468 **East Suffolk County Council**. Planning Dept. County development plan: Stowmarket and parts of Gipping Rural District, 1970, not yet approved. Written statement and town map. Ipswich, 1970

7469 **East Suffolk County Council**. Planning Dept. Stowmarket, with parts of Gipping Rural District: town-map review, and town-centre map. Ipswich, 1970

CHURCHES
7470 Short statement of the origin of the churches in Stowmarket and Stowupland,

and the consecration of the latter by the Lord Bishop of Norwich, 30 Aug 1843. [By A. G. H. Hollingsworth]. [1843]

7471 **Tymms, S.** Stowmarket church. PSIA 2, 1854/9, 248–56

7472 **Wilkes, H. E.** History of Stowmarket parish church [SS Peter and Mary]. Stowmarket, 1929

7473 Story of St. Peter and St. Mary, Stowmarket. Gloucester, 1949 and later edns

7474 **Wilkes, H. E.** List of vicars and assistant curates of the churches of St. Mary and SS. Peter and Paul (afterwards SS. Peter and Mary), Stowmarket, 1276–1898. 2 v. [1930]. MS

NONCONFORMITY

7475 **Caws, L. W.** History of Nonconformity in Stowmarket: a lecture ... at the Congregational church, Stowmarket, 9 June 1886. Ipswich, 1886. [Rp from Suffolk Chronicle]

7476 **Duncan, J.** History of the Baptist church in Stowmarket. 1966. [Typescript]. SRO/B

7477 Stowmarket: Congregational church, founded 1719; opening and dedication of new church. Stowmarket, 1955. SRO/B

7478 **Banyard, E.** The first 300 years: the unfinished story of Stowmarket Congregational church. Stowmarket, 1970

7479 **Duncan, J.** Methodists in Stowmarket. 1967. [Typescript]. SRO/B

FREEMASONRY

7480 **Prentice, J. M.** History of Phoenix Lodge, No 516, Stowmarket. SIMT, No 3913, 1931

BUILDINGS

7481 **Smith, J. T.** Fourteenth-century aisled house: Edgar's Farm, Stowmarket. PSIA 28, 1958/60, 54–61. *See also* **1623**

7482 Town and Country Planning Act, 1947. section 30. Provisional list of buildings of architectural or historic interest for consideration ... Stowmarket. nd. [Typescript]

STOWMARKET URBAN DISTRICT

7483 **Department of the Environment.** List of buildings of special architectural of historic interest: Urban district of Stowmarket, East Suffolk. 1972. [Typescript]

STOWUPLAND   *See also* **7470**

7484 Stowupland parish history. EADT 3.1.1934, Rp No 338

STRADBROKE   *See also* **1854, 2636–7**

7485 Stradbroke parish history. SC 27.7.1928, Rp No 82

STRADISHALL

7486 Stradishall parish history. EADT 23.10.1935, Rp No 414

7487 **Fleming, I. J. R.** George Chapman, parish clerk and constable of the parish of Stradishall, 1825–58. SR 2, 1963, 207–08

STRATFORD ST. ANDREW

7488 Stratford St. Andrew parish history. EADT 21.2.1934, Rp No 344

STRATFORD ST. MARY   *See also* **2802, 3326, 5345**

7489 Stratford St. Mary parish history. SC 24.4.1914, Rp No 9

7490 **Kenyon, L. R.** A Suffolk village: Stratford St. Mary, 1312–1946. Ipswich, 1951

7491 **Griffin, J. H. H.** Village of Stratford St. Mary and its church. nd. nl

7492 Parish church of Stratford St. Mary, Suffolk: reprinted with corrections and additions from ... the parish magazine. Colchester, 1885

7493 **Brewster, J. G.** Parish church of Stratford St. Mary, Suffolk. Beverley, 2nd edn 1890

7494 **Brewster, J. G.** Stratford St. Mary and its parish church, in the county of Suffolk, and the diocese of Norwich. Norwich, 3rd edn 1900

7495 **Birch, H. W.** Church notes: Stratford St. Mary. E Ang NS 12, 1907/08, 145–9, 312–13

7496 Parish magazine, 1876–1902

7497 **Benton, G. M.** Domestic wall-painting at Stratford St. Mary. Ant J 16, 1936, 213–14

7498 **Hussey, C.** Weaver's house, Stratford St. Mary. CL 98, 1945, 552–5

7499 **Thompson, L. P.** Swann Inn, Stratford, St. Mary. Ipswich, 1946

7500 **Brewster, J. G.** Alphabet in stone at Stratford St. Mary. E Ang NS 1, 1885/6, 182–3, 199

STUSTON   *See also* **2628–9**

7501 Stuston parish history. EADT 29.8.1934, Rp No 366

7502 **Mayfield, A.** Neolithic remains at Stuston. IFCJ 2, 1909, 30–33

7503 **Davenay, H.** Extracts from parish registers: Stuston. E Ang 3, 1866/8, 60–61, 89–90

STUTTON

7504 **Crisp, F. A.,** *Ed.* Some account of the parish of Stutton, near Ipswich, in the county of Suffolk. 1881. 50 copies

7505 Stutton parish history. SC 11.1.1929, Rp No 106

7506 **Whitaker, W.** Trial boring at Stutton [Eastern Counties Coal-boring Assoc.]. RBA 1895, 693

7507 Rules for the Clothing Club at Stutton. [Ipswich?], 1833. BL

7508 **Birch, H. W.** Church notes: Stutton. E Ang NS 13, 1909/10, 181–3, 205–08

7509 **Cornish, C. J.** Cavalier's moated hall [Crowe Hall]. CL 5, 1899, 20–23

7510 **N, R. G.** Crowe Hall, Stutton. CL 122, 1957, 1434–5

SUDBOURNE *See also* 3143–4, 7025, 7038

7511 Sudbourne parish history. SC 25.9.1931, Rp No 247

7512 **Baines, W.** Letter of Thomas Manning, Bishop-Suffragan of Ipswich, 1537, concerning lands at Sudbourne. E Ang NS 13, 1909/10, 81

7513 **Andrew, W. J.** Buried treasure: some traditions, records, and facts [the Sudbourne hoard]. BNJ 1st Ser 1, 1903/04, 9–59

7514 Apportionment of the rent-charge in lieu of tithes in the parish of S., in the county of Suffolk. Woodbridge, 1844. BL

SUDBURY

DIRECTORIES AND ALMANACS

7515 **Localads.** Sudbury and district directory and almanac, 1962 and later edns. Needham Market, 1962–

7516 **Regency Publicity Service.** The Sudbury book: the directory and reference guide to the commercial, business, and community activities of the borough. 1968/69–. Folkestone

7517 Burkitt's almanack, 1796–. Sudbury. nl

7518 Hill's almanack, 1823–. Sudbury. nl

GUIDES

7519 **Hodson, W. W.** Handbook and guide to Sudbury. Sudbury, 1870

7520 Mate's illustrated guides: Sudbury and district. Bournemouth, 1908

7521 Official guide. 1927 and later edns

7522 **Thompson, L. P.,** *Ed.* Sudbury and the valley of the Stour: a guide to this historic Suffolk town, with notes on the surrounding countryside. [Sudbury], [1952]. BL

GENERAL AND POLITICAL HISTORY *See also* 2405, 2411, 2423, 2499, 2614, 2902–2919, 3062, 3208, 3403, 3425

7523 **Skrimshire, A.,** *and* **W[alford], W. S.** Original documents [1397, 1576, 1577] relating to Sudbury. PSIA 1, 1848/53, 199–207

7524 **Stokes, E.,** *and* **Redstone, L. J.** Calendar of the muniments of the borough of Sudbury. PSIA 13, 1907/09, 259–310

7525 **Stokes, E.** Early Sudbury records. PSIA 14, 1910/12, 105–08

7526 **Wood, J. G.** Sudbury charters. nd. [Typescript]

7527 **Braithwaite, T. M.,** *Ed.* Sudbury common lands: a synopsis of the title deeds. Sudbury, 1911. nl

7528 **Blackwell, S. J.** Sudbury's heritage: a collection of notes and evidence and historical background to his registration of certain lands at Sudbury as town and village green. Sudbury, 1972. SRO/B. [Typescript]

7529 **Hodson, W. W.** Short history of the borough of Sudbury ... compiled from materials collected by W. W. Hodson, by C. F. D. Sperling. Sudbury, 1896

7530 **Foster, J. J.,** *and* **Croft, H.** Sudbury, the birthplace of Gainsborough. Antiquary 11, 1885, 111–15, 231, 278

7531 **Adams, O. F.** Our English parent towns: Sudbury. NEH&GR 56, 1902, 179–85

7532 Sudbury parish history, 2 pts. SC 22.5.1914, 29.5.1914, Rp No 13

7533 **Grimwood, C. G.,** *and* **Kay, S. A.** History of Sudbury, Suffolk. Sudbury, 1952

7534 **Powell, S. C.** Puritan village: the formation of a New England town [Sudbury, Massachusetts]. Middleton, Conn 1963. Sudbury, Suffolk 41–58. NCL/N

PARLIAMENTARY HISTORY *See also* **847, 857**

7535 **Gurdon, W. B.** Gurdon papers. No 6. A Sudbury election in 1699. E Ang NS 5, 1893/4, 33–5

7536 **Douglas, S.** History of the cases of controverted elections which were tried and determined during the first (and second) sessions of the fourteenth Parliament of Great Britain, 15 (and 16) Geo. III. 4 v. 1775–77. Sudbury, v 2, 129–78. BL

7537 **Philipps, J.** Election cases; determined during the first session of the fifteenth Parliament ... by committees of the House of Commons ... 1782. Sudbury, 131–216. BL

7538 Account of the vindictive conduct of the corporation party in the borough of Sudbury. Sudbury, 1832. nl

7539 Number of electors registered in the borough of Sudbury as £10 householders and as freemen. HC 1842, 33

7540 Report of the Commissioners, appointed under the Act of 6 & 7 Victoria, chap. 97, to inquire into the existence of bribery in the borough of Sudbury. HC 1844, 18; 1844, 38

7541 **Olney, R.** Sudbury, 1841–44: the end of a parliamentary borough. [c.1966]. [Photocopy]. SRO/B.

POLL BOOKS

7542 Poll ... 1826. nl

7543 Poll ... 1828. nl

7544 Poll ... 1831. nl

7545 Poll ... 1832. (2 edns) nl

7546 Poll ... 1834. nl

7547 Poll ... 1835. nl

7548 Poll ... 1837. (2 edns) nl

7549 Poll ... 1838. nl

7550 Poll ... 1841. BL

ECONOMIC HISTORY
General   See also **1358, 1385, 1393**

7551 **Workers' Educational Association.** Sudbury Branch. Sudbury survey: a history of the industries of Sudbury. [1948]. [Typescript]. SRO/B

7552 Interim report of the commissioner appointed to enquire into the affairs of the Sudbury, Suffolk, Trustee Savings Bank ... Minutes of proceedings and notes of evidence. 1894. HC 1893–4, 83. Rp Shannon, 1969

7553 **Redstone, V. B.** Early Sudbury clothiers. PSIA 14, 1910/12, 99–104

7554 Report from the select committee ... evidence ... on hand-loom weavers ... Sudbury. HC 1842, 7

7555 **Sudbury Gas and Coke Co. Ltd.** Centenary celebration, 1836–1936. Sudbury, 1936

7556 Catalogue of the Sudbury Industrial and Fine Arts exhibition ... 12 May 1875. Sudbury, 1875. SRO/B

Mint

7557 The mint at Sudbury. GM 1st Ser 27, 1757, 203–04, 258, 546–8

7558 **Gemsage, P.** Letter concerning the provenance of a Saxon coin, alleged to be from the Sudbury mint. GM 1st Ser 28, 1758, 21–2

7559 **Dolley, R. H. M.** Mints of Sudbury and Southwark at the end of the reign of Æthelræd II. BNJ 28, 1956/58, 264–9

Postal History

7560 **Wilton, H. E.** Sudbury in postal history. East Anglia Postal History Study Circle Bull 23, Nov 1967, 2–16

MUNICIPAL GOVERNMENT   *See also* **1455, 4256**

7561 **W[alford], W. S.** Note as to the mayor of Sudbury's letter in 1577. PSIA 1, 1848/53, 302–03

7562 **Hodson, W. W.** Election of mayor of Sudbury in 1665. PSIA 8, 1892/4, 9–20

7563 **Hodson, W. W.** Sudbury corporation regalia. PSIA 8, 1892/4, 1–8

7564 **Sperling, C. F. D.** Armorial insignia of the borough of Sudbury. E Ang NS 11, 1905/06, 321–2

7565 [Berry, A.] The freedom of Sudbury: a brief history. Sudbury, 1976. SRO/B

7566 **Sudbury Corporation.** Agenda, minutes, etc., 1964–74. Sudbury. SRO/B

Poor Relief

7567 Letter from the Poor Law commissioners to the Clerk of the Sudbury Union, April 1843. HC 1846, 36

Charities

7568 Sudbury charitable benefactors Rp from Suffolk and Essex Free Press, 13 Sept 1905

Public Health

7569 **Hodson, W. W.** John Colney's or St. Leonard's hospital for lepers at Sudbury. PSIA 7, 1889/91, 268–74

7570 Annual report of the Medical Officer of Health, 1889/93. Sudbury, 1890–94. BL

Education

7571 Charity schools, North Street, Sudbury. In the County Court of Suffolk, held at Sudbury, Hodson v Molyneux: A letter to the inhabitants ... concerning ... the above case, and the correspondence relating thereto, by Messrs. John James and Thomas Goldsmith, trustees of the said schools. Sudbury, 1856. SRO/B

7572 **Hodson, W. W.** Sudbury Grammar School. PSIA 7, 1889/91, 311–19

7573 **Sudbury Secondary School for Boys.** The Link [school magazine], 1923–1970. Sudbury

7574 **Sudbury Uplands Middle School** (formerly Sudbury High School for Girls). Sudbury Girls' High School magazine, 1930–39, 1956–. Sudbury

7575 **Sudbury Grammar School.** The Talbot [school magazine] 1947–71. Sudbury

Planning and Development

7576 **Jeremiah, K.** A full life in the country: the Sudbury and district survey and plan. 1949

7577 **East Suffolk County Council.** Planning Dept. Sudbury and Great Cornard: factual survey, analysis, and outline planning proposals. Ipswich, 1949. [Typescript]

7578 **West Suffolk County Council.** Planning Dept. Sudbury: report on Gaol Lane-North Street (Hillyer Parker). Bury St. Edmunds, 1962

7579 **West Suffolk County Council.** Planning Dept. Factual survey and outline plan for Sudbury, Chilton, and Cornard, including town expansion proposals. Bury St. Edmunds, 1964. SRO/B

7580 **West Suffolk County Council.** Planning Dept. Sudbury, Chilton, and Cornard town map: First review, 1965; Programme map, written statement. Bury St. Edmunds, 1965

7581 **Suffolk Preservation Society.** Sudbury: report of survey. [c.1969] [Type-script]. SRO/B

7582 **West Suffolk County Council.** Planning Dept. Sudbury town-centre report. Bury St. Edmunds, 1970

RELIGION AND CHURCHES
General See also 1812, 1835, 1843, 1874, 2405, 2411, 2423

7583 Sudbury leaflets [100 assorted, religious tracts, chiefly in verse]. Sudbury, [1861]. BL. *See also* **7603**

7584 **Maclean, H.** Sepulchral memorial to Seieve de St. Quintin found in the church at Sudbury. Arch J 5, 1848, 222–4

All Saints'

7585 **Badham, C.** History and antiquities of All Saints church, Sudbury, and of the parish generally, derived from the Harleian MSS and other sources. Sudbury, 1852

7586 All Saints' church, Sudbury. PSIA 14, 1910/12, 95–8

7587 Story of All Saints' church, Sudbury. Gloucester, 1932 and later edns

St. Gregory's See also **7775**

7588 **Hodson, W. W.** Sudbury college and archbishop Theobald [Simon of Sudbury]. PSIA 7, 1889/91, 23–32

7589 **Hodson, W. W.** S. Gregory's church and college, Sudbury. PSIA 7, 1889/91, 363–5

7590 **Hodson, W. W.** Story of old St. Gregory's, Sudbury. Sudbury, 1892

7591 St. Gregory, with St. Peter, Sudbury. Sudbury, [c.1930] and later edns

7592 St. Gregory's church, Sudbury. nd

7593 **Sparrow-Simpson, W.,** *et al.* Simon of Sudbury's head in St. Gregory's church, Sudbury. N&Q 1st Ser 1, 1852, 194–5; 3rd Ser 1, 1862, 251; 8th Ser 1, 1892, 256

7594 **Sparrow-Simpson, W.** On the head of Simon of Sudbury, archbishop of Canterbury, a relic preserved in the church of St. Gregory, Sudbury. JBAA NS 1, 1895, 126–47

St. Peter's

7595 **Oliver, B.** St. Peter's church, Sudbury. PSIA 14, 1910/12, 94–5

7596 St. Peter's church, Sudbury. nd

7597 The alderman's pall or "Burying cloth" at Sudbury. E Ang NS 9, 1901/02, 17–19

7598 St. Peter's church, Sudbury. 15th-century alderman's pall and 17th-century preaching cloth. nd

Nonconformity

7599 **Duncan, J.** Nonconformists of Sudbury. 3 v. 1968. [Typescript]. SRO/B

7600 **Hodson, W. W.** Meeting house and the manse: or, The story of the Independents of Sudbury. 1893

7601 **Fitch, S. H. C.,** *Ed.* Sudbury Quakers, 1655–1953: Extracts from various sources. Bury St. Edmunds, [1954]

LITERARY

7602 Fulcher's Sudbury Journal, 1–12, Jan–Dec 1838

7603 Sudbury leaflets: poetry, original and selected. 1864. 2nd edn 1866. 3rd edn 1873. BL. *See also* **7583**

7604 Eatanswill Gazette ... Official organ of the Eatanswill Club, Sudbury: journal devoted to Eatanswillian, Pickwickian, and Dickensian humour and research. Nos 1–4, March 1907–Jan 1908. Sudbury, 1907–08. BL. Photocopy. SRO/B

ASSOCIATIONS

7605 **Sudbury and Woodbridge Division Conservative Association.** Conservative news. v 5, no 2–. Feb–March 1955–. BL

Freemasonry

7606 **Grimwood, C. E.** History of Stour Valley Lodge, No 1224, Sudbury, 1868–1968. 1968

BUILDINGS

7607 **Hodson, W. W.** Old timbered houses of Sudbury, etc. PSIA 7, 1889/91, 1–22

7608 **Hodson, W. W.** Old Moot Hall at Sudbury. PSIA 7, 1889/91, 257–67

SUTTON   *See also* **2573, 2981**

7609 Sutton parish history. SC 1.4.1932, Rp No 266

7610 **Lewis, B.** Roman coins found near Woodbridge [Sutton]. Arch J 28, 1871, 34–40

7611 **Redstone, V. B.** Sutton, Staverton, and Butley gateway, Orford. PSIA 10, 1898/1900, 56–96

7612 **Birch, H. W.** Sutton font. E Ang NS 5, 1893/4, 334–5

SUTTON HOO   *See also* **3255, 7902**

7613 **Magoun, F. P.** Sutton Hoo ship burial: a chronological bibliography. Speculum 29, 1954, 116–24

7614 **Bessinger, J. B.** Sutton Hoo ship burial: a chronological bibliography. Supplement. Speculum 33, 1958, 515–22

7615 **Maynard, G.,** *et al.* Great archaeological find in Suffolk: details of the ship-burial near Woodbridge. EADT 29.7.1939. [First statement about Sutton Hoo ship-burial]

7616 Suffolk ship-burial find not treasure-trove: Jury's finding at Sutton inquest. EADT 15.8.1939

7617 **Maynard, G.** Sutton Hoo. EAM 4, 1939, 558–67

7618 **Birt, D. H. C.** Ancient history of the ship. Discovery NS 2, 1939, 461–7, 479–82

7619 **Kendrick,** *Sir* **T. D.,** *et al.* The Sutton Hoo finds. BMQ 13, 1939, 111–36

7620 **Kendrick,** *Sir* **T. D.** Saxon art at Sutton Hoo. Burl 77, 1940, 174–82

7621 **Kendrick,** *Sir* **T. D.,** *et al.* Sutton ship-burial. Ant 14, 1940, 1–87

7622 **Phillips, C. W.** Sutton Hoo burial ship. MM 26, 1940, 105, 345–55

7623 **Phillips, C. W.,** *et al.* Excavation of the Sutton Hoo ship-burial. Ant J 20, 1940, 149–202

7624 **Shetelig, H.** Skipsgraven ved Sutton Hoo i Suffolk: en angel-saksist kongegrave fra 600-årene. Viking 4, 1940, 167–72

7625 Sutton Hoo treasure: Anglo-Saxon finds presented to the nation. MJ 39, 1940, 479–82

7626 Kendrick, *Sir* T. D. Gourd bottles from Sutton Hoo. Ant J 21, 1941, 73–4

7627 Kendrick, *Sir* T. D. Una sepultura de rey anglo-sajon en un navio. Atlantis (Madrid) 16, 1941, 190–92

7628 Lantier, R. La tombe royale de Sutton Hoo. Revue archéologique 6th Ser 17, 1941, 46–57

7629 Phillips, C. W. Ancestor of the British navy. NGM 79, 1941, 247–68

7630 Anderson, R. C. Sutton Hoo ship. MM 28, 1942, 83–5

7631 Maynard, G. The smaller boat from Sutton Hoo. MM 28, 1942, 314–15

7632 Crosley, A. S. Survey of the 6th-century Saxon burial ship. NST 23, 1942–3, 109–16

7633 Maryon, H. Sutton Hoo shield. Ant 20, 1946, 21–30

7634 Vaufrey, R. La sépulture à barque de Sutton Hoo. Anthropologie 50, 1941/6, 295–6

7635 British Museum. Sutton-Hoo ship burial: a provisional guide, by R. L. S. Bruce-Mitford. 1947. 1951. 1956 and later edns

7636 Maryon, H. Sutton Hoo helmet. Ant 21, 1947, 137–44

7637 Bruce-Mitford, R. L. S. Sutton Hoo and Sweden. ANL 1, 1948, 5–7

7638 Bruce-Mitford, R. L. S. Sutton Hoo musical instrument. ANL 1, 1948, 11–13

7639 Lethbridge, T. C. Sutton Hoo. Archaeology 1, 1948, 8–12

7640 Lindquist, S. Sutton Hoo och Beowulf [English summary: Sutton Hoo and Beowulf]. Fornvännen 43, 1948, 94–110. Ant 22, 1948, 131–40

7641 Nerman, B. Sutton Hoo—en svensk kungs-eller hövdingsgrav? [English summary: Sutton Hoo—a grave of a Swedish king or chieftain?]. Fornvännen 43, 1948, 65–93

7642 Walker, J. W. Battle of Winwaed and the Sutton Hoo ship burial. YAJ 37, 1948/51, 99–104

7643 Bruce-Mitford, R. L. S. Sutton Hoo ship-burial: recent theories and some comments on general interpretation. PSIA 25, 1949/51, 1–78. Nature 165, 1950, 339–41. PRI 24, 1950, 440–9

7644 Anderson, R. C. Ribs of the Sutton Hoo ship. MM 36, 1950, 264

7645 Bruce-Mitford, R. L. S. New chapter in Anglo-Swedish relations. Anglo-Swedish Review, 1950, 69–72

7646 Bruce-Mitford, R. L. S. Problem of the Sutton Hoo cenotaph. ANL 2, 1950, 166–9

7647 Hill, *Sir* G. Note on the Sutton Hoo treasure trove inquest. Ant J 30, 1950, 67–8

7648 Martin-Clarke, D. E. Significant objects at Sutton Hoo. *In* Early cultures of North-West Europe, *Ed.* by C. Fox and B. Dickins. Cambridge, 1950. 107–19

7649 Phillips, C. W. Sutton Hoo ship burial. Hunter Archaeological Soc Trans 6, 1950, 322–4

7650 Phillips, C. W. Sutton Hoo. Arch J 108, 1951, 153–4

7651 **Bruce-Mitford, R. L. S.** Sutton Hoo ship-burial. *In* History of the Anglo-Saxons, by R. H. Hodgkin. 1952. 696–734

7652 **Crawford, O. G. S.** Sutton Hoo? a summary, and a rejoinder by R. L. S. Bruce-Mitford. Ant 26, 1952, 4–8, 76–82

7653 **Grierson, P.** The dating of the Sutton Hoo coins. Ant 26, 1952, 83–6

7654 **Ward, G.** Silver spoon from Sutton Hoo. Ant 26, 1952, 9–13

7655 **Cederlöf, O.** Sutton Hoo ship-burial and armour during the Vendel period. AASJ 1, 1953, 155–64

7656 **Erä-Esko, A.** Sutton Hoo and Finland. Speculum 28, 1953, 514–15

7657 **Berges, W.,** *and* **Gauert, A.** Die eiserne "Standarte" und das steinerne "Szepter" aus dem Grabe eines angelsächsischen Königs bei Sutton Hoo (650–660). *In* Herrschaftszeichen und Staatssymbolik, by P. E. Schramm. Stuttgart, 1954. 238–80

7658 **Phillips, C. W.** Excavation of the Sutton Hoo ship-burial. *In* Recent archaeological excavations in Britain, *Ed.* by R. L. S. Bruce-Mitford. 1956. 145–66

7659 **Lee, N. E.** Sutton Hoo ship built in Sweden? Ant 31, 1957, 40–41

7660 **Grosjean, P.** Le trésor mérovingien de Sutton Hoo, S. Feuillen, et S. Éloi. AB 78, 1960, 364–9

7661 **Hogg, A. H. A.** Earthwork at Sutton Hoo. Ant 35, 1961, 53–5

7662 **Green, C.** Sutton Hoo: the excavation of a royal ship-burial. 1963. 2nd edn 1968

7663 **Bruce-Mitford, R. L. S.** Excavations at Sutton Hoo in 1938. PSIA 30, 1964/6, 1–43

7664 **Hawkes, C. [F. C.]** Sutton Hoo: twenty-five years after. Ant 38, 1964, 252–7

7665 **McLoughlin, J. L. N.** Sutton-Hoo, the evidence of the documents. MA 8, 1964/5, 1–19

7666 **Cohen, S. L.** Sutton Hoo whetstone. Speculum 41, 1966, 466–70

7667 **Gamber, O.** Sutton Hoo military equipment—an attempted reconstruction. AASJ 5, 1966, 265–89

7668 **Kaske, R. E.** Silver spoons at Sutton Hoo. Speculum 42, 1967, 670–72

7669 **Bruce-Mitford, R. L. S.** Sutton Hoo excavations, 1965–7. Ant 42, 1968, 36–9

7670 **Bruce-Mitford, R. L. S.** Sutton Hoo ship-burial: a handbook. 1968. 2nd edn 1972

7671 **Bruce-Mitford, R. [L. S.],** *and* **M.** Sutton Hoo lyre, Beowulf, and the origins of the frame harp. Ant 44, 1970, 7–13

7672 **Grierson, P.** The purpose of the Sutton Hoo coins. Ant 44, 1970, 14–18

7673 **Nerman, B.** Note on the 'standard' of Sutton Hoo—a torchholder? Ant J 50, 1970, 340–41

7674 **Grohskopf, B.** The treasure of Sutton Hoo. 1971

7675 **Sherlock, D. A.** Saul, Paul, and the silver spoons from Sutton Hoo. Speculum 47, 1972, 91–5

7676 **Bruce-Mitford, R. [L. S.]** Aspects of Anglo-Saxon archaeology: Sutton Hoo and other discoveries. 1974

7677 **Bruce-Mitford, R. L. S.** Sutton Hoo ship-burial. v 1. 1975

SWEFFLING *See also* **2441**

7678 Sweffling parish history. EADT 17.5.1933. Rp No 311

7679 **Clark, P.** Roman finds at Sweffling. PSIA 13, 1907/09, 367–8

7880 **Sedge, B. W.** Some account of Sweffling (1841–1851). Sweffling, 1976

7681 **Sedge, B. [W.]** St. Mary's, Sweffling: some notes for pilgrims. Sweffling, 1977

7682 **Carnac, R.,** *and* **Farrer, E.** Ancient leather case from Sweffling church. PSIA 10, 1898/1900, 366–74

7683 **Wayman, H. W. B.** Monumental inscriptions in Sweffling. E Ang NS 12, 1907/08, 134–6, 155–7

7684 **W[ayman], H. W. B.** Monumental inscriptions remaining in the church and churchyard at Sweffling, 1907. REMI 1, 1911/12, 47–54

SWILLAND

7685 Swilland parish history. EADT 22.1.1936, Rp No 424

SYLEHAM

7686 Syleham parish history. EADT 30.5.1934, Rp No 355

7687 **Aldwell, S. W. H.** Short history of Sykeham, its manors and church. 1936. [Typescript]

7688 **Fairbrother, E. H.** Pasture of 'Frythawe' in Syleham [1583] E Ang NS 13, 1909/10, 248–50

7689 **Raven, J. J.** Syleham register extracts. E Ang NS 5, 1893/4, 123

TANNINGTON

7690 Tannington parish history. SC 24.5.1929, Rp No 125

7691 **Donnan, W. H.** Brief notes on the history of Tannington church, Suffolk. Ipswich, 1969

7692 Parish registers of Tannington, Suffolk. [*Ed.* by F. A. Crisp]. 1884. 15 copies

TATTINGSTONE *See also* **3214–15**

7693 Tattingstone parish history. SC 10.7.1914, Rp No 16

7694 **Elliot, C. L. B.** Tattingstone: some notes of the 25 years, May 1896–1921. Ipswich, 1921. nl

7695 **Birch, H. W.** Church notes: Tattingstone. E Ang NS 8, 1899/1900, 157–60

7696   Apportionment of the rent-charge in lieu of tithes, in the parish of Tattingstone. Ipswich, [1837]. BL

7697   Parish magazine, 1897–1914, *then* Samford magazine, 1914–66, *then* Parish News, Bentley with Tattingstone, 1966–

7698   Alton watermill: a rescue operation. Friends of the Abbot's Hall Museum, Stowmarket. 1974

THEBERTON   *See also* 3159–60

7699   **Doughty, H. M.** Chronicles of Theberton, a Suffolk village, ... with an introduction and notes by W. W. Skeat. 1910

7700   Theberton parish history. SC 21.12.1928, Rp No 103

7701   **Haslewood, F.** Theberton church [with Davy's notes of 1806]. PSIA 7, 1889/91, 229–37

7702   **Hampton-Wright, P.** St. Peter's church, Theberton: some historical and other notes. Leiston, [c.1958]

THEDWASTRE RURAL DISTRICT   *See also* 2406

7703   Official guide. 1961 and later edns

7704   **Thedwastre Rural District Council.** Minutes of council and committees, 1968–74. SRO/B

7705   **Thedwastre Rural District Council.** Report of the Medical Officer of Health for 1903–09. BL

THELNETHAM

7706   Thelnetham parish history. EADT 31.10.1934, Rp No 374

7707   **Murry, J. M.** Community farm [Cross Green Farm, Thelnetham]. 1952

THINGOE HUNDRED   *See also* 2406

7708   **Gage, J.** [afterwards **Rokewode, J. G.**] History and antiquities of Suffolk: Thingoe Hundred. Bury St. Edmunds, 1838

THINGOE RURAL DISTRICT

7709   Official guide. 1950 and later edns

7710   **Thingoe Rural District Council.** Report of the Medical Officer of Health for 1894–1909. Bury St. Edmunds. BL

7711   **Thingoe Rural District Council.** Report of the Medical Officer of Health for 1960–73. Bury St. Edmunds. SRO/B

THORINGTON   *See also* 2670

7712   Thorington parish history. SC 1.7.1932, Rp No 276

7713   Registers of the parish of Thorington in the county of Suffolk; with notes on the different Acts of Parliament referring to them, and notices of the Bence family, with pedigree ... *Ed.* by T. S. Hill. 1884

THORNDON

7714   Thorndon parish history. SC 15.5.1931, Rp No 228
7715   **Harris, H. A.** Thorndon before the Conquest. PSIA 18, 1922/4, 222–34
7716   **Harris, H. A.** John of Gaunt's connection with Thorndon. PSIA 23, 1937/9, 177–8
7717   **Harris, H. A.** Restoration and reconstruction of All Saints church, Thorndon. PSIA 21, 1931/3, 53–62
7718   **Harris, H. A.** "Founder's tomb" at Thorndon. E Ang NS 13, 1909/10, 243
7719   **Harris, H. A.** Thorndon lions and other symbols. PSIA 16, 1916/18, 49–64
7720   Registers of Thorndon, Co. Suffolk, with index in typescript, by H. A. Harris. nd. nl

THORNHAM

7721   Thornham Magna and Parva parish history. SC 1.11.1929, Rp No 148
7722   St. Mary, Thornham Parva: brief encounter. nd. [Typescript]. nl
7723   **Lillie, W. W.** Retable at Thornham Parva. PSIA 21, 1931/3, 153–65. Burl 63, 1933, 99–100
7724   **Farrer, E.** Portraits in Thornham Hall. Norwich, 1930

THORPE MORIEUX

7725   Thorpe Morieux parish history. EADT 21.9.193, Rp No 285

THORPENESS

7726   **Kemp, G.,** *Ed.* Concerning Thorpeness. 1912 and later edns
7727   **Ganz, C.** 'Pottering for a Galloona', the Thorpeness finds, April 1911. PSIA 14, 1910/12, 243–8

THRANDESTON.   *See also* **3325, 3327**

7728   Thrandeston parish history. SC 31.10.1930, Rp No 200

THURLESTON   *See* Whitton-cum Thurleston

THURLOW, GREAT

7729   Great Thurlow parish history. SC 2.8.1929, Rp No 135
7730   **Hughes, (–).** Antiquities found at Great Thurlow. PCAS 7, 1891/2, 252–3

7731 An idea of arithmetick at first designed for the use of the Free-school at Thurlow ... by R. B[illingsley] schoolmaster there. 1655. Wing B 2913A. O

7732 **Andrews, H. C.** Some families and brasses at Great Thurlow and Little Bradley. PSIA 20, 1928/30, 43–7

THURLOW, LITTLE *See also* 2771

7733 Little Thurlow parish history. SC 2.8.1929, Rp No 135

7734 **Dickinson, P. G. M.** Recent discoveries at Temple End, Little Thurlow. SR 1, 1957, 54–5

THURSTON

7735 Thurston parish history. SC 19.6.1931, Rp No 233

7736 **Desch, R. C.** Notes on the church. [c.1950]. [Typescript]

THWAITE

7737 Thwaite parish history. SC 9.5.1930. Rp No 175

7738 **Martin, J. S.** Supposed finds at Thwaite and Campsey Ash, 1832. BNJ 28, 1956/8, 414–16

TIMWORTH *See also* 4647

7739 Timworth parish history. EADT 19.12.1934, Rp No 380

7740 Parish register of Timworth, co. Suffolk: Baptisms, 1565-1716; Marriages, 1558–1715; Burials, 1572–1715. *Ed.* by W. Brigg. Leeds, 1909

TOSTOCK

7741 Tostock parish history. 2 pts. EADT 7.4.1937, 14.4.1937, Rp Nos 467, 468

7742 **Duncan, J.** History of Methodism in the village of Tostock. 1968 [Typescript]. SRO/B

TRIMLEY ST. MARTIN *See also* 2633–5, 4881

7743 Trimley St. Martin parish history. SC 22.6.1928, Rp No 77

7744 **Raven, A. J.** Church notes: Trimley St. Martin. E Ang NS 3, 1889/90, 340–43

7745 **Denney, A. H.,** *and* **Downes, T. R.** History of Trimley St. Martin parish church. 1956. [Typescript]

TRIMLEY ST. MARY *See also* 4881

7746 **Raven, A. J.** Some materials for a history of Trimley St. Mary. E Ang NS 5, 1893/4, 267–9

7747 Trimley St. Mary parish history. SC 22.6.1928, Rp No 77
7748 Trimley St. Martin school, 1875–1975. Trimley St. Martin, 1975
7749 **Faulconer, R. H.** Church of Trimley Saint Mary, Suffolk, a short account. [With] list of subscriptions to the restoration fund. Trimley, 1898. O
7750 **Murton, H. G.** Short history of St. Mary-the-Virgin. 1949. [Typescript]
7751 **Murton, H. G.** Story of St. Mary-the-Virgin at Trimley, in the county of Suffolk. Ramsgate, 2nd edn 1958, and later edns

TROSTON *See also* **3127–8**

7752 Troston parish history. SC 31.7.1931, Rp No 239
7753 Troston church. 1950. SRO/B

TUDDENHAM ST. MARTIN *See also* **3093, 3161, 3317**

7754 Deeds relating to Tuddenham. Frag Gen 19, 1904, 54–65
7755 **Redstone, V. B.** Tuddenham St. Martin. PSIA 11, 1901/3, 246–51
7756 Tuddenham St. Martin parish history. SC 10.2.1928, Rp No 58
7757 **Mattingly, H.,** *and* **Pearce, J. W. E.** Tuddenham hoard of *siliquae*. NC 6th Ser 6, 1946, 169–73
7758 **Birch, H. W.** Church notes: Tuddenham St. Martin. E Ang NS 6, 1895/6, 356–8
7759 **Pearson, W. C.** Extracts from the registers of Tuddenham St. Martin. E Ang NS 11, 1905/06, 165–9
7760 **Richardson, W. H.** Monumental inscriptions from Tuddenham church. MGetH NS 3, 1880, 204–05

TUDDENHAM ST. MARY

7761 Tuddenham St. Mary parish history. EADT 22.8.1934, Rp No 365

TUNSTALL *See also* **3465**

7762 Tunstall parish history. SC 28.8.1931, Rp No 243
7763 **Wayman, H. W. B.** Extracts from the parish registers of Tunstall. E Ang NS 13, 1909/10, 36

UBBESTON *See also* **2757–8**

7764 Ubbeston parish history. EADT 24.10.1934, Rp No 373
7765 Rules of Ubbeston Provident Clothing Society. Halesworth, [1833]. BL

UFFORD *See also* **7949**

7766 Admissions to the manor of Ufford. Frag Gen 6, 1901, 35–9
7767 **Maitland, R. W.** Story of Ufford. Ipswich, [c.1917]

7768 **Morley, C.** Old Ufford: its manors, chapel, chantries, church, and other antiquities. Ipswich, 1926

7769 Ufford parish history. SC 22.7.1927, Rp No 30

7770 Return of the number of acres of land, rent per acre, and tithes payable for the same, in the parish of Ufford. [1833?]. Printed form, completed in MS. BL

7771 Rules of the Ufford Clothing Club. Woodbridge, [1834]. BL

7772 Rules and regulations for the management of the Poor Allotments. 1835. Woodbridge, [1835]. BL

7773 Rules and orders for the government of the Ufford New Friendly Society. Woodbridge, 1803. BL

7774 Church of the Assumption of Our Lady, Mother of God, Ufford: a short guide. Woodbridge, 1958 and later edns

7775 **Gough, R.** Fonts at Ufford and Sudbury. Vet M 3, 1796, pl 25

7776 Inscriptions in Ufford churchyard, Suffolk. Also names of those buried in the new churchyard, without tombstones [Copied 21 and 29 August 1928, by C. P[artridge]. Revised to 31 Oct 1931, by H. D.] Woodbridge, [1931]. SRO/B

7777 Parish magazine, *extant* 1894–7. Ufford Church Messenger, 1959–71, *now* Ufford News and Views

UGGESHALL *See also* **2480, 2740**

7778 Uggeshall parish history, EADT 30.6.1937

7779 Uggeshall inclosure. State of the claims [delivered to the Commissioners]. Great Yarmouth, [1797]. BL

7780 Memoranda of Sir Lionel Playters, Bart, rector of Uggeshall, relating to the condition of the church in the seventeenth century. E Ang NS 7, 1897/8, 207

UNDLEY *See also* Lakenheath

7781 **Fowler, G.** Trial excavations in Undley ringwork. PCAS 43, 1949/50, 1

WAINFORD RURAL DISTRICT *See also* **3744–7**

7782 Official guide. 1950 and later edns

7783 Town and Country Planning Act 1947. Section 30. Provisional list of buildings of architectural or historic interest for consideration ... Wainford Rural District, Aug 1949. [Typescript]

7784 Town and Country Planning Act 1947. Section 30. List of buildings of special architectural or historic interest ... Wainford Rural District, 1 Sept 1953, 16 Dec 1969, 16 March 1972. [Typescript]. SCL/L

WALBERSWICK *See also* **2162, 3817, 6333, 7322**

7785 **Southern, W. A.** Sketches [in pencil] of Walberswick. 1877

7786 **Oakes, T. H. R.** Walberswick, the town and church. PSIA 8, 1892/4, 416–22
7787 **Christie, C.** "Ferryknoll". Walberswick notes. 1911
7788 Walberswick parish history. SC 11.11.1927, Rp No 45
7789 **Jobson, A.** Walberswick story. Lowestoft, 1953
7790 **Oakes, T. H. R.** St. Andrew, Walberswick: history of the church and list of vicars. Southwold, 1889. Rev by A. D. Thompson, 1936 and later edns
7791 Walberswick, near Southwold. CB New Issue 16, 1895, 9–14
7792 **Lewis, R. W. M.** Walberswick churchwardens' accounts, A.D.1450–99. [1947]
7793 Parish magazine, *extant* 1905–

WALDINGFIELD, GREAT

7794 Great Waldingfield parish history. SC 17.1.1930, Rp No 159
7795 **Stokes, C. A.** Great Waldingfield church. PSIA 9, 1895/7, 90–93
7796 **Haslewood, F.** Rectors of Great Waldingfield, and monumental inscriptions. PSIA 9, 1895/7, 94–110

WALDINGFIELD, LITTLE   *See also* 3055

7797 Little Waldingfield parish history. SC 27.12.1929, Rp No 156
7798 **Haslewood, F.** Little Waldingfield church. PSIA 9, 1895/7, 111–30

WALDRINGFIELD

7799 **Tye, W.,** *Ed.* Guide to Waldringfield and district. Ipswich, 1955
7800 Waldringfield parish history. EADT 1.3.1933, Rp No 303
7801 **Waller, T.** All Saints' church, Waldringfield. [c.1968]
7802 Parish magazine, 1921–, *now* Waldringfield, Hemley, and Newbourne magazine

WALPOLE

7803 Walpole parish history. EADT 20.9.1933, Rp No 325
7804 Ancient meeting-house at Walpole. CHST 3, 1908, 317–18
7805 Walpole Old Chapel tercentenary pageant, Saturday, 14 June 1947: souvenir programme [Under the patronage of the Suffolk Congregational Union]. 1947. SRO/B

WALSHAM-LE-WILLOWS

7806 Wonderfull worke of God shewed upon a chylde, whose name is William Withers, being in the towne of Walsam, within the countie of Suffolk, 1581. STC 19877. BL

7807   **Harvey, B.** Youthful memories of my life in a Suffolk village [Walsham-le-Willows]. SR 2, 1961, 198–201

7808   Walsham-le-Willows parish history. SC 10.5.1929, Rp No 123

7809   **Gordon, C. D.** Parish and parish church of Walsham-le-Willows. PSIA 10, 1898/1900, 176–82

7810   **Dymond, D. P.** Parish of Walsham-le-Willows: two Elizabethan surveys and their medieval background. PSIA 33, 1973/5, 195–211

7811   **Dodd, K. M.,** *Ed*. The field book of Walsham-le-Willows, 1577. Ipswich, 1974. SRS 17

7812   **West Suffolk County Council.** Planning Dept. Buildings of Walsham-le-Willows. [By S. Colman]. Bury St. Edmunds, 1968

7813   **Duncan, J.** Early Non-conformity in Walsham-le-Willows ... 1968 [Typescript] SRO/B

WALTON   *See also* **3346, 4881, 5453–4**

7814   Walton parish history. EADT 14.12.1938

7815   **Sage, A. R.,** *Ed*. Story of Walton parish church, Felixstowe. [1950]

7816   **West, S. E.** Excavation of Walton priory. PSIA 33, 1973/5, 131–52

WANGFORD HUNDRED   *See also* **2444**

7817   [**Kerrison, M.**] To the owners and occupiers of land, in the Hundreds of Wangford, Blithing, and Mutford and Lothingland. Bungay, [1821]. O

7818   **Prichard, M. F. L.** Early days of the Wangford Hundred workhouse. PSIA 30, 1964/6, 175–82

7819   Case [relative to the Poor House of the Hundred of Wangford]. Beccles, [1821]. BL

WANGFORD RURAL DISTRICT   *See also* **1588**

7820   **Wangford Rural District.** Annual report of the Medical Officer of Health and Sanitary Inspector for the year 1915. Beccles, [1916]. BL

WANGFORD, nr Brandon

7821   Wangford parish history. EADT 30.10.1935, Rp No 415

7822   **Chester, G. J.** Account of antiquities discovered at Wangford, near Brandon. Arch J 10, 1853, 353–5

7823   **Briscoe, G.** Combined early Iron Age and Romano-British site at Wangford, West Suffolk. PCAS 51, 1957/8, 19–29

7824   **S[perling], C. F. D.** Royal arms in churches: Wangford. E Ang NS 5, 1893/4, 383–4

WANGFORD, nr Lowestoft   *See also* **3276**

7825   A terrible thunder-clap at Wangford in the county of Suffolk, whereby 1. Knight, 1. Colonel, and a Captain of a Troop (meeting at the house of Mr. Tho. Absolon ... on Thursday the 1. of August) were much mangled by a thunderbolt ... 1661. nl

7826   **Munford, G.** Origin of the name of Wangford. E Ang 1, 1858/63, 78–9

7827   **Boyce, J.** Village ramble or a walk through Wangford, in Suffolk. Halesworth, 1854

7828   Wangford parish history. SC 19.10.1928, Rp No 94

7829   **Charles, W. B.** Wangford, village and church: a short history.. Halesworth, 1948

7830   **Waveney District Council.** Planning Dept. Wangford village plan. Lowestoft, 1976. SCL/L

7831   **Gowers, W. R.** Suffolk architectural notes. No 4. Lost arcade at Wangford. E Ang NS 5, 1893/4, 299–300

7832   Wangford and Reydon parish magazine 1886–. *afterwards* The Link, *now* The Messenger

WANTISDEN   *See also* **2441, 4452**

7833   Wantisden parish history. SC 24.6.1932. Rp No 275

7834   **Wayman, H. W. B.** Monumental inscriptions within the church and churchyard of Wantisden. E Ang NS 12, 1907/08, 66–8

7835   **W[ayman], H. W. B.** Monumental inscriptions remaining in the church and churchyard at Wantisden, 1907. REMI 1, 1911/12, 55–61

WASHBROOK

7836   Washbrook parish history. SC 23.1.1931, Rp No 212

7837   **Salter, T.** Assessment of the parish of Washbrook. 1838. MS. nl

7838   **Birch, H. W.** Church notes: Washbrook. E Ang NS 7, 1897/8, 269–70

7839   **Pipe, R. G.** Short history of Washbrook church. 1976

WATTISFIELD

7840   Wattisfield parish history. SC 2.8.1935. Rp No 405

7841   **Wacher, J. S.** Excavations at Calke Wood, Wattisfield, 1956. PSIA 28, 1958/60, 1–28

7842   **Maynard, G.,** *et al.* Reports on a Roman pottery-making site at Foxledge Common, Wattisfield. PSIA 22, 1934/6, 178–97

7843   Introducing Wattisfield ware—Henry Watson's Pottery Ltd: the renaissance of a village community. nd

7844   The potters of Wattisfield: the story of Henry Watson's Pottery Ltd. ... [195–] SRO/B

7845 **Jolly, C. A.** Story of Wattisfield Congregational church, 1654–1949. [1949] SRO/B

7846 Ancient meeting-house at Wattisfield. CHST 3, 1908, 251–6

7847 **Colman, S.** Two small medieval houses: Walnut Tree Cottage, Wattisfield, and Friar's Hall, Rattlesden. The effects of modernisation. PSIA 31, 1967/9, 64–71

WATTISHAM *See also* **840**

7848 Wattisham parish history. EADT 5.7.1933, Rp No 317

WENHAM, GREAT

7849 Great Wenham parish history. SC 14.8.1931, Rp No 241

7850 **Birch, H. W.** Church notes: Great Wenham. E Ang NS 8, 1899/1900, 196

WENHAM, LITTLE *See also* **2574, 3400**

7851 Little Wenham parish history. SC 27.1.1928. Rp No 56

7852 **Birch, H. W.** Church notes: Little Wenham. E Ang NS 8, 1899/1900, 219–22

7853 **[Crisp, F. A.]** Little Wenham Hall. [c.1920]. O

7854 **Calver, W. E.** Little Wenham Hall and church. Ipswich, nd

7855 **Jackson, S.** Little Wenham Hall. PSIA 2, 1854/9, 183–8

7856 **Tipping, H. A.** Little Wenham Hall. CL 36, 1914, 358–65

7857 **Wood, M. E.** Little Wenham Hall. Arch J 108, 1951, 190–91

WENHASTON *See also* **2277**, and Mells

7858 **Clare, J. B.** Wenhaston, Suffolk: curious parish records, including lists of vicars from 1217 and churchwardens from 1586 ... to which is appended a description of the recently-discovered ancient painting of "The Last Judgement". Halesworth, [1894]

7859 **Clare, J. B.** Wenhaston and Bulcamp, Suffolk: Curious parish records including lists of vicars from 1217 and churchwardens from 1547, description of the recently-discovered ancient painting known as "The Wenhaston Doom", old wills and law-suits of the parish, two riots at Bulcamp workhouse, and a glossary of old-fashioned words. Halesworth, 1903

7860 **Clare, J. B.** Wenhaston and Bulcamp, Suffolk, containing curious parish records. 1906. SCL/L

7861 **Becker, M. J.** Notes on the church and village of Wenhaston. Southwold, [c.1923]. SRO/B

7862 Wenhaston parish history. SC 6.1.1928, Rp No 53

7863 **Parr, R. T. L.** Sidelight on a Suffolk parish in Queen Mary's reign [Wenhaston sequestration 1554–6]. nd. [Typescript] SRO/B

7864 St. Peter's, Wenhaston. CB New Issue 20, 1899, 48–54

7865   **Keyser, C. E.** St. Peters, Wenhaston: the church and its ancient painting. Halesworth, 1906. nl

7866   **Keyser, C. E.** Recently discovered panel-painting of the Doom [in Wenhaston church]. Arch J 49, 1892, 399–401

7867   **Keyser, C. E.** On a panel painting of the Doom discovered in 1892 in Wenhaston church. Arch 54, pt 1, 1894, 119–30

7868   **Becker, M. J.** Wenhaston Doom. PSIA 19, 1925/7, 80–81

7869   **Keyser, C. E.** Panel painting of the Doom in Wenhaston church. JBAA NS 34, 1928/9, 117–20

7870   **Whitelaw, J. W.** Medieval church painting at Wenhaston. CL 129(2), 1961, 837.

WESTERFIELD   *See also* **1426, 2945, 3170**

7871   Westerfield parish history. EADT 21.3.1934, Rp No 347

7872   **Watson, S. F.** Notes on the history of Westerfield, Suffolk. 1964. [Typescript]

7873   **Pearson, W. C.** Collections on briefs made in the parish of Westerfield. E Ang NS 4, 1891/2, 186

7874   **Pearson, W. C.** Memoranda in the oldest register of the parish of Westerfield. E Ang NS 4, 1891/2, 298–9

7875   **Pearson, W. C.** Lists of confirmation candidates 1636–1763: parish of Westerfield. E Ang NS 5, 1893/4, 29–30

WESTHALL

7876   Westhall parish history. SC 2.11.1928, Rp No 96

7877   **Rudolph, L. de M.** Sherds of a Belgic vessel from Westhall. PSIA 29, 1961/3, 223–4

7878   **Harrod, H.** On horse-trappings found at Westhall. Arch 36, 1855, 454–6

7879   **Rix, S. W.** Westhall St. Andrew church. PSIA 4, 1864/74, 447–9

7880   **Smith, S.** Brief history of Westhall church in the county of Suffolk as written in its stones. Halesworth, 1913

7881   **Freeman, R.** Short guide to the church of St. Andrew, Westhall, Suffolk. Westhall, 1975. SCL/L

7882   Westhall church: appeal brochure. 1961. nl

WESTHORPE

7883   Westhorpe parish history. SC 8.2.1929, Rp No 110

WESTLETON

7884   **W.** Westleton. E Ang 3, 1866/68; 4, 1869/70, *passim*

7885   Westleton parish history. SC 11.7.1930, Rp No 184

7886 **Gay, N. S.** Short history of Westleton, Suffolk, and its parish church. Ipswich, 1942. SCL/L

7887 **Ivimey, A.,** *Ed.* Westleton from the 1830's to the 1960's: a survey of a Suffolk village. Dunwich, 1968

7888 **Haslewood, F.** Westleton church (with Davy's church notes, 1809). PSIA 7, 1889/91, 240–45

7889 Westleton church. CB New Issue 12, 1891, 11–12

7890 **Denney, A. H.** A case of delayed appropriation [Westleton]. SR 1, 1956, 11–14

WESTLEY

7891 Westley parish history. EADT 4.11.1936, Rp No 454

7892 **Prigg, H.** On a portion of a human skull of supposed Palaeolithic age ... [Westley] JRAI 14, 1885, 51–5

7893 **Baden-Powell, D. F. W.,** *and* **Oakley, K. P.** Report on the re-investigation of the Westley skull site. PPS NS 18, 1952, 1–20

WESTON *See also* **8099**

7894 Weston parish history. EADT 5.6.1935, Rp No 399

7895 **Hollis, T. K.** St. Peter's church, Weston. nd

WEST STOW

7896 West Stow parish history. SC 6.3.1931, Rp No 218

7897 **Tymms, S.** Anglo-Saxon sites from West Stow Heath. PSIA 1, 1848/53, 315–28

7898 **Tymms, S.** Some ancient fibulae and buckles from a cemetery on Stow Heath, and some leaden crosses found in Bury St. Edmunds. PSA 3, 1849/56, 165–7

7899 **Prigg, H.** Anglo-Saxon objects from West Stow Heath. JBAA 47, 1891, 94–5

7900 **Edwardson, A. R.** Beaker burial at West Stow. PSIA 29, 1961/3, 73–7

7901 West Stow: a Saxon village where sheep and their wool formed the basis of the economy. Cur A 1, 1967, 16–17

7902 Notes on finds at ... West Stow (continuing excavations); re-excavation of a burial ship at Sutton Hoo. MA 11, 1967, 268–70

7903 **West, S. E.** Anglo-Saxon village of West Stow: an interim report of the excavations, 1968. MA 13, 1969/71, 1–20

7904 **Prigg, H.** Roman pottery kilns, West Stow Heath. JBAA 37, 1881, 152–5

7905 **West, S. E.** Romano-British pottery kilns on West Stow Heath. PSIA 26, 1952/4, 35–53

7906 **Tymms, S.** West Stow Hall. PSIA 2, 1854/9, 148–50

7907 **W, I.** West Stow Hall. CL 29, 1911, 848–56

7908 West Stow parish registers, 1558 to 1850; Wordwell parish registers, 1580 to 1850. [*Ed.* by S.H.A.H(ervey)]. Woodbridge, 1903. SGB 7

WETHERDEN   *See also* 2983, 5191, 5194

7909   Wetherden parish history. SC 23.9.1927, Rp No 39
7910   **MacCulloch, N.** St. Mary-the-Virgin, Wetherden: notes for visitors. nd. [Typescript]. nl
7911   **Duncan, J.** History of the Baptist church at Wetherden. 1967. [Typescript]. SRO/B

WETHERINGSETT-CUM-BROCKFORD   *See also* 2638, 2971

7912   Wetheringsett-cum-Brockford parish history. SC 14.9.1928, Rp No 89

WEYBREAD

7913   Weybread parish history. SC 16.10.1931, Rp No 248
7914   **Dunning, G. C.** Medieval pottery roof-ventilator from Weybread. PSIA 30, 1964/6, 284–5

WHATFIELD

7915   **Clubbe, J.** History and antiquities of the ancient villa of Wheatfield, in the county of Suffolk. 1758. 1765. [A burlesque upon P. Morant's History and antiquities of Colchester, 1748]
7916   **Clubbe, J.** Miscellaneous tracts ... containing History and antiquities of Wheatfield; Physiognomy; Scattered thoughts. 2 v. Ipswich, [1770]
7917   Whatfield parish history. SC 20.7.1928, Rp No 81
7918   **J, T.** A brief description and discovery of the notorious falsehood ... contained in a book styled, The Gospel-way confirmed by miracles, published by Nicholas Ware and Matthew Hall for the use of the church of Whatfield in Suffolk ... 1649. Wing T 35. SRO/B

WHELNETHAM   *See also* 657

7919   **Collett-White, J. F. J.** Guide to the documents of the Whelnethams and Sicklesmere. [1970?]. [Typescript]. SRO/B
7920   Great Whelnetham parish registers, 1561–1850; Little Whelnetham parish registers, 1557–1850, with historical and biographical notes, illustrations, map, and pedigrees. [*Ed.* by S.H.A.H(ervey)]. Bury St. Edmunds, 1910. SGB 15

WHELNETHAM, GREAT

7921   Great Whelnetham parish history. EADT 21.8.1935. Rp No 407
7922   **Hambrook, R. J. C.** Great Whelnetham: a brief account of the fortunes of a Suffolk village from Roman times to the present day. 1970. [Typescript]
7923   **Hambrook, R. J. C.** St. Thomas a Becket's church, Great Whelnetham: a short guide. 1970. [Typescript]

7924   Powell, E. Whelnetham Magna; suit *re* advowson (1286). PSIA 15, 1913/15, 100–12

WHELNETHAM, LITTLE

7925   Little Whelnetham parish history. EADT 8.11.1933, Rp No 331
7926   **Hambrook, R. J. C.** Little Whelnetham church. 1967. [Typescript]

WHEPSTEAD

7927   Whepstead parish history. 2 pts. EADT 21.11.1934, 28.11.1934, Rp Nos 376, 377

WHERSTEAD   *See also* 3258

7928   **Zincke, F. B.** Wherstead: some materials for its history. 1887. 2nd edn 1893
7929   **Zincke, F. B.** The days of my years: a sequel to Some materials for the history of Wherstead. Ipswich, [1891]
7930   Wherstead parish history. SC 31.1.1930, Rp No 161
7931   **Eastern Electricity Board.** People and events associated with Eastern Electricity's Head Office at Wherstead, near Ipswich. 1963 and later edns
7932   **Birch, H. W.** Church notes: Wherstead. E Ang NS 13, 1909/10, 147–9
7933   Brief notes on the Ostrich Inn and village of Wherstead. Ipswich, nd

WHITTON-CUM-THURLESTON   *See also* 2569

7934   Whitton parish history. EADT 11.10.1939
7935   **Moir, J. R.,** *and* **Maynard, G.** Roman villa at Castle Hill, Whitton, Ipswich, and the Roman cemetery in Bolton and Co's brickfield, Ipswich. PSIA 21, 1931/3, 240–62
7936   **Birch, H. W.** Church notes: Whitton-cum-Thurleston. E Ang NS 6, 1895/6, 213
7937   **Swinburne, J. K.** Story of St. Botolph's, Whitton. Ipswich, 1936
7938   **Lingard, R.** Church history and notes including the churches of St. Botolph's (Whitton), St. Mary's (Thurleston), St. Mary's (Akenham), and the proposed new church of the Ascension, Thurleston. Ipswich, 1961
7939   **Pearson, W. C.** Hammond vault in Whitton church. E Ang NS 9, 1901/02, 346–8

WICKHAMBROOK   *See also* 1959, 2591, 3248–51

7940   Wickhambrook parish history. 2 pts. EADT 19.4.1933, 26.4.1933, Rp Nos 308, 309
7941   Brief history of the Dissenting interest at Wickhambrook, Suffolk, with a sketch of the rise and early progress of nonconformity. 1844

7942 **Duncan, J.** History of the Dissenters at Wickhambrook. 1968. [Typescript]. SRO/B

7943 **Duncan, J.** Badmondisfield Hall, Wickhambrook; the lords of the manor, a brief history. 1969. [Typescript]. SRO/B

7944 Giffords Hall, Wickhambrook. CL 14, 1903, 578–86

7945 **Johnston, P. M.** Giffords Hall, Wickhambrook. CL 45, 1919, 552–7, 588–93

WICKHAM MARKET   *See also* **2756, 3017, 3397**

7946 **Redstone, V. B.** Annals of Wickham Market and other papers, etc. Wood-bridge, 1896

7947 Wickham Market parish history. SC 7.8.1931. Rp No 240

7948 **Whitwell, J. R.** Bronze patera found at Wickham Market. PSIA 16, 1916/18, 179–80

7949 **Suffolk Coastal District Council.** Planning Dept. Wickham Market, Ufford, and Pettistree appraisal and policy statement. Consultation draft. [Woodbridge], 1976, SCL/L

7950 All Saints church, Wickham Market. Ramsgate, [1967] and later edns

7951 **Gunter, P.** Sermon preached in the countie of Suffolke, before the clergie and laytie, for the discouerie and confutation of certain, strange, pernicious, and heretical positions ... by a certaine factious preacher of Wickham Market ... 1615. STC 12526. SRO/B

WICKHAM SKEITH

7952 Wickham Skeith parish history. EADT 18.11.1932, Rp No 291

WILBY

7953 Wilby parish history. SC 12.7.1929, Rp No 132

7954 **Mash, N. B.** Parish church of the Blessed Virgin Mary, Wilby. [1961]

WILFORD HUNDRED

7955 [**Spurling, H.**]. Tim Digwell: an episode of the strike in Wilford Hundred in 1874. Woodbridge, 3rd edn 1874. nl

WILLINGHAM

7956 Willingham parish history. EADT 13.7.1938

WILLISHAM

7957 Willisham parish history. SC 15.7.1932, Rp No 277

WINGFIELD   *See also* 2781–5, 3287–8

7958   **Aldwell, S. W. H.** Wingfield: its church, castle, and college. Ipswich, [1925]. Abridgement 1933

7959   **P, G. R.** Wingfield college. E Ang 4, 1869/70, 145–6

7960   Wingfield parish history. SC 18.11.1927, Rp No 46

7961   Civic visit to Wingfield [Suffolk] Sunday, 7 June 1931 [for the] 600th anniversary of the granting of a charter by King Edward III to Kingston-upon-Hull, appointing a mayor, dated 6 May 1331 [Programme]. Hull, 1931. SRO/B

7962   S. Andrew's church, Wingfield. Commemoration of benefactors, Sunday, 7 June 1931: order and form of service. Beverley, 1931. SRO/B

7963   **Manning, C. R.** Wingfield church. PSIA 3, 1860/3, 331–40

7964   **J.** Wingfield castle. CL 33, 1932, 952–8

7965   **Buncombe, G. E.** Drawbridge at Wingfield. CL 121, 1957, 389

7966   **Harley, L. S.** The bricks of Wingfield college. PSIA 33, 1973/5, 86–8

WINSTON   *See also* 2486

7967   Winston parish history. EADT 29.11.1933. Rp No 334

WISSETT

7968   Wissett parish history. EADT 6.2.1935, Rp No 386

7969   **Watson, A. W. M.** Church notes: Wissett. [c.1960]. nl

WISSINGTON, WISTON   *See also* Nayland

7970   **Birch, C. E.** Brief account of the parish and church of Wiston. Colchester, [1885]

7971   Wissington parish history. EADT 23.2.1938

7972   **Birch, C. E.** Drawings of stone coffin-lids at Wiston. 1876

7973   **[Walker, J.]** House at the corner, Wiston-by-Nayland. 1920. SRO/B

WITHERSDALE

7974   Withersdale parish history. EADT 8.8.1934, Rp No 363

WITHERSFIELD   *See also* 2497

7975   Withersfield parish history. 2 pts. EADT 7.10.1936, 14.10.1936, Rp Nos 451, 452

7976   **Tymms, S.** Withersfield church. PSIA 4, 1864/74, 107–10

WITNESHAM   *See also* **3149–51**

7977 Witnesham parish history. SC 1.2.1929, Rp No 109

7978 Transcript of the Court Rolls of the Manor of Red Hall, alias Burwash, in Witnesham, 1472/3–1520, and of rentals 1581–1789. 1908. MS

7979 Transcript of the Court Rolls of the Manor of Cardon's Hall in Witnesham, Suffolk, 1502–77. MS

7980 **Trollope, M. N.** Transcripts of records and notes relating to Witnesham, with official reference to the tenure of lands and manors of associated families. nd. MS

7981 **Trollope, M. N.** Transcripts of miscellaneous records refering to the descent of Burghash, Burwash, or Burghersh manor and estates in Witnesham. nd. MS

7982 **Moore, I. E.** Witnesham flax factory. SR 4, no 2, 1973, 24

7983 **Pearson, W. C.** Memoranda in the parish registers of Witnesham. E Ang NS 5, 1893/4, 372–3

WIXOE

7984 Wixoe parish history. EADT 1.7.1936, Rp No 442

WOODBRIDGE

ALMANACS AND DIRECTORIES   *See also* **5453, 5455, 5461**

7985 Loder's household guide, and family instructor. Woodbridge, [1848?]. BL

7986 Moore's almanack with Loder's Woodbridge and Suffolk compendium, 1851, 1852. Woodbridge

7987 Woodbridge tradesmen's household almanack. Woodbridge, 1854

7988 Lambert's family almanack, 1857–1917. Woodbridge

7989 Read's family almanack and Woodbridge directory. Woodbridge, 1888

7990 Booth's illustrated almanac, 1897–1916. Woodbridge

7991 **Localads.** Woodbridge and district directory and almanac. Needham Market, 1963 and later edns

GUIDES   *See also* **2162, 5491**

7992 **Titcombe, J. C.** Fairweather's illustrated guide to Woodbridge. Woodbridge, [c.1900]. nl

7993 **Barnes, A. L.** Woodbridge and neighbourhood, its topography and history. Cheltenham, [1921]. BL

7994 **Symon, D.,** *Ed.* Woodbridge in Suffolk: a tribute. Ipswich, 1934. NCL/N

7995 Illustrated guide to Woodbridge. Woodbridge, [c.1950]

7996 Official guide. 1964 and later edns

7997 **Simper, R.** Woodbridge and beyond. Ipswich, 1972

GENERAL AND POLITICAL HISTORY   *See also* 857, 2506–08, 2624, 2647–8, 2865–2879, 3225, 3253–4

7998   Parish of Woodbridge. [Address to] Persons ... desirous of emigrating to Canada. Woodbridge, 1832. BL

7999   Ford, J. Collection of materials towards a history of Woodbridge. 2 v. [c.1840]. MS

8000   Tracts relating to Woodbridge [late 19th century]

8001   Lockwood, W. Woodbridge in olden times: being rambling reminiscences and notes on notable persons therein. Chester, [1889]. nl

8002   Redstone, V. B. Bygone Woodbridge: a contribution towards a history of Woodbridge. Woodbridge, [1893]

8003   Redstone, V. B. Woodbridge, its history and antiquity [List of rectors and curates appended]. PSIA 9, 1895/7, 345–58

8004   Woodbridge parish history. 3 pts. SC 22.3.1929, 29.3.1929, 5.4.1929, Rp Nos 116, 117, 118

8005   Carthew, P. Short history of Woodbridge. Woodbridge, [1950]

8006   Weaver, C. A., *and* M. A. Woodbridge, a short history and guide. 1976

8007   Pearce, J. W. E. Late fourth-century hoard of "Aes 4" from Woodbridge. NC 5th Ser 15, 1935, 49–53

8008   King, C. W. Jewish seal found at Woodbridge. Arch J 41, 1884, 168–70

ECONOMIC HISTORY   *See also* 1279

8009   W[oodbridge] S[avings] B[ank]. [Report for 1838] Woodbridge, [1838]. BL

8010   Jones, A. G. E. Early banking in Woodbridge. N&Q 199, 1953, 113–17

8011   Inhabitants of Woodbridge. [An address in reference to the establishment of a market]. [Woodbridge], 1851. BL

8012   Cooper, E. R. The Steelyard at Woodbridge. NST 19, 1938/40, 185–91

LOCAL GOVERNMENT AND SOCIAL SERVICES

Local Government

8013   Report of the Select Committee ... of the inhabitants of Woodbridge ... for ... taking into consideration of the best means of lighting and watching the town of Woodbridge. [Woodbridge], 1827. BL

8014   [Proceedings for lighting the town of Woodbridge with gas]. [Woodbridge], 1834. BL

Poor Relief

8015   Woodbridge Poor's Rate, 9 April—1 Oct, 1976. nd. MS

8016   Woodbridge Poor's Rate. Copy of the new and old assessments, as equalized by the Committee. [Woodbridge], 1830. BL

8017   Parish of Woodbridge. Summary of the poor rate for the first quarter 1838, ending 24 June ... [Woodbridge], [1838]. BL

Charities See also **3300–02**

8018 **Titcombe, J. C.** Short history of the Seckford Charity. Woodbridge, 1896. 3rd edn 1898

8019 **Loder, R.,** *Ed.* Statutes and ordinances, for the government of the alms-houses in Woodbridge ... founded by T. Seckford, Esq ... Notes relating to Wood-bridge priory ... [includes Seckford pedigree]. 2 pts. Woodbridge, 1792

8020 **Hart, D.,** *and* **Brook, H. W.** Seckforde hospital, Woodbridge [accounts 1849–50]. [Woodbridge], 1850

8021 Seckford charity. Amendments to the scheme for the management and regulation of the Seckford hospital at Woodbridge: in pursuance of resolutions agreed to at a public meeting 3 Aug 1860. Woodbridge, 1860

8022 Seckford charity. Report of the proceedings instituted by the churchwardens of Woodbridge on behalf of themselves and the inhabitants in the Vice-Chancellor's Court ... 8 May 1861, for securing the rights and privileges of the Charity to the town of Woodbridge. Woodbridge, 1862

8023 Seckford Charity. Scheme for the management and regulation of the Charity of Seckford Hospital and the Grammar School at Woodbridge ... directed by the High Court of Chancery, 14 June 1861, and 1864. Woodbridge, 1861. 1864

8024 Seckford Charity. Scheme for the administration of the amalgamated charity known as Seckford Hospital and Woodbridge Endowed Schools, approved by the Queen in Council, 20 Nov 1880. Woodbridge, 1881. 1891. 1937

Education

8025 **Ayres, E.** Woodbridge School, Suffolk, 1662–1962: an outline history. Ipswich, 1962

8026 Orders, constitutions, and directions to be observed for the free-school in Woodbridge ... agreed upon at the foundation, 1662. Woodbridge, 1785. O. 2nd edn 1796. 1806

8027 **J, P.** Woodbridge scholars, 1670–89. E Ang 4, 1869/70, 97–103

8028 "Liber Admissionum". Seckford Grammar School at Woodbridge, Suffolk. [*Ed.* by F. A. Crisp]. 1900. 100 copies

8029 Woodbridge Grammar School reports 1884–6, 1891–2

8030 Woodbridge Grammar School. Woodbridgian, no 1, April 1882–. Wood-bridge. CU

8031 Woodbridge School: prospectus. Ipswich, 1955

Libraries

8032 Catalogue of the library of the Woodbridge Literary and Mechanics' Institu-tion. Woodbridge, 1837. BL

8033 Second annual report of the Woodbridge Literary and Mechanics' Institution. Woodbridge, [1838]. BL. 17th report, 1852. SCL/I

8034 Seckford library catalogue. Woodbridge, 1898

8035 **Churchyard, H.** Catalogue of the Seckford Lending Library. Woodbridge, 1914

Planning and Development   See also **1642, 1646**

8036 **East Suffolk County Council.** Planning Dept. Factual survey and outline plan for the Urban District of Woodbridge. Ipswich, Rev edn. 1951. [Typescript]

8037 **East Suffolk County Council.** Planning Dept. Report on the first quinquennial review of the Woodbridge and Melton town map. Ipswich, 1958

8038 **East Suffolk County Council.** Planning Dept. Woodbridge with parts of Deben Rural District: survey and appraisal. Ipswich, 1966. SCL/L

8039 **East Suffolk County Council.** Planning Dept. Woodbridge with part of Deben Rural District: draft town-map review 1967 and draft town-centre map. Ipswich, 1967

8040 **East Suffolk County Council.** Planning Dept. Woodbridge with parts of Deben Rural District: town map. Ipswich, 1968

8041 **East Suffolk County Council.** Planning Dept. County development plan: Amendment No 5, Woodbridge and parts of Deben Rural District, written statement and town map. Ipswich, 1968. Approved 1971

8042 **Suffolk County Council.** Planning Dept. Conservation in Woodbridge: an appraisal of its townscape and a policy for future change. Ipswich, 1976

Penal Administration

8043 Rules and regulations for the good government of the House of Correction at Woodbridge. Woodbridge, 1808. O

8044 Regulations for the prison at Woodbridge in the county of Suffolk. Bury St. Edmunds, 1841. BL

RELIGION AND CHURCHES *See also* **2625–6**

Church and Priory of St. Mary

8045 Description of Woodbridge church, from Mr. Hawes's MS History of the Hundreds of Loos [sic] and Wilford, 1712. O

8046 Terrier of Woodbridge ... exhibited at the primary visitation of ... L. [Bagot] Bishop of [Norwich], to which is added the principal donations at large ... *Ed.* by R. Loder. [Woodbridge], 1787. 2nd edn enlarged 1811

8047 **[Loder, R.]** Description of Woodbridge church, in the county of Suffolk. [Woodbridge], [1790?]. BL

8048 **Dallenger, J.** A record of Woodbridge parish church as it was and is; full and complete copy of the parish terrier; account of Seckford's chapel, tomb, and charity. Woodbridge, 1875

8049 **Arnott, J.** Church and priory of S. Mary, Woodbridge. PSIA 9, 1895/7, 338–44

8050 Short guide to the church of St. Mary the Virgin, Woodbridge. Ramsgate, [c.1951] and later edns

8051 **Golding, C.** Woodbridge priory seal. PSIA 4, 1864/74, 223–4

8052 **Oliver, A.** Matrix of a brass in Woodbridge church. TMBS 2, 1892/6, 11–12

St. John's

8053   [Proposal to build a new church at Woodbridge, signed Rendlesham, with subscriptions, and a subscription card]. Woodbridge, 1840. O

8054   Church of St. John the Evangelist, Woodbridge: some notes on the foundation and first hundred years. Compiled by F. E. G[ladwell]. 1946

Roman Catholicism

8055   St. Philomena's convent, Woodbridge: its history, development, and present-day activities. Gloucester, [1937] BL

Nonconformity   See also **3048–50**

8056   **Payne, E. A.** Congregations of Sabbatarian Baptists at Woodbridge and Melton [1690]. BQ 14, 1951/2, 165

GOLF

8057   **Browning, R. H. K.** Woodbridge Golf Club. [1952]

FREEMASONRY

8058   **Bentham, R.** Freemasonry in Woodbridge a hundred years ago. SIMT No 3913, 1926

8059   **Bentham, R.** History of Doric Lodge, No 81, Woodbridge, 1824–1923. 1932. *See also* **2182**

8060   **Bentham, R.** History of Royal York Chapter, No 81, Woodbridge, 1825–1934. 1934

TIDE MILL

8061   **Weaver, M. A.** The tide mill, Woodbridge. Woodbridge, 1973. [2nd edn] 1976

WOODBRIDGE URBAN DISTRICT

8062   **Department of the Environment.** List of buildings of special architectural or historic interest: Urban district of Woodbridge, East Suffolk. 1971 [Typescript]

WOOLPIT

8063   Woolpit parish history. SC 25.11.1927, Rp No 47

8064   **Page, L. F.,** *and* **Tymms, S.** Woolpit church. PSIA 2, 1854/9, 190–202

8065   Church of St. Mary, Woolpit. 1955. SRO/B

8066   **Dow, L.** Mural inscriptions in a house at Woolpit. PSIA 29, 1961/3, 213–15

8067   **West Suffolk County Council.** Planning Dept. Buildings of Woolpit. [By S. Colman]. Bury St. Edmunds, 1968

8068   **Crossley-Holland, K.** The green children. 1966. SRO/B

WOOLVERSTONE   *See also* **2630–31**

8069   Woolverstone parish history. EADT 25.5.1927, Rp No 22

8070   Janus. Woolverstone Hall School magazine: 21st birthday issue, 1951–72. Ipswich, 1972

8071   **Birch, H. W.** Church notes: Woolverstone. E Ang NS 8, 1899/1900, 51–3

WORDWELL

8072   Wordwell parish history. EADT 18.5.1938

8073   **Paine, C. R.** Wordwell, West Suffolk: a study of village decay and depopulation ... 1968. [Typescript]. SRO/B

8074   Wordwell parish registers, 1580 to 1850. *With* West Stow parish registers ... [*Ed.* by S. H. A. H(ervey)]. Woodbridge, 1903. SGB 7

WORLINGHAM   *See also* **1227, 3113, 3335**

8075   Worlingham parish history. EADT 6.5.1936, Rp No 436

8076   Parish News, [c.1919]–

8079   **Binney, M.** Worlingham Hall. CL 147, 1970, 624–8

WORLINGTON   *See also* **1293**

8078   Worlington parish history. 2 pts. EADT 4.12.1935, 11.12.1935, Rp Nos 419, 420

8079   **Briscoe, G.** Swale's tumulus: a combined Neolithic and Bronze Age barrow at Worlington. PCAS 50, 1956/7, 101–12

8080   **Liversidge, J. E. A.** Hoard of Romano-British ironwork from Worlington. PCAS 40, 1955/6, 89

8081   **Partridge, C.** "In-bread" [term found in nave of Worlington church]. E Ang NS 10, 1903/04, 15, 80

WORLINGWORTH   *See also* **2495, 2952**

8082   Worlingworth parish history. SC 6.4.1928. Rp No 66

8083   **Cribb, N.** Worlingworth parish fire-engine. PSIA 27, 1955/7, 51–3

8084   **Ross, D.** Church of St. Mary, Worlingworth. *Ed.* by F. French. Perth, 1887. SRO/B

8085   **Donnan, W. H.** Brief notes on the history of Worlingworth church. 1964. 1972

WORTHAM   *See also* **2532**

8086   Wortham parish history. SC 19.12.1930, Rp No 207

8087   **Cobbold, R.** A few parochial features of Wortham, AD 1828–70. MS

8088   **James, C. C.** Church of St. Mary, Wortham [appeal]. 1897

8089   Hancock, W. B. Church of St. Mary the Virgin, Wortham: an outline of its history. Wortham, [c.1970]. nl

WRATTING, GREAT   *See also* 2611

8090   Great Wratting parish history. EADT 8.1.1936, Rp No 423

WRATTING, LITTLE

8091   Little Wratting parish history. EADT 12.2.1936, Rp No 427
8092   Dickinson, P. G. M. Little Wratting church. PSIA 27, 1955/7, 34–6
8093   Welch, C. E. Turnour chapel at Little Wratting. PSIA 27, 1955/7, 37–40

WRENTHAM   *See also* 2646, 3323

8094   H, M. L. Field names, Wrentham. E Ang NS 1889/90, 288
8095   Yerburgh, E. R. Notes on Wrentham. [c.1920]. [Typescript]
8096   Wrentham parish history. SC 7.11.1930, Rp No 201
8097   Wilton, H. E. Suffolk boyhood in the 1820's: the village of "D" identified [Wrentham]. SR 1, 1957, 101–03
8098   Yerburgh, E. R. St. Nicholas, Wrentham [A short guide extracted from Notes on Wrentham]. Southwold, nd
8099   Guide book to the churches of the Wrentham group of parishes [Wrentham, Benacre, Covehithe, Sotterley, Shadingfield, Henstead, Weston]. Ramsgate, [1968]. SCL/L
8100   Jenkins, T. B. Ele Bowet: a fourteenth-century lady and her sepulchral brass [Wrentham]. CA 6, 1960/1, 350–55
8101   Swetland, W. Brief history of the Congregational church at Wrentham. [c.1790]. nl
8102   Browne, J. Congregational church at Wrentham in Suffolk: its history and biographies. 1854

WYVERSTONE

8103   Wyverstone parish history. EADT 28.4.1937, Rp No 469

YAXLEY   *See also* 3313–14

8104   Charnock, R. S. Meaning of Yaxley. E Ang 2, 1864/6, 166
8105   Yaxley parish history. SC 31.8.1928, Rp No 87
8106   Royal Commission on Historical Manuscripts. Ser 13, Tenth report, Appendix 4 . . . Manuscripts of the Rev. W. H. Sewell, vicar of Yaxley. 1885. Re-issue 1906
8107   Cornelious, W. History and guide of St. Mary's, Yaxley. Palgrave, 1968. nl
8108   Woodforde, C., *and* Harris, H. A. Medieval glass in Yaxley church. PSIA 21, 1931/3, 91

8109 Restoration of Yaxley pulpit. PSIA 21, 1931/3, 170–71
8110 **Sewell, W. H.** Sexton's wheel and the Lady Fast [Yaxley]. NA 9, 1879/83, 201–14
8111 **Felgate, T. M.** Heraldic carvings in Yaxley church. PSIA 32, 1970/2, 84–7
8112 **Farrer, E.** Yaxley Hall, its owners and occupiers. PSIA 16, 1916/18, 1–28, 135–66
8113 **S, W. H.** Extracts from the parish register of St. Mary's, Yaxley. E Ang 2, 1864/6, 245–7

YOXFORD   *See also* **1729, 2593**

8114 **Scott, C.** Yoxford—the garden of Suffolk. 1890. nl
8115 **Parr, R. T. L.** Yoxford yesterday. 9 v. [Typescript]
8116 Yoxford parish history. SC 24.1.1930, Rp No 160
8117 **Delf, C.** Yoxford: a lively Suffolk village with an interesting past. Yoxford, 1971. SCL/L
8118 To the churchwardens and overseers of the poor in the parish of [Yoxford] in the Hundred of Blything [on supplying the necessitous poor with wheat at a reduced price]. Huntingfield, 1796. BL
8119 [Sequestration of the vicarage of Yoxford]. [Norwich], 1793. BL
8120 **Parr, H.,** *and* **Haslewood, F.** Yoxford church. PSIA 8, 1892/4, 37–50
8121 **Parr, R. T. L.** Brief notes on Yoxford church. Ipswich, [1946]. SRO/B
8122 **Rutton, W. L.** Carved oaken chest of Lady Katherine Grey [Yoxford]. Reliquary NS 6, 1900, 120–5
8123 **Bevan, F. B.** Cockfield Hall. CL 55, 1924, 532–8

Index

The index contains the names of authors and editors of works cited in the bibliography, together with the names of publishers, sponsors, and occasionally the titles of works when no author or editor has been named. It excludes directories listed in the general section on pp. 1–2, except when such works themselves appear as a heading later in the text. The occasional subject-headings in the index should therefore always be supplemented by reference to the appropriate divisions of the text, especially under localities.

439

Index

Turrill, W. B. 3027
Tusser, Thomas 1076–9, 3420
Tweady, J. 1694
Twichell, J. H. 3476
Twiss, *Sir* Travers 5584
Tyacke, N. C. P. 754
Tye, W. 1107, 2645, 3123, 6835, 7207, 7209, 7799
Tyllotson, William 2347–8
Tymms, Samuel 365, 513, 560, 663, 2322, 2423, 3015, 3443, 3677, 3762, 3859, 4060, 4131, 4202, 4333, 4376, 4430, 4438–9, 4524, 4566, 4651, 5057, 5171, 5181, 5226, 5247, 5366, 6286, 6292, 6514, 6517, 6527, 6888, 7003–04, 7402, 7471, 7897–8, 7906, 7976, 8064
Tyrrell-Green, E. 4777

Ubbeston Provident Clothing Society 7765
Ufford Clothing Club 7771
Ufford New Friendly Society 7773
Ufford Poor Allotments 7772
Ulph, E. C. 3730, 3742, 3749
University of East Anglia, Centre of East Anglian Studies 484–7
Unwin, F. D. 5213
Unwin, George 1176, 2021
Unwin, H. P. G. 2368

Valdar, S. 3081
Vale, Edmund 4076
Van Zwanenberg, D. F. 1554, 1572
Varden, J. T. 275
Vaufrey, R. 7634
Venables, G. 4030
Venmore-Rowland, J. 422
Venn, John 1580
Vertue, F. H. 2923, 3759, 6246
Vick, W. 3771, 5509–10, 5757
Vincent, J. A. C. 5234
Vincent, J. E. 382
Vincent, L. G. 6010
Virgoe, Roger 888, 1448

W. 3801, 3865, 6643, 7884
W, D. 3372
W, E. L. 2631
W, H. 6404
W, H. A. 4504, 4506, 4509
W, I. 7907
W, W. (1688) 1206
W, W. (1858) 3466
Wacher, John Stewart 7841
Waddington, J. A. H. 4368
Wadley, T. P. 3226
Wagner, *Sir* Anthony Richard 3498
Wagstaffe, T. 3289

Wailes, Rex 2231–2, 2235, 7240–41
Wainford Rural District 7783–4
Wait, F. W. 5186
Wake, R. 7329, 7354
Wake, T. 7399
Walcott, M. E. C. 273
Walford, W. S. 4327, 4569, 7523, 7561
Walker, H. 5963
Walker, J. (*Surveyor*) 1348, 7349
Walker, J. 7973
Walker, J. W. 7642
Walker, T. A. 2376
Wall, J. C. 562
Wall, S. D. 1218, 4897
Wallace, Doreen 401, 1877
Waller, A. J. R. 1324
Waller, J. G. 3808, 6891
Waller, T. 7801
Wallis, L. 4899
Walmsley, J. 1616
Walsh, B. D. J. 1385
Walsh, E. 2511
Walsh, N. 1086
Walsham, *Sir* John 1516
Walters, J. C. 547
"Walton, F.", *pseud.*, *see* Woolnough, F.
Wangford Rural District 7820
Wanley, Humphrey 4089
War Graves Commissions 838, 841–2
Ward, G. 3255, 7654
Ward, J. C. 2651, 3516, 4539
Ward, N. 813
Ward, S. 1689
Ward, Z. 5365
Ward Lock and Co. Ltd. 3535, 4890, 5491, 6576, 7321
Ware, S. 4537
Warman, J. P. 3861
Warner, R. S. A. 3445
Warren, *Dr.* 4200
Warren, F. E. 734, 2900, 3638, 3640–41
Warren J. 5406, 6278, 6280–83, 7080
Warren, R. 1916
Warren, W. D. 6152
Warsop, D. 6924
Warwick, M. A. S. 2528
Wase, F. W. 2107, 4731
Waterhouse, Ellis Kirkham 2911–12, 5239
Waters, R. E. C. 3486
Waters, T. F. 3477
Waterton, E. 4440
Watkins, A. A. 6907
Watkins, E. A. 2757
Watkins, W. E. 1116
Watling, H. 543, 2291, 2297, 3695, 4600, 4725, 5513, 7440, 7445

451